Using Microsoft Dynamics 365 Finance and Operations

Andreas Luszczak

Using Microsoft Dynamics 365 Finance and Operations

Learn and understand the Dynamics 365 Supply Chain Management and Finance apps

Third Edition 2026

Andreas Luszczak
Wien, Austria

ISBN 978-3-658-50562-2 ISBN 978-3-658-50563-9 (eBook)
https://doi.org/10.1007/978-3-658-50563-9

This Springer imprint is published by the registered company Springer Fachmedien Wiesbaden GmbH, part of Springer Nature.
The registered company address is: Abraham-Lincoln-Str. 46, 65189 Wiesbaden, Germany

If disposing of this product, please recycle the paper.

Preface

Reading this Book

The primary purpose of this book is to provide you with a good knowledge of the concept and functionality of Microsoft Dynamics 365 Finance and Operations. As a result, you should be able to execute business processes in the application on your own. It is primarily designed for users, students, and consultants who are interested in learning how to use the application.

Going beyond the operations on the user interface, you learn how the different parts of the application work together. For this reason, also system administrators, developers, IT executives, or consultants who do not know all the details of the application take advantage of getting to know the end-to-end concept.

The best way to learn an application is to use it. For that reason, this book includes exercises that build up on each other in a comprehensive case study. If you need support with the exercises, download the illustrated sample solutions.

Microsoft Dynamics 365 Finance and Operations is a very comprehensive business solution, which makes it impossible to explain all parts of the application in a single book. To provide a profound understanding of the core application, this book addresses the essential functionality in supply chain management (including trade and logistics, and production control) and finance management. It covers the application, but does not cover system administration and development.

Microsoft Dynamics 365 Product Version

This book is based on the product version 10.0.45 of Microsoft Dynamics 365 Finance and Operations (released in September 2025) with all features enabled. It is an update of the previous book edition on Dynamics 365 for Finance and Operations. To avoid repeating the long name, the short name "Dynamics 365" is used in most parts of this book.

New in this Edition

Apart from updates in all chapters of the book, major additional topics in this edition include the pricing management (Unified pricing) with its impact on sales order management (in particular, setting an order to complete when finishing the order entry), financial tags, options for prepayments in purchasing and in sales, DDMRP and priority-based planning, warehouse-specific inventory transactions, return orders with advanced warehouse management, item substitution in production control, and notes on topics like the Inventory visibility add-in, soft reservation, advanced quality management, and the Immersive homepage

Applicable Settings

In Dynamics 365, you can individually select the language of your user interface. Descriptions and illustrations in this book refer to the language "EN-US" (USA English). Whereas it is obvious that the Dynamics 365 client shows different labels when selecting languages like Spanish or Arabic, there are also differences if you select British English. For example, the label for the field "Sales tax" is "VAT" in British English. Other differences between your application and the descriptions in the book are possibly caused by permission settings, by local features, by settings in the feature management and in the license configuration, by later updates, or by modifications and add-ons in your application.

In order to benefit from the explanations, it is recommended to practice with Dynamics 365. A separate test application, which you can use to do the exercises, is required to avoid an impact on actual company data.

The illustrations and the exercises in this book refer to the Microsoft standard demo environment with the company "Contoso Entertainment System USA" ("USMF"). For the screenshots, the color theme "High contrast" and a small element size has been selected in the visual preferences of the user options. In order to grant a flexible choice of your training environment, the tasks in the exercises are specified in a way that you can use a Dynamics 365 test environment of your choice.

Available Support

You can download the exercise guide for the exercises in this book and other applicable resources from the online service of the publisher, or from my website:

http://D365book.addyn.com

If you have comments or questions regarding the book or the exercises, please contact me via this website or e-mail to lua@addyn.com.

Acknowledgments

Many people have been involved in finalizing this book, directly and indirectly, from the first to the current edition. Thank you to all of them. In particular, I would like to mention Christopher Weber (Arineo), Ingo Maresch (Cegeka), and Finn Nielsen-Friis (AXcademy).

Thank you also to the editor, Petra Steinmüller, and to my family—Sonja, Felix, and Caroline.

Andreas Luszczak

Competing Interests The author has no competing interests to declare that are relevant to the content of this manuscript.

Contents

What Is Microsoft Dynamics 365?

Microsoft Dynamics 365 is a cloud-based business platform that comprises the functionality of ERP and CRM solutions. Within Dynamics 365, there are several applications for the different areas of business. In that regard, Dynamics 365 Finance and Operations, the solution which is covered by this book, includes the ERP functionality for mid-sized companies and multinational enterprises. With a state-of-the-art architecture, it offers high usability and comprehensive functionality.

While Dynamics 365 Finance and Operations is a complete ERP solution, it is broken into separate applications for Finance, for Supply Chain Management, and for Commerce in terms of licensing and product management.

1.1 Dynamics 365, Dynamics AX, and Axapta

Dynamics 365 Finance and Operations was initially developed under the name "Axapta" by Damgaard A/S, a Danish software company. Before, the founders of Damgaard were co-founders of PC&C, the company that developed Navision (later "Dynamics NAV" and "Dynamics 365 Business Central").

The first official version of Axapta, version 1.0, was released in March 1998 for Denmark and the USA. Version 1.5, published in October 1998, added the country-specific functionality for several European countries. With the release of version 2.0 in July 1999 and version 3.0 in October 2002, Axapta was introduced in further countries with a wide range of functional enhancements.

Based on a merger agreement in November 2000, Damgaard A/S united with the local rival Navision A/S, the successor of PC&C. Microsoft subsequently acquired Navision-Damgaard in May 2002 and accepted the main products of this company, Navision and

© The Editor(s) (if applicable) and The Author(s), under exclusive license to
Springer Fachmedien Wiesbaden GmbH, part of Springer Nature 2026
A. Luszczak, *Using Microsoft Dynamics 365 Finance and Operations*,
https://doi.org/10.1007/978-3-658-50563-9_1

Axapta, as core business solutions in the software portfolio. Navision was positioned as the solution for small companies, and Axapta for large companies.

With version 4.0 in June 2006, Microsoft rebranded Axapta to Dynamics AX. Apart from functional enhancements, Dynamics AX 4.0 introduced a redesigned user interface with a Microsoft Office-like look and feel.

Dynamics AX 2009, which was published in June 2008, added the role centers, the workflow functionality, and substantial functional features (including the multisite foundation and new modules) that ensure an end-to-end support for the supply chain requirements of global organizations.

Published in August 2011, Dynamics AX 2012 introduced a further update of the user interface with list pages and action panes across the whole application. New features included the role-based security, the accounting framework with segmented account structures, the enhanced use of shared data structures, and further options for collaborating across legal entities within the application. Updated versions of Dynamics AX 2012 were released later: The Feature Pack in February 2012 (adding industry features for retail and process manufacturing), R2 in December 2012, and R3 in May 2014 (adding the advanced warehouse and transportation management solution).

In March 2016, the first version of the current solution—a cloud-based application with a web client—was published with the name Dynamics AX 7. In comparison to Dynamics AX 2012, the technical foundation was completely new, but initially the functionality remained unchanged for the most part. In line with the principle of a cloud-based solution, technical and functional updates have been continuously published since then. With the integration into the Dynamics 365 platform in November 2016, Dynamics AX has received the name "Dynamics 365 for Finance and Operations".

Starting in April 2019, the "one version" policy has been implemented, which means that all customers are on the current product version. In line with this policy, customer environments need to be updated to the newest version continuously. With the feature management, new functionality that is included in a product update usually remains deactivated until you activate it in the Feature management workspace.

In 2020, Microsoft officially split Dynamics 365 for Finance and Operations into separate products. The main products are Dynamics 365 Finance and Dynamics 365 Supply Chain Management, but there are further applications, including Dynamics 365 Commerce and Dynamics 365 Human Resources. From a functional, development, and administration perspective, these products are part of one common ERP solution—Finance and Operations.

> **Note**: Apart from the products on the Finance and Operations platform (based on Dynamics AX), there are Dynamics 365 products which work separately—Business Central (based on Dynamics NAV) and products for sales and marketing (based on Dynamics CRM).

1.2 Dynamics 365 Finance and Operations at a Glance

Microsoft Dynamics 365 Finance and Operations is a business solution that meets the complex requirements of multinational enterprises.

Because of its intuitive user interface, most people feel comfortable with Dynamics 365 from the very beginning. Along with the tight integration of other Microsoft cloud services, this helps to start working in Dynamics 365 easily and efficiently. Dashboards and the Immersive home page, which are the start page in Dynamics 365, grant easy and fast access to all required areas of the application.

1.2.1 Functional Capabilities

The end-to-end support of business processes across the organization enables the integration of internal organization units (including companies and departments) and external business partners (including customers and vendors).

Multi-language, multi-country, and multi-currency capabilities, the organization model with multiple hierarchies of operating units and legal entities, and the option to manage multiple sites within one legal entity, make it possible to manage complex global organizations within a common environment.

The functional capabilities of Dynamics 365 Finance and Operations include the following main areas in Finance and Supply Chain Management:

- **Sales and marketing**
- **Inventory management**
- **Procurement and sourcing**
- **Production control**
- **MRP (Material requirements planning/Master planning).**
- **Warehouse management**
- **Transportation management**
- **Finance management**
- **Cost accounting and cost management**
- **Budgeting**
- **Time and attendance**
- **Project management and accounting**
- **Asset management**

In addition to the core ERP functionality, industry-specific features for distribution, manufacturing, retail and commerce, services, and the public sector are included in the standard application and provide a broad industry foundation. Local features meet the particular requirements of different countries. By default, local features are controlled by the country in the address of the company (legal entity).

In line with the one-version policy for Dynamics 365, application and platform improvements are periodically published in a single version that includes the entire update. New features, which are covered by an update, are shown in the Feature management workspace and must be activated there to make them available.

1.2.2 Integration of AI and Microsoft Copilot

In order to support the daily work, Dynamics 365 Finance and Operations integrates AI (Artificial Intelligence) capabilities with Microsoft Copilot. The user interface in Dynamics 365 includes Copilot features in the following ways:

- **Sidecar**—Pane on the right for chats with Copilot (e.g., for user help).
- **Embedded**—Showing AI-generated content, which summarizes and classifies information, on a tab in relevant pages (e.g., in the workspace *Confirmed purchase orders with changes*).
- **Outside**—Enabling external agents to extract (chat with) Dynamics 365 data.
- Apart from Copilot features that show information to users, there are AI agents that can act autonomously. An example of this is the Supplier Communication agent, which includes the following capabilities:
- **Write emails to vendors**—Reminding them of missing order confirmations or overdue deliveries (based on Dynamics 365 data).
- **Read emails from vendors**—Updating data like the expected delivery date in the purchase order according to the information in the mail (after review).

Other examples are the Expense agent, which can create expense reports in Dynamics 365 from receipts that are scanned or electronically received, or the Time Entry agent, which creates time entries from Outlook calendars and Teams meetings.

1.2.3 Power Platform and Power Apps

Microsoft Dynamics 365 Finance and Operations is deeply integrated with the Microsoft Power Platform.

Dual-write integration enables a near-real-time synchronization of business data from Dynamics 365 Finance and Operations with Dataverse. Power Apps and Power Automate, which are low-code tools, enable creating custom apps and workflows that can work with these business data. With Power BI, you can visualize relevant business data and create interactive reports.

This book covers the functionality within Dynamics 365 Finance and Operations. You can find more information about the Microsoft Power Platform, Power Apps, Power Automate, and Power BI in the official documents of Microsoft.

1.2.4 Data Structure

ERP solutions like Dynamics 365 Finance and Operations contain data that describe transactions—for example, the inventory transactions of an item. As a prerequisite for the transactions, you need to manage data that describe the objects in the transaction—for example, the item itself. Including the data that control the configuration, there are three data types:

- **Setup data**
- **Master data**
- **Transaction data**

Setup data specify how business processes work in Dynamics 365. The setup determines, for example, whether warehouse locations or serial numbers are used. Apart from the development of enhancements, the setup is the primary way to adapt the application to the requirements of the enterprise. Setup data are specified when implementing the application. Later changes need to be checked carefully.

Master data describe objects like customers or products. They are not updated periodically, but at the time when there are changes to the object (e.g., when a customer changes the delivery address). Master data are entered or imported initially before a company starts working in the application. Depending on the business, there are only occasional updates of master data later on.

Transaction data are continuously created and updated with the activities in business processes. Examples of transaction data are sales orders, invoices, or inventory transactions. Dynamics 365 generates transaction data with each business activity. The registration and the posting of transactions comply with the voucher principle.

1.2.5 Voucher Principle

If you want to post a transaction, you have to register a voucher with a header and one or more lines. Processing a voucher includes two steps:

- **Registration**—Enter the voucher (create the initial document).
- **Posting**—Post the voucher (create the posted document).

Vouchers are based on master data—for example, the main accounts, customers, or products. It is not possible to post a voucher as long as it does not comply with the rules that are defined by setup data or given by the internal business logic of Dynamics 365 (which, for example, requires that an inventory transaction has to include a serial number if serial number control is active). Once a voucher is posted, it is not possible to change it anymore. Depending on the setup, approval in a workflow may be required before it is possible to post the transaction. Examples of vouchers are orders in sales and purchasing, or journals in finance and inventory management. The related posted documents are packing slips, invoices, ledger transactions, or inventory transactions.

> *Note*: Some minor vouchers, like quarantine orders, show an exception regarding the voucher structure—they do not consist of a header and separate lines.

1.2.6   Implementation

You can deploy Dynamics 365 Finance and Operations on Microsoft Azure in the cloud. While on-premise implementations in data centers of companies that run Dynamics 365 are still supported, it is recommended to migrate to Dynamics 365 cloud offerings.

The starting point for a Dynamics 365 implementation is the Power Platform Admin Center (which has replaced the Microsoft Dynamics Lifecycle Services)—a portal solution on Microsoft Azure that includes a collaborative environment and continuously updated services for the management of Dynamics 365 deployments.

Microsoft usually does not sell Dynamics 365 directly to customers but offers an indirect sales channel. Customers purchase licenses from certified partners, who provide their services for the implementation. These services include application consulting, system setup, and the development of enhancements.

Getting Started: Navigation and General Options

Microsoft Dynamics 365 provides an intuitive and smooth user experience. But business software supports business processes, and these processes may be quite complex. For this reason, it is important to know the basics.

2.1 User Interface and Common Tasks

Whereas the subsequent chapters give a description of the business processes in Dynamics 365, this section gives an overview of the general functionality.

2.1.1 Login and Authentication

Before you can log on to Microsoft Dynamics 365, an administrator must set up your Dynamics 365 user with appropriate permissions. In addition, a worker record ($\rightarrow$ Sect. 10.2.2) assigned to your user is required in some areas of the application.

Once your user has been set up, you can sign in with a Microsoft Entra ID account. There are different ways to access Dynamics 365 with your user:

- **Web client**—As described below, with full access to all functional areas (depending on your permissions).
- **Power Pages**—Websites for external and internal users, which you can create in the Power Platform by the use of templates (e.g., the customer portal template).

A. Luszczak, *Using Microsoft Dynamics 365 Finance and Operations*,
https://doi.org/10.1007/978-3-658-50563-9_2

- **Power Apps mobile**—Mobile apps that you can create in the Power Platform (canvas apps and model-driven apps).
- **Microsoft Excel**—With the Microsoft Office integration, you can use Excel to insert and update data in Dynamics 365.

To work with the Dynamics 365 web client, start a supported web browser like Microsoft Edge or Google Chrome and open the web address (URL) of your Dynamics 365 application. The browser shows the login dialog next, in which you enter your Microsoft Entra ID (e-mail) and password. With multifactor authentication, you have to confirm the login request with the Microsoft Authenticator app or a third-party authenticator.

Settings in your user options determine the current company (legal entity) and the language in Dynamics 365 after logging on. Parameters in the web address of the Dynamics 365 application may override these user settings, and they provide further options. For example, you can enter the web address *https://XXX.com/?cmp=FRSI&lng=fr* (*XXX.com* = Dynamics 365 URL) to access Dynamics 365 with the company "FRSI" in French.

If you want to log off, click the icon with your user initials on the right of the Dynamics 365 navigation bar and select the option *Sign out*.

2.1.2 Navigation

The Dynamics 365 web client provides the following options for accessing a page:

- **Homepage and workspaces**
- **Navigation pane**
- **Navigation search**
- **Favorites**
- **Parameter "mi" in the web address (URL)**

With the parameter "mi" in the URL, you can directly access a page within Dynamics 365. You can, for example, open the Customer list page with the web address *https://XXX.com/?mi=CustTableListPage* (*XXX.com* = Dynamics 365 URL).

Depending on the selected *Initial page* in your user options (→ Sect. 2.2.1), the *Default dashboard*, the *Immersive home* page, the *Essentials dashboard*, or one of the other pages is the homepage (initial page) which is shown by default when accessing Microsoft Dynamics 365.

The *Default dashboard* contains all workspaces that are available to the current user. In the dashboard, you can open a workspace, and in the workspace, you can subsequently access the related list pages and detail forms. The *Immersive home* page integrates AI features to support focusing on important work.

2.1.2.1 Navigation Pane

The navigation pane provides access to all workspaces, list pages, and forms for which you have appropriate permissions. The main areas in the navigation pane are the *Modules* section, which contains all your menu items, the *Workspaces* section, which contains your workspaces, and the *Favorites* section, in which you can place a limited number of menu items for frequent use.

If you want to display the complete navigation pane, press the keyboard shortcut *Alt + F1* or click the button ⊟ (*Expand the navigation pane*) in the sidebar on the left of the Dynamics 365 client. Dynamics 365 will show the following navigation elements (→ Fig. 2.1):

- **Navigation pane** [1]
- **Home** [2]—Opens the homepage (→ Sect. 2.1.3)
- **Favorites** [3]—Shows the favorites
- **Recent** [4]—Shows workspaces and pages that you have visited recently
- **Workspaces** [5]—Shows the workspaces (→ Sect. 2.1.3)
- **Modules** [6]
- **Menu for the selected module** [7]—With the buttons *Expand all* and *Collapse all* to show or hide all menu items

If you want to view the navigation pane permanently, click the button ⊞ (*Pin navigation pane open*) at the top right of the navigation pane. With the button ⊠ at the top right of the (permanently shown) navigation pane, you can subsequently collapse the navigation pane again.

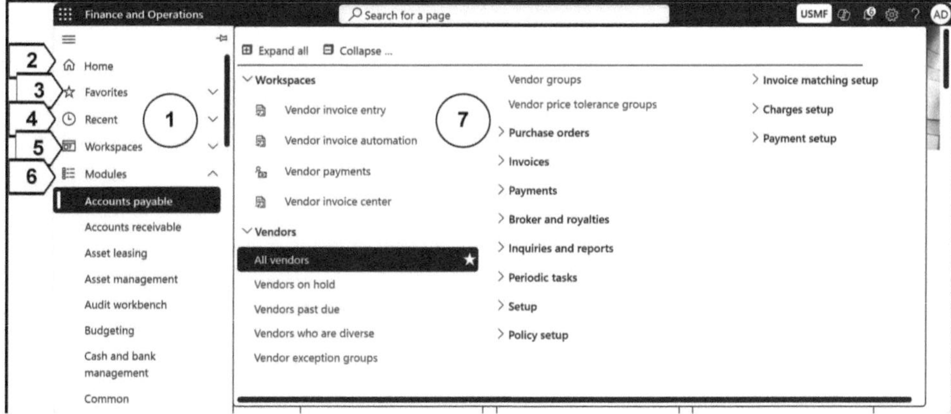

Fig. 2.1 Navigation pane and menu in Dynamics 365

2.1.2.2 Modules and Menu Structure

The structure of the modules complies with functional areas like *Accounts payable* or *Production control* and refers to standard roles in the industry. The modules *Organization administration* and *System administration* include basic settings and tasks that are not related to a specific functional area.

The *Common* module contains menu items which not related to a functional role, but which are relevant for all users. These menu items include the *Global address book* ($\rightarrow$ Sect. 2.4), the *Work items* ($\rightarrow$ Sect. 10.4.3), the *Cases* ($\rightarrow$ Sect. 10.5.2), and the *Document management* ($\rightarrow$ Sect. 10.5.1).

Within each module, the menu shows all menu items that you can access with your permissions. The menu items and folders in the menu comply with the following common structure:

The folder **Workspaces** is the first folder in the menu. It is only shown if the selected module contains one or more workspaces and contains all the workspaces of the selected module.

Below the workspaces, there are folders and menu items that provide access to **pages for frequent tasks** in the particular module (e.g., the vendor management in the Accounts payable module).

The folder **Inquiries and reports** contains menu items for analysis and reporting. Inquiries show the result directly on the screen, whereas reports generate a printout on paper. For reports, you can also select to display a print preview or to save the output to a file instead of a printed hard copy.

The folder **Periodic tasks** contains menu items, which are not in use every day—for example, the menu items for summary updates or month-end closing.

Depending on the module, one or more **Setup** folders provide access to the configuration data of the particular module. Configuration data are entered when initially setting up a company (legal entity). Later on, configuration data are only updated if changes in the business require changes in the setup. Some settings should not be changed without a deep knowledge of the Dynamics 365 functionality. For this reason, usually the permissions for the *Setup* folders are set in a way that regular users cannot edit critical configuration data.

2.1.2.3 Recent Pages

The section *Recent* in the navigation pane contains the Dynamics 365 pages and workspaces that you have visited most recently. When you access a menu item, Dynamics 365 automatically adds it to the section *Recent*. This way, you can quickly return to a form that you have opened lately.

2.1.2.4 Navigation Search

With the navigation search, you can access menu items by typing the name or part of the name (similar to the Search feature in Windows).

If you want to open the navigation search, press the shortcut *Alt + G* or click the *Search* button ⌕ in the navigation bar ($\rightarrow$ Fig. 2.2). In the *Search* field, enter the page title or a

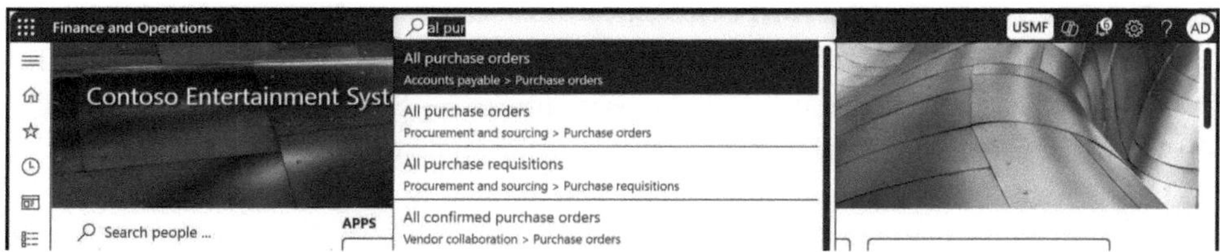

Fig. 2.2 Using the navigation search

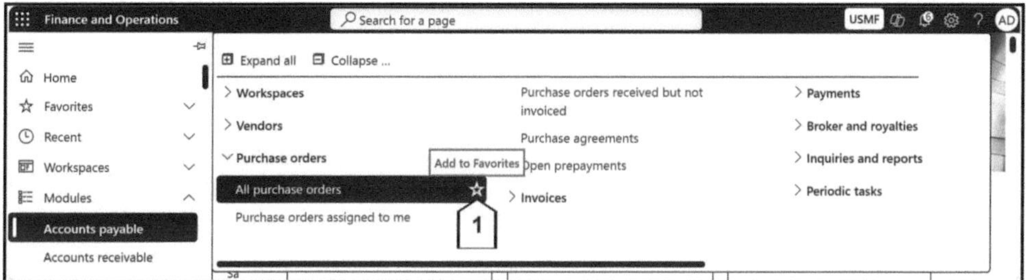

Fig. 2.3 Adding a menu item to the Dynamics 365 favorites

part of the navigation path. You can limit the text, which you enter, to the first characters of the words of the page title or the navigation path. For example, the page *All purchase orders* is shown as the first result when you type "al pur" in the navigation search. In the drop-down menu that pops up automatically, click on the respective menu item or simply press the *Enter* key to access the page.

2.1.2.5 Favorites and Shared Links

Whereas the module structure and menu items in the navigation pane are given by the system, the personal Dynamics 365 favorites provide an option to collect menu items according to the preferences of the individual user.

If you want to add a workspace or a page to your Dynamics 365 favorites, open the navigation pane and move the mouse to the menu item that you want to add to the favorites. A click on the empty star ☆, which is then shown on the right of the menu item, adds it to the favorites (→ Fig. 2.3). A full star ★ on the right of the menu item indicates that it is included in the favorites.

Once a menu item is included in the favorites, it is shown in the *Favorites* section of the navigation pane. If you want to remove an item from the favorites, click on the full star ★ that is shown on the right of the menu item.

Apart from the favorites within Dynamics 365, you can use shared links to access a page in Dynamics 365. In the action pane of all list pages and forms, there is the button *Options/ Share/ Get a link*. If you click this button, a dialog with the web address of the current form is shown. You can copy this link and send it to other users of Dynamics 365 in your enterprise, or add it to the browser start page or the browser favorites.

2.1.2.6 Switching the Current Company

You can manage multiple companies (legal entities) in a common Dynamics 365 environment. When accessing Dynamics 365, the user options ($\rightarrow$ Sect. 2.2.1) or the web address ($\rightarrow$ Sect. 2.1.1) determine the current company—the company in which you are working.

If you want to switch from one company to another at a later time, you can use the company lookup ($\rightarrow$ Fig. 2.4), which you open with a click on the company field in the navigation bar or with the shortcut *Ctrl + Shift + O*. Once you select a company in the lookup, Dynamics 365 immediately switches to this company. You are viewing and editing data in that company subsequently.

2.1.3   Elements of the User Interface

Microsoft Dynamics 365 contains the following types of standard pages, which are characterized by common elements:

- **Homepage**
- **Workspaces**
- **List pages**
- **Detail forms and transaction forms**
- **Journals, inquiries, and setup forms**

2.1.3.1 Dynamics 365 Homepage

The homepage is the initial page that is shown when accessing Microsoft Dynamics 365. With the button *Home* in the navigation pane and the link *Finance and Operations* on the left of the navigation, you can return to the homepage from every workspace or form.

One of the options for the *Initial page* (homepage), which you can select in your user options, is the *Default dashboard*. The default dashboard ($\rightarrow$ Fig. 2.5) contains all workspaces, for which you have appropriate permissions. It is designed to give an overview of your work and contains the following items:

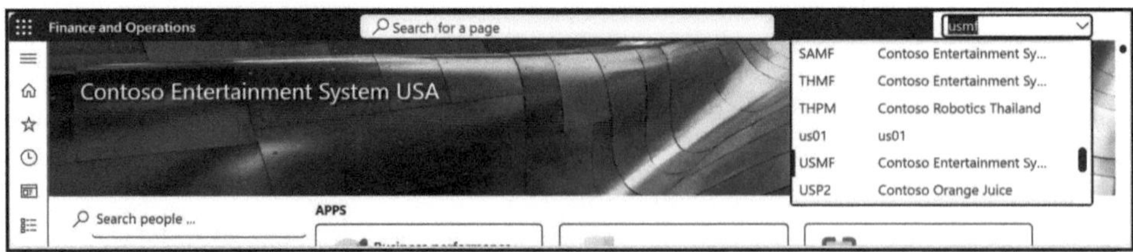

Fig. 2.4 Switching the current company

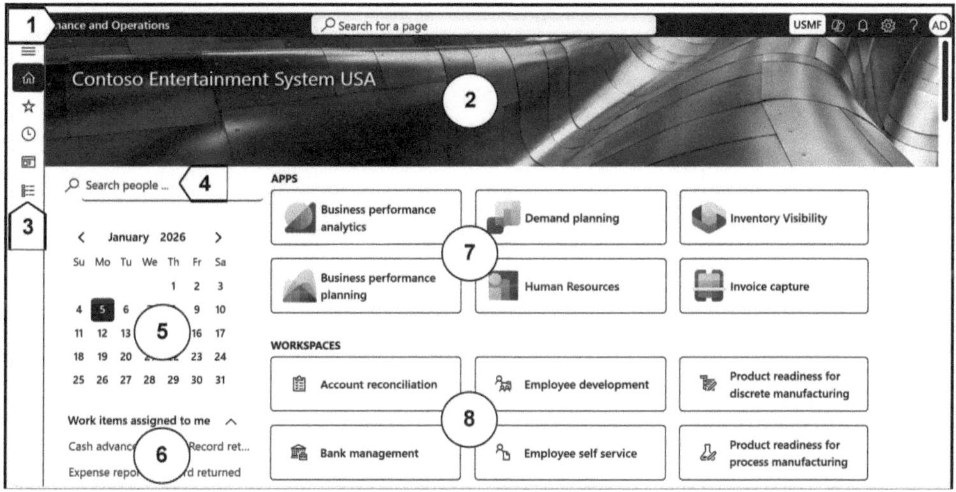

Fig. 2.5 Viewing the elements in the Dynamics 365 dashboard

- **Navigation bar** [1]—Described below.
- **Company banner** [2]—Specified in the company setup (→ Sect. 10.1.4).
- **Navigation pane** [3]—Collapsed in → Fig. 2.5.
- **People search** [4]—Search workers in Dynamics 365 Human Resources.
- **Calendar** [5]—Determines the session date.
- **Work items** [6]—Your work items from workflows (→ Sect. 10.4.3).
- **Apps** [8]—Tiles for accessing related Dynamics apps.
- **Workspaces** [8]—Tiles for accessing your workspaces in the different areas.

Workspace tiles—e.g., the tile *Bank management* in → Fig. 2.5—provide access to the related workspaces. The calendar in the dashboard highlights the *Session date* of the current session, which is the default value for the posting date in journals and orders. The initial value for the session date is the current date. If you want to set it to a different date, click on the respective date in the dashboard calendar or select it in the menu item *Common > Common > Session date and time*.

The *Immersive home* (→ Fig. 2.6) is another available option for the *Initial page* (homepage). The Immersive home page is designed to support workers doing most of the daily activities with the help of AI agents on one page. It contains a summary line at the top and an overview of the work items on the left. AI agent activities and workspaces are shown on the right.

2.1.3.2 Navigation Bar
The navigation bar (→ Fig. 2.7) at the top of the Dynamics 365 client provides access to global Dynamics 365 features.

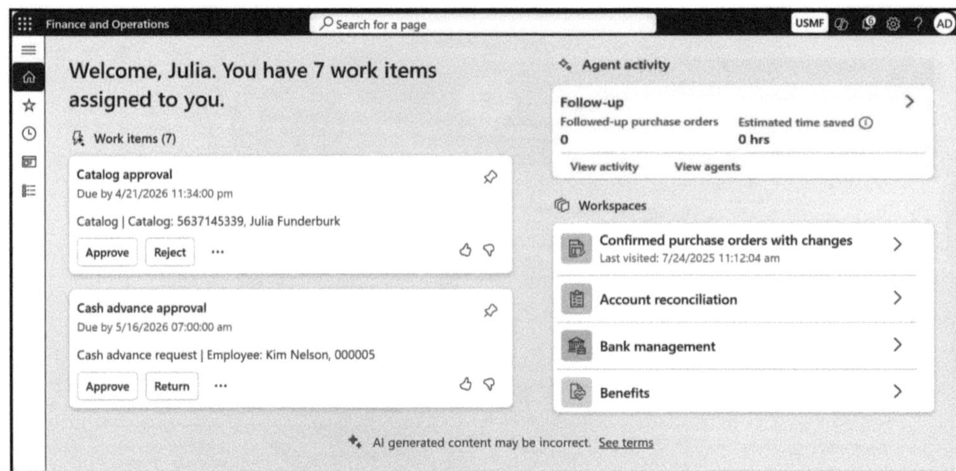

Fig. 2.6   Working with the Immersive home page

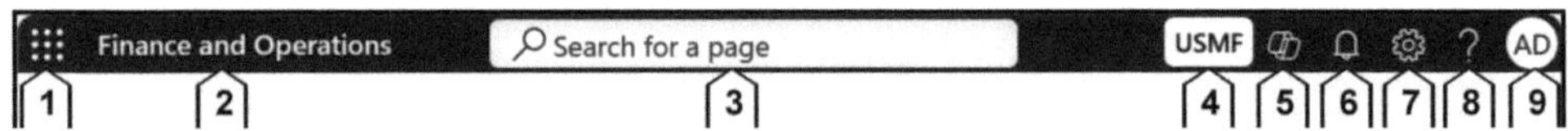

Fig. 2.7   Elements of the navigation bar in Dynamics 365

It contains the following elements:

- **Office 365 portal** [1]—Access to Microsoft Office 365.
- **Finance and Operations** [2]—Access the Dynamics 365 homepage.
- **Navigation search** [3]—Directly access a page (→ Sect. 2.1.2).
- **Company lookup** [4]—Switch between companies (→ Sect. 2.1.2).
- **Copilot** [5]—Expand the Copilot sidecar pane (→ Sect. 1.2.2).
- **Messages** [6]—View messages (→ Sect. 2.1.4).
- **Settings** [7]—User options and other general settings.
- **Help & Support** [8]—Access to help and support information.
- **User initials** [9]—Sign out.

If the browser window with the Dynamics 365 client is not wide enough to show all elements, there is the button ▪ (*More*) on the right of the Navigation bar to access the missing elements.

The options within the button ⚙ (*Settings*) [6] include the *User options* (→ Sect. 2.2.1), the *Task recorder* (→ Sect. 10.5.3), and access to the Personalization toolbar (→ Sect. 2.2.2).

Within the button ❓ (*Help & Support*) [7], you can find the buttons *Help* (→ Sect. 2.1.6), *Trace* (capture a trace for problem diagnosis and performance analysis), *About* (display product information), and buttons for submitting *Feedback* and *Ideas* to Microsoft.

Note: If the slider *Enable legacy navigation bar* in the client performance options (*System administration > Setup > Client performance options*) is set to "Yes", the navigation bar includes the navigation path and looks slightly different from the screenshots in this book.

2.1.3.3 Workspaces

The homepage—Immersive home or Dashboard—and the section *Workspaces* in the navigation pane, contain the workspaces for which you have appropriate permissions.

Workspaces are designed as a starting point for the daily work in a particular job. They are pages that collect all the information and functionality required to perform this job. In the example of the workspace *Purchase order preparation* (→ Fig. 2.8), a list of purchase orders with the status "Draft" is shown in the center. Tiles in the sections above and below the center provide access to related forms and indicate the corresponding number of records—for example, approved purchase orders without confirmed delivery date.

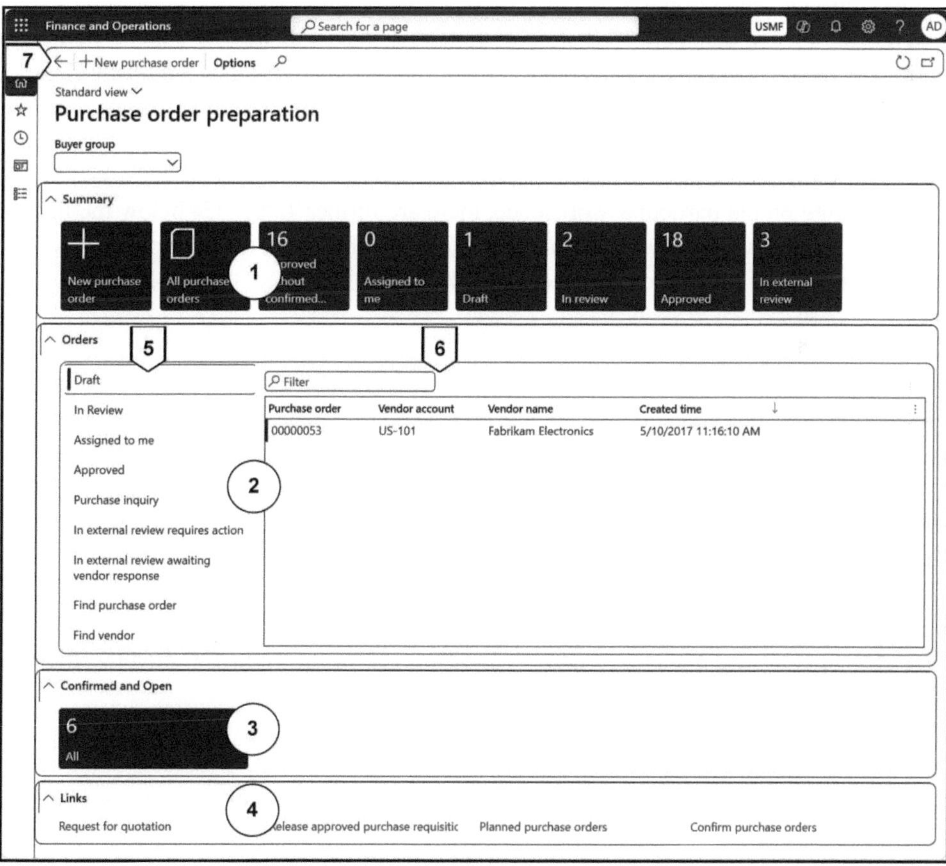

Fig. 2.8 Workspace for purchase order preparation

In general, a workspace contains the following elements:

- **Summary Table** [1]—With tiles for accessing relevant pages
- **Tabbed list section** [2]—With a list selection [5] and the grid with the selected list [6]
- **Further tabs as applicable** [3]
- **Links Table** [4]
- **Action pane** [7]

The tabbed list section [2] in the center of a workspace is the main place for the daily work. If you select a list on the left [5] of this section, the grid on the right [6] displays the related list of records. The filter field above the grid provides the option to enter a filter. A click on a key field (shown as a link) in the grid immediately opens the related form. Depending on the particular workspace, buttons in the action pane [7] and, if applicable, in the toolbar above the grid in the list section [2] (the example in → Fig. 2.8 does not include such a toolbar) provide the option to execute actions immediately.

Tiles are rectangular buttons that open pages (in the same way as a menu item), and optionally display data like counts or key performance indicators. The *Summary* Table [1] in the upper area of a workspace contains tiles that provide the option to start new tasks or to access pages that are important with regard to the selected workspace (e.g., purchase orders in → Fig. 2.8).

Depending on the particular workspace, there are further Tables [3] below the list section, which contain tiles, charts, or graphs. The *Links* Table [4] at the bottom contains links to additional pages related to the selected workspace.

2.1.3.4 List Pages

A list page shows the list of records in a Dynamics 365 table. It is primarily designed for viewing records, but you can activate the *Edit mode* to update records directly in the list page, and with the buttons in the action pane, you can execute tasks on the selected record.

While list pages have a common structure, the particular elements and features depend on the respective page. The common structure includes the following basic elements (→ Fig. 2.9):

- **Action pane [1]**—Contains the action buttons.
- **Filter button and FactBox button [2]**—Buttons on the right for showing the filter pane and the FactBoxes.
- **Quick filter [3]**—Filter field for entering a filter.
- **Grid [4]**—Displays the list of records.
- **Grid checkboxes** [5]—Select one, or multiple, or, with the checkbox in the grid header, all records.
- **Scrollbar [6]**—Scroll through records (alternatively, press the shortcuts *PgUp*, *PgDn*, *Ctrl + Home,* and *Ctrl + End).*
- **FactBoxes [7]**—Show additional information on the selected record (e.g., the primary address of the customer) in the *Related information* pane on the right.

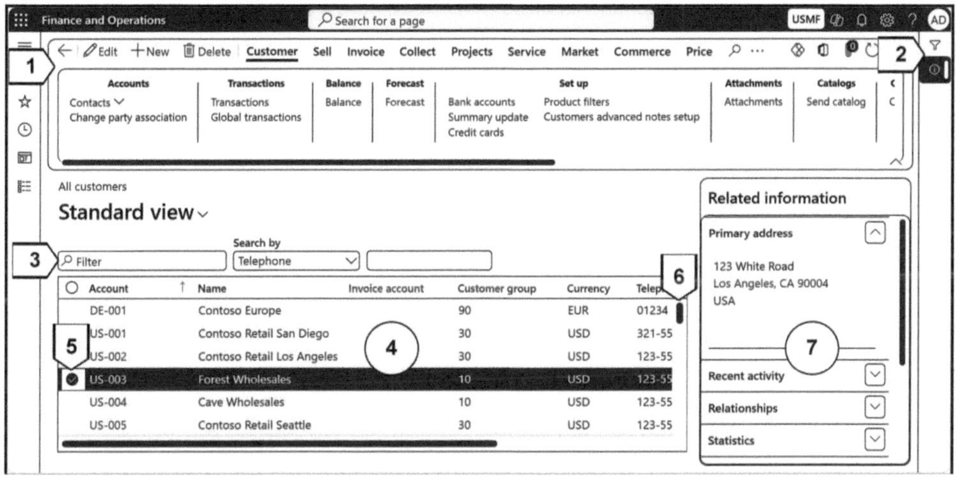

Fig. 2.9 Elements of the customer list page (in read mode)

With the button *Edit* in the action pane, you can activate the Edit mode and update record data in the list page immediately.

If a page is shown with the full action pane and you need additional space for viewing more lines in the grid, click the button ⌃ (*Collapse*) at the bottom right of the action pane. Once collapsed, the action pane automatically expands whenever you click a tab of the action pane (e.g., *Customer* in the action pane in → Fig. 2.9). If you want to show the full action pane permanently, click the button ⊞ (*Pin open*) at the bottom right of the action pane when expanded.

If the *Related information* pane is collapsed and you want to view the FactBoxes, press the shortcut *Ctrl + F2* or click the button ▣ on the right. Once expanded, you can click the button ▣ on the right again if you want to collapse the *Related information* pane. As a prerequisite for the use of FactBoxes, the FactBoxes have to be activated in the client performance options (*System administration > Setup > Client performance options*).

List pages are not automatically refreshed when data shown on the screen are updated (e.g., if somebody else is changing the records displayed in the list). To refresh a list page, press the shortcut *Shift + F5* or click the button ⋯ (*Refresh*) at the top right of the action pane.

2.1.3.5 Action Pane and Action Search

The action pane contains buttons for executing activities related to the selected record (e.g., if you want to enter a sales order from the Customer form) and buttons for accessing associated detail forms (displaying additional information). The number and functionality of the buttons, which may be shown on multiple tabs (e.g., the action pane tabs *Customer* or *Sell* in → Fig. 2.9), depend on the particular page. If the browser window is not wide enough to show all tabs of the action pane, there is the button ⊠ on the right of the action pane to access the hidden tabs.

Apart from the form-specific buttons and tabs in the action pane, there are some general buttons on the right:

- ▣ **[Power Apps]**—Add a Power App.
- ▣ **[Open in Microsoft Office]**—Export / edit data in Excel (→ Sect. 2.3.3).
- ▣ **[Attach]**—Document handling/attachment (→ Sect. 10.5.1).
- ▣ **[Refresh]**—Refresh the screen.
- ▣ **[Open in new window]**—Connected windows, as described further below.

With the button ▣ (*Back*) on the left of the action pane, you can close the current page within the Dynamics 365 client and return to the previous page.

As an alternative to the buttons in the action pane, you can use the action search to execute an activity. Click the Search button ▣ in the action pane (not in the navigation bar—this would start the navigation search) or press the shortcut *Alt + Q* for this purpose, and enter the action name or the action pane button path in the search field. Like in the navigation search, you can limit the entered text to the first characters of the words of the name. You can, for example, use the action search to access the customer balance from the Customer list page as follows: First, press the shortcut *Alt + Q*, then type "bal", and finally press the *Enter* key (you might need to wait for a second before the search result is shown).

2.1.3.6 Detail Forms for Master Data

Unlike list pages, which are primarily designed for viewing a list of records, the primary use of detail forms is to insert, modify, and view the details of individual records.

In order to access a detail form from the related list page, click on a key field in the grid of the list page or press the *Enter* key when the field is active. Key fields are shown as a link in list pages, usually in the first column of the grid (in the example of → Fig. 2.9, this is the column *Account*). The button *Options/ Page options/ Go to/ Details* in the action pane of list pages provides an alternative way to access the detail form.

Detail forms have a similar structure to list pages, and like in list pages, the elements and functions depend on the particular form. The Customer detail form (accessed from the list page *Accounts receivable > Customers > All customers*) in → Fig. 2.10 is an example of the structure of detail forms. The common structure of detail forms includes the following basic elements:

- **Action pane** [1]—Like in list pages (collapsed in → Fig. 2.10).
- **List button** [2]—In the action pane, shows the list pane with the list of records.
- **Filter button and FactBox button** [3]—Buttons on the right for showing the filter pane (→ Sect. 2.1.5) and the FactBoxes.
- **Tabs** [4]—Group fields in line with the functional area.
- **Edit button** [5]—Only shown in the Read mode when pointing at a field, activates the Edit mode (like the button *Edit* in the action pane).
- **FactBoxes** [6]—Show related information (in the same way as in a list page).

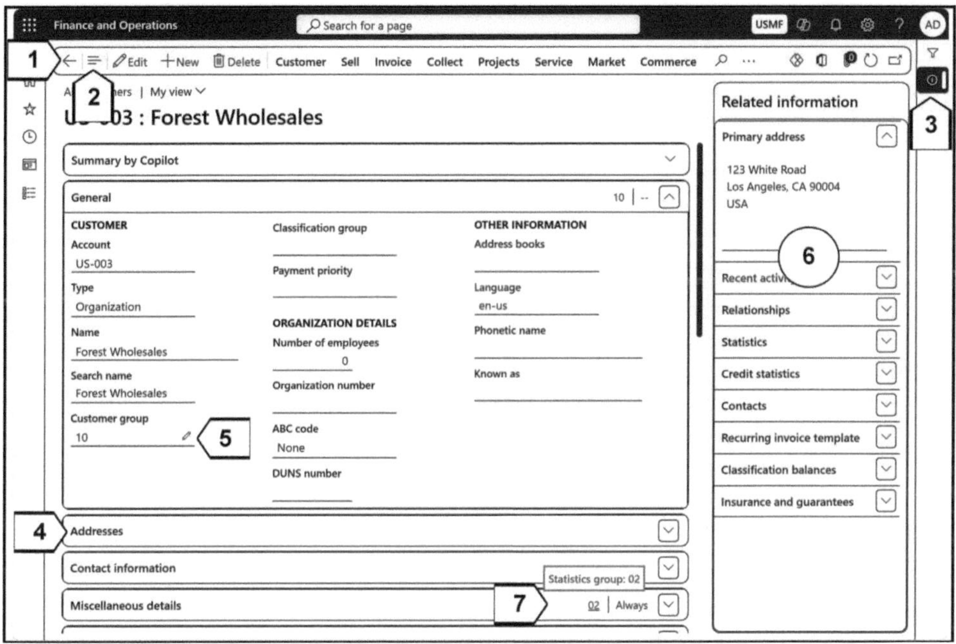

Fig. 2.10   Elements of the customer detail form (in read mode)

You can expand a tab with a click on the particular tab. If you right-click a tab, the context menu will display the options for expanding or collapsing all tabs of the form. **Summary fields** on a Table [7] show core data directly on the tab. If you want to know the field name of a summary field, hover the mouse over it. In the example of → Fig. 2.10, you can view the statistics group "02" in a summary field on the tab *Miscellaneous details*.

With the button ▭ (*Show list/ Hide list*) [2] in the action pane of detail forms, you can show the list pane with the list of records. If you select a record in the list pane, the related detail data are shown immediately, and you can use the list pane to move easily from one record to the next. If the list pane is shown and you want to hide it, click the—now acti-vate—button ▣ (*Show list/ Hide list*) again.

In → Sect. 2.1.4, you can find more details on editing records, working with tabs, and other options that are available in list pages and detail forms.

If you want to return from a detail form to the list page, click the button ▭ (*Back*) on the left of the action pane, or press the shortcut *Alt + Back arrow* or the *Esc* key, or click the *Back* button of your browser.

2.1.3.7 Detail Forms for Transaction Data

Apart from the detail forms for master data, which are described above, there are detail forms for transaction data (e.g., the Sales order form in → Fig. 2.11). Like in the master data pages, click on a key field (shown as a link) in the grid of a list page for transaction

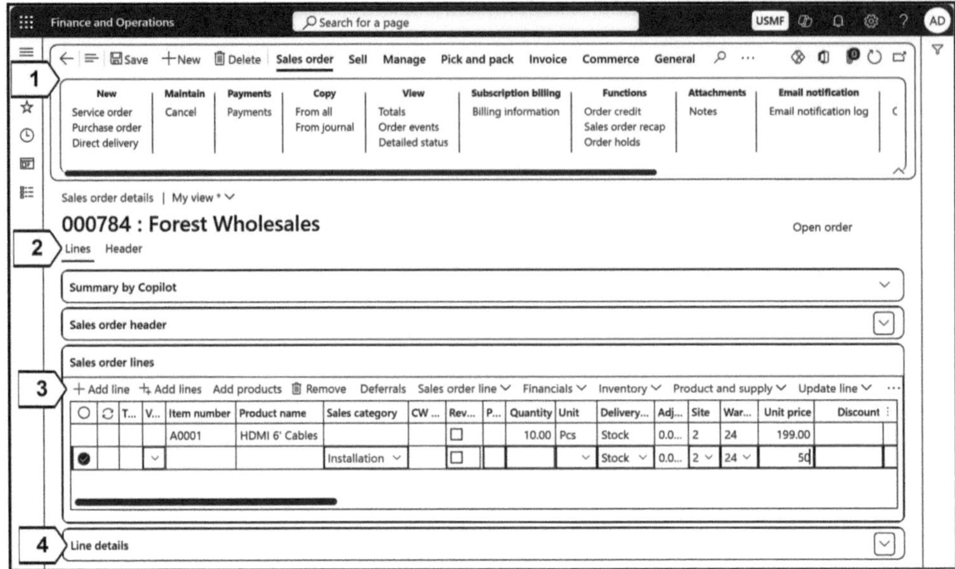

Fig. 2.11 Elements in the transaction detail form for sales orders

data to open the related detail form. When you access a transaction detail form, it is shown in the Lines view, in which you can view or edit the lines (e.g., sales order lines).

In the **toolbar** [3] above the grid with the lines, there are buttons for actions on the selected line—for example, the button *Remove* to delete the record in that line.

The **action pane** [1] at the top of the form contains the buttons for actions at the header level—for example, the button *Delete* to delete a complete order.

If you want to view or edit details that are not shown in the line grid, expand the tab **Line details** [4]. The tab *Line details* contains multiple sub-tabs that structure the fields of the line.

Some basic header data are shown on a respective tab (e.g., the tab *Sales order header* in → Fig. 2.11) in the Lines view. In order to access all available fields of the header record, open the Header view with the button **Header** [2] or with the shortcut *Ctrl + Shift + H*. In the Header view, the button **Lines** (or the shortcut *Ctrl + Shift + L*) takes you back to the Lines view.

2.1.3.8 Inquiries and Setup Forms

In comparison to detail forms, inquiries and setup forms have a simple layout. In Dynamics 365, there are the following types of simple forms:

- **Simple lists**—Contain all relevant fields directly in the grid (e.g., the form *Accounts receivable > Setup > Customer groups*).
- **Detail forms with list pane**—Detail forms, which you can directly access from the menu and which show the list pane by default, include the same functionality as the

master data detail forms described above (e.g., the form *Accounts receivable > Payment setup > Terms of payment*).

- **Parameter forms**—Show a table of contents with sections on the left and related data on the right (e.g., the form *Accounts payable > Setup > Accounts payable parameters*).

2.1.3.9 Connected Browser Windows

Connected browser windows provide the option to view connected information side by side. You can use them, for example, if you want to view the related vendor transactions when switching between vendor records.

In the example of the vendor transactions, open the Vendor list page (*Accounts payable > Vendors > All vendors*) and click the button *Vendor/ Transactions/ Transactions* in the action pane. In the vendor transactions, click the button ▣ (*Open in new window*) in the action pane. The vendor transactions are subsequently shown in a new browser window. The new browser window is dynamically linked to the main browser window, which is showing the previous form (in the example, the Vendor list page). Moving from one vendor to another in the main window automatically updates the data shown in the connected transaction window.

2.1.4   Working with Records

In Microsoft Dynamics 365, you can work with the mouse, but you can also use the keyboard for many actions. Apart from keyboard shortcuts, the navigation search and the action search enable entering data quickly without a mouse.

In the context menu, which you can open by right-clicking a control (e.g., a button or a field name) in a detail form or a list page, the option *View shortcuts* opens a window that shows all available shortcuts. In the appendix of this book, you can find an overview of the basic shortcuts in Dynamics 365.

2.1.4.1 Structure of Pages and Forms

When you open a regular form, no matter whether you access it from a tile or link in a workspace, or from a menu item in the navigation pane, Dynamics 365 shows the related list page.

List pages are the starting point for the work in a particular area. You can search and filter records in a list page, and buttons in the action pane provide the option to edit, delete, and insert data in line with your permissions. The columns in a list page only show a limited number of fields.

Detail forms include all available fields of the selected record. If you want to access the detail form from a list page, click the related key field (shown as a link in the grid of the list page, usually in the first column). In order to show the fields in a tab of a detail form, you can expand the tab with a click on the tab or—after switching to the particular tab with the *Tab* key—with the *Enter* key. If you want to collapse a particular tab, click the tab header again (or press the shortcut *Alt + 0*). All available options for expanding and collapsing tabs are shown after a right-click on a tab. If you expand all tabs, you can easily scroll the complete record (e.g., with your mouse wheel) without additional mouse clicks.

2.1.4.2 Edit Mode and Read Mode

When you open a list page or a detail form, it is, by default, shown in Read mode (also called "View mode") to prevent unintended changes to data.

In Read mode, editable fields show the icon ☑ (*Edit*) on the right when moving the mouse to such a field. If you want to switch to the Edit mode (in which you can update records), click on this icon. Apart from the icon, you can also use the *F2* key or the button *Edit* in the action pane to switch to the Edit mode. If the Edit mode is active in a list page and you open the related detail form, the detail form is also in Edit mode. If you want to return to the Read mode, press the *F2* key again (or click the button *Options/ Edit/ Read mode* in the action pane).

If you want to start a particular form in Edit mode all the time, click the button *Options/ Personalize/ Always open for editing* in the action pane of the form. You can also set your general default mode to the Edit mode or to the Read mode (setting in the field *Default view/edit mode* on the tab *Preferences* in your user options).

2.1.4.3 Inserting Records

If you want to insert a record in a list page or a detail form (e.g., a new customer in the Customer form), press the shortcut *Alt + N* or click the button *New* in the action pane. Apart from list pages and detail forms, some workspaces also contain a button in the action pane for creating new records.

In some forms, a *Quick create* dialog (→ Fig. 2.12) is shown on the right when you create a new record. This dialog contains the core fields of the record and helps in easily inserting records. Once you close the dialog with the button *Save* at the bottom, Dynamics 365 opens the related detail form in which you can enter additional data. Depending on the page, a button *Save and open* with further options is shown in the dialog. With this button, you can, for example, directly switch from the *Create customer* dialog to a new sales quotation.

If there is no *Quick create* dialog in a particular page, inserting a new record opens the detail form with an empty record, in which you can enter the required data. If you use a template (→ Sect. 2.2.3), the new record is not empty but receives default values from the template for the content of the fields.

In the lines of a transaction form (e.g., in the sales order lines), you can press the *Down arrow* key in the last line of the grid to create a new record.

If you have started inserting a record with a mandatory field and you want to cancel the action, you might need to delete the record, even if you have not entered any data. Alternatively, press the *Esc* key and close the form without saving. If you are in a *Quick create* dialog, click the button *Cancel* at the bottom.

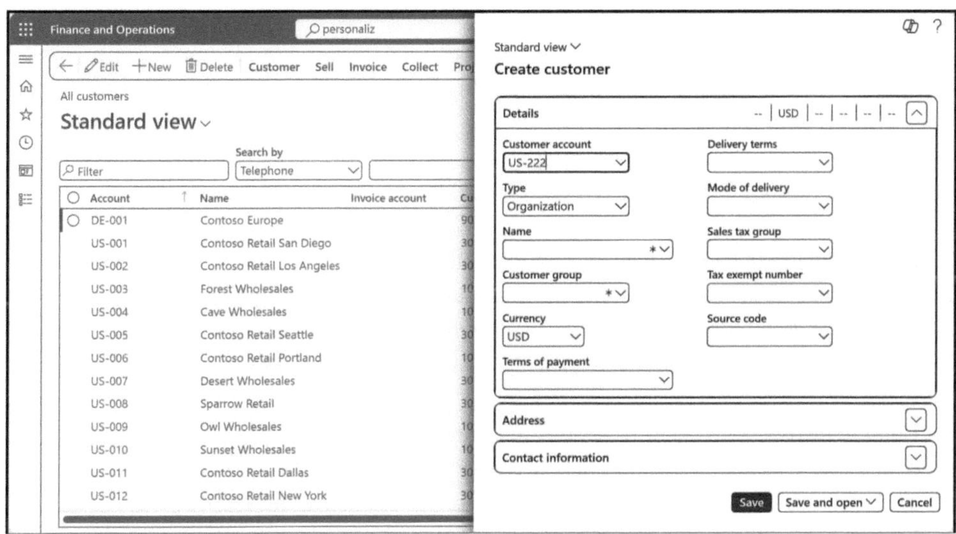

Fig. 2.12 The Quick create dialog for a new customer

> *Note*: Apart from manually inserting records field by field, there are two options to insert data from Excel—either simply copy and paste lines from Excel (→ Sect. 2.2.2) or use the option *Open in Microsoft Office* (→ Sect. 2.3.3).

2.1.4.4 Editing Data

Before you can edit a record in a list page or a detail form, you have to make sure that you are in Edit mode. In order to switch between the fields of the form, you can use the mouse, the *Tab* key, or the shortcut *Shift + Tab*.

You can manually save a record with the shortcut *Alt + S* (or *Ctrl + S*), or with the button *Save* in the action pane. But it is not required to save a record explicitly. Dynamics 365 saves every change of a record automatically when you leave the record—switching to another record or closing the form with the button ◁ (*Back*) in the action pane or with the *Back* button of the browser. If you close a form with the *Esc* key, a dialog will ask whether you want to save the changes.

If you have entered or modified data and you do not want to save the changes, press the shortcut *Ctrl + Shift + F5* or click the button *Options/ Edit/ Revert* to restore the record from the database. But this is only possible as long as the changes have not already been saved manually or automatically (e.g., by moving to another record).

Another option not to save changes is to close the form with the *Esc* key or the shortcut *Alt + Shift + Q* (as long as the changes have not been saved already).

2.1.4.5 Deleting Data

You can delete the content of an input field with the *Delete* key. If you want to delete a complete record, select the record and click the button *Delete* in the action pane (or press the shortcut *Alt + Del* or *Alt + F9*).

In some cases, Dynamics 365 is showing an error message that prevents deleting a record—for example, if you want to delete a customer with open transactions.

2.1.4.6 Elements in List Pages and Detail Forms

List pages and detail forms contain common elements. In → Fig. 2.13, you can view the Bank account detail form (*Cash and bank management > Bank accounts > Bank accounts*), which is an example of a detail form with the following elements:

- **Field groups** [1]—Group fields by functional areas.
- **Mandatory fields** [2]—Show a red frame and the icon ⊞ (*Required field indicator*). The required content must be entered before you can save the record.
- **Sliders** [3]—Sliders and checkboxes are used for a binary choice (Yes/No). If you want to select a checkbox (set a slider to "Yes"), click it with the mouse or press the *Spacebar* key while the cursor is on the field.
- **Date fields** [4]
- **Lookup fields with a fixed list of values** [5]
- **Lookup fields with a related main Table** [6]

Date fields contain a calendar icon ▦ which you can use to select a particular date. In your user options, the setting in the field *Date, time, and number format* on the tab *Preferences*

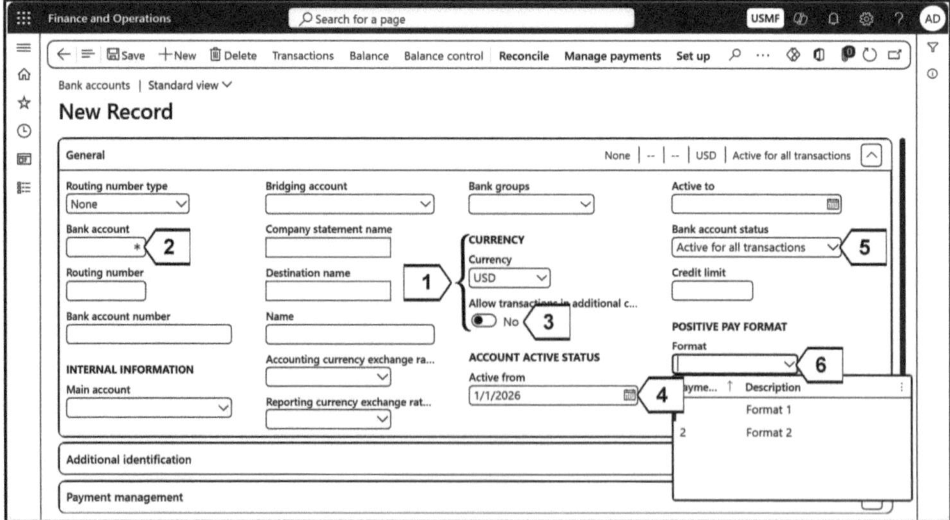

Fig. 2.13 Types of fields in the Bank account detail form

determines the format in which all date and number fields are shown in your web client. If you enter a date manually, date separators like "." or "/" are not required. For a date in the current year, you can optionally enter only day and month (e.g., "0523" if you use the US date format). If you want to insert the current date, you can enter the character "t" (or "d" for the session date) instead of a date.

Numeric fields support basic arithmetical expressions. You can, for example, type "= 55 * 1.1" instead of "60.50"to enter an amount of "55.00 plus 10 %".

2.1.4.7 Lookup Fields and Table Reference

In a lookup field, you can only enter or select a value that is included in a predefined list of values. With regard to the setup of this list of values, there are two types of lookup fields:

- **Lookup fields with a fixed list of values**, which is given by Dynamics 365 enumerable types (*Enums*)—e.g., *Bank account status* [5] in → Fig. 2.13.
- **Lookup fields with a related main table**, which contains permitted values—e.g., *Pay format* [6] in → Fig. 2.13.

In Edit mode, both types of lookup fields show the lookup button ⌄ on the right of the field. Lookup fields with a related main table are shown as a link (similar to Internet links), both in Edit mode and in Read mode. This link provides access to the corresponding main table form (in the example of → Fig. 2.13, to the Pay format form).

When you start typing characters into a lookup field, a drop-down menu (lookup) that uses the typed characters as a filter on the key field of the related table will pop up automatically. In many lookups, this filter also includes the column *Name*. If you enter, for example, the character "F" in the field *Customer account* of a sales order, the lookup that pops up automatically will show all records that start with "F" in the customer name (if there is no customer number starting with "F").

If you want to open the lookup manually, click the lookup button ⌄ on the right of the respective field (or press the shortcut *Alt + Down arrow*).

In the lookup, you can select a record with a mouse click (or with the *Enter* key once the respective line in the lookup is active). If a lookup is showing numerous lines and you want to reduce the number of lines that are displayed, you can use the grid column filter and the sorting options (→ Sect. 2.1.5). In the example of → Fig. 2.13, you can click on the column header field *Description* in the lookup to enter a filter on the field *Description* of the pay formats.

In addition to the lookup, the table reference of fields with a related main table provides the option to access the detail form of the related main table. If you want to insert a new pay format in the example of → Fig. 2.13, you can open the Pay format form directly from the field *Format*. For this purpose, the table reference is shown as a link that you can use to access the related detail form with a mouse click. Alternatively, you can access the related detail form with the option *View details* in the context menu of the field. In order to open the context menu, select the field and press the shortcut *Ctrl + F10*, or right-click the lookup button ☑ or the field label (not the field itself).

After opening the related detail form, you can edit records in the same way as after accessing the form from the navigation pane. Apart from using the table reference as an easy way to insert and edit related data, you can use it to view the details of related records—you can, e.g., click on a sales order number in the invoice inquiry to access the corresponding sales order immediately.

2.1.4.8 Product Information Dialog

If you click the link (or use the option *View details*) in the item number field, Dynamics 365 does not immediately show the Released product form (which is the form for managing items), but the *Product information* dialog. This dialog displays the core data of the item. In many cases, these core data are sufficient, and you don't need to access the details in the Released product form. But if you need to access more details, click the link in the field *Item number* of the dialog to open the related Released product detail form.

2.1.4.9 Segmented Entry Control

A special type of lookup is used in ledger account fields—for example, in the lines of financial journals. Since the ledger account is one field with multiple segments (the main account and applicable financial dimensions), there is a special control for lookup and data entry—the segmented entry control ($\rightarrow$ Sect. 9.3.1).

2.1.4.10 Message Bar and Action Center

If there is an issue with an action that you execute in Dynamics 365 (e.g., if you try to enter a main account that does not exist, or to delete a customer with open transactions), an error message is immediately shown in the message bar (below the action pane of the form).

If there is an error or a warning that is generated by an asynchronous operation (processing a batch job), the message is sent to the action center (message center). The button ▣ (*Show messages*) in the navigation bar then indicates the number of unread notifications, and you can click this button to view the recent messages.

In the example of $\rightarrow$ Fig. 2.14, you can view an error message in the message bar and, irrespective of this message, messages in the action center.

2.1.5   Filtering and Sorting

In order to work efficiently in tables with numerous records, it is important to find the right records quickly. For this purpose, Dynamics 365 offers various features for filtering and sorting in list pages and detail forms.

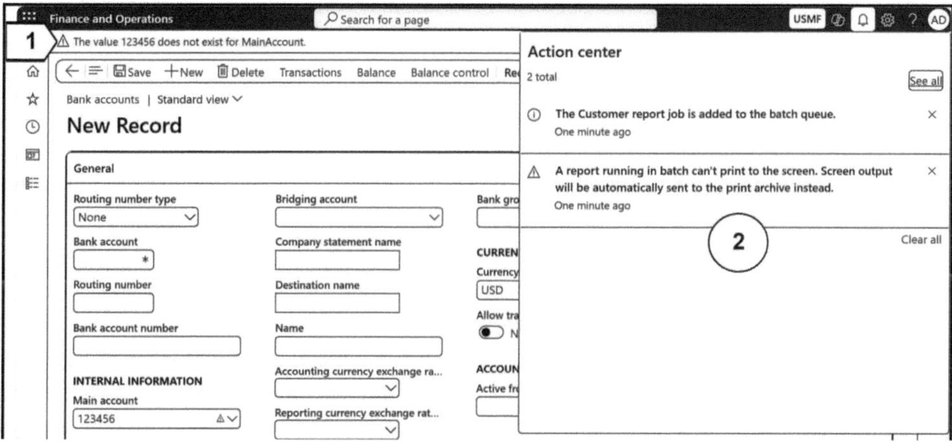

Fig. 2.14 Viewing notifications in the message bar [1] and in the action center [2]

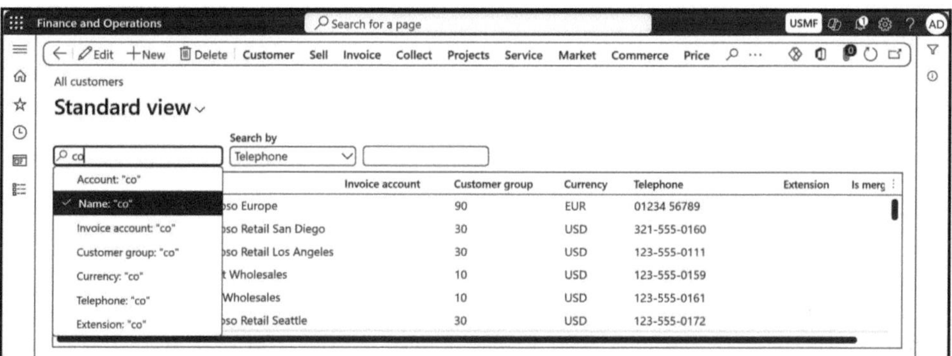

Fig. 2.15 Selecting the filter column in the lookup of a quick filter

2.1.5.1 Quick Filter

In list pages, the quick filter is the easiest way to enter a filter. When you type characters into the quick filter field, a drop-down menu, in which you select the column that you want to use for filtering, pops up automatically.

Once you have activated the filter with the *Enter* key or with the button 🔎 (*Apply filter*) on the left of the quick filter field, the page only displays records in which the content of the selected column starts with the characters entered in the quick filter field. An asterisk (*), which is shown on the right of the view name, indicates that you have modified the view (→ Sect. 2.2.2), in this case by applying a filter.

In → Fig. 2.15, which shows an example of using the quick filter, the filter on customers with a name beginning with the characters "co" is not yet executed.

If you want to clear a quick filter, remove the content in the quick filter field and press the *Enter* key.

2.1.5.2 Filter Pane

The filter pane (→ Fig. 2.16), which is not only available in list pages but also in detail forms, provides the option to apply multiple filter criteria in parallel.

If you want to show the filter pane in a form, click the filter button ▽ on the right of the form (or press the shortcut *Ctrl + F3*). Then, enter the characters that you want to use for filtering in the respective field of the filter pane. In the operator selection on the right above the filter field, you can select whether to use these characters together with the operator "begins with", "contains", "is one of", or one of the other operators. If you want to filter on additional fields, click the button *Add* at the top right of the filter pane and select the respective field. Then activate the filter with the button *Apply*.

Instead of the operator "contains", you can also use the asterisk (*) wildcard together with the "begins with" operator (which is the default operator). This way you can, for example, enter "*ab" in a filter field to filter on all records which contain "ab" in any part of the field—without the need to change the operator.

The operator "matches" provides the option to use manual wildcards and filter expressions as described further below.

If you want to hide the filter pane again, click the—now active—filter button ▽ on the right again, or click in a field in the filter pane and press the *Esc* key. Hiding the filter pane does not clear (reset) the filter. If you want to clear the filter, click the button *Reset* in the filter pane.

2.1.5.3 Grid Column Filter

The grid column filter (→ Fig. 2.17), which is available in list pages and the grid of other forms (also in the grid of lookups), is another option for filtering.

You can access the grid column filter with a click on the header field of the respective column. Alternatively, select a field in the column of the grid and press the shortcut *Ctrl + G*. In the drop-down menu, which is displayed next, you can enter the filter. The operator works the same way as described for the filter pane above.

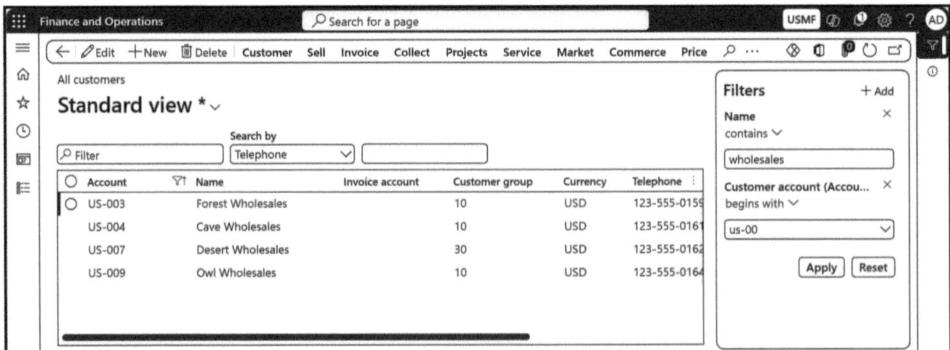

Fig. 2.16 Using the filter pane in a list page

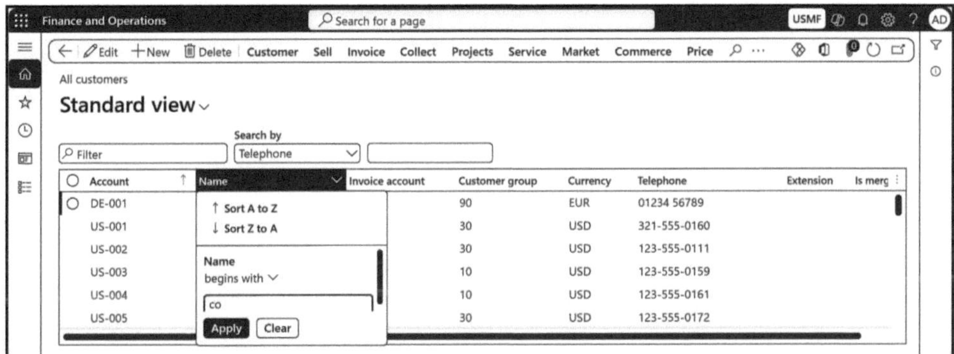

Fig. 2.17   Entering a grid column filter in a list page

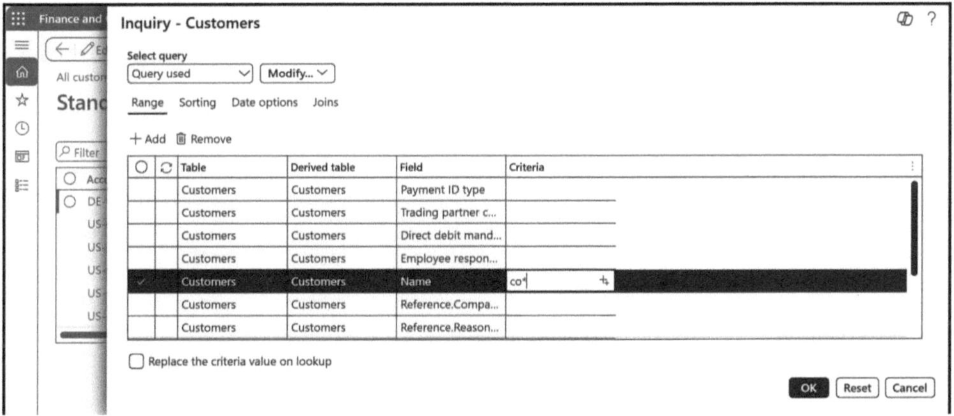

Fig. 2.18   Entering filter criteria in the advanced filter dialog

Once the grid column filter is active, the filter icon ▽ is shown next to the particular column header.

If you want to clear the grid column filter, click on the header field of the respective column to show the drop-down menu again. In the drop-down menu, click the button *Clear*. Another way to clear the filter is to open the filter pane and click the button *Reset*.

2.1.5.4 Advanced Filter

The advanced filter (→ Fig. 2.18) in list pages and in detail forms provides the option to enter more complex filter criteria. You can access the advanced filter, which is shown in a separate dialog on the right, with the shortcut *Ctrl + Shift + F3* (or with the button *Options/ Page options/Advanced Filter or sort* in the action pane). Like the filter pane, the advanced filter provides the option to set a filter on fields that are not shown in the list page or detail form.

When you open the *Advanced filter* dialog, it shows the most common filter fields of the particular form. If you need to enter a criterion on a field that is not shown in the dialog, insert a record in the dialog (press the shortcut *Alt + N* or click the button *Add*). In the new filter line, enter the filter instruction in the columns *Table, Derived table, Field,* and *Criteria.*

The fields *Table* and *Derived table* in a new line by default contain the base table of the page in which you have opened the advanced filter. In case of a simple criterion (i.e., not filtering on a related table), you don't have to change the content of these fields. In the column *Field* (you can use the lookup for the field name), select the field to which you want to apply the filter, and enter the filter criterion in the column *Criteria*. If the selected field in the filter line is a lookup field, you can use a lookup in the column *Criteria* (open the lookup with the button ⊞ on the right of the field or press the shortcut *Alt + Down arrow*). The way to enter filter expressions in the criteria of an advanced filter, which provides extensive options but is more complex, is described below.

Once you have entered the filter criteria, close the *Advanced filter* dialog with the button *OK*. The filter is active now, and the page only shows matching records.

2.1.5.5 Filter Expressions

If you use the quick filter in a list page, the page shows all records that start with the characters that you have entered in the quick filter field (in the column that you have selected for the filter).

In all other filter options, you can use further filter expressions—the filter pane and the grid column filter include the operator "matches" for this purpose. An overview of the most important filter expressions is shown in → Table 2.1.

If you want to find records with a blank value in a particular field, enter ""in the corresponding filter field.

2.1.5.6 Saving Filter Settings

If you need particular filter criteria frequently, you can save them in the *Advanced filter* dialog. For this purpose, click the button *Modify/ Save as* in the dialog and enter a filter name in a second dialog that is displayed then.

If you want to apply a saved filter, select it in the lookup field *Select query* of the *Advanced filter* dialog (→ Fig. 2.19).

In addition to the filters that you have saved manually, the filter that you have used the last time is saved automatically for every page. You can select it with the option *Previously used query* in the lookup field *Select query*.

> *Note*: Apart from explicitly saving a filter in the advanced filter, filter settings are also saved with the saved views (→ Sect. 2.2.2).

Table 2.1 Essential filter expressions

Meaning	Sign	Example	Explanation
Equal	=	EU	Field content matches "EU"
Not equal	!	!Gb	Field content does not match "GB"
Interval	..	1..2	Field content from "1" to "2" (incl.)
Greater	>	>1	Field content greater than "1"
Less	<	<2	Field content less than "2"
Is one of	,	1,2	Field content matches "1" or "2";in a filter with "not equal" criteria (e.g.,"!1,!2"), the operator AND is used
Wildcard	*	*E*	Field content contains "E"
	?	?B*	First character unknown, followed by a "B", subsequent characters unknown
2 double quotes	""""	""""	Field content is empty
Date field		<123,126	Field content less than 12/31/2026;enter a date in the filter like in any other date field, including "t" for "today";filter operators (equal, interval, greater, …) work like in any other filter field
Relative date	(day(XX))	(day(−1))	Yesterday (XX is calculated from today's date);include outer parentheses in the filter expression
Relative date range	(DayRange(XX,YY))	(DayRange(−2,1))	From the day before yesterday till tomorrow (the date range is calculated from today's date)

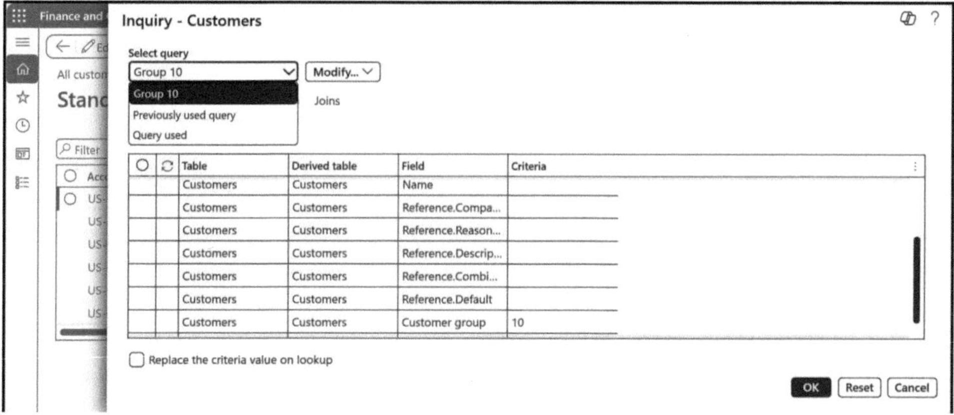

Fig. 2.19 Selecting a saved filter in the Advanced filter dialog

2.1.5.7 Sorting

The grid column filter in list pages not only provides the option to filter records, but you can also sort records. If you sort the records in a list page and open the related detail form, the detail form applies the sorting of the list page.

Alternatively, you can specify sorting criteria in the *Advanced filter* dialog, which contains the tab *Sorting* for this purpose. On this tab, you can enter sorting criteria with table name and field name in one or more lines (similar to a filter criterion).

2.1.5.8 Drop-Down Menu

You should not confuse a filter in a list page or a detail form with the drop-down menu in a lookup field ($\rightarrow$ Sect. 2.1.4). You use the drop-down menu to select the content of a field. The filter functionality, which is described in the current section, aims to select the records that are shown in the list page or detail form.

2.1.6 Help System

If you need help with the functionality, open the Dynamics 365 *Help*, which is available within the whole application. In the help pane, there are two areas:

- **Help**—Links to Microsoft help texts and videos.
- **Task Guides**—From the Microsoft Dynamics Lifecycle Services (LCS).

Whereas task guides describe how to use Dynamics 365 in business processes, the help articles explain the functionality of standard features.

Basic parameters for the help system are specified in the System parameters (*System administration > Setup > System parameters*, section *Help*).

2.1.6.1 Accessing Help

As shown in $\rightarrow$ Fig. 2.20 on the example of the *Item model group*, you can view a short help after pointing the mouse at a field label. If you want to access the full help content, click the button ▨ / *Help* in the navigation bar. The help pane subsequently displays the links to the help articles and the task guides that refer to the particular form.

2.1.6.2 Custom Help with Task Guides

The task recorder ($\rightarrow$ Sect. 10.5.3) provides the option to create recordings that are based on the particular business processes in your enterprise. If you save a recording to a Lifecycle Services (LCS) Business Process Library, which is selected in the section *Help* of the System parameters, the recording will be shown on the tab *Task guides* in the help pane of the related forms.

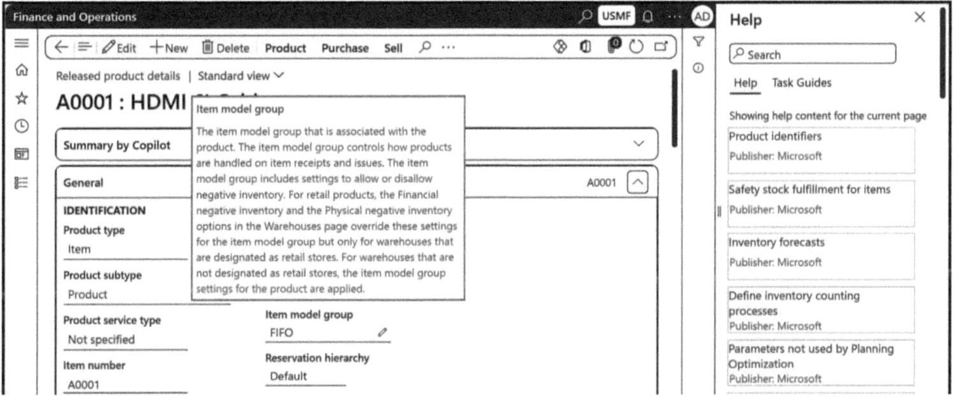

Fig. 2.20   Viewing the Dynamics 365 help in the Released product form

2.1.7   Case Study Exercises

Exercise 2.1—Login and Navigation

Your first task is to access a Dynamics 365 training environment. In this environment, switch to a company that is different from your default company.

Open the list page *All vendors*, first from the *Accounts payable* menu in the navigation pane, and then with the navigation search. Check if there are vendors with a name that starts with an "A". Then open the workspace *Purchase order preparation* and try to find a vendor with a name starting with "A".

Finally, log out of Dynamics 365.

Exercise 2.2—Favorites

Start a web client session in Dynamics 365, select the training company, and show the navigation pane. Add the list page *Released products*, which you can find in the *Product information management* module, to your favorites. Then open this page from the favorites.

Exercise 2.3—Detail Forms

Check the functionality of detail forms in Dynamics 365 in the example of the Vendor detail form, which you access from the Vendor list page (*Accounts payable > Vendors > All vendors*). Review the details of the vendor in the third line of the list page and show an example of a field group and a lookup field with and without a main table.

Then show an example of a slider and a checkbox field. What can you tell about tabs and FactBoxes? How do you proceed if you want to edit the vendor? Is there an option to edit multiple vendors in this form?

Exercise 2.4—Inserting Records

Create a new vendor with the name "##-Exercise 2.4 Inc." (## = your user ID) and any vendor group of your choice. Do not use record templates in this exercise.

> *Note*: If the number sequence for vendor accounts is set to "Manual", you have to enter the vendor number manually. If the *Sales tax group* or the *Tax exempt number* (*VAT number*) is mandatory according to the settings in the Accounts payable parameters, switch to the tab *Invoice and delivery* in the Vendor form and enter the required information.

Exercise 2.5—Lookup Fields

You want to assign a *Buyer group* to the vendor of exercise 2.4. When viewing the lookup of the corresponding field on the tab *Miscellaneous details* in the Vendor form, you notice that the required group is not there. Create the buyer group B-## (## = your user ID) with the option *View details* in this field and select this group for the vendor.

Exercise 2.6—Filtering

In order to get practice with filtering, open the Vendor list page and enter the filters given below.

Use the quick filter and the grid column filter for the first and the second filter task. For the other filter tasks, use the filter pane and the advanced filter. Clear the filter after each task. The filter tasks are as follows:

* All vendors with a name that starts with "T".
* All vendors assigned to the vendor group selected in exercise 2.4.
* All vendors with a name that contains "in".
* Vendors with a number from US-101 to US-103 or higher than US-108 (Use a similar filter if these vendor accounts do not exist).
* Vendors with a number that ends with "1" and a name that contains "of".
* Vendors with an "e" at the second position of the name.
* Vendors with no selected cash discount (the field *Cash discount* is empty).
* Vendors with a name that does **not** start with "C".
* All vendors who are **not** assigned to the *Terms of payment* "Net 30 days".

2.2   Advanced Options

In addition to the core options in the user interface, the personalization features and settings in the user options help you work efficiently in Dynamics 365.

2.2.1 User Options

The user options contain the personal settings for the user interface. They are stored for each user.

2.2.1.1 Settings in the User Options

If you want to access your user options, click the button ⚙ (*Settings*) / *User options* in the navigation bar, or open the menu item *Common > Setup > User options*. Administrators can manage the user options of all users in the user management (*System administration > Users > Users*, button *User options*).

The section *Preferences* in the User options form (→ Fig. 2.21) contains the following main settings for the user environment:

- *Company*—The company that you access when logging on.
- **Initial page**—Select the *Default dashboard*, the *Immersive home*, or a different page (e.g., the Employee self-service portal) as the start page when logging on.
- **Default view/edit mode**—Personal option to set the Read mode or the Edit mode as the default mode for all pages and forms.
- **Language**—Language of the user interface.
- **Date, time, and number format**—Personal setting for the display format of date and number fields.
- **Country/region**—Default for the country/region when entering an address.
- **Document handling**—Enable document handling for the user.

In addition, you can choose an element size and a color theme in the section *Visual*, and settings for workflow management in the section *Workflow*.

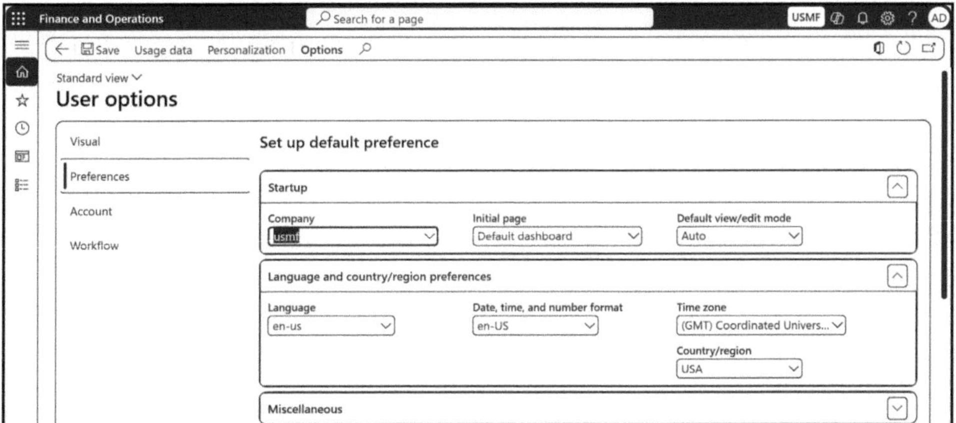

Fig. 2.21 Managing preferences in the user options form

Note: Do not confuse the language setting in the user options with the translator service in a browser like Microsoft Edge. With the translator in the browser, the translation of some labels/names of menu items and fields is different from the labels that you view when selecting the corresponding language in the user options.

2.2.1.2 Usage Data

In order to access the Usage data form with the detailed settings of the particular user, click the button *Usage data* in the action pane of the user options. The usage data, which are stored automatically or manually, include filter settings, form settings, and record templates (user templates).

In the usage data, switch from the section *General* to the other sections if you want to view the usage data of a particular area. The button *Data* provides access to the details of the selected record in the usage data. It is not possible to modify usage data, but with the button *Delete* or the shortcut *Alt + Del*, you can delete usage data records. The button *Reset* in the section *General* deletes all usage data of the user.

2.2.1.3 Personalization Data

With the button *Personalization* in the User options form, you can access the personalizations of the user.

2.2.2   Personalization and Saved Views

Apart from modifications in the development environment that affect all users, changes to the user interface are also possible at a personal level. For this purpose, each user with appropriate permissions can adjust list pages and forms according to personal preferences.

2.2.2.1 Restricted Personalization and Advanced Grid Capabilities

At the restricted personalization access level, available options include changing the column width (drag and drop the borders in the grid header), changing the settings whether the action pane, the tabs, and the FactBoxes are shown in full size or collapsed, and the advanced grid capabilities. Dynamics 365 automatically stores the selected options for each page as a personal setting.

The advanced grid capabilities include the following options:

- **Grid footer**—Displays the number of rows, and—if selected for one or more columns—the column totals.
- **Column totals**—Displays the calculated value (total sum, average, maximum, or minimum) of a numeric column in the grid footer. The option "None" is hiding the calculated value again.
- **Group by column**—Sorts and groups the lines by the content of the selected column. Together with the *Column totals* feature, you can view subtotals.

- **Freeze column**—Keep columns shown on the left when you scroll to the right.
- **Autofit column width**—Like in Excel, double-click on the right of a header field.

In order to display or to hide the **Grid footer**, click the button ⊡ (*Grid options*) on the very right in the grid header and select the option *Show footer*. The footer is automatically shown if you select to show column totals. With the option *Insert columns* in the button ⊡ (*Grid options*), you can show additional columns in the grid—e.g., if you want to display a field in the list page that you can view in the detail form (same function as the option *Add a field* in the Personalization toolbar).

If you want to use the features that refer to a particular column (**Column totals**, **Group by column**, **Freeze column**), right-click the column header field and select the respective option in the drop-down menu (→ Fig. 2.22).

2.2.2.2 Bulk Editing and Pasting from Excel

If the Bulk editing feature is enabled, you can simultaneously update the content of a selected field in multiple records. For this purpose, first select the lines that you want to update in the grid, then click the button ⊡ (*Grid options*) on the right in the grid header and select the option *Edit selected rows*. In a dialog box which is shown next, select the *Field* and the new field content (*Value*) before you click the button *Apply*. After a confirmation dialog, the selected records will be updated accordingly.

As part of the advanced grid capabilities, the option *Paste from Excel* enables copying one or more lines from Excel and pasting the lines into a new line in the grid of a page in Dynamics 365. The structure of the copied columns should match the grid, which you can easily achieve by creating the Excel sheet with an Export to Excel (→ Sect. 2.3.3).

2.2.2.3 Full Personalization

If you need enhanced options to adjust a form according to your preferences, you can use the Personalization window and the Personalization toolbar (→ Fig. 2.23). The personalization options are available in each list page and detail form.

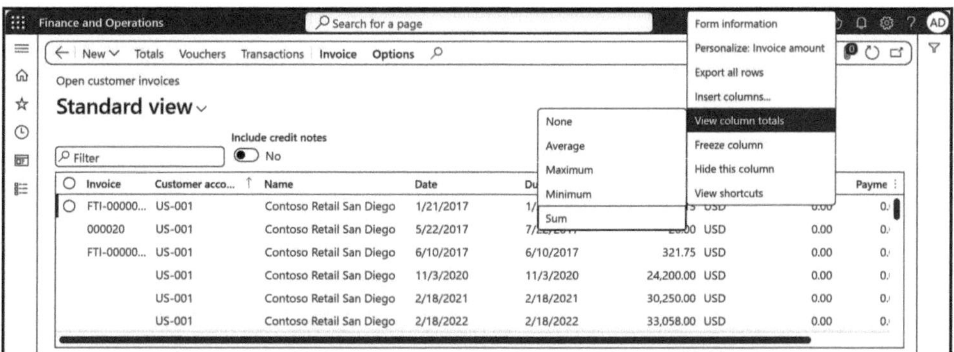

Fig. 2.22 Selecting to *view column totals* in a grid (right-click on the column header)

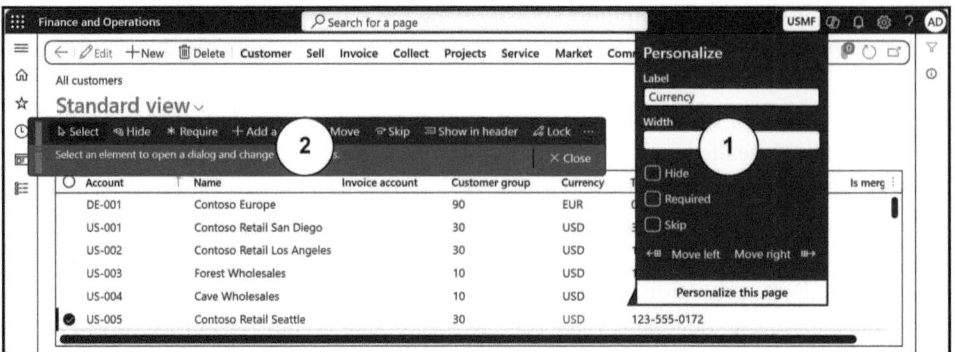

Fig. 2.23 Viewing the Personalization window [1] and the Personalization toolbar [2]

In order to access the Personalization window, select the option *Personalize* in the context menu of an element—you can open the context menu with a right-click on an element label (e.g., a field label), or with the shortcut *Ctrl + F10*. In the Personalization window of the element (field or button), you can override several standard settings—for example, by entering a personal field label, by hiding the element, or by setting a field as mandatory (required).

The Personalization toolbar, which you can access with the link *Personalize this page* in the Personalization window or with the button *Options/ Personalize/ Personalize this page* in the action pane, provides additional personalization options.

In order to adjust a form with the Personalization toolbar, click the applicable button in the Personalization toolbar first and then select the element (field, field group, tab, button) that you want to personalize. The Personalization toolbar includes the button *Select* (show the Personalization window for the selected element), *Hide* (hide the element from the page), *Require* (designate a required data entry for the field), *Add a field* (show one or more additional fields), *Move* (change the location of the element), *Skip* (skip in the tab sequence), *Show in header* (in forms with tabs, show the field as summary field on the tab), and *Lock* (prevent editing). When you click a button in the Personalization toolbar, the next step is to click the element (field or button in the page) on which you want to execute the action. If you click the button *Add a field*, select the page area to which you want to add the field first. Then select the respective field (adding multiple fields is possible) in the dialog that is shown next.

Settings in the personalization apply immediately. If you click the button ■ (*More*) on the right of the Personalization toolbar, you can access the option to reset the form to the standard layout (button *Clear*) or to import/export a personalization.

2.2.2.4 Personalization of Workspaces and the Dashboard

Apart from changing the layout of list pages and detail forms, personalization also allows adding a list page to a workspace. For this purpose, click the button *Options/ Personalize/ Add to workspace* in the action pane of the list page that you want to add, and select the appropriate *Workspace* and *Presentation* (tile, list, or link) in the related drop-down menu before you click the button *Configure* there. In the dialog that is shown next, select the applicable options for the presentation layout. Once you have finished the configuration, the list page is shown as an additional list, tile, or link in the—now personalized—workspace.

In workspaces, the Personalization window for tiles includes the option to pin a tile to the dashboard. Your dashboard then additionally contains the selected tile, and you can directly access the form that is linked to this tile from the dashboard.

It is also possible to create a new workspace via personalization. Use the option *Add a page* in the Personalization window for the *Workspaces* pane of the dashboard for this purpose.

2.2.2.5 Custom Fields

In addition to the adjustment of the layout of the user interface, the personalization includes the option to create new fields for a form. The dialog for adding fields, which you can open with the button *Add a field* in the Personalization toolbar or with the option *Insert columns* in the button ▦ (*Grid options*) of a list page, includes the button *Create new field* for this purpose (→ Fig. 2.24).

If you click this button, a second dialog is shown in which you enter the *Table name*, *Name prefix*, *Type*, and *Label* for the new field. Once you confirm the update, the new field is included in the *Insert fields* personalization dialog of the list page or detail form that you have started to personalize.

You can manage all custom fields in the menu item *System administration > Setup > Custom fields* (select the relevant *Table* in the list pane on the left).

If other users should have access to the new field, they have to use personalized views. For this purpose, it is also possible to publish, export, and import saved views.

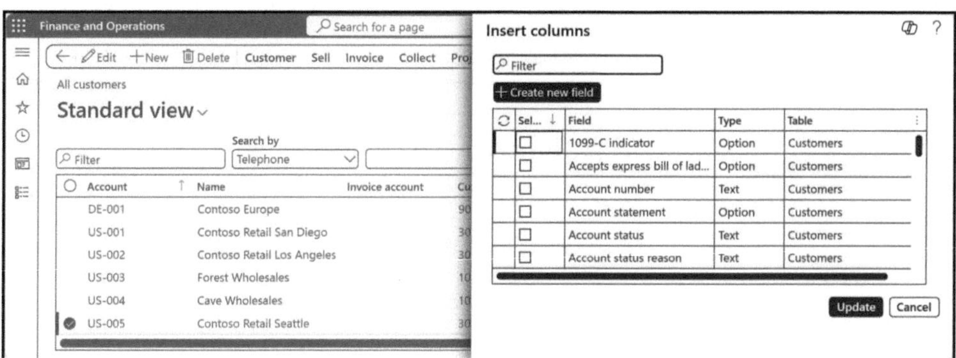

Fig. 2.24 Creating a new field with the personalization

2.2.2.6 Saved Views

With the Saved views feature, you can store one or more personalized versions of a page, a form, a workspace, or a dialog as personalized views, and use the views on your own or distribute them to other users.

The view determines the screen layout and the applied filter. When you access a form in Dynamics 365, the *Standard view* is the general default for the view name. A click on the view name (in → Fig. 2.25, on the default name *Standard view*) opens the *View selector* lookup in which you can select a different view.

If you filter or personalize a form, an asterisk (*) appears next to the current view name. In case you want to use the modified view (with its personalization and filter) again at a later time, either save the changes to the current view name (click the button *Save* in the *View selector*) or to a new view name (click the button *Save as*). When saving to a new name, a dialog is shown in which you can enter the name, a short description, and optionally set the slider *Pin as default view* (personal default) to "Yes". The section *Legal entity access* in this dialog provides the option to select whether the new view should be available in all or only in selected companies.

With the button ⊡ / *Manage my views* at the bottom of the *View selector*, you can change the initial settings later on. If you want to make a view available for others and have appropriate permissions, click the button *Publish* to release the view at the level of user roles (security roles, see → Sect. 10.2.2).

2.2.2.7 Personalization Setup

In the personalization setup (*System administration > Setup > Personalization*), settings in the section *System settings* control whether personalization is allowed in general. In the section *User settings*, there is the option to override the general settings at the level of individual users.

The section *Personal views* contains the views that have been created by the users. With the buttons in the toolbar above the grid, you can *Publish*, *Export*, or *Delete* the personal

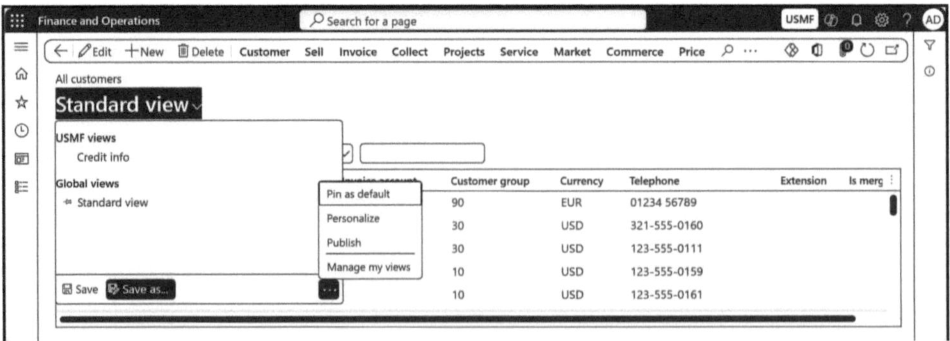

Fig. 2.25 Changing and managing personal views

views. If you want to import exported views, click the button *Import views* in the action pane.

In the section *Published views*, you can manage all views that are published. The section *Unpublished views* contains the views that are not published currently—primarily imported views, but also unpublished views (unpublish with the corresponding button in the section *Published views*).

2.2.3   Record Information and Templates

The *Record information* dialog in Dynamics 365 provides access to data and to general features that are not immediately visible in list pages or detail forms.

2.2.3.1 Options in the Record Information Dialog

In order to open the *Record information* for a record in a list page or detail form, select the record and click the button *Options/ Page options/ Record info*. In the *Record information* dialog that is shown next (→ Fig. 2.26), you can select to execute the following actions on the selected record:

- **Rename**—Change the content of the key field in the current record.
- **Show all fields** and **Database log**—View detailed data of the current record.
- **Script**—Create an insert script with data from the current record.
- **Company accounts template** and **User template**—Create a record template.

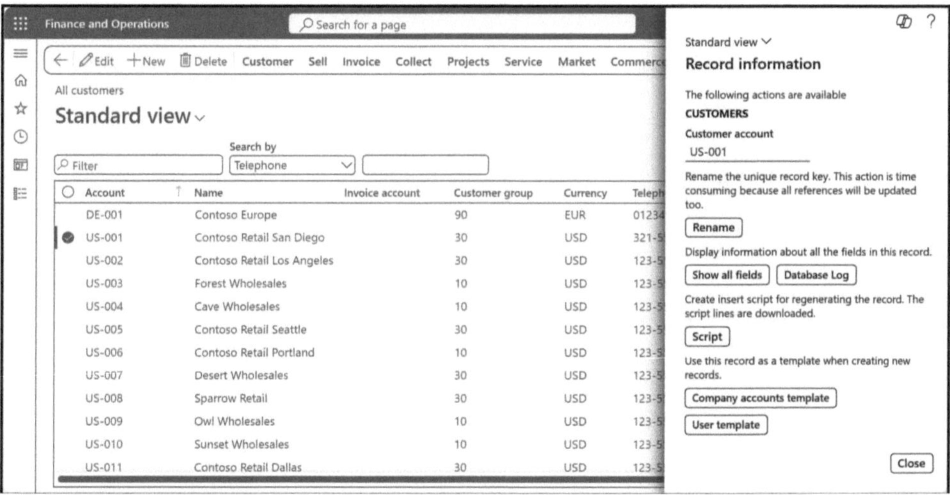

Fig. 2.26 The record information dialog in the customer list page

Note: Depending on your permissions and the Dynamics 365 configuration, not all of these options are available.

2.2.3.2 Renaming

The button *Rename* in the *Record information* dialog provides the option to change the content of the key field of the selected record. Renaming opens a second dialog, in which you enter the new field value (e.g., the new customer number).

The execution of renaming can be a time-consuming activity. The reason is that all record references within Dynamics 365 are updated in parallel. If you modify, for example, a customer number, the update does not only include the customer table itself, but also the customer transactions, the sales orders, and all other tables that contain the customer number. You should take into account that the update only includes references within Dynamics 365. Other applications and external partners (e.g., customers) have to execute the update separately.

For this reason, renaming is an exceptional activity that should be coordinated with the system administrator, and which is usually secured by appropriate permission settings.

2.2.3.3 Show all Fields and Database Log

The button *Show all fields* in the *Record information* dialog displays the content of all fields of the selected record. You can use this feature if you want to know the content of table fields that are not shown in the regular interface of a particular list page or detail form.

The button *Database log* in the *Record information* dialog opens a log file, which shows the updates on the selected record. As a prerequisite, logging for the particular table has to be enabled in the menu item *System administration > Setup > Database log > Database log setup*.

2.2.3.4 Record Templates

Based on the record that you have selected when accessing the *Record information* dialog, you can set up a template. If you subsequently create a new record in the original form, you can select this (or another) template to initialize the record with the content of the template. You can, for example, set up a template for domestic vendors and a template for foreign vendors in the Vendor form to initialize new vendors with the correct posting groups.

Within the record templates, there are the following types:

- **User templates**—Only available to the current user.
- **Company accounts templates**—Available to all users.

A user template is only available to the user who has created the template. You can create a user template with the button *User template* in the *Record information* dialog. In a second dialog, enter the name and a short description of the template. The new template is a copy of the record that you have selected when opening the *Record information* dialog.

User templates are stored in your usage data, and it is not possible to modify them. If a user template is not required anymore, you can delete it in the usage data. For this purpose, click the button ⚙ (*Settings*) / *User options* in the navigation bar, then click the button *Usage data* in the user options, and in the usage data, switch to the section *Record templates*. Alternatively, you can delete a user template with the shortcut *Alt + Del* or *Alt + F9* in the *Template selection* dialog (→ Fig. 2.27).

Company accounts templates, unlike user templates, are available to all users. You can create a company accounts template with the button *Company accounts template* in the *Record information* dialog.

If you want to view or modify a company accounts template later, open the menu item *Common > Setup > Record templates*. On the tab *Overview* in the Record template form, select the table to which the template refers. Then switch to the tab *Templates*, in which you can edit or delete the template.

If there are record templates for a particular form, they are shown in a *Template selection* dialog whenever you create a record in this form. In the example of → Fig. 2.27, you can view the *Template selection* dialog, which is displayed when you create a customer in the Customer form (in case there is a customer template).

In the *Template selection* dialog, select the appropriate template and click the button *OK* to apply it to the new record. You can recognize company accounts templates by the icon 📝 and user templates by the icon 🖳. If you do not want to apply a template, select the template "Blank". In the column on the right of the template selection, you can optionally select a template that you want to make the default template. If you set the slider *Do not ask again* at the bottom of the *Template selection* dialog to "Yes", the default template is automatically used without showing the template selection dialog when inserting a record afterward. If you want to view the template selection dialog when creating new records

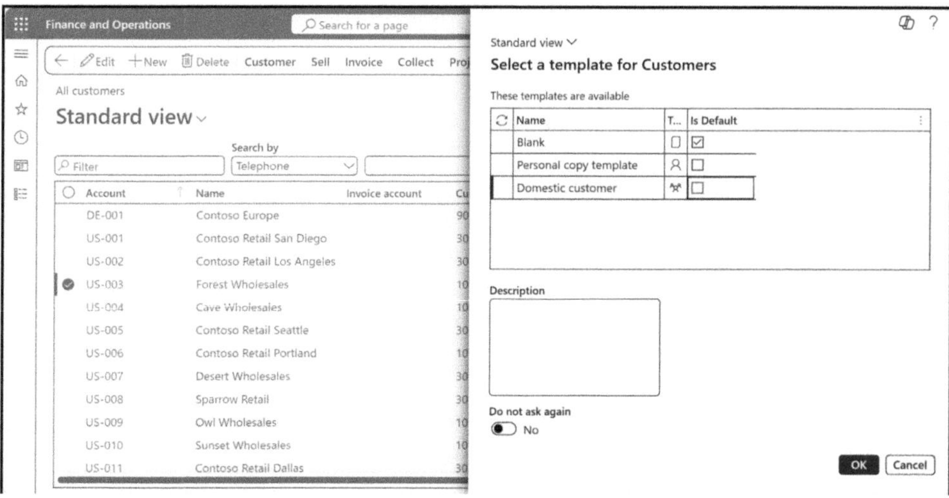

Fig. 2.27 Selecting a template in the Template selection dialog

again, click the button *Show template selection*, which is displayed in the *Record informa-tion* dialog in this case.

2.2.4   Case Study Exercises

Exercise 2.7—User Options
Review the username and other settings in your user options. In the visual options, select the dark green color theme and the small element size. Then select the training company as the company that you access when you logging on.

Exercise 2.8—Personalization
Open the Vendor list page and create a new view "My vendors" with the following personalizations:

- Show additional columns with the *Terms of payment* and the *Cash discount*
- Group the list by vendor group (column *Group*)
- Only show vendors with a cash discount (the field *Cash discount* is not empty)
- Show the number of displayed vendors in the footer

The new view should not be a default and should only be available in the current company. Once you have finished these tasks, save the view with the name given above.
   Then close the form, open it again, and select the new view.

Exercise 2.9—Record Templates
Set up a user template that is based on the vendor of exercise 2.4. Then, create a new vendor with default data from this template.

2.3   Printing and Reporting

Depending on the requirements, you have several options for viewing and analyzing data. These options include Dynamics 365 standard reports, Microsoft Office integration, and Business Intelligence tools (including Microsoft Power BI).

2.3.1   Printing Standard Reports

In Dynamics 365, there are the following options to print a report on a local or network printer, or to export it as a file in a selected format (e.g., PDF):

- **Print browser pages**—Print any list page or detail form as a web page with the page printing features of the browser.
- **Download report previews**—Print a report to the screen (print preview) and export a PDF or Word file from the preview.
- **Print reports directly**—Send a report directly to a printer.

Printing a Dynamics 365 page (i.e., the content currently shown in the browser) from the browser, which works like printing any other web page, does not require print settings in Dynamics 365. The print layout may be different in different browsers (Microsoft Edge, Google Chrome, or others).

Standard reports in Dynamics 365 are formatted documents that are generated with the Microsoft SQL Server Reporting Services (SSRS). When you print a standard report, you can either download a PDF/Word file from the print preview or send the document directly to a local printer or a network printer. If you want to send documents directly to a printer, the *Document Routing Agent* has to be installed and configured.

2.3.1.1 Network Printer Setup

In a Dynamics 365 environment, the Document Reporting Services, which are required for printing standard reports, are hosted in Microsoft Azure. If you want to connect your printers to the Azure services, install the *Document Routing Agent* on one or more computers/servers in your network.

You can download the *Document Routing Agent* from the Network printer form (*Organization administration > Setup > Network printers*). Click the button *Options/ Application/ Download document routing agent installer* in this form and install the *Document Routing Agent*. Then open the document routing agent and click the button *Settings* in the toolbar of the routing agent. In the settings, enter the *Dynamics 365 F&O URL* (web address of your Dynamics 365 application) and the *Azure AD Tenant* (Microsoft Entra ID tenant of your organization) before you click the button *OK* and *Sign In*. Finally, click the button *Printers* in the routing agent and put a checkmark in front of the printers (the form shows the printers installed on the local computer) that you want to use in Dynamics 365.

The Network printer form in Dynamics 365 then shows the printers that have been enabled in one or more *Document Routing Agents*. In Edit mode, select the option "Yes" in the column *Active* of this form for all printers that should be available in the current company.

2.3.1.2 Printing Options

In the different modules of Dynamics 365, the standard reports are included in the folder *Inquiries and reports*. In addition, some list pages and detail forms contain buttons to start particular standard reports—you can, for example, print a customer account statement with the button *Collect/ Customer balances/ Statements* in the Customer page (*Accounts receivable > Customers > All customers*).

If you start a standard report in the menu, or in a list page or detail form, the report dialog is shown first, in which you can specify filter criteria and the print destination. In the example of → Fig. 2.28, you can view the dialog of the Customer report (*Accounts receivable > Inquiries and reports > Customers > Customer report*) with a filter on the customer group.

It is not possible to enter filter criteria directly in the report dialog. Click the button *Filter* on the tab *Records to include* of the report dialog to open a filter dialog for this purpose. The filter dialog for reports works similarly to the advanced filter in list pages and detail forms. Apart from the filter criteria on the tab *Range*, you can specify sorting criteria on the tab *Sorting*. Once you close the filter dialog, the selected filter is shown in the report dialog.

On the tab *Destination* of the report dialog, the button *Change* opens the *Print destination* dialog, in which you can select the destination for the output:

- **Print archive**—Saves the report to the print archive.
- **Screen**—Shows a report preview on the screen.
- **Printer**—Prints the report on the selected printer (available printers are specified in the Network printer form described above).
- **File**—Downloads the report to a CSV, Excel, Word, HTML, XML, or PDF file.
- **E-mail**—Sends the report to an e-mail recipient.

Once you have entered the print destination and the filter criteria in the report dialog, click the button *OK* to print the report. The settings in the report dialog are automatically stored in your user options and initialize the report dialog when you print the selected report again. You can change the filter criteria and the print destination as required, then.

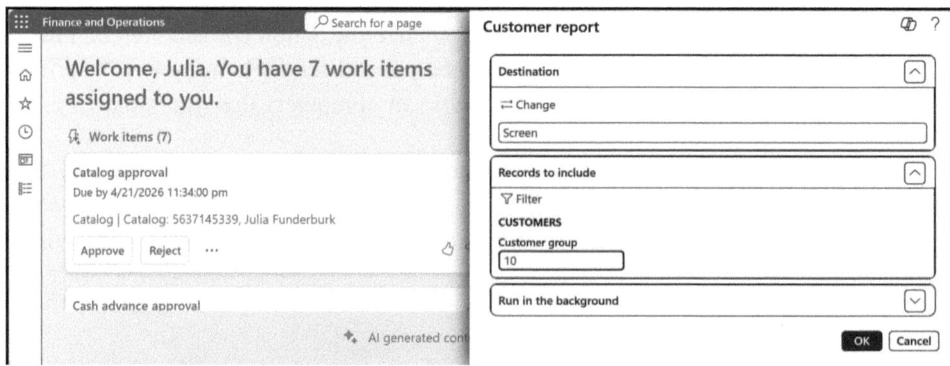

Fig. 2.28 Report dialog for the customer report

2.3.1.3 Print Preview

If you select the option "Screen" as the print destination, Dynamics 365 shows a print preview.

The print preview contains the following elements ($\rightarrow$ Fig. 2.29):

- **Export** [1]—Export the preview to different file formats (PDF, Excel, Word, CSV, XML, HTML, TIFF).
- **Show sidebar** [2]—Overview of the content of the report.
- **Find** [3]—Search text in the report.
- **Switch page** [4]—Enter the page number, or click the button for the previous page ⊡ or the next page ⊡.
- **Zoom** [5]—Zoom in and out.
- **Presentation mode** [6]—Switch to the presentation mode.
- **Print** [7]—Print the preview on a local printer of your client.
- **Download** [8]—Download a PDF file of the preview.
- **Link** [9]—Link to the detail form related to the particular field.

2.3.1.4 Print Archive

The print archive provides the option to save a report within Dynamics 365. If you want to save a report to the archive, select the print archive as the destination in the *Print destination* dialog or—if you choose a different destination—set the slider *Save in print archive* in the *Print destination* dialog to "Yes".

When saving to the archive, the report is stored in the print archive. The form *Common > Inquiries > Print archive* shows your print archive and provides the option to reprint a report later. If you want to access the print archives of all users, open the menu

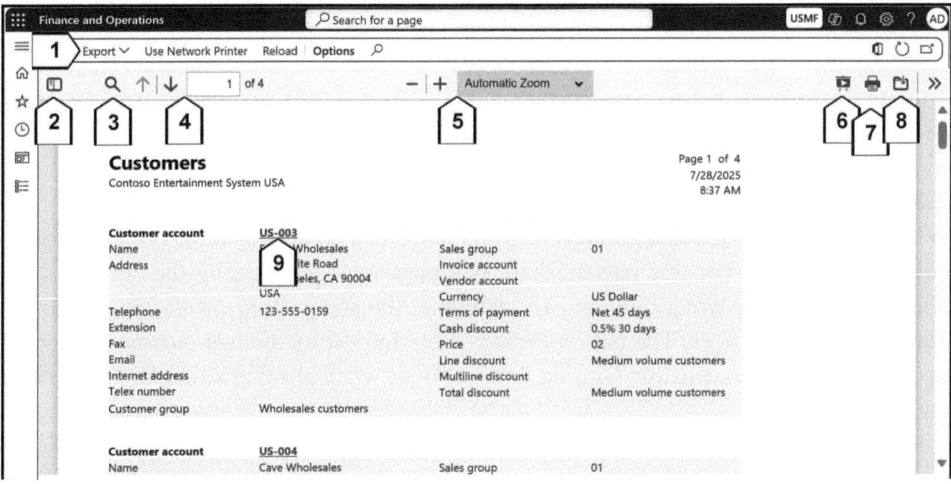

Fig. 2.29 Elements in the print preview

item *Organization administration > Inquiries and reports > Print archive* (with appropriate permissions).

2.3.1.5 Batch Processing

If you want to run a particular report (or a periodic activity) at a later time and not immediately, you can submit it to a batch process. For this purpose, expand the tab *Run in the background* in the report dialog and set the slider *Batch processing* to "Yes". Then click the button *Recurrence* on this tab to open a second dialog, in which you can enter the start time and repetitions for the batch job.

As a prerequisite for batch processing, at least one batch server has to be set up in the server configuration (*System administration > Setup > Server configuration*). If you want to categorize batch jobs, you can use batch groups (*System administration > Setup > Batch group*).

You can check and edit the status of batch jobs in the menu item *System administration > Inquiries > Batch jobs*.

2.3.2 Printing Business Documents

External documents require, in addition to the options that are available for basic reports, additional functionality for the following purposes:

- **Data storage**—Storing document data in a structured format.
- **Output**—Controlling the output.

In order to store document data (e.g., invoice data) in a structured format, core business documents like the invoice, the delivery note, or the order confirmation are posted first, and the printout is subsequently generated from the posted data. Even if you can start both steps together ("Post and print"), internally they are executed in two separate steps.

With the form setup and print management (→ Sect. 4.2.2), you can control the output destination and some basic settings for the layout of external documents.

2.3.2.1 Posting and Printing

When you post an external document (e.g., an invoice or a packing slip), you need a printout in many cases. For this reason, there is a parameter for printing the corresponding document in most posting dialogs—for example, the slider *Print invoice* in the posting dialog for sales invoices. The button *Printer setup* in posting dialogs provides the option to specify the print destination (similar to the options when printing a standard report from the menu).

You can find more details on the posting dialog in → Sect. 3.4.5.

2.3.2.2 Reprinting

If printing a posted document is required at a later time (e.g., if you have not set the slider *Print* to "Yes" when posting*)*, you can print it from the inquiry of the document. As an example, if you want to (re-)print a sales invoice, open the sales invoice journal (*Accounts receivable > Inquiries and reports > Invoices > Invoice journal*), select the invoice, and click the button *Invoice/ Document/ View/ Original.*

2.3.2.3 Modern Report Design and Electronic Reporting

With the modern report design, you can use a graphically rich design (including a flexible branding in the footer and header sections) in several business documents. The menu item *Organization administration > Setup > Document branding > Branding details* contains the settings for document branding. In order to use modern report designs, import the relevant Dataverse configuration repository into the Globalization studio workspace. As a prerequisite, the Dataverse repository needs to be linked to the Dynamics 365 environment in the Power Platform Admin Center (PPAC).

With the Electronic reporting tool, you can flexibly specify the structures of electronic formats together with the way data and rules fill these structures. Electronic reporting does not require a developer, but a regular user who does the configuration. You can use it for incoming and outgoing documents, not only for documents and file formats like a payment file in XML format, but also for generating a document like an invoice as a PDF or direct output to a printer.

More details on modern report design and electronic reporting are available on Microsoft Learn.

2.3.3 Microsoft Office Integration

The Microsoft Office integration in Dynamics 365 makes it easy to exchange data between Dynamics 365 and Office. There are two options for this data exchange:

- **Static export**—Export data from Dynamics 365 to Microsoft Excel.
- **Opening and editing**—Update Dynamics 365 data from Microsoft Office.

Apart from the standard workbooks for updating Dynamics 365 data from Office, you can use your own Excel workbooks to edit Dynamics 365 data in Excel.

In addition to the Microsoft Office integration, there are export and import features in the Data management workspace, especially for regular data export and import.

2.3.3.1 Static Export to Excel

The static export to Microsoft Excel supports copying data from the grid of a list page or detail form to an Excel sheet. Any update of data in the Excel sheet has no impact on the data in Dynamics 365.

If you want to execute a static export, open the respective page in Dynamics 365 and select the lines that you want to export. If you want to select all lines, select the checkbox on the left in the grid header, or do not select any line (if no line is explicitly selected, it also means all lines). Then click the button 🔲 (*Open in Microsoft Office*) / *Export to Excel* in the action pane (→ Fig. 2.30), or select the option *Export marked rows* in the context menu (accessed with a right-click on the grid header). In the next step, the *Export to Excel* dialog is shown. In this dialog, select to download the Excel file to your local computer, or to save it to OneDrive or SharePoint.

Note: You can set a maximum number of rows for the export in the Client performance options form.

2.3.3.2 Opening Data in Excel

Unlike the static export, which you can only use to retrieve data from Dynamics 365, the option *Open in Microsoft Office* enables the use of Excel to update Dynamics 365 data from Excel.

In order to start editing data with Excel, open the relevant list page or detail form in Dynamics 365. Then click the button 🔲 (*Open in Microsoft Office*) in the action pane and select the appropriate option in the button group *Open in Excel*. Some forms, for example, the general journals (*General ledger > Journal entries > General journals*), also contain a dedicated button in the action pane for editing in Excel.

The *Open in Excel* dialog is shown next. Select to download the Excel file to your computer, or to save it to OneDrive or SharePoint (like in the static export).

Microsoft Excel, which shows up next, includes the *Data Connector* in the task pane. Sign in to the Data Connector with your Dynamics 365 user to access Dynamics 365 data. Once the Dynamics 365 data are shown, you can edit the records and—with the button *New* in the Data Connector—insert additional records. If required, you can temporarily work offline in Excel.

If you want to retrieve current data from Dynamics 365, including new lines with new records, click the button *Refresh* in the Excel Data Connector. To transfer data from Excel to Dynamics 365, click the button *Publish*. If the Excel workbook contains incorrect data,

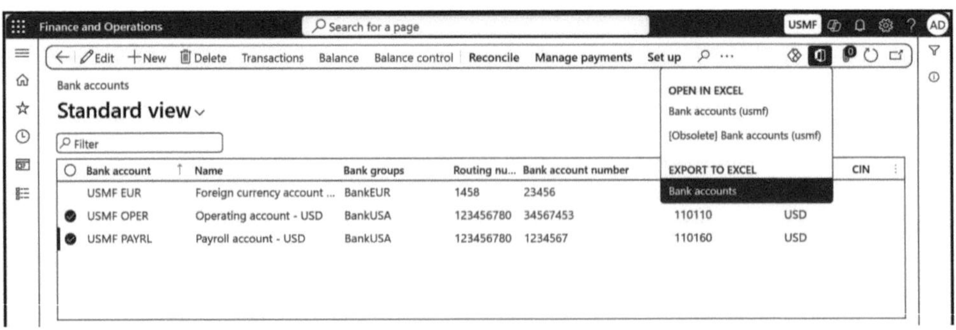

Fig. 2.30 Starting the export to Excel

an error message in the Excel Data Connector will show the issue and prevent the update. You can click the icon ⊡ at the bottom of the Data Connector to view the details of the error message.

2.3.3.3 Document Templates for Excel Integration

In addition to the standard Excel worksheets in Dynamics 365, you can create and use your own Excel workbooks to update Dynamics 365 data.

To create such an Excel workbook, open the Excel workbook designer (*Organization administration > Setup > Office integration > Excel workbook designer*) and select the Dynamics 365 table that you want to edit in Excel. In the workbook designer, move the fields, which should be included in the Excel workbook, from the pane *Available fields* to the pane *Selected fields*. Then click the button *Create workbook* in the action pane to open a dialog in which you select whether to export the Excel workbook to your local computer, to OneDrive, or SharePoint. After logging in to the Excel Data Connector, you can update Dynamics 365 data from the new worksheet (like in a Dynamics 365 standard worksheet described above).

You can save the Excel worksheet and upload it as a document template if you want to make it available as an additional option in the button ▣ (*Open in Microsoft Office*) of the related Dynamics 365 form. Open the document templates (*Organization administration > Setup > Office integration > Document templates*) for this purpose, click the button *New* in the action pane, and upload the Excel file that you have saved before.

2.3.4 Case Study Exercise

Exercise 2.10—Printing

Print a vendor list (*Accounts payable > Inquiries and reports > Vendor reports > Vendors*) and select the print preview as the print destination.

Then close the print preview and print the vendor list again. Filter on any vendor group of your choice and select a PDF file as the print destination this time.

2.4   Global Address Book

Dynamics 365 contains a common table with all business partners of your enterprise—internal and external relationships, companies, and persons. This common table is the global address book. Business partners are called "Parties" in the global address book. They are shared across your companies and include customers, sales leads, vendors, organization units, employees, and other contacts.

2.4.1　Parties and Addresses

Whenever you create a new customer, vendor, or any other kind of party, Dynamics 365 inserts a corresponding record in the global address book. A party, which may contain one or more (postal) addresses and contact data, is not the same as an address—it is an organization or person characterized by its name.

2.4.1.1 Creating Parties in the Global Address Book

Depending on the permission settings, you can manage all parties in the Global address book list page (*Common > Common > Global address book*) and in the related detail form (→ Fig. 2.31).

In order to insert a party in the Global address book page, click the button *New* in the action pane. In the new party, the *Party ID* derives from the corresponding number sequence. The party type (lookup field *Type*) with the options "Organization" and "Person"

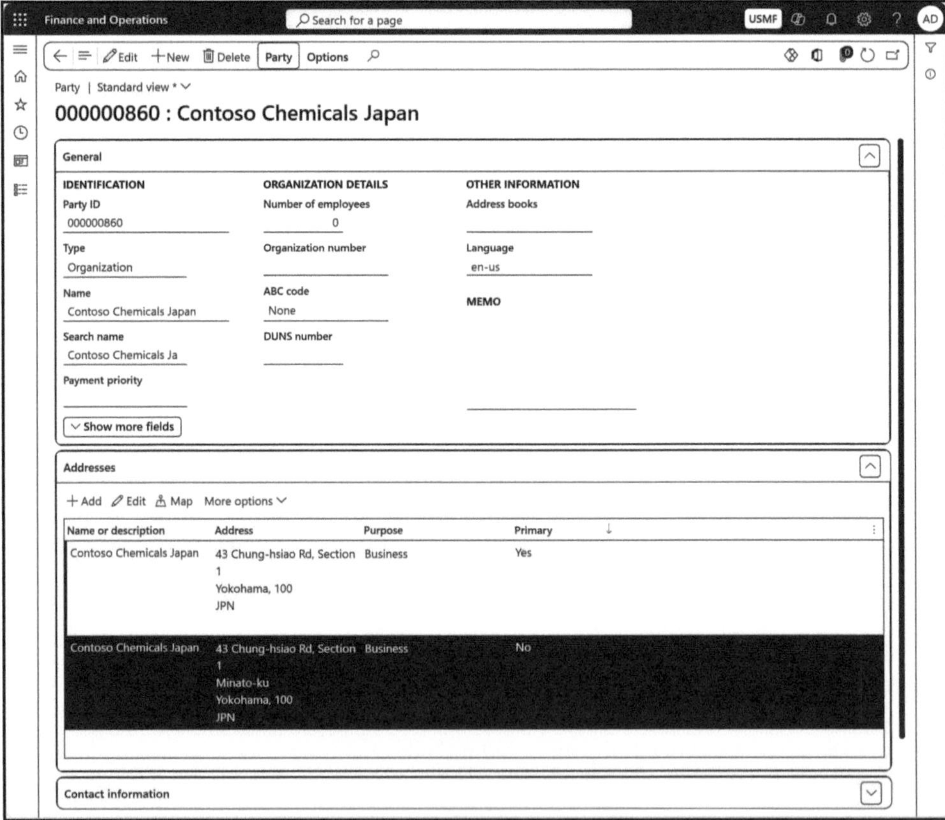

Fig. 2.31 Managing a party with multiple addresses in the Party detail form

controls the fields that are displayed in the Party form (e.g., the field *First name* is only shown for persons).

Enter the party name in the field *Name* (for an organization) or in the fields *First name* and *Last name* (for a person) before you register additional data, including the postal address on the tab *Addresses* and contact data like e-mail addresses and phone numbers on the tab *Contact information*. More details on how to manage postal addresses and contact data are given in Sect. 3.2.1 on the example of vendor management.

2.4.1.2 Indirectly Creating Parties

Apart from directly creating a party in the global address book, you can indirectly create a party by entering a customer, a vendor, or any other kind of party in any module. In all forms in which parties are created indirectly, the field *Name* is a lookup field in which you can search for an existing party. If you select a party in this field, this party receives an additional role. If you do not select a party, but type a new name, Dynamics 365 creates a new party with this name automatically.

If you insert a new customer in the Customer form and **type a name** in the lookup field *Name* of the *Create* dialog, a new party is created. However, if you **select a party** in the lookup field *Name*, the new role "Customer" is assigned to this party.

Since a party may already exist in the global address book (e.g., if a customer is already a vendor in your or an affiliated company within a common Dynamics 365 environment), you should, to avoid duplicate parties, check the existing parties before creating a new party. In case the duplicate check is activated in the Global address book parameters, and you enter a duplicate party anyhow, a confirmation dialog shows the existing party before saving the new party.

2.4.1.3 Internal Organizations

Apart from external organizations and persons, also internal organizations—e.g., the operating units and legal entities—are parties in the global address book. You can recognize internal organizations by the party type—e.g., "Legal entities". The related party types are reserved for internal organizations and not included in the options when manually entering a party in the global address book.

2.4.1.4 Changing Party Names

The field *Name* in the Party form (Global address book) is an editable field, and you can change the name of a party if applicable. Changes of a party name are stored in the name history, which you can access with the button *Party/ Maintain/ Name history* in the Party form. Old documents will print the old name, and new documents will use the new name.

> *Note*: If you want to directly access the related party from a customer or vendor, click on the field *Name* (which is a link) in the Customer or Vendor form.

2.4.2 Address Books

An address book is a collection of party records. You can set up one or more address books in the menu item *Organization administration > Global address book > Address books*—for example, one address book for sales and one for purchasing.

Independent of the individual address books, the global address book is the collection of all parties in all companies within a Dynamics 365 environment (→ Fig. 2.32).

If you want to link a party to one or more address books, open the lookup in the field *Address books* on the tab *General* in the Party detail form and put a checkmark in front of the applicable address books.

You can use address books for searching and filtering parties (e.g., with the filter field *Address books* in the Global address book list page), and as a basis for security settings (restrict access to the parties of an address book).

2.4.2.1 Party Roles

A party role—e.g., "Vendor" or "Customer"—describes the relationship between your enterprise and the party. A party can be assigned to one or more roles in one or more companies. There are two ways of assigning a role to a party:

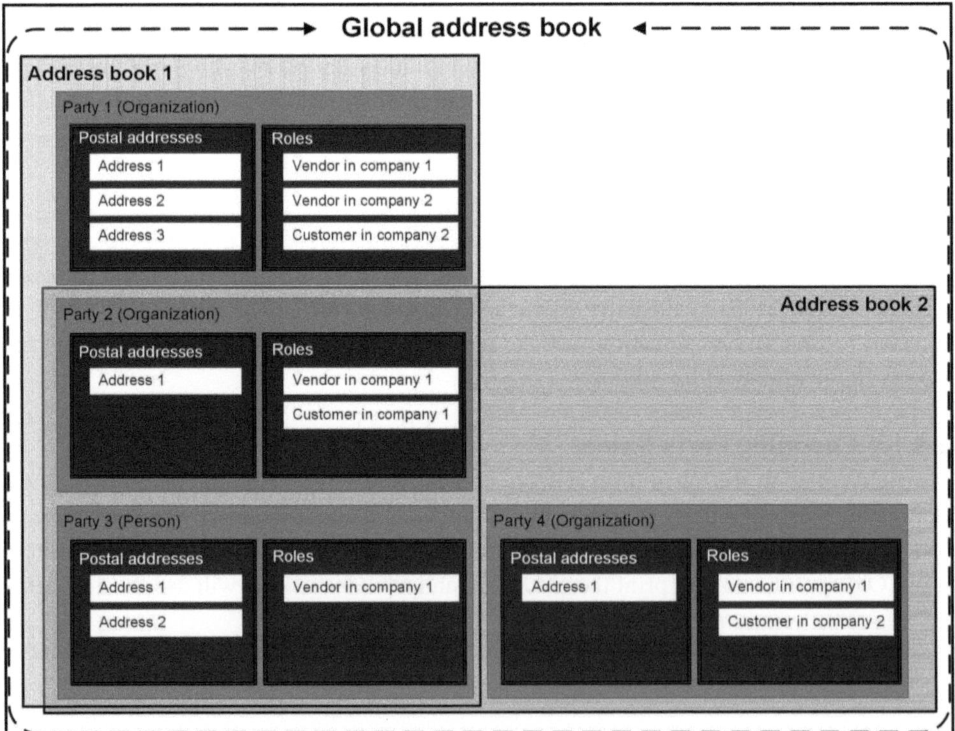

Fig. 2.32 Conceptual structure of the global address book

- **Indirectly**—Entering a record in other areas (e.g., a customer in the Customer form) automatically creates a party with the corresponding role in the global address book.
- **Directly**—Buttons in the Global address book form (e.g., *Party/ New/ Customer*) create a record in the selected area (e.g., a customer record) and assign the corresponding role to the selected party.

The roles of a party are shown on the tab *Roles* in the Party detail form.

2.4.2.2 Address Book Parameters

If the duplicate check is activated in the Global address book parameters (*Organization administration > Global address book > Global address book parameters*, slider *Use duplicate check*), a dialog shows duplicate party records whenever you try to create a party (directly or indirectly) with the name of an already existing party. In this dialog, you can select whether to use the existing party or to create a new party, which by chance has the same name as the existing party. The parameter *Check for unique DUNS number* enables using the DUNS number to avoid creating duplicate party records.

Further Global address book parameters include the default party type ("Organization" or "Person") and the name sequence for persons (first/last name).

Settings regarding the address format of postal addresses, the available ZIP/postal codes, or the available cities are specified in the Address setup form (*Organization administration > Global address book > Addresses > Address setup*). The section *Parameters* in the Address setup form contains the setting whether you can only enter ZIP/postal codes that are included in the address setup.

2.4.3   Case Study Exercise

Exercise 2.11—Global Address Book

In order to learn the functionality of the global address book, check if you can find the party that is assigned to the vendor of exercise 2.4.

Then insert a new party with the name "##-Exercise 2.11" (## = your user ID) and a postal address in London. This new party will become a vendor in your company later on. What do you do in Dynamics 365?

Purchase Management

3

The primary responsibility of purchasing is the supply of goods and services from vendors. The related processes include the following activities:

- Determine material requirements
- Process purchase requisitions, requests for quotations, and purchase orders
- Post item receipts and vendor invoices

3.1 Business Processes in Purchasing

Before we start to go into details, the lines below give an overview of the business processes in purchasing.

3.1.1 Basic Approach

As a prerequisite for procurement, correct master data are required—in particular, the vendor and the product data. For purchased services and non-inventoried commodities, it is possible to use procurement categories instead of products.

3.1.1.1 Master Data and Transactions in Purchasing

Vendors and products are master data, which are created once and only occasionally updated later. In the course of the purchasing process, planned and actual purchase orders (transaction data) receive default values from vendor and product records (master data). You can override these data in the transaction—for example, if you agree to special payment terms in a particular purchase order.

A. Luszczak, *Using Microsoft Dynamics 365 Finance and Operations*,
https://doi.org/10.1007/978-3-658-50563-9_3

If you modify data in a transaction, it does not update the related master data. If you agree on some general changes with a vendor, for example, on new payment terms, update the vendor record accordingly.

Based on correct master data, the purchasing process—along with the required predecessor and successor activities—includes the steps shown in → Fig. 3.1.

3.1.1.2 Material Requirement, Purchase Requisition, and Request for Quotation

Determining the material requirements is the starting point for the purchasing process. Depending on the particular product and the business processes, there are two alternative origins for purchase orders:

- **Planned orders**—Generated automatically from known demand within Dynamics 365 (e.g., sales orders, forecasts, or materials for production).
- **Purchase requisitions**—Entered manually for other demand.

Planned orders, which are generated in master planning (→ Sect. 6.3), require accurate figures on inventory quantity, sales orders, purchase orders, and forecasts. In addition, appropriate item coverage settings are necessary.

Purchase requisitions are internal documents that ask the procurement department to purchase specific items (like consumables and office supplies). Unlike planned orders, which are created automatically, requisitions are entered manually by the person who needs the material or service. A requisition runs through an approval workflow before it is released to a purchase order.

Requests for quotation are sent to vendors to receive information on prices and delivery times. The purchasing department enters requests for quotation manually or generates them from planned purchase orders or purchase requisitions.

3.1.1.3 Purchase Order

You can create purchase orders either manually or automatically—e.g., from a planned order, a purchase requisition, or a sales order (for direct delivery).

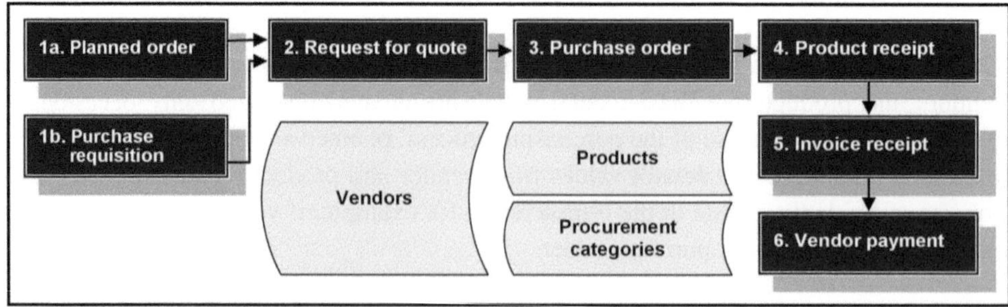

Fig. 3.1 Purchasing process in dynamics 365

A purchase order consists of a header, which contains the common data of the whole order (e.g., the vendor data), and one or more lines, which contain the ordered items. Once you have completed entering a purchase order, start the approval workflow (in case change management is active). If change management is not active, the order immediately gets the status "Approved". After approval, you can optionally post a purchase inquiry and send it to the vendor so that they can validate and confirm it.

Before you can continue with order processing and posting the product receipt, you have to post a purchase order confirmation. Posting the confirmation means to save it, optionally sending it to the vendor (electronically or as a printed document). The purchase order confirmation is stored with its original content, no matter if there is a later modification of the actual purchase order.

The status of a purchase order is indicated by the order status and the document status in the order header, and by the posted quantities of the lines. Inquiries, workspace information, and periodic reports provide the option to recognize issues like late shipments.

3.1.1.4 Product Receipt, Vendor Invoice, and Vendor Payment

Once you receive the items or services, record the product receipt. Posting the product receipt increases the physical quantity in inventory (for inventoried items) and reduces the open quantity in the purchase order.

The invoice of the vendor arrives together with the items or at a later time. When you register the invoice in the (Pending) Vendor invoice form, invoice control features support matching the invoice with the purchase order and the product receipt. If an invoice does not refer to a purchase order, there are two options: You can either enter it in an invoice journal or in the Vendor invoice form.

After posting the invoice, you can record a payment to the vendor—either manually or as a result of a payment proposal. The calculation of payment proposals is based on the due date and the cash discount period. Payment processing is independent of purchase orders and is usually a responsibility of the finance department. You can find details on vendor payments in → Sect. 9.3.3.

3.1.1.5 Ledger Integration and Voucher Principle

Based on the deep integration of finance with the business processes in all areas of Dynamics 365, the inventory and vendor transactions in purchasing are posted to ledger accounts as specified in the setup (→ Sect. 9.4).

In order to keep track of the whole business process, Dynamics 365 comprehensively applies the voucher principle to transactions: You have to register a transaction in a document (voucher) before you can post it. After posting, it is not possible to modify the document. An overview of the documents in purchase order processing is shown in → Fig. 3.2.

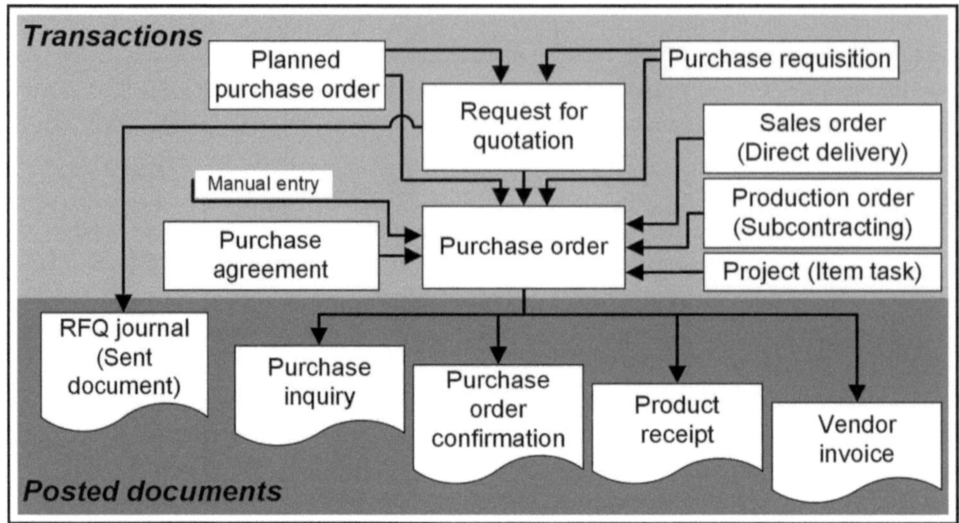

Fig. 3.2 Transactions and posted documents in purchasing

3.1.2   At a Glance: Purchase Order Processing

The following example demonstrates the main steps in purchase order processing. It starts with creating the order in the workspace *Purchase order preparation*, and shows all transactions directly in the Purchase order form. Alternatively, you can create the order from the Vendor form or directly in the Purchase order list page.

In the workspace *Purchase order preparation*, which you can access from the Procurement and sourcing module or the homepage (Immersive home or dashboard), click the button *New purchase order* in the action pane to create an order. In the *Create purchase order* dialog, which is shown next, select a vendor in the field *Vendor account* (you can trigger the search in this field by typing the first characters of the vendor name) before you click the button *OK*. Dynamics 365 then creates an order header with default data (e.g., for the language and the currency) from the selected vendor and opens the Purchase order detail form in the Lines view.

If you are in Read mode, click the button *Edit* or press the *F2* key to switch to the Edit mode. Then enter the first order line with the *Item number*, the *Quantity*, and the *Unit price* on the tab *Purchase order lines*. When you select the item number, it initializes the quantity, the price, and other fields with default values from the item. If you want to enter another line, press the *Down Arrow* key or click the button *Add line* in the toolbar of the lines. The buttons *Header* and *Lines* below the action pane provide the option to switch between the Lines view (→ Fig. 3.3) and the Header view.

If change management is activated, the *Approval status* (shown on the right above the header) is "Draft" after entering the order. In an order with this status, click the button *Workflow/Submit* (shown in the action pane) and process the approval.

Then click the button *Purchase/Generate/Confirmation* in the action pane to post the purchase order confirmation (→ Fig. 3.4). If you want to print the purchase order, do not

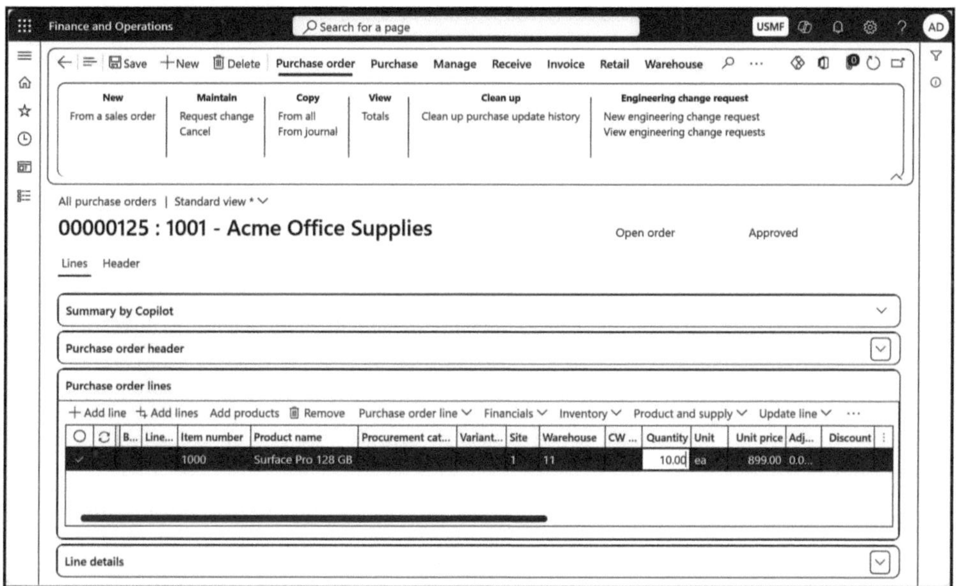

Fig. 3.3   Entering a purchase order line

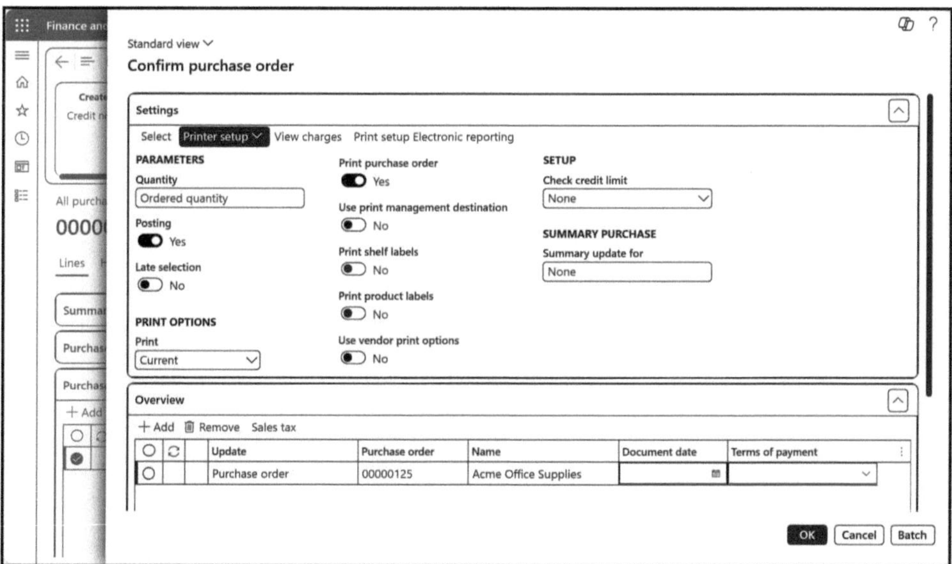

Fig. 3.4   Confirming and printing the purchase order

only set the slider *Posting* in the posting dialog to "Yes", but also the slider *Print purchase order*. The button *Printer setup* in the dialog provides the option to select a printer for the printout.

When you receive the item, click the button *Receive/Generate/Product receipt* in the purchase order to post the product receipt. Posting the receipt works similarly to the purchase order confirmation described above. But unlike an order confirmation, usually you do not print a product receipt (you receive the shipping document from the vendor). If there is no prior item arrival registration, select the option "Ordered quantity" in the lookup field *Quantity* on the tab *Settings*, and enter the vendor's packing slip number in the column *Product receipt* on the tab *Overview* of the posting dialog before you click the button *OK*. The product receipt increases the physical quantity in inventory and updates the order status to "Received".

If you want to post the vendor invoice directly from the Purchase order form, click the button *Invoice/Generate/Invoice* in this form. With an action pane and FactBoxes, the form for vendor invoice posting is different from the other posting dialogs. In a FactBox on the right, or with the button *Totals* in the action pane, you can review the totals. If the invoice matching validation is active, click the button *Update match status* to validate the invoice data against the purchase order and the product receipt. After entering the vendor invoice number in the field *Number (Invoice identification)*, click the button *Post* to post the invoice. Invoice posting generates an open vendor transaction (waiting for the payment) and updates the order status to "Invoiced".

> *Note:* If you want to quit the Pending vendor invoice form without saving, delete the invoice— do not simply close the form (this would save a pending invoice).

3.2   Vendor Management

Vendor records are required in purchasing and accounts payable. In line with the deep integration of Dynamics 365, there is one common record for each vendor, which is used in all areas of the application. If you want to restrict access to the fields and field groups of the Vendor form, you can set appropriate permissions.

3.2.1 Vendor Records

In order to check existing vendors or to create new vendors, open the Vendor list page in the Procurement module (*Procurement and sourcing > Vendors > All vendors*) or in the Accounts payable module (*Accounts payable > Vendors > All vendors*). Alternatively, use the navigation search to access this page. According to the general structure of list pages, the Vendor list page shows a list of all vendors. In the Vendor detail form, which you open by clicking the link in the field *Vendor account* of a line (→ Fig. 3.5), you can view the details of the selected vendor.

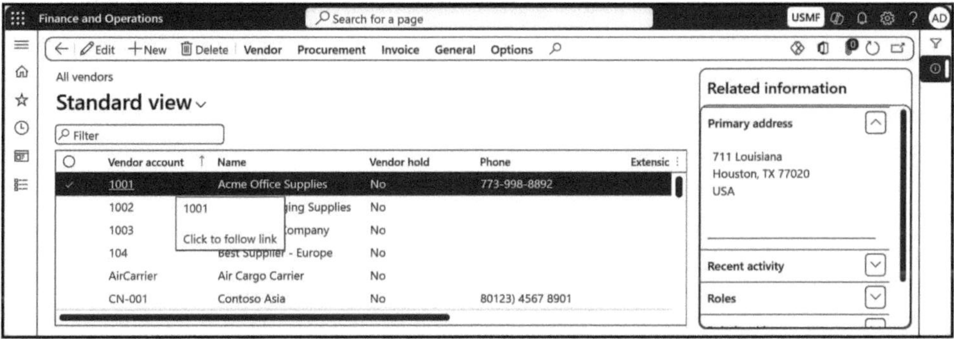

Fig. 3.5 Selecting a vendor in the vendor list page

Apart from the menu items, the workspace *Purchase order preparation* also provides access to the Vendor detail form (there is the list *Find vendor* in the list section).

If you want to update data in the Vendor detail form, switch to the Edit mode (press the *F2* key or click the button *Edit* in the action pane for this purpose). If the list page is already in Edit mode before you access the detail form, the detail form is also opened in Edit mode.

The Vendor detail form contains numerous fields. The following description covers the core data in the vendor record. More information is available in the online help.

3.2.1.1 Entering New Vendors

If you want to create a new vendor in the Vendor list page or the detail form, press the shortcut *Alt + N* or click the button *New* in the action pane. If templates for vendors are set up, you can populate the fields of the new record from a template (→ Sect. 2.2.3).

Depending on settings in the corresponding number sequence, the unique vendor number in the field *Vendor account* is assigned automatically or has to be entered manually. By default, the number sequence (→ Sect. 10.3.1) in the Accounts payable parameters is used, but you can override this number sequence in the vendor groups (personalize the Vendor group form to show the column *Vendor account number sequence*).

If you work with the same vendor in multiple companies and you want to use the same vendor number in all your companies, a setup is required that applies the same shared number sequence for vendor numbers in all companies. The way to share vendors across companies is shown further down this section.

3.2.1.2 Global Address Book Integration

The party type (field *Type* in the field group *Identification*) on the tab *General* of the Vendor detail form determines if a vendor is a company (organization) or a person. Depending on the party type, the tab *General* will show different fields—for example, the fields *First name* and *Last name* for the type "Person".

Vendors are parties in the global address book. For this reason, the field *Name* is a lookup field in which you can select an existing party from the global address book when creating a new vendor. If you enter the name of a new vendor manually, a confirmation dialog is shown in case an existing party has the same name as the new vendor (as a prerequisite, the duplicate check has to be activated in the Global address book parameters). The confirmation dialog provides the option to link the vendor to the existing party or to create a new party, which by chance has the same name.

After saving the vendor record, you can use the link (or the option *View details* in the context menu) in the field *Name* (vendor name) to access the related party in the global address book. And because of the global address book integration, it is not possible to edit the vendor name in the Vendor form—you can only change a vendor name by updating the field *Name* in the related party.

As an alternative to the Vendor form, you can create new vendors in the global address book (→ Sect. 2.4.1) in order to reduce the risk of duplicate party records. For this purpose, create a party for the new vendor in the global address book first and then assign the vendor role to the new party (click the button *Party/New/Vendor*). Before creating the new party, you can easily check if the new vendor is already a party (e.g., if the new vendor is a vendor in an affiliated company). If the vendor is a party but not a vendor in your company yet, select this party and assign the vendor role to this party.

3.2.1.3 General Data

The *Search name* in the vendor record is initialized with the vendor name. In contrast to the field *Name*, the field *Search name* is an editable field in the vendor record.

Apart from the name, mandatory data in the vendor record include the lookup field *Group* (vendor group, usually controlling the ledger integration as shown in → Sect. 3.2.3), and the *Currency* on the tab *Purchasing demographics* (initialized with the accounting currency).

Further core fields on the tab *General* are the *Language*, which determines the language for printing purchase orders or other documents, and, in case address books are used (e.g., for access control), the *Address books* linked to the vendor.

The display field *Vendor hold* on the tab *Miscellaneous details* shows whether the vendor is blocked. If you want to change the hold status, click the button *Vendor/Maintain/On hold* in the action pane. The vendor hold status "All" prevents entering or posting any purchase order or other transaction with the vendor. The options "No" and "Never" enable all transactions ("Never" prevents automatic blocking of the vendor after a period of inactivity).

3.2.1.4 Input Tax

Tax settings for the vendor have to be entered on the tab *Invoice and delivery*. The *Sales tax group* (*VAT group*, initialized from the vendor group) on this tab determines the tax duty depending on the vendor location. A correct sales tax group is necessary to distinguish between domestic vendors, who charge sales tax or VAT, and foreign vendors, who do not. The setup of the sales tax groups and the tax calculation depends on the current company and its location. You can find more information on the tax setup in Dynamics 365 in → Sect. 9.2.7.

If your company is located within the European Union and you need to record the VAT registration number of vendors for tax purposes, enter it in the field *Tax exempt number* (*VAT number*) next to the sales tax group. Since it is a lookup field, you have to insert a new tax-exempt number in the main table (use the option *View details* in the context menu, or the menu item *Tax > Setup > Sales tax > Tax exempt numbers*) before you can select it in the vendor record.

The setting in the fields *Tax exempt number requirement* and *Mandatory tax group* in the Accounts payable parameters (*Accounts payable > Setup > Accounts payable parameters*, section *General*, tab *Vendor*) determine whether the tax-exempt number or the sales tax group is mandatory when creating a vendor.

3.2.1.5 Settings for Delivery and Payment

Delivery terms and modes of delivery are a common setup for vendors and customers.

The field *Delivery terms* on the tab *Invoice and delivery* of the Vendor detail form specifies the usual delivery terms of the particular vendor. You can set up the required delivery terms, including a translation into foreign languages, in the menu item *Procurement and sourcing > Setup > Distribution > Terms of delivery*. The delivery terms reflect the agreed incoterms (standardized contractual rules that determine the tasks, costs, and risks for transportation and delivery).

The field *Mode of delivery* below the delivery terms specifies the way of delivery (e.g., "Truck" or "Parcel"). You can set up the modes of delivery in the menu item *Procurement and sourcing > Setup > Distribution > Modes of delivery*.

The tab *Payment* in the Vendor detail form contains settings on payment terms and cash discount. You can find more details on these settings in → Sect. 3.2.2.

3.2.1.6 Postal Addresses

You can manage one or more addresses of a vendor on the tab *Addresses* in the Vendor detail form. Addresses and contact data are stored in the global address book, which means that they are not directly linked to the vendor, but to the party that is linked with the vendor. Address and contact data in the global address book are shared with the other roles of the party (e.g., if the vendor is also a customer or vendor in another company in Dynamics 365).

In order to enter the postal address of a vendor, click the button *Add* in the toolbar of the tab *Addresses* in the Vendor form. In the *New address* dialog that is shown next, enter an identification (which helps to select the right address in the address search) for the address in the field *Name or description*. If the address is the primary address of the vendor, make sure that the slider *Primary* is set to "Yes" and the slider *Private* to "No". The field *Purpose* in the *Address* dialog controls which transactions should use the current address as the default value. In a primary address, select the purpose "Business". In an additional address, select an alternative purpose—e.g., the purpose "Payment" for an alternative payee address whose name is printed on checks. One postal address can have multiple purposes at the same time. If no specific address is specified for a particular purpose, the primary address is used.

The form *Organization administration > Global address book > Address and contact information purpose* shows the available standard address purposes. With the checkbox *Postal address*, you can control which purposes are available when creating an address. If required, you can set up additional purposes.

Another important setting in a postal address is the *Country/region*, which is the basis for the address format and for reports to the authorities, including sales tax and Intrastat reports.

Once you have selected the country code, only the postal codes of this country are shown in the lookup of the field *ZIP/postal Code*. Depending on the settings in the Address setup (*Organization administration > Global address book > Addresses > Address setup*, tab *Parameters*), postal codes are validated against the ZIP/postal code table when entering an address. If the ZIP/postal code validation is activated, you have to insert a new postal code in the ZIP/postal code table before you can enter it in an address. You can manage the postal codes in the Address setup form (open the section *ZIP/postal codes*), or with the option *View details* in the context menu of the ZIP/postal code field.

After closing the *Address* dialog, you can click the button *More options/Advanced* in the toolbar of the tab *Addresses* in the Vendor form if you want to access further address details. The tab *Contact information* in the Manage addresses form contains the contact data, which are specific to the particular address (e.g., the phone number of the payee address), and not the general contact data of the vendor.

If a vendor has multiple addresses with the same purpose and you want to specify a default value for a purpose, click the button *More options/Set defaults* in the toolbar of the tab *Addresses* in the Vendor form.

3.2.1.7 Contact Information

In order to enter general contact data of a vendor (e.g., the telephone number or the e-mail address of the office), click the button *Add* in the toolbar of the tab *Contact information* of the Vendor detail form.

On the tab *Purchasing demographics* of the Vendor detail form, you can select a main contact person of the vendor in the field *Primary contact*. Before you can select a person in this field, create this person with the button *Vendor/Set up/Contacts/Add contacts* in the Vendor form. If applicable, you can create additional contact persons with different functions or responsibilities. With the button *Vendor/Set up/Contacts/View contacts* in the Vendor form, you can view and edit the contact persons later.

3.2.1.8 Features in the Vendor Page

The buttons in the action pane of the Vendor list page or detail form provide access to various inquiries and activities on the selected vendor:

- **Action pane tab "Vendor":**
  - *Set up/Contacts* —Manage vendor contact persons.
  - *Set up/Bank accounts*—Manage vendor bank accounts for payment.
  - *Transactions/Transactions* —Show vendor invoices and payments.
  - *Transactions/Balance* —Show the total of open liabilities.
- **Action pane tab "Procurement":**
  - *New/Purchase order*—Enter a purchase order .
  - *Related information/Purchase orders*—View current purchase orders.
  - *Agreements/Purchase agreements*—Blanket orders .
- **Action pane tab "Invoice":**
  - *New/Invoice*—Enter a vendor invoice .
  - *Settle/Settle transactions*— Settle invoices.
  - *Related information/Invoice*—View posted invoices.

3.2.1.9 Vendor Approval

In case your company requires an approval for changing particular vendor fields (e.g., the terms of payment), you can enable vendor approvals in the Accounts payable parameters (section *General*, tab *Vendor approval*) and set up a workflow with the type "Proposed vendor changes workflow" in the menu item *Accounts payable > Setup > Accounts payable workflows*.

With this setup, updates in the selected vendor fields have to be submitted to the workflow, and only after approval, the changes are applied to the vendor. While the approval is pending, the additional button *Proposed changes* (opens a dialog in which you can view and, if necessary, discard the changes) is shown in the action pane of the Vendor form.

Similar to the approval options for the vendor, you can set up an approval requirement for vendor bank accounts in the Accounts payable parameters (along with the related workflow).

You can find details on the workflow management in → Sect. 10.4.3.

3.2.1.10 One-Time Vendors

One-time vendors provide the option to keep the master data of regular vendors separate from suppliers, from whom you purchase items only one time.

The tab *Vendor* in the section *General* in the Accounts payable parameters includes the field *One-time vendor account*, which specifies the vendor that is used as the template for one-time vendors. In addition, there is a separate number sequence for one-time vendors in the section *Number sequences* of the parameters. The settings are only required if you use one-time vendors.

If you want to apply a one-time vendor in a purchase order, do not select an existing vendor when creating the order (e.g., in the menu item *Procurement and sourcing > Purchase orders > All purchase orders*), but set the slider *One-time supplier* in the *Create purchase order* dialog to "Yes" (→ Fig. 3.6). With this setting, a new vendor is created in parallel to the order.

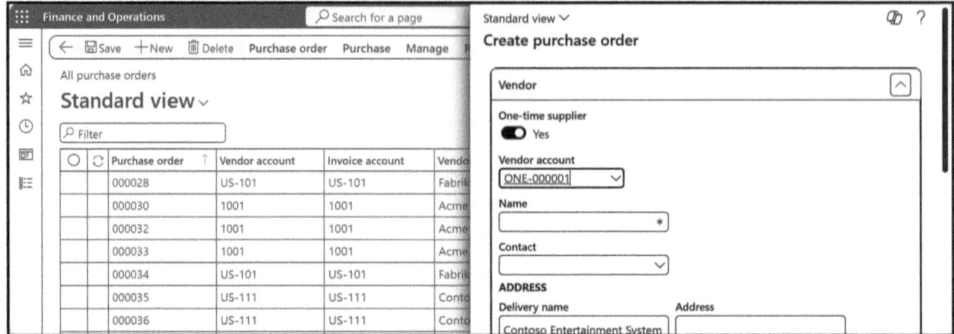

Fig. 3.6 Creating a one-time vendor in a new purchase order

The vendor account number of this vendor derives from the number sequence for one-time vendors. In addition, the one-time vendor is characterized by the checkbox *One-time supplier* on the tab *Vendor profile* in the Vendor form. If you want to convert the one-time vendor into a regular vendor, clear this checkbox (but clearing the checkbox does not change the vendor number).

3.2.1.11 Sharing Vendors Across Companies

Since vendors are parties in the global address book and the global address book is shared across companies, the party details (address and contact data) are shared automatically if you link the vendor records in two or more companies to a common party in the global address book.

The button *Vendor/Copy/Add vendor to another legal entity* in the Vendor form, which opens a drop-down in which you can select the target company, vendor group, currency, and vendor hold information, provides an easy way to create a vendor—which is linked to the same party as the selected vendor—in another company.

If you want to share the data in the vendor table (in addition to the data in the shared party table), you can use cross-company data sharing (→ Sect. 10.1.5) for the vendor table. With cross-company data sharing, make sure that the referenced data that you enter (e.g., the vendor groups) are consistent across the selected companies.

If cross-company data sharing is not enabled and you want to initialize a new vendor from the vendor record in another company, access the Vendor form in the company in which you want to create the vendor, click the button *New* and, in the field *Name* on the tab *General*, search the vendor (party) which you want to copy. If the selected party is a vendor in another company, the party lookup will show the additional slider *Existing vendor. Copy vendor?* on the right, which enables copying the vendor data. As a prerequisite, the two companies must apply the same shared number sequence for vendor numbers, which ensures a common vendor number across the companies.

3.2.1.12 Vendor Collaboration

The Vendor collaboration module in Dynamics 365 contains the menu items that are intended to be used by your vendors. This includes the *Vendor bidding* workspace (and the form *Request for quotation bid*), the *Purchase order confirmation* workspace (and the form *Purchase orders for review*), and the option to submit invoices in the workspace *Invoicing*. With vendor collaboration, your vendor can directly enter data in your Dynamics 365 environment, and you don't have to type documents that you receive.

As a prerequisite, the relevant contact persons have to be registered in the Vendor form (there is the button *Vendor/Set up/Contacts* as described above) and they have to be created as users with the respective (external) security role (→ Sect. 10.2.2).

You can activate the vendor collaboration for a vendor in the Vendor detail form—select the option "Active (PO is auto-confirmed)" or "Active (PO is not auto-confirmed)" in the field *Collaboration activation* on the tab *General*.

If a vendor uses the vendor collaboration, the following steps in purchase order processing are different from the common procedure as described in → Sect. 3.4: Instead of the (optional) purchase inquiry, you send a confirmation request to the vendor once the purchase order is internally approved—click the button *Purchase/Vendor collaboration/ Send for confirmation* in the Purchase order form for this purpose. The vendor then accepts the inquiry in the Vendor collaboration portal (*Vendor collaboration > Purchase orders > Purchase orders for review*). If the *Collaboration activation* option "Active (PO is auto-confirmed)" in the Vendor form is selected for the vendor, the purchase order confirmation is subsequently posted automatically (requires the job *Procurement and sourcing > Purchase orders > Purchase order confirmation > Confirm accepted purchase orders*, which should run as a recurring batch job).

3.2.2 Payment Terms and Cash Discounts

Unlike other business applications, which include cash discount settings in the payment terms, Dynamics 365 keeps payment terms and cash discounts separately.

Payment terms and cash discounts in Dynamics 365 are a common setup for vendors and customers. For this reason, the administration is included in both the Accounts payable module and the Accounts receivable module. The calculation of the due date and the cash discount date starts from the document date, which you can enter in an invoice. If you leave the document date empty, Dynamics 365 uses the posting date as the start date for due date calculation. But particularly in purchase invoices, the document date may deviate from the posting date.

If necessary, you can modify the due date and the cash discount date when posting an invoice or when settling it in the Settle transactions form (→ Sect. 9.3.4).

3.2.2.1 Terms of Payment

You can manage the payment terms in the Accounts payable module (*Accounts payable > Payment setup > Terms of payment*) and in the Accounts receivable module (*Accounts receivable > Payment setup > Terms of payment*).

The list pane on the left of this form displays the available payment terms with their ID and description. The settings for the due date calculation of the selected payment term are shown on the right (→ Fig. 3.7).

The lookup field *Payment method* on the tab *Setup* determines the start date for due date calculation: "Net" means starting from the document date, "Current month" means starting from the month end. The fields *Days* and *Months* determine the period length for the due date calculation.

The button *Translations* provides the option to enter a longer description (text) in different languages. When you print an external document (e.g., a printed purchase order), the text of the payment terms is printed in the language of the document. If no translation to this language has been entered for the particular payment terms, the content of the field *Description* of the payment terms is printed.

3.2.2.2 Cash Payment and Cash on Delivery

If you want to create payment terms for cash on delivery, select the *Payment method* "COD", set the slider *Cash payment* to "Yes", and select the appropriate main account for petty cash in the field *Cash*.

When you post an invoice with payment terms for cash payment (*Cash payment* = "Yes"), a payment (with the petty cash account in the payment terms) and the settlement of the invoice are posted in parallel. There is no open vendor transaction in this case.

Fig. 3.7 Settings for the due date calculation in the payment terms

3.2.2.3 Cash Discounts

Like the setup of the payment terms, the cash discount setup is included in both the Accounts payable module and the Accounts receivable module (*Accounts payable > Payment setup > Cash discounts* and *Accounts receivable > Payment setup > Cash discounts*). When you create a cash discount, some details are similar to the details in the payment terms. In addition, you have to specify the cash discount percentage and settings that control posting the cash discount to the general ledger ($\rightarrow$ Fig. 3.8).

Cash discounts are a common setup in accounts payable and accounts receivable. Nevertheless, there are different settings for posting the cash discount deduction for vendors and for customers (the settings apply when the payment is posted):

- **Accounts receivable**—Field *Main account for customer discounts*.
- **Accounts payable**—The main account depends on the selected option in the lookup field *Discount offset accounts* of the cash discount:
    - *Use main account for vendor discounts*—Posting to the *Main account for vendor discounts* specified in the field below.
    - *Accounts on the invoice lines*—Posting to the accounts of the invoice lines (offsetting part of the invoiced expense amount with the cash discount).

If required, a setup is possible that triggers posting the cash discount to ledger accounts which depend on the applicable sales tax—enter the applicable main accounts in the fields *Vendor cash discount* and *Customer cash discount* of the sales tax ledger posting groups (*Tax > Setup > Sales tax > Ledger posting groups*) for this purpose. This way, you can, for

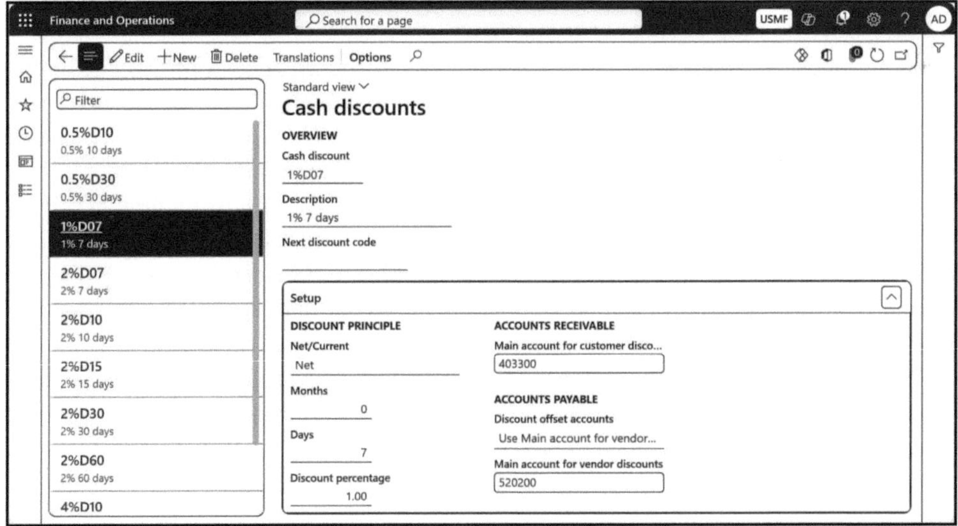

Fig. 3.8 Setting up a cash discount

example, distinguish between cash discounts that you receive from domestic vendors and from foreign vendors.

3.2.3 Ledger Integration

Whenever you post a purchase order invoice, it generates financial transactions. These financial transactions include the general ledger and subledgers for accounts payable, sales tax, inventory, and other areas as applicable.

3.2.3.1 Subledger and General Ledger

Vendor invoices, credit notes, and payments generate vendor transactions in accounts payable. In addition to these subledger postings, Dynamics 365 is posting transactions in the general ledger. There are two relevant settings for the automatic selection of main accounts in the ledger transactions:

- **Posting setup** ($\rightarrow$ Sect. 9.4.2)—Determines the applicable main accounts in the ledger transactions posted with the product (or service) receipt and the invoice (related to the vendor and the item or procurement category).
- **Vendor posting profiles**—Determine the applicable vendor summary account in the ledger transaction posted with the invoice (related to the vendor).

Both references, the reference to the item and to the vendor, are not only available at the level of individual items and vendors, but also at the group level.

3.2.3.2 Settings for Vendor Transactions

Vendor groups (*Accounts payable > Vendors > Vendor groups*) are a primary setting for vendor transactions. In addition to the ID and the description, you can optionally enter a *Default tax group* (for the input tax) in the vendor group. When you create a vendor, the default tax group of the vendor group initializes the sales tax group of the vendor.

Vendor posting profiles (*Accounts payable > Setup > Vendor posting profiles*) control the assignment of vendors to summary accounts ($\rightarrow$ Fig. 3.9). As a prerequisite for posting a purchase transaction, at least one posting profile has to be specified. In addition, the default *Posting profile* for regular purchase transactions has to be specified in the Accounts payable parameters (section *Ledger and sales tax*, tab *Posting*).

The field *Summary account* on the tab *Setup* in the posting profile determines the liability account for the assigned vendors. The assignment of summary accounts is available at three different levels, as specified in the field *Account code*:

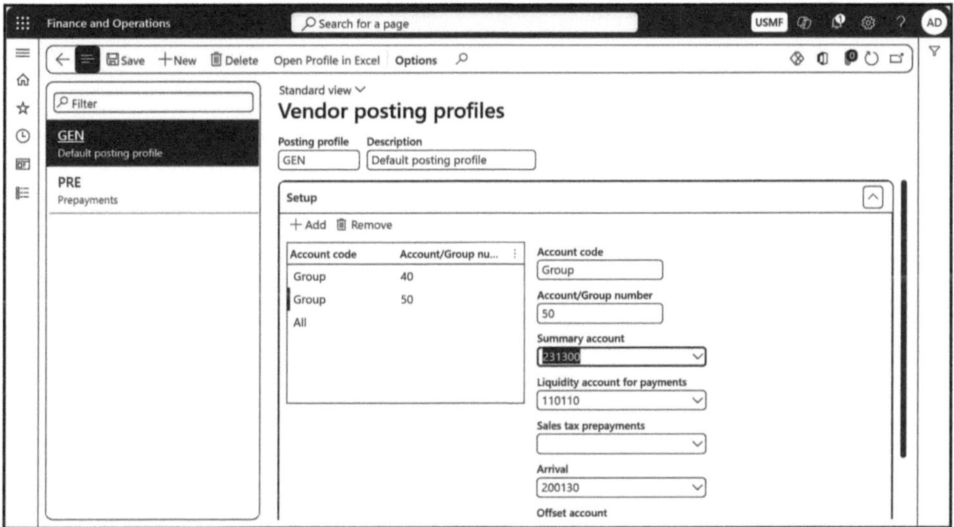

Fig. 3.9 Setting up a vendor posting profile

- **Table**—Assigns a summary account to a particular vendor (enter the vendor number in the field *Account/Group number*).
- **Group**—Assigns a summary account to a vendor group (enter the vendor group in the field *Account/Group number*).
- **All**—Assigns a general summary account (the field *Account/Group number* remains empty).

In order to facilitate reconciling the vendor transactions with the general ledger, the assignment is usually only at the group level. If there are settings at multiple levels, Dynamics 365 uses the most specific setting. The search for this setting starts with the vendor number, and the level "All" has the lowest priority.

If you want to use alternative profile settings for special purposes like prepayment, set up additional posting profiles with account assignments that are different from the settings in the default posting profile. In order to use such a posting profile in a transaction, select it in the particular transaction (e.g., in the Purchase order detail form on the tab *Setup* of the Header view). For prepayment, the posting profile is specified in the Accounts payable parameters.

3.2.4 Case Study Exercises

Exercise 3.1—Terms of Payment

New terms of payment "60 days net" are required in your company. Enter these payment terms in Dynamics 365 with a code P-## (## = your user ID).

In addition, a new cash discount D-## for "14 days with 3 percent discount" is required. Be sure to enter the details for the due date and the cash discount date calculation correctly, and select main accounts that correspond to the accounts in existing cash discounts.

Exercise 3.2—Vendor Record

A new domestic vendor is accepted. Do not use a template when you create this vendor with a name (starting with your user ID) and a primary address of your choice. Select the payment terms and the cash discount of exercise 3.1, and an appropriate vendor group and sales tax group for domestic vendors. Vendor collaboration is not used with this vendor.

> *Notes*: If the number sequence for vendor accounts is set to "Manual", you have to enter the vendor number manually. If the *Tax exempt number* (*VAT number*) is mandatory according to the settings in the Accounts payable parameters, enter the required information on the tab *Invoice and delivery* of the Vendor form.

Exercise 3.3—Ledger Integration

You want to investigate the ledger integration. Can you tell which summary account is used in ledger transactions that are posted with an invoice of the vendor of exercise 3.2?

3.3   Product Management in Purchasing

Purchased items include physical products and intangible goods (e.g., services, fees, licenses). For both types of items, you have to ensure correct and complete master data for the following purposes:

- **Identification**—Clearly describe the item to make sure that the vendor ships the right product.
- **Internal settings**—Multiple settings in the item master data control how the particular item works in Dynamics 365.

For inventoried items, required master data include the product (at the shared level) and the released product (at the company level). For intangible goods, you can also use an item (if you want to manage details like prices in the master data), which you set up in the shared and the released products, similar to an inventoried item, or, without details, a procurement category.

Along with an introduction to the basics of product management, this section primarily contains an explanation of the product data which are necessary for purchasing. In → Sect. 7.2, you can find a general description of the product management in Dynamics 365.

3.3.1   Product Categories and Procurement Categories

Product categories aim to group the products and services in a hierarchical structure. Depending on the requirements, you can set up multiple hierarchies in parallel and assign a product to a different category in each hierarchy.

The hierarchy structure of categories can be simple or complex (with multiple levels). Depending on the hierarchy type, a particular category hierarchy is only used in procurement or also in sales or other areas ($\rightarrow$ Sect. 4.8.2).

You can use categories independently of items. When you purchase a service or intangible item, which is not tracked in inventory, simply enter a procurement category (instead of an item) in the purchase order line in this case.

3.3.1.1 Category Hierarchies and Product Categories

The Category hierarchies page (*Product information management > Setup > Categories and attributes > Category hierarchies*) displays the hierarchies of categories (the different classification variants). The link in the field *Name* of a hierarchy provides access to the Category hierarchy detail form, which shows the structure of the hierarchy ($\rightarrow$ Fig. 3.10).

If you want to set up a completely new category hierarchy, click the button *New* in the Category hierarchy list page. In the *Create* dialog that is shown next, enter a name and a description for the hierarchy before you click the button *Create*. Dynamics 365 then shows the Category hierarchy detail form. If you want to add a new category or a new category folder to a hierarchy, select the parent node in the tree structure on the left and click the button *New category node* in the action pane. In the new category, enter at least the *Name*, the *Code*, and the *Friendly name*.

The purpose of a hierarchy is given by the hierarchy role. Available roles include the "Procurement category hierarchy" for purchasing and the "Sales category hierarchy" for sales. In order to assign a hierarchy to a hierarchy role, open the Category hierarchy role association form (*Product information management > Setup > Categories and*

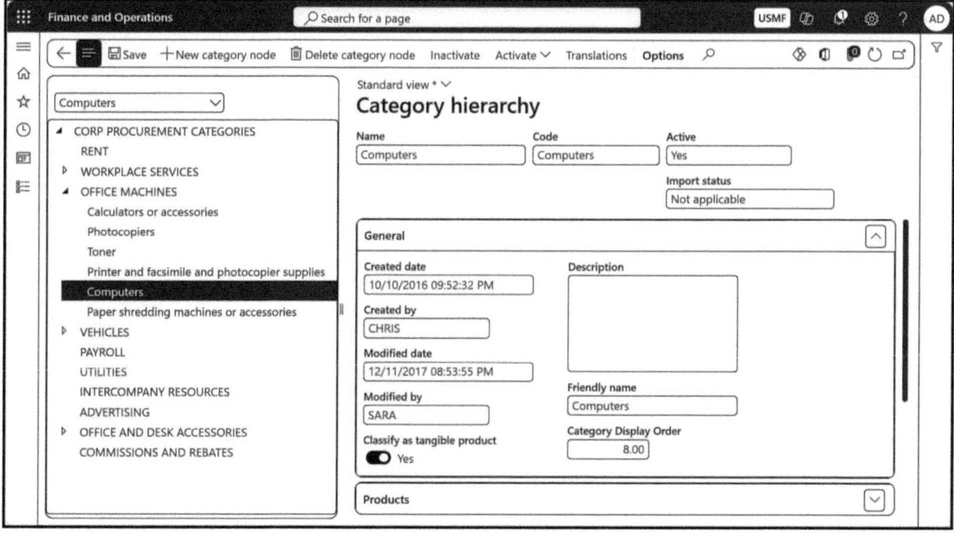

Fig. 3.10 Editing a category in the category hierarchy detail form

attributes > Category hierarchy role associations) and enter a line with a *Category hier-archy type* (select the hierarchy role) and the respective *Category hierarchy*. You can select the same hierarchy in multiple lines.

The purchasing-related data of a procurement category (a category in a hierarchy with the role "Procurement category hierarchy") are specified in a separate form, the Procurement categories form.

3.3.1.2 Procurement Categories

Procurement categories are categories that belong to the hierarchy with the type "Procurement category hierarchy". You can select a procurement category instead of a product number in the lines of purchase transactions (purchase orders, purchase requisitions, purchase agreements).

The Procurement category form (*Procurement and sourcing > Procurement catego-ries*), which shows the purchasing-related settings of these categories, includes the item sales tax group on the tab *Item sales tax groups* as a core setting.

As a prerequisite for the use of procurement categories in purchase transactions, the posting setup (→ Sect. 9.4.2) has to include settings for categories (*Cost manage-ment > Ledger integration policies setup > Posting*, tab *Purchase order*, option *Purchase expenditure for expense*).

3.3.2   Basic Product Data

In order to support multi-company organizations, the structure of product data in Dynamics 365 has two levels:

- **Products ("Shared products")**—Include the common data in all companies.
- **Released products ("Items")**—Include the company-specific data.

Shared products are a mandatory element in the data structure. But in a small enterprise with only one company, you can create products directly in the Released product form.

Notes: Creating a product works differently if your enterprise uses Engineering change man-agement (→ Sect. 7.2.5).

3.3.2.1 Shared Products

The aim of the shared products in Dynamics 365 is to establish a common table with all your products in all your companies. Apart from the product number and the name, shared products do not contain extensive information.

The All products form (*Product information management > Products > All products and product masters*) shows all items at the enterprise level—including regular products, configurable products, and service items (→ Fig. 3.11). If you want to create a new prod-uct, click the button *New* and enter the following data in the *Create product* dialog:

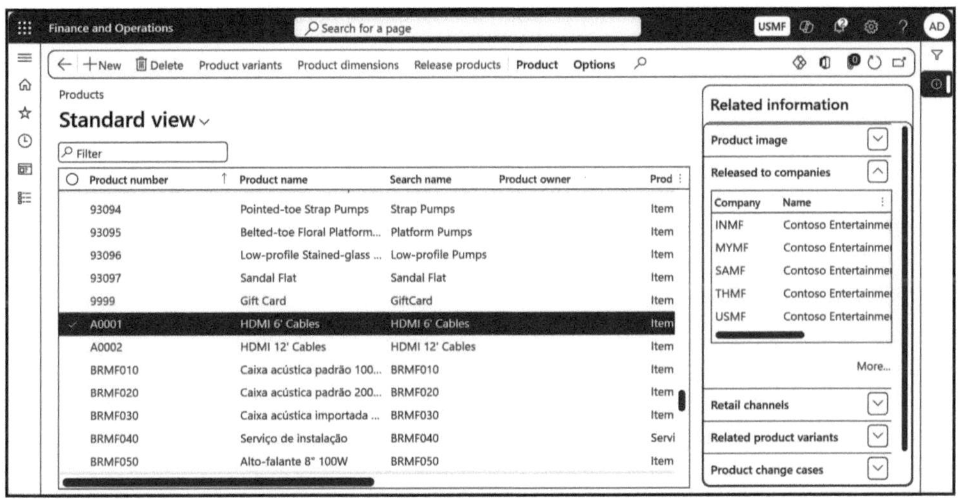

Fig. 3.11   Selecting an item in the list page *all products and product masters*

- **Product type**—"Item" for stocked products, "Service" for services.
- **Product subtype**—"Product" for regular items, "Product master" for items with variants (→ Sect. 7.2.1).
- **Product number**—Enter manually if there is no automatic number from the number sequence.
- **Product name**—Short description in system language.
- **Search name**—Internal text for searching the item.
- **Retail category** (Commerce category)—Product categorization for Dynamics 365 Commerce (including the Retail and Commerce module).
- **Catch weight**—Usually "No", only for catch weight items "Yes" (→ Sect. 7.2.1).

Note: For items with the *Product type* "Service", you can select the option "Warranty" in the additional field *Product service type* for warranty item selling in Dynamics 365 Commerce.

For a regular item that is stored in inventory, select the *Product type* "Item" and the *Product subtype* "Product". For an intangible item or a service, select the *Product type* "Service".

Note: If you select an item model group for non-inventoried products (→ Sect. 7.2.1) in the related released product later, the item is intangible, no matter if the *Product type* is "Item" or "Service".

Once you close the *Create* dialog with the button *OK*, Dynamics 365 creates a shared product and shows the (shared) Product detail form. In the detail form, you can enter further optional settings.

Apart from the fields *Product name* and *Description* in the detail form, which both have to be entered in the system language ($\to$ Sect. 10.3.4), there is a separate form for item descriptions in foreign languages (accessed with the button *Product/Languages/Translations* in the action pane).

If you want to specify the inventory dimensions ($\to$ Sect. 7.2.2), which are used for the product, at the shared level, click the button *Product/Set up/Dimension groups* in the shared product. The inventory dimensions are divided into three groups:

- **Product dimension group**—For the product subtype "Product master", specifies whether the item has versions, styles, sizes, colors, or configurations.
- **Storage dimension group**—Specifies whether the item inventory is tracked at the level of sites, warehouses, locations, inventory status, or license plates.
- **Tracking dimension group**—Specifies whether batch or serial numbers are used. The dimension "Owner" refers to vendor consignment ($\to$ Sect. 7.4.8).

The button *Product/Set up/Product categories* in the shared product provides access to the Product category form, in which you can link the product to categories. Product categories are an optional setup, which enables managing hierarchical product structures (widely used in Dynamics 365 Commerce).

Except for the product dimension group (for product masters), you do not need to enter dimension groups in the shared product. Dimension groups, which are not specified in the shared product, have to be entered in the related released product(s) at the company level. You should specify the dimension groups at the company level (in the released product, and not in the shared product) if there are different dimension settings per company (e.g., if only one company in the enterprise uses locations).

3.3.2.2 Releasing a Product

Before you can register a transaction for a new shared product, you have to release it with the button *Release products* in the action pane of the All products page (you can select multiple products at the same time). The selected product(s) are shown in the *Release products* wizard next. Once you switch to the *Select companies* page of the wizard, put a checkmark in front of all applicable companies. Then confirm the selection with the button *Finish* on the last page.

If applicable (e.g., in a single-company implementation), you can skip creating a shared product and immediately create a new product in the Released product form. If you create a product with the button *New* in the Released product form, the released product and the shared product are created in parallel.

3.3.2.3 Managing Released Products

The released product, also called "Item" in some areas of Dynamics 365, contains the item details. Apart from the Released products form (*Product information management > Products > Released products*), the workspace *Released product maintenance* provides access to the Released product form ($\to$ Fig. 3.12).

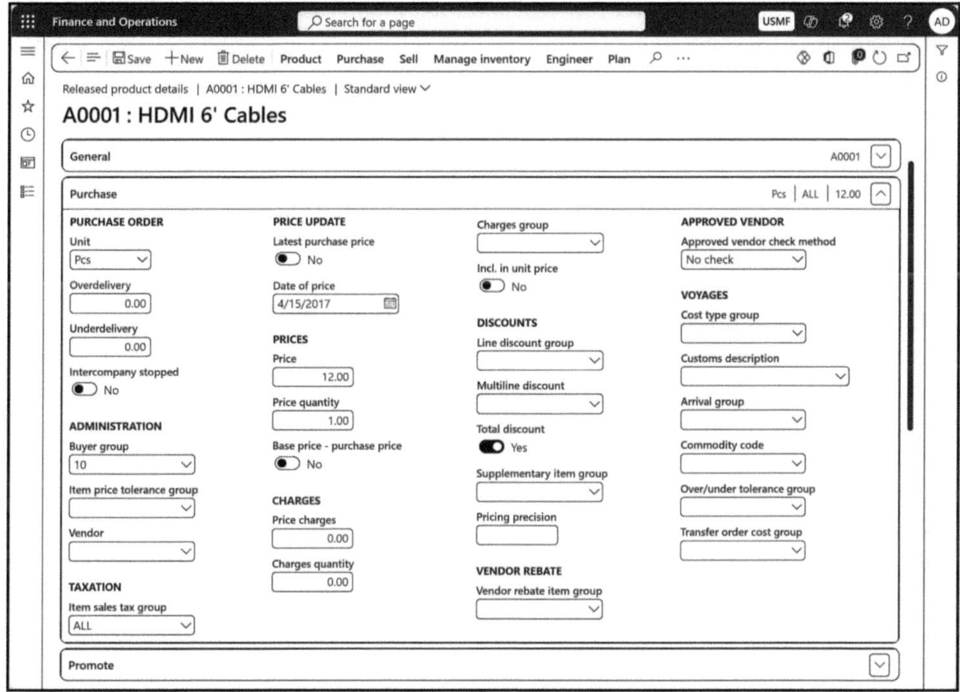

Fig. 3.12 Viewing the purchase-related product data in the released product detail form

In the shared product, you can directly access the related released product with the link in the field *Item number* on the right of the FactBox *Released to companies* (select the line with the appropriate company) and the link in the field *Item number* of the *Product information* dialog, which is shown next.

After releasing a new product, you have to populate the following mandatory fields in the Released product form:

- **Item group** (tab *Manage costs*)—Determines the main accounts for ledger integration.
- **Item model group** (tab *General*)—Determines item handling and inventory valuation.
- **Dimension groups** (button *Product/Set up/Dimension groups*)—Required if not specified in the shared product.
- **Unit of measure** —For purchasing, sales, and inventory.

The default for the inventory unit of measure (field *Unit* on the tab *Manage inventory* in the Released product form) of new items is specified in the Inventory parameters (*Inventory management > Setup > Inventory and warehouse management parameters*, field *Unit* in the section *General*). After specifying an applicable unit conversion to the inventory unit (→ Sect. 7.2.1), you can select different units for sales (on the tab *Sell*) and purchasing (on the tab *Purchase*).

In addition, you should enter the *Item sales tax group* on the tab *Purchase* and on the tab *Sell* (mandatory if the slider *Mandatory item sales tax group* in the section *General* of the Inventory parameters is set to "Yes"). A default value for the item sales tax group is specified on the tab *Setup* in the item group.

In the field *Price* on the tab *Manage costs*, you can enter a base cost price for the item. If the item applies a standard cost valuation (according to the selected item model group), click the button *Manage costs/Set up/Item price* in the action pane and enter a cost price per site (→ Sect. 7.3.3).

3.3.2.4 Purchasing Related Data and Default Order Settings

The tab *Purchase* in the Released product detail form contains core purchasing data, including the item sales tax group already mentioned. The *Buyer group* provides the option to specify the purchasing responsibility for the item. The lookup field *Approved vendor check method*, initialized from the corresponding field in the item model group, controls whether you can purchase the item only from approved vendors. If you select the option "Warning only" or "Not allowed" in this field, enter the allowed vendors in the Approved vendor page, which you access with the button *Purchase/Approved vendor/Setup* in the action pane of the Release product form.

Essential order-related settings of a released product are specified in the default order settings, which you access with the button *Manage inventory/Order settings/Default order settings* in the Released product form. In the default order settings, the record with a blank *Site* and the *Rank* "0" determines the default order settings at the company level.

The field *Default order type*, which is only editable at the company level, controls how to supply the item. The default order type "Purchase order" determines that the item is purchased externally, whereas the default order types "Production" (for discrete manufacturing and process manufacturing) and "Kanban" (for lean manufacturing) specify internal production. You can override the default order type with settings in the item coverage (→ Sect. 6.3.4).

The tab *Purchase order* in the default order settings contains the purchasing-related settings—including default values for the lot size (field *Multiple*) and the order quantity (field *Standard order quantity*). A checkmark in the checkbox *Stopped* on this tab blocks the item for purchase transactions.

If you want to specify order settings at the level of sites (→ Sect. 10.1.6), which you can use for subsidiaries, insert an additional record in the default order settings with the *Site* in the respective field. The field *Rank*, which determines the search priority within the default order settings, is automatically populated with the next number. In order to override the default order settings at the company level with settings at the level of the site, set the applicable slider *Override default settings* in the site-specific order settings to "Yes".

If the item is a product master, which is a product with variants (→ Sect. 7.2.1), you can also enter default order settings at the variant level.

When you enter an order (e.g., a purchase order), the default order settings initialize various fields in the order line (e.g., the order quantity). You can override the default values in the order line afterward.

3.3.3   Purchase Price Setup

The basic functionality for pricing (including trade agreements) in purchasing is very similar to the functionality in sales. Pricing in purchase management includes a multi-stage calculation of prices and discounts, which starts with the base price in the Released product form and continues with trade agreements at the level of vendor groups and individual vendors.

Since many companies use a more comprehensive setup for prices and discounts in sales than in purchasing, the section below only covers the base prices. You can find details on trade agreements for prices and discounts in → Sect. 4.8.1.

Apart from discounts that are deducted immediately, there is the option to manage vendor rebate contracts with a retrospective discount depending on the purchasing volume in a given period (→ Sect. 4.9.4).

3.3.3.1 Base Purchase Price

The base purchase price is specified in the field *Price* on the tab *Purchase* of the Released product form. This price is the price per purchase unit (field *Unit* on the tab *Purchase*).

The field *Price quantity* determines the quantity that is the basis for this price. Usually, the price quantity is "1", but you can, for example, enter "100" in the *Price quantity* to specify that the *Price* is a price for 100 purchase units (in order to deal with a very small unit price).

If you want to record different base purchase prices per site (subsidiary), click the button *Manage costs/Set up/Item price* in the released product to open the Item price form. In this form, you can enter and activate a price per site as described in → Sect. 7.3.3 (use the *Price type* "Purchase price").

The base purchase price is used in purchase orders if there is no applicable trade agreement for the particular vendor and item. Since prices (and price charges) in the Released product form are shown in the accounting currency of the current company, there is a conversion of the base purchase price to the currency of the purchase order if the order applies a foreign currency.

> *Note*: The Pricing management (→ Sect. 4.8.3) introduces the additional slider *Base price— purchase price* on the tab *Purchase* of the Released product form, which controls calculating base sales prices in the Pricing management.

3.3.3.2 Automatic Price Update

If the slider *Latest purchase price* on the tab *Purchase* of the released product is set to "Yes", the base purchase price in the released product is updated with the invoiced price whenever you post a purchase order invoice for the item. With this setting, not only the field *Price* on the tab *Purchase* of the released product (which is the default value for the next order if no other price is applicable) is updated with the latest purchase price, the Item price form (access with the button *Manage costs/Set up/Item price* in the released product) also shows this price update.

If you want to track the history of price updates, activate the price history (Inventory parameters, slider *Last price history* in the section *Inventory accounting*). If the price history is activated, the Item price form will insert new item price records in case of price changes (instead of updating existing item price records).

3.3.3.3 Price Charges

In order to record charges (like fees and freight), which are added to the base price, you can optionally enter *Price charges* on the tab *Purchase* of the released product.

If the slider *Incl. in unit price* is set to "No", the amount entered in the field *Price charges* is added to the total of an order line, irrespective of the quantity. An example for this setting: If an item got a *Price* of USD 3.00 and *Price charges* of USD 1.00 in the Released product form, a purchase order line with 10 units of this item will show a unit price of USD 3.00 and a line amount of USD 31.00. The price charges are not shown in a separate field on printed purchasing documents.

If the slider *Incl. in unit price* is set to "Yes", Dynamics 365 adds the price charges to the unit price. In this case, the field *Charges quantity* determines the quantity basis for allocating the price charges to the unit price. An example for this setting: If an item got a *Price* of USD 3.00, a *Charges quantity* of 0.00 (or 1.00), and *Price charges* of USD 1.00 in the Released product form, a purchase order line with 10 units of this item will show a unit price of USD 4.00 and a line amount of USD 40.00.

Apart from the general price charges in the Released product form, you can manage site-specific price charges for an item in the Item price form.

In the context of charges, do not confuse the price charges in the released product with charges codes and charges transactions, which are managed separately in orders. You can find more details on charges management in → Sect. 4.3.4.

3.3.4 Case Study Exercises

Exercise 3.4—Procurement Categories

Your company wants to purchase a new kind of service, for which you have to set up appropriate categories in the procurement category hierarchy. Enter a new category node "##-services" with the categories "##-assembling" and "##-fees" (## = your user ID). The procurement categories refer to the standard tax rate.

Exercise 3.5—Product Record

In order to process purchase orders in the following exercises, you want to set up a new product. Create a shared product with the product number I-## and the name "##-merchandise" (## = your user ID). It is a stocked product with inventory control at the level of the site and warehouse. Variants and serial/batch numbers are not required. Select the appropriate dimension groups in the shared product.

Then release the product to your test company. In the released product, select an appropriate item group for merchandise and an item model group with FIFO-valuation. The item does not require approved vendors.

The item sales tax group for sales and for purchasing should refer to the standard tax rate. The unit of measurement for the item is "Pieces" in all areas, and the main vendor is the vendor of exercise 3.2. The base purchase price and the base cost price are USD 50, and the base sales price is USD 100.

In the default order settings for purchasing and for sales, enter default quantities (*Multiple* 20, *Standard order quantity* 100) and select the main site and the main warehouse. Only in purchasing, there is a *Min. order quantity* of 40 pieces.

> *Note*: If the number sequence for product numbers is set up for automatic numbering, you don't have to enter a product number.

3.4   Purchase Order Management

An order is a firm commitment to supply and accept goods or services on agreed terms. For this reason, purchase orders have to include at least the following details: Vendor (name, address), commercial terms (currency, payment terms, terms of delivery), product (identification, quantity, unit of measure), price (price, discount), receipt date, and delivery address.

3.4.1   Basics of Purchase Order Processing

Apart from manually entering a new purchase order, there are the following options to generate an order automatically:

- **Master planning**—Generate an order from a planned order ($\rightarrow$ Sect. 6.3.5).
- **Purchase requisition**—Generate from a requisition ($\rightarrow$ Sect. 3.8.2).
- **Request for quotation**—Generate from a quotation ($\rightarrow$ Sect. 3.8.3).
- **Purchase agreement**—Generate as a release order ($\rightarrow$ Sect. 3.8.1).
- **Direct delivery**—Generate from a sales order ($\rightarrow$ Sect. 4.7.1).
- **Subcontracting**—Generate from a production order ($\rightarrow$ Sect. 5.7.2).
- **Inventory ownership change**—For consignment inventory ($\rightarrow$ Sect. 7.4.8).

- **Project accounting**—Generate from an item task in the Project module.
- **Purchase journal**—Generate from an order with the type "Journal".

Master planning generates planned purchase orders as a result. You can create actual purchase orders by firming the planned purchase orders then. Depending on the master planning setup (firming time fence), master planning may skip planned orders and immediately create actual purchase orders.

Purchase requisitions are internal documents that request the purchase of an item. They have to be entered or initiated by the person who wants the item (e.g., for items like office supplies).

Requests for quotation are required if you want to obtain and compare quotes from multiple vendors. You can create a request for quotation either automatically from a purchase requisition or a planned order, or enter it manually.

Purchase order processing related to projects is part of the Project management and accounting module.

Other ways for creating purchase orders in Dynamics 365 are automatic transfers with an import from external applications, or the intercompany functionality (purchasing from an affiliated company in a common Dynamics 365 environment).

After creating and, if required, approving a purchase order, you can process the order from the start to the end as shown in → Fig. 3.13. Confirming the purchase order and posting the vendor invoice are the only mandatory steps in standard purchase order processing. Depending on your organization and the setup, some of the other steps may also be mandatory.

If required, you can process a prepayment (→ Sect. 9.3.5) before receiving the goods and the regular invoice.

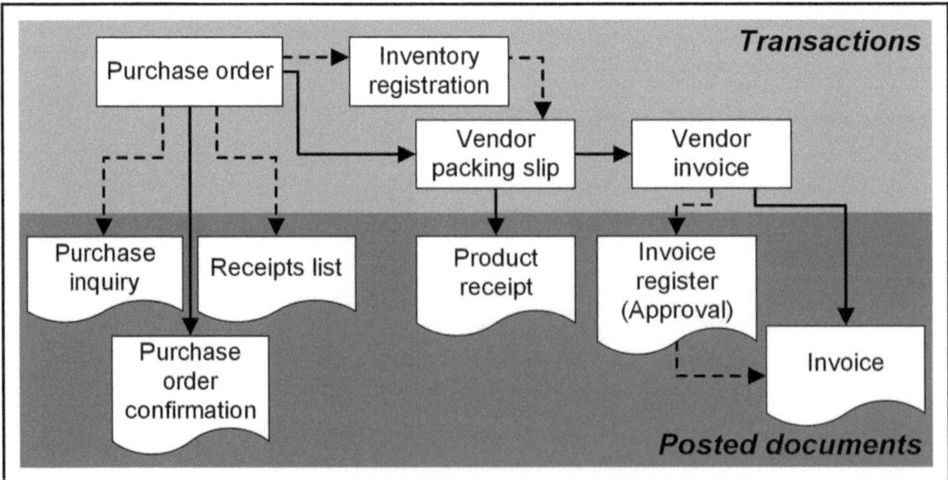

Fig. 3.13 Purchase order processing in dynamics 365

3.4.1.1 Approving and Confirming Purchase Orders

In a purchase order that is subject to change management, you have to submit the order for approval. Depending on the order and the approval workflow, there is either an automatic or a manual approval. If change management does not apply, the approval status of the order is immediately "Approved".

Once the order is approved, you can optionally post a purchase inquiry, which is a document for the vendor to review and confirm the order from their side.

The next mandatory step in order processing is the order confirmation, which usually includes sending a hard copy or electronic order document to the vendor.

3.4.1.2 Receipts List and Inventory Registration

If your warehouse requires a printed list of purchased items for information purposes and for preparing the item arrival, you can post and print a receipts list.

Unlike the receipts list, inventory registration, as the next step, updates the on-hand quantity in inventory. The inventory registration, which contains all required inventory dimensions (depending on the item, this includes the warehouse, location, serial number, or batch number), is an optional step before posting the product receipt. Depending on the business processes in the warehouse, there are the following alternatives for the inventory registration:

- **Registration form**—Inventory registration in the purchase order line.
- **Item arrival journal**—Inventory registration with a journal in inventory.
- **Mobile device transactions**—In the advanced warehouse management.

> *Note*: If the checkbox *Registration requirements* is selected in the item model group of the purchased item, inventory registration is not optional, but a mandatory step before posting the product receipt.

3.4.1.3 Product Receipts

The product receipt, which is the commercial acknowledgement that you have received the items, generates inventory transactions and, depending on the setup, general ledger transactions. You can post the product receipt either in the purchase order, in the appropriate menu item in the Procurement and sourcing module, or in the posted item arrival journal.

3.4.1.4 Vendor Invoices

Once you receive the vendor invoice, you can enter it in the Purchase order form or directly in the Pending vendor invoice form. Depending on the setup, it is not possible to post the invoice before obtaining approval in a workflow.

An alternative way for vendor invoice processing is to enter and post an invoice register and a subsequent invoice approval journal.

3.4.1.5 Physical and Financial Transactions

Inventory transactions consist of two components: The physical transaction and the financial transaction. Generally speaking, packing slips (product receipts) are physical transactions, and invoices are financial transactions. You should distinguish these transactions, in particular with regard to inventory valuation and ledger posting. You can find more details on this subject in → Sect. 7.2.4.

3.4.2 Purchase Order Registration

Like all documents, purchase orders consist of a header and one or more lines (→ Fig. 3.14). The header contains the common data of the order, including the order number, vendor, language, currency, and payment terms.

Some other fields in the order header (e.g., the *Requested receipt date*) are only a default value for the order lines—you can override them at the line level. If you modify header data after creating order lines, settings in the procurement parameters (*Procurement and sourcing > Setup > Procurement and sourcing parameters*, section *General*, button *Update order lines* in the toolbar of the tab *Default values and parameters*) control whether the present order lines are updated automatically.

The default value for the *Purchase type* in the purchase order header is specified in the section *General* of the Procurement parameters (usually "Purchase order" for regular purchase orders). There are the following options for the purchase type in a purchase order:

- **Purchase order**—Regular purchase order.
- **Journal**—Draft or template, with no impact on inventory or finance.
- **Returned order**—Credit note (→ Sect. 3.7.1).

Fields that you enter in the order lines include the *Item number* (or *Procurement category*), *Text* (initialized with the item description), *Quantity, Price, Requested receipt date*, and

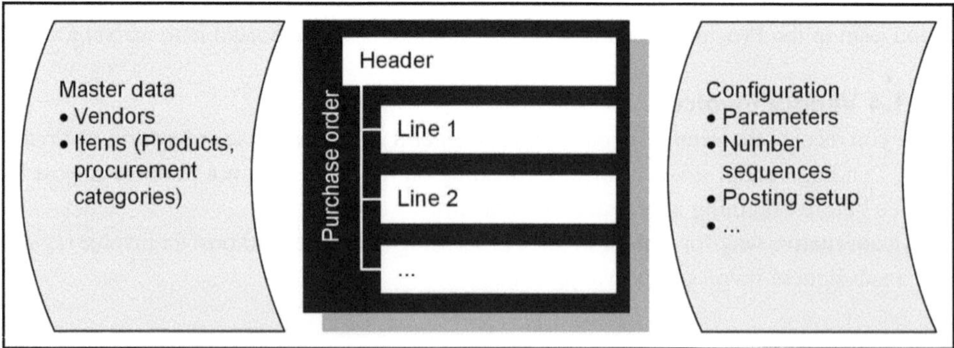

Fig. 3.14 Structure of purchase orders

other data as applicable. When ordering an inventoried item, select the item number of a released product. For non-inventoried items (e.g., services), you can enter the item number of an intangible item, or skip the item number and select a procurement category.

When you create a purchase order header or line, Dynamics 365 initializes several fields with default values from the vendor in the header and from the item in the line. Depending on your permissions, you can subsequently update the content of the fields in the purchase order. If you agree, for example, to particular payment terms in a purchase order, change the terms of payment in the order header. If the new payment terms apply to all future orders, you should also change the terms of payment in the vendor record to make sure that you receive the right default value when entering the next order with this vendor.

3.4.2.1 Entering Purchase Orders

Depending on your personal preferences, you can start from one of the following forms to create or update a purchase order manually:

- **Vendor form**—Preferably, if you want to start with a vendor search.
- **Purchase order form**—Preferably, if you want to edit an existing order (e.g., if you look for all orders that are not yet approved).
- **Purchase order preparation workspace**—Several filtered lists with orders.

In the Vendor form (*Procurement and sourcing > Vendors > All vendors*), you can click the button *Procurement/New/Purchase order* to create an order. Dynamics 365 creates a purchase order header with default data from the selected vendor and switches to the Lines view of the Purchase order detail form, in which you can enter the first order line immediately. If you want to access the current orders of a vendor from the Vendor list page or detail form, click the button *Procurement/Related information/Purchase orders/All purchase orders*. Dynamics 365 then shows the Purchase order list page filtered on the selected vendor.

The workspace *Purchase order preparation*, which you can access from the folder *Workspaces* in the *Procurement and sourcing* menu or from the homepage (Immersive home or dashboard), contains several lists with purchase orders grouped by approval status. Click on a purchase order number shown as a link in the grid if you want to view the order in the Purchase order detail form. If you want to create a new order from the workspace, click the button *New purchase order* in the action pane. The subsequent steps are the same as when creating an order from the Purchase order list page.

The Purchase order list page (*Procurement and sourcing > Purchase orders > All purchase orders*) shows a list of all purchase orders. In order to view the details of a purchase order, click the link in the field *Purchase order* in the grid.

If you want to enter a new purchase order in the Purchase order list page, press the shortcut *Alt + N* or click the button *New* in the action pane. In the *Create purchase order* dialog, select the vendor in the field *Vendor account* first (→ Fig. 3.15). You can search the

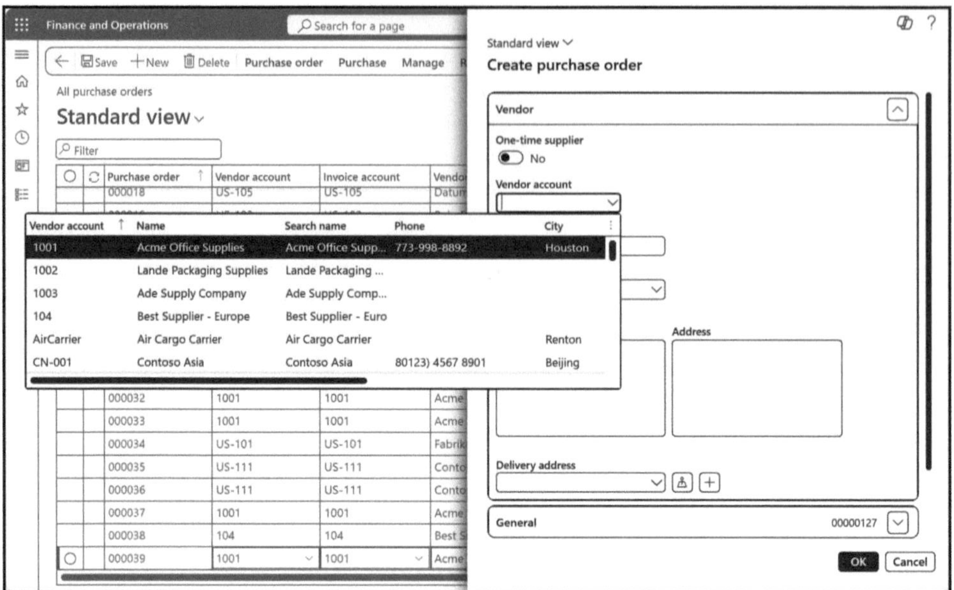

Fig. 3.15 Creating a new purchase order in the purchase order list page

vendor by typing the first characters of the vendor number (or the name), or by explicitly opening the lookup, in which you can use a grid column filter (e.g., for filtering on the column *Name* of the lookup).

Once you select a vendor, the *Create* dialog retrieves various default values from the vendor record. You can expand the tabs *General* and *Administration* in the dialog to access additional fields of the new order header. If you want to change data like the vendor number, purchase type, or currency, you can update the particular field in the dialog or, after closing the dialog, in the Header view of the Purchase order detail form.

When you close the dialog with the button *OK*, Dynamics 365 creates the order header and switches to the Purchase order detail form in the Lines view.

3.4.2.2 Purchase Order Lines

In order to create an order line in the Lines view of the Purchase order detail form, click the button *Add line* in the toolbar of the tab *Purchase order lines*, or simply click the first line in the grid and select an *Item number* (released product) or a *Procurement category*. Data in the released product initialize numerous fields in the order line—e.g., the *Quantity*, the *Unit*, the *Unit price*, or the *Site* and the *Warehouse*. If the site and warehouse are specified in the order header, they take priority over the default order settings of the item.

Trade agreements ($\rightarrow$ Sect. 4.8.1) can override the primary default for the *Unit price*, which is the base price specified in the Released product form. They also provide a default for the discount fields. The net amount in a line is calculated from the quantity, unit price, and discounts. You can update the field *Net amount* manually—Dynamics 365 clears the unit price and discount in this case.

The *Line number* is automatically populated when you save the order line. The default for line numbers derives from the field *Increment* in the System parameters (*System administration > Setup > System parameters*).

If you want to view additional line data (e.g., the receipt date), expand the tab *Line details* and switch to the respective sub-tab (→ Fig. 3.16). The *Requested receipt date* on the sub-tab *Delivery* in the line details receives its default value from the purchase order header if this date is after the lead time of the item. Otherwise, the default for the receipt date of the line is the lead time added to the session date. You can specify the purchase lead time of the item at different levels—in the default order settings of the item, in a purchase price trade agreement, or in the item coverage. Once the vendor confirms a receipt date, enter this date in the field *Confirmed receipt date* of the order line. If a confirmed date is entered, this date is used by Master planning instead of the requested date.

3.4.2.3 Inventory Transactions

When you enter a line with an inventoried product in a regular purchase order, Dynamics 365 creates a corresponding inventory transaction. You can view this transaction with the button *Inventory/Transactions* in the toolbar of the order line. The receipt status of the transaction is "Ordered" (or, for lines with a negative quantity, the issue status is "On order"), and the fields *Physical date* and *Financial date* are empty. In the course of

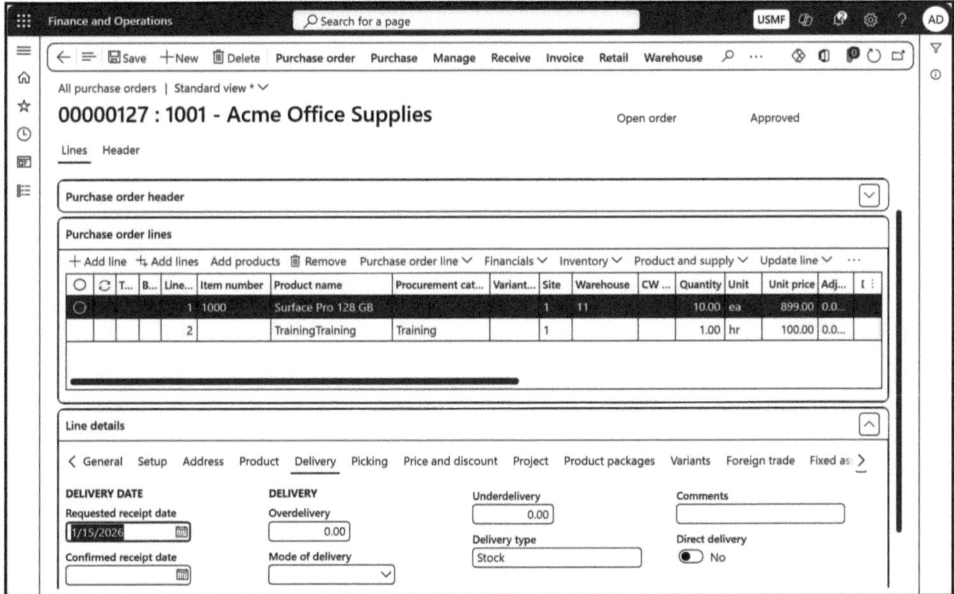

Fig. 3.16 Updating the requested receipt date in a purchase order line

purchase order processing, the product receipt and the vendor invoice update this inventory transaction ($\rightarrow$ Sect. 7.2.4).

3.4.2.4 Intangible Items and Procurement Categories

If you want to order an intangible item (e.g., a particular service), select the item number of a non-inventoried product—item with the product type "Service" and/or linked to an item model group for non-stocked items ($\rightarrow$ Sect. 7.2.1)—and enter the order line in the same way as a line with a regular inventoried item.

Alternatively, you can skip the item number field in the order line and select a procurement category. The procurement category does not include as many details as the item record. For this reason, you have to enter various details in the order line manually—e.g., the quantity, the unit, the unit price, and the line text (on the sub-tab *General*).

3.4.2.5 Delivery Addresses

You can manage the delivery address—the address to which the vendor should ship the items—on the tab *Address* in the Header view of the purchase order. The default for this address is the delivery address of the current company, specified on the tab *Addresses* in the Legal entity form (*Organization administration > Organizations > Legal entities*). If you select a site or warehouse in the order header, and an address is specified for this site or warehouse (e.g., in the form *Inventory management > Setup > Inventory breakdown > Warehouses*), this address takes priority over the company address.

There are two options to change the delivery address in a purchase order:

- **Select an existing address**—If already included in the global address book.
- **Insert a new address**—If the address is completely new.

You can select the address of the current company, the site, or the warehouse in the field *Delivery address* on the tab *Address* in the Header view of the purchase order. If you want to select another address from the global address book (e.g., a customer address), click the button ⊡ on the right of the field *Delivery address*. The *Address selection* dialog then provides the option to select an address from the global address book.

If you want to specify a completely new address, click the button ⊞ on the right of the field *Delivery address*. In the *New address* dialog that is shown next, enter the delivery address—similar to a vendor address ($\rightarrow$ Sect. 3.2.1)—and optionally set the slider *One-time* to "Yes".

If you need separate delivery addresses at the line level, open the sub-tab *Address* on the tab *Line details* in the purchase order lines. In the lines, you can select existing addresses or create new addresses (like in the header). But be aware that documents like the purchase order, which you send to the vendor, usually show the delivery address at the header level.

> **Note**: If the slider *One-time* in the *New address* dialog is set to "No" and you select the option "Delivery" in the field *Purpose* when creating a new address, the address is included in the regular receipt addresses of the current company.

3.4.2.6 Input Tax (Sales Tax)

The applicable input tax (Sales tax/VAT) depends on the vendor and the item:

- **Sales tax group**—The vendor record contains the *Sales tax group* (VAT group), which usually distinguishes between domestic vendors and foreign vendors. For companies within the European Union, "EU vendors" is another group.
- **Item sales tax group**—The item record (released product) contains the *Item sales tax group* (item VAT group), which separates items at a regular tax rate and other items, which are subject to a reduced rate (e.g., food in many countries).

Purchase order header and lines retrieve the tax groups from the vendor and the item. Based on these groups and related settings, the applicable tax is calculated automatically. You can edit the *Sales tax group* on the tab *Setup* in the Header view. The header sales tax group initializes the sales tax group in the lines. In the lines, you can edit the *Sales tax group* and the *Item sales tax group* on the sub-tab *Setup* of the tab *Line details*. If you want to view the calculated sales tax, click the button *Purchase/Tax/Sales tax* in the Purchase order form.

3.4.2.7 Charges (Surcharges)

If an order includes additional costs like freight or insurance, you can use charges at the order header level or at the line level. The functionality of charges in purchasing corresponds to charges in sales (→ Sect. 4.3.4). With the button *Purchase/Charges/Maintain charges* in the action pane of a purchase order, you can access the charges that refer to the order header. In order to access the line charges, select the respective order line and click the button *Financials/Maintain charges* in the toolbar of the tab *Purchase order lines*.

3.4.2.8 Delivery Schedule

If you have a purchase order with an item that you want to receive in multiple deliveries, enter multiple lines with the same item but different receipt dates. In order to simplify administration, you can use the delivery schedule functionality for managing order lines with common commercial conditions (price, discounts) but multiple deliveries.

Entering a delivery schedule starts by inserting a regular order line with the total quantity of all deliveries. Then click the button *Purchase order line/Delivery schedule* in the toolbar of the order lines. In the *Delivery schedule* dialog, enter the lines for the individual deliveries with quantity and receipt date. Once you close the dialog with the button *OK*, Dynamics 365 creates additional purchase order lines for the deliveries. Only these delivery lines are included in the product receipt and the invoice, and in the calculation of the item availability. The original order line can be used to manage a common price and discount for the delivery lines.

The column *Type* on the left in the purchase order lines indicates whether an order line is the total quantity line or a delivery line.

3.4.2.9 Header View and Lines View

When you access the Purchase order detail form, it is shown in the Lines view. At the top of the page, a header line displays the order number and the vendor on the left, and the order status and the approval status on the right. After expanding the tab *Purchase order header* in the Lines view, it shows selected header fields (e.g., the receipt date).

If you want to view the complete header, click the button *Header* above the tabs in the detail form, or press the shortcut *Ctrl + Shift + H*. In order to switch back from the Header view to the Lines view, click the button *Lines* or press the shortcut *Ctrl + Shift + L*.

3.4.2.10 Copying Purchase Orders

In order to support entering a purchase order that is similar to an existing order, you can copy the existing order. This order does not need to be of the same purchase type. You can, for example, copy an order with the type "Journal" into a regular purchase order.

In order to copy a purchase order into a new order, create a new order header into which you want to copy. In the new order, click the button *Purchase order/Copy/From all* in the action pane. The *Copy from other document* dialog, which is shown next, displays a list of purchase orders on the tab *Purchase orders*, and of other documents on the lower tabs. Select the checkbox in the left-most column as shown in → Fig. 3.17 to mark the records which you want to copy—entire orders in the section *Headers*, or individual order lines in the section *Lines*.

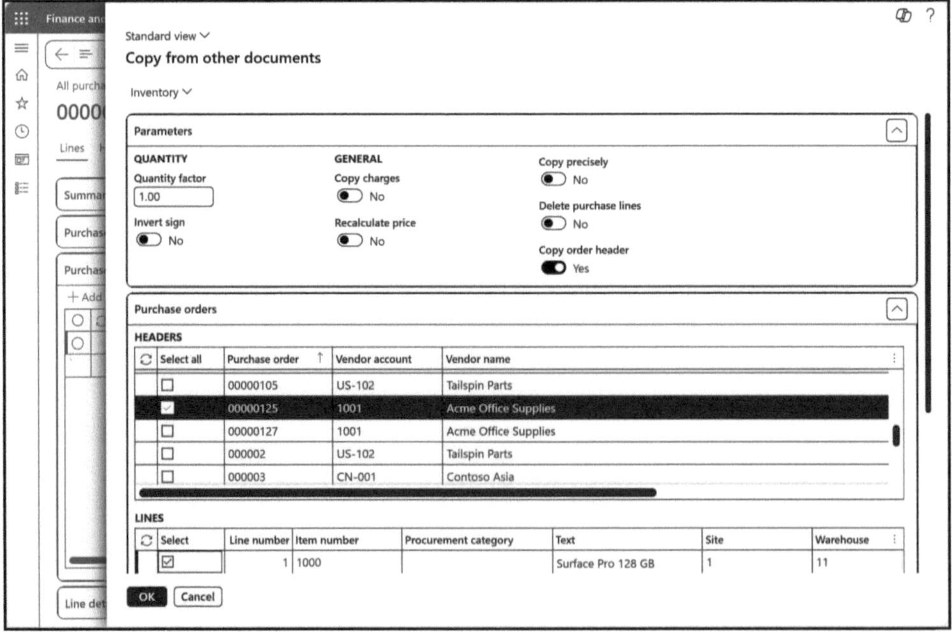

Fig. 3.17 Selecting orders and order lines in the *copy from other documents* dialog

When you copy an order, be aware of the slider *Delete purchase lines* on the tab *Parameters*. If this slider is set to "Yes", all lines of the new order are deleted before the copied lines are inserted. This does not matter for a new order, but it might be unintended if you only want to copy additional lines to an existing order.

Once you have selected the order headers and the lines (lines can refer to different headers), click the button *OK* to close the *Copy* dialog. Dynamics 365 copies the selected lines, depending on the slider *Copy order header*, including header data like the payment terms (if you want to copy header data, select one header).

In addition to the *Copy from all* button, there is another button for copying in the Purchase order form—the button *Purchase order/Copy/From journal*. You can use this button if there is a purchase order with posted documents (e.g., vendor invoices) and you want to transfer the posted lines into the order again.

In addition to the Copy buttons in the action pane, the Copy features are also available within the button *Purchase order line* in the toolbar of the order lines.

3.4.2.11 Purchase Journal Orders

Purchase orders with the *Purchase type* "Journal" are used as a draft or template. It is not possible to post a document (e.g., an order confirmation or a product receipt) in orders with this purchase type, and the order lines do not generate inventory transactions. Apart from copying a purchase journal to a regular purchase order, you can transfer a journal to a purchase order by simply changing the purchase type in the order header, or with the periodic activity *Procurement and sourcing > Purchase orders > Purchase journal > Post purchase journal*.

3.4.3   Change Management and Purchase Order Approval

Depending on the settings for change management, a purchase order has to be approved in an approval workflow after creating the order.

3.4.3.1 Change Management Settings

The Procurement parameters (*Procurement and sourcing > Setup > Procurement and sourcing parameters*) contain the core settings for purchase order change management. In the section *General* of the parameters form, the slider *Activate change management* controls whether the approval workflow is activated for all purchase orders.

If the slider *Allow override of settings per vendor* in the Procurement parameters is set to "Yes", you can enter divergent settings for particular vendors. These settings are available in the Vendor detail form on the tab *Purchase order defaults*, where you can set the slider *Override settings* in the field group *Change management for purchase orders* to "Yes" to override the general setting in either direction: Activating change management only for specific vendors (while approval is not required in general), or the other way around.

The purchase order approval process is based on the workflow system ($\rightarrow$ Sect. 10.4.2). You can manage the procurement workflows in the menu item *Procurement and Sourcing > Setup > Procurement and sourcing workflows*. Purchase order workflows are workflows with the *Workflow type* "Purchase order workflow" or "Purchase order line workflow".

3.4.3.2 Approval Status

The purchase order header contains the *Approval status*, which is displayed in a separate column in the Purchase order list page. Depending on the approval workflow, a purchase order has the following approval status:

- **Draft**—Initial approval status, before submitting for approval.
- **In review**—After submitting, while the order is waiting for approval.
- **Rejected**—After the reviewer rejects approval (resubmit or recall in this case).
- **Approved**—After approval (the next step is the order confirmation).
- **In external review**—After posting the purchase inquiry (optional step).
- **Confirmed**—After posting the purchase order confirmation.

In addition, there is the approval status "Finalized". This status, which you can set with the button *Purchase/Actions/Finalize* in the Purchase order form, is only available after posting the invoice (or canceling the order). Finalizing is an optional last step in order processing, which blocks the order from any changes. It is only necessary when working with budget control and encumbrances.

If change management is not activated for a purchase order, the approval status of the order immediately becomes "Approved", and you can continue order processing and confirm the order.

3.4.3.3 Approval Workflow for Purchase Orders

In a purchase order with activated change management, the button *Workflow* is shown in the action pane, and the initial approval status of the order is "Draft". Click the button *Workflow/Submit* to submit the order for approval after entering the order in this case. Approval is also required after modifying an order that has already been approved.

After submitting for approval, the approval status switches to "In review" and the workflow system starts processing the approval workflow in a batch process.

Because of this batch process, it is not possible to post the order confirmation for a purchase order immediately if change management is active. Even if a workflow with automatic approval applies, you have to wait until the workflow system has finished the batch process. If a manual approval is required, the responsible person has to decide whether to approve the purchase order. The work items assigned to this person ($\rightarrow$ Sect. 10.4.3) usually are the starting point for manual approvals.

3.4.3.4 Request Changes

If you want to edit a purchase order after approval, click the button *Purchase order/ Maintain/Request change* in the Purchase order form. Once you have finished the changes on the purchase order, you have to submit the order for approval again.

When deciding on the approval of a modified order, the responsible person can click the button *Manage/History/Compare to recent versions* to compare the current purchase order with the last confirmed version. With the button *Manage/History/View purchase order versions* in the Purchase order form, you can compare all precedent versions.

3.4.4   Canceling and Deleting Purchase Orders

There is a difference between canceling and deleting a purchase order: Whereas canceling removes the open quantity (the expected quantity for future product receipts), deleting eliminates the entire order or the selected order line.

Deleting an order is not possible after posting the order confirmation, or, if change management applies, after approval. But you can still cancel the order.

3.4.4.1 Canceling Purchase Orders or Order Lines

You should cancel a purchase order line if you do not expect any further deliveries for the line. For this purpose, select the respective order line and click the button *Update line/ Deliver remainder* in the toolbar of the purchase order lines. In the *Update remaining quantity* dialog, which is shown next, you can change or cancel the remaining quantity (*Deliver remainder*). If you want to cancel the deliver remainder, click the button *Cancel quantity* in the dialog. This sets the deliver remainder to zero (→ Fig. 3.18). Alternatively, you can enter zero in the field *Purchase quantity* and click the button *OK* in the dialog.

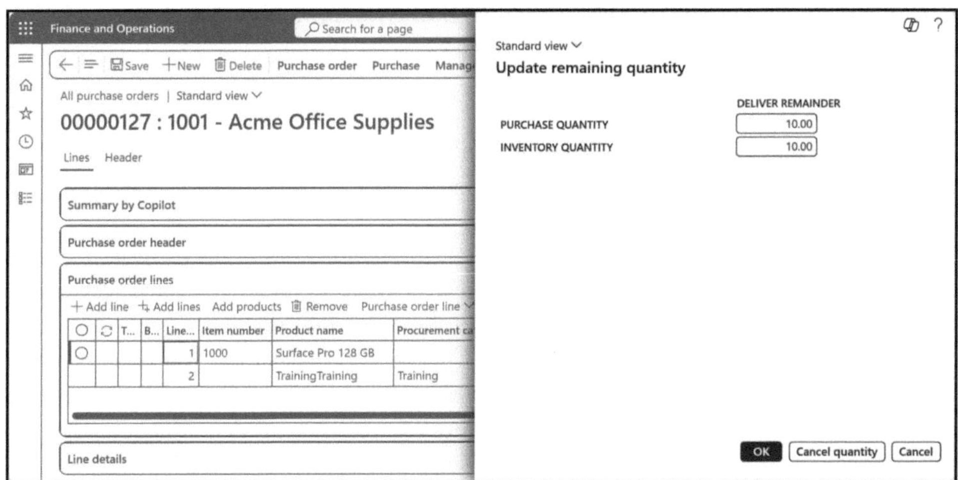

Fig. 3.18 Modifying or cancelling a remaining line quantity in the *update quantity* dialog

Once you have closed the dialog with the button *OK* or *Cancel quantity*, the deliver remainder in the order line is adjusted. If partial deliveries have been received already, canceling has no impact on these receipts—you just do not expect any further receipts.

If the purchase order confirmation has been posted already, you can cancel the complete order with the button *Purchase order/Maintain/Cancel* in the action pane of the purchase order. After canceling a complete order (that is, all lines of the order), the order status is "Canceled".

3.4.4.2 Deleting Purchase Orders or Order Lines

Unlike canceling, which reduces the open quantity of an order line, deleting a purchase order line removes it from Dynamics 365. In order to delete a purchase order line, select it and click the button *Remove* in the toolbar of the order lines (or press the shortcut *Alt + Del*).

If you want to delete a complete order, click the button *Delete* in the action pane at the top of the Purchase order form or, after selecting the order header, press the shortcut *Alt + Del*.

Once you have posted the order confirmation or submitted the order for approval, you can't delete the order completely. If you want to delete an order line in an approved order that is subject to change management (→ Sect. 3.4.3), you have to request a change with the button *Purchase order/Maintain/Request change*.

3.4.5   Purchase Inquiries and Order Confirmations

Once the order entry and—if required—the approval process is completed, the approval status of the purchase order is "Approved". In this status, you can optionally post a purchase inquiry before you post the required purchase order confirmation. If you use the vendor collaboration portal in Dynamics 365, post a *Confirmation request* (instead of the purchase inquiry) to request the vendor validation in the portal.

3.4.5.1 Purchase Inquiries

The purchase inquiry is an optional document that you can send to the vendor for validation. It does not create physical or financial transactions. Posting the purchase inquiry sets the approval status of the order to "In external review".

In order to post the purchase inquiry, click the button *Purchase/Generate/Purchase inquiry* in the Purchase order form. In the *Purchase inquiry* dialog, you can select settings for posting and printing as described below for the order confirmation.

If the vendor wants you to apply changes to the purchase order, you can update the order and—if change management is activated—approve the changes in the approval workflow before posting another purchase inquiry for the same order.

> *Note*: Purchase inquiries are available for vendors who do not use the vendor collaboration (→ Sect. 3.2.1). If vendor collaboration applies, use the option *Send for confirmation* in the Purchase order form instead of the purchase inquiry.

3.4.5.2 Purchase Order Confirmations

The purchase order confirmation is a mandatory document that you have to post before you can record a product receipt. In parallel to posting the confirmation, you usually print it (physically or electronically) and send it to the vendor.

Confirming a purchase order means to save it unchangeably and separately from the current purchase order. The confirmation shows the document that has been agreed upon with the vendor. It does not create physical or financial transactions.

In order to confirm a purchase order, select the order and click the button *Purchase/Generate/Confirmation* in the Purchase order form. Alternatively, you can click the button *Purchase/Actions/Confirm*, which executes the same functionality (without showing the posting dialog).

The option to confirm a purchase order is also available on applicable tabs in the list section of the workspace *Purchase order preparation*.

3.4.5.3 Posting Dialog for Order Updates

Whenever you post a document for a purchase order (confirming the order also is posting a document), a posting dialog with the following options is shown ($\rightarrow$ Fig. 3.19):

- **Parameters/Field "Quantity"** — "Ordered quantity" is the only option for the purchase order confirmation, posting the total quantity of all lines. Additional options are available for other transactions (e.g., for the receipts list described below).
- **Parameters/Slider "Posting"** — If set to "Yes", the document is posted. If set to "No", the output is a pro forma document.

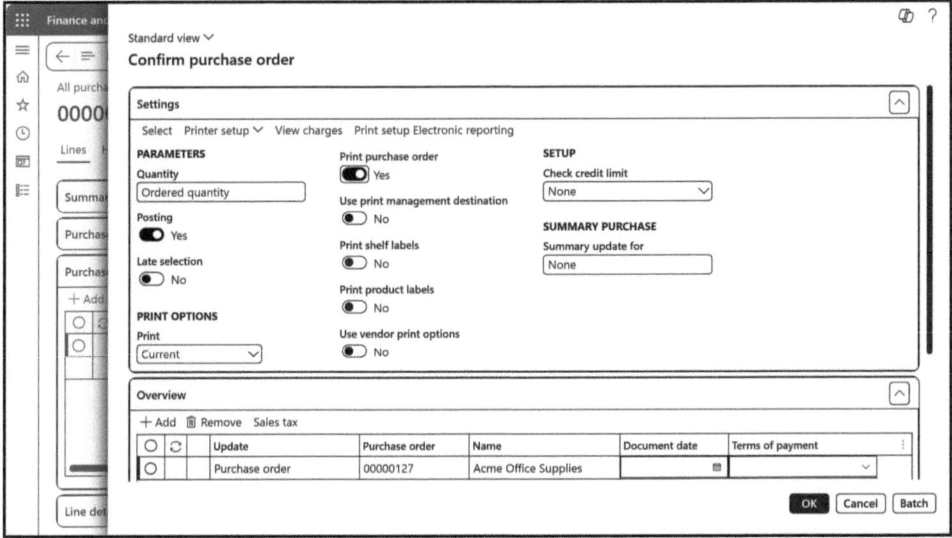

Fig. 3.19 Viewing the posting and printing settings in the *confirm purchase order* dialog

- **Parameters/Slider "Late selection"** —Relevant for the filter selection of summary updates which are submitted to a batch process (as described further below) .
- **Print options/Field "Print"** — If you select multiple orders for a summary update, the option "Current" prints each document separately while posting, whereas "After" starts printing after the last document has been posted.
- **Print options/Slider "Print purchase order"** — If set to "Yes", the document is printed. Otherwise, the document is posted without printing (reprinting is possible).
- **Print options/Slider "Use print management destination"** — If set to "Yes", the settings specified in the print management are used. Otherwise, the settings that you specify with the button *Printer setup* in the toolbar of the posting dialog apply.

If you print the purchase order without the *Print management destination* (i.e., this slider is set to "No"), you can click the button *Printer setup* to specify the destination of the print output ($\rightarrow$ Sect. 2.3.2).

You can access the print management settings in the menu item *Procurement and sourcing > Setup > Forms > Form setup* (click the button *Print management* in the section *General*) or, at the vendor level, in the Vendor form (click the button *General/Set up/Print management* in the action pane). Details on the general functionality of print management and on printing advanced notes are given in $\rightarrow$ Sect. 4.2.2.

In order to post the document finally, click the button *OK* in the posting dialog. If the slider for printing is set to "Yes" in the dialog, the document is printed on a printer, saved as a file, or shown in a print preview (depending on the selected settings for printing).

3.4.5.4 Pro Forma Documents

In the *Confirm purchase order* dialog, you can select to print a document while the slider *Posting* is set to "No". Dynamics 365 generates a pro forma document in this case. A pro forma document, which can be required for purposes like the customs declaration, is not a posted document. For this reason, it is not possible to reprint or display the document independent of the purchase order.

Instead of the regular button for posting order confirmations, you can also use the button *Purchase/Generate/Pro forma confirmation* in the purchase order to generate a pro forma confirmation. In the posting dialog for pro forma documents, the slider *Posting* is always set to "No".

3.4.5.5 Summary Updates

Apart from the button in the Purchase order form, there is another option to post a document—the corresponding periodic activity for summary updates.

The summary order confirmation (*Procurement and sourcing > Purchase orders > Purchase order confirmation > Confirm purchase orders*) opens the same posting dialog as the button for the order confirmation in the purchase order. But whereas there automatically is a filter on the current order when accessing the posting dialog from a purchase order, the summary update requires manually entering a filter. You can set this filter with the button *Select* in the toolbar of the tab *Settings* in the posting dialog. A dialog with an advanced filter, in which you can select the applicable purchase orders, is shown then. Once you close the filter dialog with the button *OK*, the selected orders are shown on the tab *Overview* of the posting dialog. If you do not want to post a particular order that is listed on this tab, delete the respective line in the dialog. Then, post the document(s) with the button *OK*.

The slider *Late selection* in the posting dialog is relevant if you submit the order confirmation to a batch *process* (→ Sect. 2.3.1): If this slider is set to "Yes", Dynamics 365 searches for orders that meet the filter criteria at the time when executing the batch process. Otherwise, posting is executed for the orders that are selected at the time when originally entering the filter (in a recurring batch process, this would mean that always the same orders are selected).

3.4.5.6 Inquiries and Document Reprint

After posting a purchase order document, the posted document is stored separately from the purchase order. Later amendments to the order have no impact on the posted document.

If you want to view a posted *Purchase order confirmation*, click the button *Purchase/ Journals/Purchase order confirmations* in the Purchase order form, or open the menu item *Procurement and sourcing > Purchase orders > Purchase order confirmation > Purchase order confirmations*.

If you want to view a posted *Purchase inquiry*, click the button *Purchase/Journals/ Purchase inquiry* in the purchase order.

The tab *Overview* in the Purchase order confirmation inquiry shows the posted purchase order confirmations (→ Fig. 3.20). Select an order confirmation header on this tab and switch to the tab *Lines* if you want to view the related lines.

If you want to display a print preview of the posted order confirmation, click the button *Preview/Print > Copy preview* or *Preview/Print > Original preview* in the toolbar of the tab *Overview* in the inquiry. From the preview, you can reprint the document. Alternatively, use the button *Preview/Print > Use print management* to print one or more order

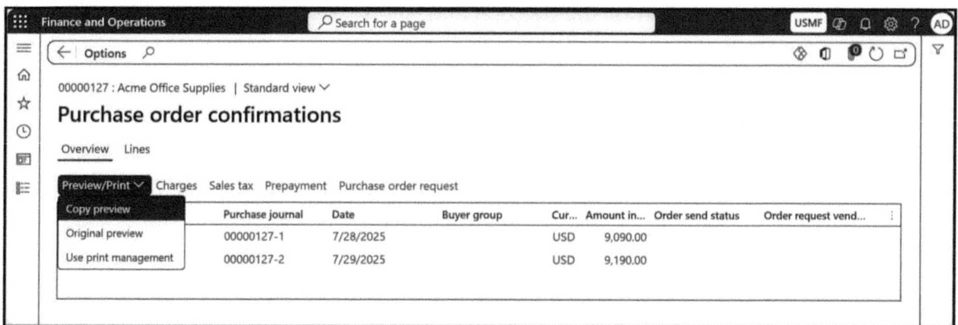

Fig. 3.20 Reprint options in the purchase order confirmation inquiry

confirmations from the Purchase order confirmation inquiry (printing to the printer specified in the print management).

3.4.6   Case Study Exercises

Exercise 3.6—Purchase Order
In order to avoid purchase order approvals, make sure that change management does not apply to the vendor of exercise 3.2.

You want to order the item of exercise 3.5 from the vendor of exercise 3.2. Enter the purchase order in the workspace *Purchase order preparation*. Which quantity and which price are shown in the order line? Then enter a second order line with two hours of the procurement category "##-assembling" (entered in exercise 3.4) for a price of USD 100.

In the next step, check all orders with the vendor of exercise 3.2. How do you proceed, and how many orders are shown?

Exercise 3.7—Order Confirmation
Post and print the purchase order confirmation for the order that you have entered in exercise 3.6. Generate a PDF file for the order confirmation.

Then change the quantity in the first line of the order of exercise 3.6 to 120 units. How do you proceed? Post the confirmation and display it as a print preview.

3.5   Item Receipt

Once an ordered item arrives in the warehouse, you post an item receipt. With the item receipt, the item is available in inventory.

3.5.1   Basics of Item Receipts

After an optional preparation of the item receipt, there are different ways to process the receipt in inventory.

3.5.1.1 Preparing the Item Receipt
The workspace *Purchase order receipt and follow-up* gives an overview of expected receipts, showing whether required items arrive on time. It displays the delayed and the pending receipts on lists in the list section, and it provides access to the related back-order lines.

Apart from the workspace, there are inquiries and reports that are designed for reviewing open purchase order lines. These inquiries include:

- **Backorder purchase lines** —List page *(Procurement and sourcing > Purchase orders > Purchase order follow-up > Backorder purchase lines)* showing open order lines with an expected receipt date (confirmed or, if empty, requested receipt date) on or before the *To date* in the filter area of the list page.
- **Open purchase order lines** — List page (*Procurement and sourcing > Purchase orders > Purchase order follow-up > Open purchase order lines*) showing all open order lines (use the filter pane, the grid column filter, or the advanced filter to select relevant records).

You can optionally print a receipts list if you need to prepare the item receipt. This list is only used for information purposes (e.g., for the responsible person in your warehouse). Apart from the receipts list, the warehouse responsible can also use the Arrival overview form for viewing and preparing expected receipts.

3.5.1.2 Processing the Item Receipt in Inventory

The item receipt in inventory includes two consecutive steps (→ Fig. 3.21):

- **Inventory registration**—You can record the inventory registration, which preliminarily increases the on-hand quantity in inventory, from the purchase order line, or in an item arrival journal, or with a mobile device transaction (with the advanced warehouse management).
- **Product receipt**—The product receipt is posting the final physical inventory transaction and, depending on the setup, general ledger transactions for the item receipt. The inventory registration before the product receipt is optional.

Whereas you can execute the inventory registration before posting a purchase order confirmation, it is not possible to post the product receipt before the purchase order confirmation.

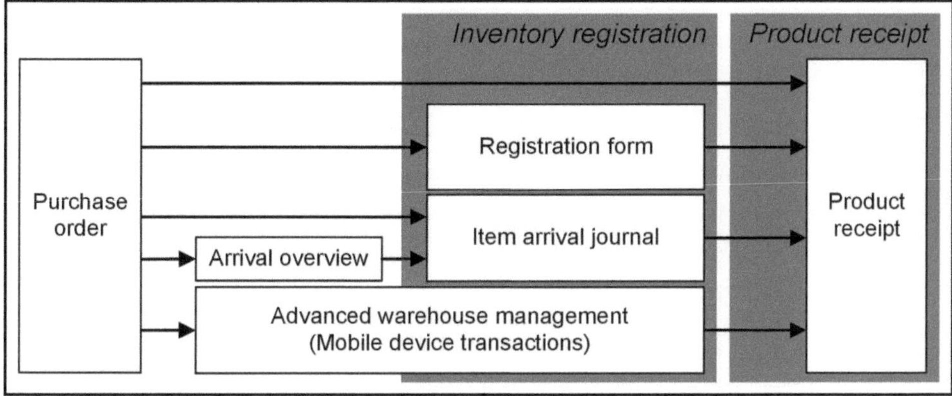

Fig. 3.21 Options for processing the item receipt

Depending on the particular requirements and on the setup, it is possible to skip the inventory registration and the product receipt for a purchase order. If you skip the product receipt, a receipt in inventory is posted when you post the vendor invoice.

3.5.2 Receipts Lists

The receipts list is an optional document that does not create transactions in inventory or finance. The way to post a receipts list is similar to posting a purchase order confirmation.

If you want to generate a receipts list, open the Purchase order list page, select the order, and click the button *Receive/Generate/Receipts list*. Alternatively, you can open the posting dialog with the menu item *Procurement and sourcing > Purchase orders > Receiving products > Post receipts list* and enter a filter with the button *Select*.

The receipts list is not a very common document, but you can use it for information purposes on expected item receipts.

3.5.3 Inventory Registration

Inventory registration is a preliminary step before posting the product receipt. The options, which are available for inventory registration, depend on the warehouse policy.

Concerning the required level of detail, there are two core warehouse policies in Dynamics 365:

- **Basic approach**—No license plate management (for pallets and other handling units) and no detailed tracking of transactions within the warehouse.
- **Advanced warehouse management**—Detailed planning and tracking of warehouse work with license plates (which represent handling units).

Depending on the warehouse policy, there are the following ways for processing the inventory registration ($\rightarrow$ Fig. 3.21):

- **Basic approach**
  - Registration form—From the order line (e.g., for entering serial numbers).
  - Item arrival journal—In inventory, separate from the Purchase order form.
  - Arrival overview—Optional prior step to the item arrival journal.
- **Advanced warehouse management**
  - Mobile device—Record transactions on the mobile device.

Inventory registration is only possible for inventoried items (product type "Item", item model group with *Stocked product* enabled). The item model group of the purchased item also controls whether you have to post a registration before the product receipt (checkbox *Registration requirements* on the tab *Inventory policies* in the item model group).

It is not possible to use the inventory registration for order lines that contain a procurement category or a non-stocked item. But you can post a product receipt for these lines.

This section explains the inventory registration in the basic approach for warehouse management. You can find details on how to process item receipts with the advanced warehouse management in → Sect. 8.1.2.

3.5.3.1 Registration from Purchase Order Lines

If it is required to register the item quantity before posting the product receipt, the usual approach is to post an item arrival journal or, in the advanced warehouse management, to register mobile device transactions.

But you can also record the inventory registration without these advanced options—for example, if you need to split the transaction of a single order line into multiple lines with different locations, batch numbers, or serial numbers.

In order to access the inventory registration from the Purchase order form, select the respective order line and click the button *Update line/Registration* in the toolbar of the tab *Purchase order lines*. The Registration form is divided into two tabs: The tab *Transactions* in the upper pane, which shows the status of the inventory transaction(s) that are linked to the selected order line, and the tab *Registration lines* in the lower pane, in which you can post the registration.

After accessing the inventory registration from a purchase order line, the tab *Transactions* initially shows a single inventory transaction, which has been created when entering the order line. This transaction is split into multiple lines if you post partial deliveries or if you split the line manually. If you want to register inventory dimensions for batch or serial numbers (if applicable), you can split a line with the button *Split* or *Create serial numbers* in the toolbar of the tab *Transactions*.

In order to record the inventory registration, insert appropriate lines on the tab *Registration lines* manually with the button *Add* on this tab, or with the button *Add registration line* in the toolbar of the tab *Transactions* (→ Fig. 3.22). You can subsequently post the registration with the button *Confirm registration* on the tab *Registration lines*.

Before posting the registration, you can change the warehouse, the quantity, and applicable inventory dimensions on the tab *Registration lines* as required. If you want to record a partial registration, enter a smaller quantity than the original quantity. In this case, the inventory transaction is split into two lines—one with the registered quantity and one with the remaining quantity.

If you have already started the registration on the tab *Registration lines* and you want to cancel it before posting, click the button *Remove all*. Removing registration lines restores the registration to the status before starting the current registration.

Fig. 3.22 Registering a receipt in the registration form

3.5.3.2 Registration Status

Once the inventory registration has been posted, the registered quantity is available in inventory, and the status of this quantity is "Registered". After registration, you can transfer, sell, or consume the registered quantity as required.

The Line quantity form (accessed with the button *General/Related information/Line quantity* in the purchase order) shows the posted quantity in the column *Registered*.

Unlike product receipt and invoice posting, which generate voucher documents with unchangeable transactions, the inventory registration is a preliminary transaction. If you reset an inventory registration (reverse it as described below), the original registration is not visible as a posted transaction anymore. The only transaction that you can still view after resetting a registration is the posted item arrival journal (if registration has been posted with an item arrival journal), or transactions in the advanced warehouse management (if the registration has been posted on mobile devices).

3.5.3.3 Item Arrival Journals

If you want to register item receipts in the warehouse separately from a product receipt posting in the office, you can use item arrival journals ($\rightarrow$ Sect. 7.4.2). Posting an item arrival journal generates the same transactions in inventory and in purchasing as the registration directly in the purchase order line.

Registering and posting an item arrival journal works similarly to the procedure in other inventory journals.

3.5.3.4 Arrival Overview

The form *Inventory management > Inbound orders > Arrival overview* gives an overview of the expected item arrivals. On the tabs *Arrival options* and *Arrival query details* of this form, you can enter filter criteria like the date range of expected receipts (*Days back, Days forward*), the warehouse, or the vendor (*Account number*). The button *Update* in the action pane then applies the selected criteria. If you want to use the same filter criteria repeatedly, create one or more profiles with appropriate filter settings (click the button *Arrival overview profiles* or *New arrival overview profile* for this purpose). On the tab *Arrival options* of the arrival overview, you can subsequently select an *Arrival overview profile name*.

Then select the receipts or lines for which you want to register an arrival (use the checkbox in the column *Select for arrival* on the tab *Receipts* or the tab *Lines*) and click the button *Start arrival* in the toolbar of the tab *Receipts*. Starting the arrival creates, but does not post, an item arrival journal for the selected lines (the journal name is given on the tab *Arrival options*).

In order to post the arrival journal, open the item arrival journals (*Inventory management > Journal entries > Item arrival > Item arrival*). Alternatively, click the button *Journals/Show arrivals from receipts* in the toolbar of the tab *Receipts* in the arrival overview after selecting the receipt, for which you have started the arrival.

With the button *Journals/Product receipt ready journals* in the arrival overview, you can show posted arrival journals, for which the product receipt (→ Sect. 3.5.4) has not been posted yet.

3.5.3.5 Reversing an Inventory Registration

If you need to reverse (cancel) a registration that has been posted in the Item arrival journal or the Registration form, select the respective order line in the Purchase order form and open the Registration form.

On the tab *Transactions* of the Registration form, click the button *Add registration line* for the particular transaction. Then post the transaction like a regular inventory registration, but with a negative quantity.

3.5.4 Product Receipts

Whereas the inventory registration is a preliminary transaction, the product receipt is the commercial acknowledgement that you have actually received the items. In line with this, posting a product receipt generates a physical inventory transaction, which finally receives the item in an unchangeable voucher document and adds the costs of the item to the (preliminary) inventory value.

3.5.4.1 Posting Dialog for Product Receipts

The way to post a product receipt is similar to a purchase order confirmation. If you want to post the product receipt from the Purchase order form, select the order and click the button *Receive/Generate/Product receipt*.

The posting dialog then shows the familiar format. In the lookup field *Quantity* on the tab *Settings*, select the applicable option depending on the prior process:

- **Registered quantity**—Select this option if an inventory registration (item arrival) has been posted before the product receipt. Dynamics 365 initializes the posting lines with the registered (not yet received) quantity.
- **Registered quantity and services**—In addition to the registered quantity for order lines with inventoried items, the receipt quantity is initialized with the deliver remainder quantity in order lines with procurement categories and non-inventoried items.
- **Ordered quantity**—Dynamics 365 inserts the total remaining order quantity.
- **Receive now quantity**—Dynamics 365 inserts the quantity of the order line column *Receive now*.

The posting quantity is shown in the column *Quantity* on the tab *Lines* in the lower pane of the posting dialog. If required, you can edit the quantities before finally posting the receipt.

The other parameters in the posting dialog are similar to the purchase order confirmation parameters (→ Sect. 3.4.5), except for the following fields/options:

- **Product receipt**—Column on the tab *Overview* of the posting dialog, in which you have to enter the packing slip number of the vendor.
- **Print product receipt**—Slider on the tab *Parameters* of the posting dialog, which is usually set to "No" because you probably don't print your own document when receiving the vendor's packing slip.

If an exclamation mark (!) is shown in front of a product receipt record on the tab *Overview* of the posting dialog, it indicates an issue with posting. A common reason is that the option "Registered quantity" is selected in the lookup field *Quantity* of the posting dialog, but there has not been an inventory registration before posting the product receipt. Depending on the circumstances, you can select the option "Ordered quantity" in the field *Quantity* of the posting dialog to solve this issue.

3.5.4.2 Product Receipts in Summary Updates and Item Arrival Journals

Similar to the options for the purchase order confirmation, the posting dialog for product receipts is also available as a periodic activity in the menu (for summary updates). If you access the posting dialog from the menu (*Procurement and sourcing > Purchase orders > Receiving products > Post product receipt*), you have to enter a filter with the button *Select*. After closing the filter dialog, you can optionally collect multiple purchase orders into one collective product receipt (click the button *Arrange* for this purpose). You can find more details on how to arrange orders into collective documents in → Sect. 4.5.2.

If an item arrival journal has been posted for the purchase order, you can also open the *Posting product receipt* dialog with the button *Functions/Product receipt* in the action pane of the item arrival journal. If a *Packing slip* number has been entered on the tab *Journal header details* of the item arrival journal before posting, it is the default value for the *Product receipt* number in the *Posting product receipt* dialog. This way, the warehouse responsible can immediately post the product receipt after the item arrival without accessing the purchase order or a separate menu item.

3.5.4.3 Canceling Product Receipts

If you want to cancel a posted product receipt, use the *Cancel* feature in the Product receipt inquiry. Open the Product receipt inquiry (e.g., with the button *Receive/Journals/Product receipt* in the Purchase order form) for this purpose and select the respective receipt. Then click the button *Cancel* in the toolbar of the tab *Overview*. If you only want to reduce the posted quantity, click the button *Correct* in the Product receipt inquiry.

Canceling or correcting a product receipt does not change the original transaction, but posts a new transaction that offsets the original one.

3.5.4.4 Ledger Integration and Settings for Product Receipt Posting

If the ledger integration is activated for the product receipt, Dynamics 365 posts general ledger transactions in parallel to the inventory transactions. These ledger transactions are reversed when posting the related invoice.

There are two relevant settings, which enable the posting of product receipts to the general ledger:

- **Accounts payable parameters**—The slider *Post product receipt in ledger* (section *General*, tab *Product receipt*) has to be set to "Yes".
- **Item model group**—The checkbox *Post physical inventory* on the tab *Costing method & cost recognition* in the item model group of the item has to be selected.

In addition to the setting on ledger integration, the item model group contains two more relevant settings for product receipts: The checkbox *Registration requirements* in the item model group controls whether you have to post the inventory registration before posting the product receipt. The checkbox *Receiving requirements* controls whether posting the product receipt is required before posting the invoice.

3.5.5 Partial Delivery, Underdelivery, and Overdelivery

You have to post a partial delivery if you do not receive the entire quantity of a purchase order line in one shipment, but if it is split into multiple shipments.

In case the slider *Prevent partial delivery* on the sub-tab *General* in the purchase order line is set to "Yes", it is not possible to post partial deliveries.

3.5.5.1 Inventory Registration of Partial Deliveries

In the inventory registration, you can record partial deliveries in the Registration form or, if the inventory registration is posted with an item arrival journal, by entering the partial quantity in the arrival journal lines (→ Sect. 3.5.3). When later posting a product receipt which refers to the inventory registration, select the option "Registered quantity" in the lookup field *Quantity* of the posting dialog.

3.5.5.2 Product Receipt of Partial Deliveries

If you do not use inventory registration, you can optionally prepare a partial product receipt by entering a *Receive now* quantity in the purchase order line.

The *Receive now* quantity is one of the rightmost columns on the tab *Purchase order lines* of the Purchase order form. Apart from the column in the purchase order lines, the *Receive now* quantity is also shown on the tab *Receive now* of the Line quantity form (→ Fig. 3.23), which you can access with the button *General/Related information/Line quantity* in the purchase order.

When posting the product receipt later, select the option "Receive now quantity" in the lookup field *Quantity* of the *Posting product receipt* dialog to refer to the previously entered *Receive now* quantity.

Alternatively, you can skip the *Receive now* quantity, but select the option "Ordered quantity" in the lookup field *Quantity* of the *Posting product receipt* dialog and enter the received quantities in the column *Quantity* on the tab *Lines* further down the posting dialog.

After posting a partial receipt, the remaining quantity for further product receipts is shown in the column *Deliver remainder* of the Line quantity form (→ Fig. 3.23). The received quantity (total of several partial receipts, if applicable) is shown in the column *Received*.

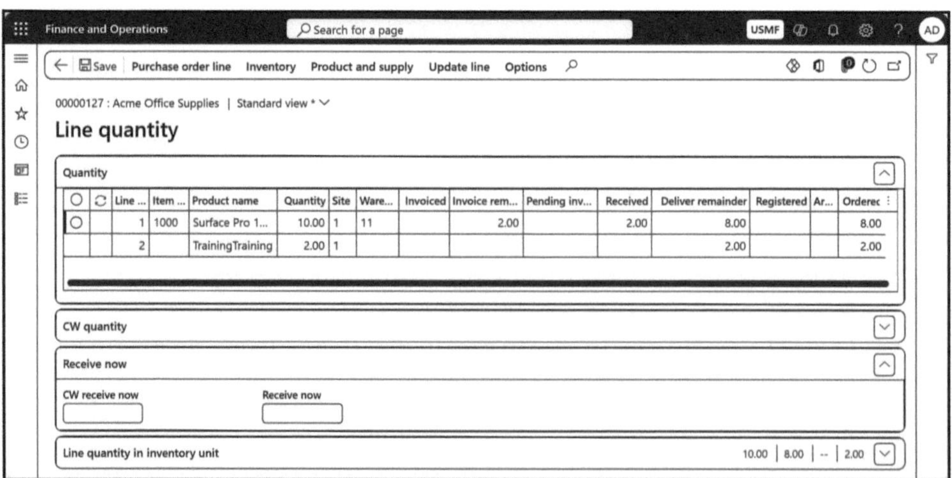

Fig. 3.23 Line quantity form for a purchase order after the receipt of a partial delivery

When receiving further partial deliveries, you can post the product receipts in the same way as described for the first delivery until the total of the received quantity matches the ordered quantity.

3.5.5.3 Underdelivery and Overdelivery

If you record a quantity in a product receipt that is less than the ordered quantity, Dynamics 365 posts a partial delivery unless you characterize the receipt as underdelivery (which means that you do not expect further receipts). In order to record underdelivery, select the checkbox in the column *Close for receipt* on the tab *Lines* of the posting dialog and enter the received quantity in the column *Quantity* ($\rightarrow$ Fig. 3.24).

As an alternative to underdelivery posting in the product receipt, you can set the open quantity to zero by canceling the deliver remainder quantity ($\rightarrow$ Sect. 3.4.4). But unlike the underdelivery option in the product receipt, canceling the deliver remainder does not execute a check whether the quantity reduction is within the allowed range for the underdelivery percentage of the order line.

If you post an item receipt (inventory registration or product receipt), the transaction is an overdelivery in case the total received quantity exceeds the ordered quantity. Dynamics 365 accepts overdelivery if the exceeding quantity is less than the allowed overdelivery specified in the overdelivery percentage of the order line.

You can only post underdelivery or overdelivery if the slider *Accept underdelivery* or *Accept overdelivery* in the section *Delivery* of the Procurement parameters is set to "Yes". In the Released product detail form (*Product information management > Products > Released products*), the maximum percentage for underdelivery and overdelivery in purchase orders and sales orders is specified on the tabs *Purchase* and *Sell*. The percentages in the released product are the default value for the order lines. In the

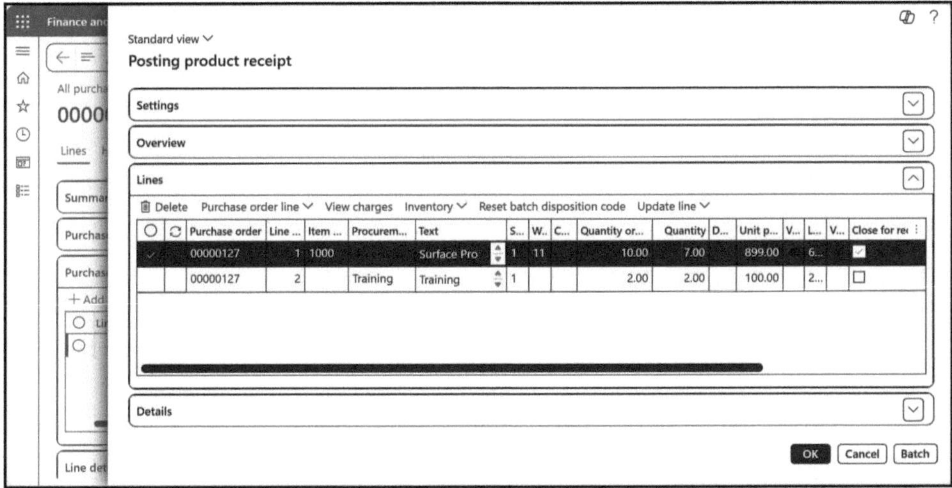

Fig. 3.24 Marking a receipt as underdelivery in the *posting product receipt* dialog

order lines, you can adjust the maximum underdelivery and overdelivery percentage as needed (on the sub-tab *Delivery* of the *Line details*).

3.5.6 Order Status and Inquiries

Posting an item receipt updates the order status and the quantity in inventory.

3.5.6.1 Purchase Order Status

The Purchase order list page contains the columns *Approval status* ($\rightarrow$ Sect. 3.4.3) and *Purchase order status*. The Header view of the Purchase order detail form additionally shows the *Document status* on the tab *General*. Whereas the order status indicates the order progress as given by the lowest status of the purchase order lines, the document status shows the highest status of a posted document.

For this reason, the order status of a purchase order may still be "Open order" while the document status is "Invoiced" (in case of partial deliveries and invoices). An overview of receipt transactions and the related status is shown in $\rightarrow$ Table 3.1.

At the line level, the status is shown in the field *Line status* on the sub-tab *General* of the order lines. In addition, the Line quantity form shows the quantity per status.

With the button *General/Related information/Postings* in the Purchase order form, you can access a dialog that shows the last document number of the posted transactions for the selected order.

3.5.6.2 Inventory Transaction Status

Both the inventory registration and the product receipt change the on-hand quantity with an inventory transaction.

When you enter a purchase order line with an inventoried item, Dynamics 365 creates an inventory transaction with the *Receipt* status "Ordered" (if change management applies, once the order is approved). You can view this transaction with the button *Inventory/ Transactions* in the toolbar of the tab *Purchase order lines*.

When you post an inventory registration, the receipt status of the inventory transaction changes to "Registered". The registration date is stored in the field *Inventory date*, which

Table 3.1 Order status, approval status, and document status for receipt transactions

Transaction	Approval status	Order status	Document status
(Approval)	Approved	Open order	None
Purchase inquiry	In external review	Open order	Purchase inquiry
Confirmation	Confirmed	Open order	Purchase order
Receipt list	Confirmed	Open order	Receipts list
Inventory registration	Confirmed	Open order	*(no change)*
Partial product receipt	Confirmed	Open order	Packing slip
Full product receipt	Confirmed	Received	Packing slip

you can view on the tab *General* of the Transaction details form (click the button *Transaction details* in the inventory transaction to access the details). If you reverse an inventory registration, the inventory date is cleared.

When you post a product receipt, with or without a prior inventory registration, the receipt status of the inventory transaction changes to "Received". The posting date of the product receipt is shown in the column *Physical date* of the inventory transaction. The *Financial date* in the inventory transaction remains empty until the vendor invoice is posted. Additional details of the transaction (e.g., the packing slip number) are shown on the tab *Updates* of the Transaction details form.

Since you can only reverse a product receipt by posting an offset transaction, the physical date in the inventory transaction never changes after posting the receipt.

If there are partial receipts, the original inventory transaction is split into two (or more) transactions with a status that refers to the respective quantity. In the example of → Fig. 3.25, you can view the inventory transactions for a purchase order line after posting the product receipts of two partial deliveries.

3.5.6.3 Product Receipt Inquiry

If you want to view the posted product receipts, open the menu item *Procurement and sourcing > Purchase orders > Receiving products > Product receipt* or click the button *Receive/Journals/Product receipt* in the Purchase order form.

Select a product receipt on the tab *Overview* of the inquiry and switch to the tab *Lines* if you want to view the related receipt lines. The button *Inventory/Lot transactions* in the toolbar of the tab *Lines* provides an alternative way to access the inventory transactions.

3.5.6.4 Ledger Transactions and Transaction Origin

If the ledger integration is activated for the product receipt, you can click the button *Ledger/Vouchers/Physical voucher* in the Inventory transactions inquiry to view the related general ledger transactions in the Voucher transactions inquiry. If you want to view all ledger transactions that refer to a product receipt, open the Product receipt inquiry and click the button *Vouchers* in the toolbar of the tab *Overview*.

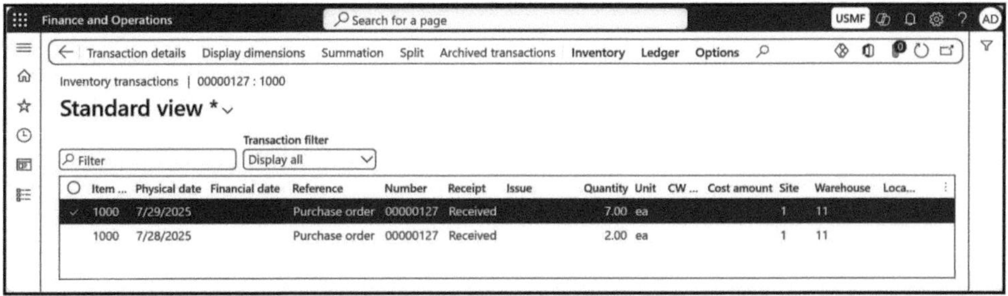

Fig. 3.25 Inventory transactions for an order line with two partial product receipts

The main accounts in the ledger transactions are given by the posting setup—for inventoried items, the accounts for the options "Cost of purchased materials received" and "Purchase, accrual" on the tab *Purchase order* of the posting setup are relevant for the product receipt (→ Sect. 9.4.2).

The button *Transaction origin* in the action pane of the Voucher transactions inquiry provides access to the Transaction origin form, which shows related transactions in all modules. Depending on integration settings, the product receipt posts transactions in inventory and in the general ledger. In the example of → Fig. 3.27, you can view the transaction origin of the voucher in → Fig. 3.26.

Note: For source documents like the product receipt, settings for subledger accounting in the General ledger parameters (→ Sect. 9.4.1) determine when the transactions are posted to the general ledger. If the Voucher transactions inquiry is empty, you can access the form *General ledger > Periodic tasks > Subledger journal entries not yet transferred*, select the product receipt, and click the button *Transfer now* to speed up the general ledger posting. In addition, you can check the form *General ledger > Periodic tasks > Documents pending accounting* and click the button *Generate accounting* there to generate the ledger transactions rapidly.

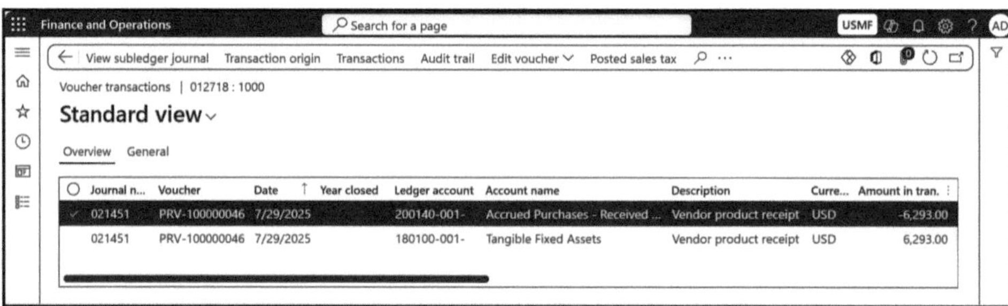

Fig. 3.26 General ledger transactions related to a product receipt

Fig. 3.27 Transaction origin form with all transactions related to a product receipt

3.5.7   Case Study Exercises

Exercise 3.8—Product Receipt
Your vendor ships the goods and services ordered in exercise 3.6 with packing slip PS308. Before posting the receipt, check the following items in the purchase order:

- Order status and document status.
- Inventory quantity of the ordered item.
- Inventory transaction for the order line of the product.

Then post a product receipt for the complete order quantity (120 units for the first line after the update in exercise 3.7) with the vendor packing slip number given above. You can post the receipt directly from the Purchase order form.

Now review the status of the items in the list above again. What is different after product receipt posting?

Exercise 3.9—Partial Delivery and Inventory Registration
You want to order the item of exercise 3.5 from the vendor of exercise 3.2 one more time, this time with a quantity of 20 units. Enter and confirm the purchase order.

With the packing slip PS309, there is a partial delivery of 10 units from the vendor. Post the corresponding product receipt.

Next, you receive a second shipment, PS309-2, with 5 units. Due to organizational reasons, you should record an inventory registration for this receipt. Open the Registration form in the purchase order line and post the registration.

Do you know how to show the remaining quantity? Check the order status, the inventory quantity, and the inventory transactions like you did in exercise 3.8. What is different in comparison to exercise 3.8?

Post the product receipt for the second shipment PS309-2 afterward.

Exercise 3.10—Product Receipt Inquiry
You are asked to review the product receipt of exercise 3.8. For this purpose, open the Product receipt inquiry, first from the Purchase order form and then from the navigation pane. Review the product receipt header and lines, and check if there are related ledger transactions.

> *Note*: If the Voucher transactions inquiry is empty, the subledger transfer probably has not been executed yet. In this case, open the form *General ledger > Periodic tasks > Subledger journal entries not yet transferred*, select the product receipt, and click the button *Transfer now* in the action pane to speed up the general ledger posting. If the ledger transactions are still empty, open the form *General ledger > Periodic tasks > Documents pending accounting* and click the button *Generate accounting* there to generate the ledger transactions rapidly.

3.6   Vendor Invoice

Together with the shipment, or at a later stage, the vendor submits an invoice. Before posting the invoice, you can check it by using the invoice matching functions, which perform a comparison with the information on the purchase order and the product receipt.

Apart from manually registering a vendor invoice, there are the following options for creating an inbound vendor invoice:

- **Vendor collaboration portal**—Enabling the vendor to enter their invoices in your Dynamics 365 environment.
- **EDI integration**—Receiving invoices in a formatted data structure (e.g., EDIFACT), and importing them (often by the use of a third-party connector).
- **Invoice capture**—Extracting invoice data from an invoice that you have received in an unstructured format (e.g., a PDF file).

Whereas product receipts update the preliminary (physical) inventory value, vendor invoices update the posted (financial) value. For this reason, posting a vendor invoice that covers the receipt of physical products not only increases the open vendor balance but also increases the financial value of inventory.

Once all lines of a purchase order are invoiced, purchase order processing is completed. The payment of vendor invoices is a separate process, which is described in → Sect. 9.3.3.

3.6.1   Processing Vendor Invoices

Related to the line content and the way of processing the invoice, there are two types of vendor invoices:

- **Invoices related to products or procurement categories**—With or without reference to a purchase order (described in this section).
- **Invoices related to ledger accounts**—For example, with reference to an expense account for office rent or legal fees.

Vendor invoices, which refer to products or procurement categories, have to be registered and posted in the Pending vendor invoices form as described below. Pending vendor invoices are not only used for invoices that refer to purchase orders, but also for invoices that do not refer to orders (these invoices may only include lines with non-stocked products or procurement categories). For inventoried items, you must process a purchase order before registering an invoice.

If a vendor invoice refers to a purchase order, you can register the invoice with reference to a prior product receipt, or, if no product receipt has been posted before, post the invoice and the receipt of the items or services at the same time (in one common step). You can post an invoice without a prior product receipt if you receive goods or services together with the invoice and do not post an item receipt in the warehouse separately. For inventoried items, the checkbox *Receiving requirements* in the item model group of the item ($\rightarrow$ Sect. 7.2.3) may not be selected in this case.

If required, you can pre-register a vendor invoice in an invoice journal (invoice register, invoice approval journal). You can find more details on invoice journals in $\rightarrow$ Sect. 9.3.2.

3.6.1.1 Vendor Invoice Registration

When you receive a vendor invoice, enter it separately from purchase orders in the Pending vendor invoice form (*Accounts payable > Invoices > Pending vendor invoices*). This form shows all vendor invoices, which have been entered but not yet posted.

In order to switch from the Pending vendor invoice list page to the related detail form, select a particular invoice and click the link in the field *Number* (invoice number) or click the button *Edit* in the action pane.

The menu item is one way to access the Vendor invoice form. Considering the other options, there are the following pages in which you can start creating a new pending vendor invoice:

- **Workspaces**—*Vendor invoice entry* and *Vendor invoice center*
- **Pending vendor invoice form**—Also called "Vendor invoice form" in some areas.
- **Vendor form**
- **Purchase order form**

The workspace *Vendor invoice entry* provides an overview of billable documents (purchase orders and product receipts) and registered invoices, which have not been posted. The workspace *Vendor invoice center* shows—in addition to manually recorded invoices— the status of invoices that are processed with invoice capture and vendor invoice automation. In both workspaces, you can create a pending vendor invoice with the button *New* (or *New vendor invoice*).

If you want to record a vendor invoice in the Pending vendor invoices form, click the button *New* in the action pane. If you would rather want to enter a new invoice in the Vendor form, click the button *Invoice/New/Invoice/Vendor invoice* in the action pane of this form.

When registering an invoice in the Vendor invoice form, select the vendor number in the field *Invoice account* first. Then select the purchase order number in the lookup field *Purchase order*. If you select the order number first, Dynamics 365 automatically retrieves the corresponding vendor.

If you are working in the Purchase order form, you can register a vendor invoice directly from the order. The button *Invoice/Generate/Invoice* in the Purchase order form opens the Vendor invoice form and creates an invoice that is already linked to the selected order. The workspaces *Vendor invoice entry* and *Vendor invoice center* provide a similar option:

Select a purchase order or a product receipt in the respective list in the list section and click the button *Invoice now* in the toolbar of the list for this purpose.

While the Vendor invoice form ($\rightarrow$ Fig. 3.28) looks different from the other posting dialogs (e.g., the product receipt), the functionality is similar. Like in the other posting dialogs, the prior business process determines which option you choose in the quantity selection (button *Default from* in the action pane of the pending vendor invoice):

- **Product receipt quantity**—Common option (for invoices linked to a product receipt).
- **Ordered quantity** or **Receive now quantity**—For invoices that are not related to a product receipt.

If you select the option "Product receipt quantity" in the drop-down menu *Default quantity for lines* (access with the button *Default from* in the action pane), the quantity that is received but not invoiced is used as the default value in the column *Quantity* on the tab *Lines* of the pending vendor invoice.

In order to review the product receipts that are covered by the invoice, click the button *Match product receipts* in the action pane of the Vendor invoice form. In the dialog that is shown next, you can view the product receipts that are available for invoicing. Select or clear the checkbox in the column *Match* of this dialog to include or exclude particular product receipts. If the vendor only invoices a partial quantity, update the column *Product receipt quantity to match* in the dialog. Then close the dialog with the button *OK* and—if

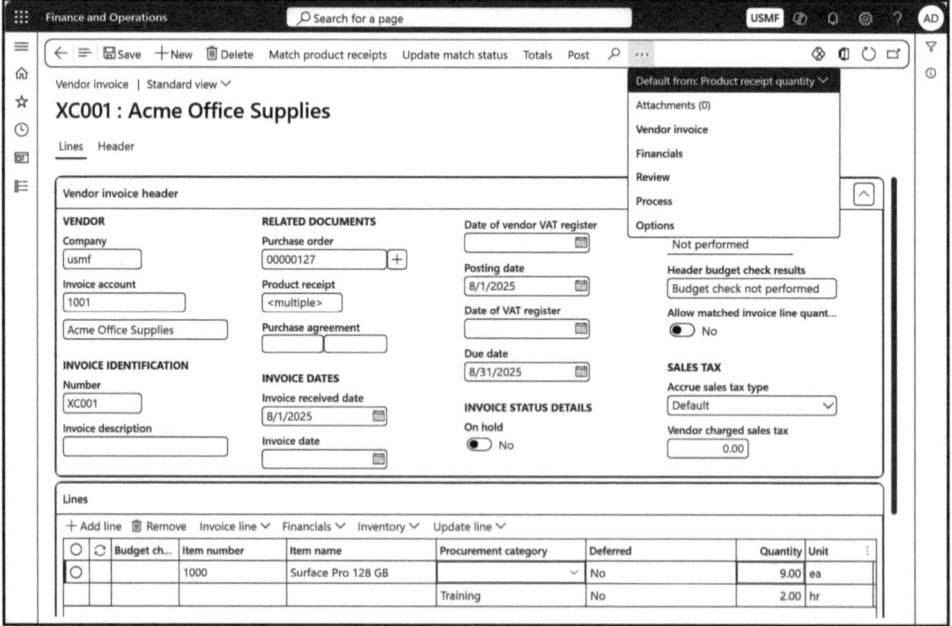

Fig. 3.28 Registering a vendor invoice for a purchase order

applicable—click "Yes" in the message box which asks whether to update the invoice quantity. The selected product receipt is shown in the invoice header and in the column *Product receipt* on the tab *Lines* ("<multiple>", if multiple receipts are assigned). If the *Product receipt quantity to match* is different from the quantity in the related invoice line, the invoice matches a receipt quantity that is different from the quantity on the invoice (e.g., in the case of a promotion "3 units for the price of 2"). A message indicates this situation.

If you want to register a vendor invoice independently of product receipts (e.g., if there is no prior item receipt), select the option "Ordered quantity" in the drop-down menu *Default quantity for lines* (or "Receive now quantity", if you have entered the invoiced quantity in the column *Receive now* of the purchase order lines). Then adjust the quantities in the invoice lines as applicable. But be aware that invoice posting, in this case, is also posting the physical receipt of any invoice quantity that exceeds the received quantity (which means receiving the total quantity if there is no prior product receipt).

The invoice number given by the vendor (mandatory field *Number* in the field group *Invoice identification*), the *Posting date* (for your ledger posting), the *Invoice date* (for the date on which the vendor has issued the invoice), and the *Due date* (receiving the default value from the payment terms calculation) are shown on the tab *Vendor invoice header*. If you want to prevent posting of the selected invoice for some time, set the slider *On hold* to "Yes".

The details, which you enter in the Vendor invoice form, have to match the invoice that you receive from the vendor. For this reason, it is useful to compare the totals on the actual vendor invoice with the totals in the Vendor invoice form—review the *Totals* dialog (access with the button *Totals*) or the FactBox *Invoice totals*—before posting the invoice. If necessary, adjust the quantities, prices, discounts, and line amounts on the tab *Lines* or *Line details* in the Pending vendor invoice detail form.

If you create an invoice and close the Vendor invoice form before posting, the invoice is stored for later posting (and approval, if applicable). You can still view and edit the invoice in the pending vendor invoices. For this reason, delete the invoice with the button *Delete* if you want to completely cancel invoice registration once you have started to enter an invoice.

> *Note*: If you simply close the Pending vendor invoice form after starting to register a vendor invoice, Dynamics 365 saves the invoice. If product receipts are assigned to the invoice, you can't assign them to a second invoice before deleting the first pending invoice.

3.6.1.2 Collective Vendor Invoices

If a vendor invoice refers to multiple purchase orders, you have to post a collective invoice. Entering collective invoices in the Vendor invoice form is different from registering collective documents for other document types (e.g., collective product receipts).

In the Vendor invoice form, click the button ⊞ next to the field *Purchase order* to open the *Retrieve purchase orders* dialog. When you select purchase orders in this dialog, pay attention to the option that is selected in the button *Default from* in the action pane of the

Vendor invoice form. This option controls whether you can select a purchase order without a prior product receipt. In addition, summary update parameters (*Accounts payable > Setup > Summary update parameters*) and settings at the vendor level determine the requirements on orders that are collected to a common invoice—similar to the options in Accounts receivable (→ Sect. 4.5.2).

3.6.1.3 Invoice Matching

Apart from manually validating a vendor invoice against the purchase order(s) and the product receipt(s), there are features for automatic invoice matching. Primary settings for invoice matching are available in the section *Invoice validation* of the Accounts payable parameters. Invoice matching is only active if the slider *Enable invoice matching validation* in the parameters is set to "Yes". In this case, the parameter *Automatically update invoice header status* controls whether invoice matching is executed automatically or if it is necessary to start it manually.

If invoice matching is active, you can specify various tolerances and types of matching in the Accounts payable parameters:

* **Invoice totals matching**—Compares invoice total fields (invoice amount, sales tax, charges) with the purchase order.
* **Price and quantity matching**
    - **Line matching policy**—"Two-way matching" compares the prices and discounts on the invoice with the order line; "Three-way matching" also compares the quantity in product receipts.
    - **Match price totals**—Tolerance ("Percentage" or "Amount") for matching the total on purchase order lines with the total on invoice lines.
* **Charges matching**—Separate settings for matching charges.

In line with the setting in the field *Allow matching policy override* on the tab *Price and quantity matching* in the section *Invoice validation* of the Accounts payable parameters, you can override invoice validation criteria at the vendor level or item level in the forms of the menu folder *Accounts payable > Invoice matching setup*. In addition, you can use business policies (menu items in the folder *Accounts payable > Policy setup*) to specify matching rules that are different from the standard invoice validation settings.

If invoice matching is activated (and not executed automatically), you have to click the button *Update match status* in the action pane of the Vendor invoice form to execute invoice matching before you can post the invoice. In case the vendor invoice exceeds the tolerances specified in the invoice matching setup, the Vendor invoice form shows the status "Failed" in the field *Match status* on the invoice header and in the related column on the tab *Lines*. Click the button *Review/Matching/Matching details* in the Vendor invoice form if you want to view the detailed results of invoice matching.

3.6.1.4 Vendor Invoice Posting

Once you have entered a pending vendor invoice, you can optionally leave it pending and post it later—for example, if you have to obtain approval in an approval workflow first.

If your enterprise wants to use approval workflows for pending vendor invoices, set up an appropriate workflow (with the workflow type "Vendor invoice workflow" or "Vendor invoice line workflow") in the menu item *Accounts payable > Setup > Accounts payable workflows*. With this setup, you can post a pending vendor invoice only after approval.

Once the vendor invoice is ready to be posted, click the button *Post* in the action pane of the Pending vendor invoice form. After posting, the invoice is not shown as a pending vendor invoice anymore. It is shown in the Open vendor invoice form (*Accounts payable > Invoices > Open vendor invoices*), which contains all invoices that are not yet paid.

Posting a vendor invoice generates general ledger transactions, inventory transactions, vendor transactions, and transactions in other subledgers as applicable (e.g., sales tax). The vendor posting profile determines the summary account that is used in the vendor transaction (→ Sect. 3.2.3). The posting setup contains the settings for the main accounts that are related to the inventory transactions (→ Sect. 9.4.2).

3.6.1.5 Invoices without Order Reference

Registering an invoice, which does not refer to a purchase order, is similar to entering an order in the Purchase order form. Once you select a vendor in the Pending vendor invoice form, the invoice retrieves numerous default values from the vendor record. You can view and edit the corresponding fields in the Vendor invoice form. But unlike purchase order lines, the lines that you enter in the Vendor invoice form may only contain non-stocked items and procurement categories.

Posting such an invoice works similarly to posting any other vendor invoice.

> *Note*: Apart from the Pending vendor invoice form, you can alternatively use journals to record invoices without an order reference (→ Sect. 9.3.2). In an invoice journal, you enter a ledger account instead of an item or a procurement category.

3.6.2 Invoice Capture and Vendor Invoice Automation

In order to record a vendor invoice that refers to a purchase order, you can manually enter it in the Pending vendor invoices form. If you want to avoid manual data entry, you can ask your vendor to use the Vendor collaboration portal in your Dynamics 365 environment and to enter his invoices there (which means that he enters the pending vendor invoices).

If you receive many invoices from particular vendors who can provide structured invoices (e.g., in the EDIFACT format), you can set up and process an automated import of invoices to the pending vendor invoices.

Another option to reduce the effort of creating pending vendor invoices is the Invoice capture solution. The *Invoice Capture for Dynamics 365 Finance* app, which needs to be installed separately, uses OCR (optical character recognition) features and AI (Artificial

Intelligence) technologies to read different invoice formats from different vendors. Based on a digital invoice document, usually a PDF file which you receive from the vendor or create by scanning a printed invoice, you can use the Invoice capture app to extract the invoice data. From the Invoice capture app, the vendor invoice is transferred to the pending vendor invoices in Dynamics 365 Finance and Operations.

In order to support the processing of the pending vendor invoices, which you have received with the Invoice capture solution, you can use the Vendor invoice automation features in Dynamics 365 Finance and Operations. They automate tasks like invoice matching, applying prepayments, and submitting the invoice to the approval workflow.

Settings for integrating the Invoice capture app with Dynamics 365 Finance and Operations are specified in the Invoice capture form (*Accounts Payable > Set up > Invoice capture*). Settings for the Vendor invoice automation are specified in the section *Vendor invoice automation* of the Accounts payable parameters.

3.6.3   Order Status and Inquiries

Similar to the product receipt, the vendor invoice updates the order status and posts inventory transactions and general ledger transactions. But an invoice additionally generates a vendor transaction.

3.6.3.1 Purchase Order Status and Transaction Status

Depending on whether you have posted a partial or a complete invoice, the purchase order has the following status:

- **Partial invoice**—*Order status* "Received" or "Open order", *Document status* "Invoice".
- **Complete invoice or last partial invoice**—*Order status* "Invoiced", *Document status* "Invoice".

If you want to view the inventory transactions that refer to an order line, select the respective line in the purchase order and click the button *Inventory/Transactions* in the toolbar of the tab *Purchase order lines*. After posting the invoice, the *Receipt* status of the inventory transaction is "Purchased", and the posting date of the invoice is shown in the column *Financial date* (→ Fig. 3.29). The invoice number is shown on the tab *Updates* of the Transaction details form (click the button *Transaction details* in the inventory transaction to access the details).

In the example of → Fig. 3.29, there are two inventory transactions that refer to one common purchase order line and are included in a posted invoice.

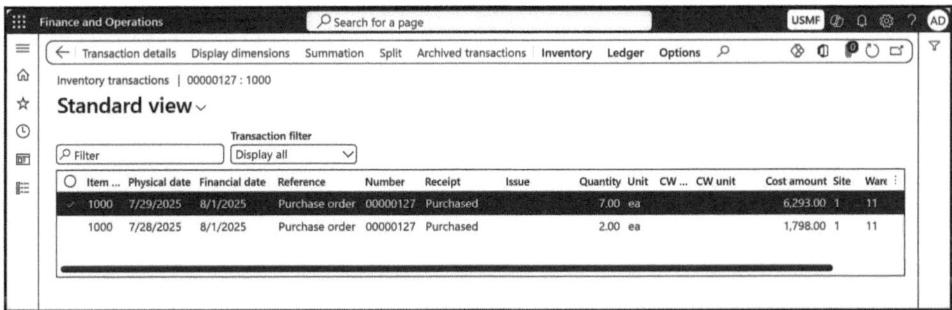

Fig. 3.29 Inventory transactions after posting the vendor invoice

3.6.3.2 Invoice Inquiry

In order to view the posted invoice, open the menu item *Accounts payable > Inquiries and reports > Invoice > Invoice journal* or click the button *Invoice/Journals/Invoice* in the Purchase order form.

Select an invoice on the tab *Overview* of the inquiry and switch to the tab *Lines* if you want to view the related invoice lines. The button *Inventory/Lot transactions* in the toolbar of the tab *Lines* provides an alternative way to access the inventory transactions described above.

3.6.3.3 Ledger Transactions and Transaction Origin

If you want to view the general ledger transactions that refer to a vendor invoice, open the Voucher transactions inquiry—click the button *Voucher* in the toolbar of the tab *Overview* in the Invoice inquiry. Alternatively, you can access the voucher transactions with the button *Ledger/Financial voucher* in the Inventory transactions inquiry (in this case, only the ledger transactions related to the particular inventory transaction are shown).

The Voucher transactions inquiry displays all general ledger transactions related to the posted invoice, including the following transactions:

- **Packing slip reversal**—Transactions that reverse the packing slip.
- **Vendor summary account transaction**—For the vendor balance (specified in the vendor posting profile).
- **Stock account transaction**—For the inventoried items (specified in the posting setup).
- **Input tax transaction**—For the sales tax, if applicable (specified in the ledger posting group of the sales tax code).

You can find more details on the setup of the vendor posting profile in → Sect. 3.2.3, and the posting setup in → Sect. 9.4.2.

The button *Transaction origin* in the Voucher transactions inquiry provides access to the Transaction origin form. This form shows the transactions in all modules which refer to the voucher—apart from the ledger transactions, this includes the vendor transactions, the inventory transactions, and the tax transactions as applicable.

> *Note*: Like for the product receipt, settings for subledger accounting in the General ledger parameters determine when the transactions are posted to the general ledger. If the Voucher transactions inquiry is empty, you can access the form *General ledger > Periodic tasks > Subledger journal entries not yet transferred*, select the vendor invoice, and click the button *Transfer now* to speed up the general ledger posting. In addition, you can check the form *General ledger > Periodic tasks > Documents pending accounting* and click the button *Generate accounting* there to generate the ledger transactions rapidly.

3.6.4   Case Study Exercises

Exercise 3.11—Purchase Order Invoice
Your vendor submits the invoice VI311, which covers the goods and services received in exercise 3.8. Before posting the invoice, check the following items:

- Order status and document status of the purchase order.
- Inventory transaction for the order line with the product.

Then, register and post the vendor invoice with the received quantity in the Pending vendor invoice page. Check the invoice total before posting the invoice.

Now review the status of the items in the list above again. What is different?

Exercise 3.12—Partial Invoice for a Purchase Order
You receive the invoice VI312, which covers the goods that you have received with packing slip PS309 in exercise 3.9. Post the vendor invoice in the Purchase order form and make sure that the posted invoice only contains the items received with the packing slip PS309.

Exercise 3.13—Vendor Invoice Not Related to an Order
Your vendor now submits the invoice VI313, which contains a line with one hour of the procurement category "##-assembling" (created in exercise 3.4) for a price of USD 105. The invoice does not refer to a purchase order.

You accept this invoice and want to register it in the Pending vendor invoice page. Check the invoice total before you post the invoice.

Exercise 3.14—Invoice Inquiry
You want to review the invoice that you have posted in exercise 3.11. For this purpose, open the Invoice inquiry, first from the Purchase order form and then from the navigation pane. Check the invoice header, the lines, and the related ledger transactions.

In exercise 3.3, you have been looking for the vendor summary account. Can you find the ledger transaction for this account? Then open the Transaction origin form and check in which modules the invoice has posted transactions.

Note: If the Voucher transactions inquiry is empty, the subledger transfer probably has not been executed yet. In this case, open the form *General ledger > Periodic tasks > Subledger journal entries not yet transferred*, select the vendor invoice, and click the button *Transfer now* in the action pane to speed up the general ledger posting. If the ledger transactions are still empty, open the form *General ledger > Periodic tasks > Documents pending accounting* and click the button *Generate accounting* there to generate the ledger transactions rapidly.

3.7   Vendor Credit Note and Item Return

If you receive a credit note from a supplier, you want to register and post it. Posting a vendor credit note works similarly to posting a vendor invoice, except that credit notes are registered with a negative quantity. Like vendor invoices, vendor credit notes are classified into the following categories:

- **Credit notes for inventoried items**—In case you want to return items to the vendor.
- **Credit notes for intangible items**—For crediting services, fees, or licenses.

For inventoried items, vendor credit notes have to be registered in the Purchase order form. Processing the purchase order includes the (negative) product receipt for the item return and the (negative) invoice for the credit note. If you do not post the item return separately, posting the invoice (credit note) posts the item return of inventoried items in parallel. If the item model group does not allow a negative physical inventory, you can only post the return if the item is still in stock.

In case you only want to reverse a product receipt, but not a vendor invoice, use the functionality for canceling product receipts (→ Sect. 3.5.4).

For intangible items, you can register a vendor credit note in the following forms (similar to invoices for intangible items):

- **Purchase order**—Order lines with non-stocked items or procurement categories and a negative quantity.
- **Pending vendor invoice**—Invoice lines with non-stocked items or procurement categories and a negative quantity.
- **Invoice journal**—Journal lines with offset ledger accounts (→ Sect. 9.3.2).

In the Purchase order form or the Pending vendor invoice form, processing a credit note for intangible items works similarly to credit notes for inventoried items, but there is no inventory transaction and no inventory value for intangible items.

3.7.1   Crediting and Returning Items

In the Purchase order form, you can process credit notes for inventoried items in one of the following ways:

- **Original purchase order**—Register a new line in the original order.
- **New purchase order**—With the *Purchase type* "Purchase order" or "Returned order".

The first option—using the original purchase order for the credit note—is not available, if the approval status of the order is "Finalized", or if the order is completely invoiced, and the Procurement parameter *Safety level of invoiced orders* (*Procurement and sourcing > Setup > Procurement and sourcing parameters*, section *Delivery*) is set to "Locked".

3.7.1.1 Credit Note in the Original Purchase Order

If you want to record a credit note in a new line of the original purchase order, open this purchase order in Edit mode and insert an order line as usual, but with a negative quantity. If you expect a replacement from the vendor, you can enter another purchase order line with a positive quantity for the replacement.

Depending on the change management settings, the purchase order may be subject to approval before it is possible to confirm it. Once you have posted the confirmation, you can optionally reserve the quantity before you post the item return with a (negative) product receipt. In the Posting product receipt dialog, enter a reference number in the column *Product receipt* on the tab *Overview* and select an appropriate option (usually "Ordered quantity") in the field *Quantity* on the tab *Settings*.

Next, you can post the credit note with the button *Invoice/Generate/Invoice* in the purchase order. In the Pending vendor invoice form, be aware of the posting quantity: If you didn't post the (negative) product receipt before, click the button *Default from* in the action pane of the Vendor invoice form and select the option "Ordered quantity". Otherwise, you can select the option "Product receipt quantity".

If there is no other order line with an open quantity apart from the line with the negative quantity, only this line is shown on the tab *Lines* of the Vendor invoice form. Otherwise, delete the lines in the posting dialog that you do not want to post. Enter the credit note number in the invoice number (field *Number* in the field group *Invoice identification*) before you finally post the credit note with the button *Post* in the action pane of the Vendor invoice form.

If the checkbox *Deductions requirement* in the item model group of the credited item is selected, you have to post a (negative) product receipt for the item return before you can post the credit note (negative invoice).

3.7.1.2 Credit Note in a New Order

If you want to use a new order for the credit note, you can enter a regular purchase order (*Purchase type* "Purchase order"), which contains lines with a negative quantity.

Alternatively, you can select the *Purchase type* "Returned order" when you create the order (the field *Purchase type* is shown on the tab *General* in the *Create purchase order* dialog). If you use the purchase type "Returned order", there are the following characteristics:

- **RMA number**—The return merchandise authorization provided by the vendor has to be entered in the field *RMA number* of the *Create purchase order* dialog.
- **Quantity**—Has to be negative in all order lines.
- **Return action**—For information purposes, displayed on the sub-tab *Setup* of the purchase order lines (you can specify a default value in the Procurement parameters).

In order to facilitate entering the credit note, you can create the order lines in the new purchase order with the button *Purchase/Create/Credit note* in the action pane of the Purchase order form, or with the button *Purchase order line/Credit note* in the toolbar of the order lines. The *Create credit note* feature is a special version of the Copy feature for purchase orders, in which you can only copy invoices or invoice lines. Compared to the regular Copy feature, creating a credit note reverses the quantity sign, creates a reservation, and applies inventory marking (exactly offsetting the inventory value of the original line).

3.7.1.3 Inventory Marking

In order to avoid unintended changes to the inventory value, you can use inventory marking to assign the value of the returned/credited item to the corresponding original receipt.

For this purpose, select the new order line (credit note line) in the Purchase order form and click the button *Inventory/Marking* in the toolbar of the purchase order lines. In the *Marking* dialog that is shown next, select the checkbox in the column *Set mark now* (marking the original order line now returned) and click the button *Apply*. The inventory value of the new line entered for crediting now exactly offsets the inventory value received from the original line. When you apply marking to a transaction which is not been posted yet, a corresponding reservation ($\rightarrow$ Sect. 7.4.5) is set automatically.

Without marking, Dynamics 365 calculates the (outbound) inventory value of the credit note according to the item model group of the item—e.g., applying a FIFO calculation for an item with a FIFO valuation model, which means that according to the FIFO principle the cost price of the oldest receipt which is still on stock will be used.

3.7.1.4 Transaction Settlement

If the original invoice has not been paid and settled yet, you can immediately close the open vendor transaction of the original invoice when posting the credit note.

For this purpose, click the button *Invoice/Settle/Open transaction* in the action pane of the crediting purchase order. In the *Settle transaction* dialog that is shown next, select the checkbox in the column *Mark* for the respective invoice and click the button *OK*. Posting the credit note then closes the open vendor transaction of the invoice.

If you do not settle the invoice when registering the crediting purchase order, the responsible person has to settle the invoice with the credit note in the open transactions later ($\rightarrow$ Sect. 9.3.4).

3.7.2   Credit Notes without Item Return

If you receive a credit note that covers a price reduction (e.g., a refund for slightly damaged goods) from a vendor, there is no actual physical return of an item.

3.7.2.1 Crediting and Re-Invoicing

The easiest way to process such a refund is to register and to post a purchase order with two lines: One line with a negative quantity and the original price (credit note) and one line with a positive quantity and the new price (invoice).

3.7.2.2 Crediting and Allocating Charges

If this is not suitable (e.g., if you have already shipped or consumed the credited item), you have to post a credit note that does not directly refer to the item. The credit amount has to be allocated to the item separately in this case. There are two ways to enter the credit note:

- **Pending vendor invoice form**—Enter an invoice line with a negative quantity and an appropriate procurement category.
- **Invoice journal**—Enter a journal line with a negative amount and an appropriate ledger account.

Once you have posted the credit note, you can, if applicable, record a charges transaction to adjust the inventory value. For this purpose, select the original invoice in the Invoice inquiry (*Accounts payable > Inquiries and reports > Invoice > Invoice journal*) and click the button *Charges/Adjustment* in the toolbar of the tab *Overview*. In the *Allocate charges* dialog that is shown next, insert a line for the charges transaction. The lookup in the field *Charges code* of this dialog only shows charges with the *Debit type* "Item" and the *Credit type* "Ledger account". You can offset the balance on the credit ledger account—select a charges code which refers to the same ledger account that you have used in the credit note. The ledger account on the credit note is either determined by the procurement category (in the Pending vendor invoice form) or entered as an offset account in the invoice journal. If the charges transaction should only cover one of the invoice lines, mark the checkbox *Show selections and clear specific lines* in the lower pane of the dialog and select the checkbox *Include* in the line of the grid which is then shown below.

You can find more details on the general use of charges in → Sect. 4.3.4.

3.7.3   Case Study Exercise

Exercise 3.15—Vendor Credit Note
The goods received with PS309 in exercise 3.9 show serious defects. You return them to the vendor and receive the credit note VC315. The vendor does not send a replacement. Which ways do you know for registering the credit note?

You decide to register the credit note in the original order. Enter the required data and post the credit note.

3.8   Purchase Agreement, Requisition, and Quotation Request

Purchase orders are the only documents that can be used as a basis for product receipts and vendor invoices in procurement. Purchase agreements, purchase requisitions, and requests for quotation (RFQ) are used in business processes that prepare a purchase order.

3.8.1   Purchase Agreements

Purchase agreements provide the option to register and to follow up on blanket orders. Apart from agreements at the level of product number and quantity, there are agreements that specify the total amount (purchase value, not the purchase quantity) per product, and agreements at the level of procurement categories or vendor totals.

When posting a product receipt or a vendor invoice, you can only reference a purchase order. For this reason, you must create release orders from the agreement for further processing. Release orders are regular purchase orders that refer to the agreement.

3.8.1.1 Managing Purchase Agreements

In order to create a purchase agreement, open the menu item *Procurement and sourcing > Purchase agreements > Purchase agreements* and click the button *New* in the action pane. In the *Create* dialog, you have to select a *Purchase agreement classification* for the new agreement. Agreement classifications (*Procurement and sourcing > Setup > Purchase agreement classification*) are only used for grouping and reporting purposes and do not refer to a particular functionality.

The field *Default commitment* on the tab *General* in the dialog determines the level of the agreement:

- **Product quantity commitment**—Item number and quantity.
- **Product value commitment**—Item and value (relevant, if there is no agreed price).
- **Product category value commitment**—Value of a product category.
- **Value commitment**—Total value for a vendor.

The fields *Effective date* (start date of the contract) and *Expiration date* (end date) in the dialog and the agreement header initialize the related fields in the agreement lines. Once you close the dialog with the button *OK*, Dynamics 365 creates the purchase agreement (header record) and switches to the Purchase agreement detail form in the Lines view (→ Fig. 3.30).

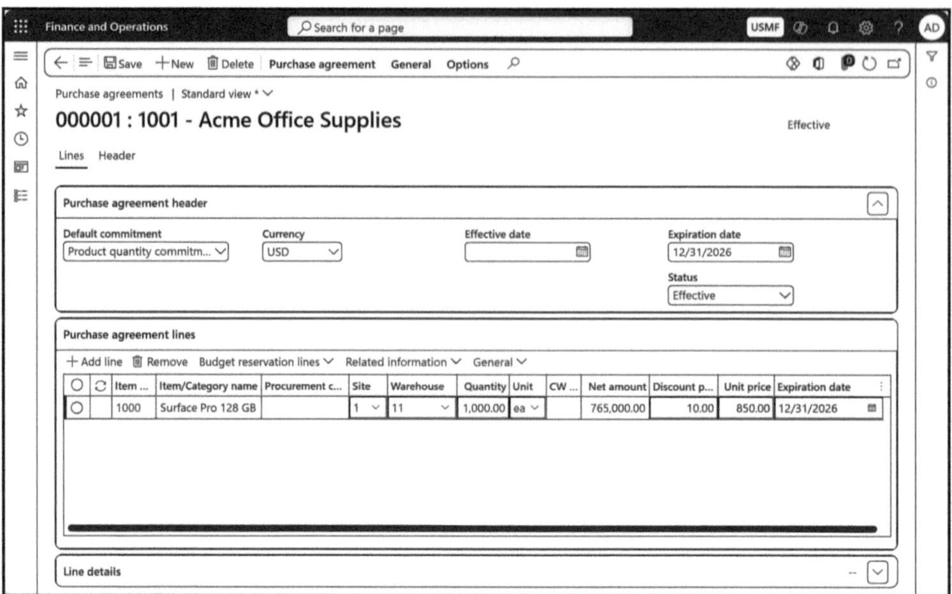

Fig. 3.30 Managing a purchase agreement

In the agreement lines, enter a new line with the *Item number*, *Quantity*, *Unit price*, and *Discount percent* (or *Procurement category* and *Net amount*, depending on the option selected in the *Default commitment*). If you want to prevent the total quantity or amount of related release order lines from exceeding the quantity or amount in the agreement line, set the slider *Max is enforced* on the sub-tab *General* of the *Line details* to "Yes".

Once you have completed the agreement lines, you can click the button *Purchase agreement/Generate/Confirmation* in the action pane to confirm the agreement. In the *Confirm purchase agreement* dialog, set the slider *Print report* to "Yes" if you want to print the confirmation. In addition, you can set the slider *Mark agreement as effective* to "Yes" if you want to set the *Status* in the agreement header to "Effective".

If you do not mark the agreement as effective when posting the confirmation, you have to manually change the *Status* in the agreement header from "On hold" to "Effective" before you can generate a release order. The status "Closed" can be used to deactivate an agreement irrespective of the expiration date.

3.8.1.2 Release Orders

Whereas the agreement is a general commitment to purchase an agreed quantity or amount in the effective period, the release order is the actual order to supply a particular quantity of an item or service at a particular date.

In order to create a release order in the Purchase agreement form, select the agreement and click the button *Purchase agreement/New/Release order*. In the *Create release order* dialog, which is shown next, select the items for the release order by entering the *Purchase quantity* and the *Requested receipt date*. Then click the button *Create* in the dialog to generate the new release order (which is a regular purchase order with the type "Purchase order").

Instead of creating a release order in the Purchase agreement form, you can start by creating a regular purchase order in the workspace *Purchase order preparation* or the Purchase order form. On the tab *General* in the *Create purchase order* dialog, select the *Purchase agreement* to indicate that the order is a release order from the respective agreement. When you enter an order line with an item that is covered by the agreement, Dynamics 365 generates a link automatically.

If you create a new purchase order in the Vendor form and there is an applicable agreement, a dialog is shown in which you can select the agreement.

In the release order, you can post the order confirmation, the product receipt, and the vendor invoice, like in any other purchase order. When you post the product receipt or the invoice, the order fulfillment in the related purchase agreement is updated. The fulfillment is shown on the sub-tab *Fulfillment* of the lines in the Purchase agreement form. If you want to check the link to a purchase agreement in the Purchase order form, click the button *Update line/Purchase agreement/Attached* in the toolbar of the purchase order line. At the order header level, there is the button *General/Related information/Purchase agreement* in the action pane.

3.8.1.3 Contract Lifecycle Management (CLM) Integration

If you manage vendor contracts in an external contract lifecycle management (CLM) system, you can use standard features in Dynamics 365 to integrate the CLM system with purchase agreements in Dynamics 365.

Once the CLM integration is configured, you can access the menu item *Procurement and sourcing > Contracts > All contracts* in Dynamics 365 to view the contracts of the CLM system. In the Purchase agreements list page, the columns *Contract ID* and *Contract status*, and in the Purchase agreements detail form, the tab *Contract* in the Header view, show data from the connected CLM system.

3.8.2   Purchase Requisitions

A purchase requisition is an internal document that asks the purchasing department to supply particular goods or services. Unlike a planned order, which is created automatically in master planning based on applicable item demand, a purchase requisition has to be entered manually.

3.8.2.1 Prerequisite Setup for Purchase Requisitions

A user who enters purchase requisitions has to be assigned to the corresponding worker record (employee or contractor) in the Human resources module ($\rightarrow$ Sect. 10.2.2). The worker is subsequently shown in the field *Preparer* of the purchase requisition.

Before you can transfer a purchase requisition to a purchase order, an approval process has to be completed. This approval process is based on the workflow management in Dynamics 365. In order to configure the purchase requisition workflow, open the menu item *Procurement and Sourcing > Setup > Procurement and sourcing workflows*. Workflows for purchase requisitions refer to the workflow type "Purchase requisition review" and, if necessary for the approval process, "Purchase requisition line review".

In the purchasing policies (*Procurement and Sourcing > Setup > Policies > Purchasing policies*), the *Policy rule* "Requisition purpose rule" of the policy that applies to your organization determines the default value for the field *Requisition purpose* in purchase requisitions with the following options:

- **Consumption**—Requisition for covering internal demand; approved purchase requisitions are directly transferred to purchase orders.
- **Replenishment**—Requisition for replenishing inventory; master planning includes this demand (similar to demand from, e.g., sales orders) in the calculation and generates purchase/production/transfer orders for approved purchase requisitions.

If the slider "Allow manual override" in this policy rule is set to "Yes", you can override the requisition purpose in the particular purchase requisition.

For purchase requisitions with the *Requisition purpose* "Consumption", available products and categories have to be registered and activated in an appropriate procurement catalog (*Procurement and Sourcing > Catalogs > Procurement catalog*). Make sure that this catalog is selected in the purchasing policies for the *Policy rule* "Catalog policy rule".

For purchase requisitions with the *Requisition purpose* "Replenishment", the *Policy rule* "Replenishment category access policy" determines the available procurement categories with the items assigned to these procurement categories.

> *Note*: A regular purchase requisition, which you enter to initiate a purchase order, has the *Requisition purpose* "Consumption". You can use the *Requisition purpose* "Replenishment" if you want, e.g., to replenish a remote location with an item and leave it to the setup whether the item is replenished with a transfer from a central warehouse or with a purchase order.

3.8.2.2 Entering Purchase Requisitions

In order to create a purchase requisition, open the menu item *Procurement and Sourcing > Purchase Requisitions > All purchase requisitions* and click the button *New* in the action pane. In the *Create* dialog, enter an explanation of the requisition in the field *Name* before you click the button *OK*.

In the requisition lines, you can enter a released product, which is included in the active procurement catalog, in the column *Item number*. In requisitions with the *Requisition purpose* "Consumption", you can also enter a *Procurement category* and a *Product name* (description) instead of an item number if you want to request a service or a product without an item number.

If external catalogs (*Procurement and Sourcing > Catalogs > External catalogs*) and integration settings with the vendor have been set up, you can click the button *External catalogs* in the toolbar of the requisition lines to access the vendor website, where you order products that are transferred to the purchase requisition.

Depending on purchasing policy settings, you can enter a requisition line on behalf of another person or organization—select the appropriate *Requester, Buying legal entity,* or *Receiving operating unit* in this case.

3.8.2.3 Approval Workflow

The initial status of a purchase requisition is "Draft". Once you have completed the purchase requisition registration, click the button *Workflow/Submit* in the action pane to start the purchase requisition workflow. The requisition status switches to "In review" and the workflow system starts processing the submitted requisition in a batch process. The further approval process depends on the workflow configuration of the purchase requisition workflow.

For a purchase requisition with the *Requisition purpose* "Consumption", you can create a related request for quotation (→ Sect. 3.8.3) with the button *Purchase requisition/New/ Request for quotation* in the purchase requisition as long as the requisition status is "In review".

3.8.2.4 Releasing Requisitions to Purchase Orders

Once a purchase requisition is approved, the status changes to "Approved", and you can release the requisition to a purchase order. If purchase requisitions are released automatically, Dynamics 365 skips the status "Approved" and sets the status "Closed" immediately.

In the purchasing policies, the *Policy rule* "Purchase order creation and demand consolidation" (in the policy for your organization) determines if purchase orders are generated automatically or if they have to be released manually. In this policy, you can also find settings that control whether the demand of different purchase requisitions may be consolidated to a common purchase order (which requires manual releasing).

If the policy specifies manual releasing, click the button *Release/New/Purchase order* in the list page *Procurement and sourcing > Purchase requisitions > Approved purchase requisition processing > Release approved purchase requisitions* to release an approved purchase requisition to a purchase order.

> *Note*: Creating a purchase order this way only works for approved purchase requisitions with the *Requisition purpose* "Consumption". For approved purchase requisitions with the *Requisition purpose* "Replenishment", master planning generates planned or actual orders in line with the settings for master planning.

3.8.3 Requests for Quotation

A request for quotation (RFQ) is an external document that asks vendors to submit a quotation. A request for quotation can include multiple vendors. Once you receive a quotation from a vendor, register it in a "Request for quotation reply" as preparation for comparing quotations. If you accept a quotation, you can transfer it to a purchase order.

3.8.3.1 Entering Requests for Quotation

You can manually create a request for quotation in the Request for quotation form, or generate it from planned purchase orders or purchase requisitions.

In the Request for quotation form (*Procurement and sourcing > Requests for quotations > All requests for quotations*), you can create a new request for quotations with the button *New*. Select the *Purchase type* "Purchase order" in the *Create* dialog, if you want to enter a request which should finally create a regular purchase order, or "Purchase agreement" if you want to prepare a purchase agreement. The *Purchase type* "Purchase requisition", which you can't select manually, indicates that the request for quotation derives from a purchase requisition. Enter the *Requested receipt date* and the *Expiration date* in the dialog before you close it with the button *OK*.

Requests for quotation consist of a header and one or more lines (→ Fig. 3.31). The header contains common data like the language and the quotation deadline (*Expiration date*). The lines contain the items with the quantity and price. Both, header and lines include the fields *Lowest status* and *Highest status*, which show the status of the request ("Created", "Sent", "Received", "Accepted", or "Rejected") and of the related quotations.

Like in the lines of purchase requisitions or purchase orders, a line in the request for quotation either contains an item number or a procurement category. In the Request for

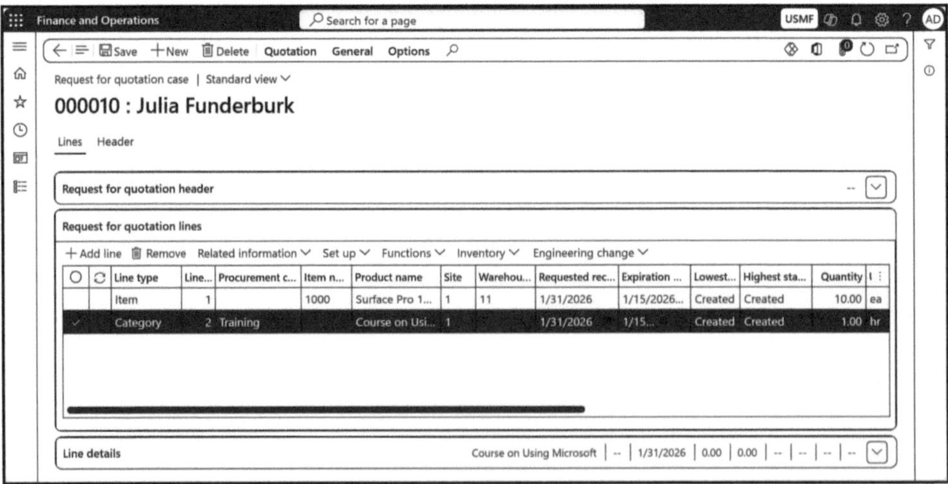

Fig. 3.31 Entering RFQ lines in the request for quotation form

quotation form, the column *Line type* controls whether the line contains an item or a procurement category. Data like the requested receipt date and the address in the lines are initialized with a default value from the header. The document management ($\rightarrow$ Sect. 10.5.1) provides the option to add details like data sheets or drawings to the request header or lines.

In order to specify the vendors who receive the request for quotation, switch to the tab *Vendor* in the Header view and insert a line for each vendor.

3.8.3.2 Sending Requests to Vendors

Once you have entered all required vendors, click the button *Quotation/Process/Send* in the action pane. In the *Sending request for quotation* dialog, which is shown next, click the button *Print* in the upper toolbar and set the slider *Print request for quotation* in the print dialog to "Yes" if you want to print the request. Then click the button *OK* in the prior dialog to post and print the request.

If you later want to view the vendors who have received the request for quotation, click the button *Quotation/Journals/Request for quotation journals* in the Request for quotation form.

3.8.3.3 Request for Quotation Replies

In order to enable regular users with appropriate permissions to register RFQ replies (vendor quotations), the slider *Purchaser can edit vendors bid* in the Procurement parameters (*Procurement and sourcing > Setup > Procurement and sourcing parameters*, section *Request for quotation*) has to be set to "Yes". Otherwise, the vendors themself should register their quotations in the Vendor collaboration portal in Dynamics 365.

The button *Quotation/Replies/Set RFQ reply defaults* in the Request for quotation form provides access to a form, in which you can specify the fields that have to be included in a reply (vendor bid). These fields are shown on the RFQ reply sheet, which you can print when sending the request for quotation (there is a corresponding slider in the printing options). Default values for the reply field settings are specified in the Procurement parameters (accessed with the button *Default request for quotation reply fields* in the toolbar of the section *Request for quotation*).

Once a vendor replies to a request by sending a quotation, open the menu item *Procurement and sourcing > Requests for quotations > Requests for quotations follow-up > Request for quotation*, select the line which shows the particular RFQ (in the column *Request for quotation case*) and vendor, and open the Reply detail form with the link in the field *Request for quotation case* or with the button *Reply/Maintain/Edit*. Alternatively, you can open the Reply detail form with the button *Quotation/Replies/Manage replies* in the request for quotation.

In the Reply detail form, click the button *Edit/Edit RFQ reply* to access the *RFQ bid*. In this form, you can enter the header and line data of the vendor quotation before you click the button *Submit* when you have finished entering the quotation. The RFQ then shows the reply status "Received".

3.8.3.4 Approving and Rejecting Replies

If you want to compare the replies (quotations) that you receive from the vendors, click the button *Quotation/Replies/Compare replies* in the Request for quotation form to access the *Compare request for quotation replies* form. In this form, you can select the checkbox in the column *Mark* and click the button *Accept* in the action pane to accept a quotation. Alternatively, you can accept a quotation in the Reply detail form (click the button *Reply/Process/Accept* in this form).

When accepting a quotation for an RFQ with the *Purchase type* "Purchase order", a purchase order is created. If you accept all lines of an RFQ, Dynamics 365 suggests rejecting the other replies for the request. But you can also reject a request with the button *Reply/Process/Reject* in the Reply detail form.

If you want to create a purchase price trade agreement (you can find details on price agreements in → Sect. 4.8.1) from a vendor quotation, click the button *General/Trade agreements/Create price agreement journal line* in the Reply detail form to generate a trade agreement journal (with a journal name specified in the Procurement parameters) which you can post subsequently.

3.8.4   Case Study Exercise

Exercise 3.16—Purchase Agreement

In a long-term contract with the vendor of exercise 3.2, you agree to purchase 500 units of the item of exercise 3.5 within the next 6 months for a price of USD 44. The contract is valid starting from today. Enter and confirm a corresponding purchase agreement.

The first release order related to this agreement is required today. Create this order with a quantity of 10 units and check the fulfillment of the agreement then.

Exercise 3.17—Request for Quotation

You want to receive vendor quotations for the item of exercise 3.5. For this purpose, enter a request for quotation with this item. The RFQ reply defaults for the request should include the header field *Reply valid to* and the line fields *Quantity* and *Unit price*. Send the request to the vendor of exercise 3.2 and another vendor of your choice.

After a while, you receive quotations with quantities and prices of your choice from both vendors. Enter these quotations in the request for quotation replies assigned to the original request. The vendor of exercise 3.2 has submitted the better quotation, which you want to accept. Reject the quotation of the other vendor.

Sales and Distribution

4

The primary responsibility in sales and distribution is the supply of goods and services to customers. In order to perform this task, the sales order process includes the order entry, picking, shipping, and invoicing.

4.1 Business Processes in Sales and Distribution

Before we start to go into details, the lines below give an overview of the business processes in sales and distribution.

4.1.1 Basic Approach

As a prerequisite for order processing, correct master data are required, in particular the customer and the product data. For services and non-inventoried items, it is possible to work with sales categories instead of products.

4.1.1.1 Master Data and Transactions in Sales

Customers and products are master data, which are created once and only occasionally updated later on. In the course of sales order processing, default values from customer and product records (master data) initialize the respective fields in sales quotations and sales orders (transaction data). You can override these data in the transaction—for example, if the customer requires a different delivery address in a particular sales order. If such an update should also apply to future orders, modify the customer record accordingly.

Since the sales process mirrors the purchasing process, sales order processing is very similar to purchase order processing. The core steps of sales order processing (with predecessor and successor activities) are shown in → Fig. 4.1.

4.1.1.2 Sales Quotation

If we disregard prior marketing activities, the sales cycle starts with a request from a prospect or customer. In the sales team, you create a quotation as an answer to this request and send it to the potential or actual customer.

4.1.1.3 Sales Order

If the customer agrees to the quotation and orders the goods or services, you create a sales order as the basis for order fulfillment. Like a purchase order, a sales order consists of a header, which contains the common data of the whole order (e. g., customer data), and one or more lines, which contain the ordered items (products or services).

Optionally, you can post an order confirmation and send it to the customer electronically or as a printed document. Posting an order confirmation stores it in a journal. Since it is stored separately, you can always view the order confirmation with its original content, no matter if the sales order has been modified later.

In order to manage long-term contracts (blanket orders), you can use sales agreements in Dynamics 365. If you later want to issue a shipment related to the blanket order, create a release order with a partial quantity of the sales agreement. Release orders are regular sales orders that are assigned to the agreement.

4.1.1.4 Picking and Shipment

Depending on the settings of the item, master planning determines the required material supply (in purchasing or production) and makes sure that you can ship the sales order in time.

Before shipping the item, you can print a picking list to prepare the delivery. After finishing the internal picking process, you can post the packing slip. If no picking list is needed, you can also post a packing slip without a prior picking list.

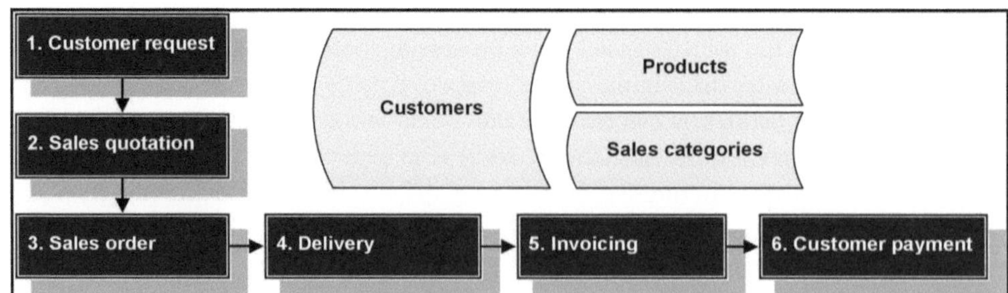

Fig. 4.1 Sales order processing in Dynamics 365

4.1.1.5 Invoicing

Once the packing slip has been posted, you can post an invoice for the sales order. If you do not require a separate packing slip, you can also post the invoice without a prior packing slip. In this case, the invoice is posting the physical and the financial transactions in parallel.

If you want to sell services or non-inventoried items, you can process a regular sales order—enter order lines with a sales category or service item for this purpose. Alternatively, you can use a free text invoice in case you just need an invoice and no other sales document. In the lines of a free text invoice, you have to enter ledger accounts instead of products or sales categories.

4.1.1.6 Customer Payment

The customer has to pay the invoice with or without cash discount deduction until the due date. You can find a description on how to post the customer payment and to settle the invoice in → Sect. 9.3.3.

If the customer does not pay on time, you can create payment reminders in Dynamics 365.

4.1.1.7 Ledger Integration and Voucher Principle

Based on the deep integration of finance with the business processes in all areas of Dynamics 365, the inventory and customer transactions in sales are posted to ledger accounts as specified in the setup (→ Sect. 9.4).

In order to keep track of the whole business process, Dynamics 365 comprehensively applies the voucher principle, which means that you have to register a document (voucher) before posting the transaction. The transactions in sales order processing are similar to the respective purchasing transactions.

For your guidance, a comparison of purchase documents and sales documents in order processing is shown in → Fig. 4.2.

4.1.2   At a Glance: Sales Order Processing

The following example demonstrates the main steps in sales order processing. It starts with creating the order in the workspace *Sales order processing and inquiry*, and shows how to post all transactions directly in the Sales order form. Alternatively, you can create an order in the Sales order form (or in the Customer form).

In the workspace *Sales order processing and inquiry*, click the button *New/Sales order* in the action pane to create the order. In the *Create sales order* dialog, which is shown next, select a customer in the field *Customer account* (you can trigger the search in this field by typing the first characters of the customer name). Once you close the dialog with the button *OK*, Dynamics 365 creates an order header with default data (e.g., for the currency) from the customer.

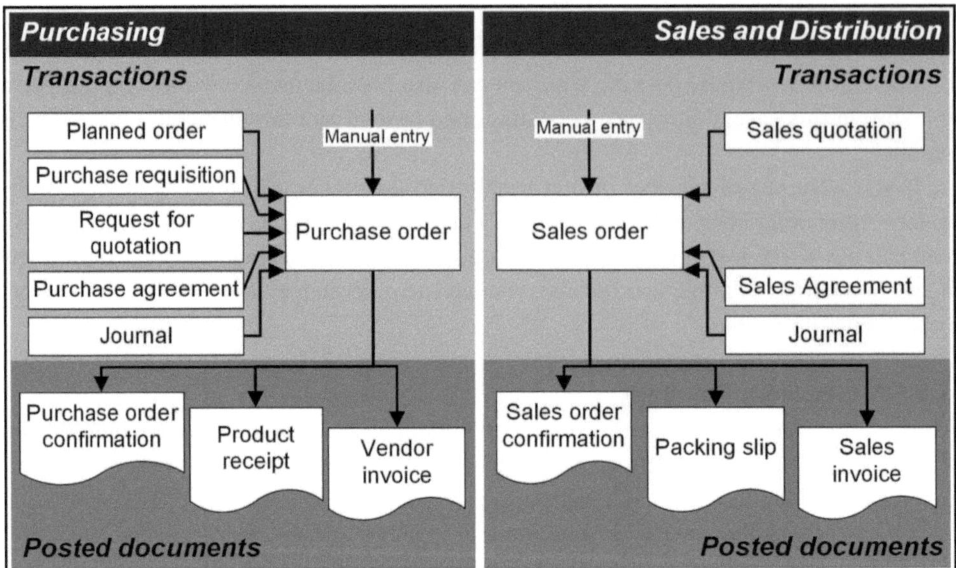

Fig. 4.2 Comparison of purchasing and sales documents

The Sales order detail form is subsequently shown in the Lines view. Enter the first order line with the item number (or sales category), the quantity, and the price on the tab *Sales order lines*. When you select the item, Dynamics 365 initializes the quantity, the price, and other fields with default values from the item. If you want to enter another line, press the *Down Arrow*, or click the button *Add line* in the toolbar. The buttons *Header* and *Lines* below the action pane provide the option to switch between the Header view (→ Fig. 4.3) and the Lines view.

If order completion is enabled, the button *Complete* is shown in the action pane. In this case, click that button (and, if shown, confirm a subsequent dialog) once you have finished entering the sales order.

You can print the order confirmation next. Click the button *Sell/Generate/Confirm sales order* in the action pane and, in the dialog that is subsequently shown, make sure that the sliders *Posting* and *Print confirmation* on the tab *Parameters* are set to "Yes". Optionally, click the button *Printer setup* in the dialog to select a printer.

Then click the button *Pick and pack/Generate/Post packing slip* in the action pane of the Sales order form to start posting the packing slip (→ Fig. 4.4). In the posting dialog, select the option "All" in the field *Quantity* to ship the entire quantity and make sure that the sliders *Posting* and *Print packing slip* are set to "Yes". Then click the button *OK* to post and print the packing slip. Posting the packing slip reduces the physical quantity in inventory and sets the order status to "Delivered".

Posting the sales invoice with the button *Invoice/Generate/Invoice* in the Sales order form is similar to packing slip posting. In order to invoice only shipped items, make sure to select the option "Packing slip" in the lookup field *Quantity* of the posting dialog. If you

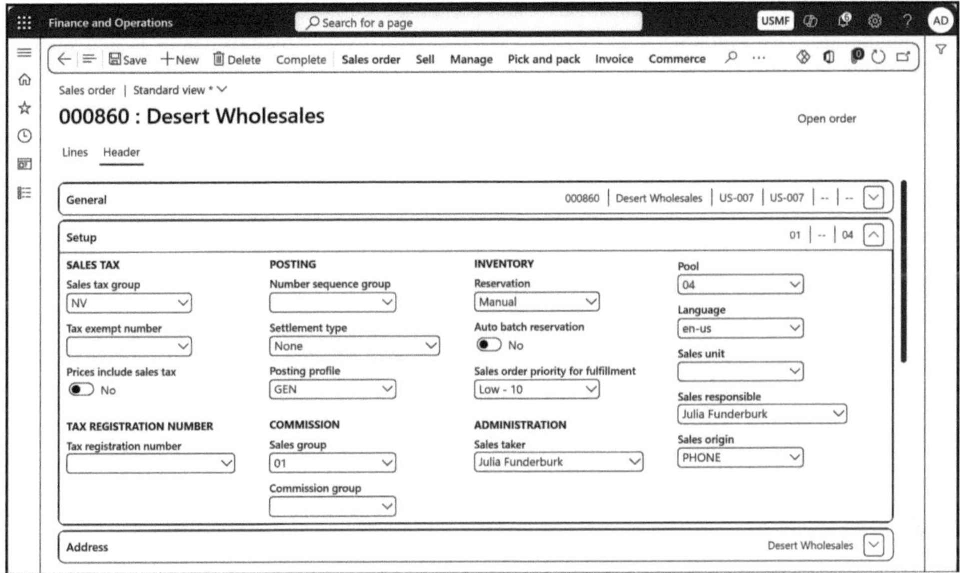

Fig. 4.3 Entering header data in the sales order Header view

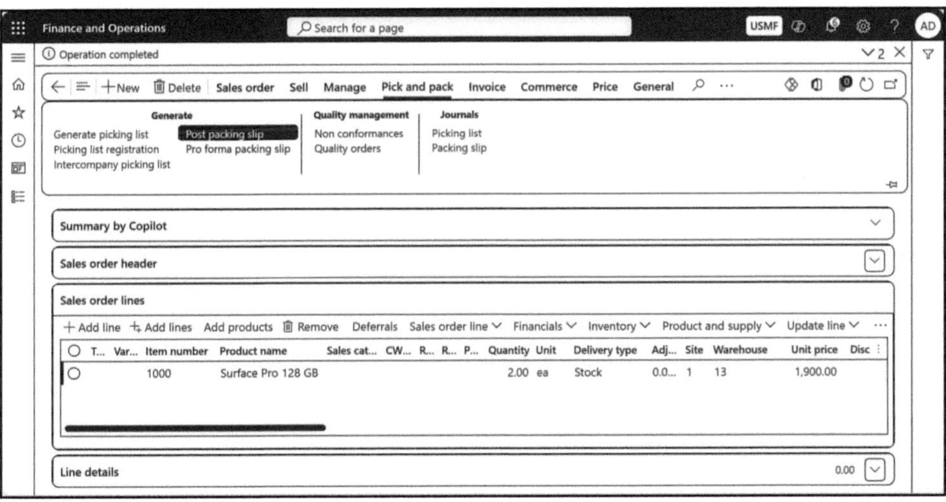

Fig. 4.4 Posting the packing slip in the sales order

select the option "All", invoice posting in parallel posts a shipment of the deliver remainder quantity (open quantity, which is not included in prior packing slips). Invoice posting generates an open customer transaction, which needs to be paid, and updates the order status to "Invoiced".

Notes: The button *Complete* and the related parameter settings in the Pricing management module are only available if the *Unified pricing management* feature has been activated. Without order completion, you might need to refresh the Sales order form with the shortcut *Shift + F5* or *Alt + S* to activate the button for the order confirmation if an order contains only one line. And depending on the requirements, you can skip transactions in the process described above. The most streamlined process is to post the invoice immediately after entering the sales order (select "All" in the field *Quantity* of the *Posting invoice* dialog in this case).

4.2   Customer and Product Management in Sales

Business partners, who receive goods or services, have to be registered as customers in Dynamics 365. As long as the business partner only receives quotations, you can optionally use a prospect instead of a customer.

Customer records in sales are similar to vendor records in purchasing, and the list pages and detail forms in both areas contain similar features. Examples of these features are one-time customers, payment terms, posting profiles, and the global address book.

Whereas the customer records are the main data source for the sales order header, products and sales categories are the main data source for the sales order line. This section primarily explains the product data which are necessary for sales and distribution. In → Sect. 7.2, you can find a general description of the product management features in Dynamics 365.

4.2.1   Customer Management

You can edit an existing or create a new customer in the Customer list page in the Sales module (*Sales and marketing > Customers > All customers*) or in the Accounts receivable module (*Accounts receivable > Customers > All customers*). In line with the general structure of list pages, the Customer page shows a list of all customers. With the link in the field *Account*, you can access the details of a customer.

4.2.1.1 Create Customer Dialog

If you want to create a new customer in the Customer page, click the button *New* in the action pane or press the shortcut *Alt + N*. In the *Create customer* dialog, which contains the core fields of the customer record, the unique customer number in the field *Customer account* is assigned automatically or has to be entered manually (depending on settings in the corresponding number sequence). By default, the number sequence in the Accounts receivable parameters is used, but you can override this number sequence in the customer groups (personalize the Customer group form to shown the column *Customer account number sequence*).

In the field *Type* below the *Customer account* (number) field, select the option "Person" (for a person with a *First name* and a *Last name*) or "Organization" (for a company or other organization). The field *Name* in the dialog is a lookup field in which you can enter a new name or—if the customer is already a party in the global address book—select an existing party. Customer records are linked to the parties in the global address book in the same way as vendor records, which is why features like the duplicate check and options to share customers across companies work similar to the options in the vendor form (→ Sect. 3.2.1).

If you want to enter a sales order immediately when creating the customer, you can click the button *Save and open/Sales order* in the dialog.

4.2.1.2 Customer Detail Form

The Customer detail form (→ Fig. 4.5) contains numerous fields, which initialize sales orders. Like the vendor group in the Vendor form, the *Customer group* on the tab *General* in the Customer form is a core setting which controls the ledger integration via customer posting profiles—similar to the vendor posting profiles (→ Sect. 3.2.3). Further important customer fields include the *Sales tax group* (*VAT group*, initialized from the customer group), the *Delivery terms* and the *Mode of delivery* on the tab *Invoice and delivery*, the *Currency* on the tab *Sales demographics*, and the *Terms of payment* on the tab *Payment defaults*.

If you want to block a customer, select the appropriate option in the lookup field *Confirmation, delivery and invoicing on hold* on the tab *Credit and collections*. Similar to

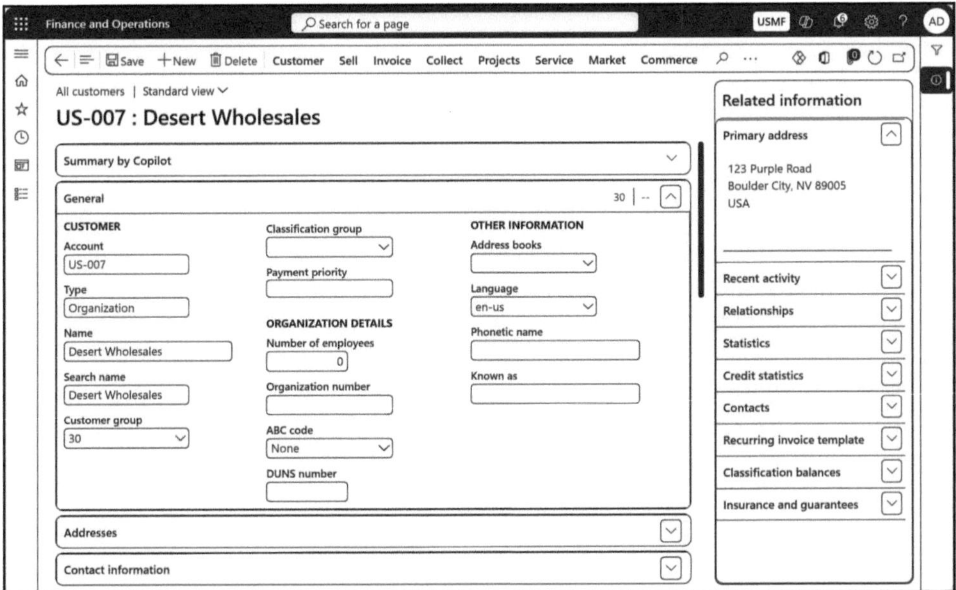

Fig. 4.5 Editing a customer in the Customer detail form

the options for blocking a vendor ($\to$ Sect. 3.2.1), the hold status "All" prevents entering or posting any sales order or other transaction with the customer.

Since the structure, the fields, and the options in the Customer form are similar to the Vendor from (corresponding to the vendor approval, there is also a customer approval), the description below only covers the differences and, in addition, the elements that are primarily relevant for customer records and have not been explained for vendor records.

4.2.1.3 Invoice Account

Sometimes it is necessary to send the invoice to a party who is not placing the order, for example, if the company headquarters of an affiliated group should receive the invoice for subsidiaries.

In order to deal with this situation, you can set up a separate customer for the party who receives the invoice—the invoice account—and enter the customer number of this party in the field *Invoice account* on the tab *Invoice and delivery* of the customer who places the order. The invoice account in the customer record (or, if empty, the original customer number) is the default for the field *Invoice account* in related sales order headers, but you can override the invoice account in the sales order. The customer in the open customer transaction is the invoice account of the sales order.

Unless chosen differently in the lookup field *Invoice address* on the tab *Invoice and delivery* in the customer record, the printed invoice shows the name and address of the invoice customer.

4.2.1.4 Alternative Addresses and Global Address Book Integration

The invoice account in the Customer form refers to another customer, who needs to be entered as a separate customer with all required details. If you only need several postal addresses for one customer, you can enter them on the tab *Addresses* of the Customer form.

Like the postal addresses for vendors ($\to$ Sect. 3.2.1), customer addresses are shared with the related party in the global address book.

In order to create a new customer address, click the button *Add* in the toolbar of the tab *Addresses*. In the *New address* dialog ($\to$ Fig. 4.6), which is shown next, enter a name for the address and select one or more purposes. If you enter the primary customer address, make sure that the slider *Primary* is set to "Yes" and the slider *Private* to "No".

If you enter an address with the purpose "Invoice", invoices for the customer show this address instead of the primary address. An address with the purpose "Delivery" is a delivery address in sales orders.

Whereas the button *Edit* in the toolbar of the tab *Addresses* in the Customer form provides access to the fields that are also shown in the *New address* dialog, the button *More options/Advanced* in the toolbar provides access to all address details. If a customer has multiple addresses with the same purpose (e.g., multiple delivery addresses) and you want to specify a default value (e.g., a default delivery address), click the button *More options/ Set defaults* in the toolbar of the tab *Addresses*.

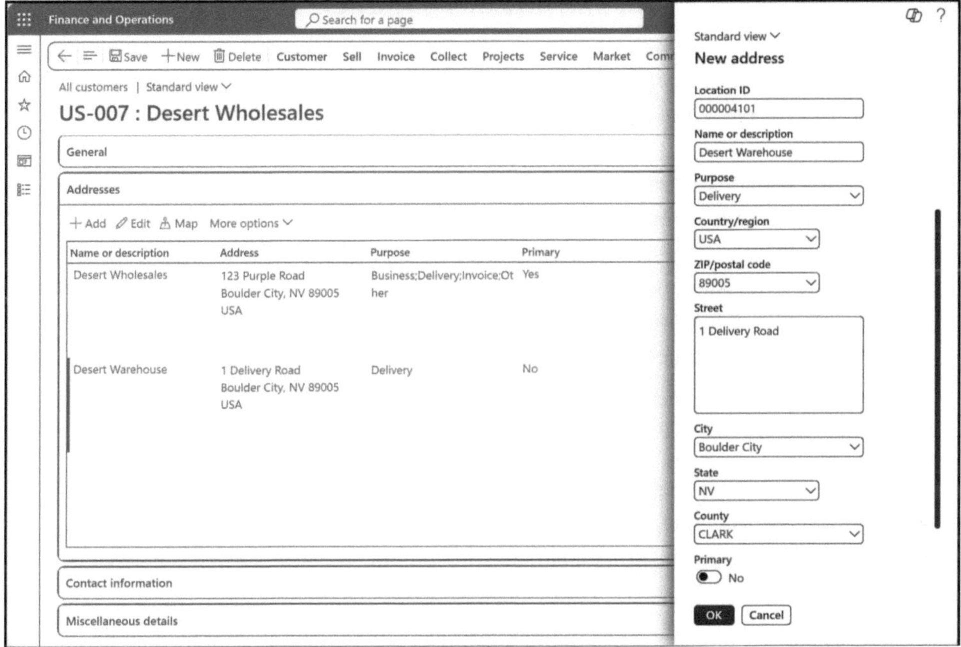

Fig. 4.6 Entering a customer delivery address in the *New address* dialog

If you want to ship a sales order to an address that is different from the default delivery address and from the primary address (which is the default if there is no particular delivery address), you can select one of the other customer addresses or enter a completely new address in the sales order.

4.2.1.5 Credit Limit

In order to reduce the risk of unpaid invoices, many companies apply credit limits to customers. For this purpose, the Credit and collections module includes detailed settings which control the usage of credit limits ($\rightarrow$ Sect. 9.2.6).

In the Customer form, the tab *Credit and collections* contains the core fields *Credit limit* (credit limit amount of the customer in the accounting currency) and *Credit limit expiration date* (validity of the credit limit) for the credit limit. Irrespective of these settings, there is no credit limit check if the slider *Exclude from credit management* for the customer is set to "Yes".

When you enter a sales order or post a transaction, there is a check whether the customer exceeds the credit limit, and, if applicable, the order is put on hold. In case of an order hold, you can click the button *Credit management/Credit management/Credit management hold list* in the Sales order form and release the hold in the hold list, similar to managing a regular order hold ($\rightarrow$ Sect. 4.3.3).

4.2.2   Print Management and Advanced Notes

Print management settings and advanced notes, which work similarly in purchasing and in sales, control the layout and the elements that are included in printed documents.

4.2.2.1 Print Management

The *Form setup* form (*Accounts receivable > Setup > Forms > Form setup*) for customer documents contains some basic settings for the layout of sales documents—for example, if you print the external item number on documents (→ Fig. 4.7). Sections like *Quotation* or *Confirmation* (for the order confirmation) on the left determine for the related document, which inventory dimensions are printed in the lines, and—in the field group *Note*— if attachments with the *Document type* which is selected in the field *Include documents of type* should be printed on the document (using the document management, see → Sect. 10.5.1).

In the Accounts receivable parameters (*Accounts receivable > Setup > Accounts receivable parameters*), the slider *Copy notes when transferring to sales order* in the section *General*, tab *Sales setup*, controls whether attachments are automatically copied from the customer or the released product to the sales order.

Base settings for printing sales documents—e.g., the destination (printer), the number of copies, or a footer text—are specified in the Print management form, which you can access with the button *Print management* in the toolbar of the section *General* in the Form setup form. If there are no settings for a particular document and you want to specify them, right-click on the respective document in the left pane of the Print management form and select the option *New* in the drop-down menu.

At the customer level, you can override these settings with the button *General/Set up/ Print management* in the Customer form. Right-click the respective Original or Copy document in the left pane of the Print management form, and then select the option *Override*

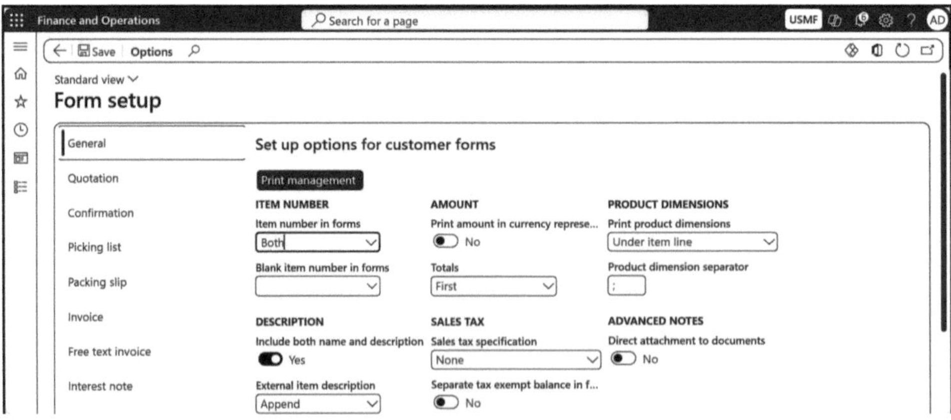

Fig. 4.7   Configuring the form setup for sales documents

in the drop-down menu before you enter the individual settings. Customer print management settings are transferred to the related sales orders. In the sales orders, you can override the settings again.

The selected option in the field *Destination* (specifying the printer or alternative output) of the Print management form is only used when printing a document, if the slider *Use print management destination* in the particular posting dialog is set to "Yes" ($\rightarrow$ Sect. 3.4.5).

If you want to include some general lines in printed documents, you can specify a standard text per document and language in the form notes (*Accounts receivable > Setup > Forms > Form notes*).

4.2.2.2 Advanced Notes

Advanced notes, which are available in sales and in purchasing, are a more detailed option for managing text elements that should be printed on documents. They specify a default text which is copied as an attachment (using the document management) to the order or directly to the posted documents.

In order to set up advanced notes for customers, open the form *Accounts receivable > Setup > Forms > Customers advanced notes setup* and create a line—per customer, per group, or for all customers—in the upper pane with the applicable text in the lower pane (select the *Restriction* "External" in the upper pane for printing on external documents). With the button *Translations* in the lower pane, you can specify language-specific texts that override the general text in the lower pane.

If you want to specify notes at the group level, create the required groups in the form *Accounts receivable > Setup > Forms > Customers advanced notes groups* and assign them to the respective customers on the tab *Sales order defaults* in the Customer form. Advanced notes at the li level can be entered on the tab *Lines* of the Advanced notes setup form.

In addition, some prerequisite settings for advanced notes are included in the Form setup form (described above). The sections for the applicable documents (e.g., *Confirmation* for the order confirmation) contain the following relevant fields:

- **Include document on sheets**—Controls whether header-level or line-level notes are included.
- **Include documents of type**—Specifies the document type that is used for attaching the advanced note to the posted documents.

On the tab *General* in the Form setup form, the slider *Direct attachment to documents* controls whether advanced notes are directly attached to the posted documents (without assigning them to the sales order before).

> *Note*: Advanced note settings for released products (notes at the order line level) and for vendors (notes in purchase orders) work similarly.

4.2.3 Products and Sales Categories

When entering a sales order line for selling a physical product, you have to select an item number. For intangible items (e.g., services, fees, licenses), you can either use items (with the product type "Service" or a particular item model group) or sales categories.

4.2.3.1 Sales Categories

A product category (→ Sect. 3.3.1) is a group of similar products or services. Sales categories are categories that belong to the hierarchy with the type "Sales category hierarchy". You can manage the sales-related settings of these product categories in the Sales category form (*Sales and marketing > Setup > Categories > Sales categories*). In this form, the item sales tax group on the tab *Item sales tax groups* is one of the core settings.

4.2.3.2 General Product Data in Sales

The product management in Dynamics 365 (→ Sect. 3.3.2 and → Sect. 7.2) has two levels: The shared products, which contain the common data of the item in all companies, and the released products, which contain the company-specific data.

Core sales data, including the *Item sales tax group* (which determines whether regular sales tax/VAT or a reduced rate applies), are available on the tab *Sell* of the Released product form.

Settings for order quantities and lot sizes are specified in the default order settings, which you can access with the button *Manage inventory/Order settings/Default order settings* in the released product. You can find the sales-related setup on the tab *Sales order* of the default order settings. A checkmark in the checkbox *Stopped* on the tab *Sales order* blocks the item for sales transactions.

In the default order settings, the record with a blank *Site* and the *Rank* "0" determines the settings at the company level. If you want to specify order settings at the level of sites, insert an additional record in which you enter the *Site* in the respective field. In order to override the default order settings at the company level with default order settings at the level of sites, set the applicable slider *Override default settings* in the site-specific order settings to "Yes".

4.2.3.3 Base Sales Prices

Apart from the base sales price in the released product, you can set up price lists and discount agreements in basic trade agreements (→ Sect. 4.8.1) and, with advanced options, in pricing management (→ Sect. 4.8.3).

The base sales price is specified in the field *Price* on the tab *Sell* of the Released product form. This price is used in sales orders with no applicable trade agreement for the respective customer and item.

It is possible to enable an automatic update of this base sales price, which is calculated from the purchase price or the cost price. The field group *Price update* on the tab *Sell* in the released product contains the settings for this price calculation. The first setting in this field group is the lookup field *Sales price model* which determines whether the price calculation refers to the field *Contribution ratio* or to the field *Charges percentage*. The *Sales price model* "None" means that there is no automatic calculation of the base sales price. The lookup field *Base price* determines the basis for the price calculation and includes two options:

- **Purchase price**—Sales price based on the base purchase price (tab *Purchase*).
- **Cost**—Sales price based on the base cost price (tab *Manage costs*).

The other settings related to the base sales price (including the price quantity and price charges) are similar to the base purchase price settings ($\rightarrow$ Sect. 3.3.3).

In addition to the base sales price on the tab *Sell* in the Released product form, you can enter base prices at the level of sites in the Item price form. In order to access the Item price form, click the button *Manage costs/Set up/Item price* in the released product. For manufactured items, you can run a price calculation ($\rightarrow$ Sect. 7.3.3) that is based on the bill of materials and the route.

4.2.3.4 Approved Customers

If enabled in the feature management as part of Advanced quality management, you can manage approved customers—for example, if a product is customer-specific and may only be sold to a particular customer. Approved customers work similarly to approved vendors ($\rightarrow$ Sect. 3.3.2), but with a more flexible setup—the Approved customer list setup form includes a Table/Group/All relation.

The field *Approved customer list check method* on the tab *Sales order defaults* in the Customer detail form controls if there is a validation of the customer against the approved customer list. In the Released product form, the field *Approved customer list check method* on the tab *Sell* controls if the item is subject to validation.

For the list check method "Warning only" and "Not allowed", you need to specify which customers are approved for which items in the Approved customer list setup form (*Product information management > Setup > Approved customer list > Approved customer list setup*). You can manage this setup at the group level (approved customer group, approved item group).

4.2.4   Case Study Exercises

Exercise 4.1—Customer Record

A new domestic customer wants to place an order. Create a record for this customer with a name (starting with your user ID) and a primary address of your choice. Select the payment terms and the cash discount of exercise 3.1, and an appropriate customer group and sales tax group for domestic customers. For this customer, the credit limit should not be checked.

The customer wants you to ship the ordered goods to a separate delivery address. Enter a domestic delivery address of your choice for this purpose, which should be the default delivery address for orders of this customer.

Exercise 4.2—Sales Categories
Your company offers installation services to the customers. For this purpose, enter a new category "##-installation" (## = your user ID) in the sales category hierarchy. The sales category should refer to the standard tax rate.

4.3   Sales Order Management

The first document in the sales cycle often is a sales quotation, which you can send to a prospect or customer in reply to a request for quotation. Once the customer orders the requested goods or services, you can enter an appropriate sales order.

With regard to the functionality and the structure of forms and list pages, sales orders work similarly to purchase orders. For this reason, this section primarily covers subjects in sales that are different from purchasing.

4.3.1   Basics of Sales Order Processing

Unlike purchase orders, which are primarily based on material requirements known within Dynamics 365, sales orders in most cases originate from sources outside the application. Apart from manually entering a sales order, there are only a few other options to generate a sales order from within Dynamics 365. These possible options for generating a sales order include:

- **Sales quotations**—After acceptance, quotations are transferred to orders.
- **Sales agreements**—Blanket orders are the basis for release orders.
- **Data import/export framework**—Exchanging data with other applications.
- **Intercompany functionality**—From purchase orders in another legal entity.
- **Project management and accounting/Project operations**—Create project sales orders or item requirements.

In Dynamics 365, blanket orders are covered by sales agreements (*Sales and marketing > Sales agreements > Sales agreements*), which not only contain contracts at the level of product number and quantity, but also at the level of the total sales amount with a product, or the level of the total sales volume with a customer. In order to ship and invoice a delivery related to a sales agreement, create a release order (a regular sales order that is linked to the sales agreement). In general, sales agreements work similarly to purchase agreements ($\rightarrow$ Sect. 3.8.1).

Once you have created a new sales order—either entered manually or by transferring a prior document like the sales agreement—and, if necessary, set the order to complete (→ Sect. 4.3.3), you can post and print the order confirmation. The further process (→ Fig. 4.8) depends on the requirements and the settings on how/which transactions should be registered in inventory and in sales.

If required, you can process a prepayment (→ Sect. 9.3.5), optionally with a prepayment invoice, before shipping items.

In the warehouse, there are the following options for processing a sales order:

- **Packing slip**—Immediately post the packing slip.
- **Picking list**—Post a picking list before posting the packing slip.
- **Picking list registration**—Confirm the picking list before packing slip posting.
- **Advanced warehouse management** (→ Sect. 8.1).

Another way to register a pick transaction is to execute picking in the Pick form (accessed from the sales order line). Usually, you work in this way if you have to register serial numbers or batch numbers, but do not process picking as a separate step in the warehouse.

After posting the packing slip, you can post the invoice. If no packing slip is required, you can also post the invoice immediately after entering the order.

4.3.2 Sales Quotations

In a sales quotation, the business partner does not need to be a customer. You can also manage a quotation for a prospect. But since sales orders require a customer, you have to

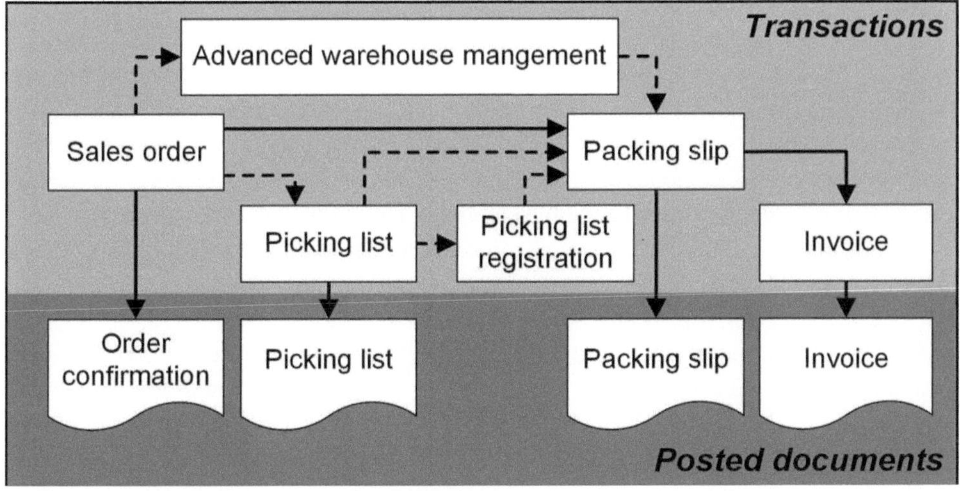

Fig. 4.8 Sales order processing in Dynamics 365

convert the prospect to a customer before you can transfer an accepted quotation to an order.

4.3.2.1 Managing Prospects

Prospects are parties—companies or persons—in sales, who are not customers yet. It is not possible to register transactions for prospects, which have an impact on the general ledger or generate customer transactions—this is only possible for customers. You can use prospects in CRM activities like mailings and marketing campaigns, and in sales quotations.

If you want to create a new prospect, open the menu item *Sales and marketing > Relationships > Prospects > All prospects* and click the button *New* in the action pane. The *Create prospect* dialog works similarly to the *Create customer* dialog (→ Sect. 4.2.1), including the integration of the global address book.

In the Prospect detail form, you can update core data like the sales tax group (VAT group) and the customer group. Some default data, like the prospect type (*Type ID* on the tab *General* in the Prospect form), derive from the Sales and marketing parameters (section *Prospects*).

If you want to convert a prospect to a customer, click the button *General/Convert/ Convert to customer* in the Prospect form. Depending on the setting in the prospect type (*Sales and marketing > Setup > Prospects > Relation types*) of the prospect, the prospect is deleted automatically after converting.

4.3.2.2 Processing Sales Quotations

In order to create a new sales quotation, open the Quotation form (*Sales and marketing > Sales quotations > All quotations*) and click the button *New* in the action pane. Alternatively, you can create a quotation with the button *Sell/New/Sales quotation* in the Customer form or the Prospect form.

If you create a quotation in the Quotation form, the *Create quotation* dialog (→ Fig. 4.9) is shown, in which you have to select the *Account type* ("Customer" or "Prospect"). Depending on the selected account type, select a customer or a prospect in the respective lookup field. The sales quotation is initialized with default values from the selected customer or prospect. Once you close the dialog with the button *OK*, Dynamics 365 creates the quotation header and switches to the Quotation detail form in the Lines view.

In the Quotation detail form, you can click the button *Add line* in the toolbar of the tab *Lines* or simply click on the first line in the grid to create a line. Then select an item number (or a sales category) and enter other line details as required.

Once you have completed the quotation lines, click the button *Quotation/Generate/ Send quotation* in the action pane to post and print the quotation (similar to an order confirmation in a sales order). Once the customer or prospect has accepted the quotation, confirm it with the button *Follow up/Generate/Confirm* in the action pane (which generates a sales order automatically). In case the customer does not accept the quotation or you

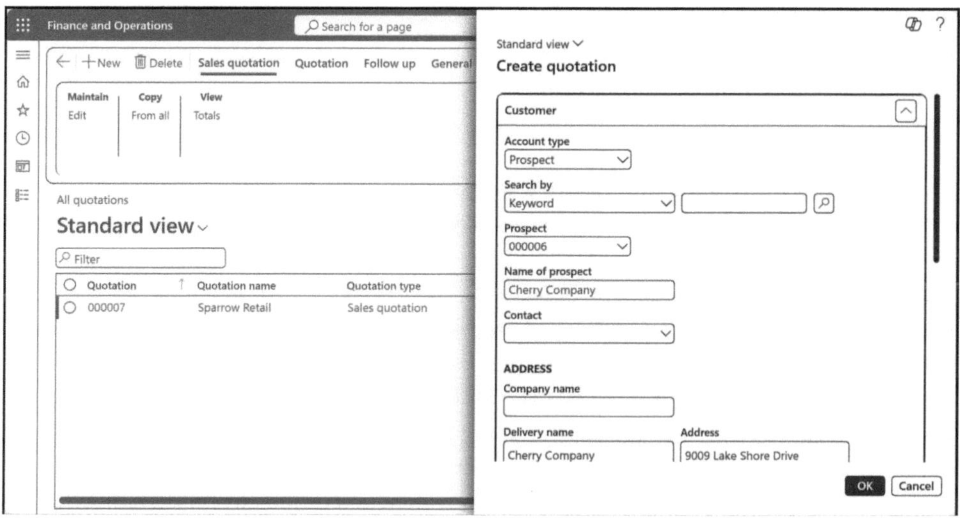

Fig. 4.9 Creating a new quotation for a prospect

want to cancel it from your side (e.g., because the *Expiration date* of the quotation has passed), click the button *Follow up/Generate/Lost quotation* or *.../Cancel*.

If the quotation refers to a prospect, you have to convert the prospect to a customer before you can create the sales order. Click the button *Follow up/Modify/Convert to customer* in the Quotation form for this purpose.

4.3.3 Sales Order Registration

Like in a purchase order, the order type is a core characteristic of a sales order. In a sales order, there are the following order types:

- **Sales order**—Regular sales order.
- **Journal**—Draft or template, without impact on inventory or finance.
- **Subscription**—Periodic order, remains open after invoicing.
- **Returned order**—Credit note (→ Sect. 4.6.1).
- **Item requirements**—Representing project demand from Project management and accounting.

It is not possible to enter a sales order with the order type "Item requirements" or "Returned order" manually in the Sales order form.

4.3.3.1 Entering Sales Orders

Depending on your personal preferences, you can manually create or update a sales order starting from one of the following forms:

- **Customer form** (*Sales and marketing > Customers > All customers*)
- **Sales order processing and inquiry workspace**
- **Sales order form** (*Sales and marketing > Sales orders > All sales orders*)

The list section in the workspace *Sales order processing and inquiry* includes a list of unconfirmed orders and a list of delayed orders. With a click on the tile *All sales orders* in the workspace, you can open the Sales order list page with all orders. If you want to create a new order in the workspace, click the button *New/Sales order* in the action pane. The following steps are the same as when creating the order in the Sales order form.

In the *Create sales order* dialog, select a customer in the field *Customer account*. You can search for the customer by typing the first characters of the customer number (or the name), or by explicitly opening the lookup. In the lookup, you can use a grid column filter, for example, on the column *Name*. The sales order then accepts various default values from the selected customer, which you can override in the dialog. When you click the button *OK* in the dialog, the sales order header is created, and the Sales order detail form is shown in the Lines view.

In the Sales order detail form, you can click the button *Add line* in the toolbar of the tab *Sales order lines* or simply click on the first line in the grid to create a line. Then select an item number (or a sales category) and enter other line details as required (→ Fig. 4.10).

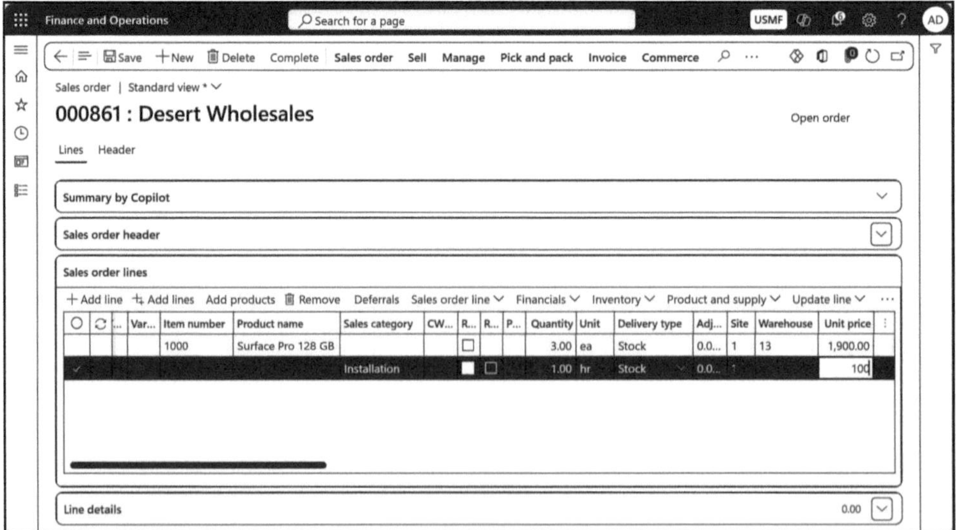

Fig. 4.10 Entering a sales order line with a sales category

Sales orders work similarly to purchase orders for the most part. For this reason, you can refer to other sections in the book on the following topics:

- **Layout and features of the order form** ($\rightarrow$ Sect. 3.4.2).
- **Sales tax/VAT**—See also $\rightarrow$ Sect. 9.2.7.
- **Delivery schedule** ($\rightarrow$ Sect. 3.4.2).
- **Order cancellation** ($\rightarrow$ Sect. 3.4.4).
- **Partial delivery, underdelivery, and overdelivery** ($\rightarrow$ Sect. 3.5.5).
- **Order status and inquiries** ($\rightarrow$ Sect. 3.5.6 and $\rightarrow$ Sect. 3.6.3).

For deleting a sales order, the following settings in the Accounts receivable parameters are relevant:

- **Mark order as voided** (in the section *General*, tab *Sales setup*)—If set to "Yes", deleted sales orders are shown in the menu item *Sales and marketing > Inquiries and reports > History > Voided sales orders*.
- **Delete order line invoiced in total** and **Delete order after invoicing** (in the section *Updates*, tab *Invoice*)—If set to "Yes", orders (order lines) are deleted when posting the invoice (but transactions in inventory and finance are kept).

Unlike purchase orders, sales orders do not include features for change management and order approval.

The prices and discounts in the sales order lines can derive from the base sales price in the released product ($\rightarrow$ Sect. 4.2.3), from basic trade agreements ($\rightarrow$ Sect. 4.8.1), and from pricing management ($\rightarrow$ Sect. 4.8.3).

4.3.3.2 Order Completion

If the setting *Skip order completion* is not activated in the Pricing management parameters ($\rightarrow$ Sect. 4.8.3), click the button *Complete* in the action pane of the Sales order form once you have finished entering a sales order. Only after a sales order is set to complete, you can continue with order processing.

And if a sales order has been set to complete, you can only change order details after resetting the status with the button *Sales order/Maintain/Modify* in the Sales order form.

> *Note:* Order completion is only available/required if pricing management is active. This is true if the *Unified pricing management* feature has been activated and the Pricing management parameter *Disable pricing management* is not set.

4.3.3.3 Keyword Search

The keyword search is an enhanced search functionality that facilitates selecting customers, prospects, and products in sales orders and quotations.

Before you can use the keyword search, the Search parameters (*Sales and market-ing > Setup > Search > Search parameters*) have to be set up. In addition, the fields that should be included in the search have to be defined in the search criteria (*Sales and mar-keting > Setup > Search > Search criteria*). Click the button *Customer* (or *Product*, or *Prospect*) in the action pane of the Search criteria form to access the search fields for the customer search, the product search, or the prospect search.

When you create a new sales order, you can select the option "Keyword" in the lookup field *Search by* of the *Create sales order* dialog to execute a customer search with the specified search criteria.

The keyword search for products is executed in a new sales order line if you enter a part of the product name, or another search field specified in the criteria, in the item number field, and press the *Tab* key (ignoring the lookup that pops up automatically). If you want to search by product name, the search criteria for products have to include the field "ProductName".

4.3.3.4 Sales Order Holds and Line Blocking

At the order line level, the slider *Stopped* on the sub-tab *General* in the *Line details* pro-vides an easy way to block transactions (picking list, packing slip, invoice). You can sim-ply set the slider *Stopped* to "Yes" to block a line (or "No" to unblock).

At the order header level, you can use sales order holds to put a complete order on hold and to give a reason for the hold. As a prerequisite, set up hold codes (*Sales and Marketing > Setup > Sales orders > Order hold codes*) which indicate the different hold reasons. If a *Role* is selected in a hold code, only users with this role can clear order holds with the respective code.

If you want to set an order hold, click the button *Sales order/Functions/Order holds* in the Sales order form. In the Order hold form, which is shown next, click the button *New* and select the respective *Hold code*. The Sales order list page then shows a checkmark in the column *Do not process* for the order. Processing the order is prevented.

In order to clear the hold, open the Order hold form again—click the button *Sales order/Functions/Order holds* in the Sales order form, or access the menu item *Sales and marketing > Sales orders > Open orders > Order holds*. In the Order hold form, click the button *Clear hold/Clear hold/Clear holds* to remove the order hold.

If you want to assign the decision to a particular user, click the button *Hold checkout/ Hold checkout/Override checkout* in the Order hold form and select the responsible user in the dialog. The selected user is then the only person who may work on the hold. If you want to transfer the checkout to another user, click the button *Override checkout* again. The checkout is cleared automatically when the responsible person clears the order hold, or the checkout (with the button *Hold checkout/Hold checkout/Clear checkout*).

4.3.3.5 Delivery Address and Invoice Address

The delivery address in a sales order is initialized with the primary address or, if specified, with the separate delivery address of the customer. Like in a purchase order, you can override the delivery address on the tab *Address* in the Header view or—at line level—on the sub-tab *Address* in the order lines. In this context, the Accounts receivable parameters (section *Summary update*, tab *Split based on*) determine whether posted documents (e.g., delivery notes) are split automatically based on different delivery addresses in the order lines.

Unlike the delivery address, the invoice address is not directly editable in a sales order. If the option "Invoice account" (which is the default value) is selected in the lookup field *Invoice address* on the tab *Invoice and delivery* in the Customer form, the name and address on the invoice is the *Invoice account* in the sales order (on the tab *General* in the Header view). The option "Order account" in the field *Invoice address* of the customer record means that the name and address of the order customer (*Customer account* in the order) is printed on the invoice.

If the customer record of the invoice account contains an address with the purpose "Invoice", this address is printed on documents.

4.3.3.6 Item Lists

If a customer frequently orders the same products, you can facilitate the order entry with the use of item lists. An item list is a copy template, and the lines of an item list contain only item numbers and quantities.

In the Item list form (*Sales and marketing > Setup > Items > Item list*), you can click the button *New* to create a new list with *Item list* ID and *Description*. Then click the button *Add* in the toolbar of the tab *Items* and add the items (including product dimensions if applicable) with the default order quantity. Alternatively, you can generate customer-specific item lists (based on past sales orders) with the button *Item list generation* in the action pane.

In order to use an item list in a sales order, click the button *Sales order line/Copy/From item list* in the toolbar of the order lines. In the *Item list* dialog, select one or more items and optionally override the quantity before you click the button *Copy and close*. If the slider *Prompt for item list* in the Accounts receivable parameters (section *General*, tab *Sales setup*) is set to "Yes", the *Item list* dialog is automatically shown when you create a sales order.

4.3.3.7 Delivery Date Control

Determining the possible ship date (delivery date) is an important task in order management. Several aspects control the calculation of delivery dates in sales:

- **Item availability**
- **Order entry deadlines**
- **Sales lead time**
- **Delivery date control settings**
- **Calendar settings**

In Dynamics 365, there is a difference between your ship date and the customer receipt date on the one hand, and between the requested and the confirmed date on the other hand. As a result, there are four different fields related to the delivery date on the sub-tab *Delivery* in the *Line details* of the sales order line.

If you want to execute an automatic calculation of the delivery date when entering a sales order line, activate the delivery date control in the Accounts receivable parameters (→ Fig. 4.11). For this purpose, you can select one of the following options in the lookup field *Delivery date control* on the tab *Delivery control* in the section *Shipments* of the parameters:

- **None**—No delivery date control.
- **Sales lead time**—Delivery date based on the lead time and calendar settings.
- **ATP** ("Available to promise")—Delivery date based on the item availability.
- **ATP + Issue margin**—Adds the safety margin for the item (specified in the coverage group) to the delivery date calculated from ATP.
- **CTP** ("Capable to promise")—Executes master planning for the selected item immediately (with Planning optimization, this is near real-time).
- **Batch CTP**—Only with Planning optimization (→ Sect. 6.3.2), executes the CTP calculation with the scheduled task of a dynamic plan.

If the option "Sales lead time" is selected, the delivery date calculation in sales order lines is only based on the applicable sales lead time and calendars (the slider *Working days* in the parameters controls whether the calculation only includes working days). The sales lead time determines the number of days that are required internally until shipping the item. A general default for the sales lead time is specified in the section *Shipments* of the Accounts receivable parameters. The lead time specified there is the default value for the

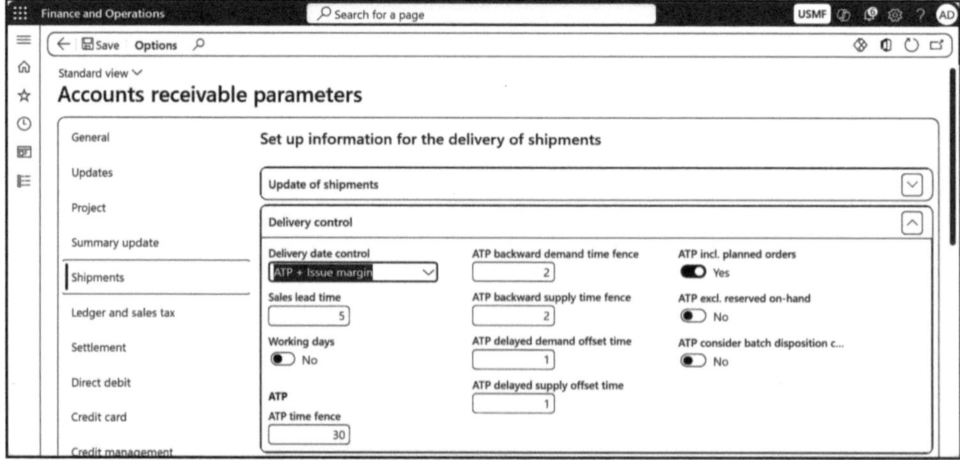

Fig. 4.11 Delivery control settings in the Accounts receivable parameters

ship date in the order header. Order lines accept the ship date of the header if the calculated ship date based on the sales lead time of the item is not after the header ship date. You can specify sales lead times at the item level in the default order settings and in trade agreements for sales prices.

If the option "ATP" is selected, the delivery date calculation is based on the item availability. The availability includes the on-hand inventory quantity and transactions (open orders) with a delivery date within the *ATP time fence* (in the field group *ATP* of the parameters). Existing planned orders are included in the ATP calculation if the parameter *ATP incl. Planned orders* is set to "Yes". If you enter a quantity in a sales order line that is not available, the ship date is the first day after the ATP time fence. In order to avoid the ship date being later than the earliest possible date, the ATP time fence should match the lead time of the item. To deal with delayed shipments and delayed receipts of open orders, the *ATP delayed demand offset time* and the *ATP delayed supply offset time* in the Accounts receivable parameters determine whether a transaction, which is scheduled for a past date (but within the *ATP backward demand time fence* and the *ATP backward supply time fence*) and has not been posted yet, is included in the calculation.

If the option "CTP" is selected, the delivery date calculation immediately executes (or, if the Planning optimization is enabled, near real-time) master planning for the selected item in the current dynamic master plan ($\rightarrow$ Sect. 6.3.1) and creates planned purchase orders and production orders as required. For planned production orders, the delivery date that results from the planned order includes the delivery time for components.

In the default order settings of the released product, the lookup field *Delivery date control* (together with the slider *Override delivery date control*) on the tab *Sales order* provides the option to override the base settings for the delivery date control in the Accounts receivable parameters. If you want to activate or deactivate delivery control in a specific sales order or sales order line, you can select the appropriate option in the lookup field *Delivery date control* on the (sub-) tab *Delivery* of the order header or line.

The calculation of the ship date in an order line includes the following calendar and transport time settings:

- **General shipping calendar of the company**—*Organization administration > Organizations > Legal entities*, tab *Foreign trade and logistics* (field *Shipping calendar*).
- **Calendar of the shipping warehouse**—*Inventory management > Setup > Inventory breakdown > Warehouses*, tab *Master planning* (field *Calendar*).
- **Receipt calendar of the customer**—*Sales and marketing > Customers > All customers*, field *Receipt calendar* on the tab *Invoice and delivery* (or a *Receipt calendar* in the delivery address details, which you access with the button *More options/Advanced* on the tab *Addresses* in the Customer form).
- **Transport calendar per delivery mode and (optionally) warehouse**—*Sales and marketing > Setup > Distribution > Modes of delivery*, button *Transport calendar*.
- **Transport days**—*Inventory management > Setup > Distribution > Transport days* (related to the delivery mode, shipping warehouse, and receipt address).

Order entry deadlines (*Inventory management > Setup > Distribution > Order entry deadlines*) determine the latest time for entering same-day shipments in sales order lines. After the deadline, the delivery date calculation starts on the next day.

In case delivery date control is activated, Dynamics 365 checks if the item in the order line is available on the entered ship date. To receive a proposal of possible delivery dates, click the link *Simulate delivery date* below the field *Requested receipt date* on the (sub-) tab *Delivery* in the order header or line.

If necessary, you can deactivate delivery date control—select the option "None" in the lookup field *Delivery date control* of the order header or line for this purpose. Once delivery date control is deactivated, you can enter a date that is not included in the regular dates for possible deliveries.

4.3.3.8 Item Availability and Delivery Alternatives

As a prerequisite for shipping a stocked product, it must be available in inventory. You can use manual or automatic reservation (→ Sect. 7.4.5) to make sure that the required quantity is reserved for the order, and it is not possible to consume it for any other purpose.

Inquiries in the Sales order form provide the option to check the item availability. If you want to view the current inventory quantity of an item with the dimensions in the order line (e.g., site/warehouse), click the button *Inventory/On-hand inventory* in the toolbar of the order line. In the *On-hand* dialog, which is shown then, you can click the button *Overview* if you want to check the item quantity in other warehouses (and further inventory dimensions). In the On-hand inventory inquiry that is shown subsequently, you can click the button *Dimensions* to select the displayed inventory dimensions.

The Net requirements form, which you can access with the button *Product and supply/ Net requirements* in the toolbar of the sales order lines, gives a more detailed view of the future availability. In the net requirements, you can start master planning (→ Sect. 6.3) for the selected item to calculate possible delivery dates.

The Explosion form shows the item availability at multiple BOM levels, which is useful if you produce an item from components. You can access this form with the button *Product and supply/Explosion* in the toolbar of the order lines.

In case there are issues to meet the required delivery date of an order line, you can search for other delivery options—warehouses, product variants (for product masters), and modes of delivery—in the *Delivery alternatives* dialog (→ Fig. 4.12). You can open this dialog with the button *Product and supply/Delivery alternatives* in the toolbar of the sales order lines. On the tab *Delivery alternatives* in the *Delivery alternatives* dialog, select a different mode of delivery (e.g., for express delivery) or a supply line with a different warehouse or variant before you click the button *OK* to transfer the selected alternative to the order line. The options in the dialog depend on the selected *Delivery date control* (sales lead time, ATP, CTP) on the sub-tab *Delivery* of the order line.

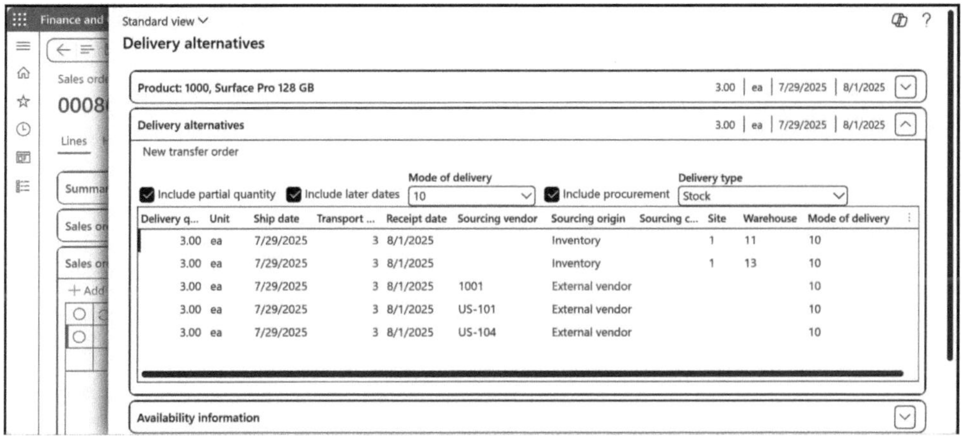

Fig. 4.12 Delivery options in the *Delivery alternatives* dialog

4.3.4 Surcharge Management

Charges in sales orders and in purchase orders are used for expenses, which are not covered by the sales price or purchase price itself—for example, fees for freight and insurance.

You can enter charges manually in a sales order or a purchase order at the header level and the line level. In addition, there are charges that automatically apply when entering an order header or line. If you want to charge a customer at the end of a period if the sales orders in the period do not meet specified criteria, you can use period charges.

Standard documents like the order confirmation only print the total charges amount, no matter whether the applicable charges refer to the header or to a line.

4.3.4.1 Charges Codes

As a prerequisite for the use of charges in orders, you have to set up the required charges codes (→ Fig. 4.13). Charges codes in sales and purchasing are independent of each other. For sales charges, use the form *Accounts receivable > Charges setup > Charges code*, and for purchasing, the form *Accounts payable > Charges setup > Charges code*.

When you create a new charges code, enter the charges code ID, the description, and—if applicable—the item sales tax group before you switch to the tab *Posting*. On this tab, you have to specify appropriate ledger integration settings.

For sales charges, select the *Debit/Type* "Customer/Vendor" and the *Credit/Type* "Ledger account" (and a related revenue account in the field *Account*) if you want to add the charges on top of the item sales amount. The charges amount is printed separately on documents (e.g., invoices).

For purchasing charges which are shown separately on the vendor invoice, select the option "Customer/Vendor" in the *Credit/Type*. In the field *Debit/Type*, select the option

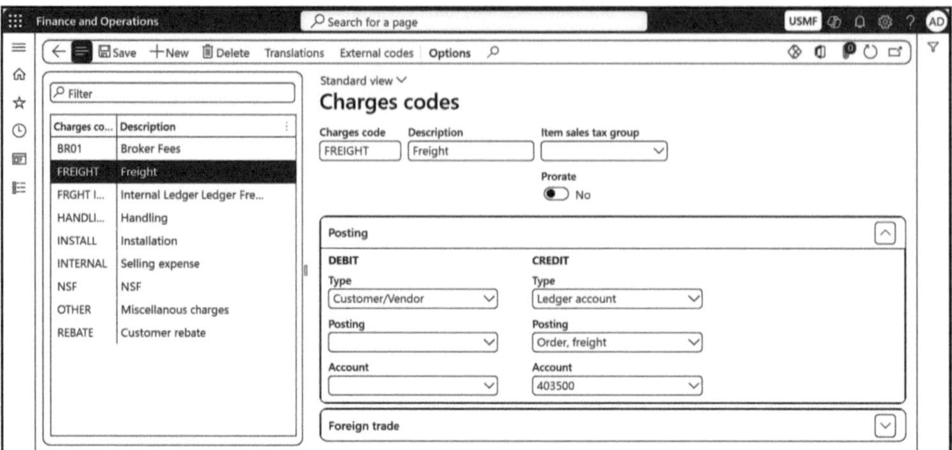

Fig. 4.13 Editing a sales charges code

"Ledger account" if you want to post the charges to a separate ledger account, or "Item" if you want to include the charges amount in the cost price (inventory value) of the item.

In addition to charges with the *Debit/Type* (or *Credit/Type*) "Customer/Vendor", which are shown separately on documents, it is also possible to set up charges codes that generate ledger transactions for internal financial purposes. The codes for these charges include the type "Ledger account" or "Item" for *Debit* and for *Credit*.

4.3.4.2 Manual Charges

If you want to enter surcharges in a sales order or in a purchase order, open the Maintain charges form. At the header level, you can access the Maintain charges form with the button *Sell/Charges/Maintain charges* in the Sales order form (or with the button *Purchase/Charges/Maintain charges* in the Purchase order form). At the line level, you can access the Maintain charges form with the button *Financials/Maintain charges* in the toolbar of the sales order or purchase order lines.

In the Maintain charges form, select the charges code first. Then, in the column *Category*, select whether the charge is a fixed total amount, or an amount per piece (sales/purchase unit), or a percentage of the line amount.

4.3.4.3 Auto Charges

If you want to apply charges to sales orders automatically, set up automatic charges (*Accounts receivable > Charges setup > Auto charges*). Auto charges initialize the charges in orders, but you can still override the charges in the order.

When setting up auto charges in the Auto charges form (→ Fig. 4.14), first select in the lookup field *Level* (in the filter pane on the left) whether the charges are specified at the order header or order line level.

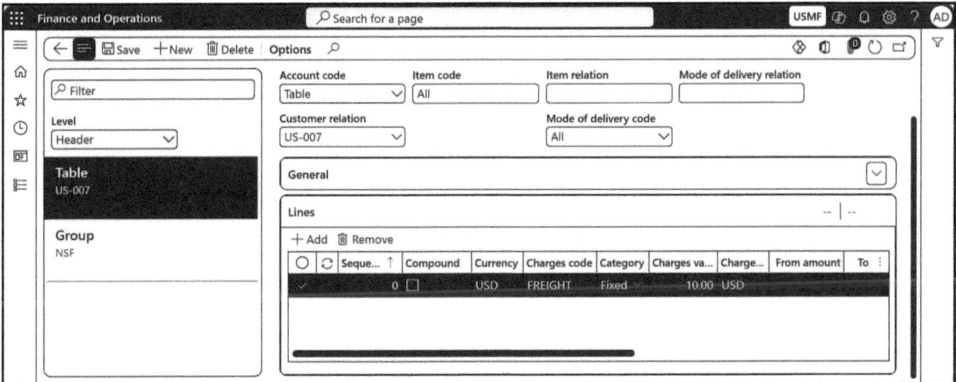

Fig. 4.14 Managing auto charges

In the right pane, the settings at the top determine the customers, the items, and the modes of delivery to which the charges apply. You can enter line charges with reference to the customer (customer number, customer charge group, or all), the item (item number, item charge group, or all), and the mode of delivery (mode of delivery, delivery charges group, or all). For header charges, the item selection is fixed to "All". To specify the calculation details for an auto charge, switch to the tab *Lines* and enter the *Charges code*, the *Category* (determining whether the charges value is a fixed amount, or an amount per sales unit, or a percentage of the line amount), and the *Charges value*.

With the columns *From amount* and the *To amount* in the *Lines* tab of header charges, you can specify that auto charges depend on the order total—e.g., granting free freight for high-value orders (order total higher than the *To amount*).

If you want to maintain auto charges at the group level, set up the *Customer charge groups*, *Item charge groups*, or *Delivery charges groups* that you want to use and assign them in the Customer form, the Released product form, or the Modes of delivery form (similar to the price/discount groups for trade agreements).

As a prerequisite for the use of auto charges in sales orders, the sliders *Find auto charges for header* or *Find auto charges for line* in the section *Prices* of the Accounts receivable parameters have to be set to "Yes".

For purchasing, the form *Procurement and sourcing > Setup > Charges > Automatic charges* and the Procurement parameters contain similar settings which control auto charges.

Advanced options for specifying auto charges in sales are available in the Pricing management module ($\rightarrow$ Sect. 4.8.3).

Note: If Unified pricing management is enabled in the Feature management, there are some settings in the Pricing management parameters that are required if you want to use the auto charges functionality described here. Basic auto charges only work with Unified pricing if either the slider *Disable pricing management* (in the section *General*) or the slider *Apply existing auto charges* (in the section *Prices and discounts*, tab *Auto charges*) is set to "Yes" in the Pricing management parameters.

4.3.4.4 Period Charges

If applicable, you can use period charges to make sure that a customer at least pays the agreed minimum charges amount per period—for example, a total of handling fees of at least USD 100 per week.

In the Accounts receivable parameters (section *Prices*, tab *Charges*), you can specify if the period calculation is based on order lines or invoices lines and, with the parameter *Required charge code match*, if there must be at least one regular sales invoice line which matches the charges code specified in the period charges rule as a prerequisite for generating the free text invoice with the period charge.

If you want to configure a period charge, open the Period charges rules form (*Accounts receivable > Charges setup > Period charges rule*) and create a rule with a name, description, and from/to invoice date. In the fields *Account code* ("Table" / "All") and *Account relation*, you specify the customers who are affected by the period charge (optionally at the level of *Site* and *Warehouse*). On the tab *Lines*, you specify whether the period charge should be generated if the customer transactions (invoice lines or order lines) are below the amount (*Type* "Monetary threshold"), or the quantity (*Type* "Quantity threshold"), or both, of the minimum which you enter in the column *Monetary threshold* or *Quantity threshold*. The column *Charges code* determines for which charge you specify the minimum. In the column *Revenue account*, enter the main account that should be used in the free text invoice for charging the difference to the agreed minimum.

Once a period has passed and the regular sales invoices have been posted, run the periodic activity *Accounts receivable > Periodic tasks > Calculate period charge*. If the charges in the regular sales invoices are below the minimum specified in a rule, a free text invoice (→ Sect. 4.5.3) is generated, which you can check and post in the form *Accounts receivable > Invoices > All free text invoices*. In the Free text invoice detail form, the sub-tab *Line invoice base* of the tab *Line details* shows the period for which the charges have been generated. With the button *Line invoice base* in the toolbar of the free text invoice lines, you can check the details.

4.3.5   Sales Order Confirmations

Printing an order confirmation requires posting it, which saves the document unchangeable and separate from the actual sales order. Within Dynamics 365, it is the evidence of the document that has been sent to the customer.

Like purchase order confirmations, sales order confirmations do not create transactions in inventory or finance.

4.3.5.1 Posting Dialog for Sales Order Confirmations

In order to generate an order confirmation, click the button *Sell/Generate/Confirmation* in the Sales order list page (or *Sell/Generate/Confirm sales order* in the detail form). The dialog for the sales order confirmation is similar to the posting dialogs in purchasing ($\rightarrow$ Sect. 3.4.5). Like in the *Confirm purchase order* dialog, you can—once you have set the slider *Print confirmation* to "Yes"—manually select the printer (click the button *Printer setup*) or use the printer specified in the print management setup (set the slider *Use print management destination* to "Yes" for this purpose). If you want to post and print the confirmation, make sure that both sliders, *Posting* and *Print confirmation*, in the posting dialog are set to "Yes" before you click the button *OK*.

Apart from the Sales order form, further options for posting the order confirmation include the workspace *Sales order processing and inquiry* (there is the button *Confirm* in the toolbar of the list *Unconfirmed* in the list section) and the summary update in the menu (*Sales and marketing > Sales orders > Order confirmation > Confirm sales order*). If you access the posting dialog from the menu, be aware that you have to enter a filter for selecting the orders that you want to confirm (click the button *Select* to open the filter dialog).

4.3.5.2 Order Confirmation Inquiry

After posting an order confirmation in the sales order, the posted document is saved. Later amendments to the order have no impact on the posted document.

If you want to view a posted order confirmation, click the button *Sell/Journals/Sales order confirmation* in the Sales order form, or open the menu item *Sales and marketing > Sales orders > Order confirmation > Sales order confirmations*.

4.3.6 Case Study Exercises

Exercise 4.3—Sales Order

The customer of exercise 4.1 orders 20 units of the item of exercise 3.5. Enter this sales order in the Customer form. Which quantity is shown by default? Where do these settings come from?

Switch to the Header view of the sales order and review the delivery address afterward.

Exercise 4.4—Surcharges

Your company wants to invoice a handling fee to customers. Create an appropriate charges code C-## (## = your user ID) with the standard tax rate, the posting type "Customer revenue", and an appropriate revenue account for credit posting.

In the header of the sales order of exercise 4.3, add this new handling fee with an amount of USD 10 as a fixed charge to the customer.

Note: If the Unified pricing management feature is activated, make sure that the slider *Apply existing auto charges* in the Pricing management parameters (section *Prices and discounts*, tab *Auto charges*), which enables basic auto charges, is set to "Yes".

Exercise 4.5—Order Confirmation
If order completion is required (i.e., if the button *Complete* is shown in the action pane), set the order to complete. Then post the order confirmation for the order of exercise 4.3 in the workspace *Sales order processing and inquiry*, and print it as a print preview.

Check the amount in the order line. In the order confirmation, where do you find the charges?

4.4   Order Picking and Shipment

Delivery management includes all activities in the process of picking and shipping the ordered items. Picking, as a preparation for shipping, is the internal process of collecting items within the warehouse.

4.4.1   Basics of Picking and Shipping

As a preparation for picking and shipping, the upcoming deliveries should be monitored continuously. For this purpose, the workspace *Sales order processing and inquiry* shows delayed orders and orders with delivery date changes in the list section.

Apart from the workspace, there are particular inquiries to review pending shipments:

* *Sales and marketing > Sales orders> Open orders > Backorder lines*
* *Sales and marketing > Sales orders > Open orders > Open sales order lines*

In addition, the pending shipments are shown in the posting dialog of picking lists and packing slips when you filter on the delivery date or the ship date.

4.4.1.1 Picking Policy
In Dynamics 365, it is not required to process picking as a separate step. Depending on the setup, you can skip picking and immediately ship an item by posting the packing slip or the invoice.

If you want to process picking, the warehouse policy, which distinguishes between the basic approach and the advanced warehouse management, determines the available options for the picking process (→ Fig. 4.15):

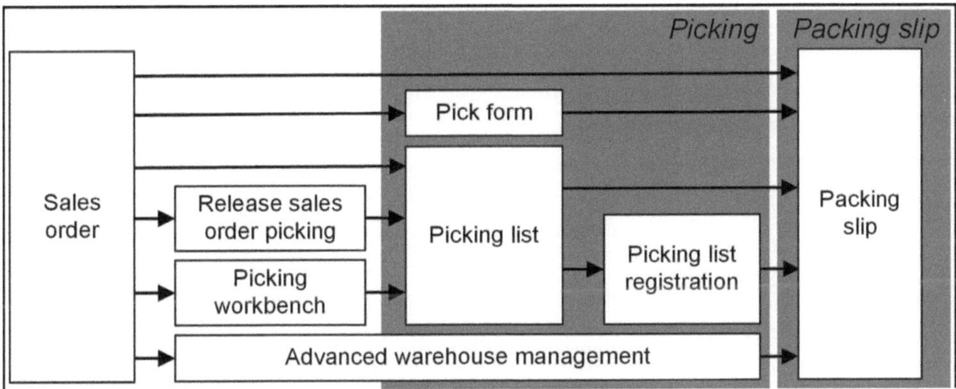

Fig. 4.15 Options for sales order picking in Dynamics 365

- **One-step picking**
  - **Pick form**—Manual recording in the Pick form.
  - **Picking list**—With automatic picking list registration.
- **Two-step picking**
  - **Order picking registration**—Picking list, followed by a picking list registration.
  - **Advanced warehouse management**—Picking wave, followed by mobile device transactions.

One-step picking is a process that includes picking but does not require a confirmation of the picked quantity. This way of picking is only used in the basic approach for warehouse management.

Two-step picking requires confirming the quantity that has actually been picked. In a warehouse with the basic approach, this is done with the picking list registration (based on the picking list that has been posted before). In a warehouse with advanced warehouse management, the confirmation is done with mobile device transactions (based on preassigned picking wave work).

This section explains the picking process in the basic approach for warehouse management. In → Sect. 8.1.2, you can find a description of how to process picking with the advanced warehouse management.

4.4.1.2 Core Settings for Picking

In the Warehouse form (*Inventory management > Setup > Inventory breakdown > Warehouses*), the slider *Use warehouse management processes* on the tab *Warehouse* controls, if the warehouse is subject to the advanced warehouse management. If this slider is set to "No", the basic approach for warehouse management applies.

In this case, the Accounts receivable parameters determine whether there is one-step or two-step picking:

- **One-step picking**—If the *Picking route status* in the Accounts receivable parameters (section *Updates*, tab *Picking list*) is set to "Completed", automatic picking list registration is enabled. In this case, the posted quantity is immediately deducted from inventory when posting the picking list.
- **Two-step picking**—If the *Picking route status* is set to "Activated", Dynamics 365 does not change the quantity in inventory when posting the picking list. In this case, only updating the →*Picking list registration* later deducts the quantity from inventory.

Picking is only possible for inventoried items (product type "Item", item model group with *Stocked product* enabled). The item model group of the item also controls whether picking is mandatory before posting the packing slip (checkbox *Picking requirements* on the tab *Inventory policies* of the item model group).

4.4.2 Pick Form and Picking List

Picking in sales matches the inventory registration in purchasing: The picked quantity reduces the on-hand inventory, and the status of this quantity is "Picked". Like the inventory registration in purchasing, picking is a preliminary transaction that is not shown separately in the inventory transaction.

4.4.2.1 Pick Form

The first option for picking, using the Pick form, is a manual registration in the sales order. The Pick form in sales works similarly to the Registration form in purchasing (→ Sect. 3.5.3). In a similar way to the inventory registration, the Pick form can be used, for example, to split the transaction of a single order line into multiple lines with different locations, batch numbers, or serial numbers.

In order to access the Pick form, click the button *Update line/Pick* in the toolbar of the order lines in the Sales order form. In the Pick form, you can register picking in the lines of the tab *Picking lines* in the lower pane. Apart from manually creating records with the button *Add* in the lower pane, the button *Add picking line* in the toolbar of the upper pane is another way to insert lines. Edit the quantity, the warehouse, or other inventory dimensions in the lower pane as applicable before you post the transaction with the button *Confirm pick all* in the toolbar of the lower pane.

4.4.2.2 Picking List

If you need a printed report for the picking work in the warehouse, post and print a picking list. In sales order processing, picking lists are another way to register a pick transaction.

There are the following ways for posting a picking list:

- **Sales order**—Sales order form, button *Pick and pack/Generate/Generate picking list* in the action pane.
- **Summary update**—*Sales and marketing > Sales orders > Order shipping > Generate picking list*.
- **Release picking**—Start from the *Release sales order picking* form, see below.
- **Picking workbench**—Group picking lists to batches (→ Sect. 4.4.3).

Posting a picking list generates a picking route with output orders (inventory orders) for the picking lines. You can view the picking route in the Picking list registration form as described below.

If the warehouse usually picks all items immediately, it is useful to enable one-step picking (the field *Picking route status* in the Accounts receivable parameters has to be set to "Completed" for this purpose). With this setup, no manual picking list registration is required, and the next step is posting the packing slip. The picking route in this case immediately shows the *Handling status* "Completed".

4.4.2.3 Picking List Registration

If two-step picking is enabled (Accounts receivable parameters, field *Picking route status* set to "Activated"), you have to record the picking list registration after posting the picking list and executing the actual picking work in the warehouse.

In order to access the Picking list registration form, click the button *Pick and pack/ Generate/Picking list registration* in the Sales order form, or open the menu item *Sales and marketing > Sales orders > Order shipping > Picking list registration*, or the menu item *Inventory management > Outbound orders > Picking list registration*.

If you access the picking list registration from the menu, the list page with all posted picking lists (picking routes) is shown, and you can enter a filter on the applicable sales order number. If you open the picking list registration from the sales order, the detail form with the picking list for the order is immediately shown. If there is more than one picking list for the order, expand the list pane (click the button ▣ in the action pane) of the Picking list registration detail form to view all posted picking lists (including the requested picking list) for the order.

On the tab *Lines* in the Picking list registration detail form (→ Fig. 4.16), select the checkbox in the column *Select* in the lines that you want to update. Before you confirm the picked quantity of the selected lines with the button *Functions/Update selected* in the toolbar of this tab, you can adjust the quantity in the column *Pick quantity* as applicable. Alternatively, you can update all lines with the button *Updates/Update all* in the action pane at the top of the form.

If you only confirm a part of the quantity on a picking list, the Inventory parameter *End output inventory order* (in the section *General* of the Inventory parameters) controls whether the picking lines (and the related output orders) are closed (if set to "Yes") or the remaining quantity is kept on the output order and the picking list (picking route) remains open. In this case, you have to register or cancel the remaining quantity on the original picking list later. Otherwise, you need to post another picking list from the sales order if you want to pick the remaining quantity.

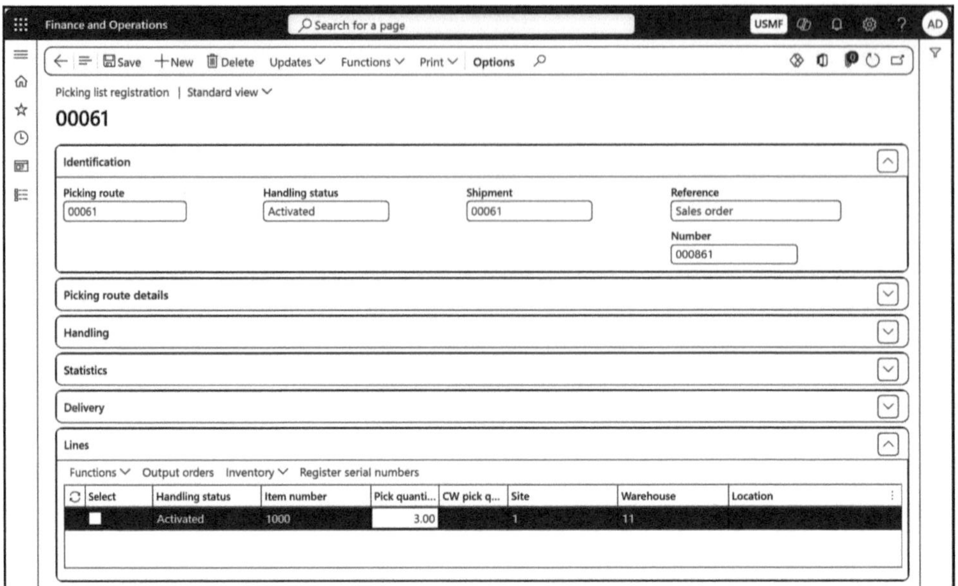

Fig. 4.16 Entering the picked quantity in the Picking list registration form

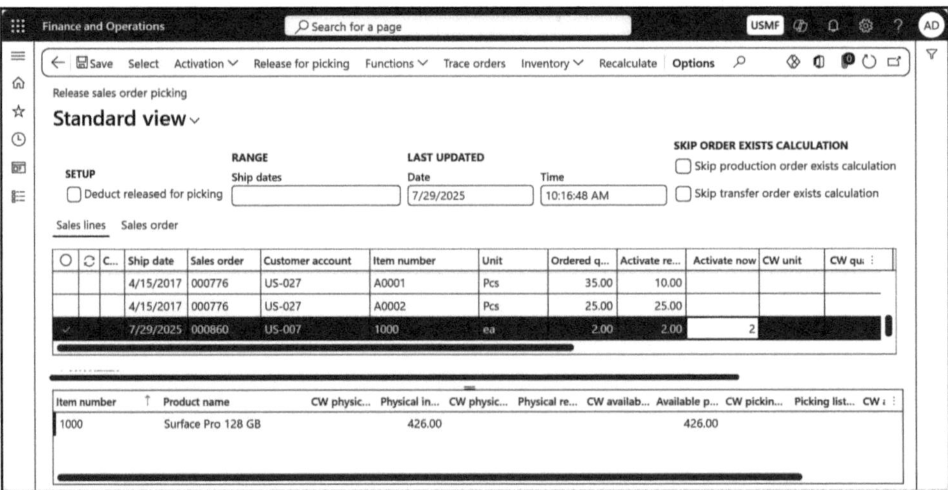

Fig. 4.17 Entering an *Activate now* quantity in the Release sales order picking form

4.4.2.4 Release Sales Order Picking

If you want to start picking from an overview that shows the order lines which are ready for shipping, use the Release picking form (→ Fig. 4.17). The Release picking form only shows items that are currently in stock.

When you open the Release picking form (*Inventory management > Periodic tasks > Release sales order picking*), an advanced filter is shown in which you can enter filter criteria on order lines. If you need to change this filter later, click the button *Select* in the action pane of the Release picking form.

In order to start the picking process, activate the items that should be picked. You can do this with the button *Activation* in the action pane (select the appropriate option within this button), or manually by entering a quantity in the column *Activate now*. Activation also reserves the respective quantity.

For the quantities in the column *Activate now*, you can subsequently post the picking list with the button *Release for picking* in the action pane. The further process with one-step picking or two-step picking is the same as when posting the picking list directly from the order.

If you want to use picking priorities for customers, you can enter a *Classification group* on the tab *General* of the Customer form. The customer classification group is shown in the left-most column of the Release picking form, and you can set a filter on this group.

4.4.2.5 Reverse Pick Transactions

If you want to reverse a pick transaction that has been posted in the Pick form or a picking list, you can use the Pick form. In the Pick form, which you can access with the button *Update line/Pick* in the toolbar of the respective sales order line, first select the transaction that you want to reverse in the upper pane and then click the button *Add picking line*. Posting the reversal with the button *Confirm pick all* works similarly to regular picking, but with a negative quantity.

If the original pick transaction has been posted with a picking list, you can alternatively use the picking list registration to reverse picking. Open the Picking list registration form from the menu or with the button *Pick and pack/Generate/Picking list registration* in the Sales order form for this purpose. In the Picking list registration form, click the button *Functions/Unpick* in the toolbar of the tab *Lines* to cancel the picking list registration. In a second step, click the button *Functions/Cancel picking route* in the action pane of the picking list registration to cancel the picking list completely. You can skip the second step if you have already set the slider *Cancel unpicked quantity* in the *Unpick* dialog to "Yes".

> *Note*: If you have posted more than one picking list for an order, expand the list pane in the Picking list registration detail form to select the picking list.

4.4.3   Picking Workbench

The Picking workbench is an enhancement for sales order picking in paper-based warehouse processes, which you can use if you need to group picking lists into batches (picking waves).

If the picking process includes putting the items into boxes, you can optionally apply a boxing logic to collect items in boxes or carts. Dynamics 365 then suggests boxes of an appropriate size for picking.

You can use the Picking workbench as an alternative to the *Release sales order picking* functionality.

4.4.3.1 Setup for the Picking Workbench

As a prerequisite for the Picking workbench, the respective number sequences have to be specified in the Inventory parameters. And if you want to use the boxing logic, the slider *Boxing logic for picking workbench* in the section *General* of the Inventory parameters has to be set to "Yes".

In the workbench profiles (*Inventory management > Setup > Picking workbench > Workbench profiles*), you can set up one or more profiles that are used as filter criteria in the Picking workbench.

In the Warehouse form (*Inventory management > Setup > Inventory breakdown > Warehouses*), the tab *Picking workbench* contains settings (e.g., the maximum number of lines per picking list) on how to split picking waves (workbench sessions).

If you want to use the boxing logic in the Picking workbench, enter the individual boxes with their physical dimensions and weight in the menu item *Inventory management > Setup > Picking workbench > Box definitions*. The slider *Active* controls whether a box is available for picking.

In the Released product detail form, the slider *Apply boxing logic for picking workbench* on the tab *Deliver* has to be set to "Yes" for items that should use the boxing logic. The selection of applicable boxes for an item is only based on the physical dimensions and the weight of the item (specified on the tab *Manage inventory* of the released product). If the slider *Ship alone* on the tab *Deliver* of the released product is set to "Yes", the item is picked separately without boxing.

4.4.3.2 Working with the Picking Workbench

The starting point for picking in the Picking workbench are sales orders that should be shipped. In the Picking workbench (*Inventory management > Outbound orders > Picking workbench*), you can start the picking process and create a new picking session with the button *New* in the action pane. In the next step, enter filter criteria (e.g., on the *Ship date* of the order line) on the tab *Criteria*, which determine the sales orders that are included in the current picking session. The field *Profile* on this tab provides the option to select a workbench profile with default values for the criteria fields.

Once you have entered appropriate filter criteria, click the button *Picking session/ Picking session/Generate picking batches* in the action pane of the Picking workbench. Depending on the criteria, on the settings for splitting picking batches in the Warehouse form, and on the settings for boxing (box size and item size/weight), Dynamics 365 creates one or more picking batches which are shown on the tab *Picking batches*. When you generate picking batches, corresponding picking lists are posted. You can view the picking lists that are linked to a picking batch on the tab *Picking list* in the workbench.

Printing the picking batch label and the picking list is a required step, which you can execute with the button *Print batch* in the toolbar of the tab *Picking batches* in the workbench (or the button *Picking session/Picking session/Print session* in the action pane). For items that apply the boxing logic, the selected box name is printed in the picking list header.

After printing all picking lists of a picking batch, select the checkbox *Complete* in the picking batch. Alternatively, set the slider *Complete* in the picking session to "Yes" to complete all picking batches of the session at the same time.

The further process with one-step picking or two-step picking is the same as when posting the picking list directly from the order (→ Sect. 4.4.2). In case of two-step picking, you can directly access the picking list registration with the button *Picking list registration* in the toolbar of the tab *Picking list* in the Picking workbench.

4.4.4   Packing Slips

Posting the packing slip (delivery note) is the last step in the picking and shipping process.

4.4.4.1 Posting Dialog for Packing Slips

In order to post a packing slip, click the button *Pick and pack/Generate/Post packing slip* in the Sales order form or open the menu item *Sales and marketing > Sales orders > Order shipping > Post packing slip*. The dialog for packing slip posting then shows the familiar format. In the lookup field *Quantity* on the tab *Parameters*, select the applicable option depending on the prior process:

- **Picked**—Select this option if picking is executed before posting the packing slip. The picked quantity then is the default for the posting quantity, but you can edit the quantity in the column *Update* on the tab *Lines* of the dialog.
- **Picked quantity and not stocked products**—Includes the ordered quantity of non-stocked products in addition to the picked quantity of stocked items.
- **All**—The total remaining order quantity is the default for the posting quantity.
- **Deliver now**—The quantity of the column *Deliver now* in the order lines is the default for the posting quantity.

If you want to post and print the packing slip, make sure that both sliders, *Posting* and *Print packing slip*, in the dialog are set to "Yes" before you click the button *OK*.

The order status and the document status in the sales order work similarly to the corresponding purchase order status (→ Sect. 3.5.6). You can also process partial deliveries, overdeliveries, and underdeliveries in the same way as in purchasing (→ Sect. 3.5.5).

4.4.4.2 Ledger Integration

If ledger integration is activated for packing slip posting, Dynamics 365 is posting general ledger transactions in parallel to the inventory transactions. These ledger transactions are reversed when posting the related invoice.

The following core settings control packing slip posting to the general ledger:

- **Accounts receivable parameters**—The slider *Post packing slip in ledger* (section *Updates*, tab *Packing slip*) has to be set to "Yes" to enable ledger posting.
- **Item model group**—The checkbox *Post physical inventory* on the tab *Costing method & cost recognition* in the item model group of the item has to be selected.

These settings work similarly to the corresponding settings for the ledger integration of product receipts in purchasing.

4.4.4.3 Transaction Inquiry

If you want to view the inventory transactions that refer to an order line (→ Fig. 4.18), select the respective line in the sales order and click the button *Inventory/Transactions* in the toolbar of the order lines. After posting the packing slip, the issue status of the inventory transaction is "Deducted". The posting date of the packing slip is shown in the column *Physical date*, whereas the *Financial date* remains empty until invoice posting. The packing slip number is shown on the tab *Updates* of the *Transaction details* form (accessed with the button *Transaction details* in the inventory transaction).

In order to view a posted packing slip, open the menu item *Sales and marketing > Sales orders > Order shipping > Packing slip* or click the button *Pick and pack/Journals/Packing slip* in the Sales order form. Select a packing slip on the tab *Overview* of the inquiry and switch to the tab *Lines* if you want to view the related packing slip lines.

You can view the related ledger transactions in the Voucher transactions inquiry, which you open with the button *Vouchers* in the action pane of the Packing slip inquiry (or with the button *Ledger/Physical voucher* in the inventory transactions).

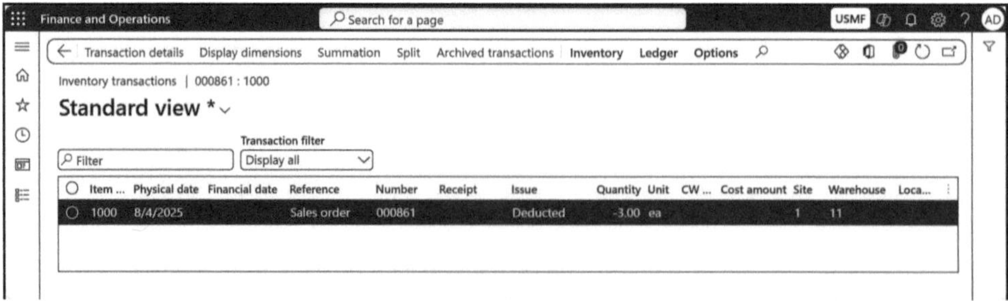

Fig. 4.18 Inventory transaction after packing slip posting

4.4.4.4 Canceling Packing Slips

If you want to cancel a posted packing slip, use the *Cancel* feature in the Packing slip inquiry. Open the Packing slip inquiry—e.g., with the button *Pick and pack/Journals/ Packing slip* in the Sales order form—for this purpose, select the respective packing slip and click the button *Cancel* in the action pane. If you only want to reduce the posted quantity, click the button *Correct*.

Canceling and correcting a packing slip does not change the original transaction, but posts a new transaction that offsets the original transaction.

4.4.5   Case Study Exercises

Exercise 4.6—Packing Slip

You are asked to review the order lines that are available for shipping. The inquiry should not be limited to your orders, but include all applicable orders in your company. Which options do you know?

Your order of exercise 4.3 is among the orders that are ready to be shipped. Check the following items in this order before you post the packing slip:

- Order status and document status.
- Inventory quantity of the ordered item.
- Inventory transactions for the order line.

Post and print a packing slip for the complete order quantity in the Sales order form and select a print preview as the print destination.

Then review the status of the items in the list above again. What is different after posting the packing slip?

Exercise 4.7—Picking List

The customer of exercise 4.1 orders another 20 units of the item that you have created in exercise 3.5. Only 10 units should be shipped at the moment.

Enter an appropriate sales order and—if required according to Pricing management parameter settings—set the order to complete. The warehouse requires a picking list this time. Post and print a picking list with 10 units of the ordered item. Can you tell which setting controls whether you need to execute a picking list registration? If required, perform the picking list registration.

Then post the packing slip for the picked items.

Exercise 4.8—Packing Slip Inquiry

Review the packing slip of exercise 4.7 in the Packing slip inquiry, which you access from the Sales order form first, and then from the navigation pane. Is it possible to update the posted packing slip (e.g., if you need to correct the posting)?

4.5   Sales Invoice

Posting the sales invoice is the last step in sales order processing. The invoice increases the open customer balance and reduces the financial value of inventory. After invoicing all lines of a sales order, the sales order is completed. The payment of invoices is processed separately in finance ($\rightarrow$ Sect. 9.3.3).

If you want to invoice a stocked product, you have to process a sales order. But it is not required to perform the complete sales process with order confirmation, picking, and shipping—you can post the sales order invoice immediately after entering the order (if no restrictions are specified in the item model group).

You can use a free text invoice if you want to post an invoice that is not related to products or sales categories. In the lines of a free text invoice, you enter ledger accounts instead of item numbers. Free text invoices have no reference to items and no impact on inventory and supply chain management.

4.5.1   Sales Order Invoices

The way to post a sales invoice is similar to posting a packing slip.

4.5.1.1 Posting Dialog for Sales Order Invoices

In order to post a sales invoice, click the button *Invoice/Generate/Invoice* in the Sales order form or open the menu item *Accounts receivable > Invoices > Batch invoicing > Invoice*.

The posting dialog then shows the familiar format. In the lookup field *Quantity* on the tab *Parameters*, select the applicable option depending on the prior process:

- **Packing Slip**—Usual option, since in most cases a packing slip is posted first, and you want to invoice the shipped quantity.
- **All** or **Deliver now**—If selected, Dynamics 365 does not initialize the column *Update* in the invoice lines with the shipped quantity, but with the open order quantity or with the quantity in the column *Deliver now* of the order lines. For any quantity not shipped yet, the physical transaction is posted in parallel to the invoice.

If you select the option "Packing Slip" in the lookup field *Quantity*, you can select or deselect particular packing slips to be included in the invoice. Click the button *Select packing slip* in the toolbar of the tab *Overview* in the posting dialog for this purpose.

Before posting, you check the totals with the button *Totals* on the tab *Overview* in the posting dialog. In order to post and print the invoice, make sure that both sliders, *Posting* and *Print invoice*, in the dialog are set to "Yes" before you click the button *OK*.

4.5.1.2 Transaction Inquiry

Posting the invoice generates general ledger transactions, inventory transactions, customer transactions, and transactions in other subledgers, like the sales tax, as applicable. Once all lines of a sales order are completely invoiced, the order status is "Invoiced".

If you want to view the inventory transactions that refer to an order line, select the respective line in the sales order and click the button *Inventory/Transactions* in the toolbar of the order lines. After posting the invoice, the issue status of the inventory transaction is "Sold", and the posting date of the invoice is shown in the column *Financial date*.

In order to view the posted sales invoices, open the menu item *Accounts receivable > Inquiries and reports > Invoices > Invoice journal* or click the button *Invoice/ Journals/Invoice* in the Sales order form. Click on an invoice number shown as a link in the grid if you want to open the related Invoice detail form. In the Invoice detail form, you can view the invoice lines on the tab *Lines*.

4.5.1.3 Ledger Transactions and Transaction Origin

If you want to view the ledger transactions that refer to a posted invoice, open the Voucher transactions inquiry with the button *Voucher* in the Invoice inquiry or with the button *Ledger/Financial voucher* in the inventory transactions.

The button *Transaction origin* in the Voucher transactions inquiry provides access to the Transaction origin form, which shows the related transactions in all modules.

The particular ledger accounts in the transactions depend on the actual procedure and on the setup. The customer summary account for the customer transaction is specified in the applicable customer posting profile, which works similarly to the vendor posting profile ($\rightarrow$ Sect. 3.2.3). The settings for the main account in the other transactions—except for the sales tax transaction—are specified in the posting setup ($\rightarrow$ Sect. 9.4.2).

4.5.2 Collective Invoices

If you want to post an invoice that covers multiple sales orders (e.g., a monthly invoice), post a collective invoice using a summary update. Collective documents are available for all document types. Apart from collective invoices, you can, for example, also post collective packing slips.

Apart from the fact that it covers multiple orders, posting a collective document is not different from posting an individual document.

The setup for summary updates at the company level and at the customer level controls whether it is possible to combine orders into collective documents.

4.5.2.1 Setup for Summary Updates

The section *Summary update* in the Accounts receivable parameters contains basic configuration settings for collective sales documents. The lookup field *Default values for summary update* in this section is a core setting for summary updates. In most cases, the option

"Automatic summary" is selected, which makes it possible to deselect orders from a collective document already in the order. If the option "Invoice account" is selected, you can only exclude a particular order by removing it in the posting dialog.

The Summary update parameter form, which you can access with the button *Summary update parameters* in the toolbar of the tab *Summary update* in the Accounts receivable parameters, contains a separate section per document type. For each document type, you can specify which fields in a sales order must have the same content to join a collective document.

If the option "Automatic summary" is selected in the parameter field *Default values for summary update*, you have to enable the automatic summary per customer (click the button *Customer/Set up/Summary update* in the Customer form). The setting in the customer is the default for related sales orders. In the Sales order form, you can access and edit this setting with the button *General/Set up/Summary*.

4.5.2.2 Posting Collective Invoices

In order to post a collective invoice, open the menu item *Accounts receivable > Invoices > Batch invoicing > Invoice*. In the lookup field *Quantity* of the posting dialog, select the option "Packing slip" if you want to make sure that the invoice only covers items that have been shipped.

Then click the button *Select* [1] in the posting dialog ($\rightarrow$ Fig. 4.19) and select applicable sales orders in the Advanced filter dialog. After closing the filter dialog, the selected orders are shown on the tab *Overview* of the posting dialog.

If there are sales orders that you do not want to include in the invoice, select the respective records on the tab *Overview* of the posting dialog and delete them (click the button *Remove* in the toolbar of this tab). Deleting a record in the posting dialog only removes the selection. It does not delete the order or the packing slip, which is why the order is shown again when you select orders for posting the next invoice.

If you want to include or exclude particular packing slips from invoice posting, click the button *Select packing slip* [2].

Once you have selected the respective sales orders and packing slips, click the button *Arrange* [3]. Arranging combines the orders into a common invoice as specified in the Summary update parameters. If the setting in the Accounts receivable parameters is not suitable for a particular invoice, you can select a different option in the lookup field *Summary update for* [4] on the tab *Parameters* of the posting dialog before arranging.

In the example of $\rightarrow$ Fig. 4.19, the *Arrange* function merges the two orders into one common line. You can subsequently post the collective invoice with the button *OK* in the posting dialog.

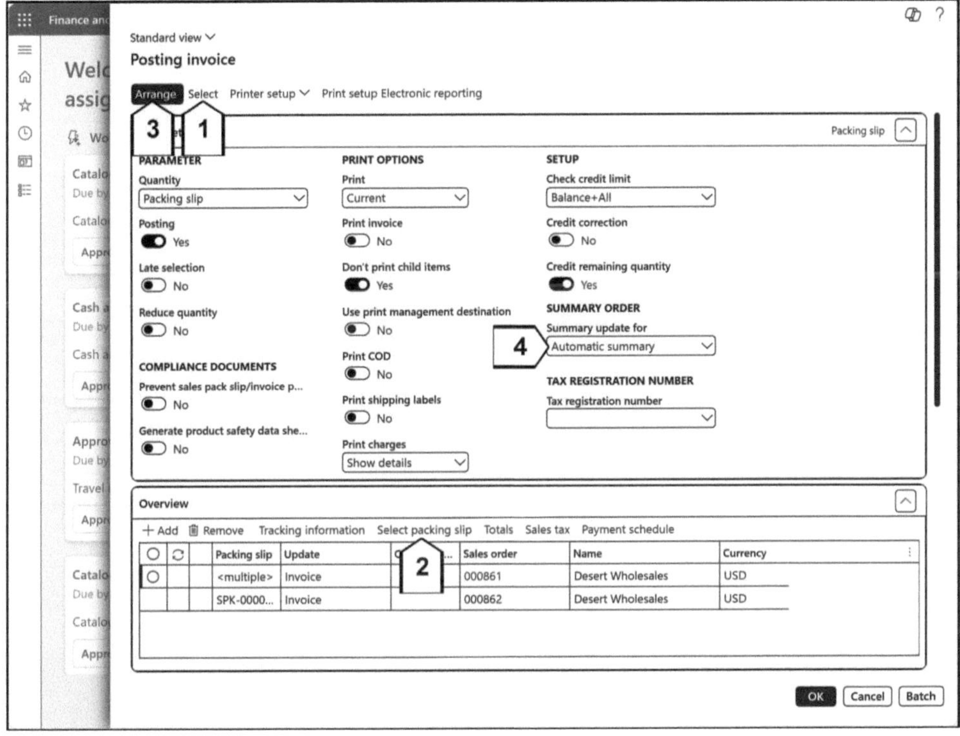

Fig. 4.19 Posting a collective sales invoice

4.5.3   Free Text Invoices

Free text invoices are independent of sales orders, shipments, and inventory. You can use free text invoices to sell intangible items or fixed assets.

The structure of free text invoices is similar to sales orders—a free text invoice consists of a header and one or more lines. Instead of product numbers and sales categories, the lines of a free text invoice contain ledger accounts.

If you want to create a credit note, enter a negative amount in the free text invoice. Item statistics and inventory valuation do not include free text invoices and free text credit notes.

Once you have entered the free text invoice, you can post and print it. The invoice is the only document that you can generate in a free text invoice. It is not possible to generate other documents (e.g., order confirmations).

4.5.3.1 Registering Free Text Invoices

In order to enter a free text invoice, open the All free text invoices form (*Accounts receivable > Invoices > All free text invoices*) and click the button *New* in the action pane. Alternatively, you can access the Customer form and create a free text invoice with the button *Invoice/New/Free text invoice* in the action pane of this form.

Unlike the Sales order form, the Free text invoice form (→ Fig. 4.20) does not open a separate *Create* dialog when you create a new record. But the fields *Customer account* and *Invoice account*, in which you select the respective customer, are not only shown in the Header view of the Free text invoice form, they are also included on the tab *Free text invoice header* in the Lines view.

After entering the header data, insert the lines with *Description, Main account*, and *Amount* (or *Quantity* and *Unit price*). If a line requires a longer description, you can use the field *Invoice text* on the sub-tab *General* of the tab *Line details*. If sales tax (VAT) applies, make sure to select the correct *Sales tax group* and *Item sales tax group*.

If you sell a fixed asset, enter the *Fixed asset number* on the sub-tab *General* of the tab *Line details*.

You can update the financial dimensions (e.g., the department or cost center) on the sub-tab *Financial dimensions line* of the tab *Line details*—enter applicable dimension values individually or select a financial dimension default template in the lookup field *Template ID*.

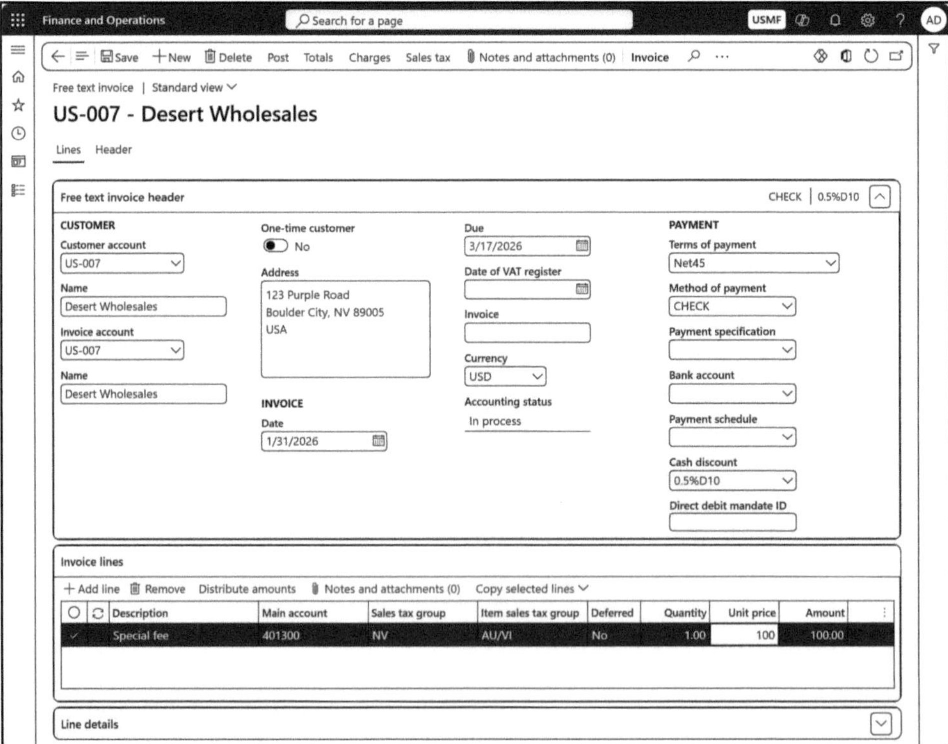

Fig. 4.20 Registering an invoice line in a free text invoice

4.5.3.2 Invoice Posting and Invoice Inquiry

In order to post the free text invoice, click the button *Post* in the action pane of the Free text invoice form. You can view the posted invoice with the button *Invoice/Related information/Invoice journal* afterward.

In the Invoice inquiry (*Accounts receivable > Inquiries and reports > Invoices > Invoice journal*), free text invoices are shown in parallel with the sales order invoices. For free text invoices, there is no order number that is shown in this inquiry.

4.5.3.3 Recurring Free Text Invoices

If you want to issue a particular free text invoice periodically, you can use recurring free text invoices. As a prerequisite for this kind of invoice, set up free text invoice templates (*Accounts receivable > Invoices > Recurring invoices > Free text invoice templates*). In the Customer form, you can assign customers to one or more templates with the button *Invoice/Set up/Recurring invoices*.

In order to generate a periodical free text invoice based on these settings, open the menu item *Accounts receivable > Invoices > Recurring invoices > Generate recurring invoices*. The periodic activity generates regular free text invoices, which you can review in the Free text invoice form before posting.

4.5.4 Case Study Exercises

Exercise 4.9—Sales Invoice
The items that you have shipped in exercise 4.6 need to be invoiced. Before posting the invoice, review the following items:

- Order status and document status of the sales order.
- Inventory transaction for the order line.

Post and print the invoice directly in the Sales order form and check the invoice total in the posting dialog.

Then review the status of the items in the list above again. What is different now?

Exercise 4.10—Partial Invoice
Invoice the items that you have picked and shipped in exercise 4.7. Post and print the invoice in the Sales order form, and make sure to invoice only the items that you have shipped.

Exercise 4.11—Shipping with Invoice
The customer of exercise 4.1 orders another unit of the product of exercise 3.5. In addition, he wants to order 1 h of the installation service of exercise 4.2 for a price of USD 110. This

time, you do not post a packing slip, but you want to consume the items when posting the invoice.

Enter an appropriate sales order, set the order to complete if required, and immediately post the invoice. After posting the invoice, review the order status, the document status, and the inventory transaction of the product.

Exercise 4.12—Invoice Inquiry
Review the invoice that you have posted in exercise 4.9 in the Invoice inquiry. Check the invoice header and the invoice lines.

Exercise 4.13—Free Text Invoice
Your company wants to invoice a service to the customer of exercise 4.1. There is no product or sales category for this service. Enter and post a free text invoice with an appropriate revenue account for this transaction.

What is the difference between a free text invoice and a sales order invoice?

4.6   Sales Credit Note and Item Return

A credit note is a document that you issue if a customer returns an item to your company and receives financial compensation. You can also post a credit note if the customer does not actually return the defective item, or if you have to credit a price discrepancy.

In order to manage customer returns, you can use the return order management in Dynamics 365. In case of a simple return process, you can alternatively use regular sales orders instead of return orders.

If a credit note does not cover inventoried items, you can use a free text invoice.

4.6.1   Return Order Management

Return orders support a proper procedure for item returns, which ensures that a customer must contact you to receive a return merchandise authorization (RMA) before returning a product.

4.6.1.1 Disposition Codes and Required Setup

As a prerequisite for the use of return orders, you have to set up disposition codes (*Sales and marketing > Setup > Returns > Disposition codes*). In the Disposition code form, the field *Action* is a core setting for the return process. It controls the handling of returned items and includes the following options:

- **Credit only**—Credit without item return.
- **Credit**—Return items and credit.

- **Scrap**—Return items and credit, scrap immediately.
- **Replace and credit** (or **Replace and scrap**)—Return items and replace.
- **Return to customer**—Do not credit.

Except for the option "Credit only", an item receipt has to be posted in all cases, no matter if the products are returned to stock or if they are scrapped. But in case of scrap, an inventory transaction for scrapping is posted parallel to the receipt of the return order.

Return reason codes (*Sales and marketing > Setup > Returns > Return reason codes*) classify return orders for statistical purposes and, if applicable, for the automatic assignment of charges. When creating a return order, reason codes are only mandatory if the slider *Require reasons for return orders* in the Accounts receivable parameters (section *General*, tab *Reason code requirements*) is set to "Yes".

4.6.1.2 Return Order Registration

Return orders (→ Fig. 4.21) are sales orders with the order type "Returned order". The sales order number of a return order is shown in the field *Sales order* of the return order header (in the Header view and on the tab *Return order header* in the Lines view). But except for return orders with the disposition code "Credit only", return orders are not shown in the regular Sales order form until the item arrival has been posted.

The workspace *Sales return processing* gives an overview of the current return orders. The tile *All return orders* in the workspace provides access to the Return order list page. If you want to create a new return order directly from the workspace, click the button *New/ Return order* in the action pane. The following steps are the same as when you create a return order from the Return order form.

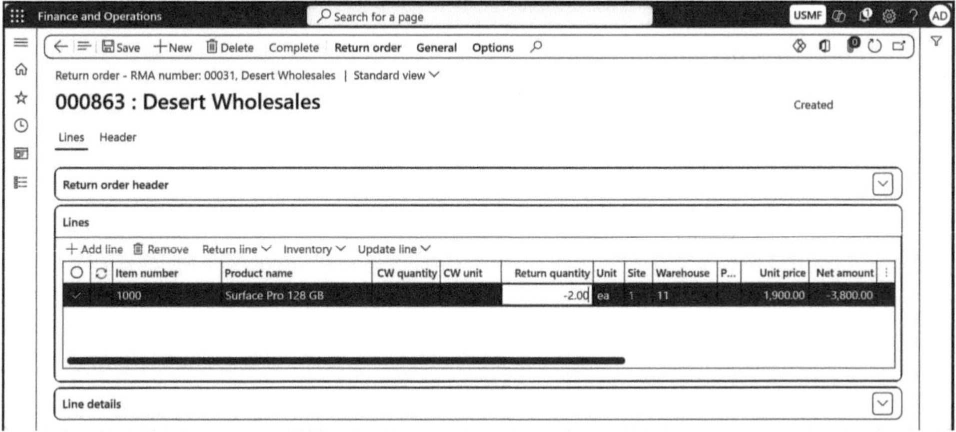

Fig. 4.21 Registering a return in the lines of the Return order form

In order to access the return orders from the menu, open the list page *Sales and marketing > Sales returns > All return orders*. When creating a new return order, you can select a *Return reason code* on the tab *General* in the *Create* dialog or the return order header.

If you want to copy the original sales order, which is sent back by the customer, to the new return order (in fact, the sales invoice lines are copied), click the button *Return order/Return/Find sales order* in the action pane. Alternatively, you can manually enter return order lines with a negative quantity. The *Disposition code* of a line is shown on the sub-tab *General* of the tab *Line details*. But except for disposition codes with the *Action* "Credit only" (crediting without physical return), you do not enter the disposition code before item arrival.

If order completion is enabled, the button *Complete* is shown in the action pane. Once you have finished entering the return order, click the button in this case.

Optionally, you can click the button *Return order/Send/Return order* in the return order to print an RMA document, which you can send to the customer.

If you want to send an up-front replacement for the returned item to the customer, click the button *Return order/New/Replacement order* in the return order to create a new sales order for this purpose.

4.6.1.3 Return Orders without Physical Return

If you do not want the customer to return the item, select a disposition code without item return ("Credit only") on the sub-tab *General* of the tab *Line details* in the return order. In this case, you can immediately post the credit note in the Sales order form (*Sales and marketing > Sales Orders > All sales orders*) or in the summary update for invoices (*Accounts receivable > Invoices > Batch invoicing > Invoice*).

4.6.1.4 Item Arrival and Credit Note for Return Orders

When you receive an item from a customer that refers to a return order, record an inventory registration. Like the inventory registration in purchasing ($\rightarrow$ Sect. 3.5.3), the registration for return orders can be done in the Registration form (accessed with the button *Update line/Registration* in the return order lines) or in an item arrival journal. In a warehouse with advanced warehouse management, you should execute the inventory registration with mobile device transactions.

If you want to use an item arrival journal ($\rightarrow$ Sect. 7.4.2), open the menu item *Inventory management > Journal entries > Item arrival > Item arrival* and create a new journal. In the Create dialog which is shown next, select the option "Sales order" in the field *Reference* and enter the *RMA number* in the respective field. You can later find these data, and the *Disposition code*, on the tab *Default values* in the Header view of the Journal form. They initialize the journal lines.

In order to create journal lines in the item arrival journal, either click the button *Functions/Create lines* in the action pane, or manually enter the lines in the Lines view of the journal.

The *Disposition code* has to be specified in the journal lines before you can post the item return. If it is not possible to decide upon the disposition code at the time when you receive the item, set the slider *Quarantine management* in the journal line to "Yes" (you can enter a default value in the journal header) and leave the disposition code empty. In this case, a quarantine order ($\rightarrow$ Sect. 7.4.6) is created when posting the item arrival, and it is not required to enter the disposition code before ending quarantine.

After posting the item arrival journal with the button *Post*, the return order lines show the *Return status* "Registered".

Once you have finished inventory registration, you can optionally print a receipt acknowledgment with the button *Return order/Send/Acknowledgement* in the Return order form.

Then post the packing slip (with a negative quantity) in the Return order form (with the button *Return order/Generate/Post packing slip*) or in the Sales order form (with the button *Pick and pack/Generate/Post packing slip*) and make sure to select an appropriate option (usually "All" since you have posted an inbound registration and not an outbound picking) in the lookup field *Quantity* of the posting dialog.

In order to credit the customer financially, open the Sales order form, select the respective order, and click the button *Invoice/Generate/Invoice* in the action pane. Alternatively, you can use the summary update for invoices (*Accounts receivable > Invoices > Batch invoicing > Invoice*).

> *Note:* With advanced warehouse management, you can register the item arrival on a mobile device ($\rightarrow$ Sect. 8.1.3).

4.6.2   Simple Credit Notes

If you do not want to process a customer return in a return order, you can use a regular sales order to credit a customer. And if it is not required to track the physical and financial process at the level of items, you can use a free text invoice.

The credit note is subsequently processed as an invoice with a negative quantity/amount.

4.6.2.1 Credit Note from Sales Orders

In the Sales order form, there are the following options for crediting:

- **Original order line**—Negative *Deliver now* quantity.
- **New order line**—Order line with a negative quantity in the original order.
- **New order**—Order line with a negative quantity in a new sales order.

The way to enter a new order or a new order line for a credit note in sales is similar to entering an order for a credit note in purchasing ($\rightarrow$ Sect. 3.7.1). But since it is not possible to select the order type "Returned order" in a sales order manually, the order header of an order that you enter for crediting in the Sales order form looks like the header of any regular sales order.

If you want to record a credit note in the original sales order line, enter a negative quantity in the column *Deliver now* in that line. When you post the credit note (by posting an invoice), select the option "Deliver now"—which refers to the column *Deliver now*—in the lookup field *Quantity* of the *Posting invoice* dialog.

> *Note:* If order completion is enabled, you can only update the original line or enter a new line in the original sales order after resetting the status with the button *Sales order/Maintain/ Modify* in the Sales order form.

4.6.2.2 Inventory Valuation for Returned Items

If you register a credit note in a new order or order line, you should select the original invoice transaction in the lookup field *Return lot ID* (on the sub-tab *Setup* of the tab *Line details*) of the order line before posting. This link to the return lot makes sure that the inventory value of the crediting line exactly matches the inventory value of the original delivery.

Dynamics 365 automatically inserts the return lot ID when you create a credit note line with the button *Return order/Return/Find sales order* in the Return order form or with the button *Sell/Create/Credit note* in the Sales order form.

If you do not select a return lot ID, Dynamics 365 uses the *Return cost price* on the sub-tab *Setup* of the crediting order line for inventory valuation.

4.6.2.3 Scrapping Items

If you do not want the customer to return a defective item that you credit to him, set the slider *Scrap* on the sub-tab *Setup* of the order line to "Yes". When you post the invoice (credit note), Dynamics 365 posts the item receipt and a related inventory loss at the same time. In return orders, the slider *Scrap* in the order line is controlled by the disposition code.

4.6.2.4 Refunds Not Related to Item Returns

The free text invoice ($\rightarrow$ Sect. 4.5.3) is another option to register and to post customer refunds. But if a refund refers to an item, you should not use a free text invoice, since this kind of invoicing is not included in item statistics and inventory valuation.

If you need to credit a price discrepancy, it is better to enter a new sales order that contains a line with a negative quantity and the old price and a line with a positive quantity and the actual price. You can link both transactions (in order to offset the inventory value) with the button *Inventory/Marking* ($\rightarrow$ Sect. 3.7.1).

4.6.3   Case Study Exercise

Exercise 4.14—Sales Credit Note
Your customer complains about defects in the items that you have invoiced in exercise 4.9. You agree to accept an item return and to credit the invoice. Enter a return order, set the order to complete if required, and post the item receipt with an appropriate disposition code. Then post the packing slip for the item return, and finally post and print the credit note.

4.7   Direct Delivery and Product Bundle

Direct delivery is the process of shipping goods directly from the vendor to the customer. This means there is no purchase receipt and sales shipment in the warehouse, which saves time and expenses for transportation and stocking.

Product bundles are an option to collect multiple items, which are separate in inventory and in the shipping process, into one order line for pricing and invoicing.

4.7.1   Working with Direct Delivery

The functionality for direct delivery in Dynamics 365 is based on a purchase order that is created from a related sales order. There are the following options for creating this purchase order:

- **Purchase order from a sales order**—Create a regular purchase order (received in your warehouse, from where it is shipped to the customer).
- **Direct delivery from a sales order**—Create a direct delivery purchase order (shipped directly to the customer).
- **Direct delivery type in a sales order line**—Automatically creates a direct delivery purchase order.
- **Direct delivery workbench**—Create a direct delivery from the workbench.

Whereas creating a regular purchase order or a direct delivery purchase order from a sales order does not require specific settings, the Direct delivery workbench requires direct delivery to be enabled in the sales order line.

> *Note:* Instead of initiating the direct delivery from sales, you can alternatively start from the purchase order and create a direct delivery sales order there.

4.7.1.1 Regular Purchase Orders from Sales Orders

You can create a regular purchase order from a sales order if you want to process the purchase order linked to the sales order (separate from other orders), but nevertheless receive and ship it in a warehouse of your company.

As a starting point, enter a regular sales order and—if order completion is required ($\rightarrow$ Sect. 4.3.3)—set the order to complete. Then click the button *Sales order/New/Purchase order* in the action pane to create a related purchase order. In the *Create purchase order* dialog, select the checkbox *Include* in the respective lines and choose a vendor (if no main vendor is specified for the item). Processing the purchase order and the sales order works like processing regular orders, including change management for the purchase order.

In the purchase order, the delivery address for the vendor is your warehouse or company address (like in any regular purchase order). You can post the product receipt in your warehouse and then perform picking and shipping to the customer. The purchase order and sales order lines are connected by marking and reservation.

4.7.1.2 Direct Delivery Purchase Orders from Sales Orders

If you want a direct delivery from the vendor to the customer, you can also start by entering a regular sales order. But it is useful to select a separate warehouse for direct deliveries to avoid confusing inventory transactions in a regular warehouse with transactions for direct delivery, which never actually affect this warehouse. If order completion is required, set the order to complete.

In order to create a direct delivery purchase order for a sales order, click the button *Sales order/New/Direct delivery* in the Sales order form. The purchase order has a tight link to the sales order (with marking and reservation). In the sales order line, the column *Delivery type* shows "Direct delivery" and the slider *Direct delivery* on the sub-tab *Delivery* of the *Line details* is set to "Yes". The delivery address of the purchase order is the customer address. Later changes of the address and of other data in the sales order, which are relevant to purchasing (e.g., the quantity or the delivery date), are synchronized to the purchase order.

After initially creating the direct delivery purchase order, and after any changes, you have to observe the purchase order change management, which at least requires confirming the purchase order.

When you post the product receipt for direct delivery in purchasing, Dynamics 365 automatically posts the related sales packing slip. If you need to print a packing slip for the customer, set the slider *Print sales documents* in the posting dialog for the product receipt ($\rightarrow$ Fig. 4.22) to "Yes".

Invoice posting in sales is independent of the purchase invoice.

4.7.1.3 Delivery Type for Direct Delivery

If you select the option "Direct delivery" in the column *Delivery type* of a sales order line (or in the corresponding field on the sub-tab *Sourcing* of the *Line details*), a direct delivery purchase order is immediately created when saving the order line. The vendor for the

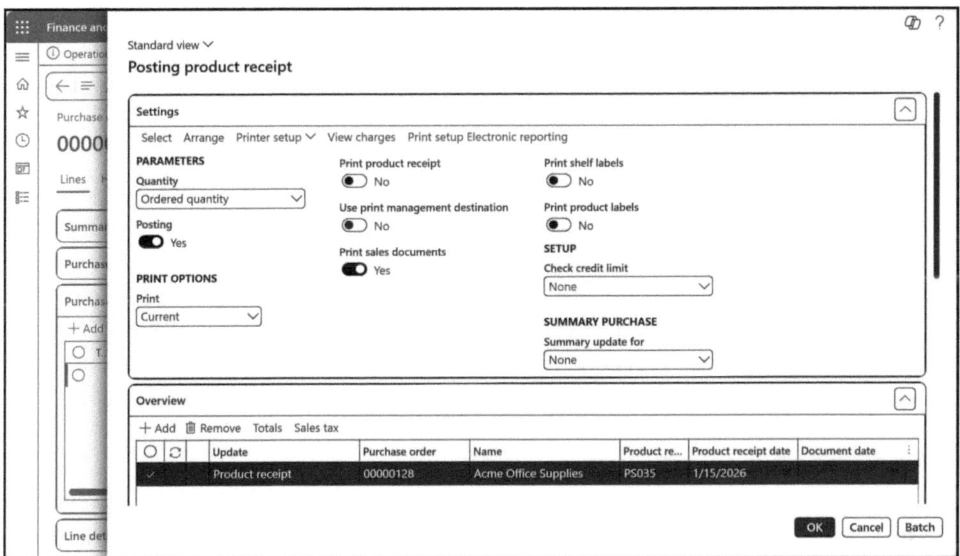

Fig. 4.22 Printing a sales packing slip for direct delivery with product receipt posting

direct delivery purchase order is specified in the field *Sourcing vendor* on the sub-tab *Sourcing* of the sales order line.

The further proceeding with product receipt and invoice posting for the direct delivery is the same as described above.

4.7.1.4 Creating Direct Delivery Purchase Orders with a Periodic Job

Instead of creating the direct delivery purchase order with the respective button in the sales order form, you can use the periodic activity *Procurement and Sourcing > Purchase orders > Direct delivery processing > Create direct delivery orders* to generate purchase orders for sales order lines with the slider *Direct delivery* set to "Yes".

Depending on the setting *Consolidate sales orders for direct deliveries* in the Procurement parameter (you might need to personalize the parameter form to show this slider), multiple direct delivery sales orders with common characteristics are consolidated into a common purchase order.

The further proceeding with product receipt and invoice posting for the direct delivery is the same as described above.

4.7.1.5 Settings in the Released Product

If an item is usually distributed with direct delivery, you can set the slider *Delivery type* on the tab *Deliver* in the Released product form to "Yes". When entering a sales order line for such an item, the setting for the *Delivery type*, the *Direct delivery warehouse*, and the main vendor in the released product initialize the column *Delivery type*, the warehouse, and the *Sourcing vendor* in the order line.

4.7.1.6 Direct Delivery Workbench

If you do not want to create direct delivery purchase orders straight from the sales orders (e.g., because the purchasing department should review direct deliveries first), you can use the Direct delivery workbench (*Procurement and sourcing > Purchase orders > Direct delivery processing > Direct delivery*).

This workbench gives an overview of all sales order lines with the slider *Direct delivery* set to "Yes". Initially, these sales orders are shown on the tab *Direct delivery*, and you can click the button *Create direct delivery* in the toolbar of this tab to create a purchase order.

This purchase order—and any other direct delivery purchase order that is created independently of the workbench—is then shown on the tab *Confirmation* of the workbench. You can post the purchase order confirmation on this tab. On the tab *Delivery* in the workbench, you can post the product receipt (together with the related sales packing slip).

4.7.1.7 Links Between Purchase and Sales Order

The field group *Item reference* on the sub-tab *Product* of a sales order line shows the purchase order, which is linked to the sales order line. The same reference is also available in the other direction, from the purchase order line to the sales order. In addition, the reference is shown in the *Related orders* dialog (accessed with the button *General/Related information/Related orders* in the action pane of the purchase order or the sales order). In the Sales order form, you can click the button *General/Related information/Purchase order* to directly access the assigned purchase order.

4.7.2   Product Bundle

Using product bundles, you can enter a sales order line with an item—the bundle item with its price—to sell a sales kit, which physically consists of multiple items. The order confirmation and the invoice only show the bundle item. The picking and shipping documents show the (physical) component items.

4.7.2.1 Managing Product Bundles

As a prerequisite for using bundles, the Product bundles feature has to be enabled. You can subsequently create a bundle item like a regular sales product (→ Sect. 4.2.3), but with the slider *Product bundle* on the tab *General* of the Released product form set to "Yes". Even if the bundle item itself is not stored in inventory (only the components are stocked items), it has to be set up as a stocked item with an approved and active BOM version (→ Sect. 5.2.2).

For the bundle components, which are included in the BOM, a base sales price (specified in the field *Price* on the tab *Sell* in the Released product form) is required as a basis for allocating the bundle price in a sales order to the components.

4.7.2.2 Using Product Bundles in Sales Orders

In order to sell a product bundle, create a sales order with an order line in which you enter the bundle item, the quantity, and the bundle price. When selecting the bundle item, the fields in the order line are initialized as for any other sales item.

When you post the order confirmation, which is a mandatory step in sales orders with bundle items, the *Line status* of the sales order line with the bundle item is automatically set to "Canceled", and the *Quantity* in this line is cleared. At the same time, new sales order lines with the component items and the quantity as specified in the BOM of the bundle item are created. The *Unit price*, *Discount*, and *Net amount* in these additional lines are calculated from the original line with the bundle item (allocated in line with the base sales price and the quantity of the components).

While picking and shipping are executed for the order lines with the bundle components, the order confirmation and the invoice only show the line with the bundle header item and its quantity, price, and applicable discount. For this reason, you can only ship full bundles (i.e., all components of a bundle together). A partial delivery is only possible with all component quantities apportioned as specified in the BOM.

4.7.3   Case Study Exercise

Exercise 4.15—Direct Delivery
The customer of exercise 4.1 orders 100 units of the item of exercise 3.5. In order to avoid stocking this large quantity in the warehouse, you want to process a direct delivery. Enter an appropriate sales order, set the order to complete if required, and create a direct delivery purchase order which you send to the vendor of exercise 3.2.

Your vendor confirms shipping the item with packing slip PS415. Post this product receipt in the purchase order. In the next step, review the status of the sales order before you post and print the sales invoice. Finally, you receive the purchase invoice VI415, which you post in the Pending vendor invoice form.

4.8   Basic Trade Agreement and Pricing Management

In a simple situation, which only requires one common sales price for all customers, you can use the base sales price in the released product ($\rightarrow$ Sect. 4.2.3).

With basic trade agreements, you can manage more detailed settings for prices and discounts. You can, for example, specify different price lists or discounts for different customer groups.

The Pricing management module, which is available with the Unified pricing feature, extends the basic trade agreements for prices and introduces discount management features in regular sales orders (in Dynamics 365 Supply Chain Management), which formerly have been only available in Dynamics 365 Commerce.

4.8.1   Basic Trade Agreements

Basic trade agreements are an option to manage price lists and discounts if you don't want to use the advanced features of pricing management ($\to$ Sect. 4.8.3). With basic trade agreements, you can manage prices and discounts in an elementary structure at the level of individual items and customers, at the group level, and at the general level (all items and customers).

In purchasing, trade agreements at the level of individual items and vendors, at the group level, and at the general level work similarly.

4.8.1.1 Required Setup for Basic Trade Agreements

If Unified pricing management is enabled in the Feature management, some settings in the Pricing management parameters (*Pricing management > Setup > Pricing management parameters*) are required if you want to use the basic trade agreements described here. Basic trade agreements for prices and discounts only work with Unified pricing, if either the slider *Disable pricing management* (in the section *General*) or the slider *Apply existing trade agreements* (in the section *Prices and discounts*, tab *Trade agreements*) in the Pricing management parameters is set to "Yes".

Independent of Unified pricing, a trade agreement is only used in the calculation of prices and discounts, if the applicable combination (Table/Group/All) is enabled in the Activate price/discount form (*Sales and marketing > Setup > Prices and discounts > Activate price/discount* for sales, and *Procurement and sourcing > Setup > Prices and discounts > Activate price/discount* for purchasing). Within the activated elements, the discount calculation searches from the specific to the general level—first the customer and item number level ("Table"), then the group level ("Group"), and finally the general level ("All").

Trade agreement journal names (*Sales and marketing > Setup > Prices and discounts > Trade agreement journal names* or *Procurement and sourcing > Setup > Prices and discounts > Trade agreement journal names*) are a prerequisite for creating a trade agreement. They are a common setup for sales and purchasing. The field *Relation* in a journal name determines the default value for the column *Relation* in the trade agreement journals.

4.8.1.2 Structure of Basic Trade Agreements

Basic trade agreements in sales determine prices and discounts depending on customers and released products. In purchasing, trade agreements with reference to vendors and released products work similarly.

In Dynamics 365, there are the following types of basic trade agreements:

- **Prices**
- **Line discounts**

- **Multiline discounts**
- **Total discounts** (Invoice discounts)

Whereas trade agreements for prices, line discounts, and multiline discounts refer to the order lines, the total discounts relate to the order header.

Basic trade agreements for prices and discounts can be specified at different levels. You can enter a line discount trade agreement for a particular customer, for a customer discount group, or all customers. In addition to the customer selection, line discount trade agreements contain an item selection (particular item, item discount group, or all items). The options for a line discount trade agreement in sales with regard to the customer and the item selection are shown in → Table 4.1.

As a result, you can, for example, enter a line discount trade agreement for a particular item and a particular customer, and another agreement for an item discount group and all customers.

For multiline discounts, the same principle is true, except that you can't enter a multiline discount at the level of an item number.

In trade agreements for prices and trade agreements for total discounts, the item selection is limited to one option: Prices are specified per item, which restricts the item selection to "Item number", and total discounts refer to the order header, which restricts the item selection to "All items".

In addition to the customer/vendor level and the item level, basic trade agreements include the following selection criteria:

- **Period of validity**—*From date* and *To date* (whether these dates refer to the order entry or the receipt date is specified in the field *Date type* in the section *Prices* of the Accounts receivable parameters and, for purchasing, the Procurement parameters).
- **Quantity**—Columns *From* and *To* (for quantity-dependent agreements).
- **Unit of measure**—Column *Unit*.
- **Currency**—Currency of the price (or a discount that is a discount amount).

Apart from the selection criteria mentioned above, inventory dimensions are another specification level for trade agreements. You can use inventory dimensions in trade agreements to specify different prices or discounts per site, or per warehouse, or with reference to product dimensions like size or color. As a prerequisite for the use of dimensions in pricing, the dimension group of the particular item has to include the selected dimensions as a price search criterion (→ Sect. 7.2.2).

Table 4.1 Selection levels for line discount trade agreements in sales

	Item number	Item discount group	All items
Customer number	X	X	X
Customer discount group	X	X	X
All customers	X	X	X

The price search runs from the most specific to the general agreement, in other words, from customer prices to customer group prices to general prices (in case of a sales price agreement). If the option *Find next* in the trade agreement line is active, Dynamics 365 searches for the lowest price in the applicable trade agreements—a lower group price overrides a higher customer-specific price in this case. You can stop this search by clearing the checkbox *Find next* (when entering the trade agreement journal line, set the slider *Find next* on the tab *Details* to "No").

For discounts, the checkbox *Find next* in the applicable trade agreements controls, if only one discount or the total of all applicable discounts is used in the respective order lines. If line discount and multiline discount apply to a particular sales order line in parallel, the Accounts receivable parameters (field *Discount* in the section *Prices*) control how to calculate the total of line and multiline discount.

An option which is only available in sales price agreements and not in purchase price agreements is the use of a *Generic currency* and an *Exchange rate type* that is specified in the Accounts receivable parameters (section *Prices*, tab *Generic currency and smart rounding*). If a generic currency is specified, prices in trade agreements with this currency (if the slider *Include in generic currency* in the agreement line is set to "Yes") are automatically converted to other currencies if there is no other applicable trade agreement when entering a sales order line.

4.8.1.3 Managing Price and Discount Groups

You can set up the discount groups for items in the Item discount groups form (*Sales and marketing > Prices and discounts > Item discount groups*). Depending on the selected option in the lookup field *Show* ("Line discount group" or "Multiline disc. group"), the line discount or multiline discount groups are shown in the grid.

In the Released product form, you can subsequently select the *Line discount group* and the group for *Multiline discount* of the item (on the tab *Sell* of the detail form). The slider *Total discount* on this tab controls it the item is included in the total discount. If this slider is set to "No", the product is excluded from the basis of the total discount calculation.

In the discount calculation, line discounts are calculated on the basis of the individual order line, whereas the calculation of multiline discounts includes all order lines with the same multiline discount group (which is relevant if the discount depends on the quantity). Total discounts (invoice discounts), which are specified at the order header level, are calculated on the order total (not including items with *Total discount* set to "No").

Price and discount groups for customers are specified in the Customer price/discount group form (*Sales and marketing > Prices and discounts > Customer price/discount groups*). Depending on the selected option in the lookup field *Show* ("Price group", "Line discount group", "Multiline disc. group", or "Total discount group"), the related groups are shown in the grid.

In the Customer form, the tab *Sales order defaults* contains the price group (the lookup field *Price*) and the discount groups (line discount, multiline discount, total discount), which you can use to group customers for pricing purposes. In sales orders, the price and discount groups of the customer initialize the related fields of the order header, but you can override the price and discount groups on the tab *Price and discount* in the Header view of the Sales order detail form.

For purchasing, settings for trade agreements are available on the tab *Purchase* in the Released product form and on the tab *Purchase order defaults* in the Vendor form.

4.8.1.4 Managing Trade Agreements for Sales Prices

If you want to record a sales price trade agreement, enter and post a trade agreement journal. You can access the trade agreement journals from the menu (*Sales and marketing > Prices and discounts > Trade agreement journals*) or with the button *Sell/Trade agreements/Create trade agreements* in the Released product form.

A trade agreement journal consists of a header and at least one line. The lookup field *Show* in the upper pane of the Trade agreement journal list page provides the option to select whether to view only open journals or to include posted journals. In order to create a new journal, click the button *New* in the action pane and select a journal name in the column *Name*. From the journal name setup, the content of the field *Relation*—e.g., "Price (sales)"—initializes the *Default relation* in the journal header, which, in turn, is the default value for the field *Relation* in the journal lines.

With the new journal selected in the list page, click the button *Lines* to access the Journal lines form with the trade agreement lines (→ Fig. 4.23). In the journal line for a sales price agreement, make sure that the option "Price (sales)" is selected in the column *Relation*. The *Party code type* determines if the price refers to a particular customer ("Table"), a customer price group ("Group"), or all customers. Depending on this selection, enter the customer or the customer price group in the column *Account selection*. In a trade agreement line for a price, you can only use the option "Table" in the column *Product code type*. Enter the item number in the column *Item relation*.

Apart from the fields in the journal lines grid, additional data of the selected line are shown on the tab *Details*. These data include the *From date*, the *To date*, the *Price unit* related to the column *Unit* in the journal line (the *Price unit* and the *Unit* in the agreement line work similar to the *Price quantity* and the *Unit* in the Released product form, see → Sect. 3.3.3), and the *Lead time*.

When entering a sales order line, the price, price unit, and lead time of the applicable trade agreement override the default values from the released product.

At the top of the Journal lines form, a message bar indicates the inventory dimensions which are applicable for prices of the selected item. In the example of → Fig. 4.23, the message tells that price agreements for the selected item can be entered at the level of site and warehouse. With the button *Inventory/Dimensions display* in the toolbar of the tab *Overview*, you can show or hide the inventory dimension columns in the journal lines.

Once you have finished entering the journal lines, click the button *Post* in the action pane to activate the trade agreement.

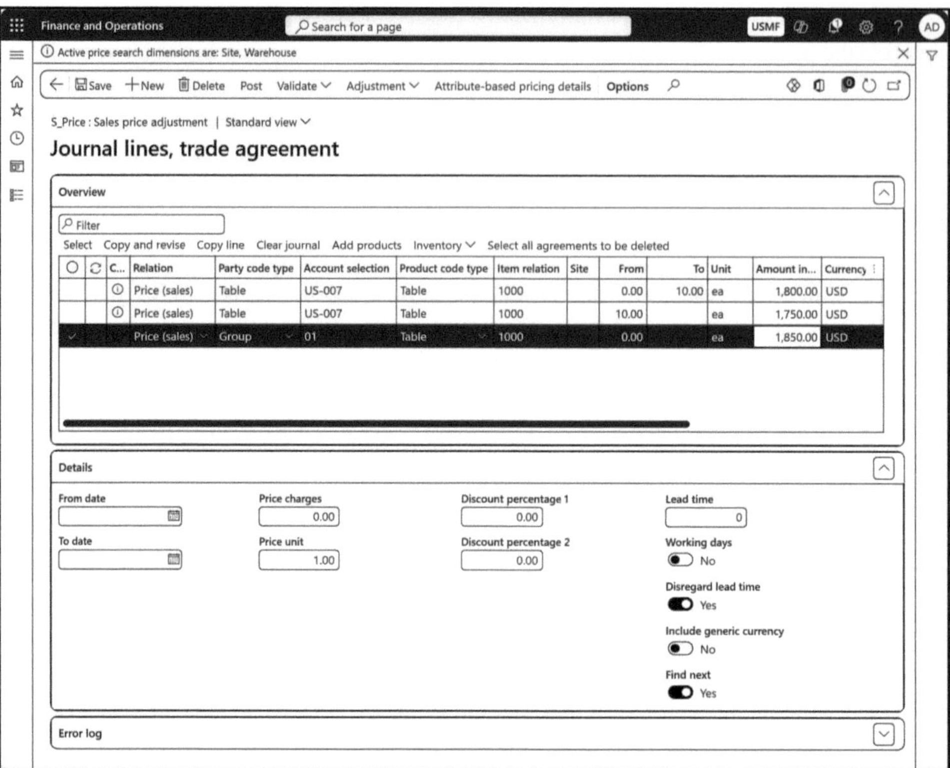

Fig. 4.23 Registering sales prices in a basic trade agreement journal (Pricing management parameter "Apply existing trade agreements" activated)

4.8.1.5 Updating or Deleting Trade Agreements

In order to record a new price for an item, you can simply enter and post a trade agreement with the new price, the from-date, and the to-date.

If you want to edit (e.g., update the to-date of the old agreement) or delete an active agreement, open the Trade agreement inquiry—for example, with the button *Sell/View/ Sales price* or the button *Sell/Trade agreement/View trade agreements* in the released product. Select one or more trade agreement lines and click the button *Edit selected lines* in the action pane next. In the confirmation dialog which is subsequently shown, select a journal name for the new journal (which is used for the update) and click the button *OK*.

The new trade agreement journal contains one line per original trade agreement line. This new line is connected to the original trade agreement. Edit the data in the line(s) as required before you click the button *Post* to update the agreement. If you want to delete the old agreement instead of updating it, click the button *Select all agreements to be deleted* in the toolbar above the grid in the new trade agreement journal lines before posting the journal.

Note: Instead of creating the new journal lines from a Trade agreement inquiry, you can alternatively start with creating a new journal directly in the Trade agreement journal form and click the button *Select* in the toolbar of the journal lines. In the Select dialog which is shown next, enter a filter for selecting the original trade agreements which you want to update.

4.8.1.6 Managing Line Discount Agreements

Like registering a price agreement, registering a line discount agreement requires entering and posting a trade agreement journal (*Sales and marketing > Prices and discounts > Trade agreement journals*). After creating a journal with the button *New* in the agreement journal header, click the button *Lines* in the action pane to access the journal lines. When entering a sales line discount in an agreement journal line, make sure to select the option "Line discount (Sales)" in the column *Relation*, and keep in mind that discount percentages are shown in the footer pane of the journal lines. If entered, a discount in the column *Amount in currency* is a discount amount.

Once you have finished entering the line discounts in the agreement journal, click the button *Post* to activate the agreement.

If you want to update or delete an active trade agreement for discounts, open the respective Trade agreement inquiry (e.g., the Line discount inquiry, which you access with the button *Sell/View/Line discount* in the Released product form), select the agreement, and click the button *Edit selected lines*. Like when updating prices, the discounts are updated or deleted when posting a new journal, which is linked to the original agreement.

4.8.1.7 Viewing Current Sales Prices and Discounts

If you want to view the sales prices of an item, which are specified in basic trade agreements, select the item in the Released product form and click the button *Sell/View/Sales price*. In the Customer form, you can click the button *Sell/Trade agreements/Sales price-Sales price* for viewing all sales prices for a customer (including the prices for the applicable price group and all customers).

Sales prices at the group level (representing price lists) are also shown in the Customer price/discount group form (*Sales and marketing > Prices and discounts > Customer price/ discount groups*). Make sure that the option "Price group" is shown in the lookup field *Show* before you select the respective *Price group* in the grid and click the button *Trade agreements/Sales/View sales prices*.

In order to view sales line discount agreements, you can access the line discounts from different menu items (depending on the basis of the discount):

- **For an item** (including the line discount group of the item)—In the Released product form, click the button *Sell/View/Line discount*.
- **For a customer** (including the line discount group of the customer)—In the Customer form, click the button *Sell/Trade agreements/Discounts/Line discount*.
- **For an item discount group**—In the Item discount group form (*Sales and marketing > Prices and discounts > Item discount groups*), make sure that the option "Line

discount group" is selected in the lookup field *Show* and click the button *Trade agreements/Sales/View line discount.*

- **For a customer discount group**—In the Customer price/discount group form (*Sales and marketing > Prices and discounts > Customer price/discount groups*), select the option "Line discount group" in the lookup field *Show* and click the button *Trade agreements/Sales/View line discount.*

In discount agreements, the column *Discount* (or *Amount in transaction currency*) specifies a discount amount—this is only the case if the discount is an amount and not a percentage. The *Discount percentage 1* is shown in a separate column and in the footer pane of the form. The *Discount percentage 2* is only shown in the footer pane. If both, the discount percentage-1 and the percentage-2, are specified in a trade agreement, the multiplied total of these discounts is transferred to the field *Discount percent* in applicable order lines. If a trade agreement contains, for example, a percentage-1 of 10% and a percentage-2 of 10%, the discount percent in the order line is 19%.

Another important setting for the discount calculation is the column *Find next* on the right of the trade agreement lines. The checkbox in this column should only be selected for discounts, which apply in addition to discounts entered at another level. In the example of the trade agreements shown in → Fig. 4.24, the discount in a sales order line with a quantity of 100 units (or more) is 17% for a customer with the applicable line discount group, if the checkbox *Find next* is marked for the 12% discount line and if the item is assigned to the item discount group with a discount of 5% in the other agreement line.

4.8.1.8 Managing Multiline Discounts and Total Discounts

Whereas the basis for the calculation of line discounts is the individual order line, the basis for the calculation of multiline discounts are all lines within a sales order, in which the

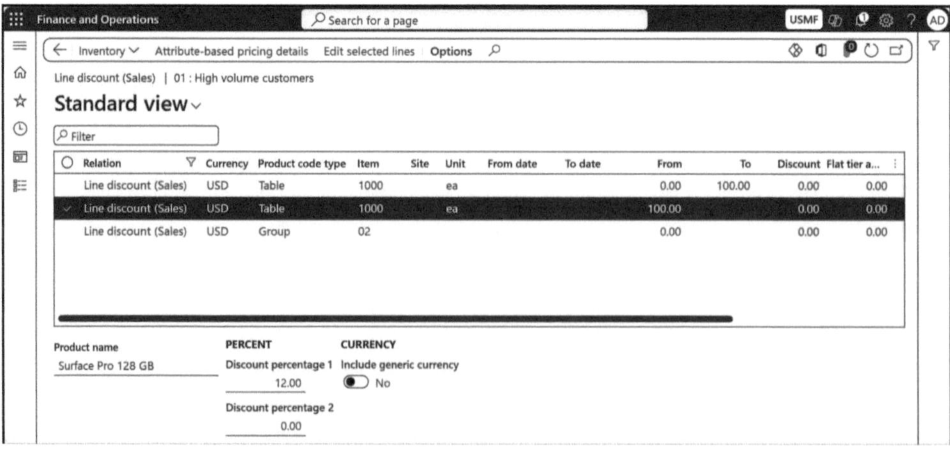

Fig. 4.24 Viewing the line discounts for a customer line discount group

items are assigned to the same multiline discount group. You can use multiline discounts if you want to grant a discount based on the total quantity of several similar items (e.g., for a discount on all items of a group "Accessories"). Managing multiline discounts works similar to managing line discounts.

Unlike line discounts, total discounts (invoice discounts) do not refer to items or item groups. Total discounts refer to a complete invoice and provide the option to enter a discount based on the invoice total.

4.8.1.9 Ledger Integration for Discounts from Basic Trade Agreements

Discounts are reflected in the financial transactions. With regard to the ledger transactions and the sales revenue calculation, you have to distinguish between line and multiline discounts on the one hand, and total discounts on the other hand.

Line and multiline discounts in sales are included in the item revenue calculation—they reduce the revenue and the gross margin. Settings for the ledger integration of line and multiline discounts control whether the discount is posted to a separate account or if it reduces the amount that is posted to the revenue account. Dynamics 365 will post to a separate account if there is an applicable main account for discounts in the posting setup (*Cost management > Ledger integration policies setup > Posting*, tab *Sales order*, option *Discount*).

Unlike line and multiline discounts, total discounts are always posted to a separate account and, at the level of items, do not reduce the revenue in sales or, in purchasing, the cost of purchased materials (which gives the inventory value). In addition, it is not possible to post total discounts to main accounts that depend on the customer. The main account for total discount transactions is specified in the accounts for automatic transactions (*General ledger > Posting setup > Accounts for automatic transactions*, line with the posting type "Customer invoice discount" and "Vendor invoice discount").

4.8.1.10 Basic Trade Agreements Prices and Discounts in Sales Orders

If pricing management (Unified pricing) is not enabled, the unit price in an order line derives from the base sales price in the released product, or from an applicable basic trade agreement. Basic trade agreements are also included in the calculation if pricing management is enabled and the Pricing management parameter *Apply existing trade agreements* is set to "Yes".

Basic trade agreements for prices at the customer level take priority over prices at the price group level. The price group (which represents a price list in Dynamics 365) of a customer is specified in the field *Price* on the tab *Sales order defaults* in the Customer form. When you enter a sales order, the price group of the customer initializes the price group in the order (shown on the tab *Price and discount* in the Header view of the Sales order form). If required, you can change the price group in the order.

In the sales order lines, you can override the calculated sales price and enter a new price in the column *Unit price* manually. If you enter a sales price or a discount manually and later modify data in the fields of the order line that are among the basis of price calculation (e.g., the quantity), Dynamics 365 may override the manual price and discount with an applicable trade agreement. A confirmation dialog is shown before overriding the manual price or discount, if specified in the Accounts receivable parameters (the dialog is shown if the source "Manual entry" is included in the list on the tab *Trade agreement evaluation* in the section *Prices*).

Apart from the basic trade agreements for prices, applicable basic trade agreements for total discounts, multiline discounts, and line discounts initialize an order line, if pricing management is not enabled in your company (or if the Pricing management parameter *Apply existing trade agreements* is active).

When you enter a sales order, the discount groups of the customer are the default for the discount groups on the tab *Price and discount* in the sales order header. If required, you can change the discount group for the line discount, for the multiline discount, and for the total discount in the order header.

Since the total discount is a discount at the header level, not only the discount group, but also the discount percentage for the total discount is included in the order header.

The percentage of a line discount is shown in the column *Discount percent* (or, for a discount amount, in the column *Discount*) of the sales order lines, if pricing management is not enabled in your company. In addition, the line discount and the multiline discount are shown on the sub-tab *Price and discount* in the order line.

If pricing management is enabled, the line discount is always shown as a calculated amount per unit in the column/field *Discount*. It is not possible to edit this discount. You can only enter a manual discount in the field *Manual discount percent* on the sub-tab *Price and discount* in the order line. Depending on the parameter *Manual line discount and system discount* (Pricing management parameters, section *Prices and discounts*, tab *Manual prices and discounts*), the manual discount is added to the calculated discount or replaces it.

The line discount in an order line is calculated when you save the line. Unlike the line discount calculation, the calculation of multiline discounts and total discounts needs to be started manually with the button *Sell/Calculate/Multiline discount* or *Sell/Calculate/Total discount* in the Sales order form.

For the total discount, you can skip the manual calculation if the slider *Calculate total discount on posting* in the Accounts receivable parameters (section *Prices*, tab *Total discounts*) is set to "Yes". In this case, the total discount is calculated whenever you print or post an order.

If the slider *Enable price details* in the Accounts receivable parameters (section *Prices*, tab *Price details*) or in the Pricing management parameters is set to "Yes", you can click the button *Sales order line/Price details* in the toolbar of a sales order line to view extended price and discount information—including the trade agreement that has been used.

> ***Note***: Do not confuse the price group in the Customer form, which can be used in basic trade agreements, with the price groups managed in the All price groups form (*Pricing*

management > During-sales pricing > Price groups > All price groups), which can be used in the extended price group functionality in pricing management and Dynamics 365 Commerce.

4.8.2   Categories and Attributes for Pricing

Products got several characteristics like weight or material, which are relevant in sales, purchasing and logistics. Apart from the product description, which usually mentions the core characteristics, some of these characteristics are stored in a structured way in applicable fields of the Released product form—e.g., the *Net weight* of the item.

In addition to these characteristics, which are relevant for most of the products, some characteristics are only relevant for some products—e.g., the cord length for wired products. In Dynamics 365, you can use attributes for such characteristics.

When working with attributes, you should keep in mind that attributes and categories are managed at a shared level in Dynamics 365, not separately per company.

4.8.2.1 Managing Attributes and Attribute Types

Attribute types (*Product information management > Setup > Categories and attributes > Attribute types*) determine the available values for attributes. The field *Type* in the Attribute type form determines if related attributes are numerical—"Integer" (without decimals) or "Decimal" –, or "Text", or "Boolean" (Yes/No).

For numerical attribute types, you can set the slider *Value range* to "Yes" and enter the *From* and *To* value on the tab *Range*, which is then shown in the form. For attribute types with the *Type* "Text", you can set the slider *Fixed list* to "Yes" and enter the valid options for the attribute value on the tab *Values*, which is then shown.

In the Attributes form (*Product information management > Setup > Categories and attributes > Attributes*), enter at least a *Name* (which initializes the mandatory field *Friendly name*) and the *Attribute type* when creating a new attribute. If you want to use an attribute as a basis for prices and discounts, set the slider *Can be used as price attribute* to "Yes" (→ Fig. 4.25). Most of the other fields are only relevant in Dynamics 365 Commerce.

With an attribute group (*Product information management > Setup > Categories and attributes > Attribute groups*), you can compile multiple attributes that you want to assign to categories and products collectively.

4.8.2.2 Assigning Attributes to Product Categories and Products

Attributes are not directly assigned to products, but the assignment is done via product categories. The category/categories of a product determine the applicable product attributes.

For this reason, category hierarchies and categories (→ Sect. 3.3.1) are a prerequisite setup. You can assign attributes or attribute groups to hierarchies with the following hierarchy role:

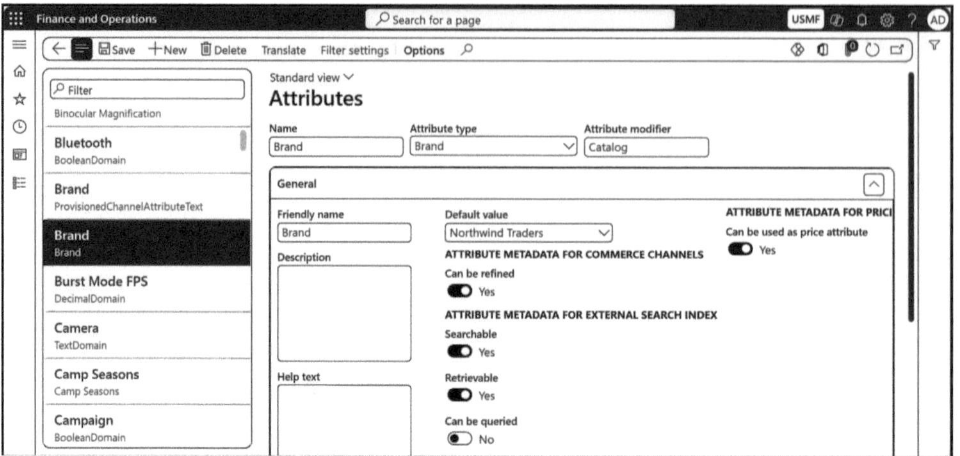

Fig. 4.25 Activating an attribute as a price attribute

- **Procurement category hierarchy**
- **Commerce product hierarchy**
- **Channel navigation category hierarchy**
- **Supplemental product category hierarchy**

If you want to use the procurement categories (categories in the hierarchy with the role "Procurement category hierarchy") for the attribute assignment, open the Procurement category form (*Procurement and sourcing > Procurement categories*), select a category in the left pane, and add the attributes for the selected category on the tab *Product attributes* on the right.

If you want to use the commerce categories (categories in the hierarchy with the role "Commerce product hierarchy") for the attribute assignment, open the Commerce product hierarchy form (*Retail and Commerce > Products and categories > Commerce product hierarchy*), select a category in the left pane, and add the attribute groups for the selected category on the tab *Product attribute groups* on the right. If applicable, you can subsequently add or remove individual attributes with the button *View attributes* in the toolbar of this tab.

In order to assign a product to a category, open the All products form (*Product information management > Products > All products and product masters*) and click the button *Product/Set up/Product categories* to access the Product categories form (→ Sect. 3.3.2). In this form, you can create one or more lines with the *Category hierarchy* (e.g., the Procurement category hierarchy) and the applicable *Category* for the product in this hierarchy. You can also enter the category assignment in the Released product form (there is also the button *Product/Set up/Product categories*), but the assignment is always at the shared level.

Once you have assigned a product to a category of a category hierarchy with the hierarchy role "Procurement category hierarchy", "Commerce product hierarchy", or one of the other roles listed above, you can enter the product attribute values for the product attributes of the category. Click the button *Product/Set up/Product attributes* in the All products form or in the Released product form to access the Product attributes values form (→ Fig. 4.26). In this form, you can enter the attribute values of the product.

4.8.2.3 Attribute Setup for Pricing Management

If you want to use product attributes as a basis for prices and discounts, make sure that the slider *Can be used as price attribute* is set to "Yes" in the applicable attributes.

In order to assign attributes to products, use the commerce categories or the supplemental product categories, which you can find in the Retail and Commerce module. From a functional view, you can also use the procurement categories, but the structure of the procurement hierarchy usually complies with the requirements in purchasing and not with the product structure in sales.

4.8.3   Pricing Management

Pricing management (Unified pricing feature) significantly increases the flexibility of the basic trade agreements for sales prices. In essence, the basic Table/Group/All option for selecting an applicable trade agreement is replaced by the option to refer to numerous fields in the customer and the order header (for the customer dimension) and in the released product and the order line (for the item dimension) for selecting an applicable trade agreement.

With regard to sales discounts, pricing management replaces the basic trade agreements for discounts in regular sales orders with the discount functionality, which formerly has only been available in Dynamics 365 Commerce. This discount functionality has also been enhanced by the option to refer to numerous fields in the customer or order header and in the released product or order line.

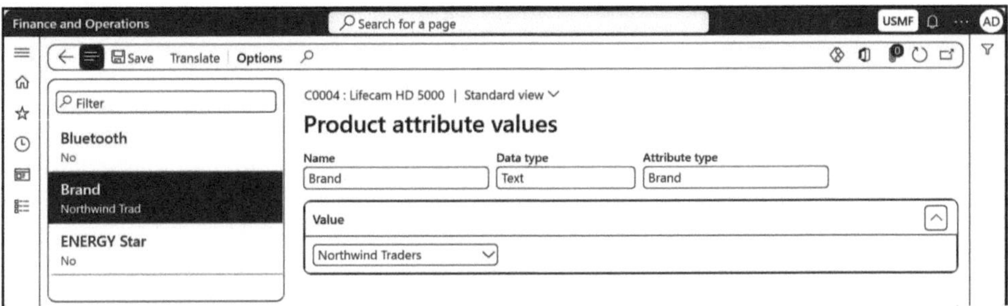

Fig. 4.26 Managing the attribute values of a product

In addition, pricing management also replaces the basic Table/Group/All relation by the option to refer to customer/header and item/line fields in auto charges and in rebate management deals (→ Sect. 4.9.5).

4.8.3.1 Prerequisite Setup for Pricing Management

In order to use pricing management, the feature "Unified pricing management" needs to be enabled in the Feature management. In addition, the slider *Disable pricing management*, the Pricing management parameters (in the section *General*) must be set to "No". The slider *Enable price details* on the tab *Price details* in this section should be set to "Yes" to enable tracking the price and discount origin in orders.

If the parameter *Apply existing trade agreements* (Pricing management parameters, section *Prices and discounts*, tab *Trade agreements*) is set to "Yes", sales prices and discounts from basic trade agreements (→ Sect. 4.8.1) are selected in order lines with no applicable trade agreement price in pricing management.

Trade agreement journal names (*Pricing management > Setup > Trade agreement prices > Trade agreement journal names*) in pricing management work similarly to the basic trade agreement journal names, but the column *Relation* is limited to the option "Price (sales)" and the checkbox in the additional column *Enable price attributes* is activated.

4.8.3.2 Price Attribute Groups and Price Component Codes

Price attribute groups (*Pricing management > Setup > Price attribute groups > Price attribute groups*) determine the fields and product attributes that should be used for selecting applicable prices and discounts. When creating a price attribute group (→ Fig. 4.27),

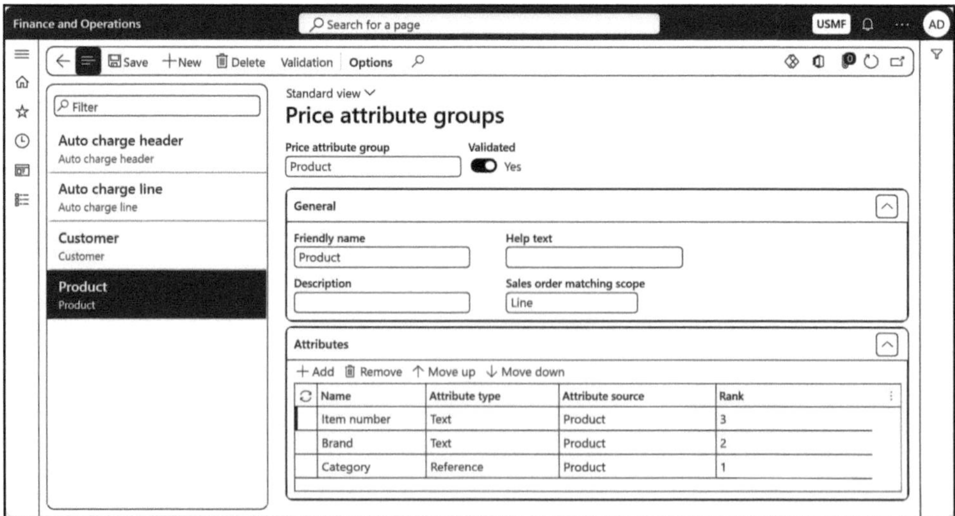

Fig. 4.27 Managing a price attribute group

first select the *Sales order matching scope* ("Header" for customer and order header fields, "Line" for item and order line fields/attributes).

After saving the record, you can add the relevant fields with the button *Add* in the toolbar of the tab *Attributes*. In the dialog, which is then shown, select the price attributes (fields in the customer/order/item tables and product attributes with *Can be used as price attribute* set to "Yes") and click the button *Update*. Once you have completed a price attribute group, click the button *Validation* to activate the group.

Price component codes (*Pricing management > Setup > Price component codes > Price component codes*) collect the price attribute groups that you want to use in pricing management. When creating a price component code, first select the *Price component* ("Sales trade agreement" for sales trade agreement prices, "Margin component" for margin price adjustments, "Discounts" for discounts). The sliders *Use all in header group* and *Use all in line group* control whether it is possible to specify a sales trade agreement price, a margin price adjustment, or a discount for all customers/orders (header attributes) or for all items/lines (line attributes).

On the tab *Header price attribute group*, you can subsequently add the price attribute group(s) at the header level (you can only select attribute groups with the *Sales order matching scope* "Header"). On the tab *Line price attribute group*, you can manage the applicable price attribute group(s) at the line level.

The price tree (*Pricing management > Setup > Price component codes > Price tree*) controls which price component is used in which sequence for searching the applicable price and discount. You can create a price tree (→ Fig. 4.28) with the shortcut *Alt + N*. In

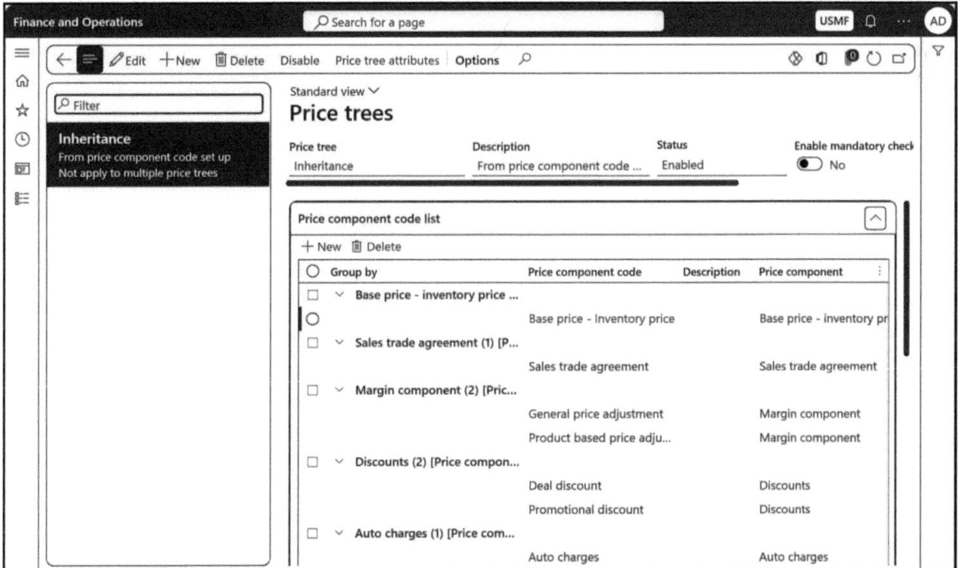

Fig. 4.28 Viewing the price tree with the applicable price component codes

the new record, enter the ID and *Description* before adding the applicable price component codes (for sales price trade agreements, margin price adjustments, discounts, and others) with the button *New* on the tab *Price component code list*. The column *Pricing sequence* on this tab determines the priority of the line. For discounts, the column *Concurrency mode across priority* determines whether multiple discounts or only the highest discount is used. Once you have completed the price tree, click the button *Enable* in the action pane to activate it. If you want to update an active price tree, deactivate it with the button *Disable* first.

If applicable, you can manage multiple parallel price trees—e.g., for a different pricing structure depending on the sales channel. As a prerequisite, particular settings in the section *Price attribute* of the Pricing management parameters are required (set the slider *Enable multiple price trees* to "Yes", select the order attribute that determines the applicable price tree in the *Price tree attribute*).

4.8.3.3 Sales Price Structure in Pricing Management

The unit price—the price in a sales order—is the total of the base price and, if applicable, a margin price adjustment.

The base price itself can derive from the following sources (listed by priority):

- **Sales agreement**—Blanket order (→ Sect. 4.3.1)
- **Trade agreement**—Managed in pricing management
- **Item base price**—Managed in the Base price version form
- **Standard cost price**—Cost price of standard cost items (→ Sect. 7.3.3)
- **Default sales price**—Specified in the released product (→ Sect. 4.2.3)

The trade agreement price, the item base price, and the standard cost price only apply if there is a related price component code that is included in the price tree.

Depending on Pricing management parameter settings (slider *Apply existing trade agreements*), basic trade agreements are also included in the price search.

4.8.3.4 Managing Sales Trade Agreement Prices

Managing a trade agreement for sales prices in pricing management works similarly to managing a basic trade agreement (→ Sect. 4.8.1), but with the option of using header and line attributes instead of the simple Table/Group/All relation.

In the pricing management trade agreement journals (*Pricing management > During-sales pricing > Sales trade agreement price > Trade agreement journals*), you can create a new journal the button *New* in the action pane. The column *Name* only accepts journal names that are configured in pricing management. With the journal selected in the list page, click the button *Lines* to access the journal lines.

Once you click the button *New* in the journal lines, the *Edit price attributes* dialog is shown (→ Fig. 4.29). On the tab *Header price attribute group* in this dialog, select the *Group type* for the header attribute ("All" only if enabled in the *Price component code* for

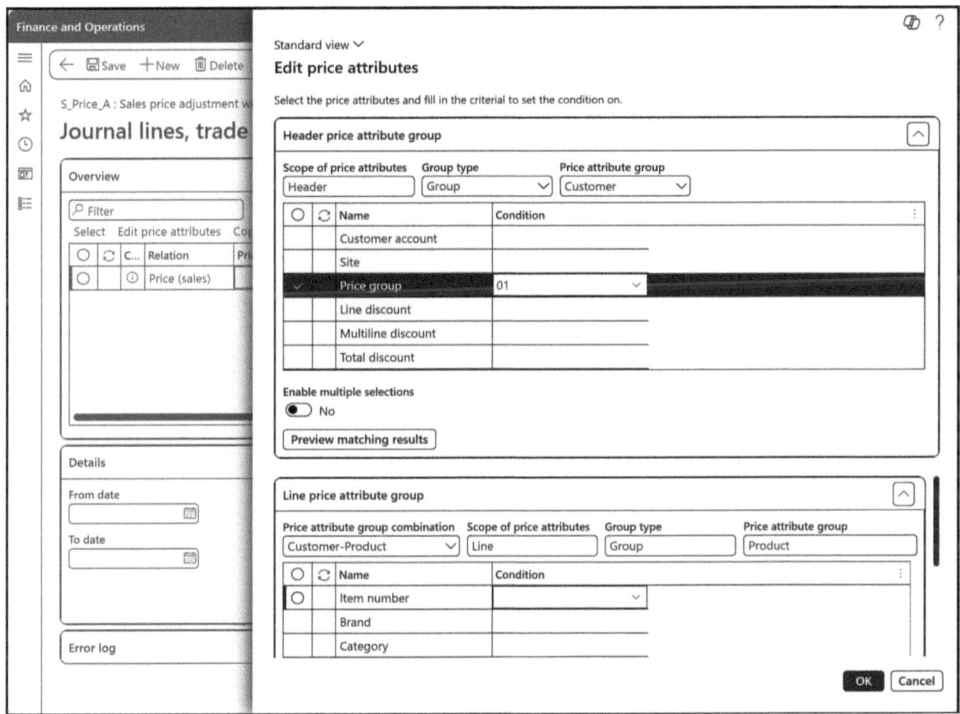

Fig. 4.29   Editing the price attributes of a sales trade agreement journal line

sales trade agreements) and, if you select the *Group type* "Group", the *Price attribute group*. The attributes (selected fields) of the selected group are then shown in a grid beneath. In the column *Condition* of this grid, select the attribute value for at least one attribute. If you set the slider *Enable multiple selections* below the grid to "Yes", you can enter multiple attribute values for an attribute (separated with a comma, like in regular filter criteria). Then, on the tab *Line price attribute group* in the dialog, select the *Price attribute group combination* and enter the attribute value for at least one line attribute in the grid beneath.

Closing the dialog with the button *OK* creates a journal line in which you can view the selected attribute values in the column *Price attribute detail*. If you want to edit the details of a journal line, click the button *Edit price attributes* in the toolbar of the journal lines to access the related dialog again.

In the journal line, you can enter the *From* and *To* quantity, the *Unit*, the *Currency*, the *Amount in currency* (price), and the *From date* and *To date*, like in a regular basic trade agreement journal. Make sure that the checkbox in the column *Allow price adjustment* is selected if you want to apply margin price adjustments. With the checkbox *Prevent discount*, you can determine that no discounts are deducted from the current trade agreement price. If you select the checkbox *Allow unit conversion* in the journal line, the sales price will be converted to other units of measurement (e.g., from pieces to pallets, based on the regular unit conversion).

Once you have completed the journal lines, click the button *Post* in the action pane to activate the trade agreement.

After posting a trade agreement journal, it is not possible to modify it. Like when updating a basic trade agreement, you can only update a sales trade agreement price in pricing management with a new journal in which the journal lines are linked to the applicable active price agreement. You can click the button *Select* in the toolbar of the journal lines in the new journal for this purpose, and, in the Select dialog that is shown next, enter a filter for selecting the original trade agreements that you want to update.

4.8.3.5 Managing Margin Price Adjustments

If you want to adjust the base price, which derives from a trade agreement or another source, you can use margin price adjustments. The unit price shown in a sales order line is the total of the base price and the margin price adjustment.

Margin price adjustments in pricing management are based on price attribute groups and price component codes, similar to the sales trade agreement prices in pricing management. In the price component codes for margin price adjustments, the option "Margin component" has to be selected in the field *Price component*. If applicable, you can set up multiple price component codes for margin price adjustments that are used in parallel. The price tree must include the relevant price component codes for margin price adjustments.

Based on this setup, you can create a margin price adjustment in the Margin component price adjustments form (*Pricing management > During-sales pricing > Price adjustments > Margin component price adjustments*). Click the button *New/Margin component price adjustments* in the action pane to create a new record in which you enter an ID and a *Name*. Then select the applicable *Price component code*.

If the price adjustment does not apply to all orders, click the button *Header price attribute group* and enter the attribute values in the *Edit price attributes* dialog, similar to the options in the sales trade agreement prices described above.

On the tab *Validation period* in the Margin component price adjustments form, you specify the *Effective date* and the *Expiration date*. When creating a line with the button *Add* on the tab *Lines*, the *Edit price attributes* dialog is shown, in which you can view the header attributes. Select the *Price attribute group combination* on the tab *Line price attribute group* of the dialog, and enter the attribute value for at least one line attribute in the grid beneath.

Closing the dialog with the button *OK* creates a price adjustment line in which you can view the selected attribute values in the column *Price attribute detail*. In the line, select the option "Percentage" or "Amount" in the column *Calculation type* and enter the percentage or amount in the respective column. In the column *Unit*, select the applicable unit of measure (in particular relevant for amount adjustments), and select the checkbox *Allow unit conversion* as applicable.

Once you have completed the lines, activate the margin price adjustment by setting the field *Status* on the tab *General* to "Enabled".

If you want to modify a margin price adjustment later on, set the *Status* to "Disabled" before you update the record.

4.8.3.6 Discounts in Pricing Management

Discounts in pricing management are based on the discount functionality in Dynamics 365 Commerce, which is different from the discount functionality in basic trade agreements. The core functionality for discounts in pricing management is the same as for margin price adjustments (see above).

Within pricing management, there are the following options for discounts:

- **Simple discounts**—Reduce the product price by a percentage or amount.
- **Quantity discounts**—Discount when purchasing a minimum quantity (quantity per order, not per line).
- **Threshold discounts**—Discount when purchasing a minimum amount (per order, not per line).
- **Mix-and-match discounts**—Discount when purchasing a combination of products.
- **Free item**—Getting items for free when meeting specified criteria (quantity or amount).

4.8.3.7 Managing Simple Discounts

Like margin price adjustments in pricing management, discounts in pricing management are based on price attribute groups and price component codes, which are included in the price tree. In the price component codes for discounts, the option "Discounts" has to be selected in the field *Price component*. If you use multiple price component codes for discounts and include them in the price tree, the column *Concurrency mode across priority* in the price tree determines whether, with the mode "Compounded", multiple discounts apply or, with the mode "Best price", only the highest discount applies.

If you want to set up a simple discount (→ Fig. 4.30), open the All discounts form (*Pricing management > During-sales pricing > Discounts > All discounts*), in which you can view all the different discounts. Alternatively, you can access the Discounts form (*Pricing management > During-sales pricing > Discounts > Discounts*), which is filtered on simple discounts. Click the button *New/Simple discount* (or *New/Discount*) in the action pane to create a new record in which you enter a *Name* for the discount. Then select the applicable *Price component code*.

If a sales order line is eligible for multiple discounts, the *Pricing priority* determines which discount applies first. The *Pricing priority* of a discount is initialized with the priority of the selected *Price component code* as specified in the price attribute group (column *Rank*), in the price component code (column *Combination rank*), and the price tree (column *Pricing sequence*). If you set the slider *Override priority* to "Yes", you can override the *Pricing priority* of the discount. The option that you select in the field *Discount*

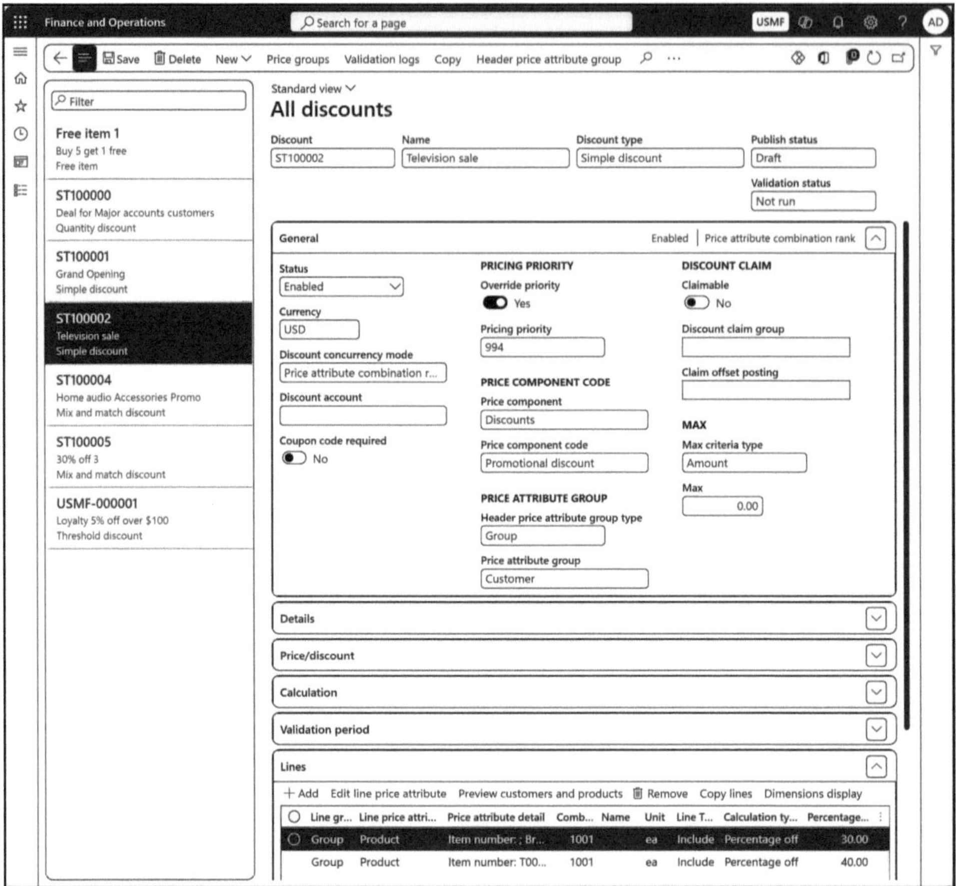

Fig. 4.30 Managing a simple discount in pricing management

concurrency mode controls the way to combine the new discount with other applicable discounts.

If the discount does not apply to all sales orders, click the button *Header price attribute group* and enter the attribute values in the *Edit price attributes* dialog, similar to the options in the sales trade agreement prices described above.

On the tab *Price/discount*, you can enter the *Percentage off*, which initializes the discount lines. The *Effective date* and the *Expiration date* for the discount are specified on the tab *Validation period*.

When creating a line with the button *Add* on the tab *Lines*, the *Edit price attributes* dialog is shown, in which you can view the header attributes. Select the *Price attribute group combination* on the tab *Line price attribute group* of the dialog, and enter the attribute value for at least one line attribute in the grid beneath.

Closing the dialog with the button *OK* creates a discount line in which you can view the selected attribute values in the column *Price attribute detail*. In the line, select the option "Percentage off" or "Amount off" (or "Unit price", if you want to enter a special price) in the column *Calculation type* and enter the percentage or amount in the respective column. In the column *Unit*, you can select the applicable unit of measure (important for "Amount off" and "Unit price" discounts). With the *Line type*, you can specify a discount at the group level in one line and exclude some items of that group in other lines.

Once you have completed the lines, activate the discount by setting the field *Status* on the tab *General* to "Enabled". If you want to modify a discount later on, set the *Status* to "Disabled" before you update the record.

4.8.3.8 Base Price Versions and Item Base Prices

If you do not manage detailed price lists, but work with common sales prices that, for example, are based on fluctuating vendor prices, you can use the item base prices. With margin price adjustments, you can add a percentage or an amount to the base price to specify the final unit price (selling price) in sales orders.

Item base prices are managed in the Base price version form, where you can optionally calculate them from a vendor list price (specified in the Vendor list price form).

As a basis for item base prices, a price component code with the *Price component* "Base price—inventory price" (or "Base price—sales price" or "Base price—purchase price") is required. The price component code needs to be included in the price tree.

You can create a new item base in the Base price version form (*Pricing management > Pre-sales pricing > Base price versions*), which works similarly to the Item price form (→ Sect. 7.3.3). In the Base price version form, select an existing version in the lines or click the button *New* to create a new version. With the button *Price/Base price* in the action pane, you can access the item base prices related to this version. To enter a new price in the Item base price form that is displayed next, make sure that the tab *Pending prices* is shown and click the button *New*. In the new base price, select the *Base price type* "Base price—inventory price" (or, depending on the applicable price component code, "Base price—sales price" or "Base price—purchase price") and enter the *Item number*, the *From date*, and the *Price*. You have to select the *Site* if it is not specified in the base price version. Once you have finished entering the pending prices, click the button *Activate* to activate them. Only active prices, which are shown on the tab *Active prices*, are used in pricing management.

If you want to create item base prices from vendor list prices, enter and enable the vendor prices in the Vendor list price form (*Pricing management > Pre-sales pricing > Vendor list price*). With the button *Calculation* in the Base price version form, you can create item base prices from the vendor list prices. In the Calculation dialog which is shown then, make sure that the slider *Delta calculation* is set to "No" if you want to create base prices irrespective of the vendor list price date. With vendor price term codes and vendor price term agreements, you can specify a percentage or an amount which is added to the vendor list price when calculating the item base price.

4.8.3.9 Pricing Management Features for Auto Charges

Charges in orders are used for additional expenses, which are not covered by the unit price itself (e.g., a fee for freight). With the auto charges functionality, specified charges automatically initialize applicable orders.

Auto charges in pricing management work similar to basic auto charges ($\rightarrow$ Sect. 4.3.4), but with the option of using header and line attributes instead of the simple Table/Group/All relation.

When setting up an auto charge in the Auto charges form in pricing management (*Pricing management > During-sales pricing > Charges setup > Auto charges*), select a *Price component code* (only price component codes with the *Price component* "Auto charges" are available) first. If the auto charge is not applicable to all sales orders, click the button *Header price attribute group* and enter the attribute values in the *Edit price attributes* dialog similar to the options in the sales trade agreement prices described above. For auto charges at the *Level* "Line", you can click the button *Default line attribute group* for the attributes at line level.

The other settings work similar to the settings in basic auto charges.

4.8.3.10 Prices and Discounts from Pricing Management in Sales Orders

With pricing management, the sales price and the discount in an order line derive from the base sales price in the released product and from the price component codes which are included in the price tree.

In the sales order lines, you can override the calculated unit price (which includes applicable margin price adjustments) and enter a new price in the column *Unit price* manually. Depending on the parameter *Apply discounts to price overrides* (Pricing management parameters, section *Prices and discounts*, tab *Miscellaneous*), a calculated discount also applies to manual prices.

Discounts in the order line are shown as an amount per unit in the column *Discount*, no matter if the discount is set up as a discount percentage or amount. It is not possible to update this discount, you can only enter a manual discount in the field *Manual discount percent* on the sub-tab *Price and discount* in the order line. Depending on the parameter *Manual line discount and system discount* (Pricing management parameters, section *Prices and discounts*, tab *Manual prices and discounts*), the manual discount is added to the calculated discount or replaces it.

If the slider *Enable price details* in the Accounts receivable parameters or in the Pricing management parameters is set to "Yes", you can click the button *Sales order line/Price details* in the toolbar of a sales order line to view the sales price trade agreement and other price components which have been included in the price and discount calculation.

> **Note**: In the Price simulator form (*Pricing management > During-sales pricing > Price simulator > Price simulator*), you can check the prices and discounts irrespective of a sales order.

4.8.4   Case Study Exercises

Exercise 4.16—Price and Discount in Basic Trade Agreements
Your company wants to use pricing management, but also basic trade agreements for prices and discounts. In addition, it should be possible to track the origin of prices and discount in sales orders. Make sure that the required setup is in effect.

An additional price list, which you want to use in basic trade agreements, is required for new sales markets. Enter a new customer price group P-## (## = your user ID) for this price list and attach it to the customer of exercise 4.1. The new price list shows a price of USD 90, which is valid from now on, for the item of exercise 3.5. Enter and post this price in a basic trade agreement journal.

In addition, you agree to a line discount of 10% on all items for the customer of exercise 4.1 which applies if the ordered quantity is 50 units or more. Enter and post a basic trade agreement with this discount.

Then enter a sales order with the customer of exercise 4.1, and a line with 60 units of the item of exercise 3.5. Check the price and the discount in the order line.

Exercise 4.17—Sales Price with Pricing Management
In sales orders with the delivery mode "60" (Pickup), there is a special price of USD 85 for the item of exercise 3.5, which is valid for all customers.

Create and validate a price attribute group that covers the header mode of delivery and include it in the price component code for sales trade agreements. Make sure that the applicable price component code is included in the price tree.

Next, enter and post the price for the given delivery mode in a sales trade agreement journal in pricing management.

Then enter a sales order with the customer of exercise 4.1, the delivery mode "60" (Pickup), and a line with 40 units of the item of exercise 3.5. Check the price and the discount in the order line.

Exercise 4.18—Simple Discount with Pricing Management
If customers pick up ordered items, your company offers a discount of 5%.

In order to set up the required discount, create a price component code "Pick up discount" for discounts, which includes the option "All" in the line group. Add the price attribute group of exercise 4.17 (for the header mode of delivery) to the header price attribute group. Then add the new price component code to the price tree (select the concurrency mode "Compounded").

Next, enter and enable a simple discount of 5% with the new price component code and the delivery mode "60" (Pickup) in the pricing management discounts.

Then enter a sales order with the customer of exercise 4.1, the delivery mode "60" (Pickup), and a line with 40 units of the item of exercise 3.5. Check the price and the discount in the order line.

4.9   Trade Allowance and Rebate Management

Apart from the prices and discounts which are immediately shown in a sales order, rebates and trade allowances, which specify a discount that depends on the sales volume in a period, have a later impact on the revenue and profitability of the order.

Customer rebates are contracts that specify a discount depending on the actual sales volume. With rebates, the customer usually receives a credit note or a payment at the end of a period if the total sales amount or quantity meets the target as agreed in the rebate contract.

In addition to customer rebates, Dynamics 365 also covers agreements with vendors, broker contracts, and royalty contracts:

- **Customer rebates**—Rebate contracts with customers.
- **Trade allowances**—Enhanced customer rebate functionality.
- **Vendor rebates**—Rebate functionality in purchasing (similar to sales).
- **Broker contracts**—Reimbursement of agents (set up as vendors) based on the sales revenue with particular customers.
- **Royalty contracts**—Reimbursement of royalty owners (set up as vendors) based on the sales volume with particular items.
- **Rebate management deals**—Extended features for customer rebates, vendor rebates, and royalties in the Rebate management module.

The Rebate management module, which covers the rebate management deals and provides extended rebate features, works independent of the customer and vendor rebates and the related setup.

In customer rebate management deals, which you manage in the Rebate management module, the basic Table/Group/All relation is replaced by the option to refer to customer/header and item/line fields if pricing management is enabled.

4.9.1   Trade Allowances

Trade allowance agreements in Dynamics 365 are used for calculating and paying rebates, and for the analysis of the profitability of promotions. You can group trade allowances in Dynamics 365 into three categories:

- **Bill back**—Allowances based on the posted invoices in a period, paid to the order customer or the invoice customer.
- **Lump sum**—Allowances paid upfront to an agent (vendor or customer).
- **Invoicing rebate**—Allowance immediately deducted from the sales invoice.

Customer rebate agreements (*Sales and marketing > Customer rebates > Rebate agreements*) with the rebate program type "Rebate" and "TMA" work similar to the bill back trade allowance agreement which is described in this section.

4.9.1.1 Required Setup for Trade Allowances

As a prerequisite for trade allowance agreements, you have to set up a customer hierarchy (*Sales and marketing > Trade allowances > Customer category hierarchy*) with the customers who use trade allowances. In order to create a hierarchy, click the button *New* in the action pane of the Customer hierarchy form. With the button *New category node* in the toolbar of the tab *Categories*, you can optionally create a multilevel hierarchy structure as applicable. Then, with the button *Add/remove customer* in the action pane, assign the customers to the top category or the lower nodes. In trade allowance agreements, you can only select customers who are assigned to a hierarchy.

In the merchandising event categories (*Sales and marketing > Setup > Trade allowance > Merchandising event category*), at least one category per trade allowance type is required:

- **Bill back**—Category with *Default type* "Bill back".
- **Lump sum**—Category with *Default type* "Lump sum".
- **Invoicing rebate**—Category with *Default type* "Off invoice".

For bill back trade allowance agreements, at least one program type with the *Rebate program type* "Bill back" has to be set up in the rebate program types (*Sales and marketing > Customer rebates > Rebate program types*).

In addition, the following parameter settings are required for trade allowances:

- **Accounts receivable parameters**—Select an *AR consumption journal* and a *Rebate accrual journal* (section *Rebate program*, tab *Journals*). Optionally set the slider *Rebates at invoicing* to "Yes" (if you want to generate a rebate claim immediately when posting an applicable sales invoice).
- **Trade allowance management parameters** (*Sales and marketing > Setup > Trade allowance > Trade allowance management parameters*)—Enter the required number sequences and optionally select a default *Customer hierarchy* and a *Default rebate program ID*. If you want to use lump sum allowances, optionally select an *Expense account* or a *Procurement category* for lump sum transactions.

4.9.1.2 Funds and Other Optional Settings

Trade allowance funds are used to specify the budget for the costs of trade allowance rebates. Although funds are not a mandatory precondition for trade allowances, it is nevertheless useful to specify the monetary funds as a basis for checking the profitability of sales promotions with rebates.

You can set up trade allowance funds in the Funds form (*Sales and marketing > Trade allowances > Funds > Funds*) with the applicable validity period (*From date* and *To date*) and the budget amount (*Fund budgeted*). Before you activate the fund (change the *Status* to "Approved"), switch to the tab *Customers* and the tab *Items*, and enter the customers and the items that are covered by the fund.

Trade allowance agreement periods (*Sales and marketing > Setup > Trade allowance > Trade allowance agreement period*) provide the option to specify date intervals that you can use as the default value when entering trade allowance agreements.

If you want to apply an approval process for trade allowance agreements, configure the required approval workflows in the menu item *Sales and marketing > Setup > Trade allowance > Trade allowance workflows*.

4.9.1.3 Managing Trade Allowance Agreements

Trade allowance agreements specify rebates for customers. In order to create a new agreement, open the Trade allowance agreements form (*Sales and marketing > Trade allowances > Trade allowance agreements*) and click the button *New* in the action pane. Then enter a description and the validity dates (mandatory fields *Order from* and *Order to*, optionally initialized from the field *Trade allowance agreement period*).

In the field group *Analysis* of the tab *General* in the Header view, select the *Unit*. Then, optionally specify the sales target of the agreement in further fields of this field group— enter the usual sales quantity without trade allowances in the field *Base units*, and the intended increase in the field *Lift percent*.

The contract customers have to be specified on the tab *Customers*. The tabs *Items* and *Funds* in the Header view of the trade allowances contain default values for the trade allowance lines.

In the Lines view of the agreement (→ Fig. 4.31), the tabs *General* and *Customers* include core header data. On the tab *Agreement lines*, the sub-tab *Merchandising events*, which contains the agreement lines with their *Category* (merchandising event category), is shown first. The other sub-tabs contain the details of each agreement line, including the allowance calculation on the sub-tab *Amounts*. The fields on this sub-tab depend on the *Category* in the agreement line ("Bill back", "Lump sum", or "Off invoice").

In a "Bill back" agreement line, the *Minimum quantity* and *Minimum amount* on the sub-tab *Amounts* determine the required minimum sales volume within the cumulating period (selected in the field *Cumulate sales by*) for being eligible to deduct a rebate. The *Payment type* determines whether the customer receives a credit note or a payment:

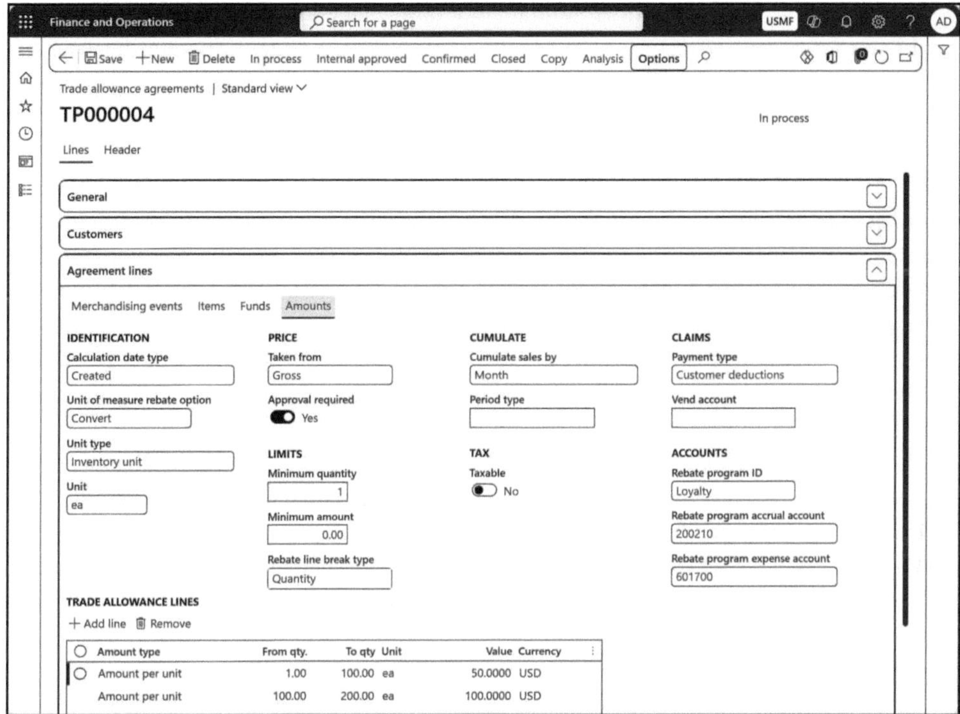

Fig. 4.31 Amount calculation settings in a bill back trade allowance agreement line

- **Payment type "Customer deductions"**—Credit note in the form of a (negative) invoice to the order customer (for orders that are covered by the agreement).
- **Payment type "Invoice customer deductions"**—Credit note to the invoice customer (for the orders that are covered by the agreement).
- **Payment type "Pay using account payable"**—Reimbursement via accounts payable, i.e., by paying the vendor in the field *Vend account* of the agreement line or the vendor who is linked to the order customer (field *Vendor account* on the tab *Miscellaneous details* in the Customer form).

The pane *Trade allowance lines* on the sub-tab *Amounts* in a "Bill back" agreement line contains the rebate calculation. The column *Amount type* in this pane specifies whether the figure in the column *Value* is an amount or a percentage. You can enter multiple trade allowance lines in case the allowance percentage or amount depends on the sales volume. The field *Rebate line break type* in the field group *Limits* determines whether the *From qty* and the *To qty* in the lines show a quantity or an amount.

Once you have completed the trade allowance agreement, click the button *Confirmed* in the action pane to activate the agreement. The trade allowance agreement subsequently shows the status "Confirmed".

If you want to set up multiple similar trade allowance agreements, you can create a template (*Sales and marketing > Trade allowances > Templates*) in a similar way to a regular trade allowance. In the template, you can click the button *Create trade allowances* to create a new trade allowance as a copy of the template.

4.9.1.4 Lump Sum Agreements

Lump sum agreements are one-time payments or credit notes, which aim to support sales promotion activities for customers or vendors. In order to set up a lump sum agreement, enter an agreement line in a trade allowance agreement as described above, but with the *Category* "Lump sum".

In a lump sum agreement line, the sub-tab *Amounts* contains—apart from the field *Amount* for the claim amount—the core fields *Payment type* and *Pay to* with the following options:

- **Payment type "Customer deductions" or "Invoice customer deductions"**—Credit note to the customer in the field *Pay to* of the agreement line (offset account is the expense account specified in the Trade allowance parameters).
- **Payment type "Pay using account payable"**—Reimbursement by a vendor invoice with the vendor in the field *Pay to* (offset account from the procurement category specified in the Trade allowance parameters).

Once you have set the status of the trade allowance agreement to "Confirmed", you can click the button *Approve* in the toolbar of the sub-tab *Amounts* to credit or pay the rebate (depending on the *Payment type* in the agreement line).

You can view the posted customer or vendor invoice for the rebate in the open transactions of the particular customer or vendor.

4.9.1.5 Processing Bill Back Agreements

Rebate claims from a confirmed bill back agreement (trade allowance agreement line "Bill back") are based on sales invoices with the customers and items that are specified in the agreement.

They are immediately created when posting a sales invoice, if the slider *Rebates at invoicing* in the Accounts receivable parameters (section *Rebate program*, tab *Invoicing*) is set to "Yes". If this slider is set to "No", execute the periodic activity *Sales and marketing > Customer rebates > Rebate update > Calculate rebates* to generate rebate claims.

The Bill back workbench (*Sales and marketing > Trade allowances > Bill back workbench*) shows the rebate claims, which refer to a bill back agreement.

For the rebate claims that have been generated, the rebate amounts need to be cumulated (based on the period revenue) at the end of each cumulating period (given by the field *Cumulate sales by* on the sub-tab *Amounts* of the trade allowance agreement line). This cumulation can be done with the button *Cumulate* in the workbench or with the periodic activity *Sales and marketing > Customer rebates > Rebate update > Cumulate rebates*.

Once the rebates are cumulated, you can approve them. Select the lines for approval in the grid of the workbench and approve the rebates with the button *Approve*. Then click the

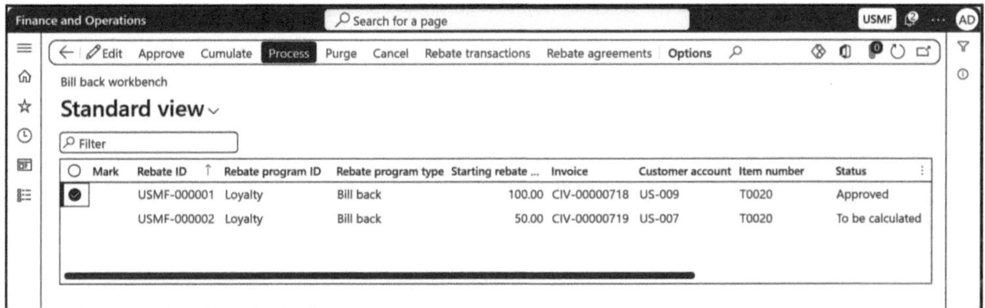

Fig. 4.32 Processing a rebate claim in the Bill back workbench

button *Process* to generate rebate transactions ($\rightarrow$ Fig. 4.32). Processing sets the rebate status to "Mark" and posts accrual transactions.

For a trade allowance agreement line, which shows a cumulating period "Invoice" (field *Cumulate sales by*) and the slider *Approval required* set to "No" (both fields on the sub-tab *Amounts*), all rebate claims are processed immediately. There is no need to cumulate, approve, and process the claims.

You can credit or pay a rebate claim in the open transactions of the customer who receives the rebate. In order to access the open transactions, click the button *Collect/Settle/ Settle transactions* in the Customer form. In the *Settle transactions* dialog that is shown next, click the button *Functions/Bill back program* to open the Rebate form in which you select the checkbox *Mark* of applicable rebate lines. Then click the button *Functions/ Create credit note* to create a sales credit note (in an *AR consumption journal* specified in the Accounts receivable parameter), or the button *Functions/Pass to AP* to create a vendor invoice which is included in the next payment proposal.

Once you have created the sales credit note or vendor invoice, the status of the related rebate claim is "Completed".

4.9.1.6 Canceling and Purging Rebates

If there is a rebate claim from a trade allowance agreement that you do not want to pay or credit, you can cancel the rebate claim after processing it (in the status "Mark"). Click the button *Cancel* in the Bill back workbench for this purpose and enter an appropriate filter in the related dialog. Canceling sets the status of the rebate claim to "Canceled" and reverses the accrual transactions.

With the button *Purge* in the Bill back workbench, you can clean up the workbench. Purging deletes all finished transactions (status "Completed" or "Canceled").

4.9.1.7 Deductions and One-Time Promotions

You can use trade allowance deductions if a customer only pays a reduced amount for an invoice and states that the deduction is an anticipation of an allowance (and the deduction will be included in the rebate payout at period end anyhow). The following setup is required as a prerequisite for deductions:

- **Deduction journal name**—Select a journal name (used for the posting of deductions) in the Trade allowance parameters.
- **Deduction types** (*Sales and marketing > Trade allowances > Deductions > Deduction types*)—Create at least one type with the related offset account.
- **Deduction denial reasons** (*Sales and marketing > Trade allowances > Deductions > Deduction denial reasons*)—If you deny deductions, a reason code is required.

Deductions are recorded together with the customer payment (→ Sect. 9.3.3) in a customer payment journal (*Accounts receivable > Payments > Customer payment journal*). Enter a payment journal line that does not fully match the invoice amount (because of the deduction) and click the button *Deductions* in the toolbar of the tab *List* in the journal lines. In the Deduction form that is shown next, insert a new line with the deduction type, the deduction amount, and the trade allowance ID. The fields in the field group *Balance* at the bottom of the Deduction form show the balance of the settled amount, payment, and deduction. After closing the Deduction form, the payment journal shows an additional line with the deduction. Posting the payment journal generates a separate transaction for the payment and for the deduction.

You can manage the open deductions after posting the payment journal in the Deduction workbench (*Sales and marketing > Trade allowances > Deductions > Deduction workbench*). When you select a deduction line in the upper pane of the workbench, the open transactions (credit notes generated in the trade allowances process) for the related customer are shown in the lower pane. In order to match a deduction with a credit transaction in the Deduction workbench, select the checkbox *Mark* in the appropriate deduction first, and mark applicable rebate transactions in the lower pane next. Then click the button *Maintain/Match* to post the match transaction.

In case a customer has applied a deduction incorrectly, click the button *Maintain/Deny* in the action pane of the Deduction workbench to reverse the deduction. The denied amount is then shown as an open customer transaction.

The button *Maintain/Split* provides the option to split a deduction line—for example, if you want to deny only part of the deduction.

A one-time deduction enables the deduction of an amount that exceeds the trade allowance agreement. You can post it with the button *Maintain/Settle deduction as one-time promotion* in the workbench. The one-time promotion is posted as a lump sum transaction (as an additional promotion) with the trade allowance template that is selected as the *One-time promotion template* in the Trade allowance parameters.

4.9.2 Broker Contracts

Broker contracts are agreements with agents (set up as vendors), which require paying the agent based on the sales volume with selected customers and items.

4.9.2.1 Required Setup for Broker Contracts

As a prerequisite for broker contracts, you have to set up at least one charges code (Ledger—Ledger) for broker charges in the sales charges (*Accounts receivable > Charges setup > Charges code*). This code is required for posting the broker charges ledger transaction when posting a sales invoice.

In the Accounts payable parameters (section *Broker and royalty*, tab *Brokerage*), select a procurement category for broker claim expenses and applicable journal names. A number sequence for the *Broker claim invoice* is required in the section *Number sequences* of the parameters.

4.9.2.2 Entering and Processing Broker Contracts

Since a broker is a vendor, the broker contracts are included in the Accounts payable module (*Accounts payable > Broker and royalties > Broker contracts*). When you set up a broker contract, select the broker and a default for the *Charges code* and the *Category* in the upper pane of the form. In the lower pane, specify the items and customers that are covered by the broker agreement. The *Break type* and *Break* in a line determine the minimum quantity or amount that is required to apply a broker charge. Depending on the *Category* in the line, the *Charges value* is a percentage or an amount. You can enter multiple lines in the lower pane in case some charges depend on the sales quantity or amount. When you are finished, select the option "Approved" in the column *Status* of the upper pane to activate the contract.

In a sales order line that is covered by a broker contract, you can click the button *Sales order line/Broker commission* in the toolbar of the lines to view the calculated broker commission. The button *Financials/Maintain charges* in the sales order line provides access to the related charges transaction. Posting the sales order invoice generates an accrual (based on the charges transaction) and a broker claim.

In the broker claims (*Accounts payable > Broker and royalties > Broker claims*), you can view the claims that are generated from sales invoices. In order to pay a claim, make sure that the checkbox *Mark* is selected in the applicable lines and click the button *Approve*. The approval is posting a reversal of the accrual and a new vendor invoice with the broker expense.

4.9.3   Royalty Agreements

Royalty agreements in Dynamics 365 support contracts with royalty owners (set up as vendors), which require paying a fee (e.g., a license fee) to the royalty owner based on the sales volume of selected items. Royalty contracts work similarly to vendor rebate agreements, but they are based on the customer invoice transactions covered by the royalty agreement.

The required setup for royalty contracts in the Accounts payable parameters includes settings in the sections *Broker and royalty* and *Number sequences*.

Based on the royalty contracts (*Accounts payable > Broker and royalties > Royalty agreements*), you can process the claims in the Royalty claims form (*Accounts payable > Broker and royalties > Royalty claims*).

4.9.4 Vendor Rebates

Rebate and trade allowance agreements are not only available in the Sales module. You can also manage rebate agreements with vendors in Dynamics 365.

Setting up vendor rebate agreements (*Procurement and sourcing > Vendor rebates > Rebate agreements*) works similarly to customer rebate agreements and trade allowance agreements. You can process the claims subsequently in the Rebate claims form (*Procurement and sourcing > Vendor rebates > Rebate claims*). The required setup for vendor rebate agreements includes the Procurement and sourcing parameters (section *Rebate program*) and the setup forms in the menu folder *Procurement and sourcing > Vendor rebates*.

4.9.5 Rebate Management Deals

The Rebate management module, which you can use instead of the trade allowances, customer rebates, vendor rebates, and royalties, provides extended features for rebates. It is shared across companies, and you can specify for each deal in which companies it should be used. Apart from a financial rebate in the form of a payment or a credit note, a rebate may also grant a free item delivery.

4.9.5.1 Setup for Rebate Management

If you want to use the Rebate management module, set in set the slider *Activate* in the section *Feature visibility* of the Rebate management parameters (*Rebate management > Setup > Rebate management parameters*) to "Yes". The applicable rebate management features are subsequently shown in all modules. The section *Rebate management* in the parameters includes further settings like the option to post rebates automatically.

Different from the trade allowance agreements with an optional approval workflow, the rebate management deals must be approved in an approval process. Configure the required approval workflows in the menu item *Rebate management > Setup > Rebate management workflows*.

Optional settings include the rebate reduction principles (*Rebate management > Setup > Rebate reduction principles*), which control how rebates are calculated if multiple rebate management deals apply to a sales transaction, and the rebate status (*Rebate management > Setup > Status > Status*), which enables characterizing the status of a deal—e.g., active or completed.

Rebate management groups for customers, vendors, and items, which you can set up and assign in the menu items of the folder *Rebate management > Rebate management groups setup*, are also optional.

The rebate management posting profiles (*Rebate management > Rebate management posting setup > Rebate management posting profiles*) control the way in which rebates are calculated and posted. The field *Module* in this form specifies whether the profile is for customer transactions or vendor transactions. The available options in the *Payment type* are similar to the options in a trade allowances bill back agreement (with the options "Customer deductions" and "Pay using account payable"), but with the additional option "Tax invoice customer deductions" for posting a free text invoice with the rebate (instead of just posting a journal with the option "Customer deductions"). The *Credit account* on the tab *Posting* is the accrual account, and the *Debit account* at the bottom of the form specifies the expense account for rebates. In the field *Use account source*, select the option "Deal line account" (and "Customer/Vendor" in the field *Type*) to award the rebate to the customer in the sales order, or the option "Fixed account" to award it to a fixed customer or ledger account irrespective of the sales customer.

4.9.5.2 Pricing Management Settings for Rebate Management Deals

If pricing management is enabled ($\rightarrow$ Sect. 4.8.3), some additional setup is required. Rebate management deals are then based on the price attribute groups and price component codes (*Pricing management > Setup > Price component codes > Price component codes*) that are included in the price tree. In the price component codes for rebates, the option "Rebate management" has to be selected in the field *Price component*.

The rebate agreement types (*Rebate management > Setup > Rebate agreement types*), which are another mandatory setup if pricing management is enabled, refer to the price component codes.

4.9.5.3 Managing Rebate Management Deals

Rebate Management deals (*Rebate management > Rebate management deals > All rebate management deals*) include customer rebates, vendor rebates, and royalties.

When you create a new deal with the button *New* in the action pane, a *Create* dialog is shown, in which you enter several fields including the *Module* ("Customer" for customer rebates), *Type* ("Rebate" for rebates), *Reconcile by* ("Line" for processing rebates at the line level; the *Posting profile* is specified on deal line level in this case). In the field *Rebate output*, make sure that the option "Financial" is selected for a rebate that is granted in the form of a payment or a credit note.

> *Note*: If pricing management is enabled, the Rebate agreement type, which controls the applicable attributes/fields for assigning deal lines to customers and items, is an additional mandatory field in the Create dialog for customer rebate deals.

In the rebate deal lines, enter one or more lines referencing the customer (customer number, customer rebate group, or all), the item (item number, item rebate group, or all), and inventory dimensions as applicable.

On the sub-tab *General* in the tab *Rebate management details* of a rebate management deal line, select the *Calculation method* and the *Basis*. Whereas the trade allowances are only based on invoices, rebate deals can also refer to orders or to deliveries—select the applicable *Transaction type* in the rebate management details. The lookup field *Posting profile* specifies the applicable settings for posting.

On the sub-tab *Dates* in the tab *Rebate management details*, enter the period of validity for the deal line.

The sub-tab *Lines* contains the rebate calculation. You can enter multiple lines on this sub-tab in case the rebate amount or, only if the field *Rebate output* in the header is set to "Financial", the percentage depends on the sales volume.

Once you have completed the rebate management deal, click the button *Workflow/ Submit*. The further approval process depends on the rebate management workflow. Once approved, the slider *Active* in the deal header is set to "Yes".

4.9.5.4 Processing Rebate Management Deals for Customers

Depending on the settings in the rebate management deal (field *Transaction type* in the deal line), rebate claims from a customer rebate deal are based on sales orders, packing slips, or invoices with the customers and the items that are specified in the deal lines. If you want to exclude a sales order line from rebate calculation, set the slider *Exclude from rebate management* on the sub-tab *Price and discount* in the line details to "Yes".

Rebate provisions are immediately created when posting an invoice or a packing slip if the slider *Process at posting* on the sub-tab *Dates* in the rebate management deal line is set to "Yes". If this slider is set to "No", you have to execute the periodic activity *Rebate management > Periodic tasks > Process > Provision* (or click the respective button in the rebate management deal).

Rebate provisions are shown in the Rebate workbench (*Rebate management > Rebate management deals > Rebate workbench*) or in the rebate transactions, which you can access with the button *Rebate management deals/Transactions/Transactions* in the Rebate management deal form. With the button *Rebate workbench/View/Source transactions* (or the respective button in the rebate transactions), you can view the basis (sales transaction) of the rebate transaction. Depending on the Rebate management settings for automatic posting, you have to post the provision (click the button *Rebate workbench/Processing/ Post*) to generate the target transaction (accrual journal).

In order to pay or refund the rebate, process the rebate with the periodic activity *Rebate management > Periodic tasks > Process > Rebate management* (or click the respective button in the Rebate workbench). When posting the rebate transaction which has been created then, a deduction journal (credit note), or a vendor invoice (for payment), or a free text invoice (credit note which can be printed) will be created as target transaction (depending on the *Payment type* in the rebate management deal line) together with a transaction which offsets the accrual.

Production Control

5

The primary responsibility of production control is to manage the manufacturing of products. In manufacturing, materials and resource capacity are consumed.

5.1 Business Processes in Manufacturing

Depending on the requirements, a company may use the following manufacturing concepts in Dynamics 365:

- **Discrete manufacturing**—Core production functionality with bills of materials (BOMs), resources, routes, and production orders.
- **Process manufacturing**—Covers the additional requirements of batch-producing industries (e.g., the chemical industry) with formulas.
- **Lean manufacturing**—Covers production flows and Kanbans (completely independent of routes and production orders).

You can apply the concepts in a mixed mode and, for example, use process manufacturing for components and lean manufacturing for finished products.

This chapter covers the core functionality in discrete manufacturing and includes an outline of process manufacturing. Before we start to go into details, the lines below give an overview of the processes in discrete manufacturing.

A. Luszczak, *Using Microsoft Dynamics 365 Finance and Operations*,
https://doi.org/10.1007/978-3-658-50563-9_5

5.1.1 Basic Approach

Like in purchasing and sales, correct master data are an essential prerequisite for order processing in production control.

5.1.1.1 Master Data and Transactions in Production Control

The released product record contains the main characteristics of an item. The composition of a finished or semi-finished item, which includes a list of components (materials or lower-level semi-finished items), is given by the bill of materials (BOM).

Resources (machines or workers) are another basic element—they provide the required capacity for manufacturing. Routes and operations, which describe the activities for manufacturing an item, determine the required resources.

Products, BOMs, resources, and routes are master data, which are created once and only occasionally updated later. In the course of production order processing, default values from the master data initialize the planned and actual production orders (transaction data). You can override these data in the transaction—e.g., if you need a non-standard bill of materials in a particular production order.

In → Fig. 5.1, you can view the main steps in production order processing.

5.1.1.2 Demand and Supply Planning

Since it calculates the required quantity of finished products, master planning (→ Sect. 6.3) often is the starting point for the manufacturing process. Depending on the settings for scheduling, the calculated item demand (required quantity) derives from sources like forecasts, sales quotations, sales orders, or a minimum stock.

5.1.1.3 Creating Production Orders

Master planning generates planned production orders, which you can convert to actual production orders. Including the option of converting planned orders, there are the following ways to generate a production order:

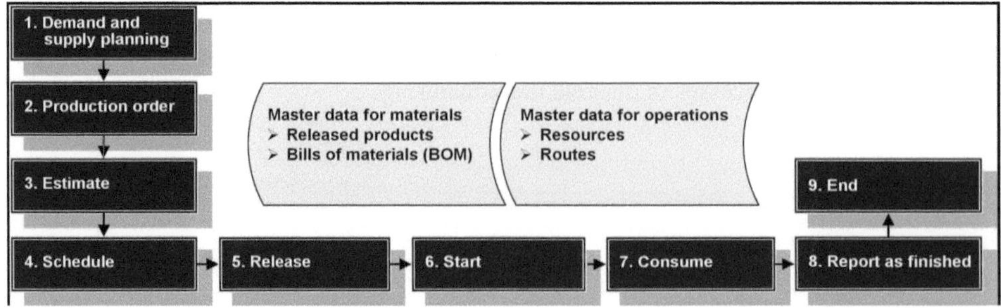

Fig. 5.1 Production order processing in Dynamics 365

- **Manual**—Enter an order in the Production order form.
- **Planned production order**—Convert/firm a planned order.
- **Sales order**—Create a production order from a sales order line.
- **Pegged supply**—Automatically creating production orders for semi-finished products (sub-production) from the production order of a finished product.
- **Project**—Create production orders from a project (Project accounting module).

A production order consists of an order header, which contains the manufactured item, and lines. Unlike purchase orders or sales orders, which only include order lines with items, a production order contains two types of lines—BOM lines with items and route operations. These different line types are shown in separate forms.

After creating a production order, you have to execute all subsequent steps—from estimating to ending—one after another. But depending on parameter settings, you can skip steps when processing a production order.

5.1.1.4 Estimation and Scheduling

Once you have created a production order, estimation is the first step in order processing. The estimation determines the quantity and the cost of items and resources that are required to manufacture the product.

Whereas the estimation calculates the item and resource demand without specifying date or time, scheduling, as the next step, determines exact production dates.

5.1.1.5 Releasing and Starting

Releasing a production order means handing it over from the front office to the shop floor. At this stage, you can print production papers as required.

Once you want to start activities on the shop floor, set the order status to "Started". You can't consume items or resources before the order has this status. When starting an order, you can print the picking list and post the automatic consumption of items and resource capacity.

5.1.1.6 Production Journals

In the manufacturing process, the shop floor consumes materials and resource capacity. This consumption is reported in production journals. Depending on the requirements, you can post the journals manually or backflush automatically (with estimation data). Alternatively, you can use Dynamics 365 Manufacturing execution features to report the consumption on terminals and mobile devices.

5.1.1.7 Reporting as Finished and Ending

Once you have produced a partial or the entire quantity of the manufactured item, post a "Report as finished" transaction. Reporting as finished increases the physical inventory of the manufactured item. Ending the production order is the last step in production order processing. It calculates the actual cost of production and posts the financial transactions to the general ledger.

5.1.1.8 Ledger Integration and Voucher Principle

Production journals, which record the consumption of materials or resources and the receipt of manufactured items, post physical transactions to the general ledger. The financial transactions are posted when ending the order (→ Sect. 9.4.3).

The voucher principle, which is the general principle for processing transactions in Dynamics 365, also applies to transactions in manufacturing: You have to register a transaction in a journal before you can post it (→ Fig. 5.2).

5.1.2   At a Glance: Production Order Processing

The following example demonstrates the main steps in production order processing. It starts with creating the order in the workspace *Production floor management* and shows how to post all transactions directly in the Production order form. Alternatively, you can create the order in the Production order form.

In the workspace *Production floor management*, click the button *Create new/Production order* in the action pane to create a regular order (for discrete manufacturing). In the *Create production order* dialog that is shown next, select the *Item number* of the manufactured item. The quantity, the BOM, and the route in the production order are initialized with default values from this item. Click the button *Create* in the dialog to create the production order with these data.

If the Production order detail form (→ Fig. 5.3) is in Read mode, click the button *Edit*, or press the *F2* key, to switch to the Edit mode. If you want to view or edit the BOM or the

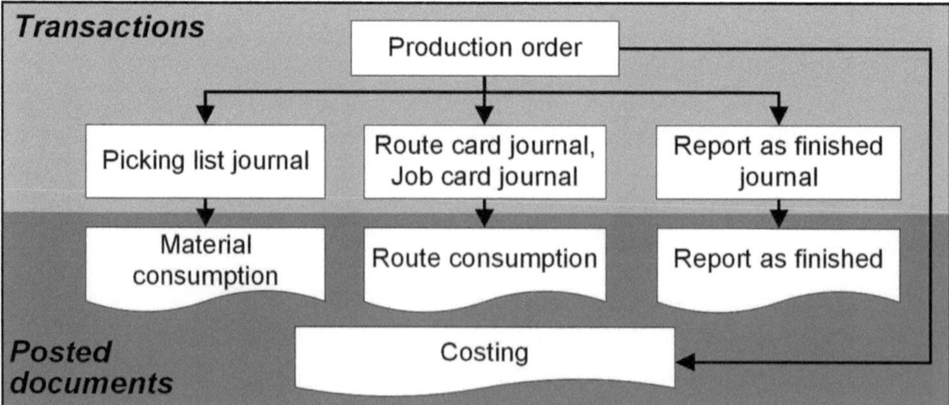

Fig. 5.2 Transactions and posted documents in production control

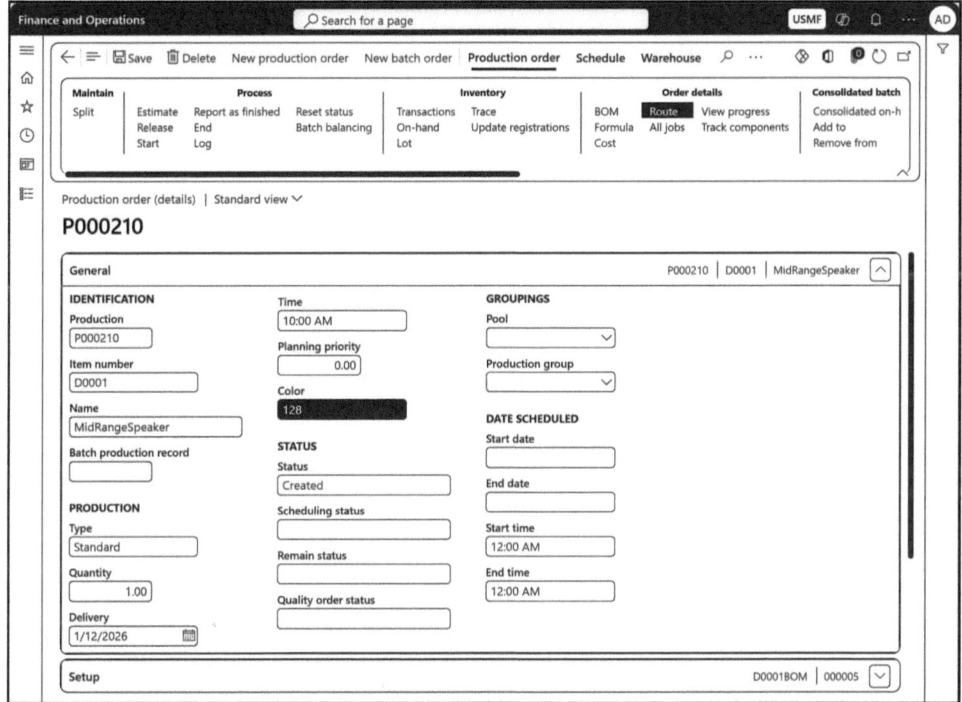

Fig. 5.3 Managing a production order in the Production order form

route of the order, click the button *Production order/Order details/BOM* or *Production order/Order details/Route* in the action pane.

In the course of processing the production order, update the order status with the following buttons in the action pane, one after another:

- *Production order/Process/Estimate*
- *Schedule/Production order/Schedule operations* or *.../Schedule jobs*
- *Production order/Process/Release*

When updating the status, you can select applicable parameters on the first tab (or on the tab *General*) of each update dialog—for example, if you want to modify the scheduling direction when scheduling, or to print production papers when releasing. If you skip a step, it is automatically executed with the next step. Once you want to execute the work for the order on the shop floor, start the order with the button *Production order/Process/Start*. Starting posts an automatic material and route consumption as applicable. In addition, you can print the picking list.

In order to record the consumption of items with the flushing principle "Manual", click the button *View/Journals/Picking list* in the production order to access the picking list journal (→ Fig. 5.4). If you want to generate a proposal with picking list lines, click the

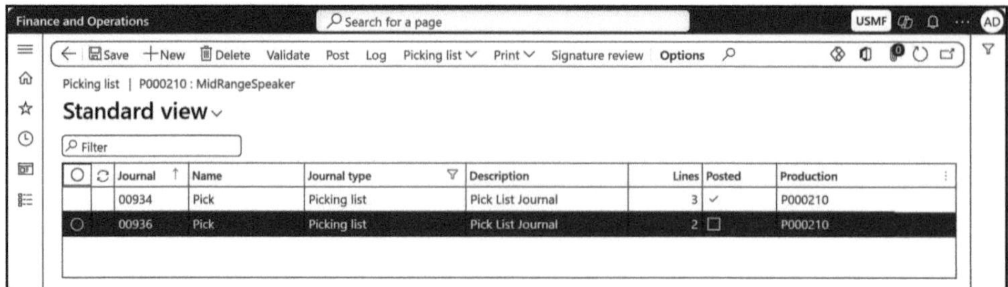

Fig. 5.4 Picking list journal page with a journal that is not yet posted

button *Picking list/Create lines* in the Journal list page. In the *Create lines* dialog, which is shown in this case, select the option "Remaining quantity" in the lookup field *Proposal* to initialize the journal lines with the open quantity. In the Lines view of the Journal detail form (shown automatically after generating the proposal, or manually with a click on the journal ID shown as a link in the list page), you can edit the quantity, the warehouse, and other data before you post the journal with the button *Post*.

Depending on the setup and on the scheduling type (*Operations scheduling* or *Job scheduling*) that you have selected when scheduling the production order, you can enter the actual working time consumption either at the route level or at the job level (click the button *View/Journals/Route card* or *View/Journals/Job card* in the order). In route card journals and job card journals, there is no proposal that initializes the lines with default values when you manually enter a journal. You can create the journal with the button *New* in the route card (or job card) journal and select the journal name in the *Create production journal* dialog before you close the dialog with the button *OK*. In the Lines view of the Journal detail form, which is shown next, enter one or more lines with the date, operation/ job number, resource, hours, and good quantity before you click the button *Post*.

In order to receive the manufactured item in inventory, click the button *Production order/Process/Report as finished* in the production order. If you want to ignore missing consumption postings, set the slider *Accept error* on the tab *General* of the dialog to "Yes". Once all transactions of the production order are posted, close the order with the button *Production order/Process/End*.

5.2 Product Management and Bill of Materials

All items, which are involved in the manufacturing process, have to be set up in the shared and the released products. Apart from inventoried items like finished products, semi-finished products, and raw materials or parts, product records are also required for phantom items or purchased services.

The bill of materials (BOM) specifies the materials that are included in a manufactured item. You can assign one or more bills of materials to an item, but you can also assign one common bill of materials to multiple items. A single item is assigned to multiple bills of materials if the applicable bill of materials is, for example, dependent on the lot size or the production date.

5.2.1   Product Data in Manufacturing

The form for shared products (*Product information management > Products > All products and product masters*) and the Released product form (*Product information management > Products > Released products*) include all products—finished products, semi-finished products, and raw materials or parts. The workspace *Released product maintenance* is another place for managing the released products.

You can find a general description of the product management in Dynamics 365 in → Sect. 7.2. The following section contains an explanation of the product data that are primarily necessary for production control. Except for the product type and the product subtype, which are specified in the shared product, these data are stored in the released product.

The engineering change management with product versions (→ Sect. 7.2.5) provides a structured way to manage the process of creating new and modifying existing products, in particular for manufacturing.

5.2.1.1 Item Model Group, Production Type, and Default Order Type

With regard to production control, a core setting for items is the *Item model group* on the tab *General* in the Released product detail form. All items that are used in production control—including finished products, semi-finished products, and raw materials or parts—have to be assigned to an item model group for stocked products (→ Sect. 7.2.1). Non-inventoried items (e.g., subcontractor work) which are included in BOM-lines also have to be assigned to an item model group for stocked products, which is why you select the *Product type* "Service" in the shared product records of non-inventoried items that you want to include in a BOM (this way avoiding inventory control for the items).

In the lookup field *Production type* on the tab *Engineer* in the Released product detail form, select the option "BOM" for finished or semi-finished products. If you select the production type "Formula" or "Planning item", you can assign a formula (related to process manufacturing) instead of a BOM to the item. The production type "None" prevents assigning a BOM to the item, and without a BOM, you can only purchase the item—not produce it. But you can also purchase an item with another production type than "None" (e.g., with the production type "BOM"), because the *Default order type*, and not the *Production type*, determines the primary sourcing strategy for the item.

The field *Default order type*, which controls item sourcing, is shown on the tab *General* in the default order settings. In order to access the default order settings, click the button *Manage inventory/Order settings/Default order settings* in the Released product form. There are the following options for the default order type:

- **Purchase order**—Purchase orders are used to supply the item.
- **Production**—Production orders are used to supply the item.
- **Kanban**—Kanbans (in lean manufacturing) are used to supply the item.

If you need to override the default order type at the level of a particular site, warehouse, or another inventory dimension, click the button *Plan/Coverage/Item coverage* in the released product to open the Item coverage form. On the tab *General* in the item coverage, you have to select the checkbox *Change planned order type* before you can select a dimension-specific order type in the field *Planned order type*.

5.2.1.2 Settings for Quantity and Price

Apart from the default order type on the tab *General*, the tab *Inventory* in the default order settings contains data which are also used for production orders—including default values for the lot size (field *Multiple*) and the order quantity (field *Standard order quantity*). You can override the default order settings at the company level (which is the record with a blank *Site*) with order settings at the site level (create additional records with the respective *Site*).

On the tab *Manage costs* in the Released product form, the field *Price* specifies the general cost price of the item. In the Item price form, which you can access with the button *Manage costs/Set up/Item price* in the released product, you can register site-specific cost prices (→ Sect. 7.3.3).

In a released product with an item model group with the valuation model "Standard cost", a cost price in a costing version with the costing type "Standard cost" has to be activated in the Item price form before you can record transactions.

5.2.1.3 Phantom Items

The slider *Phantom* on the tab *Engineer* in the Released product form determines the default for the *Line type* when inserting the item as a component in a BOM line. Phantom items are (virtual) semi-finished products with a bill of materials and (optionally) a route. When you estimate a production order, BOM lines with the type "Phantom" are exploded. The production order then contains BOM lines with the components of the phantom item (instead of a line with the phantom item itself).

You can use a phantom item to facilitate BOM management if there are manufactured items that include a lot of common components, and these components do constitute a physical semi-finished item. If you collect the common items in the BOM of a phantom item, you only need to select one phantom item instead of all concerned components in all BOMs of the manufactured items. When changing a component, you only need to modify the BOM of the phantom item later on.

5.2.1.4 Flushing Principle

The *Flushing principle* on the tab *Engineer* in the Released product detail form controls whether the respective item should be consumed automatically in production orders (if it is included in the BOM lines). There are four different options for the flushing principle:

- **Start**—Automatic consumption when starting the production order.
- **Finish**—Automatic consumption when reporting as finished.
- **Manual**—No automatic consumption.
- **Available on location**—Only used with the advanced warehouse management (automatic consumption if available on the production input location).

In the BOM lines, you can override the flushing principle specified in the released product record of the respective item.

As a prerequisite for the automatic consumption based on the flushing principle in the released product or the BOM line, you have to select the option "Flushing principle" in the dialog when starting a production order or when reporting as finished ($\rightarrow$ Sect. 5.4.3).

5.2.2 Bills of Materials (BOM)

A bill of materials (BOM), which is a list of items, specifies the components of a manufactured item (finished or semi-finished product).

5.2.2.1 Bill of Materials Structure

In Dynamics 365, the components (raw materials, parts) of a manufactured item are not directly assigned to the product, but to a bill of materials. This bill of materials is then separately assigned to the manufactured item ($\rightarrow$ Fig. 5.5). The assignment of a BOM to a manufactured item is called "BOM version" in Dynamics 365. You can assign one or more BOMs to a manufactured item.

Items in a BOM line may consist of other items and therefore refer to a lower-level BOM. Such items are semi-finished items. With semi-finished items, there is a multi-level product structure.

The BOM level shows the number of product levels between the selected product and the final finished product. Products, which are not a component in any BOM, show the level "0". Semi-finished products, which are only included in the most upper-level BOM of finished products, show the level "1".

The BOM level is relevant for master planning (should first calculate the demand for finished products, because this demand determines the demand for lower-level components) and for cost calculation (should first calculate the price of lower-level components to use already updated prices for calculating upper levels).

A product can be a component in the BOMs of multiple products with different levels. A screw, for example, may be directly used in a finished product and, in parallel, be a

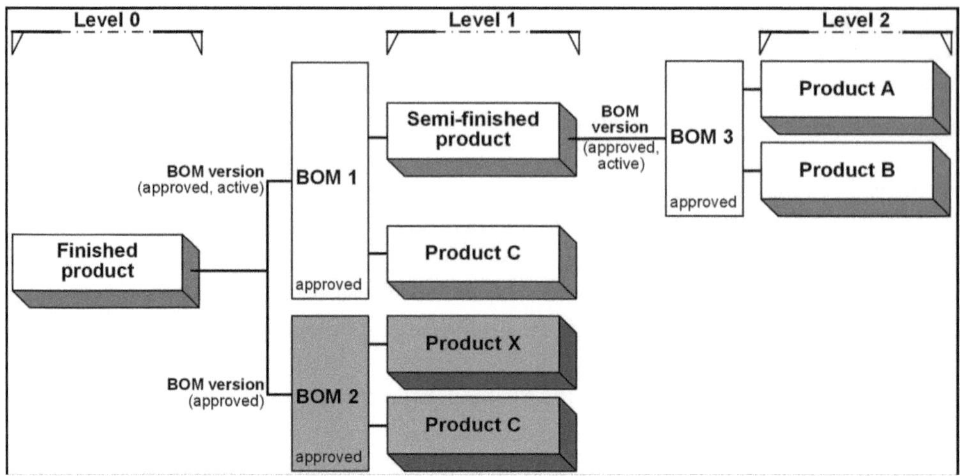

Fig. 5.5 Example of a multi-level product structure with BOMs and BOM versions

component of a semifinished product. For this reason, there are different fields for the BOM level on the tab *Engineer* of the Released product form—the *Costing level*, the *Planning level*, and the *Cost calculation level*. The difference between the *Costing level* and the *Cost calculation level* is that the *Costing level* includes production BOMs (BOMs in production orders) in the calculation, whereas the *Cost calculation level* only includes BOMs that are assigned to released products.

You can update the BOM level with the periodic activity *Product information management > Periodic tasks > Recalculate BOM levels*. In addition, the BOM level is recalculated in parallel with other relevant periodic tasks.

In order to make use of a bill of materials in production control, the BOM and the BOM version have to be approved. In addition, the BOM version has to be activated if it is to be used as the default value in production orders and in master planning. An active BOM version for an item has to be unique per date, from-quantity, and site.

5.2.2.2 Entering Bills of Materials and BOM Versions

You can access the bills of materials in the following way:

- **From the released product** (button *Engineer/BOM/BOM versions* in the Released product form)
- **From the menu** (*Product information management > Bills of materials and formulas > Bills of materials*)

The workspace *Product readiness for discrete manufacturing* is another place, from which you can access (use the link *Bills of materials* on the very right) and create (click the button *New/BOM* in the action pane) bills of materials. The BOM form is the same, no matter whether you access it from the workspace or from the menu.

Although the BOM form (accessed from the menu or the workspace) and the BOM version form (accessed from the released product) update the same BOM and BOM version data, the functionality and the structure of these forms are different.

Since understanding the data structure is easier if you start from the menu, the lines below first explain the BOM form in the menu. If you open the menu item *Product information management > Bills of materials and formulas > Bills of materials*, a list page with the bills of materials is displayed.

In order to open the BOM detail form (→ Fig. 5.6), click on a BOM ID in the first column of the list page. In the BOM detail form, the Lines view shows the BOM lines. With the button *Header* in the detail form, you can access the Header view with the BOM versions, which constitute the assignment of manufactured items to the BOM.

In order to create a new bill of materials, click the button *New* in the action pane of the BOM form. The BOM detail form then shows the Lines view with an empty record in the tab *Bill of materials header*, in which you enter the *Name* of the BOM (e.g., identical to the product name). Depending on the settings of the applicable number sequence, the BOM ID is assigned automatically or has to be entered manually.

If the bill of materials is site-specific, enter the site in the field *Site*. If you leave the site empty, it is a common bill of materials for all sites.

In order to assign a finished (or semi-finished) product to the BOM, switch to the Header view and click the button *Add* in the toolbar of the tab *BOM versions* (→ Fig. 5.6).

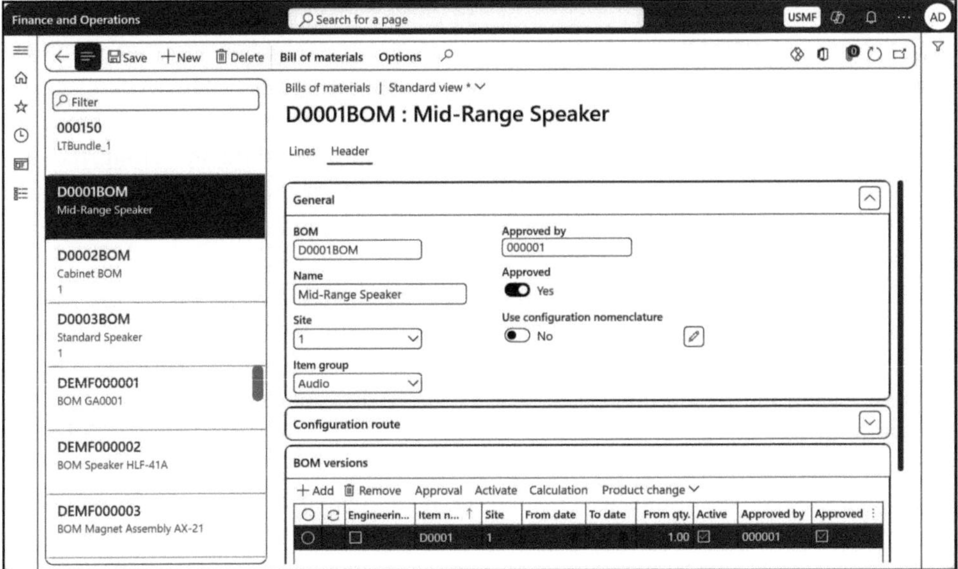

Fig. 5.6 BOM versions in the Header view of the BOM detail form

In the BOM version line, enter the *Item number* of the manufactured item. If the BOM assignment is only valid for a particular period, enter the *From date* and the *To date*. If the BOM assignment depends on the lot size, enter a *From qty*. And if the BOM assignment depends on the site, enter the *Site*.

If you want to assign the BOM to a second manufactured item in parallel (which is not very common, because it means that the other item got the same components), create another BOM version on the tab *BOM versions* for the selected BOM.

5.2.2.3 BOM Lines

In the Lines view of the BOM form, you can view and edit the components (raw materials/parts, semi-finished products) that are assigned to the bill of materials.

When you insert a new BOM line with the button *New* in the toolbar of the tab *Bill of materials lines*, enter at least the *Item number* and the *Quantity* of the component. The column *Per series* specifies the number of manufactured items which is produced with the *Quantity* of components in the BOM line—for example, 5 (*Quantity*) boxes (*Unit*) to produce 10 (*Per series*) manufactured items.

If the consumption (specified in the field *Quantity*) is independent of the production quantity, select the option "Constant" in the field *Consumption is* (instead of the default value "Variable") on the sub-tab *Setup* of the tab *Line details*. If you want to specify an additional consumption which covers inevitable scrap, enter a percentage in the field *Variable scrap*, or a fixed quantity in the field *Constant scrap*.

The *Flushing principle* (on the sub-tab *Setup*) controls automatic consumption. If the flushing principle in the BOM line is empty, the setting in the released product of the BOM line item will be used.

In a site-specific bill of materials, you can enter a picking warehouse in the column *Warehouse* of the BOM lines. In a bill of materials that is not assigned to a particular site, it is not possible to specify the picking warehouse in the BOM lines. In both cases, you can select the checkbox *Resource consumption*, which means that the picking warehouse in a production order is only determined when scheduling the order. With this setting, the *Input warehouse* (specified in the resource group or, if empty, in the production unit) of the resource/resource group in the route operation, which consumes the BOM line, is used as the picking warehouse.

The *Line type* (on the sub-tab *General* of the tab *Line details)* determines the supply strategy of a BOM line. There are the following options for the line type:

- **Item**—Semi-finished or purchased item, considered as demand in inventory.
- **Phantom**—Virtual semi-finished item, replaced by its components when estimating the production order.
- **Pegged supply**—Semi-finished or purchased item, creating a referenced sub-production or purchase order when estimating the production order.
- **Vendor**—For subcontracting, works like "Pegged supply".

BOM lines with the line type "Item" are considered as a regular demand in inventory. When creating planned production or purchase orders, master planning may consolidate the demand from different sources (orders and warehouse replenishment proposals) according to the item coverage settings. The default order type (or the order type in the item coverage) controls whether master planning creates a planned purchase order or a planned production order. Unlike the line type "Pegged supply" or "Vendor", the line type "Item" does not establish a close link between the order with the semi-finished product and the original production order with the upper-level finished product.

Production order scheduling and master planning calculate the item demand in a way that all components have to be available at the start date of the production order. If this is not necessary for some components because they are only required at a later date, you can assign components to the respective route operation (enter the operation number in the BOM line for this purpose). Available operation numbers depend on the route that is assigned to the manufactured item. For this reason, the field *Oper.No.* on the sub-tab *General* of the tab *Line details* only shows a lookup in the BOM version form, which you access from the released product.

Instead of manually entering all lines in a BOM from scratch, you can copy an existing BOM, which is similar to the new BOM, with the button *Bill of materials/Maintain/Copy* in the BOM form.

5.2.2.4 Approving and Activating Bills of Materials

In a production order, you can only use approved BOM versions. As a prerequisite for approving a BOM version, the BOM itself has to be approved.

You can approve a BOM with the button *Bill of materials/Maintain/Approval* in the action pane of the BOM form. After approving the BOM, you can approve the BOM version—click the button *Approval* in the toolbar of the tab *BOM versions* in the Header view of the detail form. If you approve the BOM version before approving the BOM itself, an additional slider, which enables approving the BOM and the BOM version in parallel, is displayed in the *Approve version* dialog.

If you want to use a particular bill of materials as a default value for production orders, for the item price calculation, and for master planning, activate the BOM version with the button *Activate* in the toolbar of the tab *BOM versions*. Active BOM versions show a checkmark in the column *Active* and have to be unique per date, from-quantity, and site.

In order to support approval and activation, the workspace *Product readiness for discrete manufacturing* includes the list *Missing active BOM versions*. This list shows items with the default order type "Production" but no active BOM version.

You can remove the activation and the approval if required. For this purpose, click the button for approval or activation again. When you remove an approval, set the slider *Remove approval* in the dialog to "Yes".

5.2.2.5 Bills of Materials in the Released Product

Apart from the menu item for bills of materials, you can also use the Released product form to access the bills of materials. Select an item with the *Production type* "BOM" in the Released product form, and click the button *Engineer/BOM/BOM versions* to open the BOM version form (→ Fig. 5.7). The BOM version form shows the bills of materials that are assigned to the selected item. In the rare case that a bill of materials is assigned to multiple items, keep in mind that modifying the bill of materials in this form also affects the other items that are assigned to the BOM.

The BOM version form has got a different structure than the BOM form accessed from the menu: Instead of a Header view and a Lines view, there is a tab *BOM version* (with the fields of the BOM version) and a tab *Bill of materials lines* (with the BOM lines of the BOM which is assigned to the BOM version).

If you want to enter a new bill of materials in this form, click the button *New/BOM and BOM version* in the action pane. In the *Create BOM* dialog, enter the *Name* of the BOM and, in case the bill of materials is site-specific, the *Site* before you click the button *OK*. The BOM form is shown next. Enter the components on the tab *Bill of materials lines* of this form. Once you close the BOM form, the BOM is shown in the BOM version form.

In the BOM version form, you can edit the details of a BOM line in a separate dialog, which you access with the button *Edit* in the toolbar of the tab *Bill of materials lines*. If you want to access the BOM form from the BOM version form, click the button *Bill of materials/Maintain BOM/Bill of materials*.

With the button *BOM version/Maintain BOM version/Approval* in the BOM version form, you can approve a BOM version (if necessary, set the slider to also approve the BOM itself in the dialog to "Yes"). With the button *BOM version/Maintain BOM version/ Activate*, you can subsequently activate the BOM version.

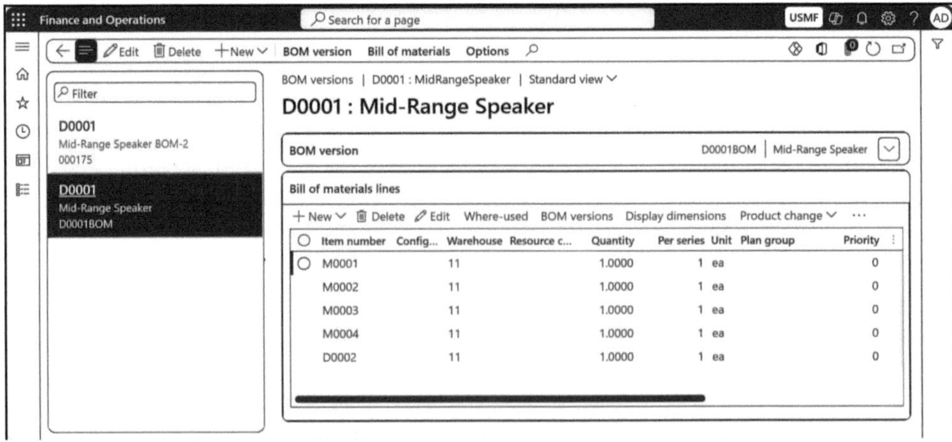

Fig. 5.7 Working in the BOM version form (accessed from the released product)

Note: Use the button *New/BOM version* (which only creates a BOM version) in the BOM version form if you want to assign the item to an existing bill of materials.

5.2.2.6 BOM Designer

The BOM designer (→ Fig. 5.8) is an alternative option for viewing and editing BOMs and BOM versions. You can access the BOM designer with the button *Engineer/BOM/Designer* in the Released product form, or with the button *Bill of materials/Maintain/Designer* in the BOM form.

The BOM designer shows a multi-level structure of the bill of materials in the list pane on the left, and related detail data in tabs on the right. In the action pane of the BOM designer, there are buttons to edit, insert, and delete BOM lines and to create new bills of materials (together with the related BOM version). On the tab *Route operations*, you can select the checkbox *Component needed at* to assign a BOM line to a route operation (which fills the field *Oper.No.* in a BOM line).

If you want to change the display settings in the BOM designer, click the button *Setup* in the action pane. In the *Setup* dialog that is shown next, select the fields that you want to view in the left pane of the BOM designer (e.g., the quantity).

The button *Filter* in the BOM designer provides access to a dialog, in which you can select the BOM/BOM version that you want to view. If you select the *Display principle* "Active" in this dialog, it is the active BOM version for the selected site, date, and quantity in the dialog (initialized with the session date and the default order settings of the item). With the *Display principle* "Selected/Active" (or "Selected"), you can view a BOM version that is different from the active BOM version. In order to select a BOM version for the display principle "Selected", click the button *BOM/BOM versions* in the BOM designer

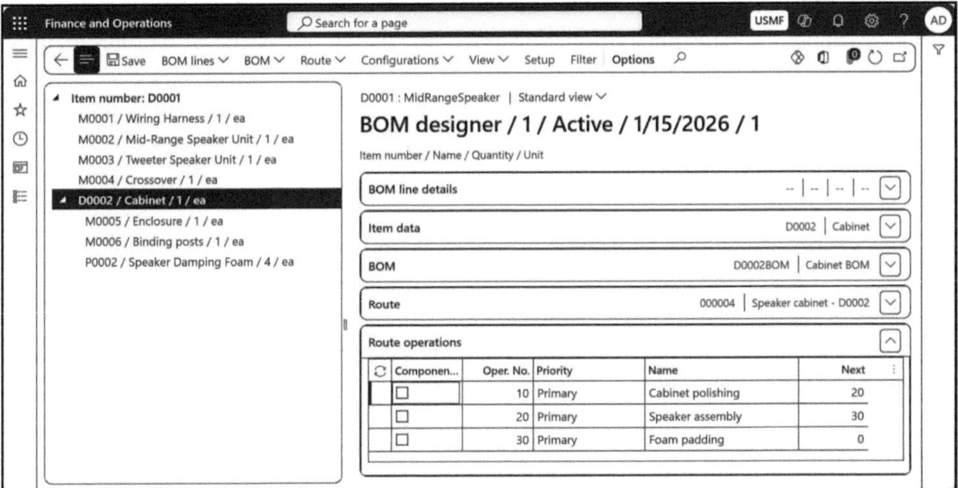

Fig. 5.8 Working with the BOM designer (accessed from the released product)

to access the BOM version selection form. In this form, highlight the BOM version that you want to view and click the button *Select* before you close the form.

5.2.2.7 Block BOM for Editing

Depending on the setup, you can update an approved bill of materials at any time. In some industries, it is required to protect an approved BOM against any changes. For this purpose, there are the following settings in the Inventory parameters (*Inventory management > Setup > Inventory and warehouse management parameters*, section *Bill of materials*):

- **Block editing**—If this slider is set to "Yes", no changes are possible once a BOM is approved (remove approval and re-approve afterward in this case).
- **Block removal of approval**—If set to "Yes" in parallel to *Block editing*, you can't change a BOM once it is approved.

5.2.2.8 Item Substitution

Originally only available in formulas (→ Sect. 5.8.1), the functionality for substituting a BOM component with another component is also available in regular bills of materials now.

Item substitution applies when firming a planned production order in master planning (→ Sect. 6.3.5): If the required quantity of the preferred component is not on hand when firming the planned order, master planning determines if a substitute is on hand. If there is, master planning supposes that this quantity will be consumed. If both the preferred component and all substitutes have no available inventory quantity, master planning generates a planned purchase or production order for the preferred component.

As a prerequisite for the item substitution, set up plan groups (*Product information management > Setup > Bills of materials and formulas > Plan groups*). Alternative items in a BOM share the same plan group. You assign the plan group to the BOM lines then (not directly to released products).

When creating a bill of materials with substitute components, enter an individual BOM line for the preferred item and each substitute item. In the BOM lines, the following columns/fields are relevant for item substitution:

- **Plan group**—Select the same plan group for the main item and the substitutes.
- **Priority**—Enter the lowest number (highest priority) for the main item and higher numbers for the alternative BOM lines.
- **Quantity**—Enter the required quantity for the main item (like in a regular BOM line) and no quantity in the BOM lines of substitutes.

5.2.2.9 Where-Used

The bill of materials shows the components of an item. If you want to know for a component, in which finished or semi-finished products it is included, access the Where-used form. For this purpose, select the respective item (component) in the Released product form and click the button *Engineer/BOM/Where-used*. If you need the where-used information across multiple BOM levels, run the report *Product information management > Inquiries and reports > Bill of materials where-used*.

5.2.3   Case Study Exercises

Exercise 5.1—Components

Your company wants to manufacture a new product which consists of two components. Create these components in the Released product form—an item with the product number I-##-C1 and the name "##-Component 1" (## = your user ID) and an item with the number I-##-C2 and the name "##-Component 2". Variants and serial/batch numbers are not required. Inventory control is at the level of site and warehouse.

For both items, choose proper settings for the product type, product subtype, dimension groups, item group (raw materials/parts), and production type. The item model group should refer to the inventory model "FIFO". Approved vendors are not required.

The base purchase price and the base cost price for both items is USD 100. Your vendor of exercise 3.2 is the main vendor for the items and the flushing principle is "Manual". For purchasing and inventory, enter the main site and the main warehouse in the *Default order settings*.

> *Note:* If the number sequence for product numbers is set up for automatic numbering, don't enter a product number.

Exercise 5.2—Finished Product

For the finished product, create an item with the product number I-##-F (if no automatic number sequence applies) and the name "##-Finished product" in the Released product form. Variants and serial/batch numbers are not required. Inventory control is at the level of site and warehouse.

Select applicable settings for the product type, product subtype, dimension groups, item group (finished product), and production type. The item model group should refer to the inventory model "FIFO". The base cost price is USD 500, and the base sales price is USD 1000. In the *Default order settings*, make sure that the appropriate *Default order type* is selected and enter the main site and the main warehouse in the settings for inventory and sales.

Exercise 5.3—Bill of Materials

After setting up the item records for the finished product and its components in the previous exercises, enter the bill of materials for the item of exercise 5.2.

Create a site-specific BOM for the main site that includes a BOM line with 2 units of the first and a BOM line with one unit of the second item of exercise 5.1. Components should be picked from the main warehouse. Once you have completed the BOM lines, approve and activate the BOM version.

5.3   Resource and Route Management

Resources include operating personnel, machines, tools, working places, and vendors (subcontractors). They execute the operations and provide the available capacity in manufacturing. Apart from calculating the item availability, order scheduling and master planning also match the available capacity of resources with the capacity demand.

Routes are the basis for calculating the capacity demand. They specify the necessary resources and the working time for producing a particular item.

Along with items and bills of materials, resources and routes are the second area of master data that are required for production control.

5.3.1   Working Time Calendars and Templates

The working time calendar of a resource or resource group determines the hours of operation. You can manage the working time calendars in the Calendar form (*Production control > Setup > Calendars > Calendars*).

If you need a new calendar (e.g., if a resource has working times that do not match any existing calendar), insert a new record with ID and name in the Calendar form. Then click the button *Working times* to access the Working times form ($\rightarrow$ Fig. 5.9). The Working times form shows the calendar days in the upper pane and the working hours of the selected day (with the start time and the end time in editable fields) in the lower pane. If you want to create working days and hours for the selected calendar, click the button *Compose working times* in the Working times form. In the *Compose working times* dialog, which is shown next, select a *Working time template* that determines the default values for the daily working hours.

The working time templates (*Production control > Setup > Calendars > Working time templates*) specify the usual working hours per weekday on the tabs *Monday* to *Sunday*.

The base calendar is an alternative way to specify the working times. In the Calendar form, you can link each calendar to another calendar by selecting the other calendar in the field *Base calendar*. With this setup, you can set the slider *Use base calendar* in the *Compose working time* dialog to "Yes". Dynamics 365 then initializes the column *Control* in the Working times form with the option "Base calendar". This option means that the working time is given by the base calendar. You can override the working times of a calendar for a day—select the option "Open" or "Closed" in the column *Control* for this purpose.

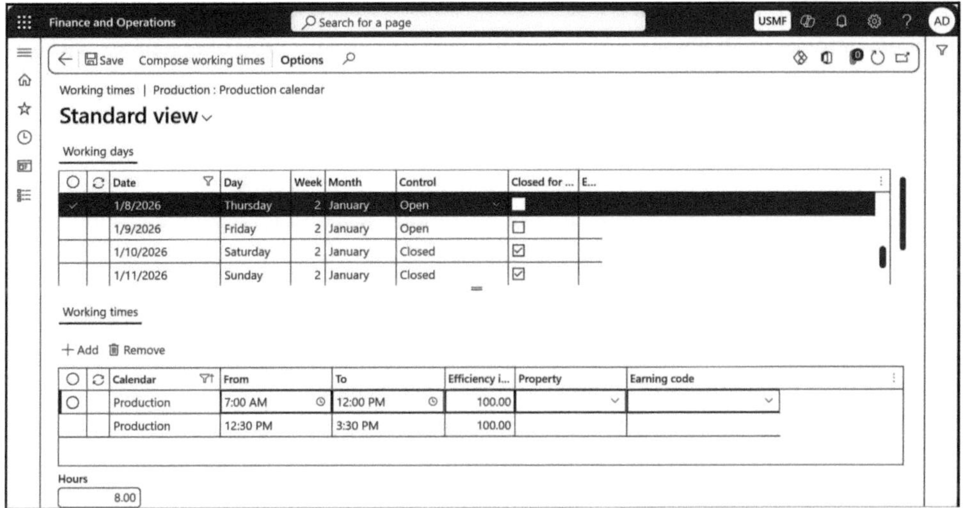

Fig. 5.9   Editing the working times in the calendar

5.3.2   Resource Groups and Resource Management

Production units represent operating plants in capacity management. Within a production unit, resource groups collect the resources according to the physical organization on the shop floor. Resources within a resource group can have different capabilities and do not need to be interchangeable.

5.3.2.1 Production Units

Production units, which are an optional setup for capacity management, are an additional organizational level below the dimension "Site". Whereas sites are also used in material management, production units are not included in the inventory transactions of items, but in the capacity reservations and route transactions of resources and resource groups. You can link multiple production units to one common site.

If you want to create a production unit, open the menu item *Production control > Setup > Production > Production units* and enter a new record with ID, name, and site. On the tab *General*, optionally enter an *Input warehouse* (the *Output warehouse* is relevant for lean manufacturing). The input warehouse of the production unit is used as the picking warehouse for BOM lines in which the checkbox *Resource consumption* is selected (in case there is no *Input warehouse* in the applicable resource group).

In order to link a resource group to a production unit, open the Resource group form and select the *Production unit* in the respective field.

5.3.2.2 Resource Groups

Resource groups in Dynamics 365 reflect the physical organization of resources. They are used for the following purposes:

- **Structuring**—Resource groups are an element in the hierarchical organization structure. They link resources to production units, sites, and warehouses.
- **Scheduling**—For capacity planning in operations scheduling, resource groups are the scheduling level.

The capacity of a resource group is the total capacity of the assigned resources. Since the assignment of resources to resource groups is date-effective, you can adjust the resource assignment in line with organizational and seasonal changes.

If a resource is not assigned to a resource group on a given day, it is not available for manufacturing on that day. Resource scheduling only includes resources that are assigned to a resource group.

You can edit the resource groups in the Resource group form (*Production control > Setup > Resources > Resource groups*). In order to create a new resource group in this form (→ Fig. 5.10), click the button *New* in the action pane and enter the ID, name, and site.

On the tab *Resources* of the Resource group form, you can manage the resources that are assigned to the resource group. If you want to assign an additional resource, click the button *Add* in the toolbar of this tab. If you want to view past assignments or to enter an assignment with a future start date (which you enter in the column *Effective*), click the button *View/All* in the toolbar of this tab.

Fig. 5.10 Editing a resource group

You can assign resources to a resource group in the Resource group form as described, but you can also work the other way around—open the Resource form and select the resource group there.

On the tab *General* of the Resource group form, you can optionally assign a production unit to the resource group. The *Input warehouse* on this tab specifies the picking warehouse for BOM lines with activated *Resource consumption* (→ Sect. 5.2.2).

If the slider *Work cell* on the tab *General* is set to "Yes", the resource group is a work cell in lean manufacturing and not available for operations and production orders in discrete manufacturing. On the tab *Work cell capacity*, you can specify the capacity of the work cell in lean manufacturing.

Settings on the tab *Operation* of the Resource group form correspond to equivalent settings on the tab *Operation* in the Resource form (see below).

The calendar of a resource group is specified on the tab *Calendars* in the Resource group form. The calendar assignment is date effective, which means that you can record a future change of the working times by entering an additional line with the start date on the tab *Calendars* of the resource group—for example, if you want to change the regular working times of the resource group from two shifts to three shifts. In order to show the required column *Effective* (for the start date), click the button *View/All* in the toolbar of this tab.

If you need to override the working times of a resource group on a given day, click the button *Resource group/Maintain/Calendar deviations* in the resource group and assign an alternative calendar for this day (e.g., a calendar without working times if a resource is not available temporarily).

5.3.2.3 Resources

Resources are the lowest level for capacity management in Dynamics 365. They are assigned to resource groups in line with the organizational hierarchy. Optionally, you can assign capabilities (which reflect the functions and skills) to resources.

In order to edit the resources, open the menu item *Production control > Setup > Resources > Resources*. When creating a new resource, be aware that the resource ID needs to be unique—not only within the resources but also within the resource groups. You can, for example, use a three-digit ID for resource groups and a four-digit ID for resources to distinguish resource groups from resources easily.

When you create a resource, select the resource type, which distinguishes the different kinds of resources, in the lookup field *Type*:

- **Machine**—General default, for production machines.
- **Human resources**—Personnel (optionally assign a worker ID).
- **Vendor**—External resource for subcontracting (optionally assign a vendor ID).
- **Tool**—Device, often subject to wear (e.g., a knife in a turning machine).
- **Location**—Represents physical space (e.g., a greenhouse), but is not linked to warehouse locations.
- **Facility**—Similar functionality to "Machine", but for a group of machines and workers.

Note: The additional type "Resource group" is reserved for resource groups and automatically assigned in the background when creating a resource group.

If you do not need to schedule and report the activities of a machine and its operating staff separately, you can use a common resource with the type "Facility" or "Machine" and avoid setting up resources with the type "Human resources". If you want to manage tools, enter the usage of a tool as a secondary operation in routes (→ Sect. 5.3.3).

On the tab *Calendars* of the Resource form, you can assign a working time calendar to the resource (similar to assigning a calendar to a resource group). The calendar, together with the efficiency percentage, determines the capacity of the resource.

On the tab *Resource groups*, you can manage the resource group to which the resource is assigned. In order to assign a resource group, click the button *Add* in the toolbar of this tab. If you want to view past assignments or to enter an assignment with a future start date (which you enter in the column *Effective*), click the button *View/All* in the toolbar of this tab.

If needed, you can assign multiple resources to a resource group in a single step: Select the resources in the Resource form, then click the button *Resource/Maintain/Add to resource group* in the action pane and select the applicable resource group in the lookup.

5.3.2.4 Resource Capacity and Operation Settings

The capacity of a resource is given by its working time calendar and efficiency percentage. For a resource group, the capacity is the total capacity of its resources. In the Capacity load form, which you can open with the button *Resource/View/Capacity load* in the Resource form, you can view the totals of available capacity and capacity reservations per day. For resource groups, a similar inquiry is available in the Resource group form.

The settings for the capacity of a resource are available on the tab *Operation* of the Resource form (→ Fig. 5.11).

In general, the time unit for resource scheduling is hours. If a different unit of time (e.g., minutes) is required for a resource, enter a conversion factor in the field *Hours/time*. In the example of minutes for the time unit in route operations, enter "=1/60" (0.0167) in the field *Hours/time*.

If the unit of measure for a particular resource is not a unit of time, select an alternative *Capacity unit* (e.g., "Strokes/hour"). The field *Capacity* then contains the conversion factor to hours. In the related route operations, refer to this capacity setting in the resource with the option "Capacity" in the field *Formula* on the tab *Setup*.

The field *Efficiency percentage* on the tab *Operation* of the Resource form enables adapting the scheduled time for route operations by a factor. The default for the efficiency percentage is 100. If, for example, a particular resource is 25 percent faster than a standard resource, enter 125 in the efficiency percentage. With this setting, the scheduled time of a route operation with 10 h (for other resources) is only 8 h (= 10 * 100/125) on this resource.

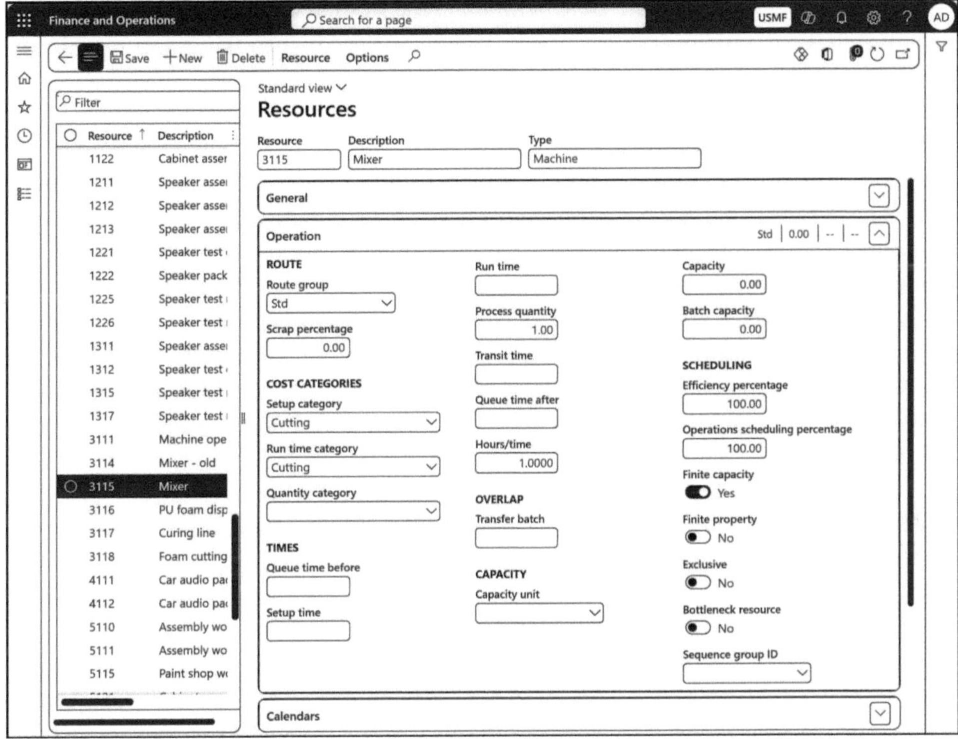

Fig. 5.11 Managing the capacity and operation settings of a resource

The slider *Finite capacity* on the tab *Operation* controls, whether capacity reservations of other production orders reduce the available capacity when you schedule an order. If this slider is set to "Yes", only one operation at a time is scheduled on this resource. Otherwise, scheduling calculates each production order separately, regardless of other orders on the same resource. In many cases, finite capacity is only used for the resources and resource groups that don't have the possibility to increase the capacity (e.g., by overtime).

In the master plan (for master planning) and the production order update dialogs (for operations scheduling and job scheduling), you can select to disregard the finite capacity setting of the resource.

The cost categories *Setup category* and *Run time category* determine the hourly rate of the resource for setup time and for run time. In the *Quantity category*, you can enter a quantity-dependent cost price (if applicable). You can find details on cost categories in → Sect. 5.3.3.

The other field groups on the tab *Operation* in the Resource form contain fields that are default values for route operations. These defaults are used when you select the resource or resource group as the costing resource in a route operation.

5.3.2.5 Resource Capabilities

Resource capabilities determine the activities that a resource is able to do (e.g., welding or cutting). You can temporarily or permanently assign one or more capabilities to a resource. The capability assignment is only available for resources, not for resource groups. In the routes, you can subsequently specify the required capabilities for the individual operations.

In order to create a capability (shared across companies), open the Resource capability form (*Production control > Setup > Resources > Resource capabilities*) and click the button *New* in the action pane. Enter the ID and description of the new capability and switch to the tab *Resources*. On this tab, assign the applicable resources to the capability ($\rightarrow$ Fig. 5.12).

It is not only possible to assign resources to a capability in the Resource capability form, but you can also open the Resource form and assign the capabilities to the resource with the button *Add* in the toolbar of the tab *Capabilities* there. If needed, you can assign multiple resources to a capability in a single step—select the resources and click the button *Resource/Maintain/Add capability* in the Resource form.

The capability assignment is date effective, which means that you can record a future capability of a resource in an additional line on the tab *Capabilities* of the resource (with a start date which you can show with the *View/All* in the toolbar of this tab). In addition, there is the field *Priority* in the assignment line: Depending on the Scheduling parameters ($\rightarrow$ Sect. 5.4.1), job scheduling searches for the applicable resources with the higher priority (this is the lower priority number; priority "1" is the highest priority) first.

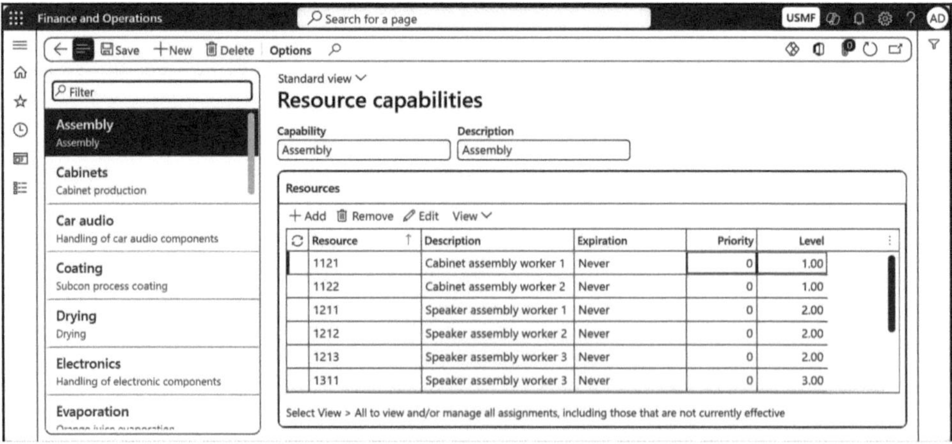

Fig. 5.12 Managing the resource capability assignment in the Capability form

5.3.2.6 Settings for Ledger Integration

The tab *Ledger postings* in the Resource form and the Resource group form contains the main accounts which are used for route consumption. When you post a route card or job card journal for a production order, the costs for the use of the resource (usually driven by the working time) are posted to the general ledger. The applicable main accounts are specified in the field group *Accounts-Physical* of the resource. When you cost and end a production order, ledger transactions are posted to the accounts in the field group *Accounts-Financial*.

The account settings in the resource only apply if the option "Item and resource" is selected in the field *Ledger posting* of the production order ($\rightarrow$ Sect. 9.4.3). If the option "Item and category" is selected, applicable main accounts derive from the cost categories.

5.3.3   Routes and Operations

Routes determine the operations that are required to manufacture an item. In addition to the bills of materials, which contain the required components, routes are the second area of required setup for production.

Like bills of materials, routes contain planned data that determine the target for production. In the course of manufacturing, the workshop reports actual figures in production journal transactions. You can subsequently compare and analyze the target and actual figures to determine possible improvements.

In order to describe the operations in manufacturing, a route has to contain at least the following data:

- **Activity**—Specified in the field *Operation*.
- **Resource**—Specified on the tab *Resource requirements*.
- **Sequence of operations**—Specified by the next operation (field *Next*).
- **Time consumption**—Specified in the fields *Setup time* and *Run time*.
- **Manufactured item**—Specified by the *Item number* in the route version.
- **Required material**—Specified in the BOM lines, optionally linked to operations.

If the workshop does not need all components which are listed in the bill of materials when starting the first operation, you can link BOM lines to the applicable route operations ($\rightarrow$ Sect. 5.2.2).

5.3.3.1 Setup of Operations

As a prerequisite for routes, you have to set up operations (*Production control > Setup > Routes > Operations*). You can use one operation in multiple routes.

Operations are separate from routes and only contain a unique ID and a name. Other details which are necessary to execute an operation (e.g., the expected time/duration, or the required resource) are not included in the operation record itself, but in the operation relations (→ Fig. 5.13).

In order to view and edit the details of an operation (specified in the operation relations), click the button *Relations* in the Operation form. Depending on the requirements, you can enter the operation relations at a general level or a route-specific level:

- **General**—For operation details at a general level, select the option "All" in the field *Item code* and *Route code* of the operation relation.
- **Route-specific**—Route-specific operation details show the option "Route" in the *Route code* and the route number in the field *Route relation*.

On the other tabs of the Operation relation form, you can enter the details of the particular operation relation (including applicable resources and times). You can find more details on the operation relations in the description of route operations further down this section.

5.3.3.2 Operation Sequence

The sequence of operations is not specified in the operation, but in the route. There are two types of operation sequences:

- **Simple sequence**—One operation after the other.
- **Complex sequence**—Multiple predecessors for an operation are possible.

Simple operation sequences (→ Fig. 5.14) are used if the slider *Route network* in the Production control parameters (section *General*) is set to "No". In this case, routes only contain operations that are executed one after another.

Fig. 5.13 Editing the general operation relation (All/All) for an operation

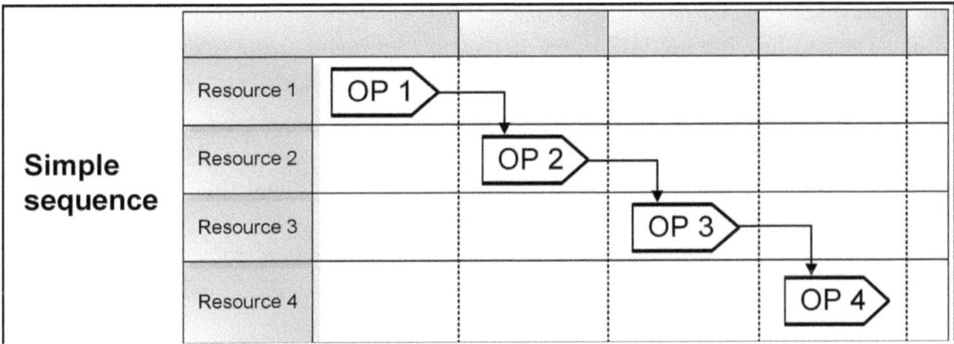

Fig. 5.14 Example of a simple operation sequence

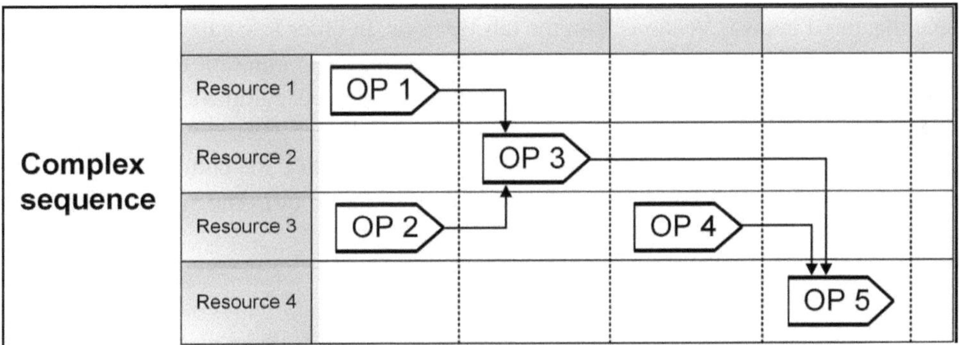

Fig. 5.15 Example of a complex operation sequence

If the parameter *Route network* is set to "Yes", you have to enter the next operation in each operation of a route. This setting enables complex operation sequences with multiple independent prior operations for a route operation (→ Fig. 5.15).

Irrespective of the setting on simple or complex operation sequences in the parameters, you can use secondary operations in routes to characterize operations that can be executed in parallel. Parallel operations got the same operation number, but a different *Priority* (see below).

5.3.3.3 Entering Routes and Route Versions

Managing routes in Dynamics 365 is similar to managing bills of materials, including how you can access the Route form:

- **From the released product** (*Product information management > Products > Released products,* button *Engineer/View/Route*).
- **From the menu** (*Production control > All routes*).

The workspace *Product readiness for discrete manufacturing* is another place, from which you can access (use the link *All routes* on the tab *Links*) and create (click the button *New/ Route* in the action pane) routes. The Route form accessed from the workspace and accessed from the menu is the same.

Although the Route form (accessed from the menu) and the Route version form (accessed from the released product) update the same route and route version data, the functionality and the structure of these forms are different.

Like the assignment of bills of materials, the assignment of routes to manufactured items is called "Version" (with the option the specify validity dates and a from-quantity). But unlike BOM versions, route versions always refer to a site.

If you open the menu item *Production control > All routes*, a list page with the routes is displayed. Click on a route number shown as a link in the grid to open the related detail form. The Route form shows the route header on the tab *General* and one or more assigned manufactured items ("Versions") on the tab *Versions*. In order to create a new route, click the button *New* in the action pane of the Route form. Depending on the settings of the applicable number sequence, the route number is assigned automatically or has to be entered manually. Enter a *Name* for the new route on the tab *General* of the Route form and switch to the tab *Versions*. In the toolbar of this tab, click the button *Add* to create a route version (assignment of a manufactured item to the route). The *Site* is a mandatory field in the route version.

5.3.3.4 Route Operations

In the Route list page or the detail form, you can access the route operations with the button *Route/Maintain/Route details* in the action pane. The Route details form then shows the sequence of the route operations in the upper pane and the operation relations (operation details) of the selected operation in the lower pane.

Click the button *New* in the action pane if you want to insert a new route operation. If required, you can override the operation number (column *Oper.No.*). Then select the applicable operation in the column *Operation*. If the Production control parameters specify complex operation sequences, you have to enter the number of the next route operation in the column *Next* of the upper pane (for the last operation, the *Next* number is "0").

If the shop floor should execute some operations in parallel (e.g., if the work of the machine and the operating personnel should be reported separately), enter two or more operations with the same operation number, but with a different *Priority*. In the example of → Fig. 5.16, there are two parallel operations with operation number 30—one with *Priority* "Primary" and one with *Priority* "Secondary 1".

In case additional time and material consumption for inevitable scrap, caused by the operation, should be included, enter a *Scrap percentage*. If there is scrap in more than one route operation, the total scrap is calculated by multiplication. If there is, for example, a route with two operations and each of them has got 10% scrap, the material and resource capacity required for the first operation is 123% of the demand without scrap: 10% scrap

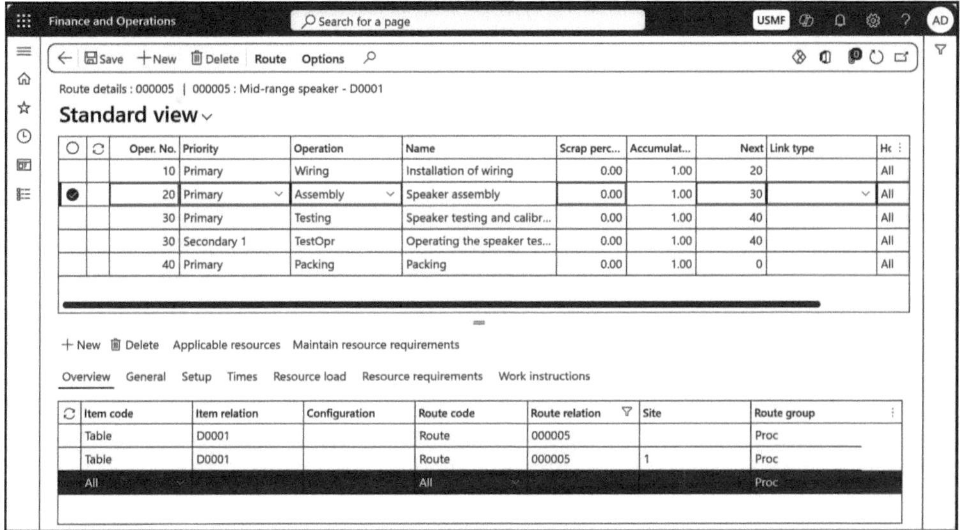

Fig. 5.16 Editing a route operation with a general operation relation (All/All)

in the first operation results in an output of 111%, which is subsequently reduced to an output of 100% by the second operation.

If the operation (in the column *Operation*) that you select in a new route operation has a general operation relation (indicated by the option "All" in the column *Route code*), this general operation relation is shown in the lower pane of the Route details form when you save the record. If you change the data of a general operation relation in the Route details form, keep in mind that these changes apply to all routes that use the selected general operation relation.

If you want to enter route-specific operation details (independent of a general operation relation), insert a line with a new operation relation in the lower pane of the Route details form. In the operation relation, select the option "Route" in the column *Route code* and enter the required data on the other tabs of the lower pane.

5.3.3.5 Route Groups

The *Route group* on the tab *Overview* (and the tab *General*) in the operation relations (shown in the lower pane of the Route details form) controls whether the resource usage is posted automatically or manually. If the resource usage for an operation should be posted automatically (actual = estimate), select a route group with settings for automatic route consumption.

In order to set up the route groups, open the menu item *Production control > Setup > Routes > Route groups*. In route groups for automatic posting, set the sliders for *Setup time*, *Run time*, and *Quantity* in the field group *Automatic route consumption* to "Yes". In addition, clear the checkboxes in the column *Job management* on the tab *Setup* for these route groups (automatic consumption is posted with route cards, not with job cards). The sliders in the field group *Estimation and costing* control, whether to include operations with this route group in estimation and cost calculation. For regular operations, set the sliders for a time-based cost calculation or the slider for quantity-based cost calculation to "Yes". If all sliders for costing are set to "No", Dynamics 365 only calculates the time, but no costs for assigned operations.

5.3.3.6 Costing Resource and Cost Categories

On the tab *Setup* in the operation relations, you can optionally select a resource or a resource group in the field *Costing resource*. Data from the costing resource initialize the fields in the field group *Cost categories* and the fields on the tab *Times* of the route operation.

Cost categories are, apart from the route group, another setting that controls cost estimation and cost calculation. You can assign different cost categories for setup time, run time, and quantity. When you assign a cost category, make sure that the related slider in the route group (the field group *Estimation and costing* controls if time or quantity are included in the calculation) is set to "Yes".

Before you can create a new cost category, you have to create a related shared category in the menu item *Production control > Setup > Routes > Shared categories*. Shared categories ensure common category definitions across companies. For categories in production control, set the slider *Can be used in Production* in the shared category to "Yes".

Cost categories for production control (*Production control > Setup > Routes > Cost categories*) contain three core settings:

- **Cost price**—Determines the hourly rate (for setup time and run time).
- **Cost group**—Classifies the cost types in the cost calculation (→ Sect. 7.3.3).
- **Ledger postings**—The settings on this tab determine the main accounts that are used for route consumption (in case the option "Item and category" is selected in the lookup field *Ledger* of the production order).

If you want to enter the cost price for a category, click the button *Category setup/Category setup/Price* in the Cost categories form to access the Cost category price form. In this form, enter a cost price with a costing version (→ Sect. 7.3.3) for the category per site or—if you leave the field *Site* empty—at the company level. Then, click the button *Activate* (which is enabled after saving the record) in the Cost category price form to activate the price.

In a production order, the (upfront) estimation applies the cost price of the cost categories in the route operation. The subsequent calculation of the actual costs applies the cost categories of the resource in the actual transaction.

5.3.3.7 Operation Times

The fields on the tab *Times* in the operation relations show the expected time for the operation. You can distinguish between the setup time, the run time, the queue times, and the transit time. The *Setup time* is the required time for preparing the operation. The *Run time* is the time it takes to produce the quantity in the field *Process qty*. This quantity refers to the manufactured product (specified in the route version).

If the *Process qty.* is 1.00, the run time is the required time in hours to produce one unit. If necessary, you can use units other than hours for the time: Enter a conversion factor *Hours/time* in the route operation or select a capacity unit in the resource ($\rightarrow$ Sect. 5.3.2) for this purpose.

The processing time of an operation is the result of the following formula:

$$PROCESSING\ TIME = \frac{Setup\ time + \left(Run\ time \times Quantity\right)}{Efficiency\ percentage\ of\ the\ resource}$$

In addition to the processing time, queue times and transit times are included in the total lead time.

5.3.3.8 Resource Requirements and Resource Load

On the tab *Resource load* in the operation relations, the field *Quantity* specifies the number of required resources (for resources that are used in parallel). The calculation of the required capacity then multiplies the operation time by the load quantity. All applicable resources must fulfill the requirements on the tab *Resource requirements*.

The settings on the tab *Resource requirements* of the operation relation determine the resources that can execute the operation. From a functional point of view, these settings are independent of the costing resource. If there are multiple lines in the resource requirements, an applicable resource must comply with all of them.

The checkboxes in the respective columns determine separate requirements for *Operations scheduling* and *Job scheduling*. In the column *Requirement type*, you can select if a requirement refers to a resource group, a resource, a resource type, or a capability. The options "Skill", "Courses", "Certificate", and "Title" are only used for job scheduling with resources of the resource type "Human resource" (related to worker data in human resource management).

If you want to view the resources that meet the requirements for a route operation, click the button *Applicable resources* in the toolbar of the lower pane in the Route details form (or in the action pane of the Operation relation form accessed from the Operations form). Since the assignment of resources to resource groups and to capabilities is date effective, you have to specify the date for which you want to view the applicable resources (today's date is the default). In addition, select whether to show the resources for operations scheduling or for job scheduling.

If you want to get an overview of all operations with the applicable resources, click the button *Route feasibility* in the toolbar of the tab *Versions* in the Route form (the button is not available in the Route details form with the operations).

5.3.3.9 Approving and Activating Routes

Like bills of materials, routes, and route versions have to be approved before you can use them in production orders. You can approve a route with the button *Route/Maintain/Approve* in the action pane of the Route form. In order to approve a route version, click the button *Approve* in the toolbar of the tab *Versions* in the Route form. If you approve the route version before you approve the route itself, a slider for simultaneously approving the route and the route version is shown in the approval dialog.

If you want to use a route as the default value for production orders, for item price calculations, and for master planning, activate the route version with the button *Activate* in the toolbar of the tab *Versions*. Active route versions show a checkmark in the column *Active* and have to be unique per date, quantity, and site.

Depending on the Production control parameters—the sliders *Block editing,* and *Block removal of approval* in the section *General* (similar to the settings for BOMs) –, you can update an approved route at any time.

You can remove the activation and the approval if required. For this purpose, click the button for approval or activation again. When you remove an approval, set the slider *Remove approval* in the dialog to "Yes".

5.3.3.10 Routes in the Released Product

Apart from the menu item for routes, you can also use the Released product form for accessing a route. Select the respective item in the Released product form and click the button *Engineer/View/Route* to open the Route version form.

The Route version form (accessed from the released product) shows all routes that are assigned to the selected item. It has a different structure than the Route form accessed from the menu—the route versions are shown in the upper pane, and the route operations with the operation number and the operation relations (operation details) in the lower pane.

If you want to create a new route in this form, click the button *New/Route and route version* in the action pane. Alternatively, click the button *New/Route version* (which just creates a route version and not a new route in parallel) if you only want to assign the item to an existing route.

In order to create a route operation for a route in the Route version form, select the route in the upper pane and click the button *New* in the toolbar of the lower pane.

If the operation (in the column *Operation*) that you select in the new route operation has a general operation relation (indicated by the option "All" in the column *Route code*), this general operation relation is shown on the tabs in the lower pane of the Route version form when you save the record. Unlike the functionality in the Route detail form accessed from the menu, overriding the data of a general operation relation in the Route version form creates a route-specific operation relation automatically—indicated by the option "Route" in the column *Route code*. You can alternatively click the button *Copy and edit relation* in the toolbar of the lower pane if you want to enter route-specific operation details, which are independent of the general operation relation (same result as simply overriding data).

If you want to delete a route-specific operation relation and apply an applicable general operation relation again, click the button *Delete relation* in the toolbar.

If there is no general operation relation for a route operation, you have to enter a new operation relation with all required data in the lower pane manually.

In the Route version form, you can approve a route version with the button *Route version/Maintain route version/Approve* (if necessary, set the slider to approve also the route itself in the dialog to "Yes"). With the button *Route version/Maintain route version/ Activate*, you can subsequently activate the route version.

5.3.4   Case Study Exercises

Exercise 5.4—Setup for Routes
In order to investigate the use of capabilities, route groups, and cost categories, you want to set up an example. As a start, create a capability C-## (## = your user ID) with the name "##-specific". Then enter a route group R-## with settings that require manually posting the actual working time. Estimation and costing should only be based on setup time and run time.

Next, set up a new cost category G-## (and the related shared category) for production. In the cost category, select an appropriate cost group of your choice and enter main accounts similar to the settings in existing cost categories. For the hourly rate, enter and activate a cost price of USD 100 at the company level (select a costing version with the costing type "Planned cost").

Exercise 5.5—Resource Groups and Resources
New resources are required to manufacture the finished product of exercise 5.2. Enter a new resource group W-## with the name "##-assembly", which is assigned to the main site and an appropriate production unit. The resource group applies the cost category of exercise 5.4 for setup time and for run time. In the resource group calendar, select a regular calendar of your choice.

Then create two new resources, W-##-1 and W-##-2, with the type "Machine". For both resources, the route group and—for setup time and for run time—the cost category of exercise 5.4 is used. Select main accounts for the resources that are similar to the settings in existing resources. Both resources are assigned to the new resource group W-##, but only the resource W-##-2 has the capability of exercise 5.4. The resources use the same calendar as the resource group.

Exercise 5.6—Operation and Operation Relations
As a prerequisite for production, a new operation is required. Create the operation O-## (## = your user ID) with the name "##-processing". In general, the setup time for this operation is 1 h, and the run time is 2 h per unit. Select the resource W-##-1 of exercise 5.5 as the costing resource that initializes the route group and the cost categories. Only

resources of the resource group W-## with the capability C-## of exercise 5.4 can execute the operation.

Exercise 5.7—Route
In order to manufacture the finished product, a new route that is based on the setup in the previous exercises is required. Select the item I-##-F of exercise 5.2 in the Released product form and access the route from the released product. Create a new route with the operation O-## of exercise 5.6 as the only route operation. There is no setup time, and the run time for the operation is 1 h per unit. The other settings in the route operation—including costing resource, route group, cost categories, and resource requirements—are the same as the applicable settings in the general operation relation, which you have entered in exercise 5.6.

Once you have completed the details, approve and activate the route and the route version. Can you check which resources can execute the route operation? Finally, check which operation relations are assigned to the operation of exercise 5.6.

5.4   Production Order Management

A production order is a request to manufacture a particular product. Apart from the item number and the quantity of the manufactured item, production orders include data on the required materials and resources.

The order status, which is updated with every step in the sequential flow of order processing, shows the progress of a production order.

5.4.1   Basics of Production Order Processing

Apart from manually entering a production order, there are the following options to create an order:

- **Sales order**—Create a production order from a sales order line.
- **Project**—Create a production order from a project (Project accounting module).
- **Master planning**—Firm a planned production order, which is generated by master planning, to convert it to an actual production order (→ Sect. 6.3.5).
- **Pegged supply**—Automatically generating a production order from the BOM line of an upper-level production order (sub-production, see → Sect. 5.4.3).

5.4.1.1 Production Order Status
When you create a production order manually, the first status is "Created". This is the only status in which you can delete a production order. If you need to delete a production order

in a later status, you have to reset the status to "Created" first. The manufacturing cycle, which updates the order status, includes the following steps:

- **Created**—Temporary status after creating a new order.
- **Estimated**—Material and resource demand is calculated.
- **Scheduled**—Start/end dates are calculated, and resources are assigned.
- **Released**—The order is transferred to the shop floor.
- **Started**—Posting of actual consumption is possible.
- **Reported as finished**—The manufactured item is received in inventory.
- **Ended**—The order is finally closed.

The order status is updated when you process the order with the corresponding button in the Production order form or with the related periodic activity in the menu folder *Production control > Periodic tasks > Production order status update*.

You can skip steps in the order processing cycle—Dynamics 365 then automatically executes the steps which you omit (applying the settings in the section *Automatic update* of the Production control parameters). If you want to reset the status of a production order, click the button *Production order/Process/Reset status* in the Production order form. Dynamics 365 then reverses all posted transactions (automatic and manual postings) that refer to the reversed status.

Settings in the section *Status* of the Production control parameters determine from which status you can move to which status. There are different checkboxes for both directions, for skipping a status, and for reversing a status.

5.4.1.2 Production Control Parameters

Unlike parameter settings in other areas, Production control parameters are not only available at the company level but also at the site level. The field *Parameter usage* in the section *General* of the Production control parameters at the company level (*Production control > Setup > Production control parameters*) determines whether the site-specific parameters are used. You can manage the site-specific parameters in the menu item *Production control > Setup > Production control parameters by site*.

5.4.1.3 Scheduling Parameters

Scheduling parameters (*Master planning > Setup > Scheduling > Scheduling parameters*) determine default values in the update dialogs for production order scheduling. Essential Scheduling parameters include the *Primary resource selection*, which determines whether capability-based scheduling is based on priority or shortest duration. Like the Production control parameters, the Scheduling parameters are available at the company level and the site level.

5.4.2 Production Order Registration

Data in a production order include the header data, the production BOM, and the production route. When you create a production order, an inventory transaction for the manufactured item with the status "Ordered" in the column *Receipt* is created (similar to the inventory transaction for a purchase order line). The inventory transactions for the components of the production order (BOM lines) are only created when you execute the order estimation. As long as the status of the production order is "Created", master planning only recognizes a supply of the manufactured item (from the inventory transaction), but there is no component demand (the corresponding inventory transactions are not created yet). For this reason, you should estimate a production order soon after creating it.

If a production order is created automatically from a planned order, settings in the applicable coverage group determine the initial status (usually "Scheduled").

5.4.2.1 Entering Production Orders

You can manually create a production order with the button *Create new/Production order* in the workspace *Production floor management* (→ Fig. 5.17). Alternatively, open the Production order form (*Production control > Production Orders > All production orders*) and click the button *New production order* there.

In a sales order, you can click the button *Product and supply/New/Production order* in the toolbar of the order lines to create a production order, which is, with reservation and marking, linked to the sales order line.

In the *Create production order* dialog, select the item number of the manufactured product first. Depending on the selected item, several fields are initialized with default values, which you can override as required (for example, if you want to select a different BOM). Once you click the button *Create* in the dialog, the production order is generated and shows the initial status "Created".

When you process the order, it switches to a subsequent status. A summary of the status updates is shown on the tab *Update* of the Production order detail form.

You can still update the settings in a production order later—for example, if you need to modify the BOM or the route in the order. If you change a production order that is already estimated or scheduled, you should run the estimation or scheduling again to ensure consistent data. If production papers have been printed already, you might need to reprint them with the updated data.

For production orders, which have not been created manually in the Production module, the tab *References* of the Production order detail form shows the reference to the origin. If the production order refers to another order, this original order is shown in the reference type and number—for example, with the reference type "Sales order" if the production order has been created from a sales order line. In a production order that has been generated as a sub-production from the BOM line of an upper-level production order, the reference type is "Production line".

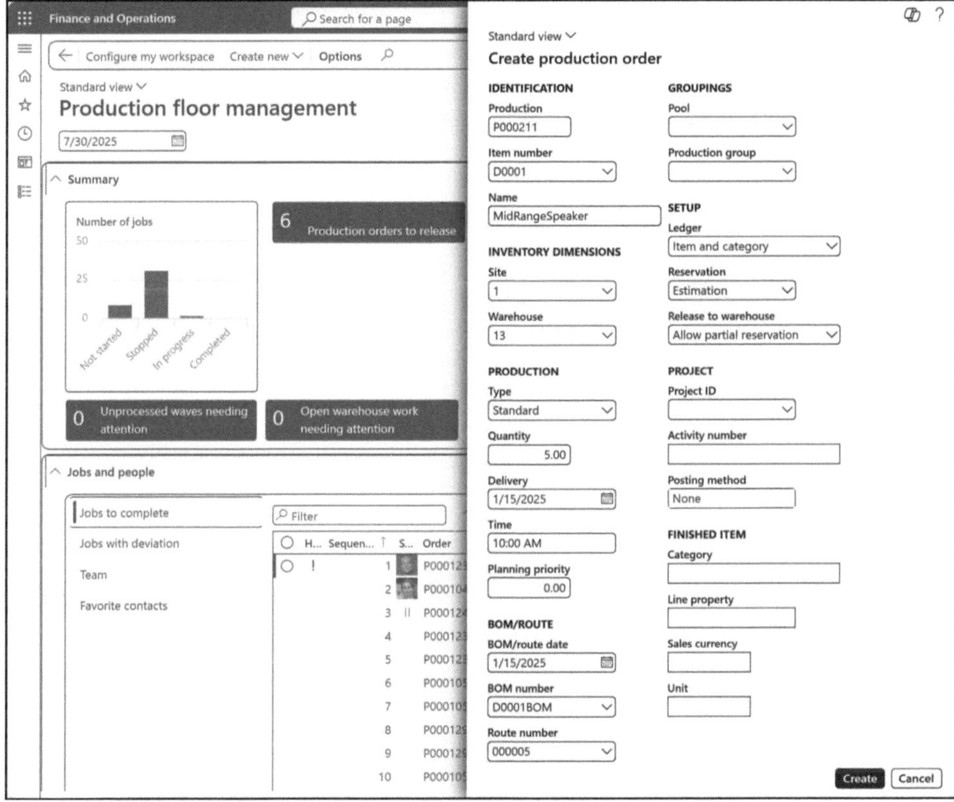

Fig. 5.17   Creating a production order in the Production floor management workspace

5.4.2.2 Production BOM and Route Basics

Like all documents, production orders contain a header with the common data of the order—including the order number, the item number of the manufactured item, the order quantity, and the delivery date. But unlike sales orders or purchase orders, production orders include two different types of lines:

- **BOM lines**—Contain the required materials.
- **Route operations**—Contain the required operations.

The Production order detail form, which you can open with a click on a production order number shown as a link in the Production order list page (*Production control > Production Orders > All Production Orders*), only shows the production order header.

In order to access the BOM lines of a particular production order, click the button *Production order/Production details/BOM* in the action pane. If you want to access the production BOM line details, click on the respective item number shown as a link in the production BOM lines.

The production route with its operations is accessible with the button *Production order/ Production details/Route* in the production order.

When you create a new production order, the production order receives a copy of the BOM and the route of the manufactured item (→ Fig. 5.18). The order subsequently has its own production BOM and route, which you can edit separately from the BOM and the route of the manufactured item.

By default, the BOM and the route that is copied into the production order are given by the active BOM version and route version for the item, site, date, and quantity of the production order. The date which is used for this BOM and route selection is specified in the field *BOM/route date* in the *Create production order* dialog (the default in this field is the delivery date).

If you do not want to use the active BOM version or route version in a particular production order, you can select any other approved BOM version or route version for the manufactured item in the *Create production order* dialog (e.g., an alternative BOM for subcontracting).

5.4.2.3 Last-Minute Changes to Production BOM and Route

Apart from manually changing a BOM item directly in the production BOM (access with the button *Production order/Production details/BOM* in the production order), you can use the feature *Change production order BOM item* to replace an item in multiple production BOMs with another item.

You can access this feature, which only updates production orders in the status "Estimated" or "Scheduled", with the button *Production order/Change/Change BOM item*

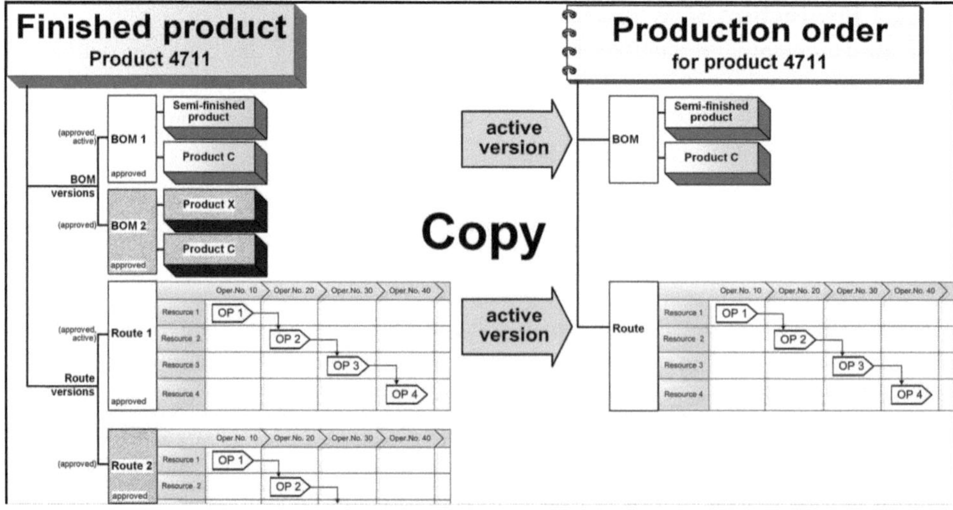

Fig. 5.18 The active BOM/route version is the default for the production BOM/route

in the Production order form, or with the periodic activity *Production control > Periodic tasks > Production order status update > Change production order BOM item.*

For production routes, the button *Production order/Change/Change route* in the Production order form and the related periodic activity provide similar options.

5.4.3   Processing Production Orders

Once a production order is created, you can prepare the order for starting the work on the shop floor in a few steps, which update the status.

5.4.3.1 Default Values in Update Dialogs

When you update the status of a production order, an update dialog is shown. In the update dialog, you can click the button *Default values* if you want to specify default values that are different from the standard defaults. In the default values dialog, you can optionally click the button *Make default for all users* to apply your customized default values to all users.

Your default values are stored in the *Usage data*, which you can access from the user options. Be aware that resetting the usage data resets your default values.

5.4.3.2 Estimation

Estimation is the first step after creating a production order. The primary task of estimation is to calculate the required material and resource capacity for the production order. The basis for this calculation is the bill of materials and the route of the order.

In order to run the estimation, click the button *Production order/Process/Estimate* in the Production order form or execute the related periodic activity.

In parallel to the calculation of the required quantities and times, estimation determines the expected costs (based on the cost price of materials and route operations). If you want to view the cost estimation subsequently, click the button *Manage costs/Calculations/View calculation details* in the Production order form. The tab *Overview estimation* in the Price calculation form shows the estimation lines. A summary according to the costing sheet setup (→ Sect. 7.3.3) is shown on the tab *Costing sheet* in the Price calculation form.

For the BOM lines of the production order, estimation creates inventory transactions that are similar to the inventory transactions of open sales order lines. You can view these transactions with the button *Inventory/Transactions* in the production BOM form (accessed with the button *Production order/Production details/BOM* in the Production order form). All inventory transactions related to a production order are shown in the inquiry, which you can access with the button *Manage costs/Cost transactions/Inventory transactions* in the Production order form.

Since there are no inventory transactions related to BOM lines before estimation, this status is the earliest order status in which you can execute a manual or an automatic reservation (→ Sect. 7.4.5).

If the *Line type* in a production BOM line is "Pegged supply", estimation creates a related order:

- **Sub-production order** (regular production order which is linked to the main production order)—For BOM lines with an item with the default order type "Production".
- **Purchase order**—For BOM lines with an item with the default order type "Purchase order".

For BOM lines with the line type "Phantom", estimation replaces the production BOM line with the components of the phantom item (and, if applicable, adds the route operations of the phantom item to the production route).

> *Note:* The expected costs are only calculated with the estimation, if enabled in the Production control parameters (slider *Price calculation* in the section *General*).

5.4.3.3 Scheduling

Production order scheduling determines the exact date and time of material and resource demand and reserves resource capacity. In Dynamics 365, there are two types of scheduling:

- **Operations scheduling**—At the level of resource groups and dates.
- **Job scheduling**—At the level of individual resources and exact times.

Depending on the setup and your requirements, you can execute either operations scheduling, job scheduling, or both (first operations scheduling, and then job scheduling).

Operations scheduling is a rough scheduling process that calculates the required time per day. Based on the resource requirements in the route operation (capabilities, resource groups, resource types), operation scheduling selects a resource group and reserves the required capacity. Only if the operation contains a resource requirement with the *Requirement type* "Resource", operations scheduling reserves capacity on the resource (and not at the group level).

The available capacity of a resource group is the total capacity of its resources. Current capacity reservations are deducted from the available capacity if scheduling is executed with finite capacity, and if the slider *Finite capacity* in the resource group is set to "Yes". Depending on the Production control parameters (slider *Planned order* in the section *General*), the deducted capacity reservations include planned orders or only actual production orders.

Job scheduling at a later stage calculates the capacity at the level of individual resources and reserves capacity with exact start and end times. In addition to the calculation of exact start and end times, job scheduling generates jobs that split the route operations of a production order into individual tasks (→ Fig. 5.19). These individual tasks show different job types, corresponding to the different time fields on the tab *Times* of the route operation (e.g., *Setup time* and *Run time*). The available job types for a particular operation are

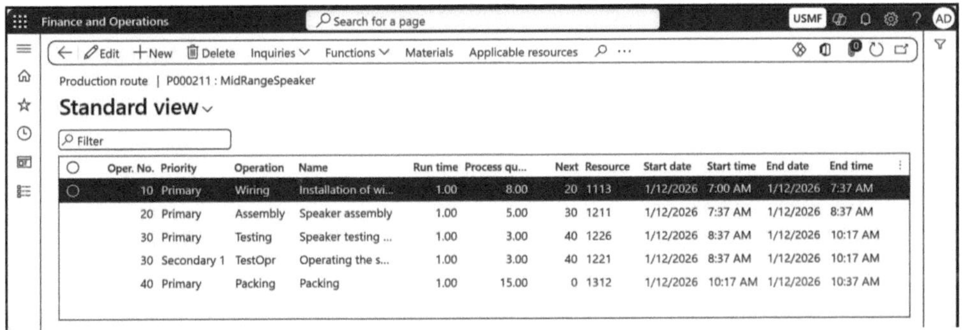

Fig. 5.19 Production route transactions after job scheduling

determined by the *Route group* of the operation (column *Job management* on the tab *Setup* in the Route group form).

Job transactions (which are generated with job scheduling) are independent of route transactions (which refer to operations scheduling). For this reason, you have to decide whether to schedule the capacity and to post the actual resource usage at the operations level or the detailed job level. There are no job transactions in a production order if you skip job scheduling.

In order to execute operations scheduling or job scheduling, click the button *Schedule/ Production order/Schedule operations* or *Schedule/Production order/Schedule jobs* in the Production order form. If you want to schedule multiple orders, execute the corresponding periodic activity in the menu folder *Production control > Periodic tasks > Scheduling*.

The tab *Scheduling parameters* of the update dialog for scheduling includes the following parameters:

- **Scheduling direction**—Select one of the various options for forward or backward scheduling ("Forward from today" is used in case the field is empty).
- **Primary resource selection** (for job scheduling)—Specifies whether a capability-based resource selection primarily searches for the shortest duration (latest start date when scheduling backward) or the highest priority (priority "1" is the highest priority).
- **Finite capacity** and **Finite material**—Observe the resource or item availability.
- **Keep warehouse from resource**—Only a resource, which is assigned to the same input warehouse as the original resource, is selected when you reschedule an order (applicable if the checkbox *Resource consumption* in the BOM lines is selected).
- **Schedule references**—Includes scheduling of sub-production orders.

If required, you can skip particular job types (set the applicable sliders in the field group *Cancellation* on the tab *Parameters per order* to "Yes"). With this setting, you can, for example, skip the setup time if you produce the same product in sequence, or skip the queue time for a production order of high importance.

If you do not execute scheduling in a separate step, it is automatically executed when you update the order to a later status (e.g., if you skip scheduling and immediately release the order). In this case, the *Scheduling method* in the Production control parameters (section *Automatic update*) specifies whether Dynamics 365 runs operations scheduling or job scheduling.

In order to view the route transactions with the scheduled dates, click the button *Production order/Production details/Route* in the production order. Jobs are recorded in a separate table, which you can access with the button *Production order/Production details/ All jobs* in the production order.

You can view the capacity reservations of resources and resource groups in various inquiries—for example, in the capacity load, which you can access with the button *Resource/View/Capacity load* in the Resource form. Capacity reservations for operations scheduling and job scheduling are shown in separate columns and as a total.

On the shop floor, the situation is continuously changing for various reasons—for example, because of delays in the supply of materials. In order to comply with these changes, you can reschedule the orders regularly. For job scheduling, use the periodic activity *Production control > Periodic tasks > Scheduling > Job scheduling* and enter a filter—e.g., on the production order status "Created .. Scheduled" (in the scheduling dialog, click the button *Filter* in the toolbar of the tab *Parameters per order* to access the filter). If you reschedule orders with the status "Released" (or a later status) and you have printed production papers, make sure to replace the papers on the shop floor with papers that show the new dates.

When you reschedule production orders, the capacity reservations of the selected orders are deleted and replaced by new reservations. If you want to lock the dates and the resource assignments for a particular order, set the slider *Locked* on the tab *Setup* in the Production order detail form to "Yes" (alternatively, click the button *Schedule/Production order/ Locked for rescheduling*) to prevent rescheduling.

If required, you can manually reassign a job to a particular resource once the production order has the status "Released". Select the job in the list *Jobs to complete* on the tab *Jobs and people* of the workspace *Production floor management*, click the button *Reassign* in the toolbar of the tab, and select the new resource.

5.4.3.4 Gantt Chart

The Gantt chart (→ Fig. 5.20) is a graphical representation of the jobs that are generated with job scheduling. It is not only possible to view the current jobs, but you can also use drag and drop features in the Gantt chart to reschedule jobs.

In order to open the Gantt chart, click the button *Schedule/View/Gantt chart* in the action pane of the production order. In the Gantt chart, you can select and move jobs as required, and you can use the buttons in the button group *Activity/Maintain* to schedule the previous and subsequent jobs automatically. Once you have finished the updates, click the button *Save* in the Gantt chart to save the updates to the jobs.

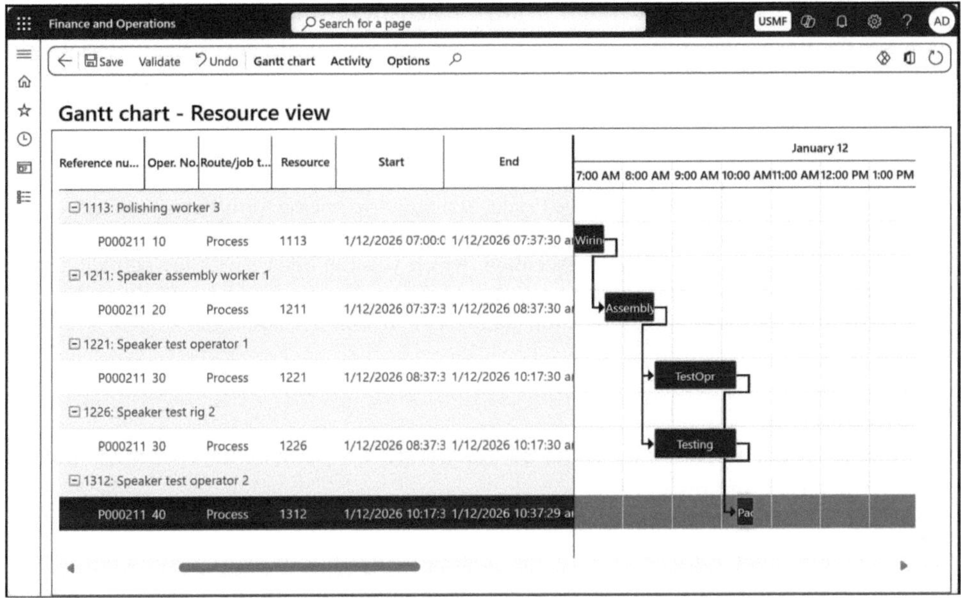

Fig. 5.20 Updating the Gantt chart for a production order

With the buttons in the button group *Gantt chart/Setup*, you can manage the layout of the Gantt chart.

It is not only possible to access the Gantt chart from the production order, but you can also use the respective button in the Resource form, or in the list *Jobs to complete* in the workspace *Production floor management*, or with the button *Gantt* in the form *Production control > Setup > Resources > Gantt chart* (in this form, first create a setup which specifies the resource groups or resources which you want to view).

5.4.3.5 Releasing

In order to transfer the production order to the shop floor, you have to release it. Once released, the production order is shown in the Dynamics 365 Production floor execution pages on terminals or devices.

You can release an order with the button *Production order/Process/Release* directly in the production order. On the tab *General* of the *Release* dialog, you can specify whether to print production papers (job or route cards). In addition, the slider *References* on this tab controls whether referenced sub-production orders are released in parallel.

The workspace *Production floor management* provides a convenient alternative to release orders: For orders with jobs on or before the date selected in the date field at the top of the workspace, you can click the tile *Production orders to release* on the tab *Summary* of the workspace to access the Production orders to release form. This form shows the production orders until the selected date, which have been job-scheduled but not yet released. Select an order in the upper pane and click the button *Material availability check* to check the item availability of the related BOM lines. The availability is then shown in the lower pane of the form. In this way, you can easily check the material availability before you release the order with the button *Release* in the toolbar of the upper pane.

> **Notes on the Production floor management workspace**: In the workspace, make sure to apply an appropriate filter (access the filter with the button *Configure my workspace*). And as a prerequisite for viewing orders in the Production orders to release form, the resource groups must be assigned to production units. The Production orders to release form uses the – separate – job table for Manufacturing execution, which you can update with the periodic task *Production control > Periodic tasks > Update entities > Synchronize job table* (usually not required, if the Manufacturing execution parameter *Job table synchronization mode* is set to "Online").

5.4.3.6 Starting

Starting the production order is a required step before it is possible to post related transactions for materials and resources.

In order to start a production order, click the button *Production order/Process/Start* in the Production order form or execute the related periodic activity. If you do not want to start the entire production quantity, you can enter a partial quantity on the tab *General* of the update dialog for starting. If you enter a *From Oper.No.* and a *To Oper.No.*, only the selected operations are started.

The automatic posting of the resource usage (working time consumption) is controlled by the field group *Route card journal* on the tab *General* of the update dialog. The field *Route card* on this tab specifies the journal name for posting. In the lookup field *Automatic route consumption*, the following options are available for automatic posting:

- **Route group dependent**—Automatic consumption depending on the route group of the operation (→ Sect. 5.3.3).
- **Always**—Automatic consumption of all route operations.
- **Never**—No automatic consumption.

The slider *Post route card now* controls whether the consumption journal is posted immediately. If automatic route consumption is selected and this slider is set to "No", a route card journal is generated, which you can edit before posting.

The automatic consumption of resource capacity is posted with a route card, which is why the route group of operations with automatic consumption should be set up in a way that jobs are not created for these operations.

The automatic BOM consumption settings in the field group *Picking list journal* of the update dialog work similarly to the automatic route consumption settings. If you want to post automatic consumption using the settings in the BOM lines, select the option "Flushing principle" (→ Sect. 5.2.1) in the lookup field *Automatic BOM consumption*. This option refers to the corresponding field on the tab *Setup* in the production BOM line details.

If you set the slider *Print picking list* in the update dialog to "Yes", the picking list is printed in parallel to starting the order. If you want to print a complete picking list, set the slider *Complete picking list journal* to "Yes". The picking list otherwise only shows the items in the picking list journal, which is generated for automatic consumption.

5.4.4 Case Study Exercises

Exercise 5.8—Production Order
Your company needs five pieces of the finished product of exercise 5.2. Enter a corresponding production order and check the BOM and the route in the order.

Exercise 5.9—Purchase Components
In order to process the production order of exercise 5.8, the required components have to be available in inventory.

Enter a purchase order with the vendor of exercise 3.2, which includes 9 units of the first and 5 units of the second item of exercise 5.1. Confirm the purchase order and post the product receipt.

Exercise 5.10—Release and Start the Order
You are asked to process the production order of exercise 5.8. Start with the estimation and check the price calculation afterward. Then execute operations scheduling and job scheduling one after another. Once you have completed scheduling, release the order from the Production order form or from the Production floor management workspace.

Finally, start the order and print the complete picking list (displayed in a print preview). You do not want to post the picking list. Is it possible to apply these settings as a default for all users?

5.5 Consumption of Material and Resource Capacity

In order to know the inventory quantity and to analyze production performance, the actual material consumption and the resource usage must be reported. This reporting is always done in production journals, but there are different ways in which you can create and post the journals:

- **Manually**—Enter and post journals in the respective forms (companies working this way usually do it in the office, based on papers from the shop floor).
- **Automatically**—Create journals automatically (e.g., when starting the order).
- **With terminals or devices**—When reporting consumption in the Production floor execution pages on shop floor terminals or mobile devices, the transactions also generate journals.

If you use the advanced warehouse management, the consumption of material and the receipt of the manufactured item are registered with mobile device transactions in the warehouse (→ Sect. 8.1.3).

Apart from the options in Dynamics 365, you can use the Manufacturing execution integration feature to integrate third-party manufacturing execution systems.

Note: The Job card terminal pages, which have been another option for registering transactions on terminals, are deprecated starting with version 10.0.41.

5.5.1   Journal Setup and Ledger Integration

In discrete manufacturing, there are the following types of production journals for posting consumption related to a production order:

- **Picking list**—Post item consumption.
- **Route card**—Post the use of resources at the level of operations.
- **Job card**—Post the use of resources at the level of jobs.

If item consumption and resource usage are posted automatically (controlled by the *Flushing principle* and the *Route group*), Dynamics 365 creates production journals automatically when starting a production order or when reporting as finished. Production journals are also automatically generated when registrations are transferred from the Manufacturing execution (Production floor execution).

For BOM lines or route operations that are not posted automatically, you have to create production journals manually and enter the transactions as described below.

5.5.1.1 Journal Setup

As a prerequisite for transactions in manufacturing, you have to set up the required journals in the menu item *Production control > Setup > Production journal names*. Picking lists, route cards, job cards, and report as finished journals refer to different journal names, which you have to set up with the appropriate *Journal type*.

The journal type "Report as finished" does not refer to item consumption, but to the receipt of manufactured items in inventory.

5.5.1.2 Ledger Integration

When you post a production journal, the consumption is posted to clearing accounts for WIP (work in progress). Posting to the final ledger accounts is done when you end and cost the production order.

As a prerequisite for posting the item consumption to WIP accounts, the slider *Post picking list in ledger* in the Production control parameters (section *General*) has to be set to "Yes". In addition, the checkbox *Post physical inventory* in the item model group of the picked item has to be selected.

Like the general ledger transactions with reference to product receipts (in purchasing) and to packing slips (in sales), which are reversed when posting the related invoice, the ledger transactions with reference to picking lists, route card journals, and job card journals are reversed when ending the production order.

5.5.2   Picking Lists

Picking list journals are used to register the item consumption related to production orders. To access the picking list journals, click the button *View/Journals/Picking list* in the Production order form or open the menu item *Production control > Adjustments > Picking list*.

Like all journals, picking lists are documents that consist of a header and one or more lines. If you access the picking list journals from the menu, the list page shows all open journals which are not been posted yet. If you want to view the posted journals, apply an appropriate filter in the column *Posted* (use the filter pane, the grid column filter, or the advanced filter). If you access the picking list journal directly from the Production order form, it shows the posted journals immediately.

5.5.2.1 Creating Picking List Journals

If you want to create a new journal, click the button *New* in the action pane of the list page. Select a journal name and click the button *OK* in the *Create* dialog. The Journal detail form with the new journal is then shown in the Lines view.

In order to facilitate the picking list registration, you can click the button *Picking list/ Create lines* instead of the button *New* in the list page or the detail form. In the *Create lines* dialog, specify how the production BOM lines should initialize the journal lines. If you want to use the open quantity as the default for the column *Proposal* in the picking list lines, select the option "Remaining quantity" in the field *Proposal* of the dialog. If you set the slider *Consumption = Proposal* to "Yes", the column *Consumption* in the journal lines is also initialized with the proposal quantity. In this case, you can immediately post the journal without manual data entry (consuming the estimated quantity).

5.5.2.2 Journal Lines

In the Journal list page, you can access the detail form with a click on a journal ID shown as a link in the list page. In the Journal detail form, click the button *Header* (below the action pane) if you want to switch to the Header view, which shows the complete journal header.

When you manually enter a line in the Lines view of a picking list journal, select the *Lot ID* (which links the consumption to a production BOM line) before you enter the *Consumption* quantity. The checkbox in the column *End* of the journal line sets the production BOM line to finished and clears the remaining quantity (select the checkbox if the final consumption is less than the estimated quantity).

If you consume an item that is not included in the BOM lines of the production order, insert a picking list line in which you enter the item number (leave the lot ID empty). Dynamics 365, in this case, automatically creates a corresponding BOM line with no estimated quantity in the production order and applies the lot ID to the picking list line.

In → Fig. 5.21, you can view an example of picking list journal lines that are generated by a consumption proposal. The column *Consumption* in the lines contains a default value for the actual quantity (the slider *Consumption = Proposal* in the *Create lines* dialog has been set to "Yes" when creating the proposal). The last line in → Fig. 5.21 shows a manual entry for an item that is not included in the BOM. The columns *Proposal* and—only before saving the line—*Lot ID* in this line are empty.

Once you have completed the picking list, you can post the journal with the button *Post* in the Journal list page or the detail form. Posting the picking list deducts the quantity from inventory (similar to the packing slip transactions in a sales order).

Inventory valuation applies a preliminary physical value when posting the picking list journal. The financial valuation is posted later when ending and costing the production order.

5.5.2.3 Inquiries and Reversal

If you want to view a posted journal, access the Picking list journal form and enter an appropriate filter in the column *Posted*. The posted journal shows a checkmark in the column *Posted* and does not allow modifications.

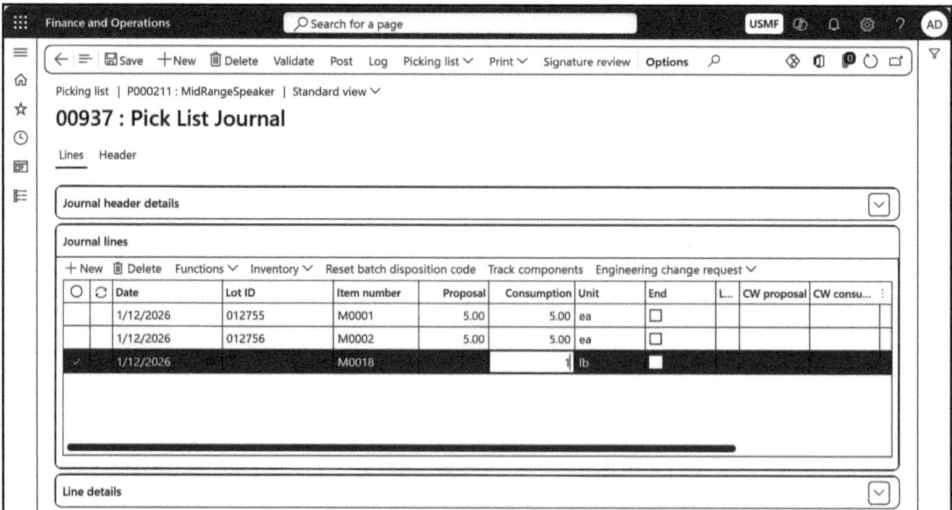

Fig. 5.21 Entering an additional picking list line in a picking list journal

Alternatively, you can view the posted transactions in the Production posting form. In order to access this form, click the button *Manage costs/Production accounting/Production posting* in the production order form or open the menu item *Production control > Inquiries and reports > Production > Production posting*.

If you want to reverse a posted picking list journal, register and post a separate picking list journal with negative quantities. You can create an appropriate picking list proposal with the button *Picking list/Create lines* in the picking list journal (select the option "Full reversal" in the field *Proposal* of the *Create lines* dialog).

5.5.3   Resource Usage

Depending on the route group settings and on the way of scheduling the order, you have to use route cards or job cards to record the usage of resources (usually measured by the working time).

Registering jobs in the Production floor execution pages on terminals or devices also creates journals (usually job card journals) for posting the consumption.

5.5.3.1 Route Cards and Job Cards

Route card journals record the use of resources at the operation level. You should use route cards if you execute only operations scheduling but no job scheduling, or if the setting in the route group (column *Job management* on the tab *Setup*) of an operation prevents the use of job cards.

Job card journals record the use of resources at the job level. Jobs are created when you execute job scheduling. Depending on the route group setting, you should use job cards instead of route cards when jobs have been created for an operation.

The automatic consumption of resource capacity when starting or reporting as finished is posted in route card journals. For registrations that are transferred from Manufacturing execution (Production floor execution pages), a parameter setting (*Production control > Setup > Manufacturing execution > Production order defaults*, lookup field *Job level* in the section *Operations*) determines whether job card or route card journals are posted.

5.5.3.2 Journal Registration of Resource Usage

In order to access the route card journals, open the menu item *Production control > Adjustments > Route card* or click the button *View/Journals/Route card* in the Production order form. For job cards, open the menu item *Production control > Adjustments > Job card* or click the button *View/Journals/Job card* in the production order.

Journal headers and lines in route card journals and job card journals work similarly to picking list journals. But except for the automatic consumption when starting or reporting as finished, there is no consumption proposal in route cards or job cards.

When you insert a journal line in a route card or job card journal, select the operation number (or the job identification) first. Then enter the resource, the task type (only in route cards, in job cards it is derived from the job), the number of hours, the produced quantity (*Good quantity*, only for the task type "Process"), and other data as applicable—for example, the scrap quantity (*Error quantity*) of the manufactured item. In a job card, you should additionally enter the start time, the end time, and the worker (if applicable). The checkbox in the column *End* of the journal line sets the route operation or job to finished and clears the remaining time and quantity (select the checkbox if the final consumption is less than estimated).

Once you have completed the journal lines, you can post the journal with the button *Post* in the Journal list page or the detail form.

If you want to view the posted journal afterward, open the route card journal or the job card journal and enter an appropriate filter in the column *Posted*. In addition, you can view the posted transactions in the Route transactions inquiry (button *Manage costs/Cost transactions/Route transactions* in the production order) or in the Production posting inquiry (*Manage costs/Production accounting/Production posting*).

5.5.3.3 Reporting as Finished in Route Cards and Job Cards

When you register the last operation or job in a journal line, you can select the checkbox in the column *Production report as finished* to post a report as finished journal for the manufactured item (*Good quantity*) in parallel to the route card or job card. The default for the report as finished setting in journal lines is specified in the Production control parameters (slider *Automatic report as finished* in the section *Journals*).

5.5.4   Case Study Exercises

Exercise 5.11—Picking List

You can pick the components of the production order of exercise 5.8 now. Enter and post a picking list journal that includes 9 units of the first component and 5 units of the second component. You do not expect any additional consumption. Pick from the warehouse in which you have received the items in exercise 5.9.

Exercise 5.12—Job Card

Record the actual working time for the operation in the production order of exercise 5.8. For this purpose, enter and post a job card that refers to this production order. Record the production of 5 units in the time between 8:00 AM and 2:00 PM. You do not want to report the order as finished in parallel.

5.6   Reporting as Finished and Ending Production

In the cycle of production order processing, reporting as finished and ending are the last steps. Reporting as finished posts physical transactions and increases the inventory quantity of the manufactured item. Ending the order then performs costing and posts the financial transactions.

5.6.1   Reporting as Finished

Reporting as finished physically receives the manufactured item in inventory. In Dynamics 365, there are the following options to report a production order as finished:

- **Order status update**—Update the status of the production order.
- **Production journal**—Post a report as finished journal.
- **Last operation**—Report as finished in parallel when posting the route card or job card for the last operation ($\rightarrow$ Sect. 5.5.3).
- **Advanced warehouse management**—Post transactions with a mobile device ($\rightarrow$ Sect. 8.1.3).

Optionally, you can use a production input journal (*Inventory management > Journal entries > Item arrival > Production input*) to post an inventory registration before reporting as finished. The production input journal works similarly to the arrival journal in purchasing ($\rightarrow$ Sect. 3.5.3).

5.6.1.1 Order Status Updates

In order to report as finished by updating the order status, click the button *Production order/Process/Report as finished* in the Production order form, or execute the periodic activity *Production control > Periodic tasks > Production order status update > Report as finished* and apply an appropriate filter when selecting the orders.

If you only want to report a part of the entire order quantity, edit the *Good quantity* on the tab *Overview* (or the tab *General*) and deselect the checkbox *End job* in the update dialog before you click the button *OK*. Select the checkbox *End job* in the dialog (which clears the remaining open quantity) in case you do not expect any additional report as finished transaction for the order.

If you are confident, that the actual consumption of items and resources has been posted completely already, and you do not want to receive messages on open consumption (estimated consumption, which has not been reported or cleared—e.g., with the checkbox *End* in the picking list line), set the slider *Accept error* on the tab *General* to "Yes".

5.6.1.2 Production Journals

Apart from the status update, reporting as finished is also possible by posting a production journal. In order to access this journal, click the button *View/Journals/Report as finished* in the Production order form or open the menu item *Production control > Adjustments > Report as finished.*

The options for registering and posting a report as finished journal are similar to the options in a picking list journal ($\rightarrow$ Sect. 5.5.2), but include the order status update settings as described above. A report as finished journal is also created and posted if you report as finished with the order status update.

Posting a report as finished journal generates transactions that are similar to product receipts in purchase orders: Inventory physically receives the item with a preliminary value and increases the on-hand quantity.

5.6.1.3 Automatic Consumption

When reporting as finished, an automatic posting of the item consumption and the resource usage is possible in the same way as when starting the production order. On the tab *General* in the *Report as finished* dialog, the field groups *Route card journal* and *Picking list journal* control automatic consumption in this context.

If you post an automatic consumption when starting and when reporting as finished, select the flushing principle "Start" in the BOM lines that should be consumed when starting the production order, and "Finish" in the BOM lines that should be consumed when reporting as finished. With this setting, you can consume some items when starting and other items when finishing the order.

Route operations do not include this option. The automatic posting is executed for all "automatic posting" operations in a production order at the same time, either when starting or when reporting as finished. In order to avoid duplicate posting, select the option "Route group dependent" in the lookup field *Automatic route consumption* only in the *Start* dialog or only in the *Report as finished* dialog—not in both dialogs.

5.6.1.4 Ledger Integration

If you want to post to clearing accounts (deducting from WIP) when reporting as finished, ledger integration has to be active for the report as finished transactions. For this purpose, the slider *Post report as finished in ledger* in the section *General* of the Production control parameters has to be set to "Yes" and the checkbox *Post physical inventory* in the item model group of the manufactured item has to be selected.

The ledger transactions related to report as finished transactions are reversed when you end and cost the production order.

5.6.1.5 Reporting Scrap

Scrap, which is specified in the BOM or in the route, is planned scrap that is included in the estimated consumption of items and resources. For this reason, the cost analysis does not show this scrap as a deviation between the estimated and the actual consumption. A deviation is only visible if the total actual consumption does not match the estimated consumption. In this context, data in the field group *Scrap* in the line details of the picking list journal are only used for information purposes and do not generate a separate transaction.

Scrapping a (partly or completely) manufactured item in the course of production order processing is unplanned scrap. You can report this scrap in the field *Error quantity* when reporting as finished. The default for the error quantity when reporting as finished is the total of the reported error quantity of all operations (entered in route card or job card journals). If the slider *Increase remain qty with err qty* in the Production control parameters (section *General*) is set to "No", the open quantity of the production order is reduced by the scrap quantity, which means that you accept a lower good quantity.

From a financial perspective, you can allocate the costs for scrapping the manufactured item to the good quantity (which means that the good quantity carries all costs of the production order). Alternatively, you can post the costs for scrapping to a separate scrap account when ending the order (you can specify a default scrap account in the section *Standard update* of the Production control parameters).

If you apply a scrap account, an inventory receipt, and an immediate consumption for scrap (crediting the scrap account) is posted when ending the order. Only when using a scrap account, you can scrap an order completely (with no good quantity).

5.6.2   Ending and Costing

Ending a production order is required for posting the final costs and closing the order. At the same time, WIP ledger transactions for production journals are reversed. The consumption of materials and resources and the receipt of the manufactured item are posted to the final ledger accounts.

You should end a production order on time. Before ending, the WIP account balance for the production order is not cleared, and the manufactured item is only included in the physical inventory, not in the financial inventory ($\rightarrow$ Sect. 7.2.4).

5.6.2.1 Ending

Ending a production order closes the order and executes costing in one step. Since it is not possible to post any further transactions for a closed production order, you should not end the order until you are confident that all transactions are posted.

In order to end the production order, click the button *Production order/Process/End* in the Production order form. If you want to end multiple orders (e.g., in a month-end procedure), execute the corresponding periodic activity in the menu item *Production control > Periodic tasks > Production order status update > End* and apply an appropriate filter (e.g., on the status "Reported as finished") when selecting the orders.

In the inventory transactions, the ending date of the production order is shown in the field *Financial date*. The receipt status in the transaction of the manufactured item is "Purchased". For consumed items (BOM lines), the issue status is "Sold".

5.6.2.2 Costing

From a financial perspective, costing a production order is the equivalent action to invoicing a purchase order or sales order. When you cost the order (which is done automatically in the course of the ending routine), Dynamics 365 calculates the actual costs of all item consumption and resource usage transactions (including indirect costs). Based on these actual costs of the production order, the cost price of the manufactured item is calculated. If the manufactured item applies a standard cost valuation, costing posts the cost price differences to variance accounts.

If you want to compare the actual and the estimated consumption, click the button *Manage costs/Calculations/View calculation details* in the Production order form. The tab *Overview costing* in the Price calculation form ($\rightarrow$ Fig. 5.22) shows—at item and operation line level—a comparison of the estimated and the actual quantity consumption, and of the estimated and the actual costs. If you want to view a summary of the estimation or the actual consumption, switch to the tab *Costing sheet*.

5.6.2.3 Ledger Integration and Inquiries

Like invoice posting in a purchase or sales order, costing a production order generates financial transactions for the items that have been consumed or reported as finished. In this context, costing reverses the WIP ledger transactions that have been posted in picking list

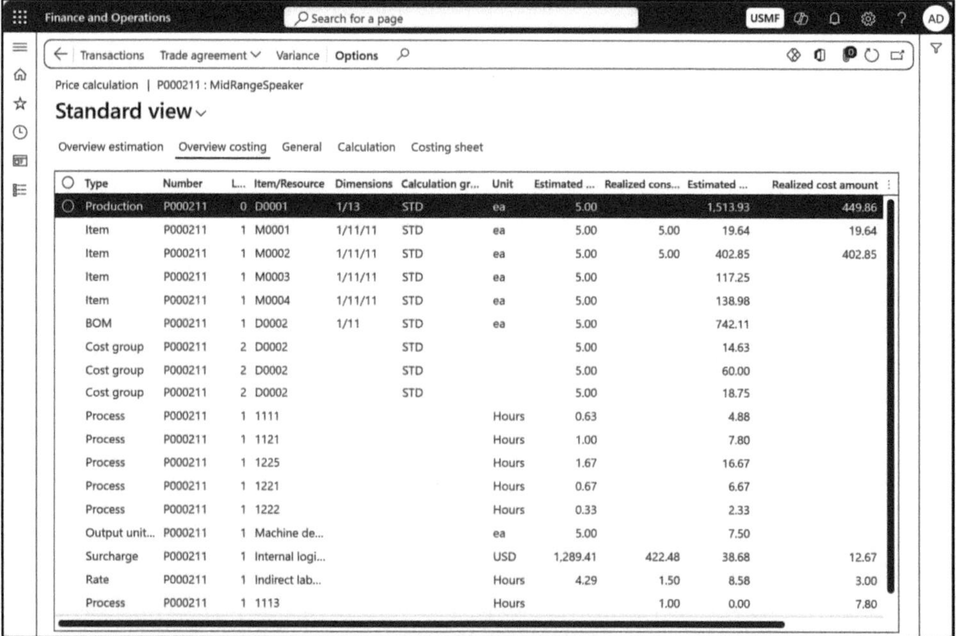

Type	Number	L...	Item/Resource	Dimensions	Calculation gr...	Unit	Estimated ...	Realized cons...	Estimated ...	Realized cost amount
Production	P000211	0	D0001	1/13	STD	ea	5.00		1,513.93	449.86
Item	P000211	1	M0001	1/11/11	STD	ea	5.00	5.00	19.64	19.64
Item	P000211	1	M0002	1/11/11	STD	ea	5.00	5.00	402.85	402.85
Item	P000211	1	M0003	1/11/11	STD	ea	5.00		117.25	
Item	P000211	1	M0004	1/11/11	STD	ea	5.00		138.98	
BOM	P000211	1	D0002	1/11	STD	ea	5.00		742.11	
Cost group	P000211	2	D0002		STD		5.00		14.63	
Cost group	P000211	2	D0002		STD		5.00		60.00	
Cost group	P000211	2	D0002		STD		5.00		18.75	
Process	P000211	1	1111			Hours	0.63		4.88	
Process	P000211	1	1121			Hours	1.00		7.80	
Process	P000211	1	1225			Hours	1.67		16.67	
Process	P000211	1	1221			Hours	0.67		6.67	
Process	P000211	1	1222			Hours	0.33		2.33	
Output unit...	P000211	1	Machine de...			ea	5.00		7.50	
Surcharge	P000211	1	Internal logi...			USD	1,289.41	422.48	38.68	12.67
Rate	P000211	1	Indirect lab...			Hours	4.29	1.50	8.58	3.00
Process	P000211	1	1113			Hours		1.00	0.00	7.80

Fig. 5.22 Viewing the estimation and the actual consumption in the price calculation

journals, route card journals, job card journals, and report as finished journals. In a second step, costing posts the following ledger transactions, which close the order financially:

- **Consumption of components**—To the stock accounts of the BOM line items.
- **Consumption of resource capacity**—To the costing accounts of the resources.
- **Receipt of the produced item**—To the stock account of the manufactured item.
- **Indirect costs**—To the financial accounts specified in the costing sheet.

For the item transactions, applicable main accounts are specified in the posting setup (*Cost management > Ledger integration policies setup > Posting*). For the resource usage, main accounts can derive from settings in the resource/resource group or in the applicable cost category. Apart from these settings, the applicable main accounts for item and resource transactions can also be derived from the production group.

The lookup field *Ledger* on the tab *Setup* of the Production order detail form (initialized from the Production control parameters) determines which of these settings for the main accounts are used ($\rightarrow$ Sect. 9.4.3).

In order to view the transactions that are generated when ending and costing the order, click the button *Manage costs/Production accounting/Production posting* in the Production order form or open the menu item *Production control > Inquiries and reports > Producti on > Production posting*. In the Production posting inquiry, the ending and costing transactions show the type "Costing". If you want to view the related ledger transactions, select the respective line and click the button *Voucher*.

5.6.3 Case Study Exercise

Exercise 5.13—End Production
Report the entire quantity of the production order in exercise 5.8 as finished. Then check the inventory quantity and the inventory transactions of the produced item. Finally, end the production order and check the Price calculation inquiry to compare estimation and costing.

5.7   Subcontracting

If it is not possible or advisable to process a particular operation internally (e.g., for technical reasons or because of insufficient internal capacity), you can subcontract the operation to an external vendor. The BOM and/or route of the manufactured item has to include the subcontracted service in this case.

Sometimes, there is a situation where you can execute an operation alternatively internally or externally—for example, small orders internally, and large quantities with a subcontractor. In order to manage these options, set up a route/BOM version for the manufactured item with the internal operation and an alternative route/BOM version with the subcontracted operation.

In Dynamics 365, there are two basic options for subcontracting:

- **External resource**—Resource with the type "Vendor" in a route operation.
- **Purchased service**—Service item with the line type "Vendor" in a BOM line.

Since a purchase order line needs to contain a physical or service item (it is not possible to purchase a route operation), a purchase order is only created with the second option ("Purchased service").

5.7.1   External Resources

You can use an external resource in an operation that is not linked to a BOM line with a service item if you do not need to generate a purchase order—for example, if there is a contract to use a fixed subcontractor capacity for a given monthly fee.

In this case, create a separate resource group and resource for the subcontractor. Set up the external resource similar to a regular internal resource ($\rightarrow$ Sect. 5.3.2), but with the *Type* "Vendor". In resources with this type, you can select the vendor number in the field *Vendor* on the tab *General* of the Resource form. In addition, make sure to select appropriate cost categories (depending on the contract, maybe only a *Quantity category*) and main accounts for subcontracting. Settings for the calendar and finite capacity depend on the contract. In the route operation, select the *Route type* "Vendor" on the tab *General* and enter the external resource in the field *Costing resource* on the tab *Setup*. On the tab *Resource requirements*, specify the requirements in a way that the external resource is selected.

Processing the operation with the external resource in a production order works similarly to processing an internal operation. There is no automatic purchase order.

5.7.2   Purchased Services

If you need a purchase order for the outsourced operation, create a service item and include it in the BOM of the manufactured item. For scheduling purposes, you can link the BOM line with the service item to an external operation.

5.7.2.1 Master Data for Purchased Services

The required service item is a product with the *Product type* "Service", an *Item model group* that generates inventory transactions ("Stocked product"), and the *Default order type* "Purchase order". In the field *Cost group* on the tab *Manage costs* of the released product, you can select a cost group with the type "Direct outsourcing". The *Flushing principle* on the tab *Engineer* should be "Finish". Other relevant settings in the released product include the item group, the cost price, the dimension groups, the units of measure, the purchase price, the main vendor, and the default order settings. In the BOM of the manufactured item, insert a BOM line with the service item and the *Line type* "Vendor" ($\rightarrow$ Fig. 5.23). You can optionally enter a *Vendor account* in the field group *Subcontractor* of the BOM line, which overrides the main vendor that is specified in the released product.

If you need an outsourced operation for scheduling purposes, you can set it up as described in the previous section. But unlike an outsourced operation which is not linked to a BOM line with a service item, this operation should contain a route group with automatic consumption and—if all subcontracting costs are included in the service item—deactivated cost calculation (the sliders in the field group *Estimation and costing* of the route group are set to "No"). In order to assign the outsourced operation (for scheduling the subcontracted activity) to the BOM line with the service item (for purchasing the subcontracted activity), select the relevant operation number in the field *Oper.No.* on the tab *General* of the BOM line, and make sure that the slider *End* is set to "Yes" (you do not consume the service item before the operation is finished).

If material is supplied to the subcontractor, assign the BOM lines of the related components to the outsourced operation in the same way as you link BOM lines to an internal operation.

5.7.2.2 Production Orders with Purchased Services

You can manually or automatically create a production order with subcontracted service items in the same way as a regular internal production order. Estimating the order creates a purchase order for the BOM line with the service item (triggered by the BOM line type

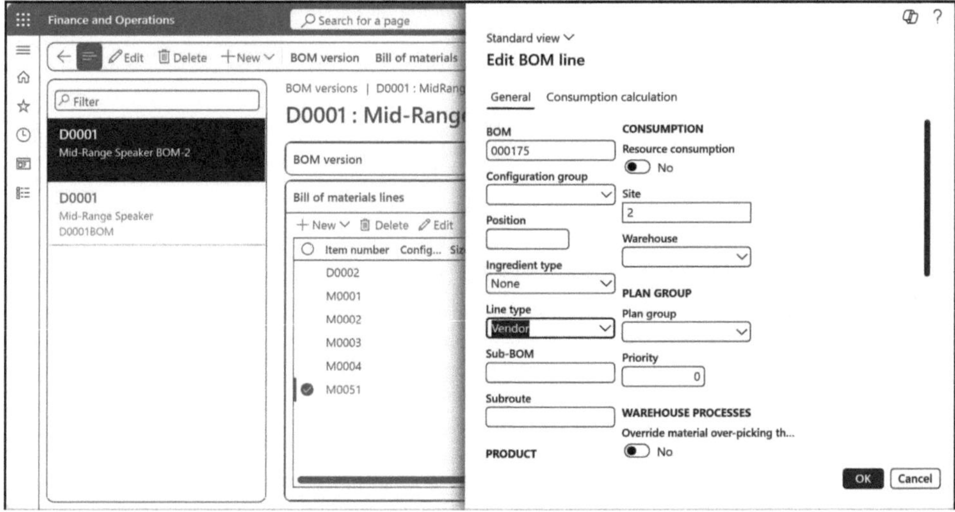

Fig. 5.23 Managing the settings in a BOM line for a subcontracted service

"Vendor" and the default order type "Purchase order"). The production BOM, which you can access with the button *Production order/Production details/BOM* in the production order, shows the reference to the purchase order in the columns *Reference type* and *Number*. Like any other purchase order, the order has to be confirmed before you can receive the service item.

Scheduling and releasing a production order with a subcontracted service is not different from the way you process an internal order.

But you can start a production order with a subcontracted service in the list page *Production control > Subcontracted work*, which includes the button *Start* in the action pane for this purpose. On the tab *General* in the *Start* dialog, make sure to apply appropriate settings for automatic consumption (when starting, do not consume the BOM lines that are consumed when you receive the purchase order). In the print options for the picking list, which you can access with the button *Print options* on the tab *General* in the *Start* dialog, you can set the slider *Use delivery note layout* for the picking list to "Yes" if you supply BOM line items to the subcontractor.

When you post the product receipt for the purchase order afterward, settings in the field group *Receive purchase order* of the Production control parameters (section *Automatic update*) determine if BOM and route consumption are posted in parallel to the product receipt. The settings have to be selected in a way that consumption is not posted two times—both when starting the production order and when posting the product receipt.

Reporting the production order as finished and ending the order works as usual.

5.7.2.3 Item Transfer to Subcontractors

If you want to keep control of the materials that are included in the production BOM and supplied from your warehouse to the subcontractor, you can set up a separate warehouse or location for the subcontractor. When you send an item to the subcontractor, register and post a transfer order or a transfer journal. The consumption of the items in the BOM lines that specify materials consumed by the subcontractor then has to be posted from the subcontractor's warehouse or location.

If you transfer a semi-finished product to the subcontractor after some internal operations, and you want to keep control of the complete material flow with the subcontractor, you have to implement additional BOM levels: Create a semi-finished item that contains all items and operations before the external operation, and a second semi-finished item after the external operation. Both items got the default order type "Production". The BOM of the second semi-finished item contains the first semi-finished item, the subcontracting service item, and—if applicable—additional materials directly supplied to the subcontractor. The BOM of the final manufactured product contains the second semi-finished item and the material required for later operations.

With this setup, master planning generates a (planned) production order for the first semi-finished item, which you receive in inventory by reporting as finished. You can use a regular transfer order to transfer the item afterward and consume it in the upper-level production order of the second semi-finished item. Processing the production order of the second semi-finished item works as described in the section for production orders with purchased services above. When you receive the second semi-finished item from the subcontractor, report it as finished and consume it in the upper-level production order for the finished product.

In order to specify that the first semi-finished item needs to be transferred to the subcontractor's warehouse, you can access the item coverage of this item and set up a record with the subcontractor's warehouse. In this record, mark the checkbox *Change planned order type* on the tab *General* and select the *Planned order type* "Transfer" and the *Main warehouse*, which is your warehouse from which you supply the semi-finished item. For the second semi-finished item, you can set up an item coverage in the other direction (with a record with your warehouse, the subcontractor warehouse is the *Main warehouse* from which the item is shipped). Based on these item coverage settings, master planning generates (planned) transfer orders for the semi-finished items. With similar item coverage settings for the materials supplied to the subcontractor, master planning also generates planned orders for these items.

5.7.3 Case Study Exercise

Exercise 5.14—Setup for Subcontracting
Because of limited internal capacity, the operation that you have set up in exercise 5.6 should be executed by a subcontractor when producing the item of exercise 5.2 with a quantity of 10 units or more.

Set up a subcontractor resource Sub-##-1 and a related resource group Sub-## (similar to exercise 5.5) with a vendor of your choice. Then create route and a route version that is an alternative to the route of exercise 5.7. This new route, in which you enter the subcontractor resource and applicable settings for subcontracting, should be the default when producing 10 units or more. When posting a route card or job card with the route operation, the good quantity should also be reported as finished.

Next, create a service item with the required settings for subcontracting and the product number I-##-SRV, the name "##-processing", the main vendor that you have selected in the resource, and a base purchase price of USD 150. Then create an alternative BOM and BOM version to the BOM of exercise 5.3, which should be the default when producing 10 units or more. Compared to the BOM of exercise 5.3, this new BOM includes a line with the subcontracting service. In order to facilitate production posting, the BOM lines with physical products in this BOM should be consumed automatically when starting a production order.

In order to avoid a duplicate posting of consumption, make sure that the Production control parameter for *Automatic BOM consumption* when receiving assigned purchase orders (in the field group *Receive purchase order* of the section *Automatic update*) is set to "Flushing principle" and for *Automatic route consumption* to "Route group dependent".

Exercise 5.15—Production Order with Subcontracting
A production order with 10 units of the finished product of exercise 5.2 is required and should be processed immediately.

Enter a corresponding production order and check the BOM and the route in the order. Then enter a purchase order with the vendor of exercise 3.2, which includes 20 units of the first and 10 units of the second item of exercise 5.1. Confirm the purchase order and post the product receipt. In the next step, estimate the production order and check the production BOM afterward. It contains a link to the purchase order for subcontracting—confirm this purchase order. In the production order, you can skip scheduling. Start the production order and check the order status and transactions afterward.

The subcontractor then completes his services, and you post the related product receipt. Check the status and the transactions of the production order again.

5.8   Formula Management and Batch Production Order

In discrete manufacturing, a distinct item is produced from multiple components. Process manufacturing, in contrast to discrete manufacturing, covers a continuous process that produces a batch-controlled item together with its co-products.

Production control in Dynamics 365 meets the requirements of process industries by the use of formulas for material management (instead of the bills of materials in discrete manufacturing). Related to resource management, process manufacturing and discrete manufacturing share the same functionality.

If you work in a discrete manufacturing environment and some requirements are covered by process manufacturing features, you can also use formulas. You can, for example, apply a formula with co-products for a cutting operation, even if the items are not batch-controlled. But it is not possible to use formulas in the product configurator.

5.8.1   Formula Management

Formula management is based on bills of materials. Formulas (with formula lines and formula versions) and bills of materials (with BOM lines and BOM versions) share the same concepts and functionality. But in addition to the functionality in bills of materials, formulas include the following core features:

- **Co-products and by-products**—Produce more than one product in parallel.
- **Catch weight items** ($\rightarrow$ Sect. 7.2.1)—Can be included as a finished product or component.

In addition, some features help to manage the quantity in formula lines (e.g., related to the columns *Scalable* and *Percent controlled*).

5.8.1.1 Product Data with Formulas

In the Released product form, items that are produced with a formula have similar settings to items that are manufactured with a BOM (including the default order type "Production"). Some settings are more common in process industry than in discrete manufacturing (e.g., weight as inventory unit), but the only mandatory difference is the setting in the field *Production type* on the tab *Engineer* of the released product. The following options in the *Production type* refer to formula management:

- **Formula**—For the main item which is produced with a formula.
- **Co-product**—Item produced with a formula in parallel to the main item.
- **By-product**—Like a co-product, but undesirable (causing costs, not value).
- **Planning item**—Virtual main item, if a formula only produces co-products.

Planning items are used if there is no clear physical main item in a formula, but co-products with similar importance (e.g., gasoline and diesel in a refinery plant).

You can assign a formula only to an item with the production type "Formula" or "Planning item". Co-products and by-products are produced in production orders of the related formula or planning item. If a co-product is always produced with the same formula or planning item, enter the respective item number in the field *Planning formula* of the co-product (on the tab *Engineer* in the released product).

5.8.1.2 Working with Formulas

You can access the Formula form in a similar way to accessing the BOM form:

- **From the released product** (*Product information management > Products > Released products*, button *Engineer/Formula/Formula versions*).
- **From the menu** (*Product information management > Bills of materials and formulas > Formulas*).

Like the assignment of BOMs, the assignment of formulas to manufactured items is called "Version". The formula version—like the BOM version—can be specified at the level of the site, date (from/to), and quantity.

In the Released product form, you can only access the formulas from items with the production type "Formula" or "Planning item". If you access the Formula form from the menu, the list page shows all formulas. Click on a formula ID shown as a link in the grid of the list page to open the Formula detail form in the Lines view, which shows the formula lines. The formula versions (assignment of formula items or planning items to the formula) are shown in the Header view, which you can access with the button *Header* in the detail form.

The field *Formula size* in the formula version initializes the column *Per series* in the formula lines, and is the default quantity for production orders with the particular product. If there are co-products and by-products, you can access them with the button *Co-products* on the tab *Formula versions* in the Header view of the Formula detail form, or with the button *Formula version/Maintain formula version/Co-products* in the action pane of the Formula version form accessed from the released product (→ Fig. 5.24). In the lower pane of the Co-product form, you can add co-products and by-products with the respective quantity. For a co-product, you can select the *Co-product cost allocation* "Manual" and enter the *Cost allocation percent*. This percentage, which is the percentage of the total production costs that is allocated to the co-product, determines the inventory value of the co-product. For a by-product, select the appropriate option for additional production costs (e.g., covering the disposal) in the *By-product cost allocation*.

Like bill of materials, formulas and formula versions have to be approved before they are available for production orders. And the active formula version is the default for production orders, the item price calculation, and master planning.

5.8.2   Batch Production Orders

Batch orders are production orders for items that are linked to a formula. There is no separate form for batch orders—they use the regular Production order form. In the Production control parameters, you can select a separate number sequence for batch orders (or use the same number sequence as for regular production orders).

The ways for creating a batch order are the same as for creating a regular discrete production order: Apart from manually entering it, you can create it automatically from master planning (including co-product demand in the calculation—select a *Planning formula*

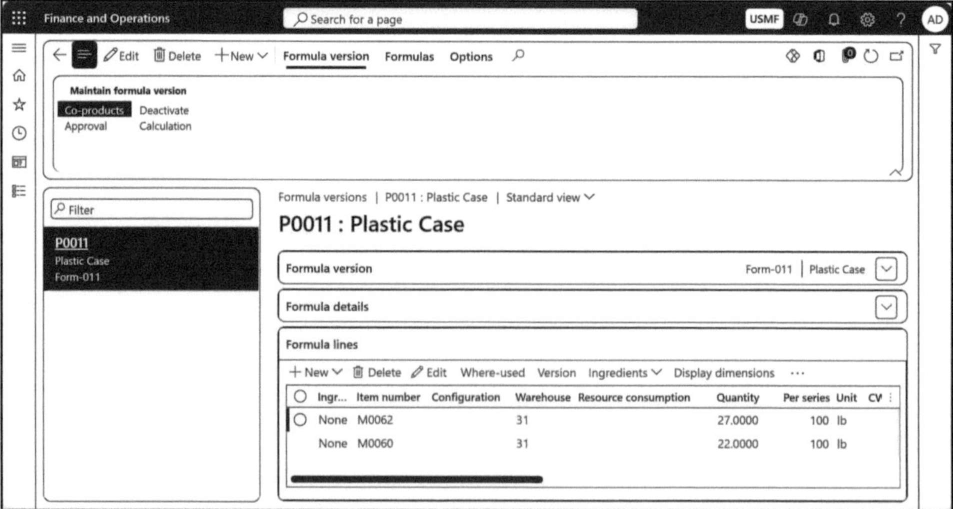

Fig. 5.24 Accessing the co-products from the Formula version form

in the planned order if not specified in the released product), from an upper-level production order (line type "Pegged supply"), or a sales order.

If you want to create a batch order manually, click the button *Create new/Batch order* in the workspace *Production floor management*, or the button *New batch order* in the Production order form. In the *Create* dialog, select the manufactured item (formula item or planning item) next. It is not possible to select a co-product in the order header—select a related formula item or planning item to produce a co-product.

When you create a batch order, Dynamics 365 copies the active/selected formula and route of the manufactured item into the order. In the production order, you can access the formula lines (which show the materials/components) with the button *Production order/ Production details/Formula* and the co−/by-products with the button *Production order/ Production details/Co-products*.

Processing the batch order—from estimation to ending—is not different from a regular production order except when reporting as finished: In addition to the formula item, you can report co-products and by-products as finished. When ending a batch order with co-products or by-products, the production costs are allocated to the co-products according to the settings in the formula, and the additional costs from by-products are posted as a route transaction with a *Burden cost category* (specified in the Production control parameters).

Forecast and Master Planning

Master planning aims to ensure item availability on the one hand and economic efficiency on the other. For this reason, master planning has to deal with the conflicting priorities of high supply readiness on the one hand and low inventory quantity and value on the other.

6.1 Business Processes in Master Planning

In Dynamics 365, the Master planning module covers managing long-term forecasts and executing the short-term master planning. To generate reliable forecasts that are processed in the Master planning module, you can use the Demand planning app.

6.1.1 Basic Approach

The task of forecasting is to identify the item demand on a long-term basis. Master planning calculates the supply and demand on a short-term basis ($\rightarrow$ Fig. 6.1).

6.1.1.1 Forecasting

Forecasting is a long-term prognosis for planning and budgeting purposes. It includes demand forecasts for sales and other demand (e.g., manufacturing materials) and supply forecasts for purchasing and other supplies. Forecast versions enable multiple parallel scenarios.

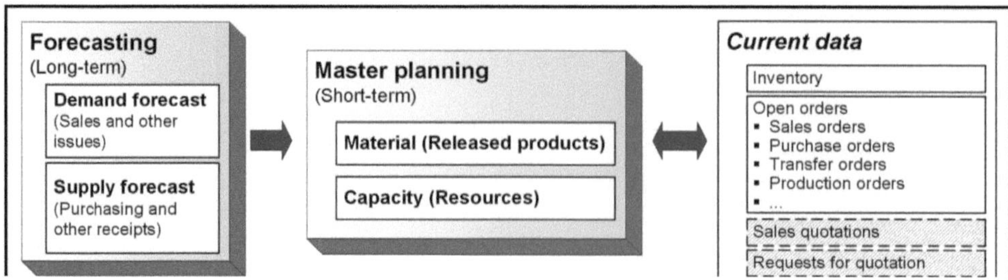

Fig. 6.1 Forecasting and master planning in Dynamics 365

6.1.1.2 Master Planning and Planning Optimization

Master planning covers the short-term planning cycle in the day-to-day business. Based on current orders, on-hand inventory, sales quotations, and forecasts, master planning calculates the item demand and supply. As a result, actual and planned orders for purchasing, transfer, and production are generated. Master planning, like forecasting, provides the option to use multiple scenarios in parallel.

With the Planning Optimization add-in, the master planning calculation is executed in a separate service. This service reduces the impact of the calculation on the performance of the transactional database and eliminates the requirement to run master planning outside the regular business hours.

6.1.2 At a Glance: Master Planning

The following example demonstrates the main steps in master planning with the example of the net requirements calculation for a manufactured item.

As a basis for the net requirements calculation, enter a sales order and an order line with a manufactured item (default order type "Production") that should be shipped today, but is out of stock. In the toolbar of the order lines, click the button *Product and supply/Net requirements* to access the Net requirements form that shows the item availability ($\rightarrow$ Fig. 6.2). In order to update the net requirements based on current data, click the button *Update/Master planning* to execute master planning for the selected item. In the described scenario, master planning generates a planned production order for the manufactured item.

You can manage several parallel scenarios in master planning—for example, a static plan and a dynamic plan. In the Net requirements form, the dynamic plan (used for simulation and order promising) is the default for the planned orders that are shown. The static plan is used for scheduling and firming orders in the planning or purchasing department. In order to switch between the different plans, select the appropriate option in the lookup field *Plan* at the top of the Net requirements form.

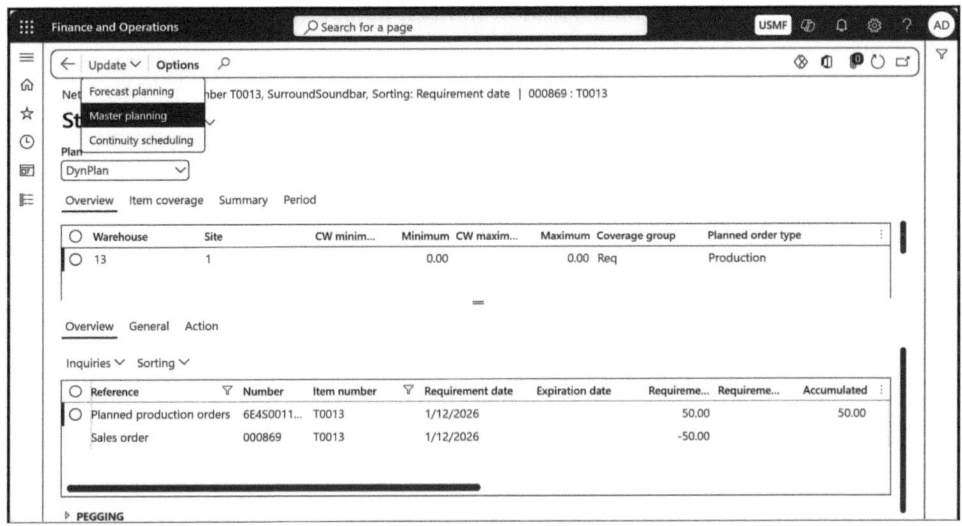

Fig. 6.2 Net requirements after executing master planning

6.2 Forecasting

A forecast is a long-term prognosis, which you use for estimating and adjusting future capacities in resource and material management. In addition, you can use forecasts as a basis for budgeting in finance. You can maintain multiple forecasts, which represent alternative scenarios for the business development, in parallel.

To generate the forecasts, which represent future item demand in Dynamics 365 Finance and Operations, you can use the Demand planning app with its advanced forecasting algorithms and models.

Forecasts in Dynamics 365 do not only include sales forecasts, but you can also include other sources of item demand. Apart from demand forecasts, you can manage supply forecasts—e.g., for a prognosis of long-term vendor contracts.

6.2.1 Basics of Forecasting

Forecast models represent the planning scenarios. When you enter or calculate a forecast in Dynamics 365, you have to select a forecast model which holds the forecast data. In master planning, you can include a forecast model as a source of supply and demand.

6.2.1.1 Demand Forecasts

Estimated sales figures are the starting point for the forecast of future demand. Apart from the sales demand, demand forecasts may also include other demand—for example, the demand for semi-finished items (instead of finished items) if it is not possible to provide reliable forecasts at the detail level of finished products.

Forecasts are based on released products. If it is not feasible or possible to specify forecasts at the level of individual items, you can use item allocation keys. An item allocation key contains several items and determines the percentage distribution between these items.

6.2.1.2 Supply Forecasts

Separately from demand forecasts, you can optionally manage supply forecasts with purchasing transactions and other types of item receipts.

6.2.1.3 Including Forecasts in Master Planning

You can include forecasts in master planning. For this purpose, settings in the master plans determine if and how to include forecasts.

The reduction key in coverage groups and the reduction principle in master plans are options to avoid a duplicate consideration of future demand. Without reduction, a duplicate consideration results from a forecast demand in upcoming periods in which there are actual sales orders already—supposing that these sales orders are part of the forecast quantity and not in addition to the forecast.

6.2.2   Basic Settings for Forecasts

Before you can start to register forecasts, you have to finish the required setup in Dynamics 365.

6.2.2.1 Forecast Models

Forecast models represent the different scenarios in forecasting. In order to use forecasts, you have to set up at least one forecast model in the Forecast models form (*Master planning > Setup > Demand forecasting > Forecast models*).

If you want to structure forecasts (e.g., for managing forecasts by region), you can configure a forecast model with submodels. Create the submodels like regular forecast models for this purpose first, and then create the main model, to which you assign the submodels (on the tab *Submodel* of the Forecast model form).

If you want to protect forecasts against changes, set the slider *Stopped* in the forecast model to "Yes". You can use blocking, for example, if you do not want any changes on an annual forecast once it is completed (use a separate forecast model per year in this case).

6.2.2.2 Parameters and Item Allocation Keys

If you do not want to manage forecasts at the level of individual items, you can use item allocation keys. With an item allocation key, you can enter a forecast total for a group of items. In order to set up item allocation keys, open the menu item *Master planning > Setup > Demand forecasting > Item allocation keys*. The tab *Item allocation* in this form contains the assigned items with their percentage.

Demand forecasting parameters (*Master planning > Setup > Demand forecasting > Demand forecasting parameters*) are required if you want to use Azure Machine Learning-based demand forecasting.

If you want to use the Demand planning app, set the Demand planning app parameters (*System administration > Setup > Demand planning app parameters*) and, in the Data management workspace, enable data imports and exports to and from the Demand planning app.

6.2.3 Managing Demand Forecasts

You can enter forecasts manually (including the option to import forecast data from Excel with the Microsoft Office integration), but it is also possible to generate demand forecasts assisted or automatically with Azure Machine Learning features or with the Demand planning app.

6.2.3.1 Manual Demand Forecasts

To enter a forecast manually, open the menu item *Master planning > Forecasting > Manual forecast entry > Demand forecast lines*. Alternatively, access the forecast lines with the button *Demand forecast* (or *Forecast*) in the action pane of master data forms—e.g., in the Released product form (button *Plan/Forecast/Demand forecast*) or in the Customer form (button *Customer/Forecast/Forecast*).

When you insert a demand forecast line (→ Fig. 6.3), select the applicable forecast model in the column *Model* first. You can record different scenarios with different models in separate lines. In the column *Date*, enter the start date of the particular forecast period—for example, the first day of a month if you enter a line per month. If you want to record a forecast per customer or customer group, select the *Customer account* or *Customer group* in the respective column. Then select the *Item number* or the *Item allocation key* before you enter the *Sales quantity* and the *Amount* (or, if it is possible to calculate the amount from the quantity and the price, the *Sales quantity* and the *Sales price*). If you want to allocate a forecast line across periods, click the button *Allocate forecast* in the toolbar of the tab *Overview* and enter the allocation details in the following dialog.

You can facilitate the manual forecast entry with bulk updates (click the button *Bulk update* in the toolbar of the tab *Overview*) or with the Excel integration. To use Excel, click the button ▣/*Demand forecast entries in Excel* in the action pane, change and add lines in Excel as appropriate, and publish the data back to Dynamics 365.

6.2.3.2 Azure Machine Learning-Based Demand Forecasting

As an alternative to the manual entry of demand forecast lines, you can create demand forecast lines with Azure Machine Learning (Azure ML). With Azure ML-based demand

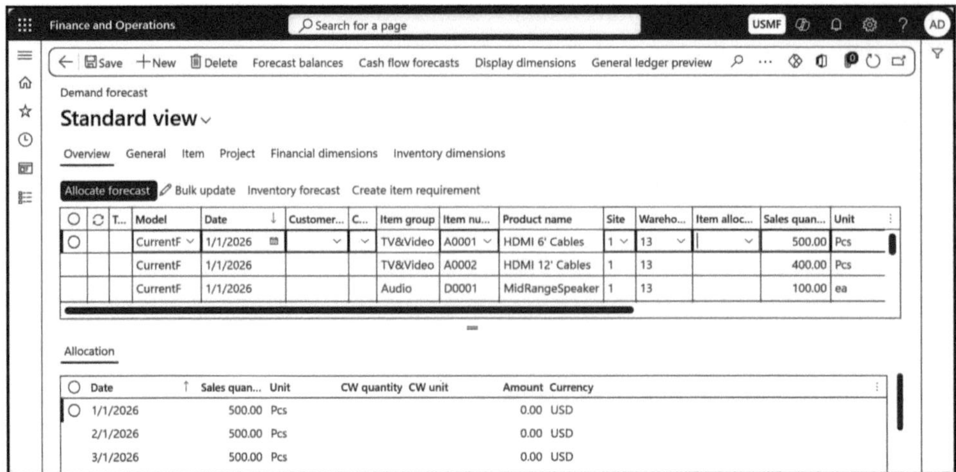

Fig. 6.3 Allocating a sales forecast line across periods

forecasting, you can calculate forecasts based on historical demand (originating from inventory transactions in Dynamics 365).

Once item allocation keys and Demand forecasting parameters are set up, you can access the Adjusted demand forecast form (*Master planning > Forecasting > Demand forecasting > Adjusted demand forecast*) and click the button *Generate statistical baseline forecast* to calculate the forecast using Azure ML. You can edit the forecast data in the Adjusted demand forecast form as required before you click the button *Authorize adjusted demand forecast* to create the actual demand forecast lines.

6.2.3.3 Demand Planning App

The Demand planning solution is another option to generate demand forecasts. With the *Demand planning* app, which needs to be installed separately, you can use advanced algorithms and customizable models for creating forecasts.

You can import master data and historical demand from Dynamics 365 Finance and Operations and other sources to the Demand planning app, execute planning there, and export the forecasts back to Dynamics 365 Finance and Operations for further use in master planning.

6.2.3.4 Supply Forecasts and Inventory Forecasts

If you want to manage a supply forecast separately from the demand forecast, for example if it is required to purchase or produce a minimum quantity per period, open the menu item *Master planning > Forecasting > Supply forecast lines* or click the button *Supply forecast* or *Forecast* in the action pane of the respective master data form (released product, vendor) and enter the supply forecast in a similar way to the demand forecast. Depending on the setup, master planning then includes the supply forecast in parallel to the demand forecast.

Inventory forecasts show the result of supply and demand forecasts at the level of item numbers and periods. You can access the inventory forecasts with the button *Inventory forecast* in applicable master data forms.

6.2.4   Case Study Exercise

Exercise 6.1—Demand Forecast
You are asked to enter a new sales forecast for items that you have set up in the previous exercises. You expect the customer of exercise 4.1 to order 200 units of the merchandise item of exercise 3.5 and 100 units of the finished product of exercise 5.2 on the first day of the next three months.

This forecast should be included in a scenario that is separate from other forecast scenarios.

In order to meet this requirement, create a forecast model F-## (## = your user ID) without submodels and enter the expected customer demand in a demand forecast with this forecast model.

6.3   Master Planning and Planning Optimization

Master planning in Dynamics 365 covers the short-term calculation of material and capacity requirements. It is the basis for the day-to-day work in purchasing and production management.

The calculation in master planning is based on data related to released products and to resources across Dynamics 365. As a result, master planning generates planned orders for purchasing, production (including Kanbans), and inventory transfer. In addition, action messages and notifications on calculated delays support the adjustment of current orders.

6.3.1   Basics of Master Planning

Depending on the setup, sales orders, purchase orders, production orders, transfer orders, and the on-hand quantity in inventory are an essential basis for master planning. In addition, master planning can include sales quotations, requests for quotation, approved purchase requisitions, and forecasts (→ Fig. 6.4).

Like in forecasting, you can maintain multiple parallel scenarios in master planning. A scenario is represented by a master plan, which contains the particular setup for the scenario. Relevant settings in the plan relate to the elements that are included in master planning and the calculation principles for planned orders.

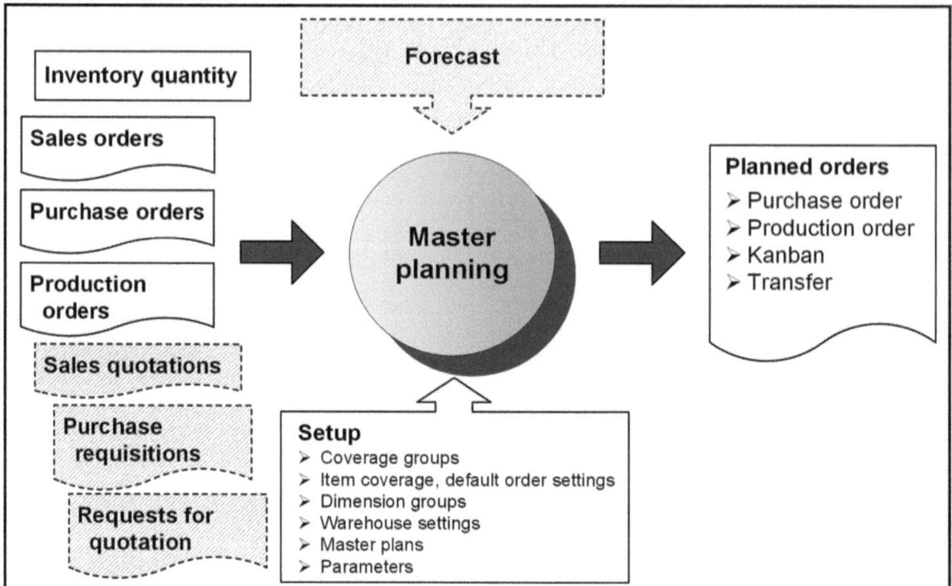

Fig. 6.4 Elements of master planning

6.3.1.1 Master Planning Strategies

In a legacy environment without Planning Optimization, master planning runs within the transactional database and puts a heavy load on the database engine. In this case, master planning is usually executed in a batch job that calculates the net requirements for all items every night. The result of this calculation is available in a scenario called "static master plan".

If you work with the Planning Optimization add-in, performance considerations are not the reason for recalculating the static plan only at night. But still, there may be organizational reasons to restrict it to a night job, avoiding planned orders in the static plan to be automatically updated during the day.

The static plan is the master plan that is used in purchasing and in production control departments for scheduling planned orders. It is the default plan that is shown when you open a Planned order form.

Apart from the master plan that is used for purchase and production scheduling, the sales department often needs to run simulations of possible delivery dates in sales orders and in quotations. This simulation requires master planning only for a particular item. The result of the simulation is available in a scenario called "dynamic master plan".

In order to meet these requirements, there are two different strategies that you can set up in the Master planning parameters:

- **One-plan strategy**—One common plan for scheduling and simulations.
- **Two-plan strategy**—Separate plans for scheduling and simulations.

If the same master plan is selected for the static and the dynamic master plan in the Master planning parameters, you run a one-plan strategy. Planned orders of current simulations in the sales department update the static plan, which is the plan used in purchasing and production control. Depending on the requirements of your enterprise, this strategy does or does not fit your business.

If you want to apply a two-plan strategy, select a different master plan for the static and the dynamic plan. If you recalculate both plans every night, the simulation in sales starts with the same data basis as purchasing and production scheduling in the morning. Simulations throughout the day do not modify the planned orders in the static plan, which avoids confusion in purchasing and production control caused by continuous changes in planned orders.

6.3.1.2 Customer Order Decoupling Point

Depending on the structure of the products, there are two key supply policies in production control for fulfilling customer demand:

- **Make-to-Stock**—Produce based on sales forecasts and historical demand.
- **Make-to-Order**—Produce based on confirmed sales orders.

In addition, there are hybrid supply strategies that apply a make-to-stock strategy for purchased or semi-finished items with a long lead time, and a make-to-order strategy for finished products. If you apply a hybrid strategy, the customer order decoupling point (push/pull point) determines the level in the product structure to which the items are built to stock.

With the use of appropriate coverage groups (→ Sect. 6.3.4), you can apply all of these strategies. In DDMRP (→ Sect. 6.3.6), identifying the decoupling points as part of inventory positioning is a core task.

In case of a simple hybrid supply strategy without using DDMRP, enter forecasts at the semi-finished product level (which is the customer order decoupling point for these items). The reduction principle (field *Method used to reduce forecast requirements*) in the master plan determines the way in which master planning offsets forecasted demand with actual orders. You do not sell the semi-finished product, which is why sales orders do not directly offset forecasts of semi-finished products. For this reason, you should select to include all inventory transactions—including BOM line demand from production orders—in the coverage groups of applicable semi-finished items. In the Coverage group form, the lookup field *Reduce forecast by* on the tab *Other* contains the required option for this purpose.

6.3.1.3 Generating Planned Orders

Master planning generates planned purchase orders, planned production orders, planned Kanbans, and planned transfers based on the item demand and settings for master planning. Apart from planned orders that cover direct demand (this is demand from sales orders, forecasts, or other sources selected in the master plan), master planning also generates planned orders for derived demand (components required in planned production orders). If a BOM includes substitute items ($\rightarrow$ Sect. 5.2.2), a planned order is only created if no substitute is available. Before creating new planned orders, master planning initially deletes existing planned orders that are not in the status "Approved".

You can review and edit the planned orders before you convert them to actual purchase orders, production orders, Kanbans, and transfer orders (or, if selected in the Site form, transfer journals).

6.3.2 Planning Optimization

The Planning Optimization add-in provides the option to execute master planning as a separate service outside the transactional Dynamics 365 environment. Unlike the built-in master planning engine, Planning Optimization this way enables running master planning at any time without a negative impact on the performance.

The Planning Optimization service replaces the built-in master planning engine, which is deprecated and does not receive updates.

6.3.2.1 Technical Overview and Differences to the Built-in Engine

Planning Optimization is a separate service which is designed for a fast calculation of large data volumes. It receives the required data and the execution trigger from the transactional Dynamics 365 environment and returns the calculation results.

As a prerequisite for Planning Optimization, it must be enabled in the license configuration. The Planning Optimization add-in, which acts as connector, must be implemented in the Power Platform Admin Center (PPAC). Subsequently, you can activate the Planning Optimization in the parameters (*Master planning > Setup > Planning Optimization parameters*).

While the technical implementation of Planning Optimization is different from the built-in master planning engine, the implemented functionality—apart from improvements and additional features in Planning Optimization—for the most part matches the built-in master planning engine.

6.3.2.2 Using the Planning Optimization

The user interface does not show a big difference between working with the Planning Optimization and the built-in master planning. You can use the same menu items for the setup and the execution of master planning, no matter if the built-in engine or the Planning Optimization service runs the calculation.

The main difference is that Planning Optimization returns the results much faster and that you can run it at any time without a negative impact on the system performance.

If you want to view the master planning job history and the Planning Optimization logs, which eventually show important warnings, open the form *Master planning > Setup > Plans > Master plans*, select the respective plan and click the button

History in the action pane. In the History form, the button *Logs* provides access to the warnings which have been generated (in case there are any).

6.3.3   Master Planning Setup

Before you can execute master planning, an appropriate setup in Dynamics 365 is required.

6.3.3.1 Master Plans

A master plan is a scenario with supply and demand calculation data which are separate from the scenarios in other master plans. Depending on the planning strategy, only one or two master plans are used. If you need more simulation scenarios, you can set up additional master plans.

You can manage the master plans in the Master plan form (*Master planning > Setup > Plans > Master plans*). Sliders on the tab *General* determine for each master plan, which items are included in the calculation (→ Fig. 6.5):

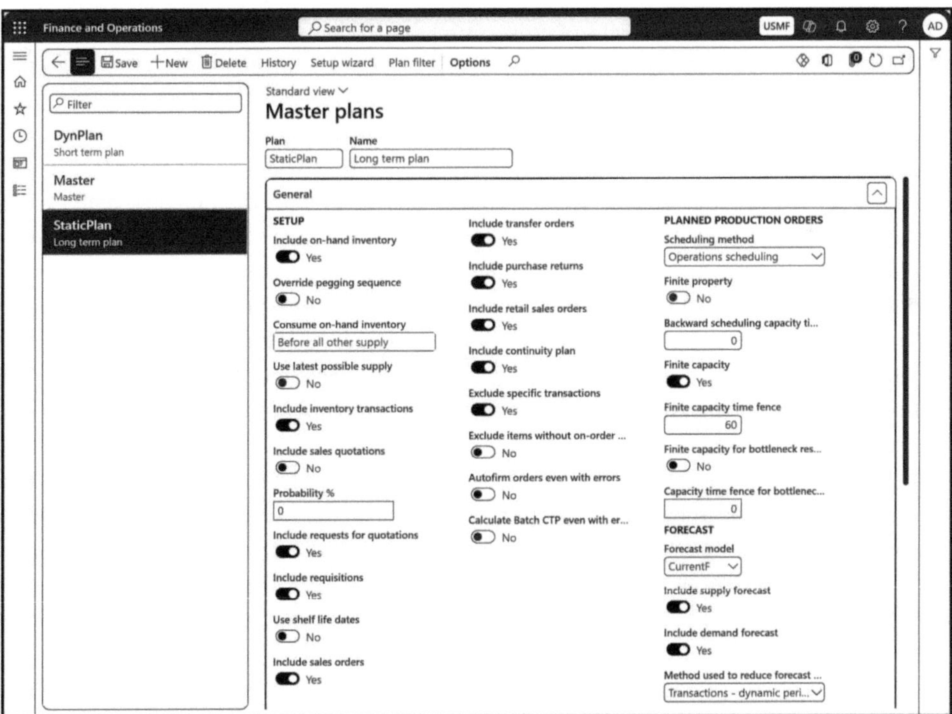

Fig. 6.5 Editing a master plan in the Master plan form

- **Include on-hand inventory**—Refers to the current inventory.
- **Include inventory transactions**—Covers "open orders" (e.g., sales orders), in connection with the sliders *Include sales orders, Include transfer orders* et al.
- **Include sales quotations**—Optionally restricted by a minimum probability.
- **Include requests for quotation**—Entered in procurement and sourcing.
- **Include requisitions**—Only approved purchase requisitions with the requisition purpose "Replenishment" (→ Sect. 3.8.2).
- **Use shelf life dates**—For batch-controlled items.
- **Include continuity plans**—Related to Retail and Commerce features.
- **Include demand forecast**—For the *Forecast model* in the master plan.

For sales quotations, you can optionally specify a minimum probability percentage. Only quotations with at least this probability are included in master planning. The probability is given by the opportunity that is attached to the quotation.

The sliders *Include sales orders, Include transfer orders, Include purchase returns*, and *Include retail sales orders* in the Master plan form provide the option to include or ignore the related order types in the calculation.

If you set the slider *Exclude specific transactions* in the Master plan form to "Yes", you can exclude selected sales orders or sales order lines from master planning. In order to exclude an order from master planning, set the slider *Exclude from master planning* in the order header or line to "Yes".

The slider *Override pegging sequence* and the related lookup field *Consume on-hand inventory* in the Master plan form control whether current inventory is kept for last-minute orders. This is in particular relevant for sales order lines with the delivery date control "CTP" (→ Sect. 4.3.3) because with this parameter, you can choose whether the item availability for a sales order is verified in the sequence of the order entry (first consuming on-hand quantity, then searching future supply which can cover the order, finally generating a planned supply order as a last resort) or in the sequence of the delivery dates (in other words, whether a later order with an earlier date may consume the inventory first). The setting in the master plan overrides the corresponding setting in the coverage group and in the item coverage.

If you want to include sales forecasts in master planning, set the slider *Include demand forecast* to "Yes" and select the appropriate forecast model in the respective field of the master plan. In order to avoid excessive demand which results from adding forecasts for a period to actual orders in the same period, you should offset the forecast by the current orders in this case—select the corresponding reduction principle in the master plan (→ Sect. 6.3.4).

The field *Scheduling method* in the Master plan form controls whether to run operations scheduling or job scheduling (→ Sect. 5.4.3) for planned production orders. Among other settings for scheduling planned production orders, there is the option to apply finite capacity.

On the tab *Time fences in days* in the Master plan form, you can override the time fences which are specified in the coverage group or in the item coverage.

The tab *Calculated delays* contains settings which specify, whether master planning may set the requirement date to a date, which is after the original requirement date in case it is not possible to meet the original requirement date (based on the applicable lead times). This setting prevents impossible dates like a delivery date in the past.

6.3.3.2 Master Planning Parameters

In the Master planning parameters (*Master planning > Setup > Master planning parameters*), there are the general settings for master planning. As a prerequisite for master planning, the slider *Disable all planning processes* in the parameters has to be set to "No".

Further core parameter settings control the planning strategy: If you want to apply a one-plan strategy, enter the same master plan in the fields *Current static master plan* and *Current dynamic master plan*. If you want to apply a two-plan strategy, select two different master plans.

> *Note:* The parameter for copying the data from the static plan to the dynamic plan is only applicable with the built-in master planning engine.

6.3.3.3 Warehouse and Site Settings

If a particular warehouse (for example, a consignment warehouse that is managed by the customer) should be excluded from master planning, set the slider *Manual* for the warehouse (*Inventory management > Setup > Inventory breakdown > Warehouses*, tab *Master planning*) to "Yes".

The tab *Master planning* in the Warehouse form also contains the slider *Refilling* and the related field *Main warehouse* which control whether the warehouse should be refilled from another warehouse (main warehouse). If selected, master planning generates item transfer proposals instead of planned purchase or production orders. As a prerequisite, the item must be assigned to a storage dimension group with the checkbox *Coverage plan by dimension* selected for the dimension "Warehouse".

If you don't need the functionality of transfer orders for transfers within a particular site, you can set the slider *Use transfer journals for movements within site* on the tab *General* in the Site form (*Inventory management > Setup > Inventory breakdown > Sites*) to "Yes". Master planning then generates a transfer journal instead of a transfer order for transfers within the site.

6.3.4   Item Coverage and Item Settings

Coverage groups and coverage settings in the released product control the calculation of the quantity and the delivery date in planned orders.

6.3.4.1 Coverage Code

The coverage principle, which is specified by the *Coverage code* in the coverage groups, is the primary setting for the item coverage. It controls the way in which requirements are summarized into a planned order.

Dynamics 365 includes the following coverage codes (→ Fig. 6.6):

- **Period**—Summarizes requirements within the coverage period (specified in the coverage group).
- **Requirement**—Creates a planned order per requirement.
- **Min./Max.**—Replenishes to the maximum quantity when inventory drops below the minimum quantity.
- **Manual**—Planned orders are not generated in master planning.
- **Priority**—Applies priority-based planning (→ Sect. 6.3.6).
- **Decoupling point**—For items that represent a decoupling point in DDMRP (→ Sect. 6.3.6).

Master planning generates a planned order if the calculated inventory at a date is below the minimum quantity (or below zero, if there is no minimum quantity in the item coverage of the released product).

Priority-based planning and DDMRP use the reorder point instead of the minimum quantity as a trigger for generating planned orders.

6.3.4.2 Managing Coverage Groups

The coverage groups (*Master planning > Setup > Coverage > Coverage groups*) determine the coverage code and further settings for calculating the quantity and the delivery date. For the *Coverage code* "Period", the *Coverage period* below this field determines the number of days for aggregating demand into a common planned order (→ Fig. 6.7).

The field *Positive days* on the tab *General* determines the time fence for including the on-hand quantity in the calculation. It should correspond to the lead time or the coverage time fence (depending on the order history).

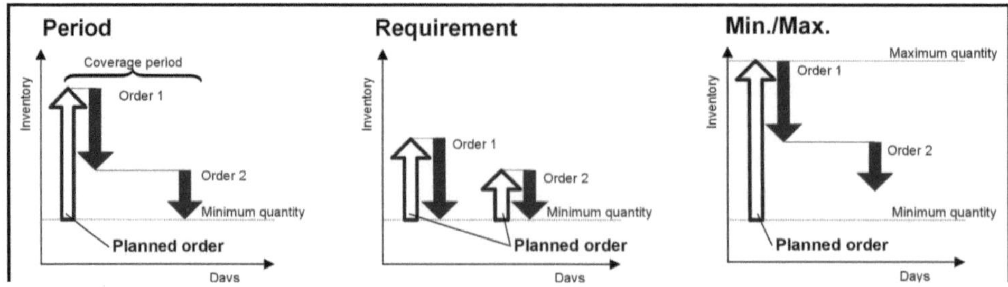

Fig. 6.6 Calculation result of coverage codes in Dynamics 365

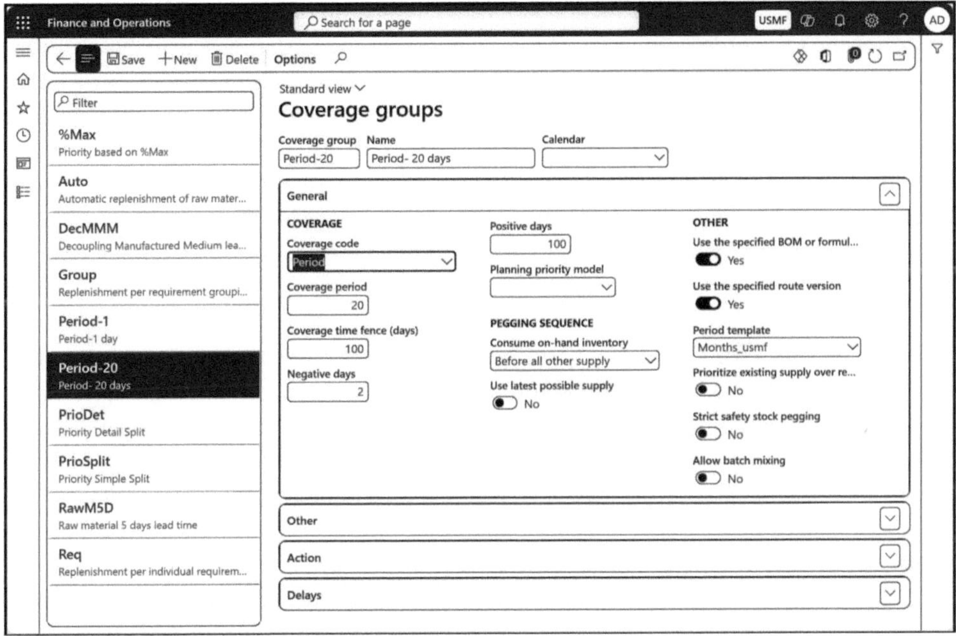

Fig. 6.7 Selecting the coverage code in a coverage group

The *Coverage time fence* on the tab *General* and the time fence fields on the tab *Other* determine the periods which are included in master planning. Depending on the planning strategy and the lead time of the items, the number of days entered in the time fence fields should cover an applicable number of weeks or months.

The *Automatic firming time fence* on the tab *Other* determines the period, in which master planning does not create a planned order but directly an actual purchase order or production order.

> *Note:* When specifying an *Automatic firming time fence*, be aware that auto-firming is based on the order date (start date) with Planning Optimization whereas it is based on the requirement date (end date) with the built-in master planning engine.

6.3.4.3 Forecasts and Reduction Keys

The *Forecast plan time fence* and the *Reduction key* on the tab *Other* of the Coverage group form determine how to include forecasts in master planning.

In the Master plan form, the reduction principle (field *Method used to reduce forecast requirements*) controls the way in which forecasts are reduced when they are included as demand. If the reduction principle in the master plan refers to a reduction key, the applicable coverage groups have to specify a *Reduction key*.

Reduction keys (*Master planning > Setup > Coverage > Reduction keys*) control the periods and percentages which are used to reduce the forecast figures in the course of time.

You can, for example, use a reduction key with a reduction of 75% for a period of 7 days, if 75% of the sales orders (in terms of the quantity) for the next 7 days usually are created already and you only want to include 25% of the forecast demand to cover short term orders.

If forecasts are entered for semi-finished items (hybrid supply strategy with a customer order decoupling point, see → Sect. 6.3.1), the reduction for the semi-finished product should not only include direct demand, e.g. from sales orders, but also demand that derives from the finished product. Select the option "All transactions" in the field *Reduce forecast by* of the coverage group to offset forecasts by all issue transactions (including production BOM line demand) in this case.

6.3.4.4 Settings for Calculated Delays and Action Messages

Action messages, which are activated on the tab *Action* in the Coverage group form, are messages from master planning which require an adjustment of actual or planned purchase and production orders. The aim of action messages is to support adjustments, which may not be done automatically—for example, postponing a purchase order that is not required at the receipt date of the order. They show optimization proposals for receipt quantities and dates. Item availability is granted, regardless of whether you disregard action messages.

Unlike action messages, calculated delays (activated on the tab *Delays* in the Coverage group form) show actual issues with the item availability. A calculated delay is created if the lead time of the required items at all BOM levels results in a necessary supply before today (which causes a delay in the order fulfillment).

If both options, calculated delays and action messages, are activated, you can select the option "Delayed date" in the lookup field *Basis date* on the tab *Action* in the coverage group. With this setting, action messages are based on the earliest possible date and not on the original—perhaps impossible—requirement date.

6.3.4.5 Assigning Coverage Groups to Items

There are three levels for the assignment of a coverage group to an item:

- **Master planning parameters**—*General coverage group* in the section *General of the parameters.*
- **Released product**—On the tab *Plan in the Released product* detail form.
- **Item coverage**—On the tab *General* in the Item coverage form (access with the button *Plan*/Coverage/Item coverage in the released product).

The coverage group controls the method for calculating order quantities. If there is a big difference in the lead time or in the cost price of the items, assign different coverage groups—based on the inventory value or the lead time—to the released products.

6.3.4.6 Dimension Group Settings

Settings in the storage and tracking dimension groups control the inventory dimensions which are kept separate in the coverage calculation. Accordingly, the dimension groups of the item determine the available dimensions in the Item coverage form and the dimensions which are calculated separately in master planning (for the supply and demand calculation per, e.g., warehouse).

You can manage the dimension groups in the menu folder *Product information management > Setup > Dimension and variant groups* (→ Sect. 7.2.2). Select the checkbox *Coverage plan by dimension* in the dimension groups of storage and tracking dimensions which should be calculated separately in master planning. Product dimensions (for product masters) and the dimension *Site* are always calculated separately.

6.3.4.7 Item Coverage

Apart from the coverage group and the dimension groups, the item coverage in the released product is another important setting for master planning.

You can access the Item coverage form with the button *Plan/Coverage/Item coverage* in the action pane of the released product. In the item coverage, you can insert records which specify a minimum and—if applicable—a maximum quantity for the item. Depending on the dimension groups of the item and the coverage settings in these dimension groups, you have to enter the item coverage per site, warehouse, or other dimensions like color or size.

The settings in the item coverage may override the settings that are specified in the item or the coverage group. You can, for example, select a coverage group for a particular warehouse that is different from the coverage group in the released product (for this purpose, select the checkbox *Use specific settings* above the field *Coverage group* on the tab *General* in the item coverage). You can also select a particular main vendor and planned order type—for example, if you purchase an item from an external vendor for one warehouse, but produce it internally for the other warehouses.

If you enter a minimum quantity, you can specify a seasonal distribution with the lookup field *Minimum key* on the tab *General*. The results of the minimum key are shown on the tab *Min./Max.* in the Item coverage form. In the minimum keys (*Master planning > Setup > Coverage > Minimum/Maximum keys*), you can specify a percentage (factor) per period on the tab *Periods*.

6.3.5   Master Planning and Planned Orders

Based on item requirements and coverage settings, master planning generates planned orders for purchasing, production, and inventory transfer.

6.3.5.1 Master Planning Execution

Master planning generates proposals for purchase and production orders in the day-to-day business of the planning department. Depending on the company size and the item structure, master planning involves extensive calculations.

In order to execute master planning, open the menu item *Master planning > Master planning > Run > Master planning* or click the corresponding tile in the workspace *Master planning*. In the following dialog, select the applicable *Master plan* (usually the current static master plan). With Planning Optimization, you can additionally set the slider *Enable auto-firming* to "Yes" or "No" for enabling or preventing the automatic firming within the corresponding time fence.

Apart from the aim of providing appropriate supply across all products, you can use master planning to check the item availability and the possible delivery dates for a particular product when entering demand data (e.g., a new sales order line). For this purpose, execute master planning directly in the Net requirements form, which you can access with the button *Plan/Requirement/Net requirements* in the action pane of the released product or with the button *Product and supply/Net requirements* in the toolbar of order lines.

The Net requirements form shows the result of the last master planning cycle (by default, for the dynamic master plan). If a one master plan strategy is in place, the net requirements lines for the dynamic plan are identical to those for the static plan (which is used in purchasing and production control). With the lookup field *Plan* in the upper pane of the Net requirements form, you can switch between the plans.

The button *Update/Master planning* in the action pane of the Net requirements form starts master planning for the selected item in the selected plan. In case you use the built-in master planning engine, take into account that not all dependencies with other items are covered by the calculation, particularly with regard to the resource capacities.

> *Note:* The demand that is included in master planning depends on the setup (e.g., the slider *Include sales orders*) of the selected master plan.

6.3.5.2 Working with Planned Orders

Master planning generates planned orders, which you can view in the list page *Master planning > Master planning > Planned orders* (→ Fig. 6.8) and in the list section of the workspace *Master planning* (e.g., in the list *Urgent*). In order to restrict the displayed

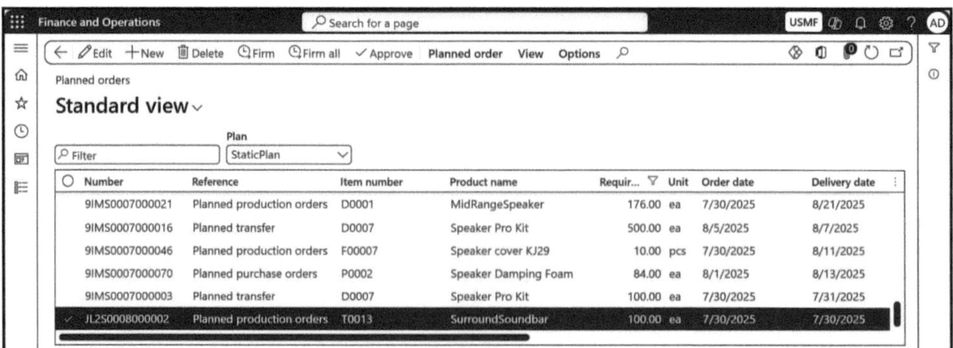

Fig. 6.8 Working with planned orders

planned orders to a particular master plan, select the master plan (e.g., the static plan) in the lookup field *Plan* at the top of the list page or the workspace.

The Planned order list page in the Master planning module and the workspace *Master planning* show planned orders in all areas—for purchasing, for production, and for inventory transfers (indicated by the column *Reference*). A filtered view of planned orders is available in all relevant modules (e.g., *Procurement and sourcing > Purchase orders > Planned purchase orders > Planned purchase orders*).

If the master planning calculation shows that it is not possible to meet a required date, and the slider *Add the calculated delay to the requirement date* on the tab *Calculated delays* in the selected master plan is set to "Yes" for the relevant order type, the *Delivery date* in the planned order is adjusted to the earliest possible date. The original—impossible—requirement date is shown in the column *Requested date*.

Apart from the delivery date and the requirement quantity, the Planned order page displays calculated delays and action messages (optimization proposals) in separate columns. The Planned order detail form, which you can open with a click on the order number shown as a link in the column *Number*, shows the details on calculated delays and action messages on the tabs *Action* and *Delays*. The tab *Pegging* in the detail form shows the demand (including sales orders, BOM lines of production orders, demand forecasts, or safety stock) that is covered by the selected planned order.

6.3.5.3 Vendor Selection in Planned Purchase Orders

When generating a planned purchase order, master planning selects the vendor that is specified in the applicable trade agreement ($\rightarrow$ Sect. 4.8.1) for the purchased item, or, if there is no vendor-specific purchase trade agreement, the main vendor specified for the item (in the item coverage or the released product). As a prerequisite for the use of vendors from trade agreements in master planning, the slider *Find trade agreement* in the Master planning parameters has to be set to "Yes".

If there is no main vendor for the item, master planning still generates a planned purchase order. But before firming the planned order, you have to select a vendor in the corresponding field of the planned order.

If you want to diversify sourcing by distributing the purchased quantity of an item to multiple vendors, you can set up multisource policies (*Procurement and sourcing > Setup > Policies > Multisource policies*). In the Multisource policy form, select the vendors and the *Target allocation (%)* on the tab *Policy rules* before you set the slider *Active* to "Yes". In order to assign a multisource policy to the relevant items, click the button *Policy assignments* to access the Multisource policy assignment form, in which you can select the items that are subject to the policy (optionally at the level of site, warehouse, and from/to date). With this setup, Planning Optimization checks the actual allocation to the vendors with each new planned order and selects the vendor that results in the smallest deviation from the target allocation specified in the multisource policy. The button *Current allocation* in the Multisource policy assignment form provides access to a comparison of the target and the current allocation.

6.3.5.4 Firming Planned Orders

On the tab *Planned supply* of the Planned order detail form, you can edit the delivery date and the quantity. For planned purchase orders, make sure that a vendor number is entered in the lookup field *Vendor*. If you want to add a planned order as an additional line to an existing purchase order (instead of creating an additional purchase order), select this order in the field *Purchase order number*.

In case you do not want to firm a planned order immediately, but together with other planned orders, click the button *Approve* or *Planned order/Process/Change status* in the action pane to change the planned order status to "Approved". Subsequent master planning does not update or delete approved planned orders. With the status "Completed", you can indicate that you do not want to approve or firm a planned order at present. Subsequent master planning will delete and regenerate the planned order (like a planned order with the status "Unprocessed").

In the next step, select one or more planned orders in the Planned order list page and click the button *Firm* in the action pane to generate corresponding purchase orders, production orders, or transfer orders. If you want to create a request for quotation ($\rightarrow$ Sect. 3.8.3) instead of a purchase order, click the button *Planned order/Maintain/Change to/Request for quotation*.

When you firm a planned production order, the initial status of the production order is given by the *Requested production status* on the tab *Other* of the applicable coverage group. When you firm a planned purchase order, the purchase order always receives the approval status "Approved" (irrespective of change management settings in procurement).

The firming history (*Master planning > Inquiries and reports > Master planning > Firming history*) displays a log of firming activities.

Apart from the Planned order form, the workspace *Master planning* also includes lists (e.g., the list *Urgent*) which you can use to edit and to firm planned orders.

6.3.5.5 Net Requirements and Explosion

To get an overview of the net requirements related to a planned order, click the button *View/Requirements/Requirement profile* in the action pane of the Planned order form. With this button, you access the Net requirements form, which you can also access from the Released product form or the order lines.

The button *View/Requirements/Explosion* in the action pane of the Planned order form provides access to another inquiry, the Explosion form. This form, which you can also access with the button *Product and supply/Explosion* in the toolbar of sales order lines, shows the item availability, including components at all BOM levels.

With the button *Setup* in the action pane of the Explosion form, you can change the display settings. The button *Explosion view* in the action pane determines the direction of the explosion: If you select "Down", the form shows the semi-finished items and components of the selected item. If you select "Up", the form shows a where-used analysis.

6.3.5.6 Action Messages and Calculated Delays

If calculated delays (which show availability issues) and action messages (which show optimization proposals that require manual decisions) are activated in the applicable coverage groups, master planning generates corresponding messages. These messages are shown in the respective columns of the Net requirements form.

The list page *Master planning > Master planning > Calculated delays* (also included as a tile in the workspace *Master planning*) gives an overview of the calculated delays. When you open this form, select the appropriate (static or dynamic) plan in the lookup field *Plan* at the top first. If you want to access a particular order, click on the order number shown as a link in the column *Number* of the list page or click the button *Calculated delays/Open/Reference*.

The list page *Master planning > Master planning > Actions > Actions* gives an overview of the action messages. Like in the calculated delays, select a plan in the lookup field *Plan* first. With a click on the order number shown as a link in the column *Number*, you can access the details of the order. If you want to execute the action message of a particular line (e.g., the action of deleting a purchase order), click the button *Apply action* in the action pane of the Action form. The button *Action graph* in the Action form provides access to a chart that shows the dependencies between related action messages.

6.3.5.7 Supply Schedule Form

The Supply schedule form (→ Fig. 6.9) contains a comprehensive view of the future supply and demand (similar to the net requirements but summarized per period and transaction type). As a prerequisite for the use of the supply schedule, set up period templates (*Organization administration > Setup > Calendars > Period templates*) with a period configuration on the tab *Periods*, which determines the columns in the supply schedule.

If you access the supply schedule from the menu (*Master planning > Master planning > Supply schedule*), a filter dialog is shown. In this dialog, enter a filter on the *Plan* (relevant for displaying planned orders), *Period template*, *Item* or *Item allocation key*, and—optionally—inventory dimensions.

Apart from the menu item, the supply schedule is also available in many other forms. These forms show a respective button in the action pane or in a toolbar—for example, the button *Plan/View/Supply schedule* in the released product or the button *Inquiries/Supply schedule* in the net requirements.

In the Supply schedule form, you can view supply and demand details on a tab at the bottom—select a cell in a period column and click the button *Expand/Collapse* in the toolbar for this purpose. With the button *New*, you can manually create planned or actual orders directly in the Supply schedule form. With the button *Master planning*, you can start master planning for the selected item.

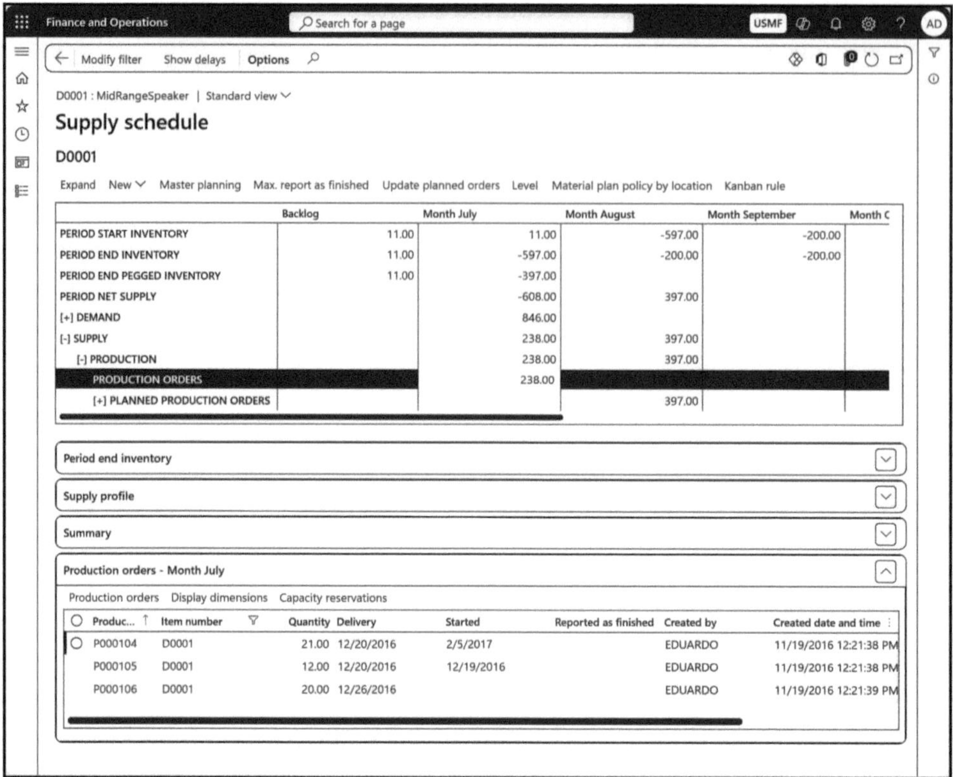

Fig. 6.9 Viewing supply details in the supply schedule

6.3.6   Priority-Based Planning and DDMRP

Priority-based planning and DDMRP are basically min./max. Coverage principles with extended functionality.

With priority-based planning, you can respect the priority of demand and schedule the supply of urgent demand first (instead of just using the sequence of requirement dates). The planning priority is based on the stock level, prioritizing the supply of items that run out of stock over the supply of items that still have a little more quantity left in stock.

Demand driven material requirements planning (DDMRP) addresses the issue of long lead times, which result from an approach of planning the entire supply chain starting at the lowest component level at the time when receiving a sales order for a finished product. With the definition of appropriate buffer quantities for relevant semi-finished products, DDMRP can significantly reduce the sales lead time while keeping the inventory quantity at an acceptable level.

Priority-based planning and DDMRP are only available with Planning Optimization.

6.3.6.1 Setup of Priority-Based Planning

With the planning priority models (*Master planning > Setup > Planning priority models*), you can determine the planning priority that is automatically assigned when master planning generates a planned order. Zero is the highest priority, 100 is the lowest priority.

In a simple scenario, you can use a planning priority model with the *Priority calculation method* "Percent of Maximum inventory quantity". This option refers to the maximum quantity (field *Maximum*) in the item coverage of the released product. With this setup, the priority is calculated by dividing the *net flow* by the maximum quantity. The *net flow* is calculated as the total of current inventory minus actual demand (e.g., sales orders) plus actual supply (e.g., purchase orders) within the planning time fence.

As an example of this *Priority calculation method*, an inventory of 30 percent of the maximum quantity with no open order gives a priority of 30 in the planned order, which is generated if the on-hand quantity is below the reorder point.

If you select the option "Priority ranges" in the *Priority calculation method* of a planning priority model (→ Fig. 6.10), you can assign priorities to quantity ranges. For this purpose, switch to the tab *Planning priority ranges* and enter planning priorities for quantity ranges, which refer to the minimum quantity, the reorder point, and the maximum quantity (fields in the item coverage). With the option "Split according to priority ranges" in the field *Planned order creation*, you can force master planning to create a separate planned order per priority (quantity range).

Once you have set up the planning priority models, you can create one or more coverage groups (*Master planning > Setup > Coverage > Coverage groups*) with the *Coverage code* "Priority" and the appropriate *Planning priority model*.

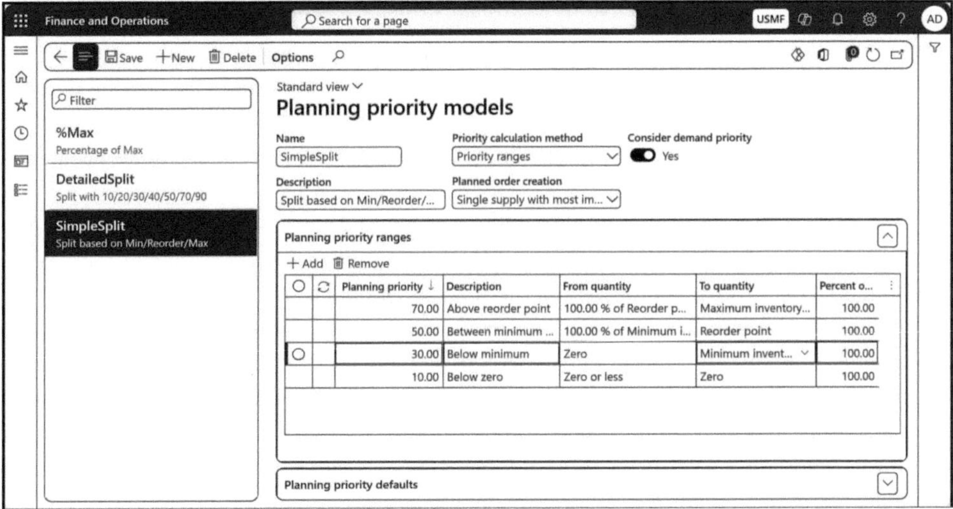

Fig. 6.10 Managing the planning priority models

For items that are subject to priority-based planning, assign the relevant coverage group in the released product or the item coverage (→ Sect. 6.3.4). In the item coverage, complete the fields *Minimum* (minimum quantity), *Reorder point* (between the minimum and the maximum quantity, triggers generating planned orders), and *Maximum* (maximum quantity).

6.3.6.2 Working with Priority-Based Planning

Planning Optimization creates planned orders, which fill up stock to the maximum quantity, for items with a coverage code "Priority", if the *net flow* (total available inventory within the planning time fence, see above) is less than the reorder point.

The field *Planning priority* on the tab *General* in the Planned order detail form is initialized in line with the setting in the applicable planning priority model of the item. When firming a planned order, the planning priority of the planned order is transferred to the actual purchase or production order. Based on the planning priority, you can prioritize planned and actual orders.

In demand forecasts and in the order lines of actual orders that constitute demand (e.g., sales orders), you can enter a priority in the field *Planning priority* on the sub-tab *Delivery* in the line details (initialized from the related field in the planning priority model of the coverage group of the item). This setting is relevant if the slider *Consider demand priority* in the applicable planning priority model is set to "Yes". In a planned order generated by Planning Optimization, the *Planning priority* will not be lower than the priority in the related demand (actual order).

6.3.6.3 Demand Driven Materials Requirement Planning (DDMRP)

The core idea of DDMRP is to decouple supply and demand. For this purpose, you define decoupling points—items for which you want to keep a buffer stock. Often, these items are semifinished products, and the buffer of the semifinished products makes sure that you have enough quantity on hand to produce finished items, which show fluctuating demand, within an acceptable lead time. In a retail company, decoupling points might be stores that need a buffer stock because the replenishment from a central warehouse takes too long to fulfill fluctuating demand in time.

In Dynamics 365, coverage groups with a coverage code "Decoupling point" identify decoupling points for DDMRP (→ Fig. 6.11). You can select such coverage groups only in the Item coverage form, not directly in the released product.

On the tab *Other* in the Coverage groups form, you can find the field groups *DDMRP parameters* and *Average daily usage*, which include the relevant fields for calculating appropriate buffer quantities. The buffer quantities are represented by the fields *Minimum*, *Reorder point*, and *Maximum*, which you can find in the Item coverage form. While you use these fields also with priority-based planning, DDMRP offers extended support to calculate the buffer quantities. The following elements are included in this calculation:

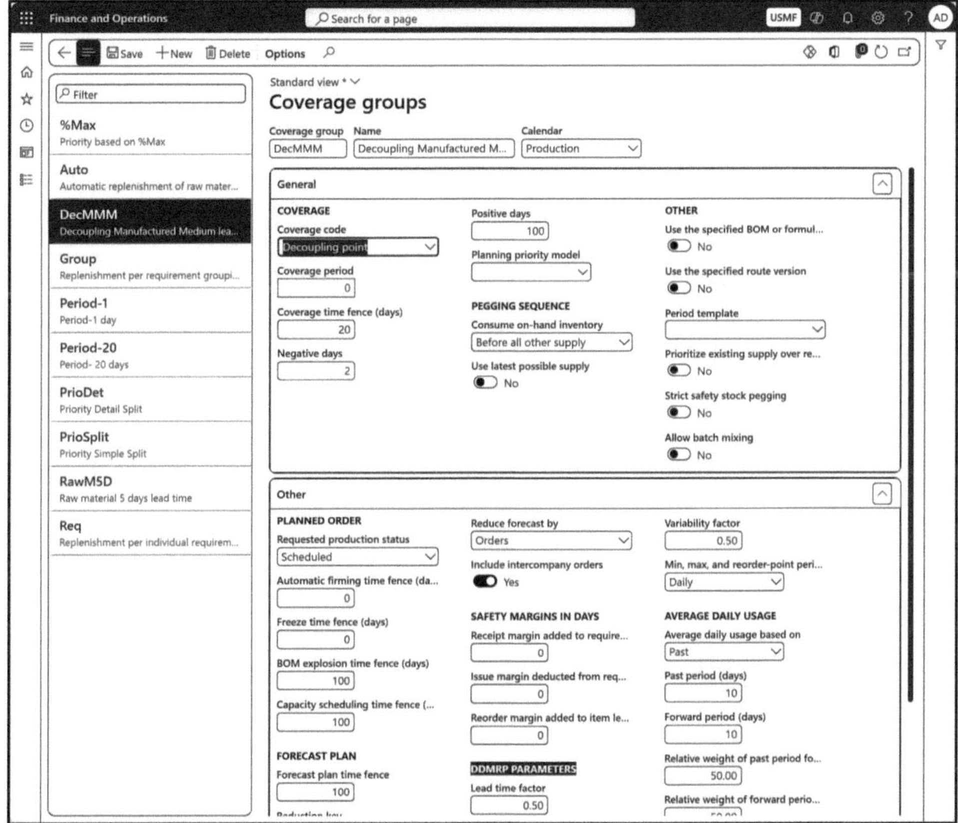

Fig. 6.11 Settings in a coverage group for DDMRP items

- **Average daily usage**—In the past and/or in the future, depending on the selected option in the field *Average daily usage based on* (the field *Min, max, and reorder-point period* controls if the average is calculated per day or week).
- **Decoupled lead time**—Lead time calculated by assuming that buffers are on stock; the *Lead time factor* is used to adjust the impact of lead time on the buffer stock
- **Demand variability**—The *Variability factor* is used to adjust the impact of demand variability on the buffer stock

In the Item coverage form, you can calculate the buffer quantities with the buttons *Buffer values/Calculate/Calculate decoupled lead time*, *Buffer values/Calculate/Calculate Average Daily Usage*, and *Buffer values/Calculate/Calculate min, max and reorder point quantities*. If you want the buffer quantities (*Minimum*, *Reorder point*, and *Maximum*) to be updated every day or every week, set the slider *Buffer values over time* on the tab *General* in the Item coverage form to "Yes". In this case, the tab *Buffer values* in the Item coverage form shows a grid with the daily or weekly buffer quantities. In order to generate the lines in the grid, you can click the button *Buffer values/Periodic setup/Add time periods*.

As an alternative to the buttons in the item coverage, you can run the periodic job *Master planning > Master planning > DDMRP > Calculate buffer values* to calculate the *Minimum, Reorder point*, and *Maximum* quantity.

Planning Optimization, with DDMRP usually executed in a daily run, creates planned orders, which fill up stock to the maximum quantity, for items with a coverage code "Decoupling point" (for DDMRP items), if the *net flow* (total available inventory within the planning time fence) is less than the reorder point.

This is similar to the calculation with priority-based planning, but the demand included in the calculation is limited to past-due demand, today's demand, and qualified order spikes in the future. The *Order spike threshold*, which is specified in the Item coverage form, indicates the daily quantity at which the demand is regarded as an additional order quantity, not included in the regular demand. The planning priority in the planned orders is calculated in line with the rules of priority-based planning.

6.3.7   Case Study Exercises

Exercise 6.2—Master Planning Including Forecasts
You want to check the impact of the forecast in exercise 6.1 on your supply chain.

For this purpose, create a master plan MF-## (## = your user ID) which only covers demand from the forecast model and the demand forecast of exercise 6.1, but no current inventory or orders.

Then execute master planning with this master plan and check the results in the net requirements of your forecasted items.

Exercise 6.3—Min./Max. Principle
A Min./Max. coverage code should be used for the finished product I-##-F of exercise 5.2. Select an appropriate coverage group in the Released product form, and enter a minimum quantity (500 units) and a maximum quantity (1000 units) in the item coverage of the item.

Then run master planning in the Net requirements form using the current dynamic plan, which is the default value. Once master planning has finished, review the result. In a second step, change the minimum quantity to one unit and execute master planning a second time. Can you explain the new result?

Exercise 6.4—Period Principle.
A coverage code that summarizes the requirements per period should be used for the item I-##-F of exercise 5.2 now. Select an appropriate coverage group in the released product and delete the Min./Max. record in the item coverage.

The customer of exercise 4.1 orders 100 units of the finished product I-##-F of exercise 5.2. Enter a corresponding sales order, but do not post the packing slip or invoice. Execute master planning in the Net requirements form and review the result.

Then enter another order of that customer with 150 units of the finished product and the same ship date as the first order. Execute master planning a second time and check the result again.

Note: As a prerequisite for including demand from sales orders, make sure that the selected master plan is configured accordingly (e.g., the slider *Include sales orders* should be activated).

Exercise 6.5—Planned Purchase Order

A minimum inventory quantity of 100 units (more than the available quantity) is required in the main warehouse for the item I-##-C1 of exercise 5.1. Enter this minimum quantity in the item coverage. Then open the Net requirements form for the item and execute master planning. What is the result?

Open the Planned purchase order form in the Procurement and sourcing module. If required, switch to the dynamic plan that you have used for master planning in the net requirements. Select the planned order which refers to the item I-##-C1 and transfer it to a purchase order.

Inventory and Product Management 7

The primary responsibility of inventory management is to manage items in the warehouse in terms of quantity and value. In order to meet this task, any update of the inventory quantity has to be registered and posted in a transaction. Most of the transactions are not a result of a business process within inventory, but derive from other areas. For example, posting a product receipt in purchasing generates an inventory transaction for the receipt.

7.1 Principle of Inventory Transactions

Before we start to go into details, the lines below show the principle of transactions in inventory management.

7.1.1 Basic Approach

Inventory management controls the inventory per product (item number). Accordingly, the most important master data in inventory management are the product records of inventoried items. Depending on the dimension groups of the particular product, the quantity and value of the item are controlled at the more detailed level of inventory dimensions. Inventory dimensions include storage dimensions (e.g., warehouse), tracking dimensions (e.g., serial number), and product dimensions (e.g., configuration).

Settings in the storage dimension group and the warehouse control, if the basic approach for inventory management or the advanced warehouse management (with license plates/pallets and mobile devices) is used. This chapter explains the basic approach for inventory management. The advanced warehouse management ($\rightarrow$ Sect. 8.1) is an extension of the basic inventory management.

7.1.1.1 Types of Transactions

In order to update the on-hand quantity, you need to post an item transaction. Depending on the direction, the transaction belongs to one of the following types:

- **Item receipt**—Inbound transaction.
- **Item issue**—Outbound transaction.

Item receipts increase the on-hand quantity. They include product receipts in purchasing, customer returns in sales, product receipts in production (reported as finished), positive adjustments in counting, and manual journals in inventory.

Item issues, which reduce the on-hand quantity, include vendor returns in purchasing, packing slips in sales, picking lists in production, negative adjustments in counting, and manual journals in inventory.

Inventory transfers, which consist of an issue from one dimension value (e.g., a warehouse) and a receipt at another (e.g., a warehouse), are registered with transfer orders and transfer journals. You use transfer orders to move items from one warehouse to another, particularly if you need a picking list. With transfer journals, it is not only possible to transfer an item from one warehouse to another, but you can also register a transfer of other dimensions (e.g., for changing a serial number in inventory).

> *Note:* Apart from regular inventory transactions, the advanced warehouse management includes warehouse-specific transactions ($\rightarrow$ Sect. 8.1.1). These transactions cover transfers at the level of storage dimensions below the dimension "Warehouse".

7.1.1.2 Transactions from Other Areas

Most of the inventory transactions are not originally registered in inventory but derive from other areas in Dynamics 365. The transaction origin in the other module (e.g., a product receipt in purchasing) needs to contain all data which are required to post the inventory transaction (e.g., the warehouse, quantity, and cost price). In a posted inventory transaction, you can view the reference to the transaction origin, including the voucher number and the date.

7.1.1.3 Inventory Quantity and Value

In order to grant an accurate inventory valuation, Dynamics 365 differentiates the physical transaction (which determines the on-hand quantity) and the financial transaction (which determines the financial value). For illustration purposes, the physical and the financial part of an inventory transaction related to a purchase order line is shown in $\rightarrow$ Fig. 7.1.

The physical transaction in Dynamics 365 causes a change in the on-hand quantity. An example of a physical transaction is the product receipt related to a purchase order. In

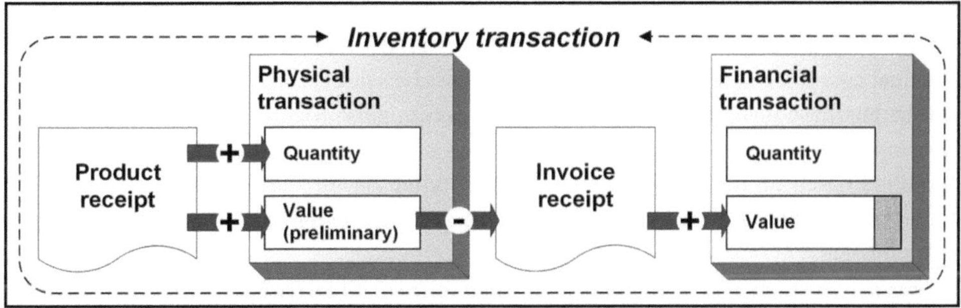

Fig. 7.1 Physical and financial transaction in inventory for a purchase order line

terms of the inventory quantity, the transaction is already completed when you post the product receipt. But from an inventory valuation perspective, the transaction only includes a preliminary cost price. For this reason, the value of the product receipt is shown in the field *Physical cost amount* of the inventory transaction details, separate from the field *Cost amount*, which contains the financial inventory value.

The second step in processing an inventory transaction is the financial transaction, which determines the cost amount for the invoiced quantity. An example of a financial transaction is the purchase order invoice. Posting the vendor invoice reverses the related posting of the preliminary cost amount of the product receipt (physical amount) and posts the final cost amount of the invoice. The invoice quantity and amount are subsequently included in the financial inventory value.

7.1.1.4 Posting Inventory Transactions

The differentiation between the physical and the financial transaction applies to each inventory transaction, no matter in which area it is generated. But the way of posting a transaction depends on the origin.

For receipt transactions in purchase orders, posting the product receipt generates the physical transaction, and posting the vendor invoice generates the financial transaction. In production, reporting the manufactured item as finished generates the physical transaction. The financial transaction is posted by ending the production order.

For issue transactions in sales orders, posting the packing slip generates the physical, and posting the invoice generates the financial transaction (similar to purchasing). In production, posting a picking list generates the physical transaction for BOM lines (materials). The financial transaction for BOM lines is posted in parallel to the financial transaction for the manufactured item when ending the production order.

Unlike the other transactions, journals in inventory management do not generate the physical and the financial transaction in two separate steps, but in parallel.

7.1.1.5 Inventory Closing

For receipt transactions, the financial value is posted finally—apart from later manual adjustments—with the invoice or with the production order ending. But for issue transactions, the financial inventory value sometimes is not known—and therefore not final—when posting the invoice. You can, for example, receive the purchase invoice with the final cost price of an item after you have posted a sales invoice for the item. If the price on the purchase invoice is different from the preliminary price in the product receipt, the final costs of the sold item, and therefore the profitability of the sales transaction, are modified based on the purchase invoice. Depending on the date of the purchase invoice receipt, it is even possible that this change is not posted in the same period as the original sales invoice.

Except for items with a standard cost price or a moving average valuation, you need to execute inventory closing to re-evaluate issue transactions. The main purpose of inventory closing, usually a month-end procedure, is to recalculate the financial value of issue transactions based on the final value of receipt transactions.

7.1.1.6 Ledger Integration

Based on the deep integration of finance with the business processes in all areas of Dynamics 365, the transactions in inventory are posted to ledger accounts in the same way as inventory transactions in other modules ($\rightarrow$ Sect. 9.4).

7.1.2   At a Glance: Inventory Journal Transactions

You use inventory journals to update the on-hand quantity of items manually, separate from orders in purchasing, sales, or production. The example below shows a manual item receipt with an inventory adjustment journal. In regular business, such transactions are an exception. The reason for receiving an item without reference to a purchase or production order may be a missing end-to-end business process or an unexpected situation like missing or wrong inventory data.

When you open the Inventory adjustment list page (*Inventory management > Journal entries > Items > Inventory adjustment*), it shows all open adjustment journals which are not been posted yet. If you want to view posted journals, adjust the filter on the column *Posted* (you can use the filter pane, the grid column filter, or the advanced filter). For journals that have not been posted yet, an icon in the column *In use* indicates if somebody is currently working in the journal. If you want to access the details of a journal, click the journal ID shown as a link in the grid.

In order to register a new transaction, click the button *New* in the action pane of the list page. In the *Create inventory journal* dialog, which is shown next, select a journal name in the field *Name* (initialized from the Inventory parameters) and optionally enter a *Site* and a *Warehouse* (used as default value for the lines). If you want to support later analysis, enter a short text that explains the use of the journal in the field *Description*. The journal number in the field *Journal* derives from the applicable number sequence.

Once you click the button *OK* in the dialog, Dynamics 365 creates the journal header and switches to the Journal detail form in the Lines view. If you want to view the complete journal header, switch to the Header view (click the button *Header* below the action pane).

In the Lines view, click the button *New* in the toolbar of the tab *Journal lines* to insert a line (→ Fig. 7.2). Select the item number in the new line before you enter the site, warehouse, and other inventory dimensions as specified in the dimension groups of the item. If you want to select the dimension columns that are displayed in the lines, click the button *Display dimensions* in the toolbar of the journal lines. You can also enter the dimension values on the sub-tab *Inventory dimensions* of the tab *Line details*. In the other sub-tabs, you can enter further details as applicable.

If you enter a positive quantity, the transaction is a receipt. A negative quantity creates an issue. Default values for the warehouse, quantity, and cost price derive from the default order settings of the released product. The default for the quantity is 1.00 if the default order settings do not specify a default inventory quantity.

Unlike a receipt transaction in purchasing, the inventory journal transaction is not split into a physical transaction (product receipt) and a corresponding financial transaction (invoice). Inventory journals generate the physical and the financial transaction in one step. For this reason, make sure that journal lines with a positive quantity (i.e., item receipts) contain the correct cost price when you post the journal.

Once you have entered the last journal line, post the journal with the button *Post* in the action pane of the Inventory adjustment journal list page or detail form.

Before posting, you can optionally click the button *Validate* to check potential issues.

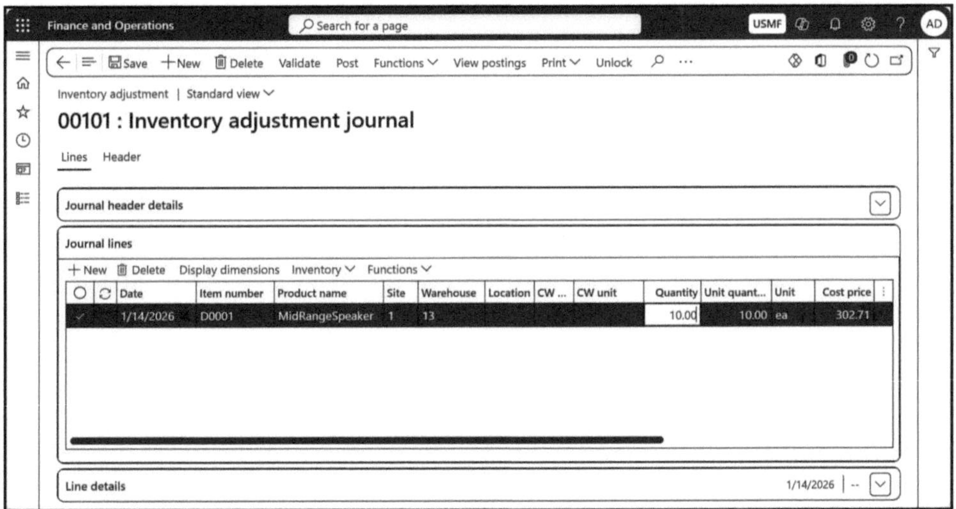

Fig. 7.2 Registering a journal line

7.2   Product Information Management

Since business processes related to inventory require inventoried products, product data represent the core area of master data in supply chain management.

The data structure of products in Dynamics 365 includes two levels: The shared products with basic item data that are common in all companies, and the released products with company-specific item data.

The product table contains all physical items—raw materials, components, semi-finished products, and finished products. But the product table also includes non-inventoried items like service items or phantom items. These items do not exist physically, but you can use them in order management or bills of materials.

If you need to manage product versioning and engineering changes, you can use engineering change management features.

In various areas of Dynamics 365, for example, in the order lines in purchasing and in sales, the label "Item" is used for released products.

7.2.1   General Product Data

Details on product data with regard to purchasing, sales, production, and master planning are included in the related Section of this book. The current Section does not include the topics that are covered in these sections. Apart from general features in the shared product and the released product, the focus in this Section is on item data in inventory and inventory valuation.

7.2.1.1 Structure of Product Data

In Dynamics 365, all products in the companies of a common enterprise are included in the shared product table. In order to be available in a company, the shared product has to be released to the particular company. It is not necessary to release a product to all companies at the same time—you can also release a product to some companies earlier and to other companies later.

The shared product table contains product data which are common in all companies. These data include the *Product number*, the *Product type* ("Item" or "Service"), the *Product subtype* ("Product" or "Product master"), the *Product name* and *Description*, and the dimension groups. Optionally, you can enter product categories and attributes ($\rightarrow$ Sect. 4.8.2) in the shared product. The dimension groups are—apart from the *Product dimension group* for product masters—not mandatory in the shared product. You can leave the dimension groups in the shared product empty and enter them at the company level in the released products.

Most product details are specified at the company level in the Released product form ($\rightarrow$ Fig. 7.3). Required fields in the released product include the dimension groups (if not

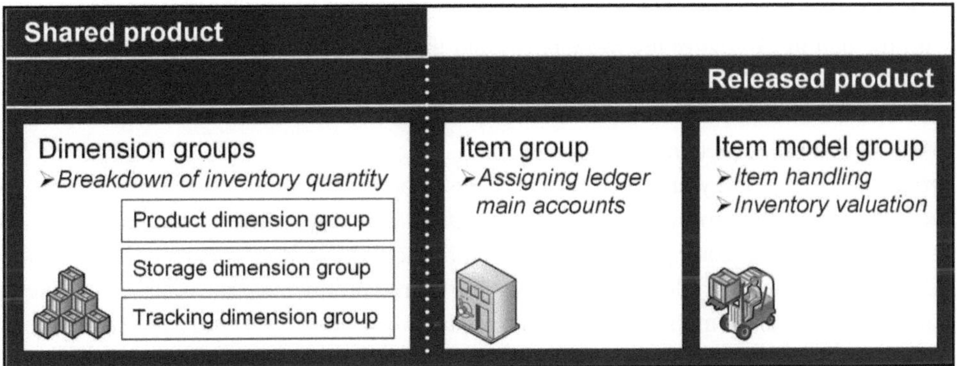

Fig. 7.3 Main control groups of a product

specified in the shared product), the item group, the item model group, and the units of measure.

7.2.1.2 Entering and Releasing Shared Products

Depending on the requirements, there are two ways of creating a product (→ Sect. 3.3.2):

- **Start with the shared product**—Create a shared product and release it.
- **Start with the released product**—Create a product in the Released product form (automatically generating a shared product in the background).

In order to view the list of all shared products, open the menu item *Product information management > Products > All products and product masters*. The list pages *Products* (for items without configurations or variants) and *Product masters* (for items with variants) show a filtered view of all shared products.

If you want to create a shared product in the All products form (*Product information management > Products > All products and product masters*), click the button *New* in the action pane. You can subsequently release the product to one or more companies—click the button *Release products* in the action pane and select applicable companies in the *Release products* wizard for this purpose.

In order to access the released products, open the menu item *Product information management > Products > Released products*. Alternatively, you can access a released product directly from the shared product. For this purpose, click the link in the column *Item number* on the right of the FactBox *Released to companies* and—in the *Product information* dialog, which is shown next—click the link in the field *Item number* there.

If you want to access the related shared product from a released product, click the field *Product number* on the tab *General* in the Released product detail form.

The workspace *Released product maintenance* is another place from which you can access released products. On the tab *Released products* in this workspace, the list *Recently released* shows the items that have been released in the past days (specify the date range with the button *Configure my workspace*) and the related validation result (missing field values).

There are two ways to create a released product: You can create and release a product in the shared products (*Product information management > Products > All products and product masters*), and you can create the released product with the button *New* directly in the Released product form. The *New released product* dialog, which includes data for both the shared and the corresponding released product (the dialog contains all mandatory fields of the released product), then creates the shared product and the released product in parallel. If there are templates for released products, the additional field *Apply template*, in which you can select an appropriate template, is shown in the dialog.

You can also apply templates for released products at a later stage—click the button *Product/Maintain/Apply template* in the released product for this purpose. The template then overrides the data in the released product with data from the template. If you want to create a template in the Released product form, click the button *Product/New/Template*.

> *Note:* Creating a product works differently if your enterprise uses engineering change management (→ Sect. 7.2.5).

7.2.1.3 Product Number, Item number, and Name

The *Product number*, which identifies the shared product, has to be unique across all companies. It is assigned automatically to new products if the number sequence for product numbers (*Product information management > Setup > Product information management parameters*, Section *Number sequences*) does not require a manual assignment.

The *Item number*, which identifies the items at the released product level, is usually identical to the shared product number. As a prerequisite, the number sequence for item numbers (*Inventory management > Setup > Inventory and warehouse management parameters*, tab *Number sequences*) must be set to "Manual" in the relevant companies.

When you create a shared product, the default for the *Search name* derives from the *Product name*, but you can override it. In addition, you can enter a longer product description in the field *Description* on the tab *General* of the (shared) Product detail form. The *Product name* and *Description* are both entered in the system language, which is the default language specified in the System parameters (→ Sect. 10.3.4). If there are different product names and descriptions in foreign languages, click the button *Product/Languages/Translations* in the shared product and enter the appropriate text in other languages.

Product name and description are only editable at the shared product level. The *Search name* in the shared product is a default for the released products, which you can override in the Released product form.

7.2.1.4 Product Type and Subtype

The *Product type* controls whether a product is an inventoried item. Whereas the product type "Item" characterizes a regular item, the product type "Service" specifies an item without inventory control in any company of the enterprise.

The *Product subtype* controls whether the item has variants. Whereas the product subtype "Product" applies to a regular standard item, the product subtype "Product master" characterizes a base item for assigned product variants.

Note: For the *Product type* "Service", you can select the *Product service type* "Warranty" for selling extended warranty in Dynamics 365 Commerce.

7.2.1.5 Product Masters and Variants

For a product with the product subtype "Product master", the product number alone does not uniquely identify the item in inventory. In transactions with this item, you have to enter the product variant that distinguishes the different versions, styles, sizes, colors, or configurations of the product.

When you create a product master (a product with the product subtype "Product master"), the *Product dimension group* (one of the dimension groups described in → Sect. 7.2.2 below) is shown in the *Create product* dialog. The product dimension group of the shared product determines which of the dimensions *Version, Style, Size, Color,* or *Configuration,* are used for the product.

The product dimension *Version* is designated for product versions in engineering change management (→ Sect. 7.2.5).

The *Configuration technology*, which is the second mandatory field when creating a product master, determines the way to create product variants.

If you select the configuration technology "Predefined variant", you have to enter the dimension values for the product variants in the Product dimension form. You can access this form, which shows the dimensions of the product (in line with the selected product dimension group) in the left pane, with the button *Product dimensions* in the action pane of the shared product.

Once you have entered the applicable product dimension values in the Product dimension form, specify the valid variants (dimension value combinations) in the Product variant form. In order to access this form, click the button *Product variants* in the shared product. The button *Variant suggestions* in the Product variant form facilitates creating new variants. If a product is not available, for example, in all colors for each size, you might want to create the variants manually. But if a product only includes one active product dimension or if all dimension combinations are valid, set the slider *Generate variants automatically* in the (shared) Product detail form to "Yes" before entering product dimension values—with this setting, you don't have to care about entering variants (dimension value combinations).

Before you can select a product variant in a transaction, you have to release the variant to the respective company. Click the button *Release products* in the action pane of the shared product for this purpose and select the variants that you want to release in the *Release product* wizard. Apart from releasing product variants in parallel to the product master, you can also release variants separately at a later stage. An alternative way for releasing a variant is to create a released product variant (based on the shared product variant) manually in the Released product variant form. You can access the Released product variant page with the button *Product/Product master/Released product variants* in the released product. On the tab *Purchase* and *Sell* in the Released product variant detail form, you can specify a variant-specific item sales tax group (which overrides the item sales tax group at the released product level).

If applicable, you can specify a default variant for order lines and transactions on the tab *Product variants* in the Released product detail form.

If there are common variants for multiple products, you can use variant groups to populate the product dimension values. Create a variant group for sizes (*Product information management > Setup > Dimensions and variant groups > Size groups*), colors, or styles with the related dimension values for this purpose, and select the size group, color group, or style group in the (shared) Product detail form. The dimension values of the variant group serve as the default value in the product dimensions of the shared product.

Default order settings for product masters are available at the level of dimension values and variants in the released product. You can, for example, specify a default warehouse for the size "Large" and a different default warehouse for the color "Red". For an item with the size "Large" and the color "Red", the priority of settings is given by the field *Rank* in the default order settings.

7.2.1.6 Core Settings in Released Products

Whereas the shared products (*Product information management > Products > All products and product masters*) only include a limited number of fields, the Released product form contains a wide range of details that characterize the item (→ Fig. 7.4).

Only a few fields in the released product are mandatory, including the unit of measure, the item group, the item model group (→ Sect. 7.2.3), and—either at shared product level or at released product level—the dimension groups (→ Sect. 7.2.2). You can click the button *Product/Maintain/Validate* in the released product to check whether a released product contains all mandatory data.

Apart from these mandatory fields, further important data in the released product include the cost price (→ Sect. 7.3.3) and the item sales tax groups.

7.2.1.7 Item Groups

The main purpose of item groups (*Inventory management > Setup > Inventory > Item groups*) is to collect products, which post to a common main account in the general ledger. For this reason, you need to set up at least as many item groups as there are different stock and revenue accounts for inventoried items. You can find more details on the posting setup in → Sect. 9.4.2.

When releasing a product, keep in mind that you should not change the item group on the tab *Manage costs* of the released product once the first transaction is registered. Dynamics 365 displays a warning on possible issues with inventory reconciliation in finance if you do not carefully check the consequences of changing the group. But you can still change the item group, if necessary.

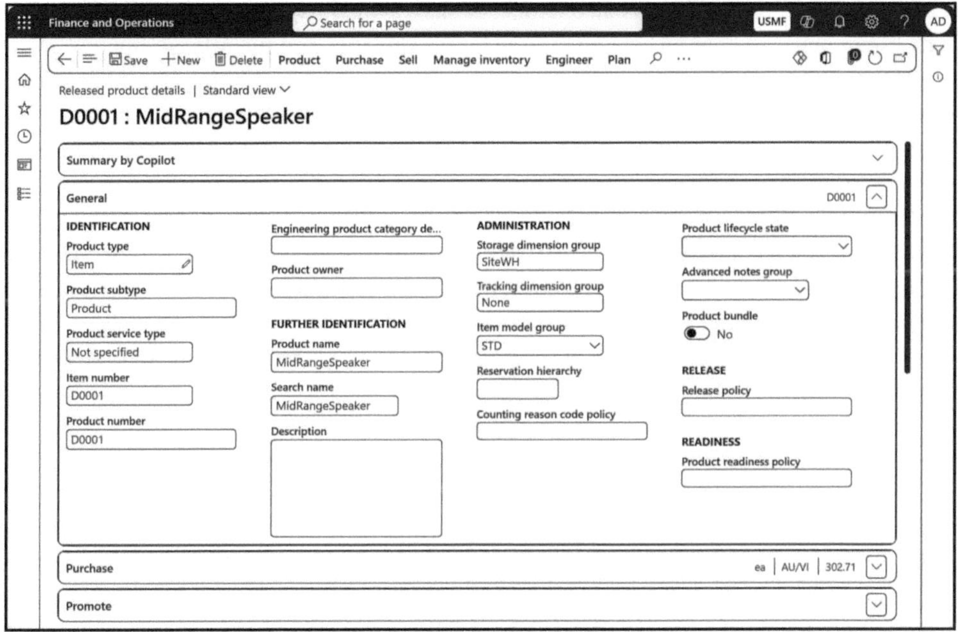

Fig. 7.4 Managing an item in the Released product form

Item groups are not only used for ledger integration settings in the posting setup, but they also serve as a filter and sorting criterion in many reports.

7.2.1.8 Units of Measure

When you release a product, Dynamics 365 applies the default unit of measure, which is specified in the Inventory parameters (field *Unit* in the Section *General*). As long as no transaction with the item has been registered, it is possible to change the inventory unit of a released product.

If an item requires different units of measure in purchasing, sales, and inventory, enter the appropriate units on the tabs *Purchase*, *Sell*, and *Manage inventory* of the Released product form (e.g., if you manage inventory in pieces, but purchase pallets). The selected unit in the released product initializes the unit in transactions with the item—for example, in a purchase order line. In the transaction, you can still override the unit. But a unit conversion between the inventory unit and the other unit needs to be specified.

Units of measure are shared across companies. If you need a new unit of measure, set it up in the menu item *Organization administration > Setup > Units > Units* before you assign it to a released product. The *Unit class* (e.g., "Quantity", "Length", "Mass") categorizes the unit of measure.

In one unit per unit class, you can set the slider *System unit* to "Yes", which means that this unit is used for quantity fields without a related unit of measure. The field *Net weight* in the Released product form is an example of such a quantity field. Order lines do not use the system unit, but contain separate fields for the quantity and the related unit.

With the slider *Base unit*, you can identify one unit per unit class that should be used as a basis for entering unit conversions. The base unit is the main unit to/from which you primarily enter unit conversions, but it does not prevent direct unit conversions between other units.

The button *Unit conversions* in the Units form provides access to the unit conversions. Conversions on the tab *Standard conversion* are independent of the product (e.g., the conversion between minutes and hours). On the tab *Intra-class conversions*, you can enter conversions per product within a *Unit class* ($\rightarrow$ Fig. 7.5), and on the tab *Inter-class conversions*, you can enter conversions across unit classes (e.g., between the weight and the quantity).

In the (shared) Product form and the Released product form, you can access the unit conversions for an item with the button *Product/Set up/Unit conversions*.

If you want to specify unit conversions at the variant level (e.g., if the number of products in a box depends on the product dimension "Size"), set the slider *Enable unit of measure conversion* in the shared product to "Yes" (applicable for product masters). For these products, you can optionally select the option "Product variant" in the lookup *Create conversion for* when setting up an intra-class or an inter-class conversion.

7.2.1.9 Non-Inventoried Items and Services

Apart from regular products, which you want to track in inventory, some items are not included in inventory—e.g., services or office supplies.

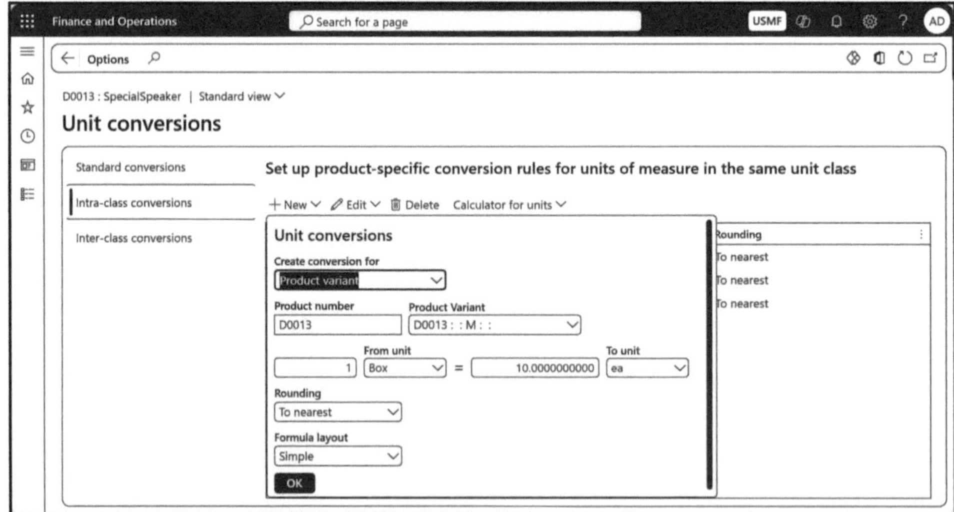

Fig. 7.5 Entering an intra-class conversion at the variant level

Table 7.1 Options for the inventory control of products

Product type Item model group	Item	Service
Stocked product	Inventory transactions, inventory quantity	Inventory transactions, no quantity
Non-stocked product	No transactions, no quantity	No transactions, no quantity

In Dynamics 365, there are two separate ways to specify whether inventory control applies to a product:

- **Product type**—Option "Item" or "Service".
- **Item model group**—Checkbox *Stocked product*.

Depending on the combination of both settings, inventory control works differently (→ Table 7.1).

The product type "Service" is used for products that do not apply inventory control in any company of the enterprise. But if the released product is assigned to an item model group for stocked products, it still generates inventory transactions. This setting is required for intangible items and services that are part of a BOM, because inventory transactions are required to establish the value chain between the consumption of the service item and the manufactured product.

If you create a released product and select an item model group in which the checkbox *Stocked product* is cleared, there are no inventory transactions for the item. Since the item model group is assigned to the released product, this setting makes it possible to deactivate inventory control for an item at the company level.

7.2.1.10 Product Lifecycle State

In the field *Product lifecycle state* on the tab *General* in the Released product form, you can select the lifecycle state of the item. For product masters, you can select the lifecycle state at the variant level in the Released product variants form.

The setup of the required product lifecycle states (*Product information management > Setup > Product lifecycle state*) includes the slider *Is active for planning*, which you set to "No" if items with the respective state should not be included in master planning (which is the appropriate setting for obsolete items).

If engineering change management (→ Sect. 7.2.5) is enabled, the Product lifecycle state form contains the additional tab *Enabled business processes*. On this tab, you can block or enable business processes for the respective lifecycle state—e.g., blocking purchase orders for obsolete items. This way, you can block engineering products at a more detailed level than the blocking option in the default order settings.

With the periodic activity *Product information management > Periodic tasks > Change lifecycle state for obsolete products*, you can update the lifecycle state—usually to a state "Obsolete"—of items that have not been created recently and which are not used in a recent transaction.

> *Note:* For engineering products (products with an *Engineering product category*), the field *Product lifecycle state* is not editable, and you can only change the lifecycle state with the button *Engineer/Engineering change management/Change lifecycle state*.

7.2.1.11 Catch Weight Products

A catch weight product (*CW product*) is an item with weight as the primary unit of measure, and a secondary unit (catch weight unit) for a countable number (e.g., pieces) in parallel. The weight per unit is variable, and as a result, there is no fixed unit conversion between the weight unit and the catch weight unit. In the order lines of purchase orders, sales orders, or batch production orders, only the catch weight quantity (the countable number) is editable. When you register an inventory transaction, both the weight and the catch weight quantity have to be entered in parallel.

The catch weight functionality originates from the process industries. Examples of catch weight products are animals (or parts of animals) in the food industry that require showing the counted number and the weight in parallel. Catch weight items usually apply batch numbers or serial numbers.

In Dynamics 365, the catch weight functionality is generally available in inventory, in purchasing, and in sales—all applicable forms contain additional fields for the catch weight. The usage in production is limited to batch orders, since only formulas, but not regular bills of materials, may include catch weight items. Because of its complexity, you should only use catch weight if you actually need to track the weight and the catch weight quantity separately.

In order to set up a catch weight item, set the slider *Catch weight (CW product)* to "Yes" when creating the shared product. Then click the button *Product/Set up/Unit conversions* in the shared product and enter an *Inter-class conversion* between the inventory unit (weight) and the catch weight unit (pieces). The catch weight unit has to be a unit without decimals (*Decimal precision* = "0" in the unit).

When you release the product, the inventory unit of the item has to be a weight unit (in applicable companies, the default unit in the Inventory parameters usually is a weight unit). On the tab *Manage inventory* in the Released product form (→ Fig. 7.6), select the catch weight unit in the field *CW unit* and enter the *Minimum quantity* and the *Maximum quantity*, which determine the range of allowed conversion (weight per unit). Then enter further data, including the item model group, the item group, and the dimension groups, in the same way as in any other product.

If you want to create a catch weight item directly in the released product form, you can also find the slider *Catch weight* in the *New released product* dialog and enter the details in the Released product form as described above.

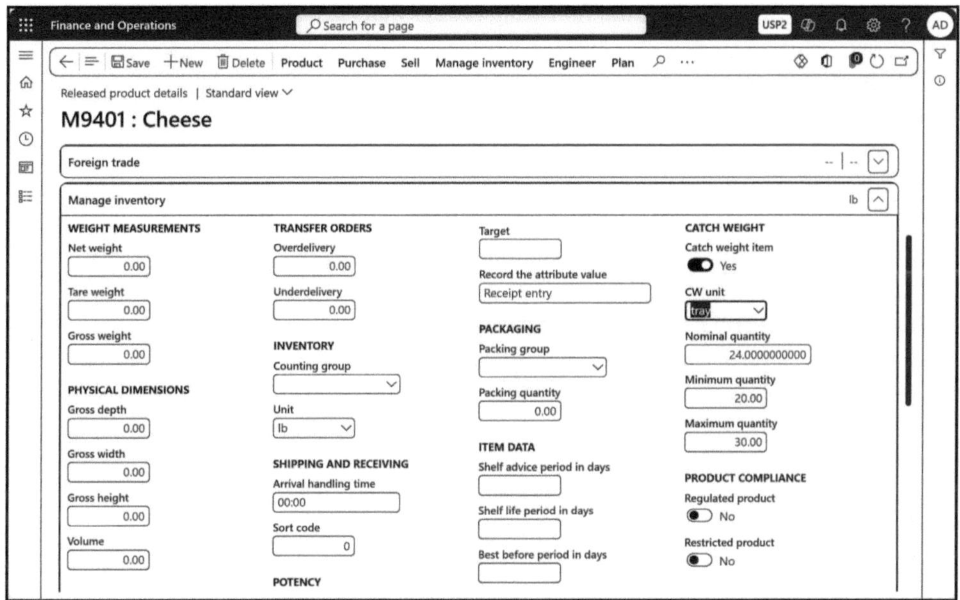

Fig. 7.6 Entering the catch weight settings in the released product

When you register a purchase order line, enter the catch weight quantity (countable number) in the column *CW quantity*. The column *Quantity*, which is not editable for a catch weight item, shows the quantity according to the regular unit conversion. When you receive the item in the Registration form or an item arrival journal (→ Sect. 3.5.3), you have to enter the CW quantity and the inventory quantity (default from the unit conversion) separately.

CW quantity and the quantity in the inventory unit have to be entered separately in all inventory transactions, including sales order picking and inventory journals. Inquiries on the current inventory show both weight and catch weight quantity.

7.2.2   Inventory Dimension Groups

Inventory dimensions control the breakdown of the inventory quantity within released products. With dimensions, you can split the inventory quantity and the transactions to a more detailed level than the item number.

7.2.2.1 Available Dimensions

The dimension groups of an item determine the inventory dimensions that you have to enter in an inventory transaction. If, for example, the dimension "Batch number" is active in the tracking dimension group of an item, you have to enter a batch number when you post a transaction with this item.

In Dynamics 365, there are the following groups that classify the inventory dimensions:

- **Product dimensions**—Version, style, size, color, and configuration subdivide an item based on product characteristics (only available for product masters).
- **Storage dimensions**—Site, warehouse, location, inventory status, and license plate represent inventory structures.
- **Tracking dimensions**—Batch and serial number control tracking options. The dimension "Owner" refers to vendor consignment (→ Sect. 7.4.8).

7.2.2.2 Dimension Groups and Settings

In order to set up a storage dimension group, open the menu item *Product information management > Setup > Dimension and variant groups > Storage dimension groups*. The menu items for product dimension groups and for tracking dimension groups are included in the same menu folder. The dimension group forms look similar, except for the applicable dimensions, which are specific to the particular form.

The example in → Fig. 7.7 shows the Storage dimension group form with the list of dimension groups in the left pane. In the right pane, you can edit the inventory dimension settings of the dimension group that is selected in the left pane.

If you need an additional dimension group, create a new record with the required inventory dimension settings (the checkbox settings are explained in → Table 7.2).

In storage dimension groups, the dimension *Site* (→ Sect. 10.1.6) is always active, which is why you must specify the site in each inventory transaction. On the tab *Warehouse specific setup*, the slider *Mandatory* controls whether the warehouse has to be entered

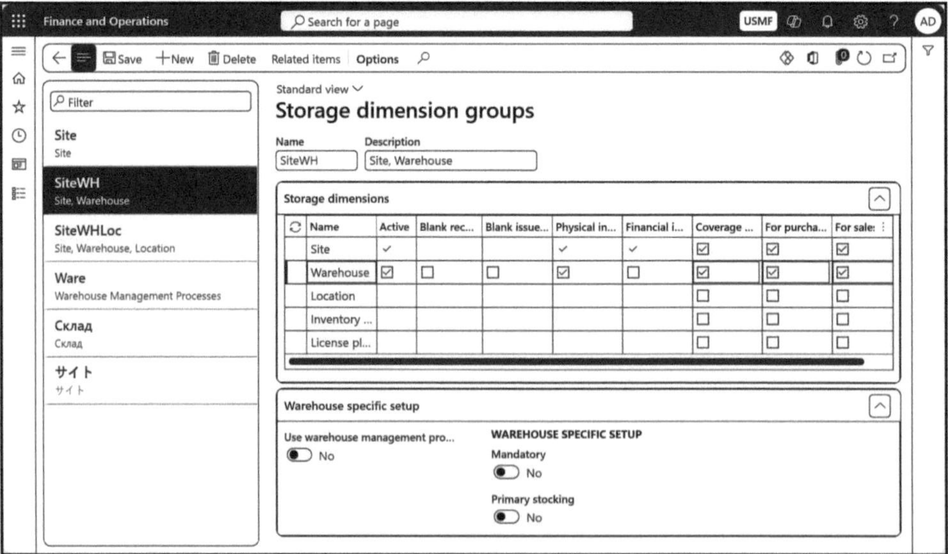

Fig. 7.7 Managing a storage dimension group

Table 7.2 Overview of the settings in the dimensions of a dimension group

Parameter	Explanation
Active	Dimension is used in transactions of the item
Active in sales process	Only in tracking dimension groups, for simplified serial number control in sales
Primary stocking	Dimension is mandatory in reservations; displayed as the default dimension in the On-hand inventory inquiry
Blank receipt allowed	Dimension is not mandatory in receipt transactions
Blank issue allowed	Dimension is not mandatory in issue transactions
Physical inventory	Item availability per dimension value (depending on the item model group, no negative inventory per, e.g., batch number)
Financial inventory	Inventory value per dimension value (necessary for calculating the value and cost price per, e.g., warehouse)
Coverage plan by dimension	Separate item coverage in master planning per dimension value ($\rightarrow$ Sect. 6.3.4)
For purchase prices	Dimension available for purchase price agreements
For sales prices	Dimension available for sales price agreements ($\rightarrow$ Sect. 4.8.1)
Transfer	Only in tracking dimension groups, for consignment inventory ($\rightarrow$ Sect. 7.4.8)

already when entering an order line (or any other transaction), or if the warehouse may remain empty until posting. The slider *Use warehouse management processes*, which activates the inventory dimensions *Inventory status* and *License plate*, controls whether the products in this group use the advanced warehouse management.

Product dimension groups only include the columns *Active*, *For purchase prices*, *For sales prices*, and the column *Display order* (controlling the sequence in which the product dimensions are shown in general forms).

When creating a product, select dimension groups with dimension settings that are in line with your requirements. You can, for example, only view the on-hand quantity per location if the dimension *Location* is active for the respective item. If you need a particular dimension for some, but not for all transactions of an item, a possible way is to use a dummy dimension value for transactions in which the dimension is not applicable. If locations are only used in some warehouses, you can use dummy locations as a default value in all warehouses without locations.

7.2.2.3 Dimension Groups in the Released Product

In order to assign the applicable inventory dimensions to a released product, click the button *Product/Set up/Dimension groups* in the Released product form. A dimension group, which has been entered in the shared product, is not editable in related released products.

In order to avoid invalid dimension values in posted transactions, it is not possible to change inventory-related settings in a dimension group once a transaction refers to the dimension group (or to change the dimension group of an item if the quantity is not zero and there are no open transactions).

If you need to change the dimension settings of an item, post transactions that completely consume the current inventory physically and financially. Before you can assign the new group, you still have to execute inventory closing.

7.2.2.4 Number Groups for Tracking Dimensions

In the released product, the *Tracking dimension group* controls whether the item uses batch numbers or serial numbers. For items with batch numbers or serial numbers, you need to record the batch or serial number in all transactions. As a prerequisite to enter a batch or serial number in a transaction, this number has to be included in the batch number table (*Inventory management > Inquiries and reports > Tracking dimensions > Batches*) or the serial number table.

If your company is in charge of assigning the batch or serial numbers to the physical products (e.g., if you produce the item), you can set up tracking number groups (*Inventory management > Setup > Dimensions > Tracking number groups*) to generate batch or serial numbers automatically. On the tab *General* in the Tracking number group form, you can specify the structure of the batch/serial numbers and select a *Number sequence code* for the automatic numbers (if you want to use a number sequence, set the slider *Number sequence No.* to "Yes"). If you set the slider *Reference No.* to "Yes", the order number—usually the production order or the purchase order—related to a product receipt will be included in the respective serial or batch number. Settings on the tab *Activation* determine which transactions generate numbers. In order to assign a tracking number group for batch or serial numbers to an item, select it in the field *Batch number group* or *Serial number group* on the tab *Manage inventory* in the Released product form.

If you generate batch or serial numbers, make sure to attach a label with the serial or batch number to the physical product in order to be able to physically track the item with the serial or batch number.

7.2.2.5 Simplified Serial Number Control in Sales Processes

If you need to track serial numbers along the whole supply chain, the tracking dimension *Serial number* has to be active. For items that are linked to a tracking dimension group with this setting, inventory transactions are split by serial number (which causes a high number of transactions). If serial number tracking is only required for warranty purposes in sales, there is no need to split inventory transactions by serial number in purchasing and other areas.

In this case, you can simplify the inventory processes by tracking serial numbers only in sales. With the sales serial number feature, there is only one inventory transaction record for all serial numbers in a transaction. The serial numbers of the transaction are stored in a separate table, which is linked to the inventory transaction. Sales serial numbers are only available for sales orders and return orders, not for other transactions (e.g., transfer orders). Serial number labels are physically attached to the item in inventory, but not tracked within Dynamics 365 until the order is shipped to or returned from the customer.

The sales serial number functionality is controlled by the tracking dimension group. If you want to use sales serial numbers, set up a dimension group in which the checkbox *Active in sales process* is selected for the dimension *Serial number*.

You can register sales serial numbers when you post the picking list registration, the packing slip, the sales invoice, or—in the advanced warehouse management—a sales transaction on the mobile device.

If you want to register serial numbers for items with sales serial number control when posting the packing slip, open the *Packing slip posting* dialog (e.g., with the button *Pick and pack/Generate/Post packing slip* in the Sales order form). On the tab *Lines* of the posting dialog, click the button *Update line/Register serial numbers* to access the Serial numbers form. In the Serial numbers form, which supports the use of scanners, enter or scan the serial numbers one by one. If a serial number label on the physical item is missing or not readable, click the button *Not readable* for the particular item. Once you have registered all serial numbers, close the registration form and post the packing slip.

If you work with two-step picking (→ Sect. 4.4.2), you can also use the button *Register serial numbers* on the tab *Lines* in the Picking list registration form.

If you do not post a picking list or packing slip, but ship the item with the sales invoice, open the serial number registration from the *Posting invoice* dialog.

If you want to know which serial numbers have been shipped, open the Serial number inquiry in the related journal. In case of a packing slip, click the button *Inquiries/Serial numbers* in the toolbar of the tab *Lines* in the packing slip journal. Tracking of sales serial numbers is also possible in the Item tracing form (→ Sect. 7.2.4).

7.2.2.6 Dimension Display Settings

The primary setting for the display of dimension columns in the grid of forms is specified on the tab *Inventory dimensions* in the parameters of each relevant module. For example, the default inventory dimensions in the sales order lines are specified in the Accounts receivable parameters (*Accounts receivable > Setup > Accounts receivable parameters*, Section *Inventory dimensions*).

In all forms that contain inventory dimension columns, an appropriate button—e.g., the button *Sales order line/Display/Dimensions* in the toolbar of the sales order lines, or the button *Display dimensions* in the toolbar of the inventory journal lines—provides access to a dialog that controls the dimensions that are displayed. In the *Dimension display* dialog, the slider *Save setup* provides the option to apply the current dimension settings as the default for the respective form.

If you display an inventory dimension in an inquiry that shows the inventory quantity or value, take into account that the result is only reliable if the selected dimensions comply with the dimension setup. You should, for example, only report the inventory value and the cost price per warehouse if the checkbox *Financial inventory* is selected for the dimension *Warehouse* in the applicable storage dimension group. If there is a different setting, inventory valuation does not offset the item issue transactions with the receipt transactions at the warehouse level, which is why there is no correct cost price at the warehouse level in this case.

7.2.3 Item Model Groups

Item model groups ($\rightarrow$ Fig. 7.8) contain settings on the valuation method and on item handling. The number of required item model groups depends on the requirements for processing items. In a usual Dynamics 365 implementation, there are at least two groups—one for inventoried items and one for service items. In the item model group for service items, the ledger integration should be deactivated.

If you change the settings in the field *Inventory model* or the field group *Ledger integration* of an item model group after posting related item transactions, the reconciliation of inventory and finance might become difficult. Before you modify any of these settings, you should carefully consider the consequences.

In the Item model group form (*Inventory management > Setup > Inventory > Item model groups*), the list pane on the left displays the list of available groups. In the right pane, you can edit the settings of the group that is selected in the left pane.

7.2.3.1 Settings on Item Handling

In item model groups for inventoried items, the checkbox *Stocked product* needs to be selected. Products that are assigned to a group, in which this checkbox is cleared, do not generate inventory transactions. For non-inventoried products like service items (except for subcontracted production services), this is a valid option.

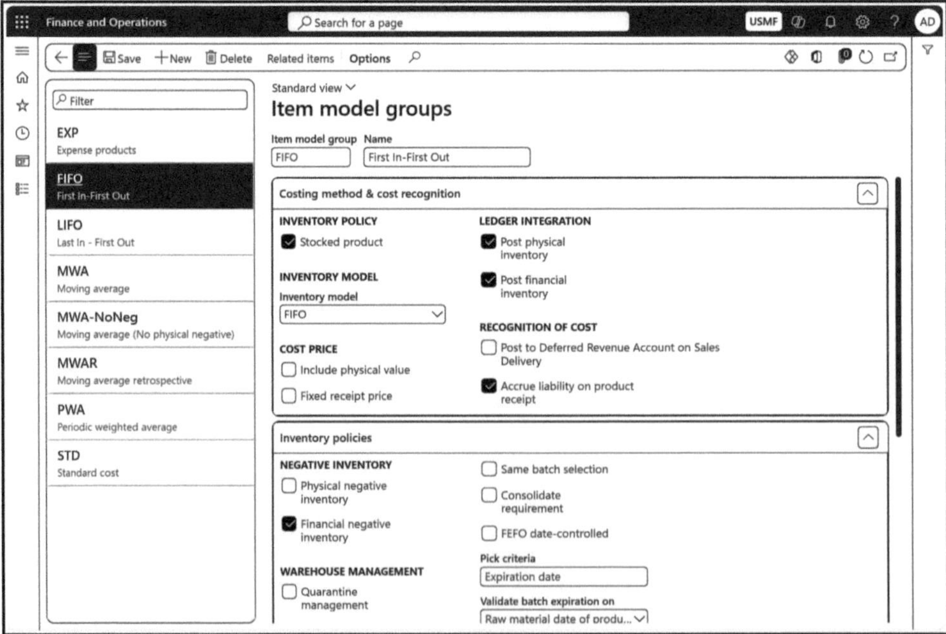

Fig. 7.8 Settings in the item model group

On the tab *Inventory policies*, the checkbox *Quarantine management* controls whether quarantine orders ($\rightarrow$ Sect. 7.4.6) are created automatically when posting an item receipt.

The checkbox *Registration requirements* on this tab controls if you have to post an inventory registration (in the Registration form, or an item arrival journal, or a mobile device transaction) before posting a product receipt in purchasing ($\rightarrow$ Sect. 3.5.3). The checkbox *Picking requirements* in a similar way controls posting the pick transaction before posting the packing slip in sales.

The checkboxes *Receiving requirements* and *Deduction requirements* control if you have to post a product receipt in purchasing or a packing slip in sales before posting the invoice.

7.2.3.2 Negative Inventory

In most cases, you do not allow a negative physical inventory for inventoried items, but you do accept a negative financial inventory. A negative financial inventory is a result of posting a sales invoice before posting the purchase invoice.

Settings on negative inventory in the item model group depend on the dimension group settings: Dynamics 365 controls negative physical (or financial) inventory only at the level of the inventory dimensions, for which the checkbox *Physical inventory* (or *Financial inventory*) is selected.

7.2.3.3 Inventory Model

The selected option in the field *Inventory model* (FIFO, LIFO, weighted average, moving average, or standard cost) determines the inventory valuation method. The valuation method is how issue transactions offset related receipt transactions in terms of valuation.

You can find more details on inventory valuation methods in $\rightarrow$ Sect. 7.3, and more details on the ledger integration in $\rightarrow$ Sect. 9.4.2.

7.2.4   Transactions and Inventory Quantity

Buttons for accessing transaction inquiries and inventory quantity inquiries—e.g., the button *Inventory/Transactions* or *Inventory/On-hand inventory* in the toolbar of the sales order lines—are included in various forms. Examples of these forms are the Released product form, the *Lines* tab in the Sales order form or the Purchase order form, or the journal lines in Inventory journals.

7.2.4.1 Inventory Transactions Inquiry and Cost Entries

The list page *Inventory management > Inquiries and reports > Transactions* gives an overview of the inventory transactions of multiple items (selected in a filter dialog).

If you want to view the inventory transactions of an item in the Released product form, click the button *Manage inventory/View/Transactions* in the Released product form. The

Inventory transactions inquiry then shows all transactions of the selected item ($\rightarrow$ Fig. 7.9). The columns *Reference* and *Number* display the original voucher.

In order to view the details of a transaction, click the button *Transaction details* in the action pane.

In addition to posted transactions, the Inventory transactions inquiry also shows future transactions which are not been posted yet. These transactions include quotation lines and order lines in sales, purchasing, and production, for which no packing slip/product receipt or invoice has been posted. You can recognize such lines by the receipt status "Ordered" or the issue status "On order" ("Reserved physical" in case there is a reservation) and by the empty physical and financial date.

The cost entries of an item show a cost-oriented view of inventory transaction data. You can access the cost entries with the button *Manage costs/Cost transactions/Cost entries* in the released product. The date filter above the grid determines the date range for displaying the cost entries.

> *Note:* Apart from regular inventory transactions, there are warehouse-specific transactions (for transfers at the level of storage dimensions below the warehouse) in the advanced warehouse management ($\rightarrow$ Sect. 8.1.1).

7.2.4.2 Physical and Financial Transaction

When you post a product receipt in purchasing, a packing slip in sales, a picking list in production, or a report as finished journal, Dynamics 365 populates the *Physical date* in the inventory transaction with the posting date. In parallel, the status of the transaction changes to "Received" or "Deducted". In the Transaction detail form, the field *Physical cost amount* on the tab *Updates* shows the preliminary inventory value of the transaction.

The *Financial date* in an inventory transaction is updated when you post the related invoice in purchasing or sales, or when you end the production order. The status of the transaction then changes to "Purchased" or "Sold", and the inventory value of the transaction is shown in the column *Cost amount*.

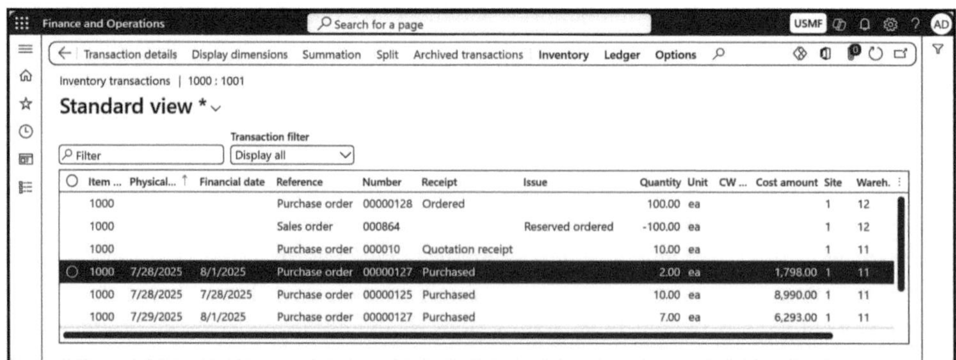

Fig. 7.9 Inventory transaction form with the transactions of an item

Dynamics 365 does not change the posted financial cost amount anymore. If there is a later adjustment of the inventory value, which is posted with inventory closing or a manual adjustment, the posted difference is shown separately in the field *Adjustment* on the tab *Updates* of the Transaction detail form.

7.2.4.3 Inventory Picking and Registration

Inventory registration in purchasing ($\rightarrow$ Sect. 3.5.3) and picking in sales ($\rightarrow$ Sect. 4.4.2) are additional steps in inventory when processing an order. They update the on-hand quantity of the item and the status of the inventory transaction, but unlike product receipt and packing slip transactions, inventory registration and picking do not generate an unchangeable voucher.

The date of the inventory registration (or picking) is shown in the field *Inventory date* on the tab *General* in the Transaction detail form, and it remains there when posting the packing slip in sales or the product receipt in purchasing. But if you do not proceed the regular way (post a product receipt after registration, or post a packing slip after picking), but cancel the registration, it is not possible to view the original picking or registration transaction in the inventory transactions anymore.

7.2.4.4 Transaction Details and Ledger Integration

Further details on the inventory transaction are shown on the tab *Updates* of the Transaction detail form ($\rightarrow$ Fig. 7.10). The fields on this tab are separated into the field groups *Physical*, *Ledger*, *Financial*, and *Settlement*.

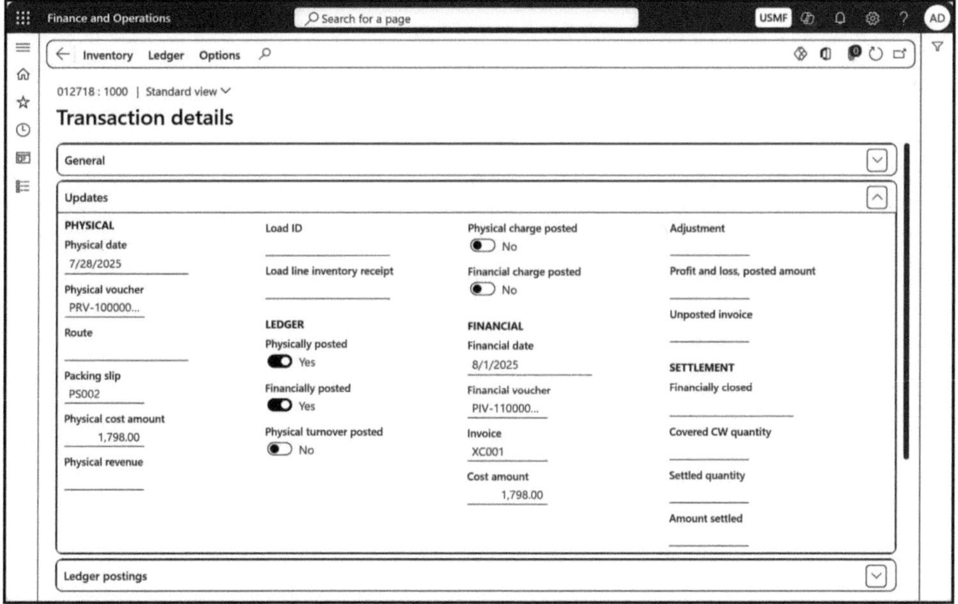

Fig. 7.10 Physical and financial data in the inventory transaction details

The field group *Physical* includes the date, number, and preliminary value of the product receipt or packing slip. Invoice data are shown in the field group *Financial*.

If the value of a transaction is modified after posting the invoice (as a result of inventory closing, or with a manual adjustment), the value difference is shown in the field *Adjustment*. The original financial *Cost amount* does not change anymore—all later adjustments are added in the field *Adjustment*.

The field group *Settlement* indicates if an inventory transaction is already settled by inventory closing. If the quantity of a transaction is completely settled with offsetting item issues or receipts, inventory closing populates the field *Financially closed* with the closing date and closes the transaction (the field *Value open* on the tab *General* then shows "No"). Registering a manual adjustment of a closed transaction reopens it.

The slider *Physically posted* on the tab *Updates* of the transaction details shows if the product receipt or packing slip has been posted to the general ledger. As a prerequisite, ledger integration for physical transactions has to be activated in the item model group of the particular item.

If ledger integration is activated for financial transactions, the option "Yes" in the slider *Financially posted* indicates that the invoice related to the inventory transaction has been posted. For purchase invoices, the slider is set to "Yes" after invoice posting, even if ledger integration is not active for an item. This has got the reason that a purchase invoice for items always generates a ledger transaction: To a stock account (for the receipt transaction in case ledger integration is active) or to an expense account (for immediate financial consumption otherwise).

7.2.4.5 On-Hand Inventory Inquiry

The list page *Inventory management > Inquiries and reports > On-hand list* gives an overview of the on-hand quantity for multiple items (selected in a filter dialog). In order lines or journal lines, you can click the button *Inventory/On-hand inventory* in the toolbar of the lines to view the on-hand quantity of the selected item and dimension values (for primary dimensions) in the line.

In order to view the current inventory quantity of an item in the Released product form, click the button *Manage inventory/View/On-hand inventory*. The related list page ($\rightarrow$ Fig. 7.11) shows a list with the inventory quantity of the item on the different sites (or other inventory dimensions that are selected as primary dimensions for the item). For a catch-weight item, you can select the option "Catch weight quantities" instead of "Inventory quantities" in the lookup field above the grid if you want to view the quantity in catch weight units.

If you want to view the quantity at a level other than the primary dimensions, click the button *Dimensions* in the action pane of the On-hand inventory inquiry to open the

Dimension display dialog ($\rightarrow$ Sect. 7.2.2), in which you can select dimensions that you want to view as columns in the inquiry. If you select, for example, the batch number in this dialog, the inquiry lines display the quantity per batch number.

7.2.4.6 On-Hand Inventory Details

In order to view the details of a line in the On-hand inventory inquiry, open the On-hand detail form by clicking the field *Search name* in the respective line of the list page. Apart from the *Physical inventory*, which is the current quantity in inventory, the detail form shows the item availability and the current cost price (average cost price, except for items with a standard cost price or a fixed receipt price).

The physical inventory of an item is the total of the transactions with the following status:

- **Posted quantity**—Invoiced quantity (purchase invoices minus sales invoices).
- **Received**—Product receipts in purchasing, added to the posted quantity.
- **Deducted**—Packing slips in sales, deducted from the posted quantity.
- **Registered**—Registration and item arrival, added to the posted quantity.
- **Picked**—Picking in sales, deducted from the posted quantity.

Apart from transactions in purchasing and sales, the transactions with the related status in production and all other areas are also included in the calculation.

All data shown in the On-hand detail form refers to the dimension selection of the line in the list page from which you open the detail form. In $\rightarrow$ Fig. 7.12, the applied dimension values are site "1" and warehouse "11" as selected in the list page ($\rightarrow$ Fig. 7.11). In line with this selection, Dynamics 365 will apply a filter on this site and warehouse when you access the related on-hand details to view the detailed quantity and cost amount information. When you review the cost price and the cost amount, take into account that data on item costs are only valid for dimensions with separate financial inventory (according to the dimension group settings).

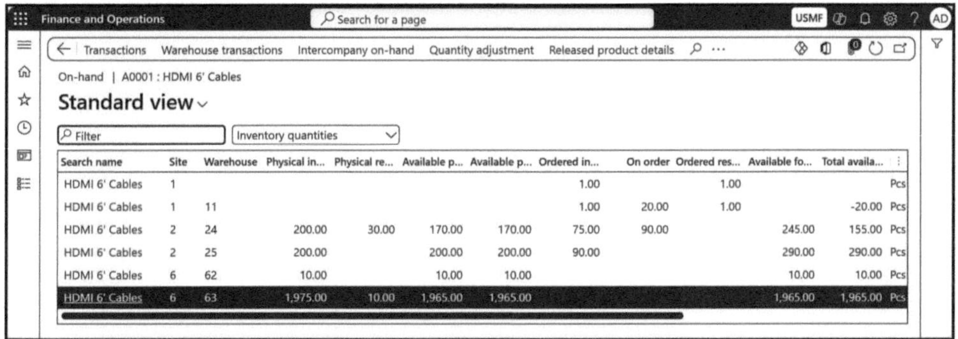

Fig. 7.11 On-hand overview with the inventory quantity of an item

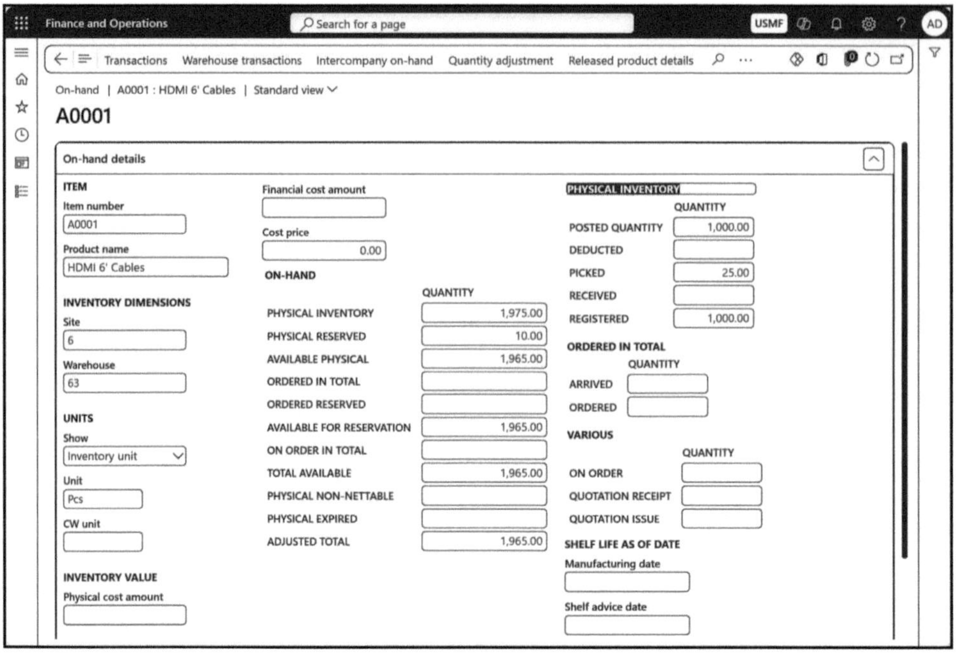

Fig. 7.12 Viewing the on-hand details of an item

7.2.4.7 On Hand Inventory in the Past

If you want to view the physical inventory on a date in the past, print or view the report *Inventory management > Inquiries and reports > Physical inventory reports > Physical inventory by inventory dimension*.

7.2.4.8 Item Tracing for Serial and Batch Numbers

When working with batch numbers and serial numbers, it is sometimes necessary to trace them back to the origin or forward to the usage.

With backward tracing, you can check the source—the purchase order or, for manufactured items, the production order with the consumed materials (including the batch/serial numbers of the materials) in a multi-level structure.

With forward tracing, you can check the consumption until the sales order or, for production materials, the production order and the manufactured item (including the batch/serial number) which has been produced with the traced batch/serial number in a multi-level structure.

You can access the Item tracing form directly from the menu (*Inventory management > Inquiries and reports > Tracking dimensions > Item tracing*) or with the button *Trace/Trace/Item tracing* in the Batch inquiry (*Inventory management > Inquiries and reports > Tracking dimensions > Batches*), which you can also access from the Released product form. For serial numbers, you can use the Serial number inquiry (*Inventory management > Inquiries and reports > Tracking dimensions > Serial numbers*).

In the dialog which is shown when accessing the Item tracing form, select the *Item number*, the *Batch number* or *Serial number*, and the *Trace direction* ("Forward" or "Backward") and click the button *OK*. The Item tracing form then shows the multi-level origin or usage in a tree with the on-hand quantity of the traced item, with the batch or serial number in the top node.

7.2.4.9 Soft Reservation and Inventory Visibility Add-In

Based on inventory data in the whole enterprise, which include inventory management data in Dynamics 365 and possible other logistic data (e.g., from third-party WMS or ERP systems), the Inventory Visibility add-in is an independent microservice in Microsoft Dataverse which enables third-party solutions to view inventory and to post inventory changes in real time, independent of a later transaction posting in Dynamics 365.

In this context, third-party solutions (but also sales orders in Dynamics 365) can place soft reservations in the Inventory Visibility add-in to avoid overselling.

A soft reservation reduces the available inventory that is shown in the Inventory Visibility add-in. It is removed by offsetting the soft reservation with a regular hard reservation in Dynamics 365 ($\rightarrow$ Sect. 7.4.5) or by consuming the reserved quantity—e.g., with a packing slip.

If you want to use the Inventory Visibility add-in, install it from the Power Platform admin center and, in order to integrate Dynamics 365, configure the Inventory Visibility Integration parameters (*Inventory Management > Setup > Inventory Visibility integration parameters*).

7.2.5 Engineering Change Management

The Engineering change management module supports the versioning of products and the management of engineering changes.

Different from the standard way for creating a product, you start from the released product—and not from the shared product—when creating an engineering product. The shared product is automatically created in parallel (like for a regular released product). If you want to release an engineering product to other companies, you do not start from the shared product, but from the released product in the engineering company (or from an engineering change order).

Product versions of an engineering product are managed with *Engineering versions*. If it is necessary to know the product version in inventory and in the inventory transactions, the engineering product has to be set up as a product master with an active product dimension "Version".

7.2.5.1 Setup for Engineering Change Management

As a prerequisite for using the engineering change management, it must be enabled in the license configuration. If you want to use the product dimension "Version", also enable the "Product dimension version" in the license configuration.

Engineering companies, in which engineering products are created initially, are set up in the Engineering organizations form (*Engineering change management > Setup > Engineering organizations*).

If product versions should be tracked in inventory, you need a product dimension group with an active dimension "Version" ($\rightarrow$ Sect. 7.2.2). With version number rules (*Engineering change management > Setup > Product version number rule*), you can specify how to generate version numbers. If the option "Auto" is selected in the field *Number rule* of the Product version number rule form, version numbers are automatically created as specified in the field *Format*. If the option "List" is selected, consecutive version numbers have to be specified on the tab *Version* that is shown then.

The product lifecycle state ($\rightarrow$ Sect. 7.2.1) enables tracking the item status and controlling the allowed transactions (blocking the item). For engineering products, there are more detailed options than for regular products.

Product release policies (*Engineering change management > Setup > Product release policies*) specify for each company to which you release engineering products, if the BOM and the route should be copied (not available if you select the *Production type* "None" in the release policy), and if or which item should be used as a template. For engineering products, the template item in the product release policy replaces the regular product template ($\rightarrow$ Sect. 7.2.1) for populating default data in a new released product.

Different from product release policies, the product readiness policies (*Engineering change management > Setup > Product readiness policies*) are not mandatory. You can use a product readiness policy to make sure that particular checks, which you specify on the tab *Readiness control* of the Product readiness form, are executed automatically or manually before activating a product version. The columns *Owner type*—with the option "Team" ($\rightarrow$ Sect. 10.1.2) or "Person"—and *Owner* determine who should execute the check. The responsible workers can view their open checks in the menu item *Engineering change management > Common > Product readiness > My open readiness checks*.

The engineering product categories (*Engineering change management > Setup > Engineering product category details*) contain the core settings for engineering change management. When creating an engineering product, the settings in the selected engineering product category determine core item characteristics like the product type, the product subtype, the product dimensions, the version number rule, the product readiness policy, and the product release policy. If the slider *Track version in transactions* is selected in the category, only *Product dimension groups* with an active dimension "Version" are available. The field *Engineering organization* in the upper pane of the Engineering product category form determines the company in which you can use the category. If no engineering product category is assigned to a company, it is not possible to create engineering products initially in that company—you can only release engineering products from another (engineering) company to this company.

Engineering change priorities (*Engineering change management > Setup > Engineering change management > Engineering change priorities*) and engineering change categories (*Engineering change management > Setup > Engineering change management > Engineering change categories*) serve grouping and sorting purposes. Change priorities are mandatory in engineering change orders.

Optionally, you can set up product owners (*Engineering change management > Setup > Product owners*). Product owners are groups of workers—selected on the tab *Members*—who are responsible for particular products. If a product owner is assigned to an engineering product, only the members of this group can release the product. As a precondition, the selected workers need to be assigned to users (→ Sect. 10.2.2).

In the Engineering change management parameters, the lookup field *Product acceptance* controls whether it is necessary to accept products, BOMs, and routes after they have been released from an engineering company. The parameter of the receiving company is relevant in this case.

7.2.5.2 Creating Engineering Products

It is not possible to create an engineering product starting from a shared product. In order to create an engineering product, open the Released product form in an engineering company (engineering organization) and click the button *Product/New/Engineering product* in the action pane.

In the *New product* dialog (→ Fig. 7.13), select the *Engineering product category*, which determines core item characteristics like the product type or the initial version (from the version number rule). Depending on the settings in this category, the product may be a product master with a product dimension group that applies the product dimension "Version" (for tracking the version in inventory transactions). Further relevant settings in the *Engineering product category* include the *Product release policy*, which controls whether item data (including BOM and route) from the template item in the release policy are copied to the new product, and the *Product readiness policy*, which controls the readiness checks which have to be executed before you can activate the new engineering version and use the product (not required, if the readiness policy in the category is empty). You can only edit the product release policy and readiness policy in the shared product. The related fields in the Released product form are display fields.

If a *Product readiness policy* is assigned to the new product, execute the readiness checks for the new product and the new engineering version (which is created automatically with the product). For checks at the level of engineering versions (as specified in the column *Apply checks on* in the readiness policy), click the button *Engineer/Engineering change management/Engineering versions* in the Released product form to access the Engineering version form, and click the button *Product/Checklist/Readiness checks* in the engineering version to access the checks. For checks at the product level, click the button *Product/Readiness checks/Readiness checks* in the Released product form to access the

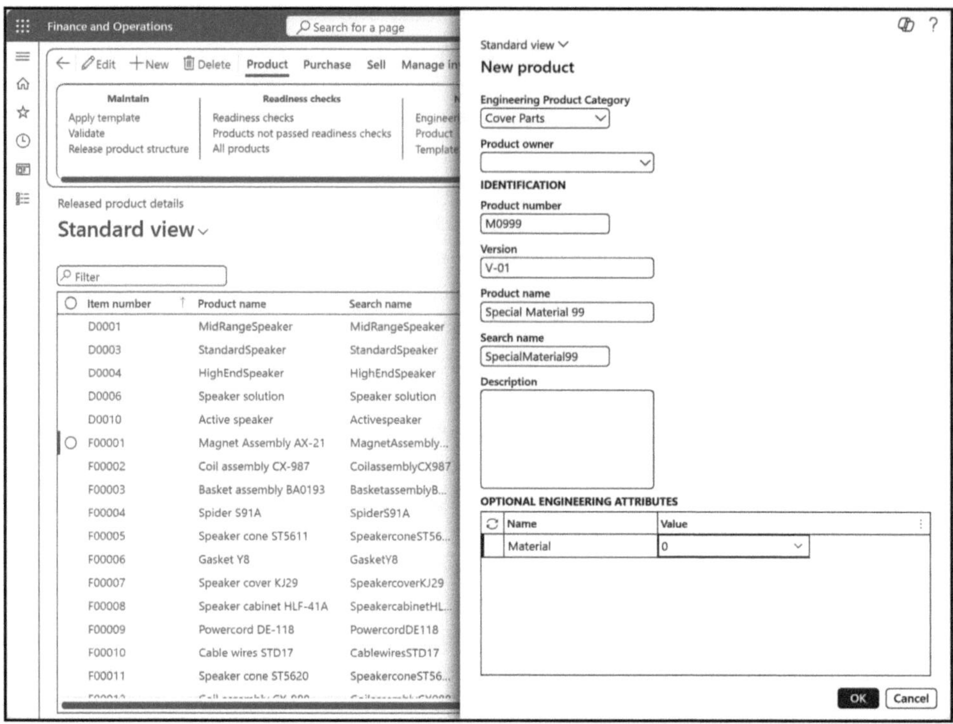

Fig. 7.13 Creating an engineering product in the demo-company DEMF

related checks. Once you have finished the readiness checks, click the button *Activate version* in the Engineering version form. The new version is then active, and you can use the product.

Apart from the settings that derive from the engineering product category, you can manage the released product with the other fields and settings like a standard product, including the BOM and the route as applicable.

If you want to use the product not only in the engineering company, but also in other companies of your enterprise, release the product to the relevant companies. For this purpose, click the button *Product/Maintain/Release product structure* in the Released product form. In the wizard which is shown next, select the applicable product (mark in the column *Select*) and optionally check the details (including BOM and route) with the button *Release details* on the first page. Then select the applicable companies on the next page before you confirm releasing. Depending on the Engineering change management parameter *Product acceptance*, the released product (including BOM and route, depending on the product release policy) is immediately available in the other companies, or only after the receiving company has approved it in the form *Engineering change management > Common > Product releases > Open product releases*.

7.2.5.3 Working with Engineering Products

The product lifecycle state of an engineering product, which you can update with the button *Engineer/Engineering change management/Change lifecycle state* in the Released product form, controls which transactions are enabled for the engineering product (e.g., if sales orders are possible).

If the *Engineering product category* of the item determines that the product is a product master with an active product dimension "Version", the version has to be specified in all transactions and order lines—similar to the other product dimensions (e.g., the size).

7.2.5.4 Change Orders and New Versions of Engineering Products

The engineering versions of a product, which you can access with the button *Engineer/Engineering change management/Engineering versions* in the Released product form, apply to simple products without version control in inventory, and to product masters with an active product dimension "Version". Simple products are easier to work with, but only the product dimension "Version" provides full control of the version in inventory and in transactions (e.g., if you want to know which version has been shipped to a customer in case two product versions are available in inventory at the same time).

If there are changes to the product design (e.g., when replacing a component in the BOM), create a new product version (engineering version). For this purpose, enter and process an engineering change order. The engineering change request, which you can process as a prior step, is optional.

You can start an engineering change request in several forms—for example, in the engineering versions of a released product. In order to create the change request, click the button *Product/Engineering change request/New engineering change request* in this form. In the Change request form, enter a *Title* and a *Priority*, and make sure that the respective product (including applicable product dimension values) is added to the tab *Products* of the form after saving the record. The default values for the *Priority* and the optional field *Category* (Engineering change category) are specified in the Engineering change management parameters.

If the change request should result in a change order, enter an explanation as a note on the tab *Information* before approving the request (with the button *Change request/Change status/Approve*) and creating the change order (with the button *Change request/Engineering change order/Copy link and products*). In the following dialog *Add the engineering change request to an engineering change order,* click the button *New* in the header area for creating a new change order.

The change order (→ Fig. 7.14), which you can also create directly in the form *Engineering change management > Common > Engineering change management > Engineering change orders*, enables managing the release of new product versions in a structured way. In the Engineering change order form, you can add and edit concerned

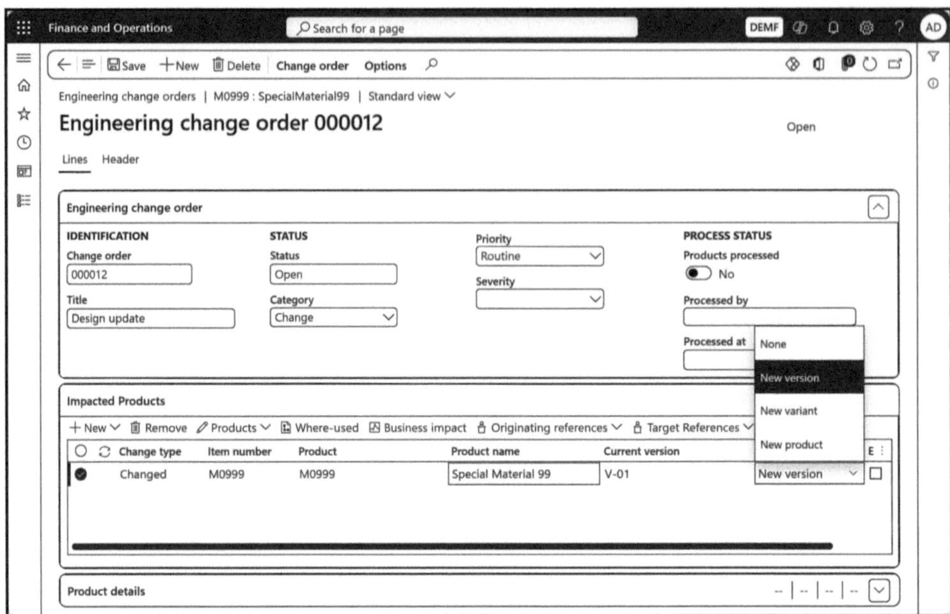

Fig. 7.14 Managing an engineering change order

products on the tab *Impacted products*. The column *Impact* on this tab controls whether to create a new version or a new product. The new version or product is shown on the tab *Product details* (which includes the field group *Impact*). On the sub-tab *Bill of materials* and *Route*, you can manage the BOM and the route for the new version or product.

In order to create the new version or product (as specified in the column *Impact*), approve and process the change order with the button *Change order/Change status/ Approve* and *Change order/Change status/Process*.

If a *Product readiness policy* is assigned to the product, execute the readiness checks for the new engineering version (e.g., with the button *Product/Checklist/Readiness checks* in the Engineering version form accessed from the released product) and activate the engineering version (with the button *Activate version* in the Engineering version form).

In the next step, the product (including BOM and route, depending on the product release policy) can be released to other companies, like when initially creating an engineering product, but this time with the button *Change order/Product releases/Release product structure* in the Engineering change order form.

> *Note:* If there is a workflow with an active workflow version for engineering change requests or change orders in the engineering workflows (*Engineering change management > Setup > Engineering workflows*), you have to process the workflow for approval instead of simply clicking the button *Approve* in the change request or the change order.

7.2.6 Case Study Exercises

Exercise 7.1—Dimension Groups

In order to review the functionality of dimension groups, create a new storage dimension group DS-## and a tracking dimension group DT-## (## = your user ID). Set up the dimension groups in a way that the dimensions *Site*, *Warehouse*, and *Batch number* are required in each transaction. The financial inventory value and the cost price should be tracked at the level of warehouses.

Exercise 7.2—Item Model Group

As a preparation for the next exercise, create a new item model group T-## (## = your user ID) with FIFO valuation (inventory model "FIFO"). The ledger integration for physical and financial inventory should be active. The item model group is used for stocked products, and a negative financial inventory is allowed. All other checkboxes remain cleared. Approved vendors are not required.

Then set up a second item model group S-## with standard cost valuation, which has the same settings as the first group, except that the inventory model is "Standard cost" and a negative physical inventory is allowed.

7.3   Inventory Valuation and Cost Management

Based on the deep integration of the entire application, Dynamics 365 provides a very accurate calculation of the inventory value. In addition to the valuation methods for moving average and standard cost, there is the option to use an end-to-end FIFO or LIFO valuation.

Relevant modules in this context are the Inventory management module, which contains all data on inventory quantity and value, and the Cost management module with forms and features related to inventory costing and valuation.

7.3.1 Valuation and Cost Flow

Inventory transactions update the physical inventory quantity and the financial inventory value.

In addition to the transaction in the Inventory management module, which contains the complete physical and financial record, the transaction also generates a cost entry, which only contains cost-related data. Cost entries are not generated for inventory transfers with no impact on the inventory value.

7.3.1.1 Basics of Inventory Valuation

The basis for inventory valuation is a simple principle:

- **Receipt costs**—The value of receipts is specified in the receipt transaction.
- **Issue costs**—The value of issues is calculated according to the valuation model.

The receipt transactions determine the cost price of related consumption (issue transactions). The principle for linking issue and receipt transactions is given by the valuation model (FIFO, LIFO, average cost). It is not possible to enter the cost price or the cost amount in an issue transaction.

The standard cost price, which specifies an inventory value regardless of the actual costs, is an exception to this principle. In Dynamics 365, there are two options for standard cost valuation:

- **Standard cost**—Inventory value according to a predefined item cost price.
- **Fixed receipt price**—Similar to standard cost, but specifying the receipt price.

The option "Fixed receipt price" is available in combination with the valuation methods FIFO, LIFO, and average cost. The fixed receipt price sets the cost price for receipts to a predefined value, which means that the cost price does not change with an actual transaction.

Unlike the fixed receipt price, the inventory model "Standard cost" constitutes a true standard cost valuation. The standard cost price of an item is immediately used in all issue and receipt transactions.

The main difference between the methods "Standard cost" and "Fixed receipt price" is given when changing the standard cost price of an item. With the standard cost method, an adjustment of the current inventory value is immediately posted. With the fixed receipt price method, there is no adjustment of the current inventory value. The new price is only used for later receipts, and the current inventory is issued with the old price until it is completely consumed.

The valuation method for an item is given by the field *Inventory model* in the item model group of the item. In the inventory model, the following options for the valuation method are available:

- **FIFO**—First in, first out (the value of the first receipt is consumed first).
- **LIFO**—Last in, first out (the value of the last receipt is consumed first).
- **LIFO date**—LIFO, consuming only receipts with a posting date before the issue.
- **Weighted average**—Average of receipts per period, calculated at the time of inventory closing/recalculation.
- **Weighted average date**—Average price per day.
- **Standard cost**—Predefined standard cost price.
- **Moving average**—Keeps the average cost price.

7.3.1.2 Valuation of Item Receipts

The final value of an item receipt is set by the related financial transaction (invoice). Except for items with standard cost or fixed receipt price valuation, which use a predefined cost price, the cost price in the receipt transactions is calculated as follows:

- **Purchase order receipt**—Amount of the invoice line, including related item charges (→ Sect. 4.3.4). If specified in the costing sheet (→ Sect. 7.3.3), indirect costs are added.
- **Production receipt**—Cost amount of the production order (total costs of BOM item consumption and resource utilization, including applicable indirect costs).
- **Sales return**—Original value of the returned item (if assigned to an original sales order), otherwise the return cost price that is entered in the return order.
- **Other receipt**—Cost amount entered in the journal line.

7.3.1.3 Valuation of Item Issues

When you post an item issue (e.g., a sales packing slip), the (preliminary) cost price of the issue is given by the current average cost price (except for items with a standard cost price or a fixed receipt price). You can view the current average cost price in the field *Cost price* of the On-hand detail form (→ Sect. 7.2.4)—for a valid result, make sure to select appropriate inventory dimensions ("Financial inventory").

Depending on the setting in the checkbox *Include physical value* of the respective item model group, the current average cost price is only based on financial transactions (invoices), or it includes the preliminary value of item receipts that are not invoiced yet.

The valuation method is used with inventory closing. Based on the assigned receipts, inventory closing calculates the exact cost price of the issue transactions. For this reason, the issue price and amount are not final until you have posted the financial transaction (invoice) of all assigned receipts and inventory closing has been executed. The assignment of issues to receipts is determined by the inventory model—FIFO, LIFO (date), or weighted average (date).

In general, the financial date (invoice date) is the basis for the chronological assignment of issue and receipt transactions. The physical date is used for items with the inventory model FIFO or LIFO (or LIFO date), if the checkbox *Include physical value* in the respective item model group is selected.

In order to determine the correct cost price and inventory value, inventory closing is required for all items except for items with the following valuation methods:

- **Standard cost price**—The standard cost price is immediately used in issue and receipt transactions.
- **Moving average**—Keeps the cost price of issue transactions (current average cost price at the time of posting) and does not require inventory closing.

These two valuation methods determine the final cost price of consumption already when posting the consumption.

Note: For items with the inventory model "Weighted average" or "Weighted average date", the checkbox *Include physical value in weighted average recalculation* in the item model group controls whether the *Recalculation* ($\rightarrow$ Sect. 7.3.2)—but not the inventory closing itself—includes transactions which are only physically updated (not yet financially). As a prerequisite for this option, the related feature must be enabled.

7.3.1.4 Standard Cost Price

Items with the inventory model "Standard cost" do not require inventory closing because all receipt and issue transactions immediately apply the standard cost price that is specified in the Item price form ($\rightarrow$ Sect. 7.3.3).

When you activate a new standard cost price, Dynamics 365 immediately posts an adjustment of the current stock value in inventory and the general ledger. Therefore, the new standard price is immediately used in issues of the current stock.

7.3.1.5 Fixed Receipt Price

The checkbox *Fixed receipt price* in the item model group is only used in combination with the valuation methods FIFO, LIFO (date), or weighted average (date). With a fixed receipt price, the cost price entered in the Released product form or in the Item price form specifies the fixed cost price for receipt transactions. The cost price in issue transactions is calculated in line with the valuation method. But as long as you do not change the item cost price, this cost price will match the fixed receipt price of the item.

When you change the item cost price, issue and receipt transactions apply the new cost price immediately. But since there is no revaluation of the current inventory when you change a fixed receipt price, the financial value of the current inventory still complies with the old price. As a result, inventory closing is required for the option "Fixed receipt price" to adjust the cost amount of issue transactions to the old price according to the valuation method (until the inventory that has been received with the old price has been consumed completely).

7.3.1.6 Moving Average Price

For items with the inventory model "Moving average", receipt transactions are posted with the cost price of the transaction. When you post a vendor invoice, the financial transaction depends on whether the quantity that is covered by the invoice is still on hand:

- **Complete quantity still on hand**—The total amount of the purchase invoice—including possible differences to the order—is posted as the financial cost amount in inventory.
- **Part of the quantity already consumed**—For the quantity that is not in stock, the difference between the physical cost amount and the financial cost amount is posted as an adjustment to a price difference account.

When you post an issue transaction (e.g., a sales packing slip), the average cost price at the time of posting is used. This cost price does not change anymore, which is why inventory closing is not required.

7.3.1.7 Inventory Value Calculation

The available valuation methods in Dynamics 365 are shown in → Table 7.3.

In the following example, you can view the cost price calculation for the valuation methods that are based on the actual costs. Standard cost valuation with a pre-defined item price (independent of actual receipts) is not included in the example.

The basis of the example are three receipt transactions with different cost prices and an issue transaction in between, as shown in → Table 7.4. The cost amount of the issue transaction after inventory closing is shown in → Table 7.5. This cost amount depends on the valuation method.

7.3.1.8 Financial Inventory Dimensions and Inventory Marking

In addition to the inventory model, the inventory dimension settings have an impact on the cost calculation of item issues. An assignment of an issue to a receipt is not possible across dimensions with a separate financial inventory (according to the dimension group settings).

If a separate financial inventory is, for example, activated for the dimension *Warehouse*, issues of a warehouse "20" are only assigned to receipts in warehouse "20" (including transfers). If a separate financial inventory is not activated for the dimension *Warehouse*,

Table 7.3 Inventory models with the valuation methods in Dynamics 365

Inventory model	Explanation
FIFO (First In First Out)	Item issues are assigned to the oldest item receipt still in stock
LIFO (Last In First Out)	Item issues are assigned to the newest item receipt in stock (including all transactions before the inventory closing date)
LIFO date	Like LIFO, limiting the assignment of issues to receipts before the particular issue
Weighted average	The cost price of item issues in a period is the average cost price of all receipts (including the beginning balance) in this period, calculated when executing inventory closing
Weighted average date	The cost price of item issues is the average cost price, calculated separately for each day
Standard cost	The cost price of item issues and receipts matches the active standard cost price of the item
Moving average	The cost price of item issues is the average cost price of the inventory quantity at the time of posting the issue

Table 7.4 Posted transactions for the comparison of valuation methods

Date	Transaction	Quantity	Cost amount
July 1	Receipt	10	100
July 2	Receipt	10	200
July 3	Issue	−10	(to be calculated)
July 4	Receipt	10	300

Table 7.5 Valuation of the item issue in → Table 7.4

Inventory Model	Amount	Explanation
FIFO	100	From the receipt on July 1
LIFO	300	From the receipt on July 4
LIFO Date	200	From the receipt on July 2
Weighted average	200	Average of all receipts
Weighted average date	150	From the receipts on July 1 and July 2
Moving average	150	Current average when posting the issue

the assignment only complies with the date sequence, irrespective of the warehouse in the transactions. For this reason, a valid cost price is only shown per site, not per warehouse in this case.

Marking is another option with an impact on the automatic assignment according to the inventory model. Marking works as a batch for inventory valuation and assigns the cost amount of a particular receipt to a specific issue. You can use it, for example, in vendor returns (→ Sect. 3.7.1). If you want to mark a transaction, click the button *Inventory/ Marking* in transactions inquiries, order lines, or journal lines.

7.3.1.9 Inventory Value Report and Cost Explorer

The inventory value report is a configurable report with the option to set up multiple report versions. As a prerequisite for this report, you have to set up at least one value report version with the report layout (*Cost management > Inventory accounting policies setup > Inventory value reports*). The settings in the layout determine which inventory value data are shown in the columns and lines of the report version. When you print the inventory value report (*Cost management > Inquiries and reports > Inventory accounting—status reports > Inventory value*), select the report layout in the field *ID* of the print dialog.

The cost explorer is an inquiry that shows the assignment and the adjustments (posted with inventory closing) of issues and receipts. In order to open the cost explorer, click the button *Inventory/Costing/Cost explorer* in an inventory transaction that has been financially posted (invoiced). You can access the inventory transactions in various ways, for example, with the button *Manage inventory/View/Transactions* in the Released product form.

7.3.2   Inventory Closing and Adjustment

At the time when you post an issue transaction, Dynamics 365 always applies the current average cost price (except for items with a standard cost price or a fixed receipt price). In order to calculate the final cost price and the inventory value according to the valuation method of the item, you have to close inventory. Only items assigned to the inventory model "Standard cost" or "Moving average" are not included in inventory closing.

7.3.2.1 Inventory Closing

You need to close inventory periodically—usually in the course of month-end closing in finance—in order to show correct item costs in finance and to close the inventory transactions. After inventory closing, it is not possible to post inventory transactions in the closed period. If you have to post a transaction in a closed period, the only option is to reverse inventory closing.

Inventory closing is executed in the form *Inventory management > Periodic tasks > Closing and adjustment* (→ Fig. 7.15), which by default shows the active (i.e., posted) closings. To close a period, usually the past month, click the button *Close procedure* in this form. The first and the second option in the close procedure, the check of open quantities and the check of cost prices, generate reports that help to assess inventory transactions. You can run these reports to take corrective actions (e.g., resolve issues with missing or wrong transactions) before you actually close the period. But it is not required to complete these steps. With the button *Close procedure/Close inventory* in the Closing and adjustment form, you finally execute and post inventory closing. Depending on the number of transactions, it might be useful to run closing as a batch job in the nighttime.

As a prerequisite for closing a period in inventory, the accounting period in the ledger calendar has to be open. As far as possible, you should post all vendor invoices that refer to item receipts in purchasing, and end all production orders that are reported as finished. The corresponding product receipts in purchasing and in production then already include the financial cost amount (instead of the physical cost amount, which is shown before invoicing), which minimizes the number of open transactions.

Once you have finished inventory closing, you can view the posted adjustment transactions with the button *Details/Settlements* in the Closing and adjustment form. If you have to reverse inventory closing, click the button *Reverse* in the Closing and adjustment form.

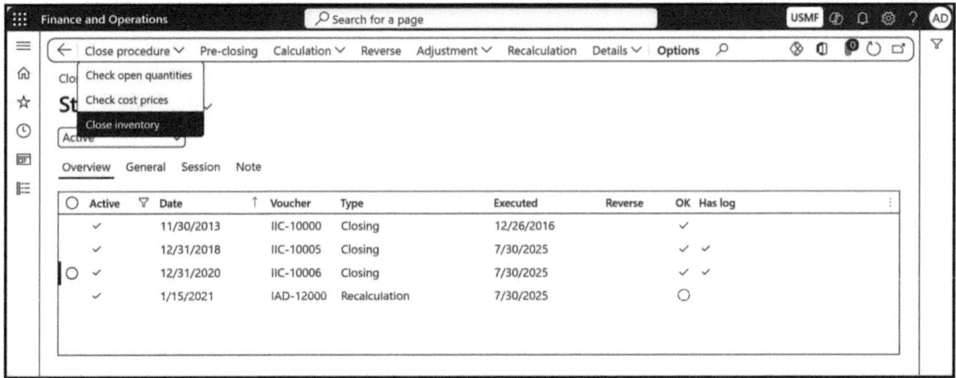

Fig. 7.15 Closing inventory for a past month in the Closing and adjustment form

7.3.2.2 Recalculation

Sometimes, you want to execute the calculation and posting of inventory closing without actually closing a period—in particular, if you don't want to wait for the month-end closing to get to know the final inventory value and cost margins in line with the inventory model of the items. For this purpose, you can click the button *Recalculation* in the Closing and adjustment form.

7.3.2.3 Manual Adjustment of Inventory Value

If you want to adjust the inventory value of an item manually, use the *Adjustment* feature, which includes the following options:

- **Adjustment/On-hand**—Adjusts the cost price and cost amount of the current financial inventory at the level of inventory dimensions (e.g., for a warehouse).
- **Adjustment/Transactions**—Adjusts the cost amount of particular, financially posted, receipt transactions.
- **Adjustment/Revaluation for moving average**—Adjusts the cost price and amount of the financial inventory for items with a moving average valuation.

In the Adjustment form, which you access with the related buttons in the Closing and adjustment form, click the button *Select* to open the filter dialog in which you select the respective items or transactions for the adjustment. Then enter a positive or negative adjustment amount in the column *Edit now* of the Adjustment form, or retrieve an adjustment proposal with one of the options in the button *Adjustment*. Finally, click the button *Post* in the Adjustment form to post the adjustment.

7.3.3   Product Cost Management

The financial value of inventory is a result of the quantity and the cost price of products. In order to support inventory cost management, the Cost management module, with the workspaces *Cost administration* and *Cost analysis*, collects relevant information on item costs.

7.3.3.1 Item Base Cost Price

The base cost price of an item is specified in the Released product form (field *Price* on the tab *Manage costs*). This base cost price is used as a default value for the cost price of item receipts in inventory journals and in counting journals (in case there is no site-specific cost price in the Item price form). In order to avoid transactions without (or with a wrong) cost price, make sure that the base cost price is correct.

If the slider *Latest cost price* on the tab *Manage costs* of the released product is set to "Yes", the base cost price in the released product is updated with each financial receipt transaction (e.g., purchase order invoice) of the item. In addition to the cost price in the

Released product form, the Item price form (accessed with the button *Manage costs/Set up/Item price* in the released product) also shows this price update. If you want to track the history of price updates in the Item price form, activate the price history (Inventory parameters, slider *Last price history* in the Section *Inventory accounting*).

The base cost price is not used for items with the valuation method "Standard cost". Standard cost price items require an active cost price in the Item price form.

7.3.3.2 Costing Versions and the Item Price Form

You can manage the cost price per site (in parallel to the purchase price and the sales price per site) in the Item price form, which you access with the button *Manage costs/Set up/ Item price* in the Released product form.

Before you can enter a record in the Item price form, an appropriate costing version has to be configured in the Costing version setup form (*Cost management > Predetermined cost policies setup > Costing versions*). Costing versions contain separate versions of prices and provide the option to set up different calculation principles. Items with standard cost valuation use a costing version with the *Costing type* "Standard cost". The costing type "Planned cost" refers to the other valuation methods. You can set up additional costing versions—for example, if you need to calculate prices in a simulation with other settings. In order to enter a new cost price in the Item price form, switch to the tab *Pending prices* and click the button *New*. In the new cost price, select the *Price type* "Cost" and, in the column *Version*, the applicable costing version. You have to select the *Site* if it is not specified in the costing version. Apart from the *Price* itself, the Item price form contains additional details like the *Price quantity* and the *Price charges*, which work similarly to corresponding settings in the Released product form ($\rightarrow$ Sect. 3.3.3).

For manufactured items with a bill of materials, you can click the button *Calculate item cost* in the Item price form to run a cost calculation. Once you have entered or calculated the pending price, click the button *Activate pending price(s)* to activate it ($\rightarrow$ Fig. 7.16).

Only active prices serve as the cost price for inventory valuation. They are shown on the tab *Active prices* in the Item price form.

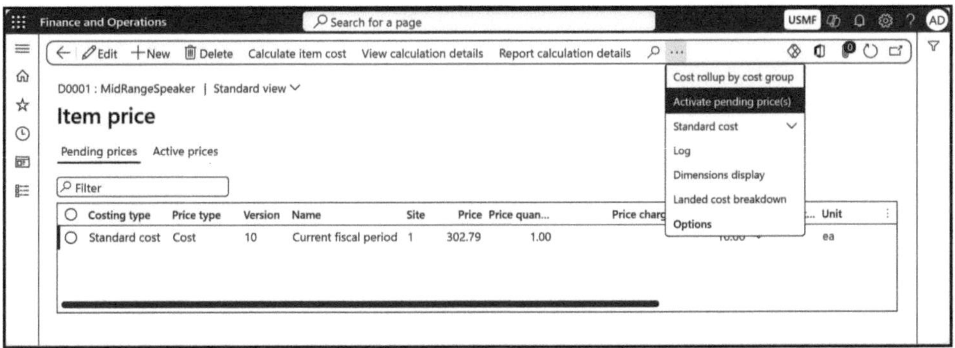

Fig. 7.16 Activating a pending price in the Item price form

For product masters, cost prices are available at the product variant level, if the slider *Use cost price by variant* on the tab *Manage costs* in the released product is set to "Yes".

7.3.3.3 Calculation Groups

Calculation groups (*Cost management > Predetermined cost policies setup > Calculation groups*) determine the basis for calculating cost prices and sales prices.

In this context, the selected option in the field *Cost price model*—"Item cost price", "Item purchase price", Trade agreements", or "Inventory price"—specifies for materials (purchased items), which price should be used for calculating the cost price of the manufactured item. The *Alternate cost price model* applies if the cost price in the selected *Cost price model* is zero. The *Sales price model* controls whether the sales price of a manufactured item is calculated from the cost price of the components (including the profit percentage in the cost group) or from the sales price of the components.

The default calculation group is specified in the Inventory accounting policy parameters (*Cost management > Inventory accounting policies setup > Parameters*, field group *Calculation*). At the item level, you can select a *Calculation group* on the tab *Engineer* in the Released product form.

7.3.3.4 Cost Groups

Cost groups (*Cost management > Inventory accounting policies setup > Cost groups*) classify the different types of costs in the cost calculation on the one hand, and specify different margins for the sales price calculation on the other hand.

When creating a cost group, enter the ID, the *Name*, and select the appropriate *Cost group type*. The cost group type determines the basic costing structure, with the following options:

- **Direct materials**—For material consumption.
- **Direct manufacturing**—For route operations (consumption of resource capacity).
- **Direct outsourcing**—For purchased subcontracting services.
- **Indirect**—For overhead margins.
- **Undefined**—For unspecific cost classifications.

For each cost group type, you can specify a default cost group—set the slider *Default* in one cost group per *Cost group type* to "Yes" for this purpose.

Margins for the sales price calculation are specified on the tab *Profit* in the Cost group form—you can enter up to four lines with the *Profit-setting* (in general, "Standard" is selected as the default value in the Cost management parameters) and the *Profit percentage*. When you execute a cost calculation or estimate a production order, you can select the *Profit-setting* in the calculation dialog—for example, if you do not want to use the default profit setting because you need to apply a lower margin for competitive reasons.

In the Released product form, you can select a cost group in the field *Cost group* on the tab *Manage costs*. For items that are not assigned to a particular cost group, the default cost group for the cost group type "Direct materials" is used.

For route operations (consumption of resource capacity), the applicable cost group is not directly assigned to resources or operations, but to a cost category ($\rightarrow$ Sect. 5.3.3).

7.3.3.5 Costing Sheet

The costing sheet (*Cost management > Ledger integration policies setup > Costing sheets*) is there to establish a clear structure of item costs. It is used for estimation (cost estimation in production orders) and for costing (when ending production orders and in the general item price calculation), and has two different purposes:

- **Cost classification**—Classification by cost groups.
- **Overhead costs**—Specification of rules for the calculation of overhead costs (used for both, manufactured and purchased items).

For classification purposes, the costing sheet constitutes a multi-level structure of the different costs. Apart from the cost groups, which are the bottom level in the structure, the costing sheet can contain nodes for totals at multiple levels.

Directly below the node *Root*, you can set up two primary nodes with the *Node type* "Price"—one with the *Type* "Cost of goods manufactured" (for manufactured items) and one with the *Type* "Costs of purchase" (for purchased items).

When you set up the costing sheet ($\rightarrow$ Fig. 7.17), make sure that the cost groups, which are assigned to manufactured items, are below the node with the *Type* "Cost of goods

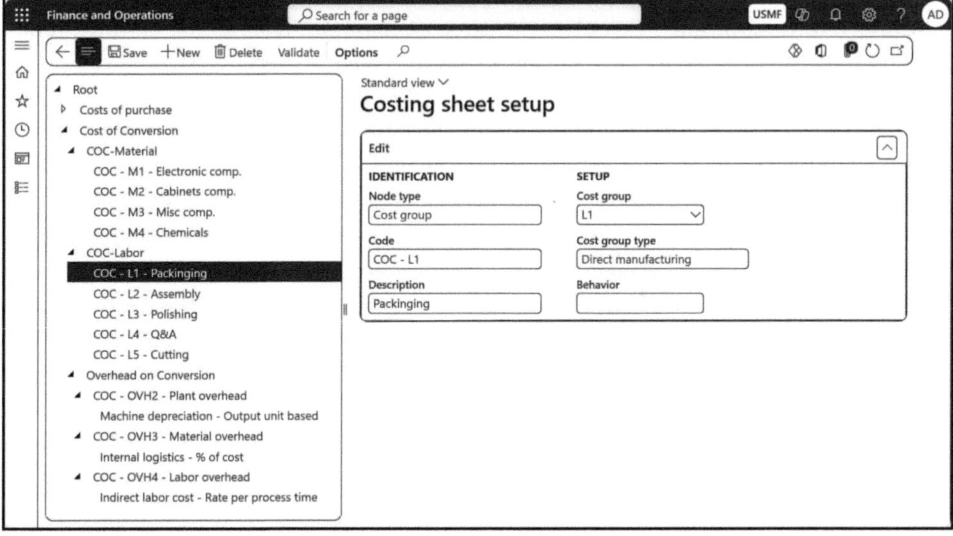

Fig. 7.17 Editing the costing sheet

manufactured". The node with the *Type* "Costs of purchase" and the elements below are an optional structure, which you can use to add indirect costs in the costing sheet to the item cost price in purchase orders.

If you want to enter a new node in the costing sheet, select the higher-level node and click the button *New* in the action pane. The nodes that are assigned to a cost group constitute the lowest level in the costing sheet. When you can create a node for a cost group, select the option "Cost group" in the field *Select node type* of the *Create* dialog. Then select the appropriate *Cost group* on the tab *Edit* in the new node.

If you want to define overhead costs in the costing sheet, select or create a node with a *Cost group* that refers to the *Cost group type* "Indirect". Sub-nodes of such a node determine the calculation rules for overhead costs. When you create a sub-node for overhead cost calculation, select the applicable *Node type* ("Surcharge", "Rate", "Output unit based", or "Input unit based") in the dialog before you specify the basis for the calculation on the tab *Absorption basis* in the new sub-node. For a node with the type "Surcharge", enter the percentage for indirect costs on the tab *Surcharge*. For the other node types, enter an amount for indirect costs on the tab *Rate*. Then activate the indirect costs with the button *Activate* in the toolbar of this tab. The main accounts for the general ledger transactions for the indirect costs have to be entered on the tab *Ledger postings*.

Before closing the costing sheet, save the changes with the button *Save*.

7.3.3.6 Item Price Calculation

For manufactured items, you can run a price calculation that is based on the bill of materials and the route. There are two different options to execute this calculation:

- **Item-specific calculation**—Calculate the price of an item in the Item price form (e.g., when entering a new item).
- **Collective calculation**—Calculate the price of multiple items in the Costing version form (e.g., if you want to calculate all item prices once a year).

To calculate the price of a particular item, open the Item price form with the button *Manage costs/Set up/Item price* in the released product, switch to the tab *Pending prices*, and click the button *Calculate item cost*. For a collective calculation of multiple (or all) items, open the Costing version inquiry (*Cost management > Inventory accounting > Costing versions*), select the line with the appropriate costing version, and click the button *Calculation*.

In the calculation dialog, which is shown next, you can select the *Site* and the *Calculation date* (if not specified in the costing version), which determine the applicable active BOM and route of the released products. If you start the calculation in the Item price form, you can override the *Quantity* (the default is specified in the default order settings) or select a particular *BOM* and *Route number* in the dialog. If you start the calculation in the Costing version inquiry, you can specify an item filter on the tab *Records to include* in the dialog. On the tab *Price recordings in version* of the dialog, you can specify whether to calculate the cost price and/or the sales price (the price type needs to be allowed in the costing version setup).

Click the button *OK* in the dialog to start the calculation. Once the calculation is finished, you can view the result on the tab *Pending prices* in the Item price form (in the Costing version form, click the button *Price/Item price* to access this form). If you want to check the calculation, click the button *View calculation details* in the Item price form to view the price structure. In order to activate a price finally, select the respective pending price in the Item price form and click the button *Activate pending price(s)*.

7.3.4   Case Study Exercises

Exercise 7.3—Product Records
As a basis for viewing the impact of settings in the dimension groups and the item model group, create the following items in the Released product form:

- Item I-##-S with standard costs (item model group S-## of exercise 7.2).
- Item I-##-T with FIFO valuation (item model group T-## of exercise 7.2).

For both items, select the product subtype "Product" and the storage/tracking dimension group that you have set up in exercise 7.1. Enter an item group for merchandise and select an item sales tax group for purchasing and for sales that refers to the standard tax rate. The unit of measurement is "Pieces". The base purchase price and the base cost price are USD 50. The base sales price is USD 100. For purchasing, inventory, and sales, enter the main site and the main warehouse in the *Default order settings*.

For the item I-##-S, you have to enter and activate a standard cost price. Specify a standard cost price of USD 50 for the main site in the Item price form.

> *Note:* If the number sequence for product numbers is set up for automatic numbering, don't enter a product number.

Exercise 7.4—Inventory Value of Receipt Transactions
Enter a purchase order with the vendor of exercise 3.2. In order to facilitate the tracking of inventory valuation, select a tax-exempt sales tax group in the order header. The order includes 100 units of the first item and 100 units of the second item of exercise 7.3, both at a purchase price of USD 60.

Confirm the purchase order and check if you can post a product receipt without a batch number. Then open the batch table (use the option *View details* in the batch number column) and create the batch B001 for both items. Insert this batch number in both purchase order lines.

In the next step, post the product receipt and the invoice receipt for the complete quantity. If you look at the item transactions and the on-hand quantity, can you explain the different cost amount and cost price of the two items?

Exercise 7.5—Valuation after a Second Purchase Order

You want to receive 100 units of the first and the second item of exercise 7.3 from the exercise 3.2 again. Create an appropriate purchase order and enter the batch number B001 and a purchase price of USD 80 in both order lines.

Select a tax-exempt sales tax group in the order header and confirm the order. Then post the product receipt before you post the vendor invoice with the entire quantity. In the *Product receipt date* (on the tab *Setup* of the Posting product receipt dialog), and the *Posting date* (in the vendor invoice), enter the day after the posting date of exercise 7.4 (e.g., July 2, if you have posted the transactions in exercise 7.4 with July 1).

Once you have posted the invoice, check the inventory transactions, the inventory quantity, and the inventory value (cost amount) of the two items.

Exercise 7.6—Valuation of Sales Orders

The customer of exercise 4.1 orders 150 units of the first and the second item of exercise 7.3. Enter a corresponding sales order with the batch number B001 in both order lines. If required, set the order to complete. Then post the invoice for the entire order. In the *Invoice date* on the tab *Setup* of the posting dialog, enter the day after the posting date of exercise 7.5 (e.g., July 3, if you have posted the transactions in exercise 7.5 with July 2).

Once you have posted the invoice, check the inventory transactions, the inventory quantity, and the inventory value (cost amount) of the two items again.

Exercise 7.7—Inventory Closing

Run a *Recalculation* in the Closing and adjustment form to calculate the correct inventory value according to the valuation method. In the Recalculate inventory dialog, set the recalculation date to the posting date of exercise 7.6 (e.g., July 3) and enter a filter that restricts the calculation to the two items of this exercise.

For the selected items, check the cost price and the inventory value (cost amount) in the inventory transactions and the on-hand inventory. Which changes are caused by the recalculation? Can you explain the result?

7.4   Business Processes in Inventory

The only way to change the inventory quantity of an item is to post an inventory transaction. Business processes, which change the inventory quantity and do not originate in inventory management, but in other functional areas like purchasing, sales, or production, generate these transactions automatically in the background.

Business processes in other areas are covered in the corresponding chapter of this book. The lines below cover the business processes within inventory in the basic inventory management, which is also the basis for the advanced warehouse management (→ Sect. 8.1). With the advanced warehouse management, workers usually register inventory transactions on mobile devices, but you can, if you enter all required inventory dimensions, get a similar result by posting a transaction with an inventory journal.

7.4.1 Inventory Structures and Parameters

As a prerequisite for inventory transactions, the setup in inventory management and product management has to be finished.

7.4.1.1 Warehouse Setup

Dynamics 365 includes three storage dimensions that group the inventory according to the physical warehouse structure within the company—*Site*, *Warehouse*, and *Location*. Depending on the applicable dimension group, you need to record these dimensions in each inventory transaction.

In order to set up a new warehouse (→ Fig. 7.18), open the Warehouse form (*Inventory management > Setup > Inventory breakdown > Warehouses*) and click the button *New*. In the new record, enter the warehouse ID, the *Name*, and the *Site*. The site (→ Sect. 10.1.6) is a mandatory field that groups the warehouses within the company from a geographical and financial point of view.

Fig. 7.18 Editing a warehouse in the Warehouse form

The lookup field *Type* determines whether the warehouse is a regular warehouse (*Type* "Default"), a quarantine warehouse, or a transit warehouse. Transit warehouses are used in transfer orders (→ Sect. 7.4.4), and quarantine warehouses in quarantine orders (→ Sect. 7.4.6).

The slider *Use warehouse management processes* on the tab *Warehouse* of the Warehouse form controls, whether the selected warehouse is subject to the advanced warehouse management. If it is, a further breakdown of the warehouse with the storage dimension *Location* is required (→ Sect. 8.1.1).

> *Note:* In addition to the warehouse types which are described above, there are the types "Goods in transit" and "Under delivery" used in the Landed costs module.

7.4.1.2 Storage Dimensions

When you set up the warehouse structure, be aware that the storage dimension groups of the released products control the required inventory dimensions in an inventory transaction. If you need locations in a particular warehouse, the storage dimension groups of all concerned items have to contain an active dimension *Location*. Since this setting requires locations for all warehouses, you need to set up at least one (dummy) location for each warehouse in this case.

7.4.1.3 Inventory Parameters and Journal Setup

If you want to enter a manual transaction in inventory, you have to use an inventory journal (→ Sect. 7.4.2). Apart from sites and warehouses, inventory journal names are another required setup for the use of inventory journals. You can divide the journals in inventory into two groups:

* **Inventory journals**—For general transactions.
* **Warehouse management journals**—For receipts that are related to orders.

Inventory journals are used for registering general transactions in inventory, not related to an order, including quantity adjustments, item transfers, and inventory counting. In order to set up the inventory journals, open the menu item *Inventory management > Setup > Journal names > Inventory* and enter at least one journal name for each *Journal type* that your company uses in transactions. The number sequence in the lookup field *Voucher series* provides the option to apply a separate number sequence per journal.

Warehouse management journals are in use for order-related item receipts and include two journal types: Item arrival journals (for the receipt of purchase orders and customer returns) and production input journals (for the receipt of manufactured items in production). In order to create the warehouse management journals, open the menu item *Inventory management > Setup > Journal names > Warehouse management*.

Inventory parameters (*Inventory management > Setup > Inventory and warehouse management parameters*) contain settings for the number sequences, the default unit of measure, and default journal names. In the Section *Inventory dimensions*, you can select the dimensions that should be shown by default in the inventory journals.

7.4.2 Inventory Journals

Inventory journals are required to record a transaction that is independent of other functional areas, like purchasing, sales, or production. If your company uses advanced warehouse management, transactions are usually recorded on mobile devices, but you can still use inventory journals to post inventory transactions.

Warehouse management journals (including item arrival journals) enable registering an item receipt related to an order in the basic inventory management.

> *Note:* Inventory journals only create inventory transactions, not warehouse-specific transactions (→ Sect. 8.1.1).

7.4.2.1 Journal Structure

Since inventory transactions have an impact on finance, the voucher principle applies: You have to enter a journal completely before you can post it in a second step.

There are different journals for general inventory transactions, for item arrivals, and for item counting. They have a common structure, but are divided among the following journal types:

- **Inventory adjustment**—Manual updates of the on-hand quantity.
- **Movement**—Like inventory adjustment, but with a user-defined offset ledger account.
- **Transfer**—Between warehouses or other inventory dimensions.
- **Bill of materials**—Consume components and receive the manufactured item.
- **Inventory ownership change**—Financial transfer of consignment stock.
- **Counting**—Register the actual on-hand quantity and post adjustments.
- **Tag counting**—Tags as preparation for counting.
- **Item arrival**—Receipt related to a purchase order or sales return order.
- **Production input**—Receipt of manufactured items related to a production order.

The journal name setup in inventory management includes two more journal types, which refer to other modules: The journal type "Project" for item consumption journals in the Project accounting module, and the journal type "Fixed assets" for journals that transfer items from inventory to fixed assets in the Fixed assets module.

When you open an inventory journal, the related list page with the open—not yet posted—journals is shown. If you want to view the posted journals, apply an appropriate filter in the column *Posted* (you can use the filter pane, the grid column filter, or the advanced filter). You can open the Journal detail form, which contains a Header view and a Lines view, by clicking the journal ID shown as a link in the grid.

7.4.2.2 Movement Journals and Inventory Adjustment Journals

If you want to record manual changes of the item quantity in inventory, you can use a journal with the type "Movement" or with the type "Inventory adjustment". The difference between movement journals and inventory adjustment journals is the assignment of the offset account.

Movement journals show the field *Offset account*, in which you select the expense account for the item consumption (or the revenue account for the item receipt). In inventory adjustment journals, the offset account derives from the posting setup and is not shown in the journal lines. You can use movement journals, for example, if you want to apply a particular expense account for consuming an item in a department for testing or demonstration purposes. Since you can enter a default offset account in the journal setup (journal names), you can set up multiple journal names with the related offset account for the different use cases to facilitate registration.

The example in → Sect. 7.1.2 at the beginning of the current chapter describes registering and posting a transaction in a journal with the journal type "Inventory adjustment".

The list page *Inventory management > Journal entries > Items > Movement* shows the journals with the journal type "Movement". In order to register a new movement journal, click the button *New* on this page and select a *Name* (journal name) in the *Create* dialog. In the field *Offset account* on the tab *General* of the dialog, optionally enter a default for the offset account in the journal lines before you close the dialog with the button *OK*. In the detail form that is shown in the Lines view next, enter one or more journal lines with the posting date, item number, appropriate inventory dimension values, and quantity (a negative quantity for item issues). In the receipt transactions (with a positive quantity) of items that are not subject to a standard price valuation, the cost price is editable (default value is the base cost price in the released product or the applicable active price in the Item price form). Make sure to select an appropriate main account in the column *Offset account* before you post the movement with the button *Post* in the action pane.

7.4.2.3 Transfer Journals

Unlike movement journals and inventory adjustment journals, which record item issues and receipts, transfer journals are used to register the transfer of inventory from one dimension value to another. In most cases, this is the transfer from one warehouse or location to another. But you can also use a transfer journal to change batch numbers, serial numbers, or product dimension values (e.g., the color).

In order to register an item transfer, open the menu item *Inventory management > Journal entries > Items > Transfer* and create a journal with one or more journal lines (similar to an adjustment journal). But in addition to the data entered in the inventory adjustment journal lines, you have to enter the applicable inventory dimensions to which the item should be transferred.

The *Quantity* should be entered with a negative sign to issue the item from the "from-dimensions" and to receive it at the "to-dimensions".

Once you have completed the journal lines, post the journal with the button *Post* in the action pane of the Journal list page or detail form.

Although you enter only one line for a transfer in the transfer journal, there are two posted inventory transactions—one for the issue and one for the receipt. A transfer between warehouses, for example, creates one transaction for the item issue from the shipping warehouse and one transaction for the item receipt at the receiving warehouse.

7.4.2.4 BOM Journals

Bill of materials journals (BOM journals) enable posting the receipt of a manufactured item together with the consumption of the components. You can use such a journal instead of a production order in a simple scenario (e.g., when assembling a kit), if you don't need the extensive functionality of manufacturing.

It is also possible to use a BOM journal the other way around—to record the disassembly of a manufactured item together with the receipt of the components. But be aware that the cost price of the components is not adjusted in this case.

In order to register a regular BOM journal, open the menu item *Inventory management > Journal entries > Items > Bills of materials* and create a new journal. In the lines of a BOM journal, you can enter a journal line with the manufactured (received) item and a positive quantity and one or more journal lines with the materials (which show a checkmark in the column *BOM line* and a negative quantity).

But it is not required to enter BOM journal lines manually—you can click the button *Functions/Report as finished* in the action pane of the BOM journal to create the journal lines. In the *Report as finished* dialog (→ Fig. 7.19), insert a line with the manufactured item that you want to receive in inventory. If the checkbox in the column *Post now* is selected, the BOM journal is posted immediately after closing the *Report as finished* dialog with the button *OK*. If the checkbox *Post now* is cleared, the manufactured item and its component are transferred to the BOM journal lines, and you can subsequently edit the journal lines before you post the journal with the button *Post*.

7.4.2.5 Item Arrival Journals

Item arrival journals enable posting the initial item receipt related to a purchase order (→ Sect. 3.5.3) or a customer return (→ Sect. 4.6.1) in the basic inventory management. Production input journals, which work similarly to item arrival journals, can be used to post the receipt of manufactured items related to a production order.

You can register an item arrival journal in the menu item *Inventory management > Journal entries > Item arrival > Item arrival* and create a journal similar to an adjustment journal. In order to specify the reference to a purchase order, switch to the tab *Default values* in the *Create* dialog (or in the Header view of the detail form), and select the option "Purchase order" in the lookup field *Reference* before you enter the order number in the field *Number*. For customer returns, select the *Reference* "Sales order" and enter

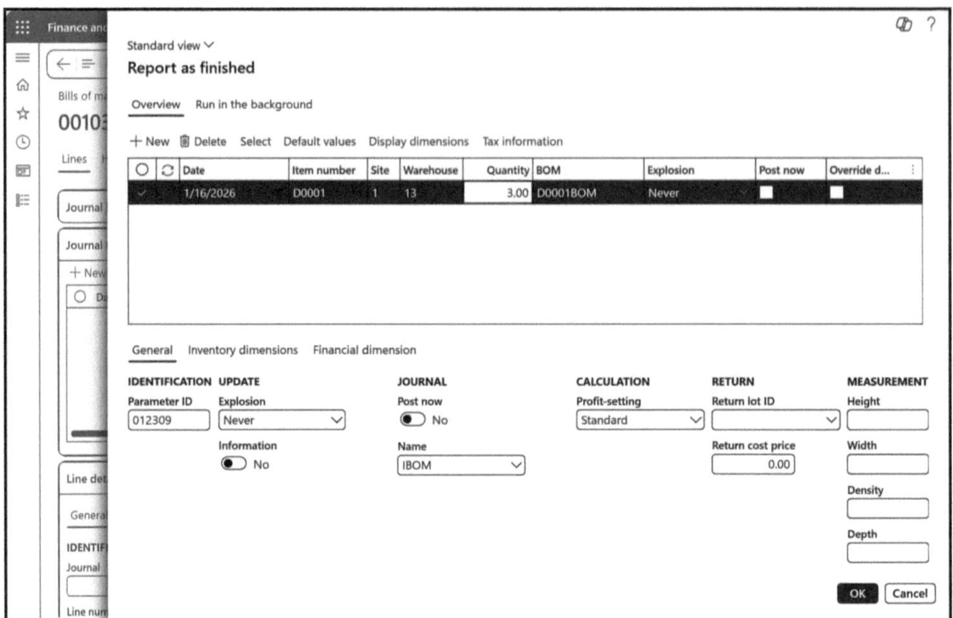

Fig. 7.19 Report as finished dialog, accessed from the bill of materials journal

the *RMA number*. If you want to use quarantine management, make sure that the applicable slider in the field group *Mode of handling* is set to "Yes".

Once you have created the journal header, you can optionally click the button *Functions/ Create lines* in the action pane of the list page or detail form to retrieve journal lines with default values for the item numbers, the inventory dimensions, and the open quantity from the purchase order lines (or the return order lines).

In order to post the arrival journal finally, click the button *Post* in the action pane of the Journal list page or detail form. Unlike inventory journals, which immediately post the physical and financial transaction, arrival journals require posting the product receipt and the invoice of the corresponding purchase order (or return order) to generate physical and financial transactions.

7.4.3   Inventory Counting

In order to determine the actual quantity in inventory, you have to execute physical inventory counting (stocktaking) in the warehouse. Depending on legal and other requirements, periodical counting is necessary to make sure that the posted quantity in Dynamics 365 is in line with the actual on-hand quantity as physically counted.

In Dynamics 365, you can either use inventory journals with the type "Counting" or, in the advanced warehouse management, mobile device transactions (→ Sect. 8.1.4) for item counting.

When you post an item counting journal, the difference between the counted quantity and the quantity in Dynamics 365 is posted as an item issue or receipt—similar to the transactions in an inventory adjustment journal. The basic posting setup, which determines the stock account and the offset account (expense account for a negative discrepancy or revenue account for a positive discrepancy), is the same as for adjustment journals, but you can override the offset account with a reason code (see below).

Since the counting difference is calculated as of the counting date, you do not need to stop other transactions in inventory while counting. But if required for organizational reasons, you can lock inventory—set the slider *Lock items during count* in the Section *General* of the Inventory parameters to "Yes" for this purpose. In this case, a lock is set at the level of warehouse items.

7.4.3.1 Counting Journals

In order to register a counting journal, click the button *New* in the list page *Inventory management > Journal entries > Item counting > Counting*. On the tab *Counting by* in the *Create* dialog, select the inventory dimensions that you register in the counting journal. Once you have created the journal header, there are two ways to create the journal lines for inventory counting:

- **Manually**—Enter counting journal lines manually.
- **Automatically**—Create counting journal lines from a proposal.

You can manually enter the counting journal lines (→ Fig. 7.20) with the counting date (in the column *Date*), item number, site, warehouse, and other inventory dimensions as required. The counted quantity has to be entered in the column *Counted*. In the column *On-hand*, you can view the corresponding inventory quantity in Dynamics 365 as of the counting date. The discrepancy between the counted and the on-hand quantity is shown in the column *Quantity*. This quantity is posted as an adjustment when posting the counting journal, depending on the sign with an issue or with a receipt transaction. In case of a positive adjustment (receipt transaction), you should review the *Cost price* in the line details, which you can update if required (except for items with standard cost valuation).

If you want to create the counting lines automatically, click the button *Create lines/ On-hand* (which creates lines for items and related inventory dimension values that are, or have been, on hand) or the button *Create lines/Items* (which creates lines for all items) in the action pane of the counting journal. In the *Create* dialog, specify a filter on the tab *Records to include* (e.g., for counting a particular warehouse). Other parameters in the dialog provide the option to restrict counting on items or on inventory dimensions (e.g., in combination with a filter on a warehouse) with an inventory transaction after the last inventory counting.

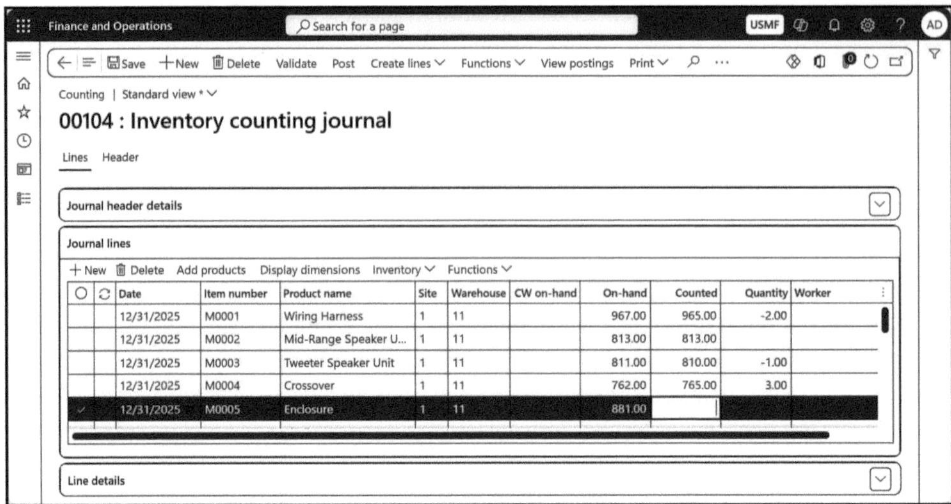

Fig. 7.20 Entering the counted quantity in a counting journal line

After creating the counting journal lines manually or automatically, you can optionally print a counting list with the button *Print/Counting list* in the action pane of the counting journal. For review, you can print the counting list again later—after entering the counted quantity in the journal –and in this case, set the slider *Print on-hand* in the Counting list dialog to "Yes" for printing both the counted quantity and the quantity which should be on-hand (according to the data in Dynamics 365).

Once you have completed the registration and the review of the counting journal, post it with the button *Post* in the action pane of the Journal list page or detail form.

7.4.3.2 Warehouse Items

Warehouse items are the level at which the counting status is tracked and at which items are blocked while counting (in case locking is activated in the Inventory parameters). If there are multiple warehouses and you want to lock inventory while counting, you might want to create a warehouse item per released product and warehouse.

You can access the warehouse items of a released product with the button *Manage inventory/Warehouse/Warehouse items* in the Released product form. A warehouse item at the general level (with empty inventory dimensions) is automatically created when you create a released product. In order to create a warehouse item for an item and a particular warehouse, click the button *New* in the Warehouse item form and select the warehouse on the tab *General*. If you create a counting journal line with this item and warehouse later on, the counting journal is shown on the tab *Counting status* of the warehouse item until the journal is posted. If there is no warehouse item for the respective warehouse, counting is tracked in the warehouse item at the general level (with empty inventory dimensions).

7.4.3.3 Counting Groups

In order to support selecting the items in the dialog for creating counting lines, you can filter on counting groups. Counting groups (*Inventory management > Setup > Inventory > Counting groups*) are not only used for grouping and sorting purposes, but they also contain particular settings for counting. A core setting is the *Counting code*, which controls when to execute counting (periodically, when equal to or below minimum stock, or when there is no stock). You can assign a counting group at the level of the released product (on the tab *Manage inventory*) or in the warehouse item.

If you want to apply the counting code when creating counting lines, set the slider *Activate counting code* in the dialog for creating counting lines to "Yes".

7.4.3.4 Reason Codes for Counting

You can use reason codes to classify the causes of counting discrepancies and to specify particular offset accounts for posting the discrepancy in the general ledger.

If you want to use reason codes, first set up the required reason codes with ID, *Description*, and (optionally) *Offset account* in the Counting reason codes form (*Inventory management > Setup > Inventory > Counting reason codes*). Then create one or more reason code policies (*Inventory management > Setup > Inventory > Counting reason code policies*), in which you select whether a reason code is optional or mandatory, and assign the relevant reason code policy to the warehouses (click the button *Warehouse/Set up/ Counting reason code policy* in the Warehouse form) or to the released products (click the button *Product/Set up/Counting reason code policy* in the Released product form).

If counting reason codes are set to be mandatory, you have to select a reason code in the counting journal lines.

7.4.3.5 Tag Counting

Tag counting (*Inventory management > Journal entries > Item counting > Tag counting*) is an option to pre-register counting lines. The principle of tag counting is to attach numbered tags to the physical warehouse locations. When you execute counting, write the item number, quantity, and applicable inventory dimensions (e.g., warehouse and serial number) on each tag. Then collect the tags and register them in the tag-counting journal. When you post the tag-counting journal, there is no posting of inventory transactions, but a transfer of the lines to a regular counting journal.

7.4.4 Transfer Orders

Whereas inventory transfer journals post the transfer of items immediately and without shipping documents, transfer orders provide the option to manage transport times, to track the quantity that is in transit, and to print shipping documents.

7.4.4.1 Setup for Transfer Orders

As a prerequisite for the use of transfer orders, you have to set up at least one warehouse with the type "Transit" in the Warehouse form. This transit warehouse holds the items for the time of transportation. In addition, you have to assign a transit warehouse to each regular warehouse, from which you issue transfer orders.

If the dimension *Location* is activated in the applicable storage dimension groups, specify a *Default receipt location* and a *Default issue location*, usually a dummy location, in the transit warehouse (on the tab *Inventory and warehouse management* of the Warehouse form).

Delivery date control is an optional feature in transfer orders, which works similarly to the delivery date control options in sales orders (→ Sect. 4.3.3).

7.4.4.2 Processing Transfer Orders

You can manually create a transfer order in the Transfer order form (*Inventory management > Inbound orders > Transfer order* or *Inventory management > Outbound orders > Transfer order*) with the button *New* in the action pane.

In a sales order, you can click the button *Product and supply/New/Transfer order* in the toolbar of the order lines to create a transfer order that is linked to the sales order line.

The transfer order (→ Fig. 7.21) consists of a header, in which you enter the *From warehouse* and the *To warehouse*, and lines, which contain the items that are transferred from one warehouse to another.

When you select the *From warehouse* in the header, the transfer order retrieves the related transit warehouse (shown on the tab *General* in the Header view). In the transfer

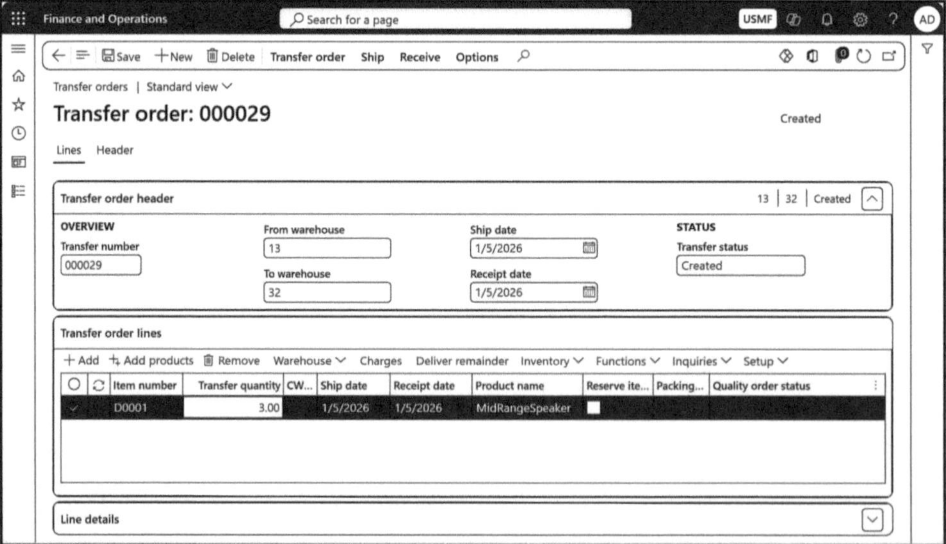

Fig. 7.21 Entering a line in a transfer order

order lines, enter one or more records with the item number, transfer quantity, and inventory dimensions as applicable.

Similar to sales order processing, you can execute transfer order picking with the basic inventory management processes (→ Sect. 4.4.2) or with the advanced warehouse processes (→ Sect. 8.1.2). If picking is not mandatory (depending on the setup), you can immediately post the shipment.

In order to post the shipment (corresponding to a packing slip in sales), click the button *Ship/Operations/Ship transfer order*. In the upper pane of the *Shipment* dialog, select the option "All" in the column *Update* to ship the complete quantity (depending on the prior steps, you can alternatively select the picked quantity or the ship-now quantity). The checkbox *Print transfer shipment* provides the option to print a shipping document. When you click the button *OK* in the dialog, a transfer to the transit warehouse is posted.

When you receive the item at the destination warehouse, post the receipt. You can optionally post an inventory registration or an item arrival—similar to the options in a purchase order (→ Sect. 3.5.3)—before posting the receipt.

In order to post the transfer receipt finally (corresponding to a product receipt in purchasing), click the button *Receive/Operations/Receive* in the Transfer order form. In the *Receive* dialog, select the option "All" in the column *Update* (depending on the prior steps, you can alternatively select the registered quantity or the receive-now quantity). Then click the button *OK* in the posting dialog to post a transfer from the transit warehouse to the destination warehouse.

> *Note:* If you don't want to post the receipt at the destination warehouse in a separate step, select the checkbox *Autoreceive* in the Shipment dialog to receive the item at the other warehouse immediately when posting the shipment.

7.4.5   Item Reservation

Master planning should make sure that there is sufficient inventory to cover the future demand for products in sales orders, production orders, and other issue transactions at the time when needed. But in some cases, the supplied quantity is not enough to cover a changing demand. This can occur, for example, if a short-term sales order consumes inventory that is already allocated to another order.

You can use reservations to prevent such a situation. Reservations are primarily used for sales order lines and BOM lines in production orders, but you can also use them for any other issue (e.g., vendor returns or transfer orders). Apart from manual reservations, there are automatic reservations.

Reservation, which helps to ensure that an item is available for the selected future consumption, works separately from marking (→ Sect. 3.7.1), which connects transactions for valuation purposes. But when you apply marking in an issue transaction (e.g., a vendor return) which is not been posted yet, it creates a corresponding automatic reservation.

7.4.5.1 Setup for Reservation

Reservation works at the item number and inventory dimension level. Dimensions that are selected as *Primary stocking* in the dimension group ($\rightarrow$ Sect. 7.2.2) of the respective item have to be specified when entering a reservation. A reservation at the lower level of further active inventory dimensions is optional, and you can still change reservations at that level later. With advanced warehouse management, additional settings in reservation hierarchies are required ($\rightarrow$ Sect. 8.1.1).

Apart from the reservation of current on-hand quantity, reservations may refer to future receipts of purchase orders or production orders. As a prerequisite for reserving quantities that are not in stock yet, the reservation of ordered items must be enabled in the Inventory parameters (slider *Reserve ordered items* in the Section *General*).

If you enter a sales order line with the setting "Automatic" in the field *Reservation* on the sub-tab *Setup*, there is an automatic reservation. The default for the reservation setting in a sales order line is specified in the item model group (field *Item sales reservation*) of the item. If the selected reservation setting in the item model group is "Default", the reservation setting in the order line receives the default from the corresponding field in the order header, which again receives its default from the Accounts receivable parameters (Section *General*, tab *Sales default values*, lookup field *Reservation*).

For the BOM lines in a production order, automatic reservation is controlled by the lookup field *Reservation* on the tab *Setup* in the production order header. The related default value is specified in the Production control parameters (on the tab *General*), but it is possible to override this general default with a default from the item model group (checkbox *Override item production reservation*) of the manufactured item. Unlike sales order lines, production BOM lines are not reserved automatically when creating the order, but when estimating, scheduling, releasing, or starting (depending on the reservation option that is selected in the order header).

7.4.5.2 Working with Reservations

If you want to create a manual reservation in a sales order, click the button *Inventory/ Reservation* in the toolbar of the sales order lines.

In the Reservation form ($\rightarrow$ Fig. 7.22), which is shown next, you can manually enter the reserved quantity in the column *Reservation*. Alternatively, you can create the reservation with the button *Reserve lot* in the action pane of the Reservation form. With the button *Display dimensions* in the toolbar of the tab *On-hand quantities*, you can show applicable inventory dimensions for a more detailed control of the reservation at the dimension level. If required, you can change or delete the quantity in the column *Reservation* and enter a quantity in another reservation line. Depending on the related Inventory parameter setting, you can only reserve from the current on-hand inventory or also from open purchase orders (or other receipts).

Automatic reservations are generated in the background, but you can edit the reservation in the Reservation form in the same way as a manual reservation. If you enter an order line with automatic reservation and the available quantity is not sufficient to cover the automatic reservation, the *Autoreservation* dialog immediately shows the problem.

After reservation, the reserved quantity is shown with the status "Physical reserved" ("Ordered reserved", if a future receipt is reserved) in the inventory transaction and the On-hand inventory inquiry. The reserved quantity is not available for any other transaction.

7.4.5.3 Removing Reservations

If the On-hand inventory inquiry is showing a reserved quantity that you need for any other purpose, you can remove the reservation. In the On-hand inventory inquiry (*Inventory management > Inquiries and reports > On-hand inventory*), which you can also access with the button *Overview* in the *On-hand* dialog of transaction lines (e.g., the sales order lines), you can open the inventory transactions with the button *Transactions* in the action pane. Select the respective inventory transaction with the issue status "Reserved physical" and click the button *Inventory/View/Reservation* to access the Reservation form, in which you can update the reservation as required (e.g., set the reserved quantity in the column *Reservation* to zero).

7.4.6   Quarantine and Inventory Blocking

If you want to exclude a particular quantity of an item from the available stock (e.g., because of the test results in quality control), you can alternatively use the following options:

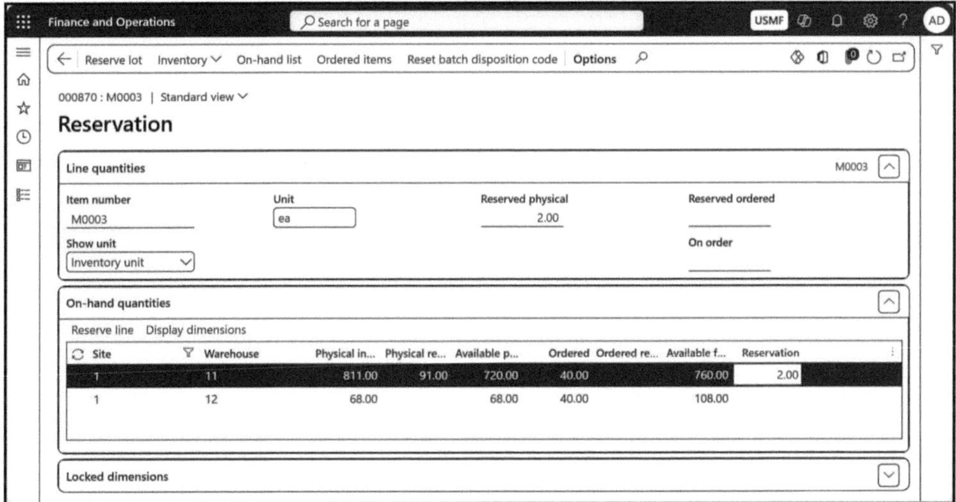

Fig. 7.22 Reserving inventory for a sales order line in the Reservation form

- **Inventory blocking**—Temporary blocking (e.g., for the time of quality testing).
- **Quarantine management**—Transfer to a quarantine warehouse.

Inventory blocking, which is primarily used with quality inspection, generates a temporary inventory transaction for blocking.

Quarantine management is based on quarantine orders, which post a transfer to a quarantine warehouse. You can create quarantine orders manually whenever necessary, or automatically with each item receipt. When working with quarantine warehouses, keep in mind that only the quarantine order blocks inventory. Just posting an item transfer to a quarantine warehouse does not block inventory.

In the advanced warehouse management, quarantine orders are only available for customer returns.

> *Note:* Technically, it is the reservation that is set by inventory blocking and by quarantine orders, which blocks the quantity.

7.4.6.1 Setup for Quarantine Management

As a prerequisite for the use of quarantine management, set up at least one warehouse with the *Type* "Quarantine" in the Warehouse form. If you want to use automatic quarantine for item receipts, select the applicable *Quarantine warehouse* in each regular warehouse that applies quarantine.

Automatic quarantine applies to released products, which are assigned to an item model group with a checkmark in the checkbox *Quarantine management*.

7.4.6.2 Manual Quarantine

The Quarantine order list page (*Inventory management > Periodic tasks > Quality management > Quarantine orders*) shows the open quarantine orders. If you also want to view ended quarantine orders, select the checkbox *View ended* above the grid (→ Fig. 7.23).

In order to create a new quarantine order, click the button *New* in the action pane and enter the item number, quantity, site, warehouse, and other inventory dimensions as

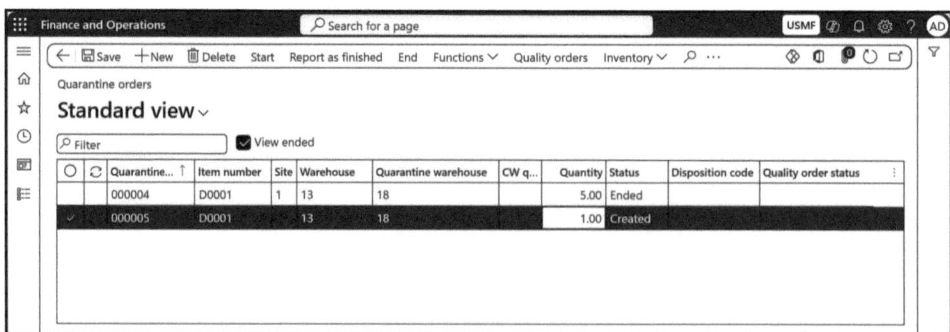

Fig. 7.23 Managing quarantine in the Quarantine order form

applicable. On the tab *Quarantine inventory dimensions*, the default for the quarantine warehouse is the quarantine warehouse of the initial warehouse in the quarantine order. The other quarantine inventory dimensions receive the default from the initial dimension values of the quarantine order.

In the next step, click the button *Start* in the Quarantine order form to transfer the quantity to quarantine. Starting quarantine includes transferring the item to the quarantine warehouse, generating inventory transactions for the future transfer back to the initial warehouse, and, in order to block other consumption, reserving the item for the transfer back.

If you want to scrap the quarantined quantity partly or completely, click the button *Functions/Scrap* in the Quarantine order form.

In order to end quarantine, with or without prior scrapping of a partial quantity, click the button *End* in the Quarantine order form. Ending quarantine posts the transfer back to the initial warehouse and makes the quantity available again.

If you want to post the completion of inspections as an intermediate step, click the button *Report as finished* in the quarantine order. The item is not available in inventory before ending the quarantine order, which is why reporting a quarantine order as finished is usually only done if the transfer back to the initial warehouse should be posted separately.

7.4.6.3 Automatic Quarantine

When you post an item arrival journal, a production input journal, or a product receipt, Dynamics 365 automatically creates and starts a quarantine order for items that are assigned to an item model group with selected *Quarantine management*. The further processing of quarantine works similarly to manual quarantine.

7.4.6.4 Inventory Blocking

Inventory blocking is typically used in combination with quality orders (→ Sect. 7.4.7) and the advanced warehouse management. But you can also use inventory blocking manually, independent of quality management and advanced warehouse management.

In order to manually block the inventory of an item, open the menu item *Inventory management > Periodic tasks > Inventory blocking* and click the button *New* in the action pane. In the blocking record, enter the item number, the quantity, and—on the tab *Inventory dimensions*—the applicable inventory dimensions. If you expect the item to become available again (like in a quarantine order), set the slider *Expected receipts* to "Yes". Depending on the setting for the expected receipt, Dynamics 365 generates one or two inventory transactions that show "Inventory blocking" in the column *Reference*. If you want to end inventory blocking, simply delete the line in the Inventory blocking form.

7.4.7   Quality Management

Quality management in Dynamics 365 is integrated into the supply chain and helps to manage quality processes and issues. It consists of the following components:

- **Quality control**—Manage quality orders with quality tests.
- **Non-conformance** and **CAPA management**—Manage quality issues.

With the Advanced quality management features (if enabled in the feature management), the quality management functionality has been significantly enhanced. Among other items mentioned below, the advanced quality management includes the CAPA (Corrective and Preventive Actions) management, which is based on the case management functionality ($\rightarrow$ Sect. 10.5.2) and which you can use instead of the non-conformance functionality (*Inventory management > Periodic tasks > Quality management > Non conformances*) in the basic quality management.

    The focus in this book is on quality orders and quality control.

7.4.7.1 Basic Setup for Quality Control

As a prerequisite for using the quality control functionality, quality management has to be enabled in the Inventory parameters (slider *Use quality management* in the Section *Quality management*).

    For the tests in quality control, the following setup is required:

- **Tests**—Measure individual characteristics of the tested quantity.
- **Test variables**—Only for tests with results from a list of values.
- **Test groups**—Sequence of tests that have to be executed in a quality order.

To set up a test, open the Test form (*Inventory management > Setup > Quality control > Tests*) and insert a line with test ID, *Description*, *Type* ("Fraction" for numbers with decimals, "Integer" for whole numbers, "Option" for distinct values), and *Unit* (for the *Type* "Fraction" or "Integer"). For tests with the *Type* "Option", create a test variable (*Inventory management > Setup > Quality control > Test variables*) with the list of possible results, which you enter in the test variable outcomes (access with the button *Outcomes* in the Test variable form).

    Once the tests and the applicable test variables are set up, you can create one or more test groups (*Inventory management > Setup > Quality control > Test groups*).

    For a test group entered in the upper pane of the Test group form ($\rightarrow$ Fig. 7.24), assign the individual tests in the lower pane. When you enter a test with the type "Option" in the lower pane, select the *Test variable* and the *Default outcome* on the tab *Test* in this pane. For the other test types, specify the standard value and the tolerances in the field group *Test measurement values* on this tab. The *Acceptable quality level* in the field group *Action on*

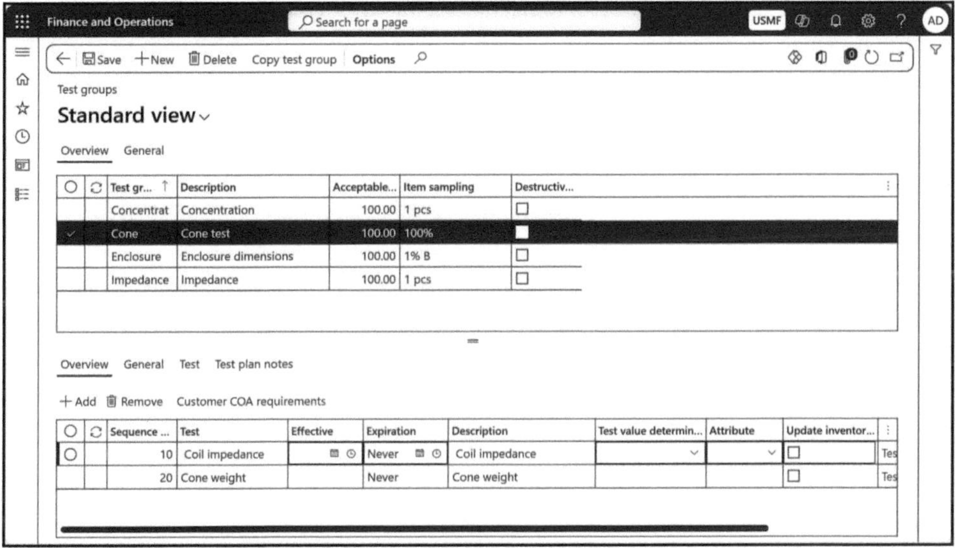

Fig. 7.24 Setting up a test group

failure controls whether you accept a quantity if less than 100% of the tested quantity passes the test.

If it is not possible to utilize the tested quantity after the test, select the checkbox *Destructive test* in the upper pane of the Test group form.

> *Note:* Optionally, you can set up test instruments (*Inventory management > Setup > Quality control > Test instruments*) and, in the Test form, select a test instrument for the applicable tests. The advanced quality management adds features for managing the calibration of test instruments based on test instrument tags.

7.4.7.2 Item Sampling Setup

If it is required to generate quality orders automatically, set up item sampling and quality associations.

Item sampling (*Inventory management > Setup > Quality control > Item sampling*) determines the test quantity when automatically generating a quality order. In the field *Quantity specification*, you can select to test a percentage (less than 100% if you want to test only samples) or a fixed quantity. As long as a quality order is not finished, the test quantity is blocked by inventory blocking ($\rightarrow$ Sect. 7.4.6). Set the slider *Full blocking* on the tab *Process* of the Item sampling form to "Yes", if it is required to block the complete quantity of a transaction, irrespective of the percentage which is actually tested (i.e., the quantity in the quality order).

Once you have completed the item sampling setup, you can assign item sampling to test groups (in the column *Item sampling* of the Test group form).

Quality associations (*Inventory management > Setup > Quality control > Quality associations*), which are based on items and test groups, control the automatic generation of quality orders. When you set up a quality association, select the *Reference type* (e.g., "Purchase" for purchase receipts, or "Sales" if you want to execute tests before sales shipping), the item selection (with the options "Table"/"Group"/"All"), and the *Test group* (on the tab *Specifications*). The fields *Event type* and *Execution* on the tab *Process* determine the trigger for generating a quality order. On the tab *Conditions*, you can restrict the quality association to vendors, customers, or other applicable characteristics.

If you want to set up a quality association for a group of items, create quality groups (*Inventory management > Setup > Quality control > Quality groups*) and—based on the *Item quality groups*, which you can access with the button *Items* in the Quality group form—assign the respective items to one or more quality groups. Alternatively, you can assign quality groups to an item with the button *Manage inventory/Quality/Item quality groups* in the Released product form.

> *Note:* With the advanced quality management, you can set up flexible sampling plans (*Inventory management > Setup > Quality control > Flexible sampling plans*), which you select in the quality associations to adjust the tests and test quantity based on the test results in quality orders.

7.4.7.3 Creating Quality Orders

If you want to create a quality order manually, open the Quality order form (*Inventory management > Periodic tasks > Quality management > Quality orders*) and click the button *New* in the action pane. In the *Create* dialog, select the *Reference type* ("Inventory" is the default value) and, if applicable, further reference data before you enter the *Item number*, *Test group*, *Quantity*, and the required inventory dimensions. The quality order header is subsequently shown in the upper pane of the detail form, and the tests as specified in the test group in the lower pane. The tested quantity is blocked by inventory blocking.

If there is an applicable *Quality association*, quality orders are automatically generated when posting the related event (e.g., a product receipt). The *Item sampling* in the quality association determines the quality order quantity. Depending on the setting *Full blocking* in the item sampling, the complete quantity, or only the quality order quantity is blocked.

7.4.7.4 Processing Quality Orders

Once you have finished a test in a quality order, click the button *Results* in the toolbar of the lower pane of the Quality order form and enter the *Result quantity* and the related result (*Outcome* for the test type "Option", otherwise the *Result value*) in one or more lines of the Results form. Depending on the results of the particular test and on the *Acceptable quality level*, which is specified on the tab *Test* of the quality order (initialized from the test group), the column *Test result* on the tab *Overview* in the lower pane of the quality order indicates whether the test is passed or not.

Once the last test is finished, click the button *Validate* in the action pane of the quality order. Depending on the results, the column *Status* in the quality order header then shows "Pass" or "Fail". Inventory blocking is removed, and the quantity is available again (in case the test is non-destructive).

If the transaction quantity (which is, if testing a sample, not only the quantity in the quality order) should be blocked further on in case of a failed test, select an appropriate action when validating the quality order. For this purpose, there are the following options depending on whether the item is subject to advanced warehouse management (and the dimension *Inventory status* is active for the item):

- **Quarantine**—For items with basic warehouse management.
- **Inventory status**—For items with advanced warehouse management.

If you use quarantine for blocking, set the slider *Quarantine upon validation failure* in the Validate dialog (initialized from the quality association) to "Yes". A related quarantine order, which blocks the transaction quantity, is generated with the validation in this case.

If blocking should be set by the inventory status in case of a failed test, the test group needs to be configured accordingly—the slider *Update inventory status* on the tab *General* in the Test group form (in combination with a passed and a failed inventory status) has to be set to "Yes" for this purpose. In this case, the slider *Update inventory status* in the dialog when validating a quality order is set to "Yes", and the transaction quantity is updated with the specified inventory status.

> *Note:* The advanced quality management enhances the Quality order form with a *Quick results entry* (button in the action pane) and the option to skip individual tests (button in the toolbar of the lower pane).

7.4.8 Consignment Inventory

The consignment inventory feature in purchasing helps to manage the inventory of items that are still owned by a vendor, but physically stored in your warehouse. For this purpose, the following items cover the business processes in consignment inventory:

- **Consignment replenishment orders**—For the initial product receipt.
- **Inventory ownership change**—Journal for the transfer of the ownership from the vendor to your company.

The consignment inventory feature is only available for items with the inventory model "Standard cost" or "Moving average" (models without inventory closing). Catch weight is not supported, and restrictions apply to master planning, advanced warehouse management, and reservation (only possible after ownership change).

Consignment inventory in sales—inventory stored at the customer site but still owned by your company—does not require consignment inventory features. For sales consignment, you can simply set up a warehouse "Warehouse at customer site" which you replenish with a regular transfer order.

7.4.8.1 Setup for Consignment Inventory

As a prerequisite for vendor consignment inventory, the inventory dimension *Owner* has to be activated in the tracking dimension groups of the relevant items. In addition, create a record in the menu item *Inventory management > Setup > Dimensions > Inventory owner* for each vendor who supplies consignment inventory (with the vendor number in the column *Vendor account*). A record with an empty vendor account is created automatically for the current company.

In the inventory journals (*Inventory management > Setup > Journal names > Inventory*), at least one journal name with the *Journal type* "Ownership change" is required.

7.4.8.2 Consignment Replenishment Orders

A consignment replenishment order (*Procurement and sourcing > Consignment > Consignment replenishment orders*) with the respective vendor, which works similarly to a purchase order, is the basis for the physical receipt of consignment inventory. But different from purchase orders, consignment replenishment orders have to be manually entered since it is not possible to generate such an order in master planning. For this reason, assign a coverage group with the coverage code "Manual" (→ Sect. 6.3.4) to the items with consignment inventory if you do not want master planning to generate regular purchase orders.

When you create a consignment replenishment order (→ Fig. 7.25), enter the order lines with the item number, quantity, site, warehouse, and other inventory dimensions as applicable. At the time when you receive the items, you can optionally post the inventory registration in an item arrival journal (or with the button *Inventory/Registration* in the toolbar of the replenishment order lines). Once you post the product receipt with the button *Consignment replenishment order/Generate/Product receipt* in the action pane of the replenishment order, the *Order status* in the Header view shows "Completed".

The product receipt of a consignment replenishment order does not generate ledger transactions. In the on-hand inquiry and the inventory transactions, consignment inventory is shown as available quantity with the vendor as *Owner* (in the applicable tracking dimension) and no inventory value. In the vendor collaboration portal, the list page *Vendor collaboration > Consignment inventory > On-hand consignment inventory* (in a filtered view also available for applicable vendors) gives an overview of the current consignment inventory.

Before posting an inventory ownership change, the use of consignment quantity is restricted to picking list journals in production orders.

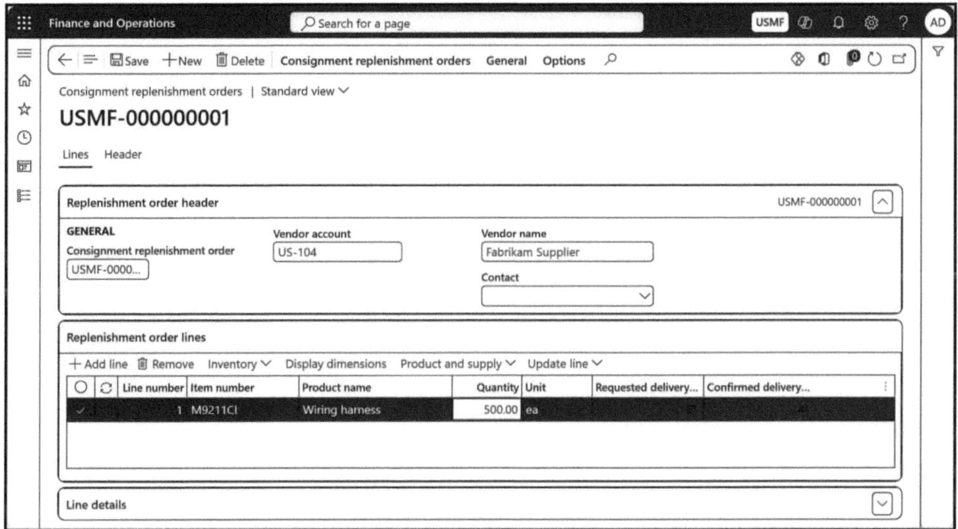

Fig. 7.25 Entering a consignment replenishment order

7.4.8.3 Consignment Inventory Ownership Changes

In order to post the inventory ownership change, open the menu item *Inventory management > Journal entries > Items > Inventory ownership change* and create an ownership change journal, which works similarly to a transfer journal ($\rightarrow$ Sect. 7.4.2). Select the applicable vendor number in the column *From owner* of the journal lines. The current company is shown in the column *To owner*. If you have already consumed vendor-owned consignment inventory for production, you can generate the ownership change journal lines based on the picked quantity (click the button *Functions/Create journal lines from production orders* in the action pane of the ownership change journal).

Posting the ownership change journal posts a transfer of the tracking dimension *Owner* to the current company and generates a purchase order with the status "Received", which is the basis for the later vendor invoice.

Similar to the situation after posting a regular product receipt in a purchase order, the on-hand inquiry and the inventory transactions show the status "Received" for the related quantity, and ledger transactions for the physical receipt are posted (if ledger integration is activated for product receipts in purchasing).

7.4.9   Case Study Exercises

Exercise 7.8—Journal Transaction
You find 100 units of the item I-## of exercise 3.5 in the main warehouse. Post an appropriate transaction in an inventory adjustment journal and check the posted transaction afterward.

Exercise 7.9—Transfer Journal

The quantity that you have received in exercise 7.8 is transferred to another warehouse. Register and post this transaction in an inventory transfer journal. Then check the transactions and the quantity of the item in the selected warehouse.

Exercise 7.10—Inventory Counting

You are asked to execute inventory counting for the item I-## of exercise 3.5 in the main warehouse. The counted quantity is 51 units. Create a counting journal with a line, which you either insert manually or generate automatically (with a filter on the item and the main warehouse). Once you have entered the counted quantity, post the journal and check the on-hand quantity.

Exercise 7.11—Transfer Order

A transfer of 60 units of the item, which you have moved to the other warehouse in exercise 7.9, back to the main warehouse is required. This transfer should be processed in a transfer order.

Before you create the transfer order, make sure that a transit warehouse is assigned to the warehouse from which the item is shipped. Then enter the transfer order and post the shipment. After the shipment, check the inventory transactions and the inventory quantity of the item in all warehouses. Finally, receive the item transfer in the main warehouse.

Exercise 7.12—Manual Quarantine

Because of reported quality issues, you want to block the quantity in the main warehouse that you have transferred in exercise 7.11. Enter a manual quarantine order and select an appropriate quarantine warehouse. Check the on-hand quantity of the item and start the quarantine order.

After some time, you get to know that there is no problem with the item. End the quarantine and check the inventory quantity before and after ending.

Exercise 7.13—Manual Quality Order

In order to prevent further quality issues, you want to perform quality tests. Create a new test T-## to measure the length of items in centimeters (including decimals). Then create a test group G-## which only includes this test. The standard length is 100 cm with a tolerance of 10% above and below.

Enter and process a quality order with this test to examine 10 units of the item I-## of exercise 3.5 in the main warehouse. The length of all tested items is 105 cm.

Warehouse and Transportation Management

8

Depending on the requirements, your company may want to use mobile devices in the warehouse and track the transactions in detail. For this purpose, advanced warehouse management in Dynamics 365 provides the necessary functionality.

Transportation management helps to manage carriers and external transports. It is linked to advanced warehouse management, but can be used independently.

In this chapter, you get to know the core functionality of the advanced warehouse and transportation management. There are additional features for a variety of further processes—e.g., packaging and containerization, shipment consolidation, cross-docking, short picking, label printing, or quality management.

8.1 Advanced Warehouse Management

The advanced warehouse management in Dynamics 365, which enables registering warehouse transactions with pallets or boxes on mobile devices, is an enhancement of the basic warehouse management. Compared to the basic warehouse features, advanced warehouse management adds the following functionality:

- **Mobile device support**—*Warehouse Management* app for mobile devices.
- **Detailed tracking**—Using transactions within the warehouse.
- **Flexible setup**—Based on location directives and work templates.
- **Picking waves**—Combine warehouse work for shipments.
- **Flexible reservation**—With reservation hierarchies.
- **Packing**—Special features for item packing.
- **Inventory status**—Storage dimension for the status of units (e.g., "Damaged").
- **License plate**—Storage dimension for handling units (e.g., pallets).

© The Editor(s) (if applicable) and The Author(s), under exclusive license to
Springer Fachmedien Wiesbaden GmbH, part of Springer Nature 2026
A. Luszczak, *Using Microsoft Dynamics 365 Finance and Operations*,
https://doi.org/10.1007/978-3-658-50563-9_8

Apart from transactions within the warehouse, transactions covered by advanced warehouse management include the inventory registration (item arrival) in purchasing, picking in sales, and similar transactions in production and transfer orders. In the entire business process, these transactions are prior steps to the physical transaction with the product receipt or the packing slip ($\rightarrow$ Sect. 7.2.4).

Transactions within the warehouse are recorded in warehouse-specific transactions or, depending on the transaction type and settings in the Warehouse management parameters, in regular inventory transactions.

If activated in the license configuration, you can use the Material handling equipment interface module to connect an external automated storage system to the advanced warehouse management.

And if you want to integrate companies which run their core business in other ERP systems (e.g., Business Central), the feature *Warehouse management only mode*, which you can set up in the menu items of the folder *Warehouse management > Setup > Warehouse management integration*, enables using advanced warehouse management in a dedicated company, which is not configured for other business processes. Menu items related to shipment orders (*Inbound shipment orders*, *Outbound shipment orders*, *External warehouse shipment orders*) cover business processes that are part of the *Warehouse management only mode*.

8.1.1 Core Setup for Warehouse Management

Before you can use advanced warehouse management, you have to complete the related setup (in addition to the setup of the basic inventory management).

Advanced warehouse management is only used if both conditions are met: The item is assigned to a storage dimension group, in which advanced warehouse management processes are enabled, and the warehouse is also enabled for advanced warehouse management processes.

> *Note*: In order to facilitate comprehensive warehouse implementations, the Warehouse management initiation wizard supports the setup.

8.1.1.1 Parameters and Mobile Device Access

As a preparation for registering warehouse transactions on a mobile device, install the *Warehouse Management* mobile app for Dynamics 365 on your device (available for Android, iOS, and Windows). In the app, enter the required settings for the connection to the applicable Dynamics 365 environment.

For testing purposes, you can emulate the mobile app with the address *https://XXX.com /?mi=action:WHSWorkExecute&cmp=YYY* (*XXX.com* = Dynamics 365 URL,

YYY = Company) in the web client. The web client requires signing in with a regular Dynamics 365 user before the separate login for a warehouse work user is shown.

The Warehouse management parameters (*Warehouse management > Setup > Warehouse management parameters*) contain basic settings for the Warehouse management module, including the number sequences in warehouse management.

8.1.1.2 Inventory Status

The storage dimension "Inventory status" indicates the status or condition of inventory (e.g., "Good", "Damaged", or "Used"). It is only available for items with a storage dimension group, in which advanced warehouse management processes are enabled. In warehouses with advanced warehouse management processes, the inventory status is the usual way for blocking inventory of items (quarantine management is not generally available for these warehouses).

As a minimum setup, a status for available inventory has to be created in the Inventory status form (*Warehouse management > Setup > Inventory > Inventory statuses*). This status is required even if there is no need to block inventory with the inventory status. Optionally, set up further status values as required. The checkbox *Inventory blocking* in the Inventory status form controls whether the status blocks inventory (you can still move the blocked quantity within the warehouse).

You can specify a default value for the inventory status of transactions at multiple levels: At the company level (in the Warehouse management parameters, section *General*, tab *Inventory status*), at the site level (in the Site form), at the warehouse level (in the Warehouse form), and in the Default item status form (*Warehouse management > Setup > Inventory > Default item status*).

Blocking via inventory status is making use of the regular blocking feature in inventory (→ Sect. 7.4.6). Details on how to change the inventory status for blocking or unblocking an item are provided in → Sect. 8.1.4.

8.1.1.3 Warehouse-Related Settings

In order to create a warehouse that applies advanced warehouse management processes, the following setup is required:

- **Location formats**—Specify the structure of location IDs.
- **Location types**—Indicate the purpose of a location.
- **Location profiles**—Core setting for locations.
- **Sites, warehouses, locations**—Show the physical structure of the warehouses.
- **Warehouse groups**—Only required if you want to manage location directives or wave templates for warehouses at the group level.

Location formats (*Warehouse management > Setup > Warehouse > Location formats*) provide a flexible setup for the structure of location IDs. You can, for example, compose the location ID as a combination of the aisle, rack, and position ID. Since it is a required setup, you need to create at least one format with its segments.

Location types (*Warehouse management > Setup > Warehouse > Location types*) are used for filtering and grouping purposes. At least a location type for final shipping locations, which has to be selected in the Warehouse management parameters (field *Final shipping location type* in the section *General*, tab *Location types*), is required. If you use staging or packing, additionally set up the related location types and select them in the Warehouse management parameters. Other location types are optional.

Location profiles (*Warehouse management > Setup > Warehouse > Location profiles*) group locations with common characteristics. These characteristics include the location format and settings on license-plate tracking, mixed items, mixed inventory status, and cycle counting.

When you create a location profile (→Fig. 8.1), select the applicable *Location format*. In location profiles for regular locations, the slider *Allow cycle counting* should be set to "Yes" to make counting possible. In location profiles for locations in which you want to track the quantity per license plate (e.g., for pallets), the slider *Use license plate tracking* needs to be set to "Yes". For the assigned locations, all receipt and issue transactions have to include the license plate.

The location profile for user locations is selected in the Warehouse management parameters (section *General*, tab *Location profiles*). Location profiles for shipping or for staging locations have to include the *Location type* for shipping or for staging (as selected in the Warehouse management parameters).

Warehouses (*Warehouse management > Setup > Warehouse > Warehouses*) and the settings in the Warehouse form are discussed in →Sect. 7.4.1. In addition to the general

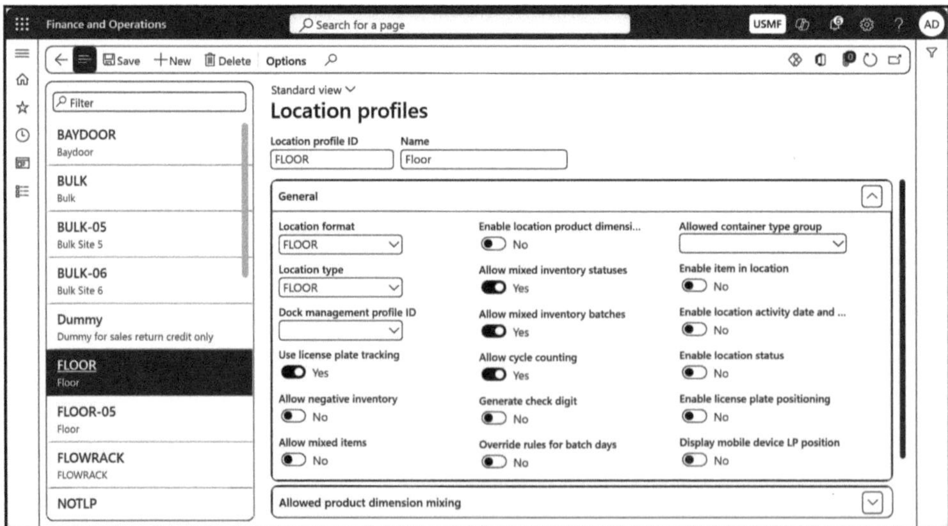

Fig. 8.1 Setting up a location profile

settings, the tab *Warehouse* contains the settings for advanced warehouse management. In order to create a warehouse that uses advanced warehouse management processes, insert a record in the Warehouse form and set the slider *Use warehouse management processes* to "Yes" before saving the record. Then open the related warehouse locations with the button *Warehouse/View/Inventory locations* in the Warehouse form.

In the Location form, you can click the button *Location setup wizard* to create multiple locations conveniently. For each location, the selected location profile determines the characteristics of the location (e.g., the format of the location ID, the location type, and whether to allow different items in one location).

In a typical warehouse, you can find at least the following types of locations:

- **Receiving location**—Intermediate location for purchase receipts.
- **Shipping location**—Last location for sales shipping (bay door).
- **Buffer locations**—Storage locations for pallets and bulk items (bulk area).
- **Floor locations**—Storage locations for single items (picking area).

If there is a need to prepare shipments at separate locations before transferring to the shipping location, set up one or more staging locations with the appropriate location type.

User locations are automatically generated when you create a warehouse user. They are used as intermediate locations for the time between picking from one location and putting to the other location (handling time, e.g., for forklift driving).

Once you have completed the location setup, close the Location form and select a *Default receipt location* for the warehouse on the tab *Inventory and warehouse management* in the Warehouse form.

In the Site form (*Warehouse management > Setup > Warehouse > Sites*), set the slider *Allow users on mobile devices to receive at another warehouse* to "Yes" if it should be possible to receive purchase orders in a warehouse which is different from the warehouse specified in the order line (within the same site).

Warehouse groups (*Warehouse management > Setup > Warehouse > Warehouse groups*) are an optional setup, which enables managing some warehouse settings (e.g., location directives or wave templates) at the group level. You can assign a warehouse to several warehouse groups, if applicable.

8.1.1.4 Basic Setup for Warehouse Work

Activities in the warehouse are reflected by "warehouse work" in Dynamics 365. In general, warehouse work consists of a pair of activities—picking from one location and putting to another location. There are two basic types of warehouse work in Dynamics 365:

- **Predefined work**—For predefined activities, like processing a sales shipment, work is generated in advance (based on work templates). Warehouse workers report the actual execution of the planned work later.

- **Unprompted work**—Unprompted work, like a manual quantity adjustment, is created and reported at the time you execute the activity.

Unprompted work does not require a specific setup. For predefined work, the following setup is necessary:

- **Work classes**—Group and characterize work.
- **Work templates**—Determine what to do (e.g., "Pick" or "Put").
- **Location directives**—Determine where to pick or put (e.g., location "01–001").

Work classes (*Warehouse management > Setup > Work > Work classes*) for predefined work represent the different types of work that are processed on mobile devices. The field *Work order type* groups the work classes by source document type (e.g., "Raw material picking"). The work classes link mobile device menu items with work templates:

- **Mobile device menu items**—In mobile device menu items for work registration, the work class determines which work you can register with the menu item.
- **Work templates**—In the work templates for predefined work, the work class is a mandatory field that links the work template to mobile device menu items.

Work templates (*Warehouse management > Setup > Work > Work templates*) are the basis for automatically generating predefined work. When you open the Work template form (→ Fig. 8.2), first select a *Work order type* (e.g., "Purchase orders" for item arrivals related to purchase orders) in the lookup field at the top of the form. If you want to create a new work template, click the button *New* in the action pane. The upper pane subsequently shows a new record with the next available *Sequence number*. If you need to specify filter criteria, which are used for selecting a work template when automatically creating predefined warehouse work, click the button *Edit query*. Since the sequence number, which is an editable field, determines the search sequence for the applicable template when creating work, templates with more specific criteria should be first in the sequence.

Once you have saved the work template header, switch to the tab *Work template details* and enter a line with the *Work type* "Pick" and a line with the *Work type* "Put". If required, you can enter additional lines—e.g., with the *Work type* "Print".

8.1.1.5 Location Directives

Location directives (*Warehouse management > Setup > Location directives*) determine the location for executing the warehouse work. Examples are the location directives for the *Work order type* "Purchase orders" and the *Work type* "Put", which determine the location to which to put an item after receiving a purchase order in the warehouse.

In the Location directive form (→ Fig. 8.3), select the relevant *Work order type* at the top of the list pane on the left first. The related location directives are subsequently shown below. The field *Work type* on the tab *Location directives* in the right pane determines if

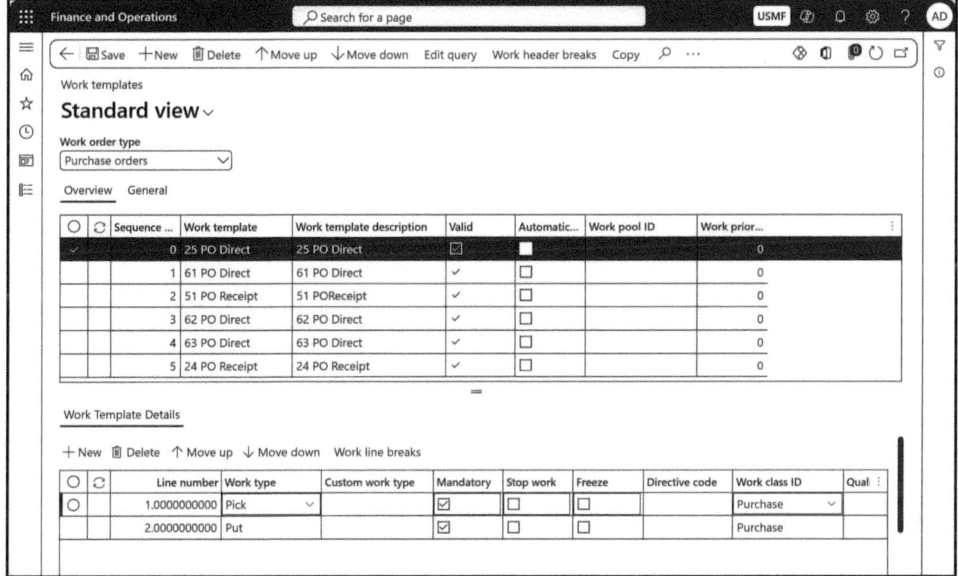

Fig. 8.2 Setting up a work template for purchase put-away

the location directive selected in the left pane controls pick or put work. On the tab *Warehouse selection*, you specify whether the location directive relates to an individual warehouse, to a warehouse group, or to all warehouses.

Apart from the work order type, the work type, and the warehouse selection, the filter criteria in the dialog, which you can access with the button *Edit query* in the action pane, control which location directive is selected automatically when generating work for a source document (e.g., a purchase order line with its warehouse and item).

On the tab *Lines*, you can enter an additional filter on the quantity and unit. The column *Unit* refers to the from/to quantity columns. If you want to set up a directive for a particular unit, select the checkbox *Restrict by unit* and enter the unit in the form, which you access with the button *Restrict by unit* in the toolbar of the tab *Lines*. In this way, you can, for example, enter a line for moving full pallets to buffer locations and another line for moving individual units to floor locations.

The tab *Location Directive Actions* contains the setting, to which location(s) to put (in directives with the *Work type* "Put") or from which to pick (in directives with the *Work type* "Pick"). The filter criteria, which determine these locations, have to be entered in the filter dialog, which you access with the button *Edit query* in the toolbar of this tab. In the filter dialog, you can also specify sorting criteria on the tab *Sorting* (e.g., referring to the column *Sort code* in the warehouse locations).

If there are products with batch numbers, select the checkbox *Batch enabled* in the location directive action of directives for the work type "Pick" (in an additional line, if you have some items with and other items without batch control).

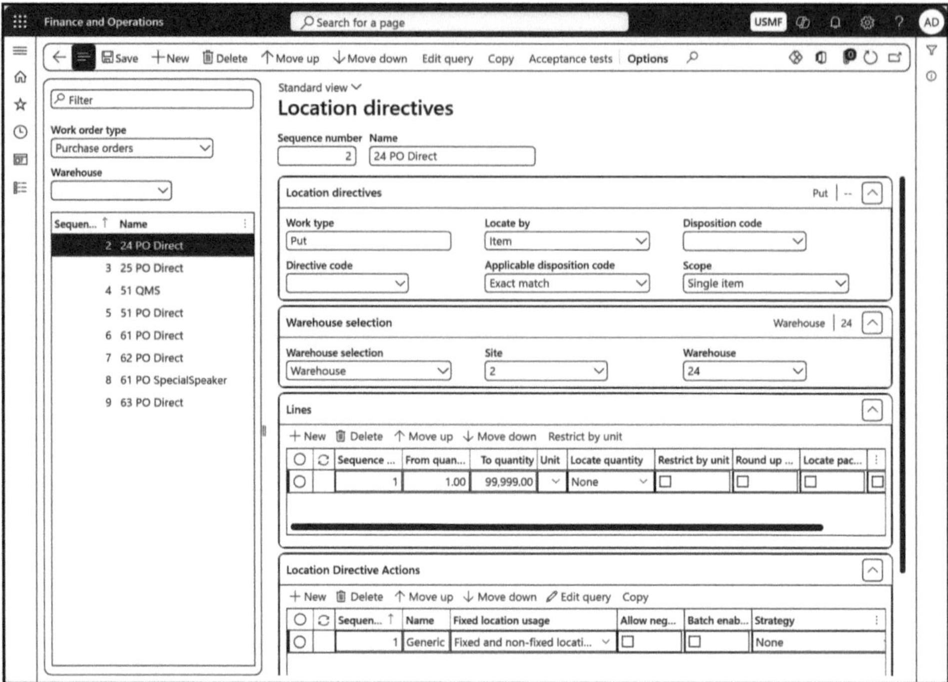

Fig. 8.3 Setting up a location directive for purchase put-away

The *Sequence number* of the location directives (and of the *Lines* within a directive, and of the *Location directive actions* within a line) is an editable field that determines the search sequence for the applicable record when automatically creating work. For this reason, directives, directive lines, and location directive actions with more specific criteria should be first in the sequence.

8.1.1.6 Basic Setup for Shipments

Load templates (*Warehouse management > Setup > Load > Load templates*) represent transportation units (e.g., the different container sizes). In transportation management, the load template initializes restrictions on the weight or equipment of the related loads in the Outbound load planning workbench (→ Sect. 8.2.2). In warehouse management, they are the basis for generating a load in an outbound shipment.

Waves collect orders that are commonly released for picking in the warehouse. The required setup for waves includes the wave process methods and the wave templates.

Wave process methods (*Warehouse management > Setup > Waves > Wave process methods*), which are generated by the application, determine the available steps for wave processing. In a new company or after implementing additional methods, initialize the methods with the button *Regenerate methods* in the Wave process methods form.

Wave templates (*Warehouse management > Setup > Waves > Wave templates*) contain settings for the picking work that refer to the grouping of work, to automated steps, and to applicable methods. On the tab *Warehouse selection* of the Wave templates form ($\rightarrow$ Fig. 8.4), specify whether the wave template relates to an individual warehouse, to a warehouse group, or to all warehouses. In wave templates that specify an automatic wave creation (the slider *Automate wave creation* in the template is set to "Yes"), you can click the button *Edit query* to specify filter criteria that are used for searching the applicable template when automatically creating a wave. For these templates, the sorting (field *Wave template sequence*) controls the search priority (like in work templates and location directives).

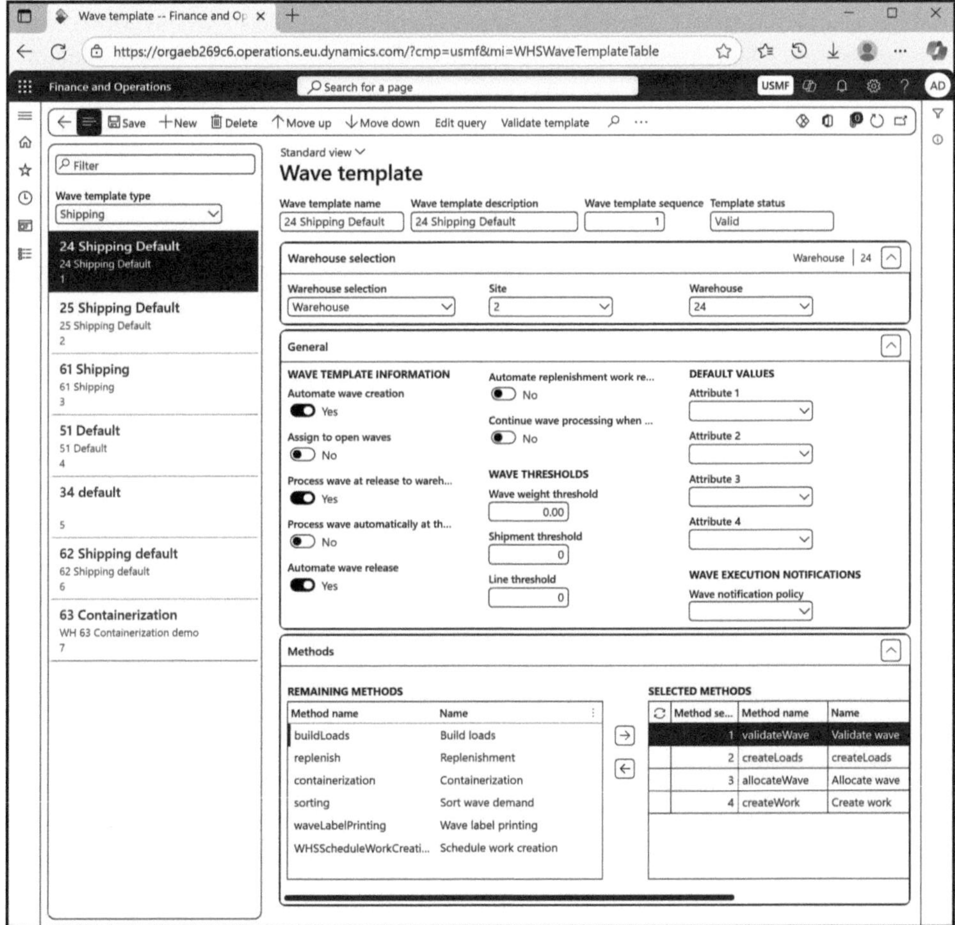

Fig. 8.4 Managing a wave template

8.1.1.7 Setup for Mobile Devices

Before you can view menus and menu items in the Warehouse Management app on mobile devices, the corresponding setup needs to be completed. You can set up multiple menus and submenus in line with the requirements in the warehouse, and assign each warehouse worker to a respective menu.

The required mobile device setup in Dynamics 365 includes the following items:

* **Mobile device menu items**—Determine the available forms on mobile devices.
* **Mobile device menus**—Determine the menu structures.

Mobile device menu items (*Warehouse management > Setup > Mobile device > Mobile device menu items*) determine the forms that are available on mobile devices. The primary setting for a menu item is given by the lookup field *Mode*: The mode "Work" refers to warehouse work (the registration of transactions), the mode "Indirect" includes inquiries and common features (like logging off).

For menu items with the mode "Work" (→ Fig. 8.5), the slider *Use existing work* determines whether the menu item serves to register predefined work (existing work, which has already been created on the basis of a work template before) or unprompted work.

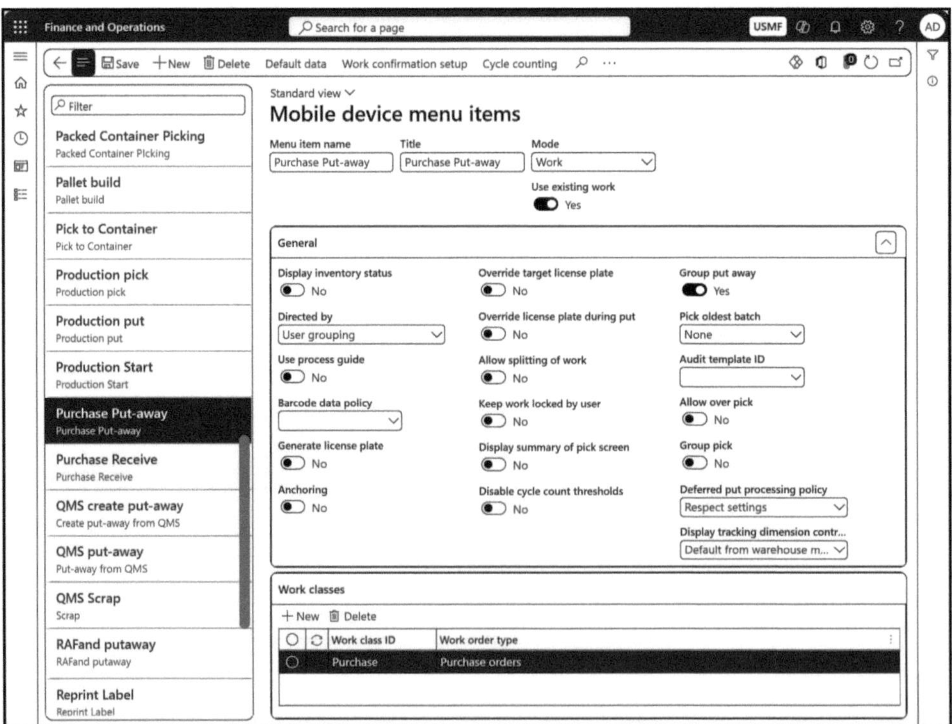

Fig. 8.5 Setting up a mobile device menu item for purchase put-away

In a menu item that creates work (unprompted work which is not predefined), set the slider *Use existing work* to "No" and select the applicable work item in the field *Work creation process* on the tab *General* (e.g., "Adjustment in").

In menu items for existing work (required to execute predefined work), set the slider *Use existing work* to "Yes". The lookup field *Directed by* in this case controls whether the system (*Directed by* = "System directed") or the warehouse worker (*Directed by* = "User directed") selects which work to execute. For *User directed* work, the warehouse worker has to enter or scan the work ID of the executed work (which means that he does the selection), whereas for *System directed* work, the device (mobile device menu item) shows which work to do next. With reference to the option "System directed", you can click the button *System directed work sequence queries* to enter sorting and filtering criteria for the work.

In case the option "User grouping" or "System grouping" is selected in the field *Directed by*, the worker can register multiple work lines with pick-transactions on the mobile device, then click the button *Done*, and finally register one common or multiple separate put-transactions (controlled by the slider *Group put away*).

The work classes selected on the tab *Work classes* in menu items for existing work determine the work that you can register with the particular menu item. If there is, for example, only one line with a work class "Purchase" on this tab, you can only execute work that is generated from a work template line with the work class "Purchase" (and not a "Sales" work).

Mobile device menus (*Warehouse management > Setup > Mobile device > Mobile device menu*) control the menu structure of the mobile device menu items. You can set up multiple menus and submenus.

> *Note*: In addition to the core setup, you can manage the mobile devices and the menu item layout with the Warehouse management setup forms *Mobile device brands*, *Mobile device user settings*, *Warehouse app field names*, and *Warehouse app field priority*. In addition, the *Mobile device steps* form provides the option to show menu-specific instructions on the mobile device and to add menu-specific overrides—e.g., adding a detour which shows a location inquiry for selecting a location to a menu item on the mobile device.

8.1.1.8 Warehouse Workers and Work Users

As a prerequisite for using the Warehouse Management app with the (required) user-based authentication, the warehouse worker needs a Dynamics 365 user account (with the role "Warehouse mobile device user role") and an assigned worker/employee record ($\rightarrow$ Sect. 10.2.2).

Based on the worker record in human resources, you can create the company-specific warehouse workers in the Work user form (*Warehouse management > Setup > Worker*). Click the button *New* in the action pane of the Work user form for this purpose, and select the worker/employee in the field *Worker*.

For the worker, enter one or more work users on the tab *Users* (→ Fig. 8.6) subsequently. The *User ID* and the password of the work user are used for the login on the mobile device. The *Default warehouse* determines the assigned warehouse, and the *Menu name* the available menu and menu items. If you select the checkbox *Default user* for a *User ID*, the Warehouse Management app logs in automatically with this user (on a device connected to the Dynamics 365 user account that is assigned to the respective worker record).

If you create multiple users for a worker, you can assign different menus and warehouses to the worker (who has to log in with the respective User ID in this case). For work users who should switch between warehouses, click the button *Warehouses* in the toolbar of the tab *Users* to open the Allowed warehouses form, in which you enter the warehouses.

Creating a work user automatically creates a location (used as an intermediate location while executing warehouse work) in the warehouses of the user.

8.1.1.9 Product-Related Settings

In the released product, the following setup is required for advanced warehouse management:

- **Storage dimension group**—Enables advanced warehouse management.
- **Reservation hierarchy**—Controls the inventory dimensions for reservation.
- **Unit sequence group**—Controls the available units of measurement for warehouse transactions.

The storage dimension group in the released product controls whether the item is subject to advanced warehouse management. At least one storage dimension group (*Product*

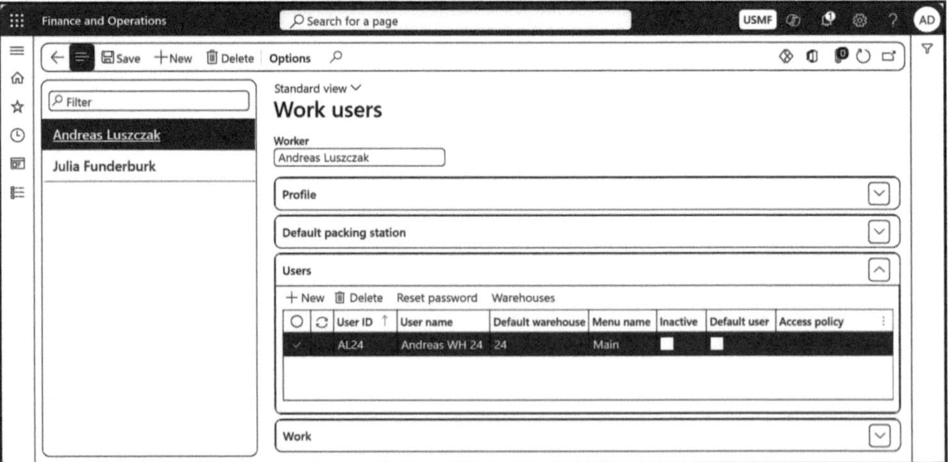

Fig. 8.6 Setting up a warehouse worker

information management > Setup > Dimension and variant groups > Storage dimension groups), in which the slider *Use warehouse management processes* on the tab *Warehouse specific setup* is set to "Yes", is required for advanced warehouse management. This setting activates the inventory dimensions *Inventory status* and *License plate*.

Reservation hierarchies (*Warehouse management > Setup > Inventory > Reservation hierarchy*) determine for products that use advanced warehouse management, which inventory dimensions are available for reservation in sales orders, transfer orders, shipments, and other outbound transactions:

- **Dimensions for order reservation**—Dimensions above the dimension *Location* in the reservation hierarchy are subject to a reservation in order lines.
- **Dimensions for warehouse reservation**—The location and the dimensions below the location in the reservation hierarchy are subject to a reservation in the warehouse (reserving when generating warehouse work).

When creating a new reservation hierarchy, a dialog is shown in which you can select applicable inventory dimensions and change the sorting of the dimensions.

The selected dimensions in the reservation hierarchy of an item have to comply with the active storage and tracking dimensions of the item. For this reason, the setup of the reservation hierarchies depends on the inventory dimensions that are used. The reservation hierarchy is primarily important for items with batch or serial numbers because it controls whether you reserve the batch or serial numbers already in the order line (in the hierarchy, the batch/serial number is above the location), or later in the warehouse (the batch/serial number is below the location). For batch-controlled items, you can additionally select the checkbox in the column *Allow reservation on demand order* of the reservation hierarchy if you want to enable optionally reserving a batch number in an order line (relevant for hierarchies with the batch number below the location).

Unit sequence groups (*Warehouse management > Setup > Warehouse > Unit sequence groups*) control for the assigned items, which units of measurement you can use for moving and storing the product within the warehouse. The available units in a unit sequence group have to be entered on the tab *Line details* of the Unit sequence group form ($\rightarrow$ Fig. 8.7). The checkboxes *Default unit for purchase and transfer* and *Default unit for production* in the unit sequence group determine the unit that is used as the default value when receiving an assigned item. With the default unit, you can, for example, specify to receive a particular item in pallets. The checkbox *License plate grouping* controls whether a separate license plate per unit (e.g., pallet) or one license plate for the whole quantity (in the selected unit) is generated when receiving an item. As a prerequisite for the use of this grouping, the slider *License plate grouping* has to be set to "Yes" in the applicable mobile device menu items.

When you create a released product (*Product information management > Products > Released products*) that should use advanced warehouse management, select an appropriate storage dimension group (for advanced warehouse management), a

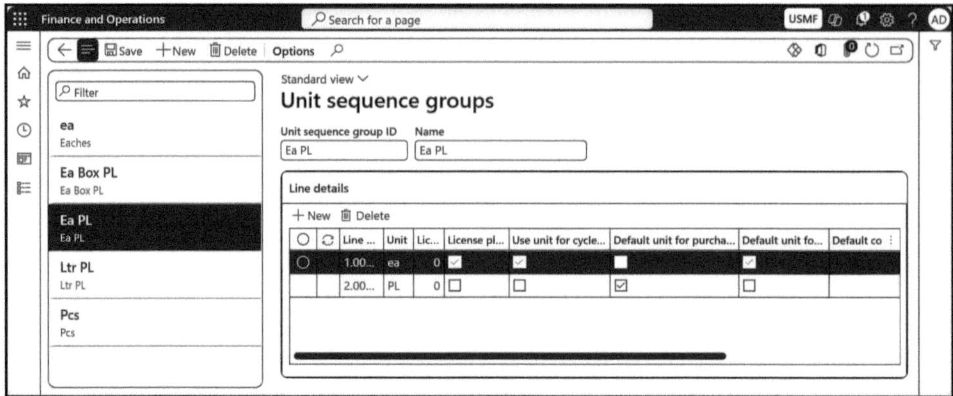

Fig. 8.7 Setting up a unit sequence group with the units "ea" and "PL"

reservation hierarchy (edit with the button *Product/Set up/Reservation hierarchy*), and a unit sequence group (field *Unit sequence group ID* on the tab *Warehouse*). Depending on the units in the selected unit sequence group, related unit conversions are required for the item.

Apart from the weight and the physical dimensions (depth, width, height) on the tab *Manage inventory* in the released product, there is the Physical dimension form (access with the button *Manage inventory/Warehouse/Physical dimensions* in the released product) in which you can enter the physical dimensions of the item in the different units (in particular, the units of the unit sequence group). Weight and physical dimensions can be used to calculate the utilization of location capacity and transportation loads.

> *Note*: If activated in the license configuration, you can use advanced warehouse management also for catch weight items.

8.1.1.10 Warehouse-Specific Inventory Transactions

Warehouse management generates a large number of transactions, which may cause performance issues in case they are posted as regular inventory transactions. In order to avoid these issues, there is a separate table for transactions within the warehouse—the warehouse-specific transactions (applicable for transactions in advanced warehouse management).

In the Warehouse management parameters, section *General*, settings on the tab *Warehouse inventory transaction mechanism* control which *Warehouse scenario* (type of transaction) creates warehouse-specific transactions (checkbox *Use warehouse inventory transactions*). In a new Dynamics 365 implementation, enabling warehouse-specific transactions in all scenarios is mandatory.

With warehouse-specific transactions, the on-hand quantity at the level of storage dimensions below the warehouse is not only given by regular inventory transactions, but also includes the warehouse-specific transactions.

In the On-hand inquiry (*Inventory management > Inquiries and reports > On-hand list*), which you can also access from the Released product form (button *Manage inventory/View/On-hand inventory*), you can click the button *Warehouse transactions* to access the Warehouse transaction inquiry that displays both regular inventory transactions and warehouse-specific transactions. This is different from the Inventory transaction inquiry, which only shows regular inventory transactions and, for this reason, misses the warehouse-specific transactions that are relevant if you want to track transactions at a storage dimension level below the warehouse.

8.1.2   Core Warehouse Processes

Warehouse transactions include inbound processes (e.g., purchase order receipts, transfer order receipts, receipts of customer returns, or receipts of manufactured items in production) and outbound processes (e.g., sales order shipments, transfer order shipments, or material picking in production).

An overview of the warehouse layout and the structure of the warehouse work, which is used as a basis for the warehouse transactions, is shown in → Fig. 8.8.

In the overall process, the mobile device transactions are another way for recording the inventory registration in purchasing (→ Sect. 3.5.3), the picking list in sales (→ Sect. 4.4.2), and equivalent transactions in production and transfer orders.

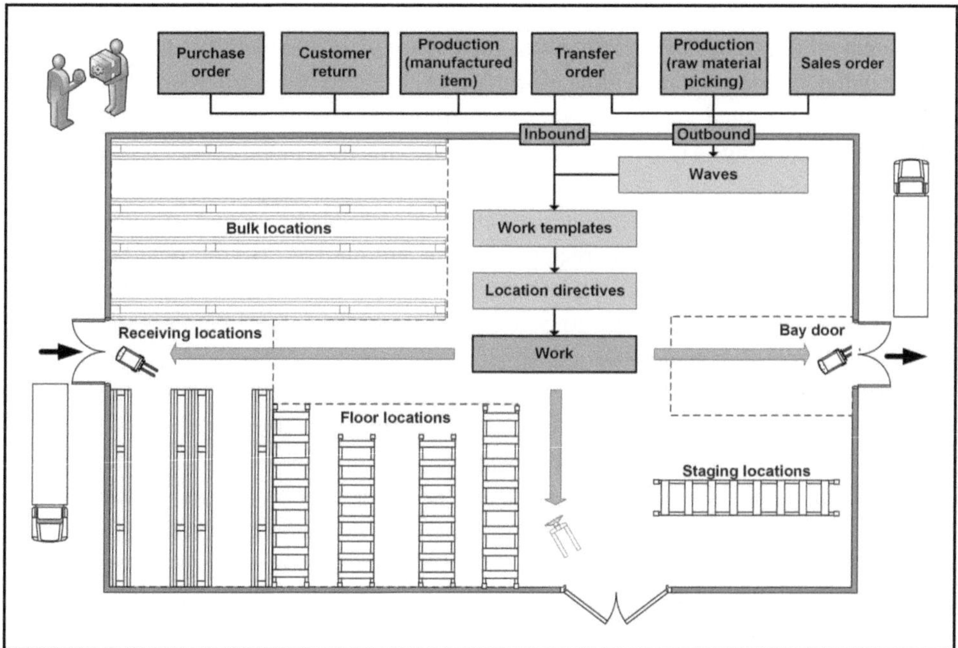

Fig. 8.8 Warehouse layout and the structure of warehouse work

8.1.2.1 Purchase Order Receipt

The starting point for a purchase order receipt in the warehouse is a purchase order line with a product and a warehouse, which both are enabled for advanced warehouse management.

The receipt process then includes the following steps:

- **Initial receipt** (on a mobile device)—Receive the item in the receipt location.
- **Put away** (on a mobile device)—Move the item to the final location.
- **Product receipt**—Commercial acceptance of the receipt (→ Sect. 3.5.4).

You can find a description of further options for purchase order receipts on the mobile device in → Sect. 8.1.3.

The initial receipt of a purchased item is not based on work that is created upfront, but generates work when posting the receipt. Applicable mobile device menu items include the following settings: *Mode* = "Work", *Use existing work* = "No", *Work creation process* = "Purchase order line receiving" (register the order number and line number when receiving) or "Purchase order item receiving" (register the order number and item number when receiving).

On the mobile device, you can record the initial receipt in the warehouse in such a menu item. Enter or scan the purchase order number and the line number (or the item number) there. The default for the *Unit* in the receipt is specified in the unit sequence group of the item, but you can select a different unit that is included in the unit sequence group, and you can reduce (split) the quantity. Depending on settings in the mobile device menu item (slider *Generate license plate*), the license plate that identifies the handling unit (e.g., a pallet, a box, or an individual piece) has to be entered/scanned manually in the field *LP* (from a pre-printed tag), or is generated from a number sequence (which eventually requires printing a tag). Dynamics 365 then receives the item in the default receipt location of the warehouse.

Posting the initial receipt generates warehouse work for the second step, the put-away work (picking the item from the receipt location and putting it to the final bulk or floor location). The applicable work template and location directive determine the details of this work. The work lines, which are to be registered on a mobile device, are shown in the menu item *Warehouse management > Work > All work*.

In order to register the put-away work on a mobile device, open an applicable menu item on the device (→ Fig. 8.9). The required settings for this menu item are: *Mode* "Work", *Use existing work* "Yes", *Work class* as specified in the work template that has been automatically selected when generating the work. Depending on the setting in the field *Directed by* of the menu item, the mobile device displays the next work (if "System directed"), or you have to enter/scan the work ID or the license plate (if "User directed") of the put-away work. When you have finished picking at the receipt location, the mobile device shows the put location (based on the location directive). Depending on settings for

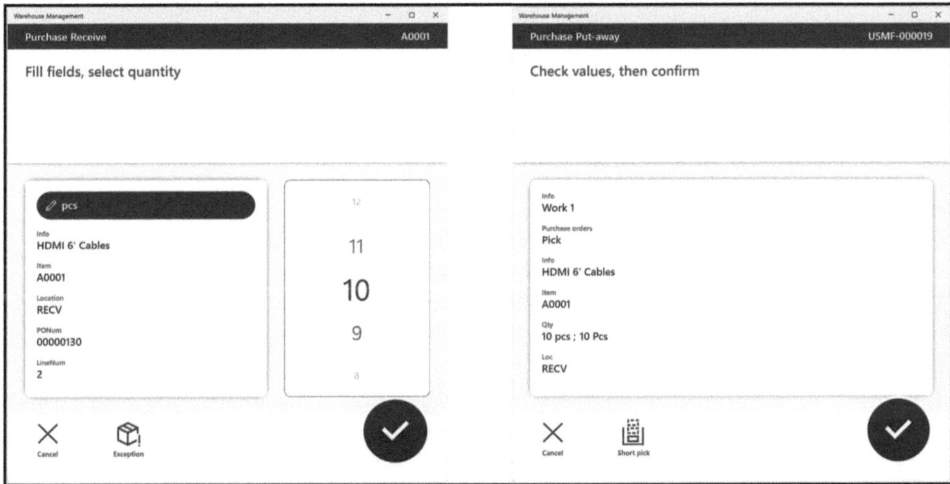

Fig. 8.9   Registering the initial receipt and picking for the separate put-away in the mobile app

the work user (slider *Allow put location override* on the tab *Work* in the Work user form), you can override the put location.

Once the registration of the inbound transactions on the mobile device is finished, the product receipt has to be posted manually in the Dynamics 365 web client or, related to an inbound load, with a batch process. Whereas a purchase order confirmation is not required for the inventory registration, the order has to be confirmed before you can post the product receipt.

When you post the product receipt in the purchase order or a summary update ($\rightarrow$ Sect. 3.5.4), select the option "Registered quantity" or "Registered quantity and services" in the lookup field *Quantity* of the posting dialog to make sure that the product receipt refers to the quantity that has been registered on the mobile device. Apart from the options for posting the product receipt in the Procurement module, which require entering a *Product receipt* number in the *Posting product receipt* dialog, you can use the periodic activity *Warehouse management > Periodic tasks > Update product receipts*, which you can submit to a batch process. This periodic task does not require entering a product receipt number, but a load ID must be assigned to the order line (if applicable, you can activate the slider *Automatically create at purchase order entry* in the section *Loads* of the Warehouse management parameters to create a load per purchase order automatically).

8.1.2.2 Sales Order Shipment

The starting point for a sales order shipment in the warehouse is a sales order line with a product and a warehouse, which both are enabled for advanced warehouse management. If order completion is required according to the Pricing management parameters ($\rightarrow$ Sect. 4.3.3), set the sales order to complete.

The basic shipment process then includes the following steps:

- **Reservation**—Reserve the item before shipment.
- **Shipment**—Create a shipment and include the item ("Release to warehouse").
- **Load**—Create a load for external transportation (before or after the shipment).
- **Wave**—Create and release a picking wave with the shipment.
- **Warehouse work**—Execute the picking work on a mobile device.
- **Confirm shipment**—Close the shipment.
- **Packing slip**—Post the packing slip (manual or with a periodic job).

A shipment is collecting one or more lines of one or more orders with the same destination address within a load. A load consists of one or more shipments with a common transport (e.g., truck).

Before processing a shipment in advanced warehouse management, you have to make sure that the item is reserved. The inventory dimensions for the reservation in the sales order are controlled by the reservation hierarchy of the item. You can manually reserve an item in the Reservation form, which you can access with the button *Inventory/Reservation* in the toolbar of the order lines in the Sales order form. Depending on the settings for reservation, there is an automatic reservation ($\rightarrow$ Sect. 7.4.5).

Shipments (*Warehouse management > Shipments > All shipments*) represent separate deliveries within a load. If you want to ship a complete sales order, you can create the shipment with the button *Warehouse/Actions/Release to warehouse* in the Sales order form. Alternatively, you can use the Release sales orders to warehouse form (*Warehouse management > Release to warehouse > Release sales orders to warehouse*), which gives an overview of orders to be released, or the periodic job *Warehouse management > Release to warehouse > Automatic release of sales orders*. The setting for the *Sales order fulfillment policy* in the Accounts receivable parameters (section *Warehouse management*) and in the Customer detail form (on the tab *Warehouse*) are the minimum criteria for releasing. Creating the shipment sets the *Release status* of the sales order (shown in the corresponding column of the Sales order list page) to "Released".

If, e.g., the transportation planning department has created a load already before you create the shipment, open the Outbound load planning workbench and create the shipment from the load ($\rightarrow$ Sect. 8.2.2).

A load (*Warehouse management > Loads > All loads*) represents an inbound or outbound transportation unit (e.g., a container or a truck). It consists of one or more shipments. You can also split a single order line into multiple shipments and loads—for example, if the transportation unit is too small for the complete quantity of the order line. For creating a load, there are the following options:

- **After creating the shipment**—Create the load in the Shipment form.
- **Before creating the shipment**—Create the load in the Outbound load planning workbench.
- **Skip creating the load**—Processing the wave in a later step creates the load automatically in this case.

Another option is to create loads automatically when entering a sales order (configured in the section *Loads* of the Warehouse management parameters).

If you want to create a load from a shipment, click the button *Shipments/ Shipments/ Transfer shipment to new load* in the Shipment form ($\rightarrow$ Fig. 8.10). In the dialog that is shown next, select the load template that characterizes the transportation unit for the load (e.g., the container size) before you click the button *OK*. If you want to ship multiple orders together, add them to a common load (click the button *Shipments/Shipments/ Transfer shipment to existing load* in the Shipment form).

A wave (*Warehouse management > Outbound waves > Shipment waves > All waves*) is a group of shipments that are to be processed together in the warehouse. Depending on settings in the applicable *Wave template*, waves are created and processed automatically.

If you need to create a wave manually, click the button *New* in the Wave form and select a wave template in the *Create* dialog. Then click the button *Wave/Wave/Maintain shipments* in the Wave form to open the *Maintain shipments* form. The tab *Shipments not on a wave* in the Maintain shipments form shows all shipments that you can add to the wave. Click the button *Add to wave* in the toolbar of this tab to add a shipment to the wave. Shipments, which are already included in the selected wave, are shown on the tab *Wave lines* in the Maintain shipments form and in the Wave detail form (you might need to refresh the form to display a new shipment).

The workspace *Outbound work planning* is another place for creating a wave. For the *Warehouse* which you select in the upper pane of the workspace, shipments without wave assignment are shown in the list *Shipments needing attention* in the list section. Select one

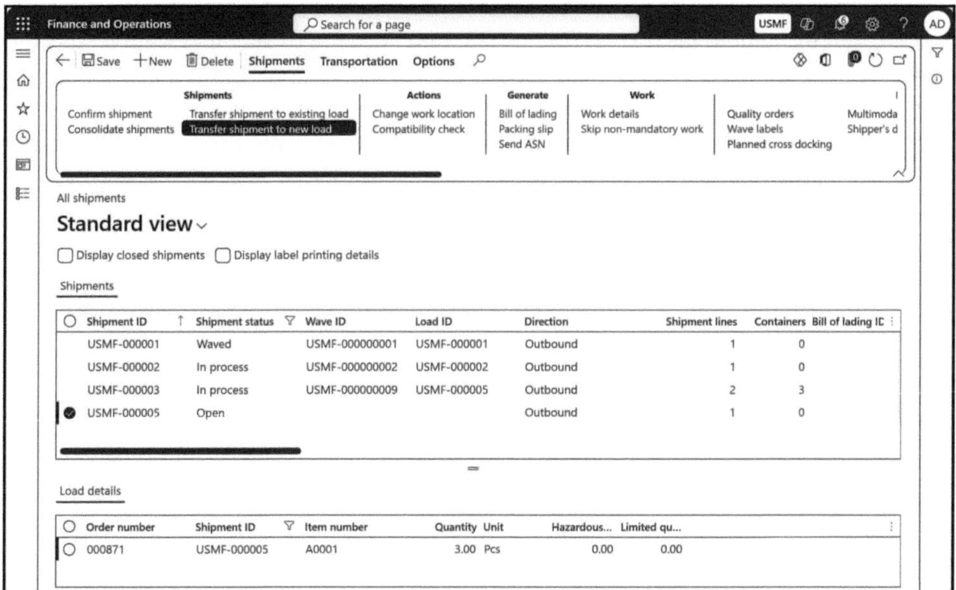

Fig. 8.10 Creating a load in the Shipment form

or more shipments and click the button *Add to new wave* in the toolbar of the list to create a wave with these shipments.

Once you have created a wave and added the shipment, process the wave in the next step. If wave processing is not executed automatically (specified in the wave template), click the button *Wave/Wave/Process* in the Wave form (→ Fig. 8.11). Depending on the parameter *Process waves in batch* (Warehouse management parameters, section *General*, tab *Wave processing*), processing is done in a batch job.

Processing a wave generates warehouse work. You can view this work in the Work form (*Warehouse management > Work > All work*), which you can also access with the button *Wave/ Related information/ Work* in the Wave form. But at this stage, the *Wave status* of the wave is "Held", and the work is blocked (shown in the column *Blocked* of the Work list page). Before you can start executing the actual warehouse work, you have to release the wave with the button *Wave/Wave/Release* in the Wave form.

Depending on the wave template, some or all of the steps for creating and processing a wave are executed automatically and are not to be done manually for this reason. In case of errors in wave processing (e.g., because of a missing location directive), the list page *Warehouse management > Work > Work exceptions log* will show the relevant messages.

In order to process the wave in the warehouse, open a menu item for sales order picking on the mobile device (→ Fig. 8.12). The required settings for this menu item are: *Mode* "Work", *Use existing work* "Yes", *Work class* as specified in the work template that is selected automatically when processing the wave. Depending on settings in the work template (field *Directed by*), the next picking work is shown (if "System directed"), or you have to enter or scan (e.g., from a printed work list) the work ID of the work. After picking the item from the displayed location (specified in the location directive for the work type "Pick"), put the item to the displayed final shipping location or staging location (specified in the location directive for the work type "Put"). Depending on the settings specified in

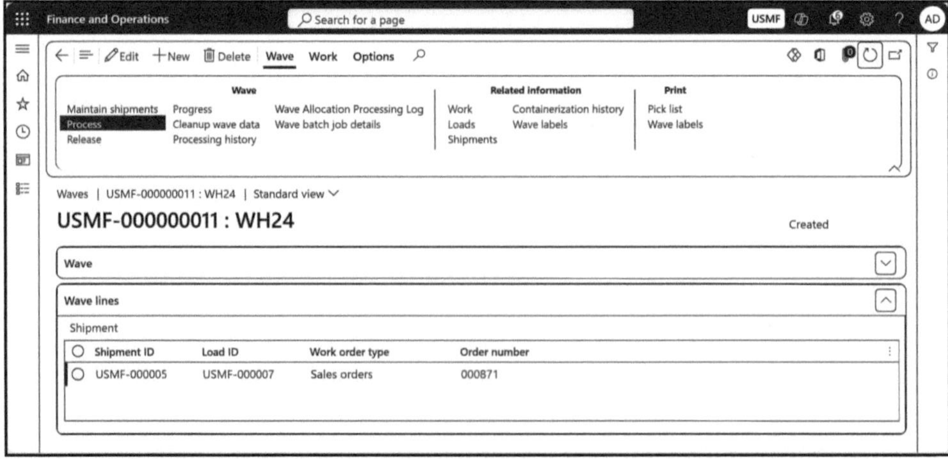

Fig. 8.11 Processing a shipment wave

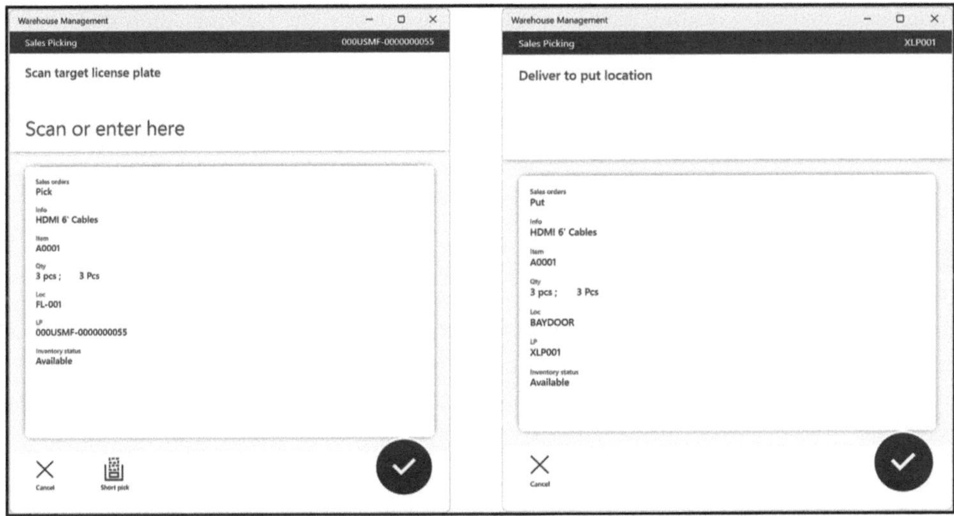

Fig. 8.12 Registering the pick transaction and the put transaction in the mobile app

the Work user form, you can override the pick location and the put location. Settings in the work template and in the wave template control whether there are additional steps for staging or for replenishment. Putting an item to the final shipping location as the last step on the mobile device sets the status of the inventory transaction to "Picked" (deducting the quantity from the on-hand inventory).

Once you have finished the warehouse processes on the mobile device, confirm the shipment. Confirming closes the shipment and the load. Apart from automatically confirming (→ Sect. 8.1.3), you can manually confirm a shipment in one of the following pages:

- **Shipment form**—Button *Shipments/Shipments/Confirm shipment* (if the load does not contain multiple shipments).
- **Load form**—Button *Ship and receive/Confirm/Outbound shipment.*
- **Outbound load planning workbench**—Button *Ship and receive/Confirm/Outbound shipment* in the toolbar of the tab *Loads*.
- Once the shipment is confirmed, the last step is posting the packing slip. You can post the packing slip manually in one of the following pages:
- **Shipment form**—Button *Shipment/Generate/Packing slip* (select the checkbox *Display closed shipments* if the shipment is not shown).
- **Load form**—Button *Ship and receive/Generate/Packing slip.*
- **Outbound load planning workbench**—Button *Generate/Packing slip* in the toolbar on the tab *Loads*.
- **Sales and marketing module**—Various options for posting a packing slip with reference to the picked quantity (→ Sect. 4.4.4).

Apart from manually posting the packing slip, you can post the packing slip for confirmed shipments with the periodic job *Warehouse management > Periodic tasks > Load packing slip posting*. As a prerequisite, Packing slip posting parameters (*Warehouse management > Setup > Inventory > Packing slip posting parameters*), which control printing and other options, need to be set up.

8.1.3 Advanced Options for Inbound and Outbound Processes

In addition to the basic process for purchase order receipts and sales order shipments, there are variants of these processes, including the option to automate steps. Transfer orders, customer returns, and production orders are further variants of the inbound and outbound processes.

8.1.3.1 Task Automation

Apart from manually executing activities, you can perform tasks automatically. Depending on the setup, the following options are available:

- **Work execution**—Automatically execute warehouse work.
    - **Automatically process**—Select the checkbox *Automatically process* in the work template to execute the work automatically when releasing a wave (e.g., for bulk items not tracked in detail).
    - **Work confirmation setup**—Click the button *Work confirmation setup* in the respective mobile device menu item to open the Work confirmation form, in which you can select the checkbox *Auto confirm* in lines with the *Work type* "Put" (you only register the pick work on the mobile device in this case).
- **Picking process**—Automatically create/release shipments/loads/waves.
    - **Release to warehouse**—Automatically create shipments with the periodic job *Warehouse management > Release to warehouse > Automatic release of sales orders* (specify the required *Fulfillment policy* on the tab *Warehouse* in the Customer form or, at a general level, in the section *Warehouse management* of the Accounts receivable parameters).
    - **Automatically create waves**—The slider *Automate wave creation* in the wave template controls automatic wave creation when releasing to the warehouse.
    - **Automatically process waves**—Sliders in the wave template control automatic wave processing when releasing to the warehouse or when reaching the threshold in the wave template (online or in a batch job, as specified with the Warehouse management parameter *Process waves in batch*).
    - **Automatically release waves**—The slider *Automate wave release* in the wave template controls automatic wave releasing.

- **Automatically create loads**—Slider in the section *Loads* of the Warehouse management parameters; independently of this parameter, loads are created automatically when processing a wave for which no load has been created before.
- **Confirming shipments**—Automatically confirm outbound shipments.
  - **Work audit template**—Using a work audit template (see below).
  - **Periodic task**—Execute the task *Warehouse management > Periodic tasks > Process outbound shipments* (enter a filter on the *Load status* = "Loaded").

Depending on the general parameters for reservation ($\to$ Sect. 7.4.5), there is an automatic reservation when entering a sales order line. Apart from the general settings, the tab *Warehouse* in the Warehouse form includes the sliders *Reserve inventory at load posting* (reserving when releasing to warehouse from the Outbound load planning workbench) and *Reserve when orders are released by a batch job* (reserving in parallel to releasing with the periodic task *Warehouse management > Release to warehouse > Automatic release of sales orders*) which provide further options for the automatic reservation in advanced warehouse management.

With work audit templates (*Warehouse management > Setup > Work > Work audit template lines update*), you can assign additional actions to a mobile device menu item. If you select an audit template that contains a line with the *Function* "Event" and the *Event* "Shipping confirmed" in a mobile device menu item for sales shipments, each shipment for which you execute the warehouse work with this menu item is automatically confirmed. Further features in the audit template lines include the option to display and print data.

8.1.3.2 Options for Purchase Receipts

In advanced warehouse management, there are the following options for purchase order receipts:

- **Two-step order receipt**—Receive with reference to a purchase order number and execute the put-away work in a second step ($\to$ Sect. 8.1.2).
- **Load item receipt**—Receive with reference to a load (instead of the order).
- **License plate receipt**—Receive with reference to a license plate (preferably if you import a vendor ASN with, e.g., pallet numbers).
- **One-step receipt**—Receive and put away in one step.

A load item receipt is based on an inbound load, which includes one or more purchase orders. As a prerequisite for load item receipts, set up a mobile device menu item with the *Work creation process* "Load item receiving" and include it in the mobile device menu. If you enter a purchase order and create a load in the Inbound load planning workbench, you can select the *Load ID* (instead of the purchase order number) when registering the receipt with this mobile device menu item. Receiving generates put-away work, which has to be executed in the same way as a purchase order receipt.

Apart from the two-step receipt, which requires posting the initial receipt (on the default receipt location) and the put-away (to the final location) in two separate menu items on the mobile device, you can execute a one-step receipt to move the item to the final location immediately. As a prerequisite for one-step receipts, create a mobile device menu item with the *Work creation process* "Purchase order item receiving and put away", or "Purchase order line receiving and put away", or "Load item receiving and put away". With these menu items, receiving and putting away are done in one common transaction.

> *Note:* If you want to leave the items on the (default) receipt location and prevent generating and executing work for putting them to a final location (based on work templates and location directives), set up a work policy (*Warehouse management > Setup > Work > Work policies*) with the *Work order type* "Purchase orders", the applicable *Work process* (e.g., "Purchase order item receiving (and put away)"), the *Work creation method* "Never", and, on the tab *Inventory locations*, the (default) initial receipt location(s).

8.1.3.3 Storage Utilization and Limits

When Dynamics 365 searches a location for a put transaction (e.g., for the put away of a purchase receipt), it selects the first location with available storage capacity. The search sequence is specified on the tab *Sorting* in the query that is assigned to the applicable location directive (on the tab *Location Directive Actions*). For the definition of the capacity of a location, there are two different options:

- **Location stocking limits**—In the menu item *Warehouse management > Setup > Warehouse > Location stocking limits*, you can enter the maximum quantity of a unit (unit in the unit sequence group) per location. This maximum quantity can be specified at various levels—e.g., for a location profile (this record determines the maximum quantity for all locations with that profile).
- **Dimension settings in the location profile**—On the tab *Dimensions* in the location profile, you can specify the capacity of the locations in terms of weight and physical dimensions (depth, width, height).

If the dimension settings in the location profile are used, the available capacity of locations and the required capacity of released products—weight/volume, specified on the tab *Manage inventory* or in the Physical dimension form (→ Sect. 8.1.1)—are the basis for calculating if there is capacity on a location for storing a product.

Other settings in the location profile (e.g., the slider *Allow mixed items*) control whether it is possible to put an item to a location with current on-hand inventory.

If you want to get an overview of the available capacity, run the report *Warehouse management > Inquiries and reports > Warehouse monitoring reports > Warehouse utilization*.

8.1.3.4 Location Status

In the location profile, the sliders for the location status (*Enable item in location, Enable location activity date and time, Enable location status*) control whether the related fields (*Item number, Last activity date and time, Aging date, Location status*) in locations with this location profile are updated with the item, date/time, and status (empty/picking/storage) when posting a warehouse transaction.

If enabled, you can refer to the location status fields when setting up filters (*Edit query*) in the location directives.

8.1.3.5 Directive Codes

When generating warehouse work, Dynamics 365 searches for the applicable work template and the location directive separately. With directive codes, you can link a work template to a location directive. This is useful, for example, if some items should be subject to a work template that includes staging as a separate step that has to be done in a special location.

The following setup is required for the use of directive codes:

- **Directive code** (Warehouse management > Setup > Directive codes)—Create a code.
- **Work template**—Select the Directive code in applicable work template lines (only in "Put" work template lines of outbound processes).
- **Location directive**—Select the Directive code in location directives as needed.

When you create work that is based on a work template with an assigned directive code, Dynamics 365 searches the location directive with the same directive code.

8.1.3.6 Staging

Staging, an optional step after picking, enables collecting and preparing shipments in separate locations (staging locations) before transferring them to the final shipping location, where you execute loading (e.g., loading a truck).

In addition to the basic configuration for sales order shipments, the following setup is required for staging:

- **Directive code**—Additional directive code for staging.
- **Work template**—With work lines for staging and for loading (→ Fig. 8.13).
- **Location directive**—Location directive to put the items to the staging location.
- **Mobile device menu items**—With the *Work class* of the work template lines.

In order to link the "Put" work template line for staging to the related location directive, enter a directive code in this work template line. In the "Pick" line below this "Put" line, select the checkbox *Stop work* to prevent picking from the staging location shown as the next activity on the mobile device immediately after putting to the staging location.

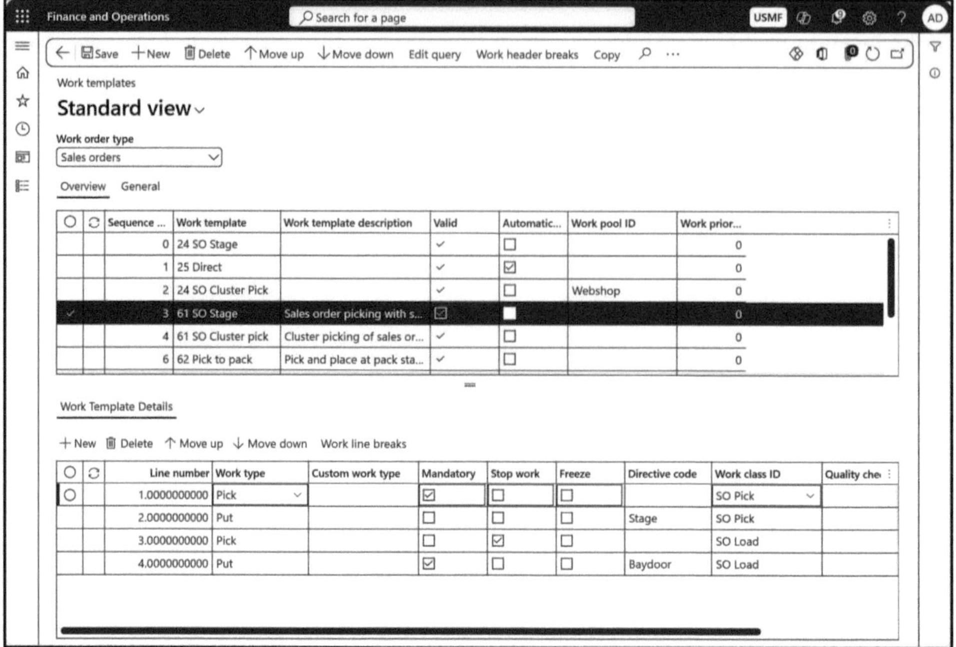

Fig. 8.13 Work template for staging

In addition to the work template, set up a location directive (with the directive code of the "Put" work) for putting to the staging location.

If there is no common location directive (without directive code) for putting to the final shipping location, which you can use after staging, create a separate directive code and location directive for this final put work.

In a similar way to the sales order picking process without staging, you can execute the outbound process with staging: Create the shipment, the load, and the wave, and release the wave (applying the work template for staging). The work created from the wave includes four steps in case of staging: Picking from the storage location, putting to the staging location, picking from the staging location, and putting to the final shipping location. On the mobile device, the warehouse work for staging (pick from the storage location and put to the staging location) and for loading (pick from the staging location and put to the final shipping location) has to be registered in two separate steps.

Anchoring is an additional option for staging and loading: In the Mobile device menu item form, you can set the slider *Anchoring* to "Yes" and subsequently set the option *Anchor by* to "Shipment" (or to "Load"). With anchoring, the warehouse worker can override the staging or loading location, and all remaining open put transactions for the same shipment (or load) will be directed to the new location.

8.1.3.7 Work Pools

Work pools are an option to group the work, for example, if you need to collect all work in a particular warehouse zone. In order to use work pools, the following setup is required:

- **Work pool** (Warehouse management > Setup > Work > Work pools)—Create a pool.
- **Work template**—Select the Work pool ID in applicable work templates.
- **Mobile device menu items**—Create or adjust menu items for using work pools (Directed by = "System grouping", System grouping field = "WorkPoolId").

In the work records (*Warehouse management* > *Work* > *All work*), the work pool is an editable field that is initialized from the work template.

On the mobile device, the work pool (instead of the work ID) is shown when opening a menu item that is configured to use work pools. The work is grouped by work pool in this case.

8.1.3.8 Transfer Orders

Transfer orders ($\rightarrow$ Sect. 7.4.4) are used to move items from one warehouse to another. While you can process transfer orders from and to a warehouse with or without advanced warehouse management, the way to process the transfer order is different for the different scenarios. Shipping a transfer order from a warehouse with advanced warehouse management works similarly to shipping a sales order, and receiving a transfer order in a warehouse with advanced warehouse management works similarly to receiving a purchase order.

In order to process transfer orders in a shipping or receiving warehouse with advanced warehouse management, the following setup is required (similar to the setup for purchase order receipts and sales order shipments):

- **Item, warehouse(s)**—Enabled for advanced warehouse management (for a transfer between two warehouses with advanced warehouse management, a transit warehouse with advanced warehouse management is required).
- **Work classes, work templates, location directives** ($\rightarrow$ Fig. 8.14)—For the work order types "Transfer issue" (in the from-warehouse) and "Transfer receipt" (in the to-warehouse).
- **Mobile device menu items**—for work on the mobile device.
  - **Transfer issue**—*Mode* = "Work", *Use existing work* = "Yes", work class for transfer issue.
  - **Transfer receipt**—*Mode* = "Work", *Use existing work* = "No", *Work creation process* = "License plate receiving" or "License plate receiving and put away" ("Transfer order line receiving", if advanced warehouse management is not enabled for the from-warehouse).
  - **Transfer receipt put-away**—*Mode* = "Work", *Use existing work* = "Yes", work class for transfer receipt (only required for two-step receipts).
- **Wave template**—In case you don't want to use the template for sales shipments.

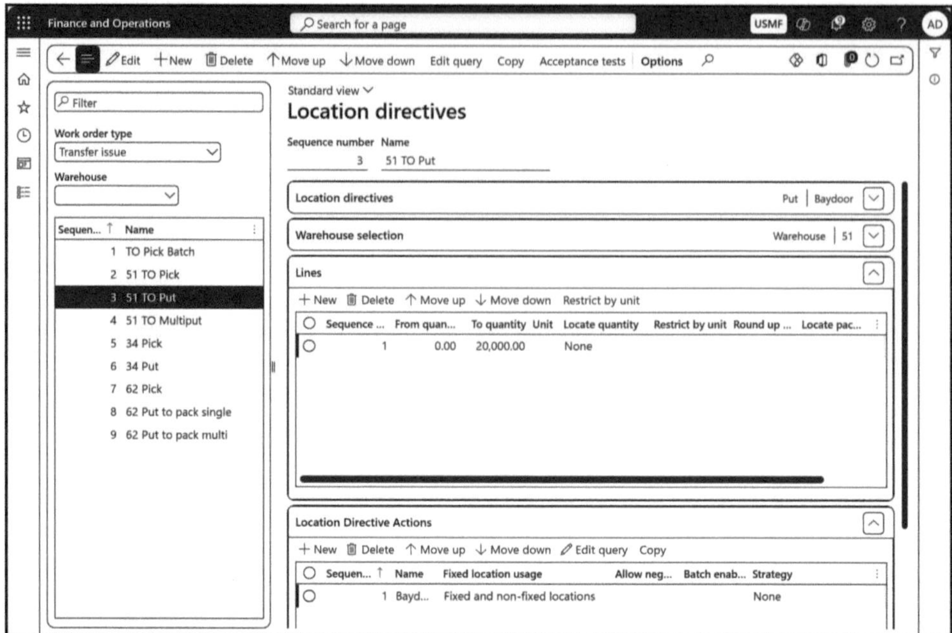

Fig. 8.14 Location directive for transfer issues ("Put" work to the shipping location)

The transfer order process in advanced warehouse management starts with creating a transfer order (*Inventory management > Inbound orders > Transfer order*) that ships from or to a warehouse with advanced warehouse management.

If advanced warehouse management is enabled for the from-warehouse, the first step is to reserve the item (automatically or manually). Then create a shipment (similar to sales order shipments) by releasing the transfer order to the warehouse—automatically with the periodic job *Warehouse management > Release to warehouse > Automatic release of transfer orders*, or manually (e.g., with the button *Ship/Operations/Release to warehouse* in the Transfer order form). Create the load and the wave next, assign the transfer order, process the wave, and release the wave (depending on settings in the wave template, the steps are executed automatically). On the mobile device, you can subsequently execute the picking work in the from-warehouse (including putting to the final shipping location).

Confirming the shipment in advanced warehouse management, which closes the shipment and the load, posts a transfer to the transit warehouse.

In order to receive the item in the to-warehouse, the warehouse worker has to log on to the appropriate warehouse on the mobile device. Executing the transfer receipt work on the mobile device works similarly to the receipt of a purchase order. If you receive a transfer from a warehouse with advanced warehouse management, use a menu item for "License plate receiving", which requires entering or scanning the license plate(s) that have been assigned to the item in the prior shipping process. If advanced warehouse management is not enabled for the from-warehouse, use a menu item for "Transfer order line receiving" (or "Transfer order item receiving"), which requires entering or scanning the transfer order number.

If you ship from a warehouse for which advanced warehouse management processes are not enabled, you have to execute the standard transfer order process there. If advanced warehouse management is not enabled for the to-warehouse, the standard transfer order process has to be executed for receiving.

Note: With a mobile device menu item with the *Mode* "Indirect" and the *Activity code* "Create transfer order from license plates", you can initiate transfer orders from a mobile device. The transfer orders are finally created with the subsequent job *Warehouse management > Periodic tasks > Process warehouse app events*.

8.1.3.9 Production Orders

In a production environment, you can use advanced warehouse management for material picking and the receipt of manufactured items.

As a prerequisite for processing production orders with advanced warehouse management, the following setup is required (similar to the setup for purchase order receipts and sales order shipments):

- **Items**—Materials and manufactured items enabled for advanced warehouse management.
- **Warehouse**—Enabled for advanced warehouse management; one or more warehouse locations in the production area.
- **Production input location**—*Input location* of the resource or resource group that consumes material, or *Default production input location* in the warehouse (specifies the location from which raw material is consumed, which means that this is the "Put" location for warehouse work).
- **Production output location**—*Output location* in the resource or resource group of the last operation, or *Default production finished goods location* in the warehouse (specifies the location which originally receives the manufactured item when reporting as finished, which means that this is the "Pick" location for put-away warehouse work).
- **Work classes, work templates**—For the work order types "Raw material picking" and "Finished goods put away".
- **Location directives**—For the *Work order type* "Raw material picking" and the *Work type* "Pick", and for the *Work order type* "Finished goods put away" and the *Work type* "Put".
- **Wave template**—Separate from the sales shipment templates (select the option "Production orders" in the left pane of the Wave template form).
- **Mobile device menu items**—for work on the mobile device.
- **Material picking**—*Mode* = "Work", *Use existing work* = "Yes", work class for "Raw material picking".

- **Report as finished** (if production orders are reported as finished on a mobile device in the warehouse)—*Mode* = "Work", *Use existing work* = "No", *Work creation process* = "Report as finished" (or "Report as finished and put away").
- **Finished goods put-away** (for two-step receipts, or if production orders are first reported as finished on Production floor execution terminals or in the Dynamics 365 web client)—*Mode* = "Work", *Use existing work* = "Yes", work class for "Finished goods put away".

In order to use advanced warehouse management in manufacturing, create and process a production order (*Production control > Production Orders > All production orders*) as described in → Sect. 5.4.2. Depending on the settings for automatic reservation (field *Reservation* on the tab *Setup* in the Production order detail form, initialized from the Production control parameters), you might need to reserve the raw materials manually after estimation.

Once the production order is released, you can immediately create a production wave (*Warehouse management > Outbound waves > Production waves > All waves*), assign the BOM lines of the production order (button *Wave/ Wave/Maintain productions*), process the wave, and release the wave. Depending on settings in the applicable production wave template, these steps are executed automatically. Processing the wave creates warehouse work for raw material picking, which you can view with the button *Wave/ Related information/Work* in the Wave form. Separately creating a shipment (button *Warehouse/Actions/ Release to warehouse* in the Production order form) before creating a wave is only required if you need additional materials for a released production order.

On the mobile device, you can execute the warehouse work for raw material picking (transfer to a *Production input location*) in the next step. Depending on the setting for the *Issue status after raw material picking* (field on the tab *Inventory and warehouse management* in the Warehouse form), the material is immediately consumed (issue status "Picked") or only reserved (issue status "Reserved physical") after putting the item to the production input location.

After starting the production order, you can subsequently post a picking list in the Dynamics 365 web client. The picking list posts the physical transaction (→ Sect. 7.2.4) related to the registered warehouse work, depending on the *Issue status after raw material picking* updating the issue status from "Picked" to "Deducted", or initially posting the consumption and updating the issue status from "Reserved physical" to "Deducted".

In order to report the production order as finished and to receive the manufactured item, open a menu item for "Report as finished" or—for one-step receipts—"Report as finished and put away" on the mobile device (which works similarly to a purchase order receipt). The mobile device transaction posts a report as finished journal in production, and receives the product in the *Production output location*. In case of a one-step receipt ("Report as finished and put away"), the product is directly received on the final floor or bulk location. In case of a two-step receipt, the initial receipt on the mobile device generates warehouse work for the put-away to the final location, which has to be executed in a separate menu item on the mobile device.

If you report as finished on a mobile device in the warehouse, you need to update the production order status to "Reported as finished" subsequently—e.g., with the button *Production order/Process/Report as finished* in the Production order form.

Instead of reporting a production order as finished on the mobile device, you can also update the production order status to "Reported as finished" first—e.g., on a Production floor execution terminal when reporting the last operation. Reporting as finished this way receives the manufacturing item initially and, based on the work template for "Finished goods put away", creates warehouse work for the put-away to the final bulk or floor location.

8.1.3.10 Customer Returns

Based on a return order (→ Sect. 4.6.1), which you enter in the Sales and marketing module, you can register the receipt of the returned item in the warehouse on a mobile device.

As a prerequisite for processing customer returns with advanced warehouse management, the following setup is required (similar to the setup for purchase order receipts):

- **Work class, work template**—For the *Work order type* "Return orders".
- **Location directive**—For the *Work order type* "Return orders" and the *Work type* "Put", usually directing to particular return locations.
- **Mobile device menu item**—With the *Mode* = "Work", *Use existing work* = "No", *Work creation process* = "Return order receiving" (or "Return order receiving and put away").
- **Mobile device disposition code**—With reference to a *Return disposition code*.
- **Warehouse management parameters**—Item arrival journal (*Default return order journal*) in the section *General*, tab *Returns*.

Mobile device disposition codes (*Warehouse management > Setup > Mobile device > Disposition codes*), which you can select on a mobile device when registering a transaction, are separate from the disposition codes for return orders (→ Sect. 4.6.1), which control the handling of returned items. But the column *Return disposition code* in the Mobile device disposition code form (→ Fig. 8.15) enables assigning a return disposition code. Apart from the *Return disposition code*, you can also assign an *Inventory status* for blocking purposes to a mobile device disposition code (→ Sect. 8.1.4).

When you receive a returned item with reference to a return order in the warehouse, open a menu item for "Return order receiving" or—for one-step receipts—"Return order receiving and put away" on the mobile device. In the menu item, register the RMA number, the item number, the license plate (like in a purchase receipt, if not generated automatically), the quantity, the unit, and the (mobile device) disposition code.

The mobile device posts an inventory registration (item arrival with the *Default return order journal* in the parameters) for the return order and receives the item in the default

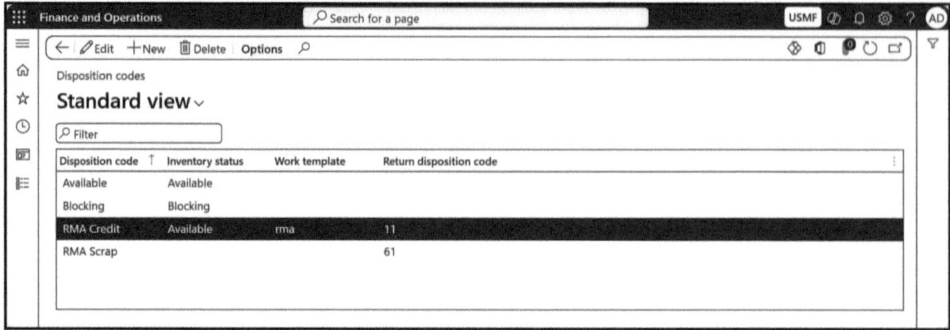

Fig. 8.15 Managing a mobile device disposition code

receipt location of the warehouse (or, in case of a one-step receipt, directly in the return location specified in the location directive). In case of a two-step receipt, the initial receipt on the mobile device generates warehouse work for the put-away to the return location, which has to be executed in a separate menu item on the mobile device.

Once you have finished the work on the mobile device (which replaces the item arrival journal transactions in a basic warehouse), you can process the return order as usual and credit the customer if applicable.

If enabled in the Warehouse management parameters (slider *Enable return order creation from mobile device* in the section *General*, tab *Returns*), you can also process unannounced customer returns—with return details (in case you ship items already with a return label) and blind returns. You can—based on the setup for Return item policies (*Warehouse management > Setup > Return items > Return item policies*) and Return item receiving policies (*Warehouse management > Setup > Mobile device > Return item receiving policies*)—register blind returns with a mobile device menu item for "Return item receiving" (*Mode* = "Work", *Use existing work* = "No"). Closing the menu item with the button *LP Complete* immediately creates the return order and registers the initial receipt. Otherwise, open the Mixed license plate receiving form (*Warehouse Management > Inquiries and reports > Mixed license plate receiving*) and click the button *License plate/Complete license plate* for this purpose.

> *Note:* Apart from the option of simply using a return location for inspection (specified in the location directive) or applying a particular inventory status (specified in the mobile device disposition code), you can also use quick quality checks and regular quality orders in advanced warehouse management.

8.1.3.11 Canceling Warehouse Work

If warehouse work is still open, you can cancel it with the button *Work/ Work/Cancel work* in the Work form (*Warehouse management > Work > All work*). In case you only want to block a particular work temporarily, click the button *Work/Work/Block work* in this form.

You can also cancel open work on the mobile device. For this purpose, create a mobile device menu item with the *Mode* "Indirect" and the *Activity code* "Cancel work" and include it in the mobile device menu.

Once the warehouse work has been executed (*Work status* = "Closed"), it is not possible to cancel it in the Work form or on the mobile device. Administrators can use the menu item *Warehouse management > Periodic tasks > Clean up > Cancel work* to cancel work that is in progress or closed.

After loading a sales order shipment, it is possible to reverse the warehouse work with the button *Loads/Work/ Reverse work* in the Load form if the load has not been confirmed yet (*Load status* = "Loaded")—in a subsequent dialog, you can select in which location the items are received back. If it has been confirmed, you can reverse the confirmation with the button *Ship and receive/ Reverse/ Reverse shipment confirmation* in the Load form. And if the packing slip has been posted already, you can cancel it with the button *Ship and receive/Reverse/Cancel packing slips* in the Load form (which sets the status back to a confirmed load with *Load status* = "Loaded").

8.1.4 Tasks within the Warehouse

Apart from inbound and outbound transactions, warehouse operations include internal transactions (like counting and movements between locations), internal tasks (like inventory blocking), and inquiries.

8.1.4.1 Inventory Blocking

The purpose of inventory blocking is to stop transactions—e.g., prevent shipping a pallet (license plate) with quality issues. In advanced warehouse management, you can block inventory by changing the dimension value of the storage dimension *Inventory status* for an on-hand quantity. This blocking applies the inventory blocking functionality in inventory management (→ Sect. 7.4.6).

Changing the inventory status, which blocks or unblocks inventory, generates a transaction that you can view later on.

After blocking a quantity in inventory, outbound transactions are not possible. If you receive a purchase order line with the status "Blocked", the quantity is blocked after receipt.

In order to use the inventory status for blocking, the following setup is required:

- **Inventory status**—Status value with "Inventory blocking" (→ Sect. 8.1.1).
- **Mobile device disposition code**—For status changes in parallel to warehouse transactions.
- **Mobile device menu items**—For changing the inventory status/disposition code on the mobile device.

If you want to be able to change the inventory status in a separate step on the mobile device, create a mobile device menu item with the setting *Mode* = "Work", *Use existing work* = "No", *Work creation process* = "Inventory status change", and include it in the mobile device menu.

It is not possible to directly update the inventory status in parallel with a warehouse transaction on the mobile device, but you can use a Mobile device disposition code (*Warehouse management > Setup > Mobile device > Disposition codes*) for this purpose. The disposition code can be assigned to an inventory status. If you want to be able to update the inventory status (via the disposition code) when registering the initial receipt in an inbound arrival, set the slider *Display disposition code* in the applicable mobile device menu items to "Yes". If the location for the put-away of the received items depends on the disposition code, create a particular location directive with the respective disposition code (e.g., a location directive for the *Work order type* "Purchase orders" and the *Work type* "Put" to store damaged items in separate locations).

Apart from changing the inventory status with a mobile device menu item on the mobile device, you can update the inventory status in the Dynamics 365 web client:

- **Inventory status change** (Warehouse management > Periodic tasks > Warehouse management inventory status change)—With flexible filter options.
- **Warehouse status change** (Warehouse management > Periodic tasks > Warehouse status change)—For blocking/unblocking at the warehouse level (select the warehouse and the new status (field Change status to) in the upper pane of this form, then click the button Details to access the individual items or locations).
- **On-hand inquiry** (Warehouse management > Inquiries and reports > On hand by location)—Button Inventory status change in the toolbar of the tab On hand in the on-hand inquiry by location.
- **Quality order**—Automatically change the inventory status from a quality order if specified in the test group (Inventory management > Setup > Quality control > Test groups, slider Update inventory status on the tab General).

On a license plate, a mixed inventory status with partly blocked and partly unblocked inventory is not possible. If you want to block a partial quantity of a license plate, move the required quantity to another license plate and block it there. For locations, you can specify in the location profile whether a mixed inventory status is allowed.

8.1.4.2 Movements and Adjustments

Movements and adjustments are manual transactions in inventory. Apart from registering these transactions on a mobile device, you can use regular inventory journals (which only generate inventory transactions, not warehouse-specific transactions) and enter all required inventory dimensions manually ($\rightarrow$ Sect. 7.4.2).

Warehouse adjustments are used for manual changes of the item quantity. In that respect, adjustments generate inventory counting journals that post the inventory transaction. The journal name for these journals is specified in the adjustment type (*Warehouse management* > *Setup* > *Inventory* > *Adjustment types*).

The following setup is required for registering adjustments on the mobile device:

- **Adjustment types**—For grouping purposes, specify the inventory journal name and control whether existing reservations are removed.
- **Mobile device menu item**—*Mode* = "Work", *Use existing work* = "No", *Work creation process* = "Adjustment in" or "Adjustment out".

The default value for the field *Adjustment type*, which is displayed later on the mobile device, is specified in the mobile device menu item, a general default in the Warehouse management parameters (section *General*, tab *Adjustments*).

In order to record an adjustment on the mobile device, select the menu item for "Adjustment in" or "Adjustment out" and register the quantity by which you want to change inventory. The quantity is always a positive number—in case of an item issue, select a menu item with the *Work creation process* "Adjustment out".

Whereas adjustments change the on-hand quantity, movements register manual transfers from one location to another (→ Fig. 8.16). As a prerequisite for registering

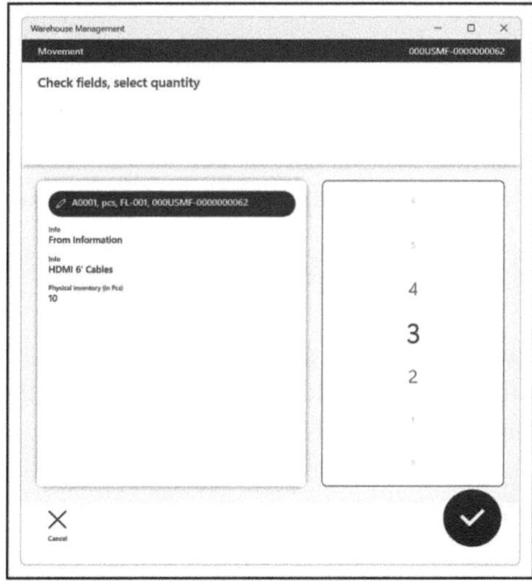

Fig. 8.16 Registering a movement in the mobile app

movements on the mobile device, a mobile device menu item with the required settings (*Mode* = "Work", *Use existing work* = "No", *Work creation process* = "Movement") has to be set up and included in the mobile device menu.

If required, you can use location directives to suggest the put location in a movement (e.g., for the movement from a quality test location to a storage location). For this purpose, the following setup is required:

- **Mobile device menu item for creating work**—*Mode* = "Work", *Use existing work* = "No", *Work creation process* = "Movement by template", *Create movement* = "Yes".
- **Work class, work template, location directives**—For the work order type "Inventory movement".
- **Mobile device menu item for executing work**—*Mode* = "Work", *Use existing work* = "Yes", work class for inventory movement.

> *Note:* Apart from transfers within a warehouse, you can also register transfers between different warehouses with a simple movement (mobile device menu item with *Mode* = "Work", *Use existing work* = "No", *Work creation process* = "Warehouse transfer") if you don't need a transfer order for the transfer.

8.1.4.3 Inventory Counting

The purpose of counting is to audit the physical quantity of items and to adjust the on-hand quantity in Dynamics 365 to the counted quantity in case of discrepancies. The discrepancies, which are calculated based on the counting transactions on the mobile device, are posted in a regular inventory counting journal. The Warehouse management parameters determine the adjustment type, and with the adjustment type, the journal name for the counting transaction.

In advanced warehouse management, there are the following options for counting:

- **Periodic counting**—In a periodic interval (e.g., annual stocktaking).
- **Threshold counting**—Counting when inventory reaches the threshold limit.
- **Spot counting**—Ad-hoc counting on the mobile device.

The following setup is required for inventory counting on mobile devices:

- **Location profile**—In the location profile of all locations that are subject to counting (e.g., not for user locations), set the slider *Allow cycle counting* to "Yes".
- **Warehouse management parameters**—In the section *Cycle counting* of the parameters, enter a default work class and a default adjustment type. Select the checkbox *Remove reservations* in the settings of this adjustment type if you want to avoid counting to be blocked by reservations in sales orders (and other issue transactions).
- **Unit sequence group**—Controls the available units for counting.

Periodic counting has the purpose of creating and executing counting work at a regular interval. In addition to the general setup for counting on mobile devices, the following setup is required for periodic counting:

- **Mobile device menu item**—*Mode* = "Work", *Use existing work* = "Yes", work class for cycle counting, additional settings (e.g., the field *Number of attempts*, which controls how often to re-count in case of a discrepancy) with the button *Cycle counting* in the action pane (→ Fig. 8.17).
- **Warehouse worker**—On the tab *Work* in the Work user form, select the limits for counting discrepancies that the worker can post without approval (if the worker is a supervisor, no approval is required to post discrepancies).

The first step in the process of periodic counting is to generate the counting work. You can create this work with the periodic activity *Warehouse management > Cycle counting > Cycle count work by location* or *Warehouse management > Cycle counting > Cycle count work by item*. The open counting work that has been generated is shown in the Open cycle count form (*Warehouse management > Cycle counting > Open cycle work*).

Based on the created counting work, you can execute counting on the mobile device with the menu item that is set up for cycle counting. Register the quantity (including "0") in all counting units per item and location, and confirm the quantity in case of discrepancies (depending on the settings in the menu item). Depending on settings in the work user,

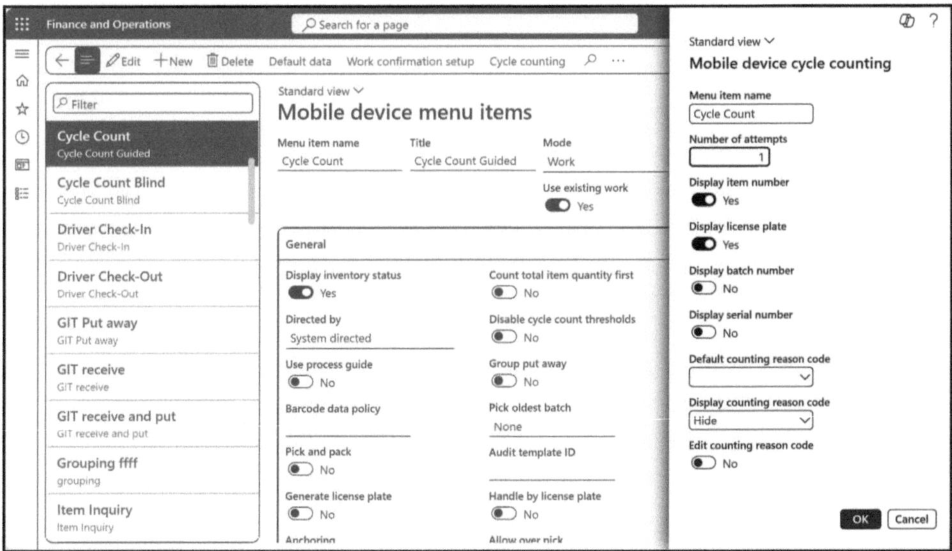

Fig. 8.17 Settings for cycle counting in the mobile device menu item

discrepancies between the counted quantity and the current quantity in Dynamics 365 are posted immediately in order to adjust the current quantity. Discrepancies, which are not posted immediately, are shown in the menu item *Warehouse management > Work > Warehouse > Cycle count work pending review*. In this form, the button *Work/Work/Cycle counting* provides access to the Cycle counting transactions form, in which you can click the button *Accept count* to post the inventory adjustment (if applicable).

Threshold counting is a strategy to execute counting automatically when the inventory reaches the threshold limit. As a prerequisite for threshold counting, set up a cycle counting threshold (*Warehouse management > Setup > Cycle counting > Cycle count threshold*). With the buttons *Select items* and *Select locations*, you can specify filter criteria for the threshold. Registering an outbound transaction on the mobile device (e.g., picking) then triggers threshold counting if the quantity on the location reaches the cycle counting threshold. If the slider *Process cycle counting immediately* in the cycle counting threshold is set to "No", Dynamics 365 generates cycle counting work that has to be executed later on the mobile device (similar to periodic counting work). If this slider is set to "Yes", a dialog for counting is immediately shown when registering an outbound transaction.

Spot counting is an ad-hoc counting on a mobile device. As a prerequisite for spot counting, a mobile device menu item (required settings: *Mode* = "Work", *Use existing work* = "No", *Work creation process* = "Spot cycle counting", additional settings with the button *Cycle counting*) needs to be set up. With this menu item, you can execute spot counting in a similar way to periodic cycle counting (but you can select any location). Posting the counting transactions and resolving discrepancies works similarly to periodic counting.

> *Note:* Optionally, you can use cycle count plans (*Warehouse management > Setup > Cycle counting > Cycle count plans*) as a structured basis for periodically creating counting work (in the menu item *Warehouse management > Cycle counting > Cycle count scheduling*).

8.1.4.4 Replenishment and Warehouse Slotting

Replenishment within the warehouse aims to prepare an efficient picking process by moving the required items from buffer locations to picking locations. In Dynamics 365, there are two basic strategies for replenishing locations:

- **Based on minimum/maximum quantities**—Uses minimum and maximum stocking limits at the location level.
- **Based on demand**—Replenishing required quantity on picking locations, triggered by the picking process for outbound orders.

Minimum/maximum replenishment is used to fill a location to the maximum if the current quantity is below the minimum (e.g., as the first work in the morning). For a minimum/maximum replenishment, the following setup is required:

- **Replenishment template** (*Warehouse management* > *Setup* > *Replenishment* > *Replenishment templates*)—Replenishment type "Minimum or maximum" (→ Fig. 8.18), one or more template details lines with the min/max quantity for the selected items and locations (buttons *Select products* and *Select locations to replenish*).
- **Work class, work template, location directives**—For the work order type "Replenishment".
- **Fixed locations for items** (*Warehouse management* > *Setup* > *Warehouse* > *Fixed locations*)—Required if you want to refill empty locations.
- **Mobile device menu item**—*Mode* = "Work", *Use existing work* = "Yes", work class for replenishment.

If you use minimum/maximum replenishment, run the replenishment batch job (*Warehouse management* > *Replenishment* > *Replenishments*) to generate replenishment work. In the warehouse, execute the replenishment on the mobile device with the menu item for replenishment.

Wave demand replenishment—unlike minimum/maximum replenishment, which is refilling locations independently of current picking processes—refills locations when processing a wave. Wave demand replenishment is only created if there is no available quantity at the location that is selected by the location directive for picking.

If you want to use wave demand replenishment, the following setup is required in addition to the regular setup for sales shipments:

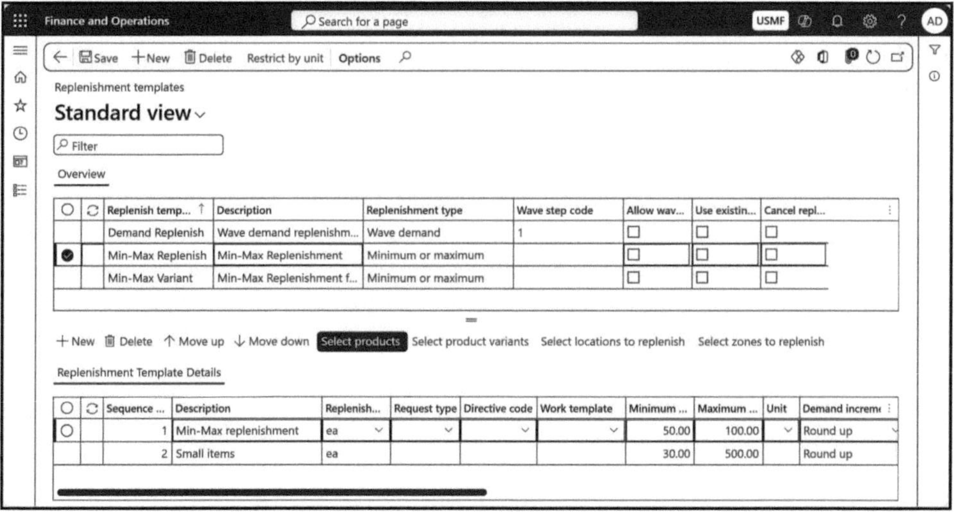

Fig. 8.18 Setting up a min/max demand replenishment template

- **Replenishment template**—With the *Replenishment type* "Wave demand" and a *Wave step code*.
- **Wave template**—With the additional method "replenish" and the wave step code of the replenishment template.
- **Work class, work template, location directives**—For the work order type "Replenishment" (match "Put" locations in the replenishment location directive with "Pick" locations in the sales order picking location directive).
- **Mobile device menu item**—*Mode* = "Work", *Use existing work* = "Yes", work class for replenishment (you can use the same menu item as for minimum/maximum replenishment).

If the wave template for sales order shipments is set to automatically release waves, set the slider *Automate replenishment work release* in the wave template to "Yes" (replenishment has to be released and executed before sales picking).

In order to execute wave replenishment, create the shipment, the load, and the wave for sales order picking (applying the wave template for replenishment), assign the sales order, process the wave, and release the wave (depending on settings in the wave template, the steps are executed automatically). If no quantity is available on the picking location, a replenishment wave with replenishment work is created when processing the wave for sales order picking. The sales order wave is automatically blocked until the replenishment work is finished. On the mobile device, execute the replenishment work before sales picking and loading.

Apart from the wave demand replenishment, load demand replenishment is another type of demand replenishment. The difference between these two replenishment types is that wave demand is processed automatically (if specified in the wave template), whereas load demand replenishment needs to be calculated with a batch job that can sum the demand for several loads.

Warehouse slotting, which is another option to refill locations in preparation for picking, is a replenishment before releasing orders to the warehouse—in contrast to the wave demand replenishment, which creates the replenishment not before the picking wave is released. For warehouse slotting, a slotting template (*Warehouse management > Setup > Replenishment > Slotting templates*) for each respective warehouse is required. In order to generate the replenishment work for the slotting template, execute the batch job *Warehouse management > Replenishment > Run slotting* (in the dialog, set the sliders *Generate demand*, *Locate demand*, and *Create replenishment work* to "Yes") or click the corresponding buttons in the Slotting template form (*Generate demand*, *Locate demand*, and *Run replenishment*).

8.1.4.5 Warehouse Inquiries and Work Lists on Mobile Devices

In the Dynamics 365 web client, the inquiry *Warehouse management > Inquiries and reports > On hand by location* is one of the main pages for viewing the current inventory in advanced warehouse management. In order to show the locations with the item quantities, select a warehouse and refresh the page (or select the checkbox *Refresh across locations*). If you want to change the inventory status of a selected quantity, click the button *Inventory status change* in the toolbar of the tab *On hand*.

On the mobile device, there are also inquiries that display the current quantity in inventory. In order to set up a mobile device inquiry showing the on-hand quantity per item (or per location), create a mobile device menu item with the *Mode* "Indirect" and the *Activity code* "Item inquiry" (or "Location inquiry") and include it in the mobile device menu. You can access the respective inquiry on a mobile device. In the item inquiry, enter or scan the item number to view the quantity of the item at the different locations.

Another useful inquiry on mobile devices is the "Open work list". You can set up one or more menu items with the *Mode* "Indirect", the *Activity code* "Display open work list", and the work classes that you want to view with the respective menu item. With the buttons *Field list* and *Edit query* in the Mobile device menu item form, you can specify the displayed fields and add filter criteria. On a mobile device, an open work list displays the open work (assigned to the selected work classes), which you can further filter and sort. Apart from viewing open work, you can click on a work header in the work list on a mobile device to register the execution.

8.1.5   Case Study Exercises

Exercise 8.1—Warehouse Setup
In order to investigate the options for the warehouse setup, create a new location format L-## (## = your user ID) with two segments: A segment with a length of one digit, followed by the separator "-" and a 3-digit segment.

Then set up a location profile F-## for floor locations and a location profile B-## for bulk locations. Both location profiles refer to the new location format L-## and allow cycle counting, but only floor locations use license plate tracking. Accept the default settings in the other fields of the Location profile form.

Once the basic setup is done, create a warehouse WH-## which applies advanced warehouse management processes. This warehouse has the receiving location "RECV", the shipping location "SHIP", three floor locations ("F-001" to "F-003"), and six bulk locations ("1-001" to "2-003"). Floor locations and bulk locations refer to the appropriate location profiles that you have created before. The location "RECV" is the *Default receipt location* in the warehouse.

Exercise 8.2—Work Template, Location Directive, Wave Template
The purchase put-away work for the warehouse WH-## of exercise 8.1 should be registered in separate menu items on the mobile device. Create a new work class PO-## for this purpose.

Then create a work template for purchase orders with one line for pick work and one line for put work, which only refers to the warehouse WH-## and this new work class. In addition, create a work template for sales orders that is only used in this warehouse and contains one line for pick work and one line for put work (no staging). The work template lines refer to an existing sales order work class.

In order to use the warehouse in purchasing and sales, related location directives are required. Create a location directive for the warehouse WH-##, which specifies putting purchase order receipts to bulk locations in case of full pallets and to floor locations otherwise. Then enter a location directive for sales picking, which should pick full pallets from bulk locations. Other units should be picked from floor locations first, and in the second line from bulk locations (if all floor locations are empty). The sales order directive should put items to the location "SHIP".

Finally, set up a wave template T-##, which does not apply any automatic action, for the warehouse WH-##.

Exercise 8.3—Mobile Device Menu and Work User

A new mobile device menu is required for the warehouse work in the following exercises. Create the following mobile device menu items for this purpose:

- Menu item "##-PO-Receive" for the initial receipt of purchase shipments (with the *Work creation process* "Purchase order line receiving").
- Menu item "##-PO-Put" for the transfer from the default receipt location to the final location in purchase receipts (referring to the work class created in exercise 8.2 and *Directed by* = "User directed").
- Menu item "##-SO-Direct" for sales order picking (referring to the sales order work class selected in exercise 8.2 and *Directed by* = "User grouping").

Then set up a new mobile device menu "##-Main" with these menu items. In addition, the menu should include a menu item "About" and a menu item for logging off.

In the next step, set up a warehouse worker who is linked to the worker/employee assigned to your Dynamics 365 user account. On the tab *Work users* of the Work user form, enter a user with the user ID X-##, the menu name which you have created in the current exercise, and the warehouse WH-## of exercise 8.1.

Exercise 8.4—Warehouse Management Settings in the Released Product

In order to apply advanced warehouse management to a product, you need an appropriate storage dimension group, a reservation hierarchy, and a unit sequence group. In this exercise, you can use an existing storage dimension group. But you want to create a new reservation hierarchy R-##, which does not contain tracking dimensions, and a unit sequence group U-##, which includes pieces and pallets (pallets are the default unit for purchasing).

Then create the item I-##-W with the name "##-AdvWarehouseMgmt" in the Released product form. It is a stocked product without variants or batch numbers, but you want to use the advanced warehouse processes. Select an item group for merchandise and an item model group with FIFO-valuation. The item does not require approved vendors. The base purchase price and the base cost price are USD 50. The base sales price is USD 100. The unit of measurement for the item is "Pieces" in all areas except purchasing. In purchasing, the default unit for the item is pallets (1 pallet = 10 pieces). Make sure to choose the same units of measurement that you have selected in the unit sequence U-##. Assign the new item to the unit sequence group U-## and the reservation hierarchy R-##.

> *Note:* If the number sequence for product numbers is set up for automatic numbering, don't enter a product number.

Exercise 8.5—Warehouse Management Processes in Purchasing

Enter a purchase order with 34 units of the item I-##-W of exercise 8.4 and any vendor (e.g., the vendor of exercise 3.2) for a receipt in the warehouse WH-## of exercise 8.1. Confirm the order and check the inventory transaction that refers to the purchase order line.

Log on to the mobile device with the work user X-## of exercise 8.3. Open the menu item for receiving the purchase order and post the receipt for the complete quantity of the purchase order.

Which status do the inventory transactions and the warehouse transactions of the item show afterward? Open the inquiry "On hand by location" in the *Warehouse management* menu, select the warehouse WH-##, and take note of the license plate with the posted quantity.

In the next step, open the mobile device menu item for the put-away of the purchase receipt and post the transaction (refer to the license plate shown in the previous inquiry).

If you review the inventory transactions, the warehouse transactions, and the inquiry "On hand by location" for the warehouse WH-## again, what is different now? Finally, post the product receipt based on the mobile device transactions of the current exercise.

> *Note*: To register transactions on the mobile device, use the *Warehouse Management* app (make sure that the *Connection settings* in the app provide access to the training company), or use the form *WHSWorkExecute*, which you can access with the web address *https://XXX.com /?mi=action:WHSWorkExecute&cmp=YYY* (*XXX.com* = URL of the Dynamics application, *YYY* = Training company).

Exercise 8.6—Warehouse Management Processes in Sales

A customer (e.g., the customer of exercise 4.1) orders 12 units of the item I-##-W, which you have purchased in the previous exercise. Enter an appropriate sales order that is shipped from the warehouse WH-##, reserve the quantity, and create the shipment. What is the status of the inventory transactions and the warehouse transactions now?

Create a load for the shipment. Then enter, process, and release a wave which is based on the wave template T-## of exercise 8.2. Take note of the *Work ID* of the warehouse work that has been generated when processing the wave. Check the inventory transactions and the warehouse transactions of the item again. What is different now? Review the inquiry

"On hand by location" for the warehouse WH-## and take note of the license plate shown for the floor location.

In the next step, log on to the mobile device with the work user X-## of exercise 8.3 and open the mobile device menu item for sales order picking. Post the pick transaction that is related to the work ID and, when you pick from the floor location, to the license plate noted before.

Check the inventory transactions, the warehouse transactions, and the on-hand quantity in the warehouse WH-## again. What is different now? Finally, post the packing slip for the sales order based on the mobile device transactions of the current exercise.

8.2 Transportation Management

The purpose of transportation management in Dynamics 365 is to select external freight carriers for inbound and outbound shipments and to manage these inbound and outbound shipments. Transportation management is based on advanced warehouse management, but it is also possible to use it independently.

Based on the load (e.g., a truckload), the origin address, and the destination address, you can run a calculation of transportation routes and rates, and create a route based on this calculation (or enter it completely manually). Transportation tenders, dock appointments, and the reconciliation of the freight invoice with the route are further options in the transportation management (→ Fig. 8.19).

Note: For inbound shipments, you can use the Landed cost module instead of the transportation management if you got goods in transit and take ownership of the items before receiving them in the warehouse (which is a common practice in international trade).

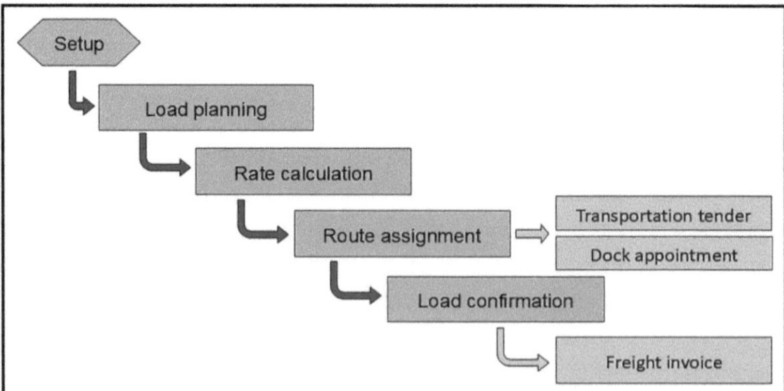

Fig. 8.19 Overview of the transportation management functionality in Dynamics 365

8.2.1   Core Setup for Transportation Management

Before you can perform the processes in transportation management, you have to complete the required setup.

8.2.1.1 Transportation Engines

Transportation engines, which include rate engines and transit time engines, are calculation routines that compute the price and the time for transportation. Engines include a .NET assembly and work like plug-ins for the individual carrier contracts. While it is easy to integrate additional transportation engines, the standard application includes a few default engines.

The engines are divided into the following types:

- **Rate engines**—Calculate the transportation cost.
- **Generic engines**—Simple engines that calculate the result (e.g., the distribution of costs for a load) based on call parameters. They are used by other engines.
- **Mileage engines**—Calculate the distance between origin and destination.
- **Zone engines**—Calculate the zone of the origin and the number of zones between the origin and destination.
- **Transit time engines**—Calculate the transportation time.
- **Freight bill types**—Used for automatic freight bill reconciliation.

Rate engines (*Transportation management > Setup > Engines > Rate engine*) are the core engines for calculating transportation costs. They can refer to sub-engines like the mileage engines.

Rating metadata (*Transportation management > Setup > Rating > Rating metadata*) determine the lookup criteria for calculating the rates of a shipping carrier. These lookup criteria are fields that are relevant for the transport—for example, the postal code of the destination address. They are used as parameters for the different rate engines and have to match the internal requirements of the respective rate engine. Basic metadata are generated when initializing the base engine data in the Transportation management parameters.

Mileage engines (*Transportation management > Setup > Engines > Mileage engine*) *determine the distance between the origin and destination addresses, typically* based on postal codes. You can enter or import the distance between the postal codes of the relevant origin and destination addresses on the tab *Details* of the mileage engines (→ Fig. 8.20). The button *Metadata* provides access to the definition of available and mandatory fields for entering distances. If you add or change a field in the metadata, the related column is subsequently shown in the mileage engine. But be aware that the field selection has to match the requirements of the engine.

Transit time engines (*Transportation management > Setup > Engines > Transit time engine*) determine the required time for the transport between addresses. The setup is

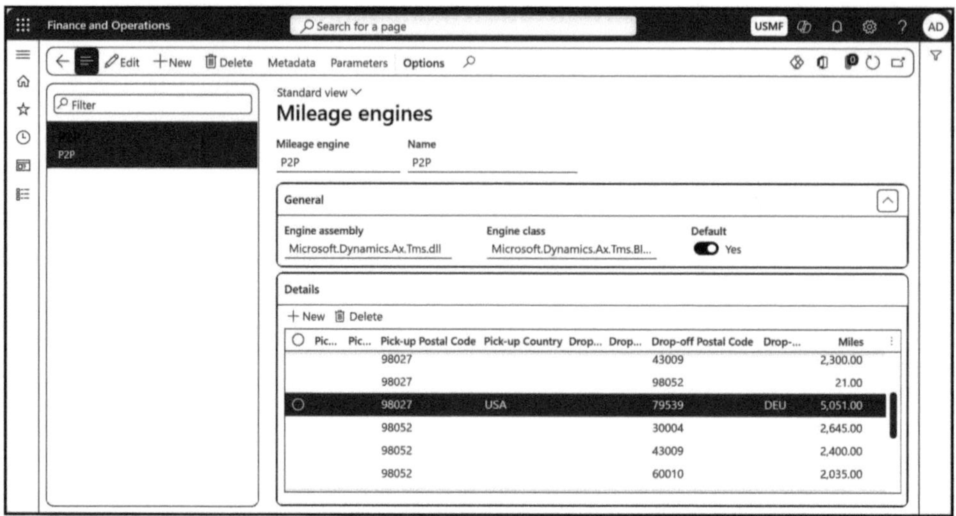

Fig. 8.20   Entering distances in the mileage engine

similar to the mileage engine, except that you enter days (instead of miles in the mileage engine), and that transit time depends on the carrier service.

8.2.1.2 Transportation Methods and Shipping Carriers

Transportation methods (*Transportation management > Setup > Carriers > Transportation methods*), which include categories like "Air" or "Ground", classify transportation. The *Transportation method* is a required field in the shipping carrier service. Modes (*Transportation management > Setup > Carriers > Mode*) categorize carriers. When setting up a carrier, you can select a mode in the field *Mode* of the Carrier form.

If you want to set up a shipping carrier, open the Carrier form (*Transportation management > Setup > Carriers > Shipping carriers*) and insert the carrier (→ Fig. 8.21). In order to activate the carrier for transportation, set the sliders *Activate shipping carrier* and *Activate carrier rating* to "Yes". The field *Vendor account* assigns the carrier to a vendor for freight invoice matching and posting (→ Sect. 8.2.2). On the tab *Services* in the Shipping carrier form, enter one or more transportation services that are provided by the carrier. When you insert a carrier service, a new *Mode of delivery* is created automatically in the line.

8.2.1.3 Break Masters, Rate Masters, and Rating Profiles

Break masters, rate masters, and rating profiles are the core setup for calculating the carrier rates.

Break masters (*Transportation management > Setup > Rating > Break master*) determine the steps (intervals) and the unit (e.g., miles) for the rate (→ Fig. 8.22). If there is, for

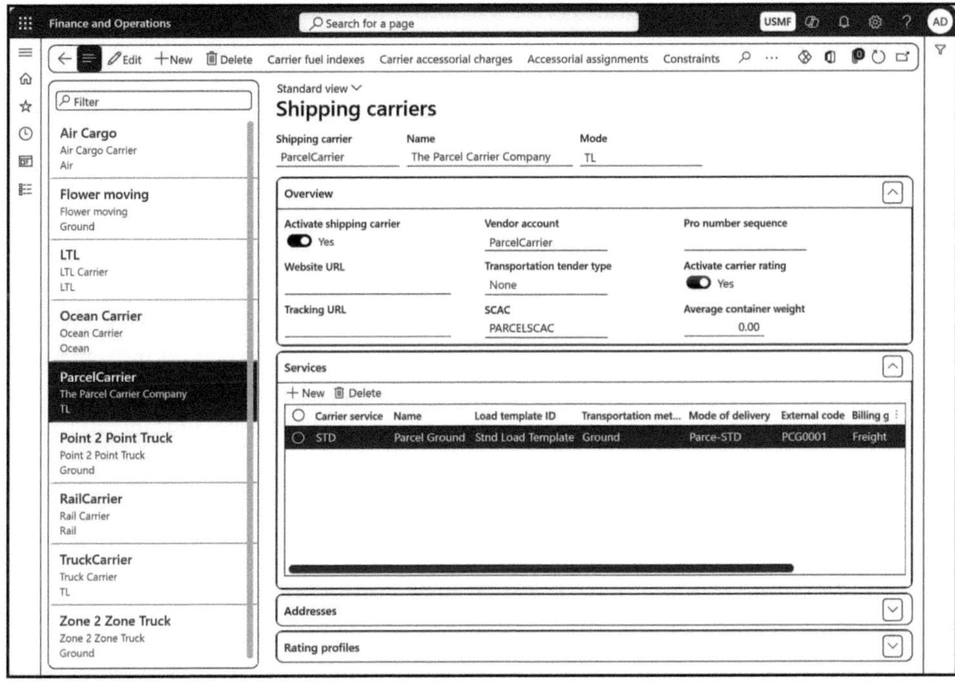

Fig. 8.21 Entering a carrier with his service

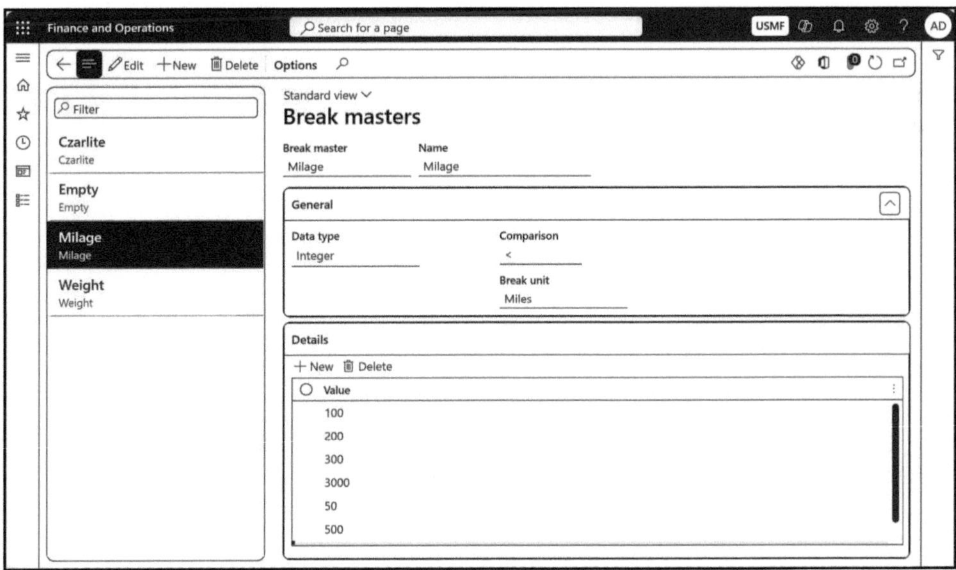

Fig. 8.22 Setting up a break master

example, a different price for transports up to 100 miles and for longer distances, enter a break master with a step "100" and a step "9999" (or another maximum distance).

Rate masters (*Transportation management > Setup > Rating > Rate master*) contain the pricing structure and the prices of the particular carriers. When you create a rate master (→ Fig. 8.23), select the *Rating metadata ID* (which determines the columns on the tab *Rate base assignments*) on the tab *Overview*. Then click the button *Rate base* and enter the rate bases for the rate master (→ Fig. 8.24). Rate bases contain the prices of the rate master. They use the steps or intervals of the *Break master* (selected on the tab *General* in the rate base) as columns on the tab *Details*, in which you can enter the respective prices.

Once you have finished the setup of the rate base, return to the Rate master form and, on the tab *Rate base assignment*, enter lines with the rate base (created for the rate master as described above) and the origin/destination address area. The selected *Rating metadata ID* in the rate master controls the columns (e.g., postal codes or zones) for the origin/destination address areas on this tab.

The rate base assignment makes the rate master available for calculating the transportation price from/to the applicable addresses.

Rating profiles (*Transportation management > Setup > Rating > Rating profile*) link the shipping carrier with the *Rate engine*, the *Rate master*, and the *Transit time engine*. With this link, the rating profiles control which prices and transport times are applicable for the particular transports. If a carrier applies different rate masters for different services, there are multiple rating profiles for one carrier. As an alternative to the separate menu item, you can access the rating profiles of a carrier on the tab *Rating profiles* in the Shipping carrier form.

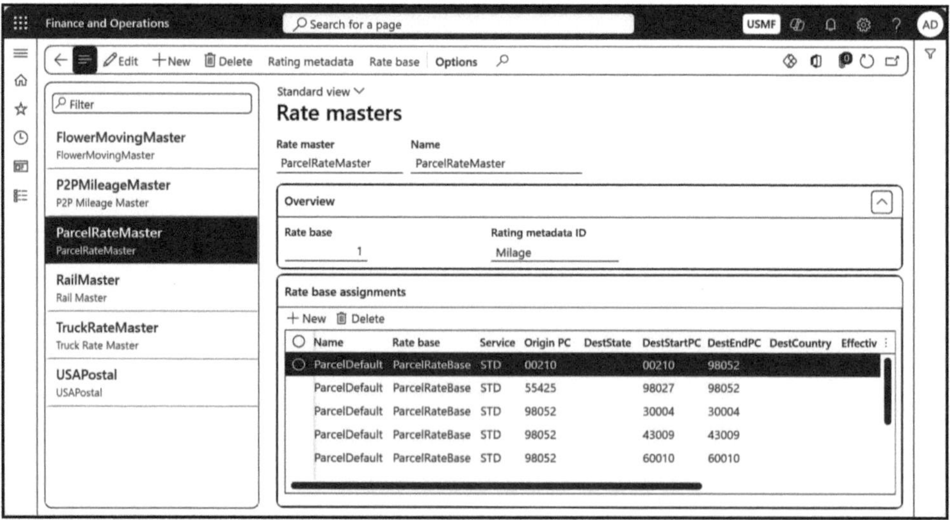

Fig. 8.23 Setting up a rate master

Fig. 8.24 Entering the rate base for the rate master

8.2.1.4 Transportation Management Parameters

The Transportation management parameters (*Transportation management > Setup > Transportation management parameters*) contain basic settings for transportation management, including the applicable number sequences. The button *Initialize base engine data* in the toolbar of the tab *General/Engines* in the parameters provides the option to initialize the engine setup data for the available base engines.

8.2.1.5 Load Templates and Load Posting Methods

Load templates (*Transportation management > Setup > Load building > Load templates*), which are also required for advanced warehouse management, represent the different inbound and outbound transportation units (e.g., regular vs. refrigerated trucks, or different container sizes).

If you want to specify a default load template that is used when creating a load, open the form *Warehouse management > Setup > Load > Item load mapping* and enter the default *Load template ID* for each applicable item group there.

Load posting methods (*Warehouse management > Setup > Load posting methods*) are a prerequisite for generating shipment waves from the Outbound load planning workbench. In a new company or after implementing additional methods, initialize the methods with the button *Regenerate methods* in this form.

8.2.1.6 Settings in the Released Products

In the Released product detail form, the slider *Use transportation management processes* on the tab *Transportation* controls whether transportation management is used for the item. This slider is always set to "Yes" if the item is subject to advanced warehouse management (as specified by the storage dimension group).

For items that use basic warehouse management, the slider *Use transportation management processes* is initialized with "No", but you can manually change it to "Yes".

8.2.1.7 Check of the Rate Calculation

You can check the rates for transportation, which are calculated with the selected transportation settings, in the Rate route workbench (*Transportation management > Planning > Rate route workbench*). Enter a From-address and a To-address on the tab *Criteria* and click the button *Rate shop* in the action pane to view all available transports with the related price on the tab *Route results*. If you deselect the checkbox *Hide Exceptions* on this tab, transport options that are not available with the selected settings are also shown. For these transports, you can click the button *View exception details* to view details on the missing setup.

8.2.2   Managing Transportation Processes

Transportation management can be used in inbound and outbound processes. Apart from sales orders, it covers purchase orders and transfer orders.

8.2.2.1 Core Transportation Process

The starting point for the transportation process is a sales order, a purchase order, or a transfer order with a product that is enabled for transportation management. If order completion for sales orders is required according to the Pricing management parameters, the sales order has to be set to complete.

For sales orders and transfer order shipments, the next step is planning the transportation in the Outbound load planning workbench (*Transportation management > Planning > Outbound load planning workbench*), which you can also access with the button *Warehouse/Loads/Outbound load planning workbench* in the Sales order form. For purchase orders and transfer order receipts, use the Inbound load planning workbench, which works similarly.

In the Outbound load planning workbench, select the respective order line(s) on the tab *Sales lines* and—with the button *Supply and demand/ Add/ To new load* in the action pane—add it to a new load (→ Fig. 8.25) or—with the button *Supply and demand/Add/ To existing load*—to an existing load, which you select in the lower pane first. If you add it to a new load, a dialog is shown in which you select an applicable load template. In the lower pane of the dialog, you can edit (reduce) the *Quantity* that you ship with the load (e.g., if the quantity in the order line is more than the load capacity) and, on the other tabs, view the required and the remaining load capacity in terms of weight and volume. Once you create the load with the button *OK* in the dialog, the new load is shown in the lower pane of the Outbound load planning workbench.

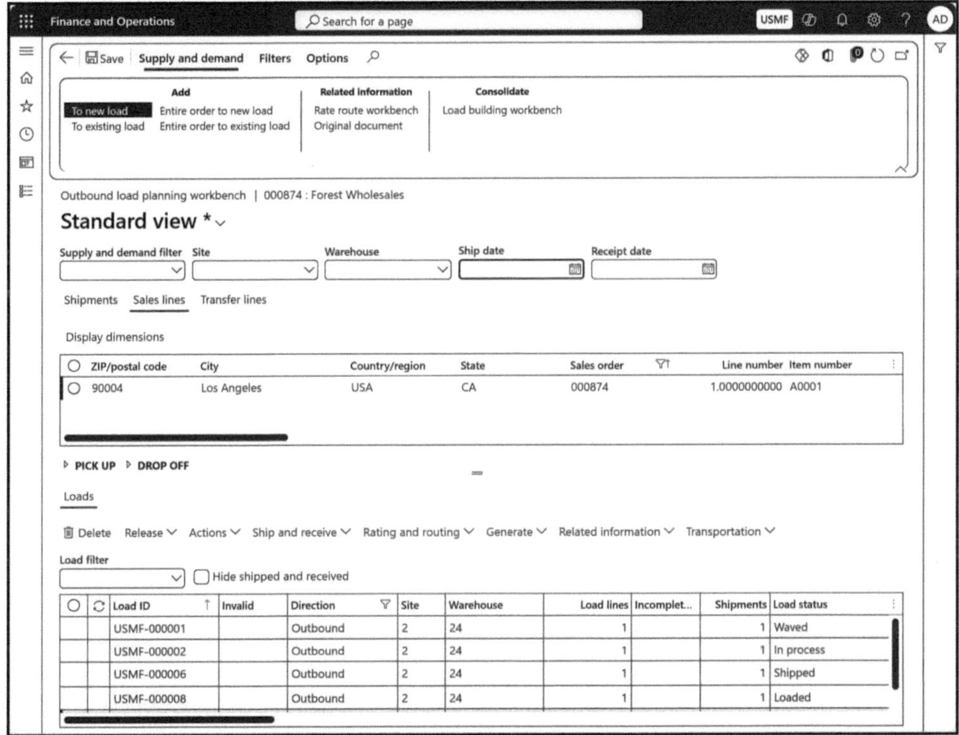

Fig. 8.25   Adding an order line to a new load in the Outbound load planning workbench

If the slider *Plan by shipment* in the Transportation management parameters (section *General*, tab *Shipment*) is set to "Yes", the tab *Shipments* is shown in the Outbound load planning workbench. In this case, you can add a sales order line to a load also after it has been released to the warehouse—in other words, add the shipment for a sales order line to a load.

In order to calculate the rate and the time for transportation, select the respective load on the tab *Loads* in the lower pane of the Outbound load planning workbench and click the button *Rating and routing/Rate route workbench* in the toolbar of this tab to access the Rate route workbench.

In the Rate route workbench (→ Fig. 8.26), click the button *Rate shop* to calculate all available transport options with the particular prices (the button *Rate* only shows the least expensive transport). Once you have decided on the transport, select the respective line on the tab *Route results* and click the button *Assign* in the toolbar of this tab. Assigning creates a route and links this route (which you can also view in the menu item *Transportation Management > Planning > Routes*) to the load.

If you want to create a route with a manual price (instead of calculating the price in the Rate route workbench), click the button *Rating and routing/Manual rating* in the toolbar of the lower pane in the Outbound load planning workbench.

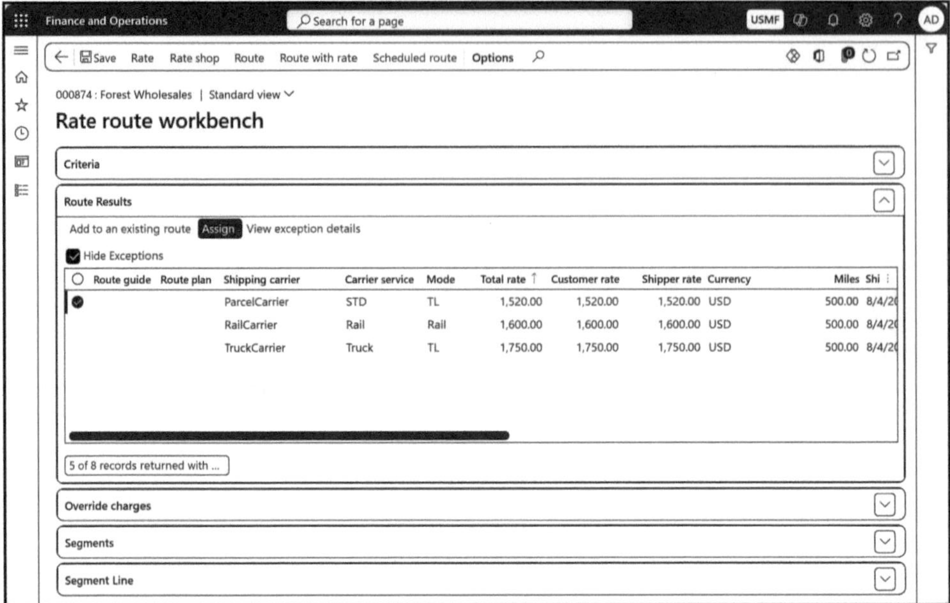

Fig. 8.26 Assigning a route in the Rate route workbench

In order to initiate warehouse picking next, select the load on the tab *Loads* in the lower pane of the workbench and create the shipment with the button *Release/Release to warehouse* in the toolbar of this tab.

Once all warehouse processes are finished, and the items are received at the final shipping location, you can confirm the shipment and the load ($\rightarrow$ Sect. 8.1.2). The confirmation tells the carrier that the load has been shipped. The load status changes to "Shipped", and by default, the load is not shown in the Outbound load planning workbench anymore.

8.2.2.2 Transportation Tenders

A transportation tender is an agreement with a carrier for a particular transport. It includes the transportation date and the rate. In the Shipping carrier form (*Transportation management > Setup > Carriers > Shipping carriers*), the field *Transportation tender type* on the tab *Overview* controls whether transportation tenders are updated manually or via EDI.

When managing transportation, you usually access the transportation tender from the respective route in the Route form (*Transportation Management > Planning > Routes*, button *Transportation tenders*), or from the load in the Load form (*Transportation Management > Planning > Loads > All loads*, button *Transportation/Transportation tenders*). In order to create a new tender, click the button *New* in the Transportation tender form. You can subsequently update the status of the tender with the button *Update status/Submit* when submitting it to the carrier, *Update status/Confirm* when it is confirmed by the carrier, and *Update status/Accept* when it is finally accepted from your side.

If you want to view all transportation tenders, open the menu item *Transportation management > Planning > Transportation tenders*.

8.2.2.3 Transportation Constraints

Transportation constraints restrict the available options for transportation, for example, to prevent a particular carrier from transporting a particular item number.

In order to set up transportation constraints, open the menu item *Transportation management > Setup > Routing > Constraints* and enter the disallowed combinations of items, shipments, and carriers. The field *Constraint action* controls whether to create a warning or an error.

When routes are calculated in the Rate route workbench, a constraint (disallowed combination) that applies to a particular transport generates an exception. The exceptions are shown in the column *Constraints*.

8.2.2.4 Segmented Transports

Segmented transports apply if you want to change the carrier within a transport. Hub masters represent the hubs where you can switch carriers for this purpose.

As a prerequisite for segmented transports, the following setup is required:

- **Hub types** (*Transportation management > Setup > Routing > Hub types*)—Different types of hubs (e.g., harbors or airports).
- **Hub masters** (*Transportation management > Setup > Routing > Hub masters*)— Places with an address (e.g., different harbors), on which you can switch carriers.
- **Route plans** (*Transportation management > Setup > Routing > Route plans*)— Sequence of transports from the origin to the first hub, from the first hub to the next hub, and between all following hubs. The rate per segment is the result of the regular rate calculation based on the hub addresses, or, if applicable, a spot rate that you enter for the segment (click the button *Spot rates* on the tab *Details*).
- **Route guide** (*Transportation management > Setup > Routing > Route guides*)—With criteria for the *Origin* and *Destination*. Enter the route plan on the tab *Result*.

In order to calculate rates with segmented transports, click the button *Route with rate* in the Rate route workbench. If you want to view the transport segments with the rate, select the route on the tab *Route results* and switch to the tab *Segments*.

8.2.2.5 Customer Rate Adjustment

Rate engines calculate the base rate for transportation as described above. If you want to charge a freight rate to a customer that is different from the base rate calculated by the rate engine, there are the following options:

- **Freight discounts**—For the *Discount type* "Customer".
- **Override charges**—Customer rate independent of the actual transport.
- **Transportation templates**—If selected in the Rate route workbench.

With freight discounts (*Transportation management > Setup > Rating > Discounts*), you can adjust the rates that derive from the base rate. The discounts are available for the rate paid to the carrier (*Discount type* "Shipper") and for the rate charged to the customer (*Discount type* "Customer"). When you set up a freight discount, select the *Discount type* and, on the tab *Dates*, the start/end date. Additional fields in the Discount form enable restrictions that serve as a filter—for example, if a discount should only apply for a particular *Shipping carrier*. In order to enter the discount value, expand the tab *Discount*, select the *Result type* ("Percentage" or "Amount"), and enter the rate discount percentage or the rate discount amount. Positive discounts reduce the freight rate, and negative discounts increase the rate. When calculating a rate in the Rate route workbench, the amounts in the columns *Customer rate* and *Shipper rate* deduct the discount from the base rate (*Total rate*).

With override charges (*Transportation management > Setup > Rating > Override charges*), you can enter a fixed price or apply the charges of a fixed carrier regardless of the selected route. For a fixed price, set the slider *Manual* on the tab *Charge* of the Override charges form to "Yes" and enter the price on the tab *Charge manual rates*, which is subsequently shown. If you want to apply the charges of a fixed carrier, regardless of the actual carrier (e.g., if the customer pays only truck charges), select the *Shipping carrier* on the tab *Charge*. When you calculate the freight rate for the customer in the Rate route workbench, the *Customer rate* shows the rate as specified in the override charges.

Transportation templates (*Transportation management > Setup > Carriers > Transportation templates*) work similarly to override charges, but the rate calculation only respects a transportation template if it is selected in the respective field on the tab *Criteria* in the Rate route workbench.

8.2.2.6 Charging Freight to the Customer

If applicable, you can automatically include transportation costs in sales orders. For this purpose, the following setup is required:

- **Charges code** (*Accounts receivable > Charges setup > Charges code*)—Set up a charges code with the posting type combination *Customer—Ledger* (for adding the charges to the order total) or *Ledger—Ledger* (for internal posting).
- **Charges assignment** (*Transportation management > Setup > Rating > Miscellaneous charges*)—Create a miscellaneous charges assignment with the *Miscellaneous charge type* "None" which links the miscellaneous charges code in accounts receivable with freight charges in transportation management.
- **Delivery terms** (*Sales and marketing > Setup > Distribution > Terms of delivery*)—Delivery term(s) with the slider *Add transportation charges to orders* set to "Yes".

In order to generate the charges in a sales order, enter the order, create the load, calculate the rate, and create/assign the route. Then create the shipment ("Release to warehouse") and execute the warehouse processes. When you confirm the shipment, the freight charges are added as miscellaneous charges to the order line.

8.2.2.7 Freight Invoice Matching

When receiving a freight invoice from a carrier, you can enter or import it and match it with the related route(s). As a prerequisite for freight invoice matching, the following setup is required:

- **Bill types** (*Transportation management > Setup > Freight reconciliation > Freight bill type*)—Required to link freight invoice processing to the transportation engine, define the parameters that control the mandatory fields for finding a match.
- **Bill type assignments** (*Transportation management > Setup > Freight reconciliation > Freight bill type assignments*)—Assign bill types to carriers and transportation modes.
- **Reconciliation reasons** (*Transportation management > Setup > Freight reconciliation > Reconciliation reasons*)—Are used when there is no exact match to a freight bill. For the deviation, they categorize reasons and specify the ledger posting.
- **Audit masters** (*Transportation management > Setup > Freight reconciliation > Audit master*)—For automatic freight reconciliation (optional for manual reconciliation), contain tolerances and reconciliation results.
- **Billing groups** (*Transportation management > Setup > Freight reconciliation > Billing groups*)—Group carrier services for billing purposes. Select the respective *Billing group ID* per service in the Shipping carrier form.
- **Transportation management parameters** (section *General*)– Slider *Enable Freight Reconciliation* on the tab *Freight reconciliation* , and settings on the tab *Vendor invoice* .

In the transportation process, freight invoice matching is based on routes that have been completed (the shipment/load is confirmed).

If you want to manually register the freight invoice that you receive from the carrier, open the Load form, deselect the checkbox *Show closed*, and select the respective load before you click the button *Transportation/Related information/Freight bill details* to access the Freight bill details form. In the Freight bill details form, select the applicable freight bill in the list pane on the left before you click the button *Generate freight bill invoice* and enter the invoice number in the subsequent dialog.

Alternatively, you can record a freight bill from the Outbound load planning workbench (click the button *Related information/Freight bill details* in the toolbar of the tab *Loads* to access the Freight bill details form, similar to the process in the Load form), or in the Freight invoice details form (*Transportation management > Inquiries and reports > Freight invoice details*), where you can enter the invoice with the header and line details manually.

To match and approve the freight invoice subsequently, click the button *Match freight bills and invoices* in the Freight invoice details form. In the form *Freight bill and invoice matching* that is shown next, switch to the tab *Unmatched freight bill details*, select the respective freight bill, and click the button *Match* in the toolbar of this tab. Close the *freight bill and invoice matching* form and, back in the Freight invoice details form, click the button *Submit for approval* in the action pane (if the freight invoice matches the details of the route).

After approval, you can click the button *Vendor invoice journals* in the Freight invoice details form (deselect the checkbox *Hide approved* to view the approved invoice) to access and, if necessary, to post the vendor invoice journal that has been created for the freight invoice.

8.2.2.8 Transportation Management with Basic Warehouse Management

If the slider *Use transportation management processes* is set to "Yes" for an item with basic warehouse management (as specified by the storage dimension group), you can use the transportation management functionality.

In order to use transportation management when processing a sales order without advanced warehouse management, create and confirm a shipment (without a wave) for a warehouse that is enabled for advanced warehouse management. In the Outbound load planning workbench, execute rating and routing as usual.

8.2.3 Case Study Exercises

Exercise 8.7—Shipping Carrier and Transportation Method
You want to manage the transportation from warehouse WH-## of exercise 8.1 to the customers. As a prerequisite, enter an address for the warehouse.

A new shipping carrier that offers transportation by drones is accepted. Set up a transportation mode M## (## = your user ID) with the name "##-Drone carrier", and a transportation method T## with the name "##-Drone service".

Next, create a vendor for the carrier with any name (starting with your user ID), a primary address of your choice, and an appropriate vendor group for domestic vendors. Then create the shipping carrier C## with the transportation mode M##. The carrier name should match the name of the vendor that you have created before. Activate the carrier and the carrier rating, and link the carrier with the corresponding vendor. Finally, enter a service S## with the transportation method M## and the billing group "Freight" for the carrier.

> *Note*: To prepare freight invoice matching, additionally enter a freight bill type assignment with the transportation mode and the carrier.

Exercise 8.8—Shipping Rates

The carrier of exercise 8.7 offers transportation by drone for USD 5 per mile for distances up to 100 miles, and for USD 3 for longer distances.

Create a break master D## (## = your user ID) with the name "##-Drone price steps" for this pricing. Next, set up a rate master DR## with the name "##-Drone pricing" and the rating metadata "Milage" for this offer. In the rate bases for this rate master, insert a rate base DB## with the break master D## and the given prices. Then enter a rate base assignment with this rate base, the service S## of exercise 8.7, the postal code of the warehouse W-## of exercise 8.7 as origin, and the postal code of the customer of exercise 4.1 as destination. Assign the new rate master to the carrier of exercise 8.7.

Exercise 8.9—Mileage and Transit Time Setup

The distance from warehouse W-## of exercise 8.7 to the customer of exercise 4.1 is 2300 miles. The transit time for a truck is 5 days. A transport by drone takes 1 day. Enter the required settings for transporting from the postal code of the warehouse to the postal code of the customer in the transportation management setup.

Then check the results for a shipment from the warehouse to the customer in the Rate route workbench.

Exercise 8.10—Transportation Process

The customer of exercise 4.1 orders one unit of the item I-##-W of exercise 8.4. The item should be shipped from the warehouse W-## of exercise 8.7 with delivery terms "FOB" (or other delivery terms in which the slider *Add transportation charges to orders* is set to "Yes"). Enter a sales order, check the available quantity in this warehouse, and reserve the item.

Then start transportation planning: Create a load, execute the rate calculation, and create the route. Because of the short transit time, the carrier of exercise 8.7 should do the transport. In the next step, release the load to the warehouse (which creates the shipment). Then enter, process, and release a wave for the shipment as required and execute the warehouse work (like in exercise 8.6). Finally, confirm the shipment and post the packing slip.

Exercise 8.11—Freight Bill

The carrier of exercise 8.7 transmits the freight invoice "FR001" for the transportation of exercise 8.10—Transportation Process. Enter and process the carrier invoice until it is ready for payment.

Finance Management

9

The primary responsibility of finance and accounting is to control and analyze the transactions that change the financial value in any area of the enterprise. These transactions are generated in business processes all over the organization.

Finance management is the core area of business management solutions. In Dynamics 365, there is a deep integration of finance with all business processes. As a result, accurate financial figures are immediately available all the time.

9.1 Business Processes in Finance

Before we start to go into details, the lines below give an overview of the business processes in finance.

9.1.1 Basic Approach

The core task of finance and accounting is to manage the general ledger with its accounts, which is the basis for the balance sheet and the income statement (profit and loss statement). Apart from the general ledger, there are subledgers—e.g., accounts receivable, accounts payable, fixed assets, projects, and inventory. These subledgers contain detailed data for the related transactions in the general ledger. Inventory management, for example, includes the inventory transactions that reflect the details of changes for the stock accounts in the general ledger.

Whenever you post a subledger transaction that has a financial impact (e.g., an invoice in sales, or a counting difference in inventory), there is a transaction in the general ledger.

If you post a sales order invoice which includes a stocked item, there are transactions in, at least, the following ledgers:

- **Inventory**—Financial value (in the transaction and the on-hand quantity).
- **Accounts receivable**—Customer debt (customer transaction).
- **General ledger**—Stock account, revenue account, COGS account (cost of goods sold), customer summary account.

The ledger integration is one of the core characteristics of Dynamics 365. It provides traceability of all financial vouchers back to the origin in other modules. Depending on the settings for subledger batch transfer in the General ledger parameters, subledger transactions are immediately posted to the general ledger.

The processing of transactions in Dynamics 365 follows the voucher principle: In all areas of the application, you have to register a voucher before you can post it. After posting, it is not possible to modify a voucher anymore. If you want to cancel a transaction, you have to post a reversing transaction.

9.1.2 At a Glance: Ledger Journal Transactions

In order to record a manual ledger transaction in Dynamics 365, you use a journal. The lines below show how to post a single-line transaction in a general journal.

In the General journal list page (*General ledger > Journal entries > General journals*), which shows the open journals that are not posted yet, click the button *New* to create a new journal header. Alternatively, you can open the workspace *General journal processing* and create a journal header with the tile *New journal* there.

In the next step, select a journal name for the new journal in the column *Name* of the Journal list page and optionally enter a text that explains the transaction in the column *Description*. If the transaction is subject to sales tax or VAT, the slider *Amounts include sales tax* on the tab *Setup* of the journal header controls whether the debit (or credit) amount in the journal lines includes tax.

In order to switch to the journal lines, click the button *Lines* in the action pane (or click the *Journal batch number* shown as a link in the grid of the list page). In the journal lines (→ Fig. 9.1), leave the default option "Ledger" in the column *Account type* if the transaction that does not refer to subledgers, and select the account number with the financial dimensions in the column *Account* (using segmented entry control). If you want to post to a subledger, select the respective *Account type* (instead of the type "Ledger") and enter the related account number in the column *Account*—e.g., the vendor number in a line with the *Account type* "Vendor".

In a single-line transaction, you enter the account and the offset account (including applicable financial dimensions) in a common journal line. Once you have completed the line, post the journal with the button *Post* in the action pane of the journal header or lines.

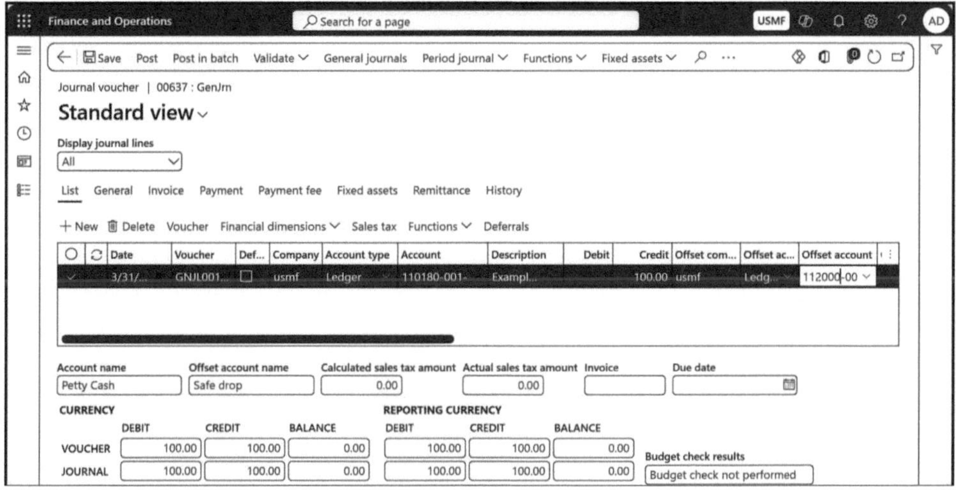

Fig. 9.1   Registering a journal line in a general journal

9.2   Core Setup for Finance

Since settings in finance are a core prerequisite for the whole application, you have to complete the basic financial configuration before you can set up other modules and before you can post a transaction in any part of the application.

The basic configuration in finance includes the following items:

- **Fiscal and ledger calendars**—Specify the financial periods.
- **Currencies and exchange rates**—Specify the monetary units.
- **Charts of accounts**—Specify the ledger accounts.

Charts of accounts, fiscal calendars, currencies, and exchange rates are shared across companies. The Ledger form determines the accounting currency, the chart of accounts, and the calendar that is used in the current company. If you want to manage a separate chart of accounts or calendar per company, set it up and assign it accordingly in the Ledger form of each company.

9.2.1   Fiscal and Ledger Calendars

Fiscal calendars determine the fiscal year. Within a fiscal year, the financial periods are specified with a start date and an end date. The ledger calendar, which is based on a fiscal calendar, controls at the company level which financial periods are open for transactions.

9.2.1.1 Fiscal Calendars

Fiscal calendars are shared across the companies within a common Dynamics 365 environment. The field *Fiscal calendar* in the Ledger form (*General ledger > Ledger setup > Ledger*) determines the applicable fiscal calendar for the current company. Selecting the fiscal calendar is part of the initial company setup.

Within the fiscal years of a fiscal calendar, there are accounting periods with a start date and an end date. The length of the individual accounting periods depends on the reporting requirements of the company.

You can edit the fiscal calendars in the Fiscal calendar form (*General ledger > Calendars > Fiscal calendars*). If you want to create a new fiscal calendar, click the button *New calendar* and enter the calendar ID together with the settings for the first fiscal year—start date, end date, name, period length, and unit ("Months" in case of monthly periods)—in the drop-down menu for the calendar.

If you want to add a fiscal year to an existing fiscal calendar, select the calendar in the lookup field *Calendar* at the top left before you click the button *New year* in the action pane. In the related drop-down menu, select to copy the settings from the last year (set the slider *Copy from last fiscal year* to "Yes"), or—if you choose not to copy—manually enter the end date, the period length, and the unit for the new year. Then click the button *Create* in the dialog to create the new year with its accounting periods.

9.2.1.2 Opening Periods and Closing Periods

Apart from regular operating periods (with the *Type* "Operating"), there are two period types which are not available for regular transactions—the types "Opening" and "Closing". If required, you can attach multiple closing periods to a regular operating period.

Closing periods contain period-end or year-end transactions. You can only register and post these transactions in a closing sheet (*General ledger > Period close > Closing period adjustments*) in the course of period closing.

Opening periods contain the opening transactions for a fiscal year. Once the previous year is closed, you can create the opening transactions in the menu item *General ledger > Period close > Year end close* based on the closing transactions.

9.2.1.3 Ledger Calendars

As a prerequisite for posting a transaction in Dynamics 365, the posting date of the transaction has to be included in a ledger period with the period status "Open". The required period status is controlled at the company level in the ledger calendar, not in the shared fiscal calendar.

The ledger calendar (*General ledger > Calendars > Ledger calendars*) contains the periods of the fiscal calendar that is assigned to the current company (selected in the Ledger form). For the (fiscal) *Calendar*, the *Fiscal year*, and the period that is selected on the left of the Ledger calendar form (→ Fig. 9.2), the tab *Legal entities* on the right shows all assigned companies with their period status. You can open or close periods for

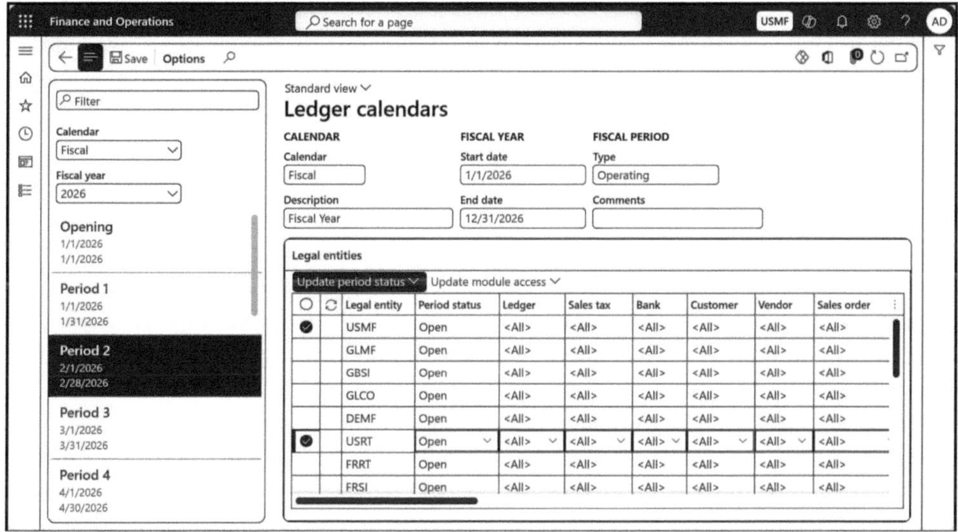

Fig. 9.2 Managing the period status in the ledger calendar

individual companies (select the respective option in the column *Period status*) or in common (select the applicable companies and click the button *Update period status*).

If the period status is "Open", you can post transactions in that period. The period status "On hold" blocks posting. The status "Permanently closed" also blocks posting, but whereas it is possible to reopen periods that are on hold, this is not possible for permanently closed periods. For this reason, only close a period permanently when it is definitely closed in accounting (after reporting to the authorities).

With the button *Update module access* and the related columns, you can set a module-specific blocking of transactions and exclude user groups from blocking.

Before actually closing a period in the ledger calendar, several tasks in finance have to be accomplished. In order to support this process, the workspace *Financial period close* shows a list of tasks. You can set up these tasks in the menu item *General ledger > Period close > Financial period close configuration*.

9.2.2   Currencies and Exchange Rates

The value and the amount in financial transactions—general ledger transactions and sub-ledger transactions (e.g., inventory or customer transactions)—refer to currencies. A transaction is always recorded in the accounting currency of the company, and, if applicable, additionally in a foreign currency. For this reason, the setup of currencies is a prerequisite for posting any transaction in Dynamics 365.

9.2.2.1 Currencies

In order to facilitate currency management in multi-company organizations, the currency table is shared across all companies within a common Dynamics 365 environment. For the currency that you select in the list pane on the left of the Currency form (*General ledger > Currencies > Currencies*), the tabs on the right show the related settings for this currency. This includes the definition of the rounding precision on the tab *Rounding rules*.

9.2.2.2 Exchange Rates

Exchange rate types (*General ledger > Currencies > Exchange rate types*) enable multiple parallel exchange rates between currencies. You can use two exchange rate types, for example, if you want to apply a different exchange rate for budget entries and for current transactions.

To access the Currency exchange rates form, click the button *Exchange rates* in the Exchange rate types form, or open the menu item *General ledger > Currencies > Currency exchange rates*. For the *Exchange rate type* selected at the top left in the Currency exchange rate form (→ Fig. 9.3), the related currency relations are shown in the list pane below. If you need an additional relation (e.g., for a currency which has not been used before), click the button *New* in the action pane and enter the details in the upper area of the right pane. The *Conversion factor* specifies the applicable factor for the exchange rate calculation.

The tab *Add or remove exchange rates* on the right shows the exchange rates for the currency relation that is selected in the list pane on the left. The filter *From date* and *To date* determines the date range for displaying exchange rates. In order to enter an exchange rate for a new date, click the button *Add* in the toolbar of the tab. The column *Exchange value* shows the conversion result. In daily business, enter or import (*General*

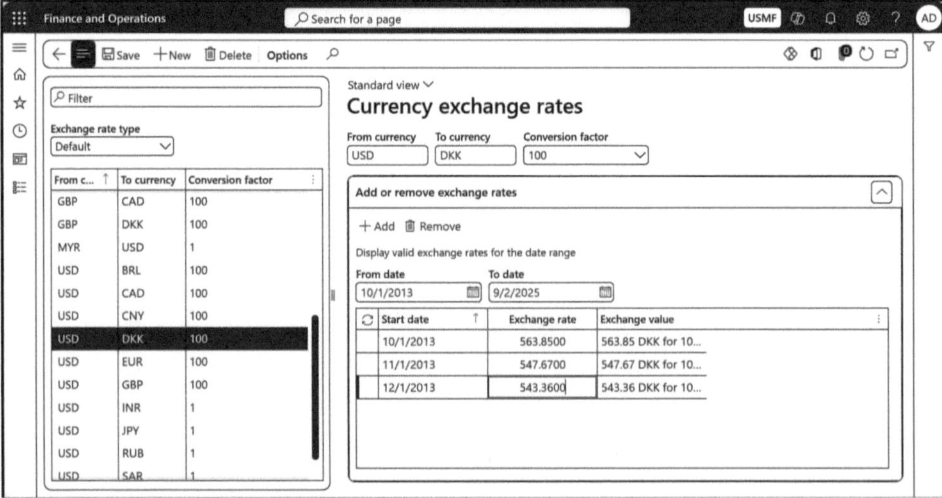

Fig. 9.3 Managing exchange rates in the Currency exchange rate form

ledger > Currencies > Import currency exchange rates) new exchange rates regularly to use a correct conversion of foreign currency transactions.

Currency exchange rates and exchange rate types are shared across all companies. If you need to keep separate exchange rates per company, select a different exchange rate type for each company in the Ledger form.

9.2.2.3 Currency Settings in the Ledger Form

The *Accounting currency* on the tab *Currency* in the Ledger form (*General ledger > Ledger setup > Ledger*) determines the local currency of the current company. This currency is used in all financial transactions. If required for reporting purposes, you can additionally select a *Reporting currency* in the Ledger form. It is not possible to change the accounting currency or the reporting currency of a company once transactions are registered.

The *Accounting currency exchange rate type* in the Ledger form determines the default exchange rate type for foreign currencies in regular transactions. In addition, there are separate exchange rate types for the reporting currency and for budget transactions.

The main accounts for exchange rate gains and losses in the current company are specified on the tab *Accounts for currency revaluation* in the Ledger form.

9.2.3   Financial Dimensions and Financial Tags

In addition to the main accounts, which are specified in the chart of accounts, the financial dimensions (like "Cost center" or "Department") are further levels in the structure of the ledger accounts in financial transactions. The required financial dimensions in a ledger transaction depend on the account structures that are assigned to the current company.

Financial reporting is not only possible at the level of the company and the main account, but also at the level of financial dimensions. This is, apart from other reporting purposes, also useful with reference to the multisite functionality: If you assign a financial dimension to the inventory dimension "Site" ($\rightarrow$ Sect. 10.1.6), you can, for example, report the income statement per subsidiary within a legal entity.

In parallel to financial dimensions, you can use financial tags to include additional data when posting a transaction—e.g., to keep the order number in ledger transactions related to sales. Whereas financial dimensions are included in a ledger transaction (which is used for external reporting and not editable in a posted transaction for this reason), financial tags are kept separate from the ledger and only serve internal purposes, which means that you can also edit them after posting.

In general, you use financial dimensions for static data (like cost centers), which may be part of external reporting, whereas you use financial tags for nonrecurring data like order numbers, which are only included in internal reporting.

9.2.3.1 Setup of Financial Dimensions

In Dynamics 365, financial dimensions and dimension values are shared across the companies within a common Dynamics 365 environment.

Financial dimensions are not limited to standard dimensions like department, cost center, and purpose, but you can set up your own financial dimensions. Taking the ease of use and the probability of wrong entries into account, you should not set up more dimensions than are effectively required.

If you want to set up a new financial dimension, open the Financial dimension form (*General ledger > Chart of accounts > Dimensions > Financial dimensions*) and click the button *New*. Then select the origin of the dimension values for the new financial dimension in the lookup field *Use values from*:

- **<Custom dimension >** – Create a dimension without reference to other tables.
- **One of the other options**—Link the dimension to other entities in the application (e.g., customers, item groups, or departments).

If you select, for example, the option "Departments" in the field *Use values from*, the financial dimension is linked to operating units with the type "Department". In this case, each department that you enter in the organization management (*Organization administration > Organizations > Operating units*) is synchronously available as a financial dimension value for this dimension.

If you select the option "<Custom dimension>" in the lookup field *Use values from*, you need to enter the financial dimension values manually.

Once you have created a new dimension, a system administrator or a user with appropriate privileges has to activate the dimension (click the button *Activate* in the Financial dimension form).

After activation, you can optionally set the slider *Copy values to this dimension* to "Yes" if the dimension is linked to an entity like the customer table. In this case, Dynamics 365 not only creates a dimension value with each new record in the respective main table (e.g., a new customer), but also assigns the dimension value as a default value to the new record (e.g., for customers on the tab *Financial dimensions* in the Customer form). This way, you can run financial reporting on, e.g., customer numbers without manually creating or assigning a financial dimension value to new customers.

> *Note:* You can only activate financial dimensions when the environment is in maintenance mode.

9.2.3.2 Financial Dimension Values

You can access the dimension values of a financial dimension with the button *Financial dimension values* in the Financial dimension form. For custom dimensions, you have to create the *Dimension values* manually. For other financial dimensions, you can edit the dimension value details, but you cannot create records (since the dimension values derive from a different table).

In the Financial dimension values form (→ Fig. 9.4), the right pane shows the related details of the dimension value that you select in the list pane on the left. The tab *General* on the right contains shared settings that apply to all companies that use the dimension. If you want to block future transactions that refer to the selected dimension value, set the slider *Suspended* to "Yes" or enter applicable dates in the field *Active from* or *Active to*. On the tab *Legal entity overrides*, you can enter further blocking at the company level.

9.2.3.3 Using Financial Dimensions

Before you can use a financial dimension in transactions and inquiries, it has to be included in the account structures or the advanced rule structures that are assigned to the current company. Settings in the applicable account structure or advanced rule structure also determine if and which dimension value is optional or required when posting to a particular account.

In master data forms (e.g., in the Customer form or in the Released product form), the tab *Financial dimensions* shows all financial dimensions that are included in the account structures and the advanced rule structures of the current company. A dimension value, which you enter on this tab in the master data, is used as the default dimension value when registering a related order or journal header, or line.

In the ledger journal lines and all other forms with a ledger account field, financial dimensions are not shown as separate fields. Using segmented entry control (→ Sect. 9.3.1), the financial dimensions are to be entered together with the main account in one segmented field.

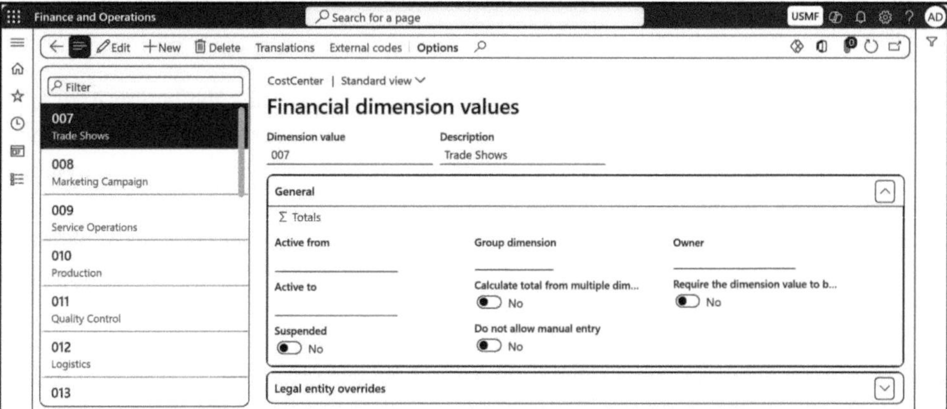

Fig. 9.4 Managing the dimension values for a financial dimension

9.2.3.4 Financial Dimension Sets

Based on the financial dimensions, you can set up financial dimension sets (*General ledger > Chart of accounts > Dimensions > Financial dimension sets*). A dimension set is a list of one or more financial dimensions (usually starting with the main account) that determine the dimensions shown in reports and inquiries that use the dimension sets—e.g., the trial balance (→ Sect. 9.2.4).

In order to ensure displaying results quickly, Dynamics 365 calculates and stores ledger balances at the level of dimension sets.

9.2.3.5 Financial Tags

For internal analytics and information purposes, you can use financial tags to add information to ledger transactions. Financial tags are a more flexible option than financial dimensions for this purpose. Different from financial dimensions, they are managed at the company level.

In the General ledger parameters, the *Financial tags segment delimiter* in the segment *Financial tags* has to be selected before you can set up financial tags.

Once the delimiter is specified, you can manage the financial tags in the Financial tags form (*General ledger > Chart of accounts > Financial tags > Financial tags*). If you want to create a new tag, click the button *New* and enter the *Financial tag* name. In the lookup field *Value type*, select the origin of the tag values for the new tag:

- **Text**—Free text can be entered in the tag when registering a transaction.
- **List**—Tag values are given by the table selected in the column *Use values from*, but you can manually enter other tag values in a transaction.
- **Custom list**—Tag without reference to other tables (similar to a financial dimension "<Custom dimension>"), but applying the values entered in the Tag value form (access with the button *Tag values* in the Financial tag form).
- **Fixed list**—Like "List", but restricting tag values to the referenced table.
- **Fixed custom list**—Like "Custom list", but restricting tag values to the specified tag values.

Once you have created the tags and tag values as applicable, click the button *Activate or deactivate tags* to activate the tags. In the dialog that is shown next, move the tags from the left pane (*Inactive financial tags*) to the right pane (*Active financial tags*) as applicable before you click the button *OK*.

In journal and order headers, and order lines, active tags are shown on a separate tab (*Financial tags*), where you can edit the tag values. In journal lines, there is a separate column *Financial tags* instead of a tab. In the posted ledger transactions, financial tags are shown in separate columns on the right. With the button *Edit voucher/Edit internal voucher data* in the Voucher transactions inquiry (*General ledger > Inquiries and reports > Voucher transactions*), which you can also access with the respective button in various forms, you can update tag values in a posted transaction.

9.2.4   Account Structures and Chart of Accounts

Account structures, charts of accounts, and main accounts determine the core structure in finance. They are shared across companies in Dynamics 365. In a company, the chart of accounts that is selected in the Ledger form determines the applicable main accounts. The applicable financial dimensions are controlled by the assigned account structures.

9.2.4.1 Ledger Account and Main Account

The ledger account field in a financial transaction includes the main account and the applicable financial dimensions. The account structure, which is assigned at the level of the company and main account, controls the financial dimensions that are included in the ledger account.

9.2.4.2 Chart of Accounts

Depending on the structure of your organization and the number of legal entities, there is one common or multiple independent charts of accounts. The Chart of accounts form (*General ledger > Chart of Accounts > Accounts > Chart of Accounts*) displays all available charts of accounts in the list pane on the left. For the chart of accounts that you select on the left, the main accounts are shown on the right (→ Fig. 9.5). If you show the *Related information* pane with the FactBoxes on the right, you can view the ledgers and legal entities (companies) that use the selected chart of accounts in the FactBox *Ledgers*.

If you want to create a completely new chart of accounts, click the button *New* in the action pane. To create a main account, click the button *New* or *Edit* in the toolbar of the tab *Main accounts*. In the Main accounts form, which is shown then, you can insert or modify the main accounts of the selected chart of accounts.

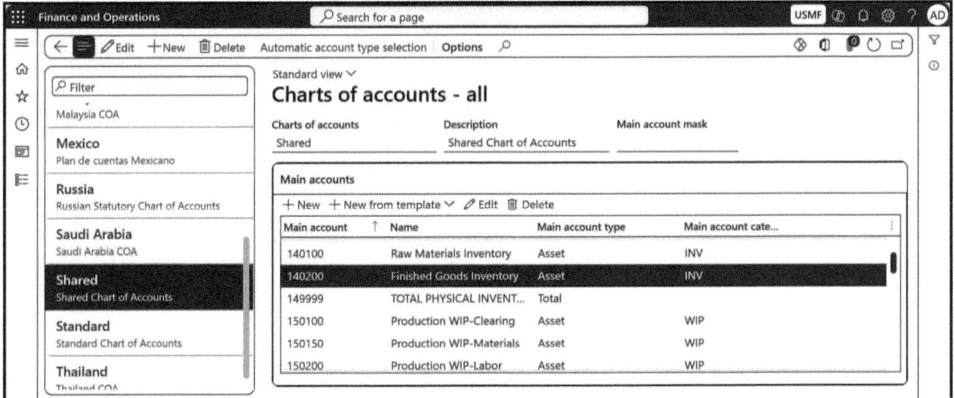

Fig. 9.5 Editing a chart of accounts

9.2.4.3 Settings in the Ledger Form

Settings in the Ledger form (*General ledger > Ledger setup > Ledger*) determine the chart of accounts and the account structures that are assigned to the current company. These settings are required before you can register any transaction.

You can use one common chart of accounts in multiple companies—select the same *Chart of accounts* in the respective field of the Ledger form in all applicable companies. Once the first transaction has been posted in a company, it is not possible to change the assignment of the chart of accounts anymore.

The tab *Account structures* in the Ledger form contains the account structures that are assigned to the current company. To add an account structure, click the button *Add* in the toolbar of this tab. Since the account structures determine the available financial dimensions when posting to a ledger main account, each main account, which is included in the chart of accounts, has to be uniquely assigned to one account structure without overlapping or missing assignments.

9.2.4.4 Account Structures

The Account structures form (*General ledger > Chart of Accounts > Structures > Configure account structures)* shows all account structures of the enterprise. If you want to access the details of an account structure, click the respective field *Name* shown as a link in the grid. Alternatively, open the Account structures detail form with the button *Configure account structures* in the toolbar of the tab *Account structures* in the Ledger form.

If you want to create a new account structure (i.e., a segment combination that consists of the main account and financial dimensions), click the button *New* in the Account structure list page. In the drop-down menu that is shown next, the slider *Add main account* usually remains set to "Yes" in order to include the main account as the first segment. You can set this slider to "No" if you want to use a financial dimension, and not the main account, as the first segment—e.g., if your organization has divisions and you want to apply the division as the first segment in transactions. Once you click the button *Create* in the dialog, the Account structures detail form with the new account structure is shown.

When you create a new account structure or edit an existing one, it has the status "Draft". In order to add dimensions to the account structure, click the button *Add segment* in the toolbar of the upper pane in the detail form. Then select a segment (financial dimension) in the *Add segment* dialog. Once you close the dialog with the new segment, the related column is shown in the upper pane of the detail form. You can subsequently enter a filter for the segment (an advanced filter in the field itself, or, in an easier way, on the tab *Allowed value details*). If you select the checkbox *Blank values are allowed* for a segment, the dimension is optional, and you are not required to select a dimension value when entering a transaction for a ledger main account that is covered by the account structure.

In the example of → Fig. 9.6, you can view an account structure for the main accounts "100,000" to "399,999", which contains the financial dimensions "BusinessUnit" and "Department" and does not restrict the available dimension values for the dimension "BusinessUnit".

Fig. 9.6 Configuring an account structure in the detail form

If applicable to the account structure, you can add one or more lines for a segment—including the segment with the main account—with appropriate filters that prevent overlapping definitions. In this way, you can specify multiple allowed dimension value combinations.

Once you have finished the setup of an account structure, click the button *Activate* to enable the updated account structure. The status is "Active" then. If you want to edit an account structure later, click the button *Edit* in the action pane. The account structure status then switches to "Draft". For transactions that are posted until the new draft is activated, the settings in the account structure before you switched to the draft status are still in place. If you edit the account structure in the draft status and do not want to activate the changes, click the button *Delete draft*. The previously active status will remain active in this case.

9.2.4.5 Advanced Rule Structures

Advanced rules and rule structures are an optional setup that you can use to apply an additional financial dimension only to transactions of one or a few particular accounts. An example is the use of the financial dimension "Campaigns" in combination with a particular marketing account in order to track campaigns.

In the Advanced rule structures form (*General ledger > Chart of Accounts > Structures > Advanced rule structures*), you can create an advanced rule structure with the button *New* in the action pane. Then enter the applicable financial dimension(s) in a similar way to the setup of an account structure (described above).

As a prerequisite for using an advanced rule structure, an advanced rule has to be created. For this purpose, open the Account structures form (*General ledger > Chart of*

Accounts > Structures > Configure account structures) and select the respective account structure (if the account structure has got the status "Active", click the button *Edit* to switch to the status "Draft") before you click the button *Advanced rules*. In the Advanced rules form, click the button *New* and enter the ID and name for the new advanced rule in the drop-down menu. In order to specify the main accounts which are assigned to the advanced rule, click the button *Add new criteria* on the tab *Advanced rule criteria* of the Advanced rules form.

Then click the button *Add* on the tab *Advanced rule structures* to assign the advanced rule to an advanced rule structure. Activating the account structure, to which the advanced rule is assigned, activates the advanced rule in parallel.

9.2.4.6 Main Accounts

The structure and the format of the main accounts in the chart of accounts is only depending on the internal requirements of your company.

For reporting purposes (balance sheet, income statement, and other reports in finance), you can set up and use financial reports (*General ledger > Inquiries and reports > Financial reports*) with a structure that is separate from the structure of the chart of accounts.

If you want to edit the main accounts, open the Main accounts form (*General ledger > Chart of accounts > Accounts > Main accounts*) and click the button *Edit*. Alternatively, you can edit the main accounts with the button *Edit* in the toolbar of the tab *Main accounts* in the Chart of accounts form.

If accessed form the menu, the Main accounts form (→ Fig. 9.7) shows the chart of accounts which is assigned to the current company. The name of this chart of accounts is shown in the header on the right. In case this chart of accounts is assigned to multiple companies, keep in mind that changes on main accounts in this form also affect the other companies.

If you want to create a new account, click the button *New* in the action pane and enter a unique *Main account* number, a *Name*, and a *Main account type*. If you want to enter a translation of the account name, click the button *Name Translations* in the action pane.

In the structure of the main accounts, you have to distinguish between transaction accounts and auxiliary accounts. The core difference between transaction accounts and auxiliary accounts is that you can only use a transaction account in a financial transaction. Auxiliary accounts serve to establish a clear structure of the chart of accounts, but they are not necessarily required.

The *Main account type*, a lookup field in the Main accounts form, divides the accounts into transaction accounts and auxiliary accounts shown in → Table 9.1.

Transaction accounts include balance accounts and profit and loss accounts. From a functional point of view, these two account types work differently when closing a fiscal year: Whereas the balance of profit and loss accounts is zero in the opening transactions of the next year, balance accounts keep the balance.

Within the balance accounts, you can optionally distinguish between asset accounts and liability accounts. These subcategories are only used for filtering and sorting purposes.

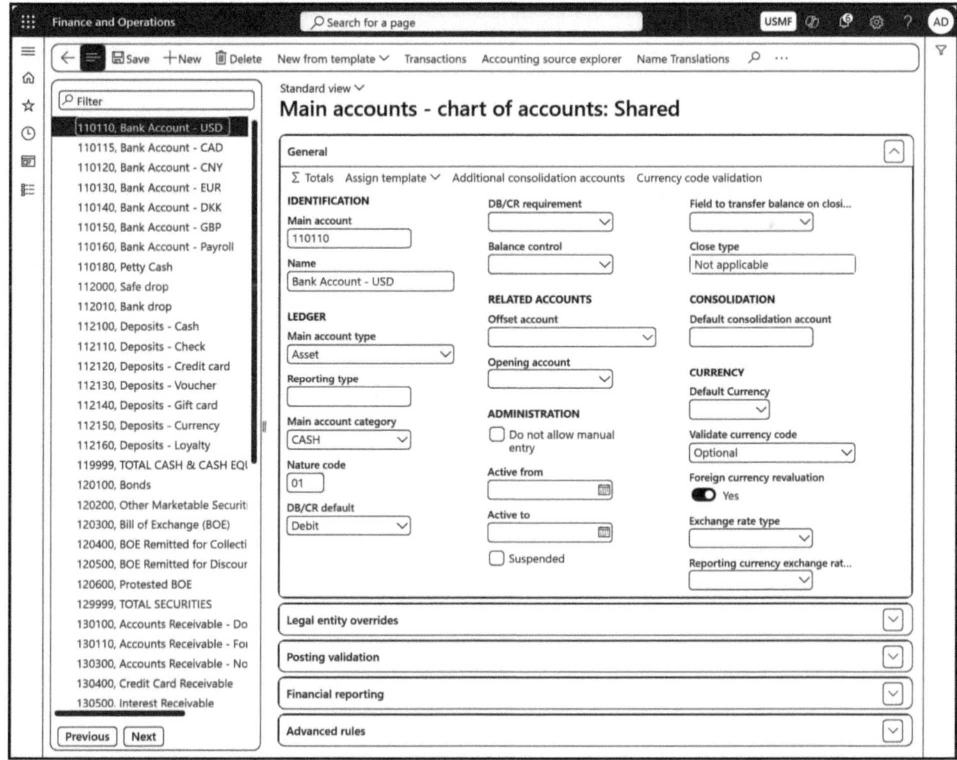

Fig. 9.7 Editing a ledger main account

Table 9.1 Structure of main accounts

Type		Main account type in Dynamics 365
Transaction accounts	Balance accounts	• Balance sheet • Asset • Liability • Equity
	Profit and loss accounts	• Profit and loss • Expense • Revenue
Auxiliary accounts		• Reporting (used for printing, options in the related field *Reporting type* are "Header", "Empty header", and "Page header") • Total • Common (required in China)

The same way in which you can subcategorize balance accounts, you can split profit and loss accounts into expense accounts and revenue accounts.

Accounts with the *Main account type* "Total" are optional auxiliary accounts which you can use to display subtotals in inquires. In order to specify the accounts which are added up, click the button *Total accounts* in the action pane.

In addition to the main account type, the lookup field *Main account category* on the tab *General* of the Main accounts form provides another classification of main accounts. Main account categories (*General ledger > Chart of accounts > Accounts > Main accounts categories*) can be used as a basis for financial reports.

When setting up a ledger main account which receives transactions from other modules (e.g., a summary account for vendor liabilities), select the checkbox *Do not allow manual entry* to block manual transactions on this account.

In further fields on the tab *General* in the Main accounts form, and on the tabs *Posting validation* and *Financial reporting*, you can specify default values and restrictions for transactions. On the tab *Legal entity overrides*, you can block a ledger main account or enter default values for financial dimensions at the company level.

9.2.4.7 Voucher Transaction Inquiry and Trial Balance

The Voucher transaction inquiry (*General ledger > Inquiries and reports > Voucher transactions*) shows all posted ledger transactions as selected in the filter dialog. In the Main accounts form, you can click the button *Transactions* in the action pane to view the ledger transactions of the selected account. A button for viewing related ledger transaction is also available in other forms—e.g., in the Trial balance form.

In the Voucher transactions inquiry, the following buttons provide access to further details:

- *Voucher*—Shows the complete voucher (all general ledger transactions that are posted with the selected voucher number).
- *Transaction origin*—Shows the related transactions in all modules.
- *Original document*—Access to the original document (invoice, packing slip, order), which you can reprint from there.
- *Audit trail*—Shows the user and the actual time of posting.

If you want to view the balances of the ledger accounts, open the Trial balance form (*General ledger > Inquiries and reports > Trial balance*) and, in the *Parameters* pane at the top of the form, specify the *Financial dimension set* (determining the displayed dimensions) and the period for which you want to calculate the balances. Then click the button *Show balances* in this pane to execute the calculation and to show the results. With the trial balance snapshots, which you can access with the button *Trial balance snapshots* in the Trial balance form, you can calculate and store trial balances for dimension sets and fiscal years, which you can open in Excel or access from external applications.

9.2.4.8 Accounts for Automatic Transactions

Settings in the Accounts for automatic transactions form (*General ledger > Posting setup > Accounts for automatic transactions*) control ledger transactions that are posted automatically and for which there is no other setting—e.g., for invoice discounts.

If you want to enter a new account for automatic transactions, open the Accounts for automatic transactions form and insert a record with the *Posting type* and the assigned *Main account*. You can generate a basic set of posting types, for which you enter the default accounts, with the button *Create default types*. Core settings in the accounts for automatic transactions include:

- **Error account**—Used in case of missing account settings.
- **Penny difference in accounting currency**—For small payment differences.
- **Year-end result**—Account for profit/loss when closing the fiscal year.
- **Order invoice rounding**—Sales invoice rounding.
- **Vendor invoice rounding-off**—Purchase invoice rounding.
- **Vendor invoice discount**—Main account for purchase order total discounts.
- **Customer invoice discount**—Main account for sales order total discounts.

If the slider *Interrupt in case or error account* in the General ledger parameters is set to "Yes", Dynamics 365 will display an error message instead of posting to the error account (in case there is a transaction for which no main account is specified in the integration settings).

9.2.4.9 Default Descriptions

Default descriptions (*General ledger > Journal setup > Default descriptions*) determine a default text for transactions which are posted automatically (based on the ledger integration). If you want to enter a default description, select the transaction type in the field *Description* first. Then enter the *Language* ("user" for a generic description) and the *Text*. The *Text* may include variables—available variables are shown at the bottom of the right pane.

9.2.5   Vendors, Customers, Bank Accounts, and Petty Cash

When entering a ledger transaction in a journal line, you can—apart from a ledger account—select a customer, a vendor, a fixed asset, a project, a bank account, or a petty cash account in the account field and in the offset account field.

9.2.5.1 Vendors

In order to manage vendors in Dynamics 365, open the Vendor form (*Accounts payable > Vendors > All vendors*) and edit the vendor data (including shared vendor data) as described in → Sect. 3.2.1. If you want to view the vendor transactions (invoices and payments), select the vendor and click the button *Vendor/Transactions/Transactions* in the action pane of the Vendor form. If the vendor is shared across companies, click the button *Vendor/Transactions/Global transactions* to view the vendor transactions in all companies.

Apart from the invoice or payment amount in the column *Amount*, the column *Balance* in the Vendor transactions form shows the open, not yet settled amount. You can settle invoices with payments in the *Settle transactions* dialog (→ Sect. 9.3.4).

9.2.5.2 Customers

You can find details on customer records (*Accounts receivable > Customers > All Customers*) in → Sect. 4.2.1. The way to execute transaction inquiries and to settle transactions for customers is similar to the procedures in vendor management.

9.2.5.3 Bank Accounts

The Bank accounts form (*Cash and bank management > Bank accounts > Bank accounts*) shows the bank accounts of your company. In order to create a new bank account, click the button *New* and enter the (internal) bank account ID, the *Routing number* (identifying the bank), the *Bank account number* (as specified by the bank), and the *Name* for the bank account. In the field *Main account*, enter the main account which is assigned to the particular bank account.

The field *Currency* specifies the currency of the bank account. If you want to enable transactions in multiple currencies, set the slider *Allow transactions in additional currencies* to "Yes". The tab *Additional identification* contains the fields for the IBAN and the SWIFT/BIC.

If your company has got multiple bank accounts at a particular bank, you can create a bank group (*Cash and bank management > Setup > Bank groups*) with general bank data like the routing number, address, and contact information. If you select a bank group in the related field on the tab *General* of the Bank accounts form, the bank account is initialized with these data.

In the Cash and bank master data change setup (*Cash and bank management > Setup > Cash and bank master data change setup*), you can enable an approval workflow for creating or editing bank accounts—similar to the vendor approval workflow (→ Sect. 3.2.1). If enabled, set up the related workflow with the type "Workflow for proposed bank account change" in the Cash and bank management workflow page (*Cash and bank management > Setup > Cash and bank management workflows*).

Transactions on a bank account are posted in a separate subledger, the bank transactions, and, applying the main account selected in the bank account, in the general ledger.

9.2.5.4 Petty Cash

With the optional petty cash functionality, you can also manage cash transactions in a separate subledger.

As a prerequisite for using the petty cash features, they must be enabled in the parameters (*Cash and bank management > Setup > Cash and bank management parameters*, section *Cash*). You can subsequently specify additional required cash parameters, including the default posting profile in the field *Cash posting*, and the number sequences.

Different to the setup of bank accounts, the ledger integration of cash accounts is not established by a field for the main account in the main table, but by cash posting profiles (*Cash and bank management > Setup > Cash posting profiles*).

Once the setup is finished, you can create cash accounts in the Cash accounts form (*Cash and bank management > Petty cash > Cash accounts*) with the cash ID, the name, and the currency.

In order to post cash transactions with a cash account, you can use a slip journal, or, selecting the *Account type* "Petty cash", a general journal (→ Sect. 9.3.1). Slip journals (*Cash and bank management > Petty cash > Slip journal*), which are specific for registering cash transactions, work similarly to general journals, but restrict the account type to "Petty cash" and require approving a transaction with the button *Document approval/ Approve* before posting it. As a prerequisite for using slip journals, a journal name with the Journal type "Cash" is required.

9.2.6   Credit Management

The Credit and collections module includes the credit management for the credit limit of customers and the collections management for payment reminders.

Below you can find a description of the core functionality for credit management. The credit management adds various enhancements to basic customer credit limits, including the option to flexibly manage holds for sales order, or features for credit limit adjustments and shared credit limits.

9.2.6.1 Credit Management Setup

Blocking rules (*Credit and collections > Setup > Credit management setup > Blocking rules*), which control the credit holds for orders (similar to regular order holds, see → Sect. 4.3.3), are a core setting for credit management. The different areas or triggers for blocking are reflected in the sections on the left of the Blocking rules form (→ Fig. 9.8)— e.g., blocking based on overdue invoices or on the total amount of the sales order.

Apart from blocking rules with the *Rule type* "Blocking", you can enter blocking rules with the *Rule type* "Exclusion"—e.g., to prevent blocking of low-value orders. If you select the checkbox in the column *Release sales order* (only available for the *Rule type* "Exclusion"), applicable sales orders will be released regardless of any other rule that may block the order.

In addition to the blocking rules, which set credit holds as applicable (including holds with the trigger "Credit limit used"), the Credit and collections parameters (*Credit and collections > Setup > Credit and collections parameters*, section *Credit*, tab *Credit limits*) include another setting which can block transactions when exceeding the credit limit. If the parameter *Check credit limit for sales order* is set to "Yes" and the parameter *Message*

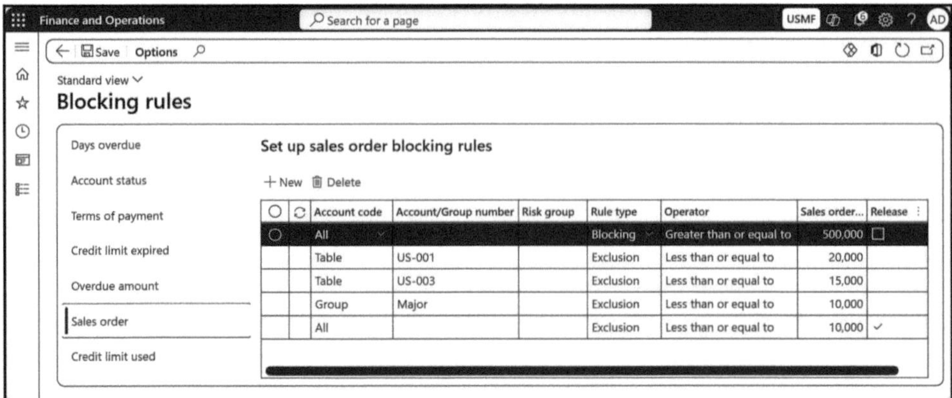

Fig. 9.8 Setting up a blocking rule for high-value sales orders

when exceeding credit limit is set to "Error", an error message will prevent posting the order confirmation or other documents when exceeding the credit limit. Depending on the parameter *Credit limit type*, this credit limit check only includes unpaid invoices, or also open packing slips, or additionally open orders.

Settings on the tabs *Credit holds* and *Credit management checkpoint* of the Credit and collections parameters control how blocking rules are processed.

A credit management reason (*Credit and collections > Setup > Credit management setup > Credit management reasons*) with the *Reason type* "Hold", "Release", or "Status" is mandatory when manually setting or releasing a credit hold, and optional when updating the account status.

The account status (*Credit and collections > Setup > Credit management setup > Account statuses*) is an optional setting that characterizes the credit standing of customers and that you can use as trigger in the blocking rules. In the column *Invoicing and Delivery on Hold* of the Account status form, you can specify a blocking option which is transferred to the customer (field *Confirmation, delivery and invoicing on hold* in the Customer form) when selecting the account status.

If enabled in the Credit and collection parameters (Section *Credit*, tab *Credit holds*, slider *Check customer credit groups credit limit*), you can specify a common (shared) credit limit for customers by the use of customer credit groups (*Credit and collections > Customers > Customer credit groups*). If a credit limit is also specified on the individual customer, the lower of both will be used for the customer—except if the customer has got unlimited credit limit (the result is unlimited credit limit), or if the customer credit limit is zero and the slider *Mandatory credit limit* for the customer is set to "No" (the result is the credit limit of the group).

In the Customer detail form, settings on the tab *Credit and collections* (→ Sect. 4.2.1) include the options *Unlimited credit limit* and *Exclude from credit management*, the *Credit management group*, the *Credit limit*, the *Credit limit expiration date*, and the *Account status*. For the credit limit and other core customer fields, you can enable an approval process which is similar to the vendor approval ($\rightarrow$ Sect. 3.2.1).

9.2.6.2 Working with Credit Holds

When you post a sales document—e.g., a sales order confirmation—and this document is defined as a checkpoint in the Credit and collections parameters (*Credit and collections > Setup > Credit and collections parameters*, section *Credit*, tab *Credit management checkpoint*), a credit hold will be set automatically if a blocking rule with the with the *Rule type* "Blocking" applies.

You can view this hold in the Credit management hold list (*Credit and collections > Credit management hold list > Open credit holds*), which you can also access with the button *Credit management/Credit management/Credit management hold list* in the Sales order form. In the Credit management hold list, you can check the *Blocking reasons* in the related FactBox (alternatively, click the button *Blocking reasons*).

If you want to manually release blocking, click the button *Release* in the Credit management hold list and select a *Release reason* in the related drop-down ($\rightarrow$ Fig. 9.9). If you select the *Release action* "With posting", the posting that has triggered the hold will be executed when releasing the hold. Otherwise, only the hold is released and posting the original document has to be executed separately. As an alternative to manually releasing, you can click the button *Evaluate for release/Process blocking rules* in the Credit management hold list to execute a check whether the original blocking reason is still valid. If the circumstances have changed accordingly (e.g., due to a customer payment), the hold will be released automatically—with or without posting, depending on the Credit and collection parameters (field *Automatically release* in the section *Credit*, tab *Credit holds*).

If you want to manually set a credit hold in a sales order, click the button *Credit management/Credit management/Force credit hold* in the Sales order form and select the hold reason in the following dialog.

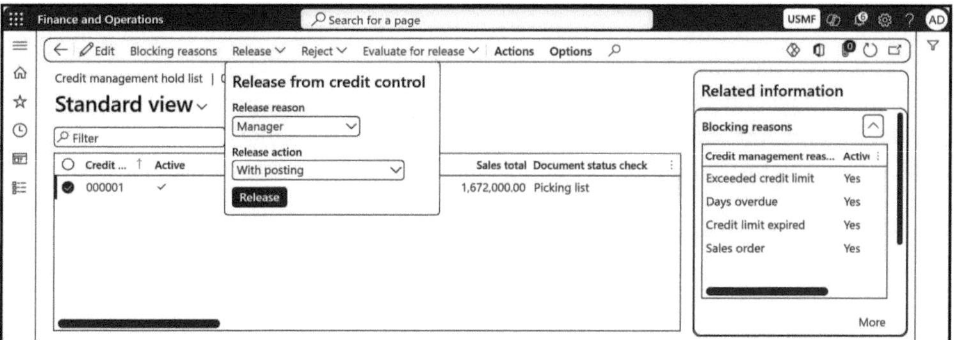

Fig. 9.9 Releasing a credit hold

9.2.6.3 Adjusting the Credit Limit

If enabled in the Credit and collection parameters (slider *Allow manual editing of credit limits* in the section *Credit*, tab *Credit limits*), you can manually edit the field *Credit limit* in the Customer detail form, which automatically populates the field *Credit limit change date* accordingly.

Unlike the regular credit limit, the temporary credit limits, which you can access with the button *Credit management/Related information/Temporary credit limits* in the Customer form, are not editable. You can only update temporary credit limits with a credit limit adjustment journal.

Credit limit adjustment journals (*Credit and collections > Credit limit adjustments > Credit limit adjustments*) are used to insert or update the regular credit limit or a temporary credit limit. In a similar way to managing a trade agreement journal ($\rightarrow$ Sect. 4.8.1), you can create a new journal with the button *New* in this form. Then select the *Credit limit adjustment type* ("Credit limit" or "Temporary credit limit") and click the button *Lines* to access the Journal lines form. In the journal lines, you can manually enter a new credit limit or a temporary credit limit per customer or customer credit group. Alternatively, you can click the button *Generate* to populate the lines with an adjustment of the current credit limit (fixed amount or percentage). Posting the journal with the button *Post* updates the current credit limit of customers or customer credit groups (or creates a temporary credit limit).

9.2.7 Sales Tax/VAT Settings

The sales tax/VAT functionality supports various tax regulations, including the sales tax in the United States and the value added tax in Europe.

Sales tax codes, which determine the tax rate, are the basis for the sales tax calculation. In an invoice line, the applicable sales tax code is depending on both, the item sales tax group of the item and the sales tax group of the customer or vendor.

9.2.7.1 Sales Tax Parameters

A primary setting for the tax calculation is whether sales tax is used: If your company is subject to taxation with sales tax (and not with VAT), set the slider *Apply sales tax taxation rules* in the General ledger parameters (*Tax > Setup > Parameters > General ledger parameters*, section *Sales tax*) to "Yes". Further parameter settings for sales tax include a default *Item sales tax group* or the setting whether cash discounts reduce sales tax.

9.2.7.2 Sales Tax Authorities

In the setup of sales tax calculation, enter the authorities (*Tax > Indirect taxes > Sales tax > Sales tax authorities*) with ID, *Name*, and *Report layout* for tax reporting first.

9.2.7.3 Sales Tax Settlement Periods

Applicable periods for tax reporting (usually monthly periods) are specified in the menu item *Tax > Indirect taxes > Sales tax > Sales tax settlement periods*.

When you create a settlement period definition with ID and description, assign the applicable *Authority* and enter the period length (*Period interval unit* and *Period interval duration*) on the tab *General*. Then switch to the tab *Period intervals* and click the button *Add* in the toolbar to enter the first period manually (e.g., Jan 1 – Jan 31). You can subsequently use the button *New period interval* in the toolbar of this tab to create further periods.

9.2.7.4 Ledger Posting Groups

Sales tax ledger posting groups control the main accounts for sales tax transactions (depending on the sales tax code of the invoice transaction).

In order to create a sales tax ledger posting group, open the menu item *Tax > Setup > Sales tax > Ledger posting groups* and click the button *New*. Enter the group ID and description before you select the main account for the *Sales tax payable*, for the *Sales tax receivable*, for the *Use tax expense*, and the *Use tax payable* as applicable. The *Settlement account* specifies the balance account for the payment to the authorities.

> *Note:* Depending on the option *Apply sales tax taxation rules* in the General ledger parameters, not all fields in the Ledger posting groups form are shown.

9.2.7.5 Sales Tax Codes

Sales tax codes (*Tax > Indirect taxes > Sales tax > Sales tax codes)* control the tax rate and the calculation basis. On the tab *General* in the Sales tax code form (→ Fig. 9.10), assign the *Settlement period* and the *Ledger posting group*. Detailed calculation parameters are available on the tab *Calculation*. In order to specify the tax rate, click the button *Sales tax*

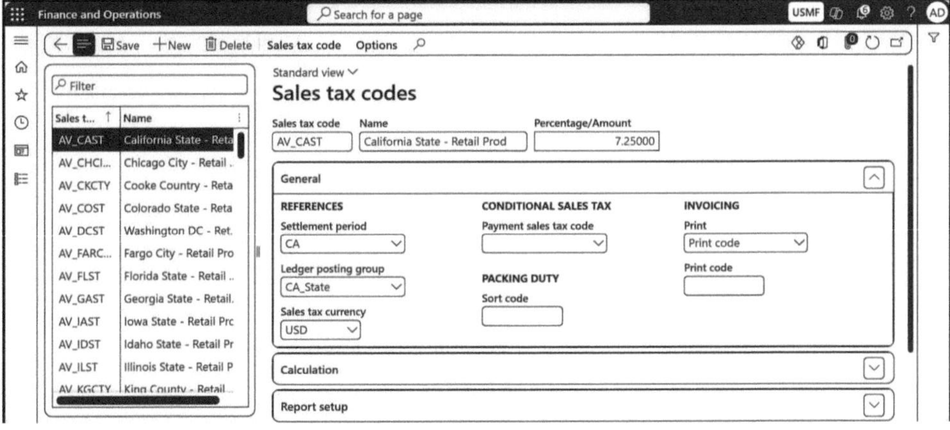

Fig. 9.10 Managing the sales tax codes

code/Sales tax code/Values in the action pane and enter the applicable rate in the column *Value* of the Sales tax code values form.

Once you have created a sales tax code, assign it to applicable sales tax groups and item sales tax groups. Dynamics 365 determines the sales tax code of an invoice line from the sales tax code, which is included in the settings of both—the item sales tax group of the item, and the sales tax group of the customer or vendor.

In order to apply, for example, a tax code "AV_CAST" to a sales invoice line, the line has to comply with both of the following conditions:

- **Item sales tax group**—The item sales tax group of the item contains the sales tax code "AV_CAST".
- **Sales tax group**—The sales tax group of the customer contains the sales tax code "AV_CAST".

9.2.7.6 Sales Tax Groups and Item Sales Tax Groups

If you want to set up a new sales tax group, open the Sales tax groups form (*Tax > Indirect taxes > Sales tax > Sales tax groups*) and click the button *New*. Enter the ID and the description on the tab *Overview* before you switch to the tab *Setup*. On this tab, insert all applicable sales tax codes for the customers or vendors in this group.

In order to assign the sales tax group to a customer or vendor, open the Customer form (or the Vendor form) and select the *Sales tax group* on the tab *Invoice and delivery* in the detail form, usually when creating a customer or vendor. Default values for the sales tax group are specified in the customer group (or vendor group).

In the Item sales tax groups form (*Tax > Indirect taxes > Sales tax > Item sales tax groups*), you can manage the item sales tax groups that refer to the released products. Setting up an item sales tax group (→ Fig. 9.11) works similarly to setting up a sales tax group.

Fig. 9.11 Managing the item sales tax groups

In order to assign item sales tax groups to an item, open the Released product form and select the *Item sales tax group* for sales (on the tab *Sell*) and for purchasing (on the tab *Purchase*) in the detail form. Default values for the item sales tax groups in the released product are specified on the tab *Setup* in the Item group form. If you use product categories in order lines, assign the applicable item sales tax group to the categories in the Procurement category form and in the Sales category form.

> *Note:* For product masters, you can specify variant-specific item sales tax groups in the Released product variant form.

9.2.7.7 Sales Tax Transactions

When you enter a transaction in a journal line or an order line, Dynamics 365 initializes the sales tax code based on the item and the customer/vendor. In order to view the calculated tax before posting, click the button *Sales tax* in the action pane or in the toolbar. This button is available in journal lines, sales and purchase order headers or lines, and posting dialogs (e.g., for the sales invoice).

If necessary, you can change the sales tax groups or the sales tax code in a journal line or order line before posting. When posting an invoice, Dynamics 365 generates a transaction for the sales tax in the general ledger (according to the ledger posting group assigned to the sales tax code) and a sales tax transaction in the tax ledger.

9.2.7.8 Tax Calculation Service

The tax calculation service provides the option to execute the tax calculation as a separate service on Microsoft Azure. For this purpose, configure the Tax Calculation add-in in the Globalization studio workspace. As a prerequisite, the relevant Dataverse repository needs to be linked to the Dynamics 365 environment in the Power Platform Admin Center (PPAC). Then enable the service in the parameters (*Tax > Setup > Tax configuration > Tax calculation parameters*).

If the tax calculation service is enabled, transactions like a sales order initially receive the sales tax group, the item sales tax group, and the tax code from within the transactional Dynamics 365 environment. When the tax calculation is triggered, for example, with the button *Sell/Tax/Sales tax* in the Sales order form, the required data are sent to the tax calculation service, which calculates the tax amount and, if applicable, overrides the tax group, the item tax group, and the tax code.

> *Note:* When using the tax calculation service, you can manage multiple VAT registration numbers (registration numbers in different countries) for customers, vendors, and your own company.

9.2.8   Basic Setup for Journal Transactions

In addition to the basic setup in finance, the journal names have to be configured before you can register a journal transaction in the general ledger.

9.2.8.1 Journal Names

All ledger journals show a common structure, which is independent of the journal type. But the different journal types enable different fields in the related journals. In addition, some journals include additional features—e.g., the payment proposal feature in the vendor payment journal.

Journal names (*General ledger > Journal setup > Journal names*) classify transactions by subject matters. The lookup field *Journal type* in this form controls, in which journal you can use the selected journal name. The most common journal types are:

* **Daily**—General journal.
* **Periodic**—Periodic journal.
* **Vendor invoice recording**—Invoice journal in accounts payable.
* **Vendor disbursement**—Vendor payment.
* **Customer payment**—Payment of customers.

Depending on the transactions in your company, journal names with further journal types are required—e.g., a journal with the journal type "Post fixed assets" for fixed asset transactions. If you want to use the invoice register and the invoice approval journals in accounts payable, you need a journal name with the journal type "Invoice register" and a journal name with the journal type "Approval".

If you select different number sequences in the field *Voucher series* of journal names, you can distinguish different journals by the voucher number. The default for the offset account in journal lines is specified in the fields *Account type* and *Offset account* of the journal names. Another important setting in the journal names is the slider *Amounts include sales tax*. If this slider is set to "Yes", amounts that you enter in the journal lines include sales tax or input tax (if applicable). Otherwise, the entered line amount is a net amount to which Dynamics 365 adds the sales tax.

9.2.8.2 Journal Approval

There are two options in the journal name setup which enforce an approval of journals before posting:

* **Journal approval system**—Enabled in the field group *Approval.*
* **Approval workflow**—Enabled in the field group *Approval workflow.*

If you want to activate the simple journal approval system (→ Sect. 9.3.1) for a journal name, set the slider *Active* in the field group *Approval* to "Yes". Then select the responsible user group for approval in the related lookup field *Approve*.

If you want to apply the other option for approval, the approval workflow, an appropriate general ledger workflow has to be configured in the menu item *General ledger > Journal setup > General ledger workflows*. The workflow type "Ledger daily journal workflow" determines approval workflows for daily journals. You can find more details on workflows in → Sect. 10.4.

9.2.8.3 Posting Layers

When you create a journal name, the default value for the field *Posting layer*, which determines the posting layer of transactions with this journal name, is "Current". If you need to keep particular ledger transaction separate (e.g., to cut off transactions that refer to local tax regulations), you can create journal names with the posting layer "Operations", or "Tax", or one of the custom layers.

You can subsequently select the appropriate posting layer in the closing sheet (when executing the fiscal year closing) or in a journal transaction (by selecting a suitable journal name) to record transactions, which should not be included in regular reports that are based on the layer "Current". In order to analyze and to report the transactions in the other layers, you can set up additional versions of financial reports which include the transactions in these layers.

9.2.8.4 General Ledger Parameters

The General ledger parameters (*General ledger > Ledger setup > General ledger parameters*) contain further settings for journal transactions. One of these settings is the parameter field *Check for voucher used,* which you should not set to "Accept duplicates" in order to avoid confusion with the voucher number of documents.

In the section *Chart of accounts and dimensions* of the parameters, you can set up the delimiter between the segments in the ledger account field (used in the segmented entry control).

9.2.9   Case Study Exercises

Exercise 9.1—Main Accounts
The following main accounts are required in your company (## = your user ID):

- Main account 111C##, Name "##-Petty cash", Account type "Balance sheet".
- Main account 111B##, Name "##-Bank", Account type "Balance sheet".
- Main account 6060##, Name "##-Consulting", Account type "Expense".
- Main account ZZ##, Name "##-Account structure test", Account type "Balance sheet".

Create these accounts in the chart of accounts of your training company.

Exercise 9.2—Account Structures
Unlike the other main accounts that you have created in exercise 9.1, the main account ZZ## is not included in an account number range which is covered by any account structure. For this reason, set up a new account structure which only refers to this main account.

Create and activate a new account structure ZS## with two segments—the main accounts and the financial dimension for business units. The main account ZZ## is the only applicable main account in this account structure. Assign the account structure to your company.

Exercise 9.3—Bank Accounts
Your company opens a new bank account. Create a bank account B-## with any routing number and bank account number of your choice. Assign the main account 111B## of exercise 9.1 to this bank account.

Exercise 9.4—Journal Names
You want to register the transactions of the next exercises in your own journals. For this purpose, create a journal name G-## (## = your user ID) with the type "Daily", a journal name I-## with the type "Vendor invoice recording", and a journal name P-## with the type "Vendor disbursement". Select an existing number sequence in all these journal names.

9.3 Transactions in Finance

Each business process with an impact on financial values generates general ledger transactions. Most of the ledger transactions are not initially created in accounting but derive from transactions in other areas like purchasing, sales, or production. Transactions in these areas generate ledger transactions in the background.

Apart from the derived transactions, some ledger transactions originate from activities in accounting. You can record these ledger transactions in a journal in the General ledger module.

9.3.1 General Journals

If you want to post manual transactions in the general ledger, use a general journal (*General ledger > Journal entries > General journals*).

General journals refer to the journal type "Daily". Apart from the general journals, there are financial journals that are assigned to other journal types—for example, the invoice journals in the Accounts payable module, or the payment journals in the Accounts payable and the Accounts receivable module. If you do not need the advanced functionality of a specific journal (e.g., payment proposals in payment journals), it does not matter whether you register a transaction in the specific journal or in the general journal.

9.3.1.1 Journal Header

Journals are vouchers and therefore consist of a header and at least one line. The header contains common settings and default values for the corresponding lines. In each line, you can subsequently override the default values that derive from the corresponding header field (e.g., the offset account).

The selected option in the lookup field *Show* at the top of the General journal list page (→ Fig. 9.12) determines whether open or posted journals are shown. In order to register a new journal, click the button *New* and select a journal name.

On the tab *Setup* of the journal header, you can override the default values which derive from the journal name (e.g., the offset account). The columns *In use* and *In use by* in the journal header display if somebody is currently working in the lines of the particular journal.

9.3.1.2 Journal Lines

In order to switch to the journal lines, click the button *Lines* in the action pane or click the *Journal batch number* shown as a link in the grid of the Journal list page. In a new line, the default for the posting date is the current session date. The voucher number derives from the number sequence of the journal name which you have selected in the header. Depending on the option which you select in the column *Account type*, enter a ledger account, a

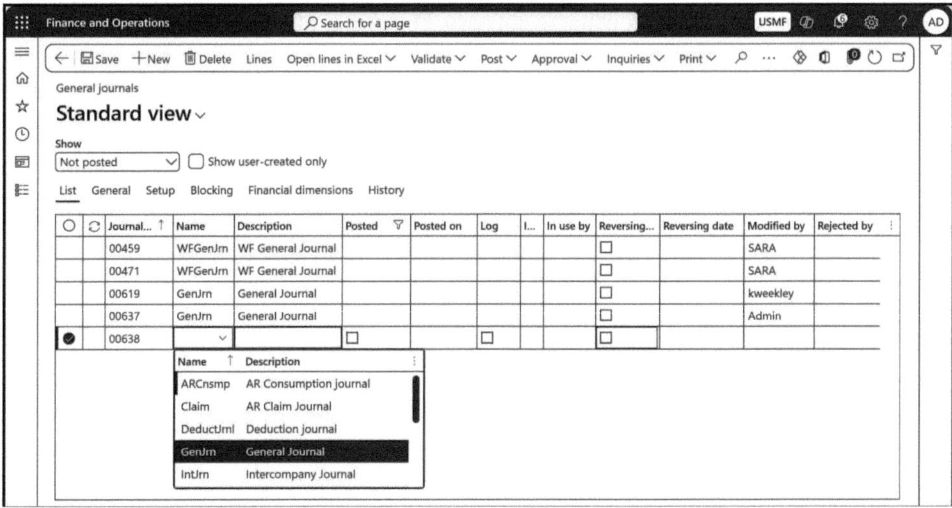

Fig. 9.12 Selecting a journal name in a new general journal header

vendor, a customer, a bank account, a cash account (if enabled), or a fixed asset in the column *Account*.

If you enter a ledger account in the field *Account*, segmented entry control applies (see below). With segmented entry control, the main account usually has to be entered in the first segment of the ledger account field. If and which financial dimension segments are available and need to be entered is depending on the applicable account structure for the selected main account. The lookup in the account field shows the available values for the segment which is currently selected.

Once you have registered the account, you can enter the amount in the column *Debit* or *Credit*. In a single-line transaction, which applies the same amount (with a different sign) to the debit and the credit account, enter the *Offset account type* and the *Offset account* (including segments for financial dimensions as applicable) in the appropriate columns of the journal line.

The columns *Company* and *Offset company* provide the option to register intercompany transactions. As a prerequisite, intercompany accounting (*General ledger > Posting setup > Intercompany accounting*) has to be configured for the respective companies.

In order to support data entry, a separate pane at the bottom of the lines shows the voucher balance of the selected line and the balance of the complete journal. Before you can post a journal, the balance of the individual vouchers (lines with the same voucher number) and the balance of the complete journal have to be zero.

If you prefer entering data in Excel over the Journal line detail form, you can use the Office integration: Click the button *Open lines in Excel* in the journal header and enter or edit the journal lines in Excel.

In case you need to enter a transaction with more than one offset account, you can record one voucher in multiple lines ($\rightarrow$ Fig. 9.13). In this case, do not enter an offset account in the first line, but in one or more separate journal lines for the offset transactions. As long as the balance of the voucher is not zero, Dynamics 365 retrieves the same voucher number as in the previous line. Once the voucher balance is zero, the next line shows a new voucher number (as a prerequisite, the option "In connection with balance" has to be selected in the field *New voucher* of the journal name).

> *Note:* If the "One voucher" requirement is active (which means that the slider *Allow multiple transactions within one voucher* in the section *Ledger* of the General ledger parameters is set to "No"), it is not possible to post one common voucher for multiple lines with different sub-ledger accounts (e.g., different customers).

9.3.1.3 Segmented Entry Control

When you enter a ledger account in an account field, segmented entry control applies. Since the main account and applicable financial dimensions are merged into a single ledger account field, this field includes the complete posting information as required by the account structure.

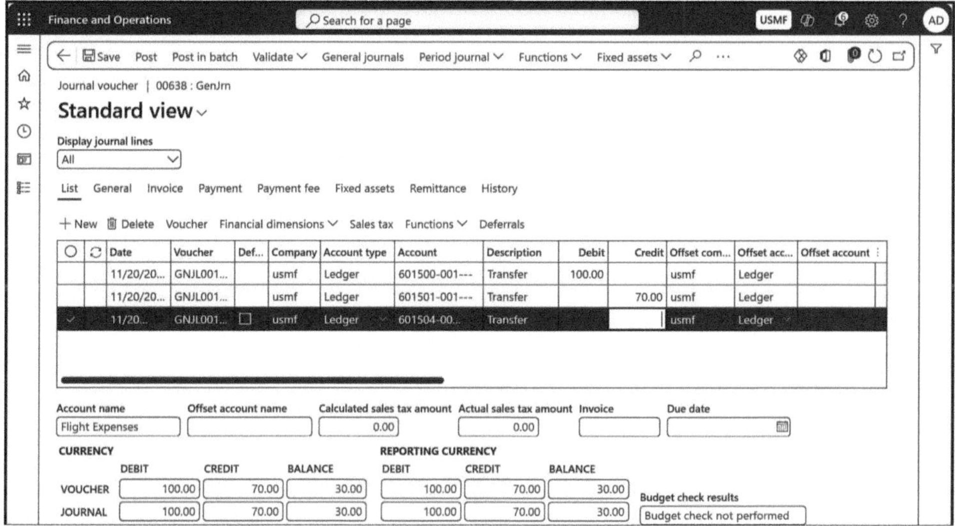

Fig. 9.13 Registering the journal lines of a voucher with multiple offset lines

The lookup when entering a ledger account refers to the currently active segment of the ledger account field. In order to search a segment value, enter the search content—the first characters of the identification or the name—in the applicable segment of the ledger account field before or after opening the lookup with the lookup button or the shortcut *Alt + Down*.

In the example of → Fig. 9.14, you can view the segment lookup that is shown after entering the characters "sp" in the second segment of the ledger account field. This lookup contains the list of business units that start with the characters "sp" in the ID or the name.

The sequence and the number of segments is depending on the account structure that is assigned to the selected main account (→ Sect. 9.2.4). If the account structure allows a blank for a particular segment (or does not include any financial dimension), it is not required to enter a corresponding segment value.

9.3.1.4 Posting Financial Journals

Once you have completed the journal lines, you can post the journal with the button *Post* or *Post/Post* in the action pane of the journal header or lines. If there are issues, an error message is shown, and it is not possible to post the transaction.

If you click the button *Post/Post and transfer* (instead of *Post/Post*) in the journal header, only vouchers with correct data are posted. Vouchers in the journal with incorrect data are transferred to a new journal, in which you can enter corrections.

Optionally, you can check the journal with the button *Validate/Validate* before posting. The button *Validate/Simulate posting* starts a more in-depth validation of the journal, which covers all checks that are executed when posting.

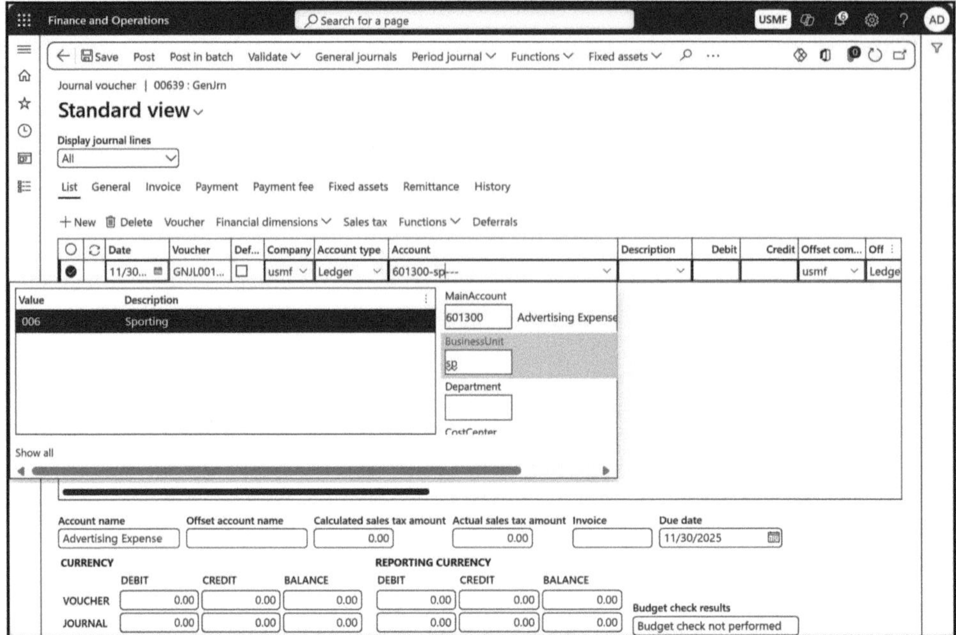

Fig. 9.14 Segmented entry for the main account and applicable financial dimensions

9.3.1.5 Using Financial Tags

If you use financial tags (→ Sect. 9.2.3), you can enter tag values, which are a default for the journal lines, on the tab *Financial tags* in the journal header. In the journal lines, you can edit the tag values in the column *Financial tags* and *Offset financial tags*.

9.3.1.6 Global General Journals

If you want to view the general journals across companies, open the menu item *General ledger > Journal entries > Global general journals*. In the Global general journals list page, the first column shows the company in which the respective general journal has been registered. If you click the button *New journal* in this form, a drop-down is shown in which you select the company and the journal name for the new general journal.

9.3.1.7 Journal Approval System

If a journal approval—either with the journal approval system or with the approval workflow—is activated for the selected journal name, it is not possible to post the journal before obtaining the required approval.

In case of the journal approval system, you can click the button *Approval/Report as ready* in the journal header to request approval. The responsible person for approval (member of the user group for approval selected in the journal name) then clicks the button *Approval/Approve* to release the journal for posting.

9.3.1.8 Periodic Journals and Voucher Templates

If you need to register a particular transaction repeatedly, you can use one of the two options for a recurring registration:

- **Periodic journals**—If the transaction recurs on a regular basis.
- **Voucher templates**—If you only want to use a copy template.

Periodic journals are used to register transactions which are repeated on a regular basis (e.g., office rent, or monthly installments). In order to create a periodic journal, open the form *General ledger > Journal entries > Periodic journals* and enter a journal header and journal lines (similar to a general journal). An alternative way for creating a periodic journal is to copy a general journal to a periodic journal (click the button *Period journal/Save journal* in the lines of a general journal). The column *Date* in the lines of a periodic journal determines the start date for the periodic transactions. The frequency of the transaction (e.g., monthly) has to be specified in the columns *Units* and *Number of units* (also shown on the tab *Periodic*).

In order to post the transactions for a periodic journal, you have to create related general journals on a regular basis.

In the lines of such a common general journal, click the button *Period journal/Retrieve journal* to retrieve the periodic journal. In the Period journal dialog which is shown then (→ Fig. 9.15), select the periodic journal, enter the *To date* until which you want to generate journal lines, and leave the option "Copy" in the field *Copy or move journal*. Once the periodic journal lines are transferred to the general journal, you can edit and post the lines in the general journal as usual. In the periodic journal, the column *Date* in the lines is—at the time when you retrieve the journal lines—updated with the next posting date. This date

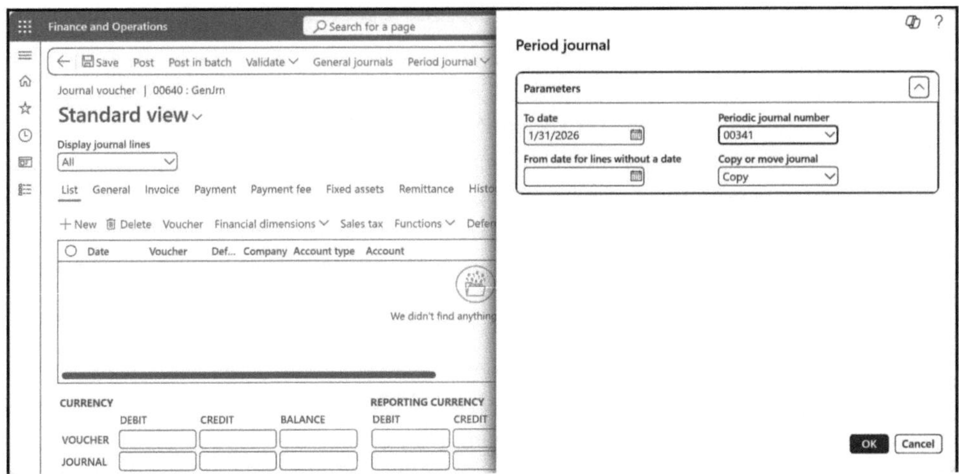

Fig. 9.15 Retrieving a periodic journal into the lines of a general journal

is calculated by adding the frequency period to the last posting date that has been retrieved. The column *Last date* in the periodic journal lines shows the date on which the journal has been retrieved the last time.

Apart from periodic journals for general journals, you can also use periodic journals as a basis for invoice journals in accounts payable.

Unlike periodic journals, voucher templates are templates for simply copying journals, without a periodic interval. In order to create a voucher template, select a journal line in a general journal (or in an invoice journal) and click the button *Functions/Save voucher template* in the toolbar of the journal lines. The template will include all journal lines with the same voucher number as the selected line. In the dialog that is shown when saving the template, select the *Template type* "Percent" in case you want to apply a proportional distribution of line amounts.

If you select this voucher template in the template dialog that you open with the button *Functions/Select voucher template* in a journal, a second dialog is shown in which you can enter the amount that you want to distribute across the lines according to the proportion in the template.

9.3.2 Invoice Posting

Depending on the particular invoice, there are different ways for registering and posting the document. In Dynamics 365, there are the following options for invoice posting:

- **Sales order invoice**—For items shipped to customers ($\rightarrow$ Sect. 4.5.1).
- **Free text invoice**—For sales invoices not related to items ($\rightarrow$ Sect. 4.5.3).
- **(Pending) Vendor invoice**—For items or procurement categories received from vendors, with or without reference to a purchase order.
- **Vendor invoice journal**—For invoices not related to items or categories.
- **General journal**—For manual purchase or sales invoices (not to be printed).

9.3.2.1 Invoices in the General Journal

If you want to register a vendor invoice which refers to a particular offset account (e.g., an invoice for an expense), the easiest way is using a vendor invoice journal. For customer invoices which refer to a particular offset account (revenue account), use a free text invoice.

Alternatively, it is possible to register an invoice in a general journal. This is, for example, an option for sales invoices which are not originally created in Dynamics 365 (e.g., invoices from an external cash register).

If you enter a sales invoice in a general journal, select the *Account type* "Customer" and enter the customer number in the column *Account* of the journal lines. In the column *Offset account*, enter an appropriate revenue account. On the tab *Invoice*, enter the invoice number (in the field *Invoice*), the payment terms, and the cash discount as applicable. Before posting, you can check the sales tax groups on the tab *General*. With the button *Sales tax* in the toolbar of the tab *List*, you can check the sales tax calculation. In order to post the journal, click the button *Post* or *Post/Post* in the action pane of the journal header or the journal lines.

Registering a vendor invoice in a general journal works similar to the sales invoice—for a vendor invoice, select the *Account type* "Vendor" (instead of "Customer").

9.3.2.2 Options for Vendor Invoice Posting

Depending on whether a vendor invoice refers to a purchase order or not, there are the following ways to process a vendor invoice (→ Fig. 9.16):

- **Purchase order invoice**—Register a pending vendor invoice (the lines only include both, stocked or non-stocked products, or procurements categories).
- **Invoice without order assignment**—Depending on whether you want to enter the offset ledger account number, there are two types:
  - **With non-stocked products or procurements categories**—In the pending vendor invoices (similar to purchase order invoices, but without purchase order assignment).
  - **With ledger accounts**—Register and post an invoice journal, usually for particular subjects like office rent or legal services.

You can register a vendor invoice—with or without reference to a purchase order—in the Pending vendor invoice form (*Accounts payable > Invoices > Pending vendor invoices*) as shown in → Sect. 3.6.1. Apart from manually entering the invoice with its lines, you can use the vendor collaboration, or an automated import, or the Invoice capture solution (→ Sect. 3.6.2) to create pending vendor invoices.

The invoice lines in a pending vendor invoice usually derive from the invoiced purchase order(s) and contain stocked and non-stocked items, and procurement categories. If you record an invoice in the Pending vendor invoice form which does not refer to a purchase

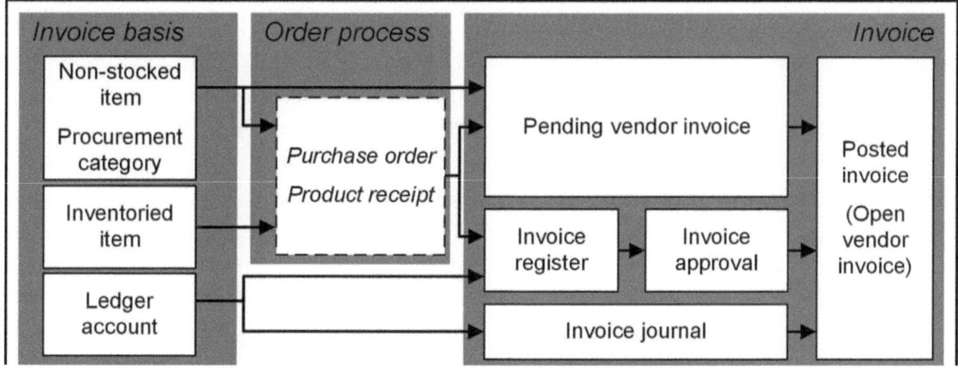

Fig. 9.16 Options for processing vendor invoices

order, enter the lines manually in which you select non-stocked items and procurement categories.

In order to register a vendor invoice that does not refer to an item number or a procurement category, but directly to a ledger account (e.g., for office rent) or to a fixed asset (acquisition), enter a journal transaction. In the Accounts payable module, the following journals are available for recording an invoice:

- **Invoice journal**—Main form for vendor invoices in accounts payable.
- **Global invoice journal**—Like the invoice journal, but across companies.
- **Invoice register**—In conjunction with the *Invoice approval journal*.
- **General journal**—As described above.

If you want to apply an approval workflow to invoice journals, set up an appropriate workflow with the workflow type for the respective journal type in the menu item *Accounts payable > Setup > Accounts payable workflows* and assign it to the journal name.

For purchase order invoices, there are two options for recording and processing an invoice that requires approval:

- **Approval workflow in the Pending vendor invoice form**—Enter and post the invoice in the Pending vendor invoice form, with activated approval workflow.
- **Invoice register journal**—As a prior step to the Pending vendor invoice form, you can first post the invoice to interim accounts in the invoice register journal, followed by recording an invoice approval journal (or an invoice pool) which finally opens the Pending vendor invoice form.

From a financial perspective, the main difference between the vendor invoice approval workflow and the invoice register journal is, that the invoice register journal already posts an invoice, which is subject to tax calculation, when starting the approval process.

The Open vendor invoice page (*Accounts payable > Invoices > Open vendor invoices*) shows all invoices which are not yet paid, irrespective of the way in which the invoice has been posted. In the action pane of this form, the options in the button *New* provide an alternative way to access the different vendor invoice journals and the Pending vendor invoice form. Similar options are available in the workspaces *Vendor invoice entry* and *Vendor invoice center*, and in the Vendor form (on the action pane tab *INVOICE*).

9.3.2.3 Invoice Journals

The invoice journal (*Accounts payable > Invoices > Invoice journal*), which you can also access from the workspace *Vendor invoice entry*, is the main form in the Accounts payable module for registering invoices which do not refer to a purchase order.

In order to register an invoice in the invoice journal (→ Fig. 9.17), create a header record in the list page before you switch to the lines. Enter the invoice lines with the vendor number (in the column *Account*), vendor invoice number (column *Invoice*), transaction

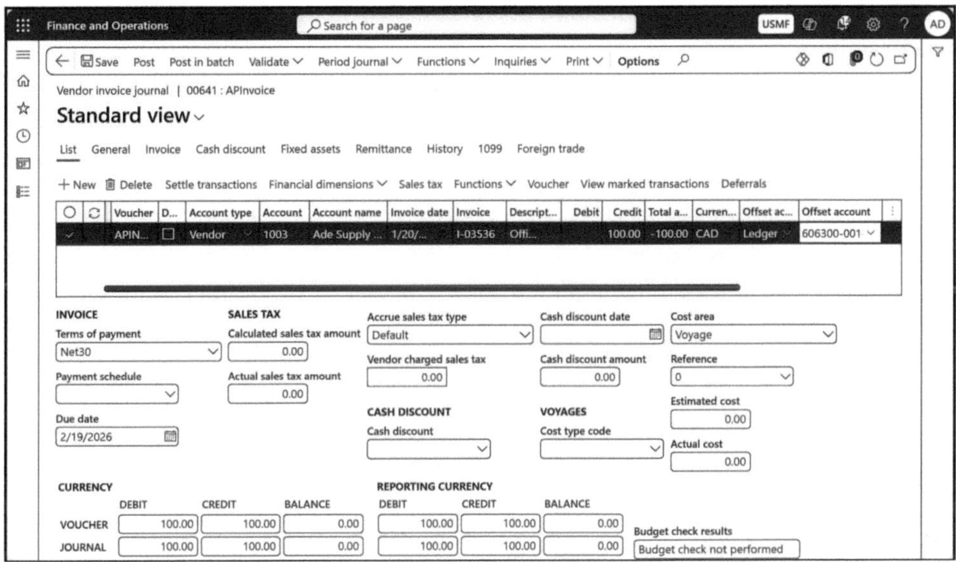

Fig. 9.17   Registering an invoice journal line

text, amount (for an invoice, in the column *Credit*), offset account, terms of payment, approver (*Approved by* on the tab *Invoice*) and other data like sales tax and cash discount as applicable. The column *Total amount* shows the total amount including tax—depending on the setting of the slider *Amounts include sales tax* in the journal header (on the tab *Setup*), the sales tax is added or the amount entered in the column *Credit* already includes the tax.

Once you have completed entering the invoice, post it with the button *Post* or *Post/Post* in the action pane of the journal header or lines.

9.3.2.4 Invoice Registers

The invoice register (*Accounts payable > Invoices > Invoice register*) provides the option to pre-register vendor invoices. Posting an invoice register includes posting the vendor transaction, the ledger transactions (to interim accounts), and, depending on the Accounts payable parameters (field *Time of sales tax posting* in the section *Ledger and sales tax* on the tab *Sales tax*), the applicable sales tax transactions. If the sales tax is not posted with the invoice register, it is posted later with the invoice approval.

The structure of the invoice register with journal header and lines is similar to the structure of the general journals, but the account type is restricted to "Vendor". In the journal lines, enter the responsible employee for approval (*Approved by* in the lower pane of the journal lines), the terms of payment, the cash discount, and sales tax groups as applicable. If the invoice refers to a purchase order, select the purchase order number in the column *Purchase order* of the journal lines to facilitate later approval. In order to post a journal in the invoice register, click the button *Post* or *Post/Post* in the action pane of the journal header or lines.

Posting a journal in the invoice register creates a regular vendor transaction, which you can access with the button *Vendor/Transactions/Transactions* in the Vendor form. The slider *Approved* on the tab *General* of this transaction is set to "No", which is why the invoice is not included in payment proposals.

The ledger transactions of the invoice register are posted to interim accounts. These interim accounts are specified in the vendor posting profile (*Accounts payable > Setup > Vendor posting profiles*, field *Arrival* and *Offset account* on the tab *Setup*).

> *Note:* Depending on the Accounts payable parameters (section *Invoice*, tab *Invoice register*, field *Approved by*), the approver (field *Approved by*) in invoice register lines is mandatory or optional.

9.3.2.5 Invoice Approval Journals

Once an invoice is posted in an invoice register, the responsible person for approval can approve it in the invoice approval journal.

In order to start processing the invoice approval, create a new header in the invoice approval journal (*Accounts payable > Invoices > Invoice approval*). Then switch to the journal lines and click the button *Find vouchers* in the action pane to retrieve a posted invoice register. The *Find vouchers* dialog shows all not yet approved invoice registers in the upper pane. With the button *Select* in this dialog, you can select one or more invoices for approval. Once you close the dialog with the button *OK*, the selected invoice(s) are transferred to the approval journal lines.

If the approver has not been selected in the invoice register that has been transferred, select the approver in the column *Approved by* of the invoice approval journal. The following steps depend on whether the invoice refers to an order:

- **Not related to a purchase order**—In this case, select a ledger account (e.g., an expense account) in the lower pane of the invoice approval journal lines (first line in the lower pane of → Fig. 9.18). If multiple expense accounts apply, enter multiple lines that share the total amount. In order to post the approval, click the button *Post*.
- **Related to a purchase order**—In this case, click the button *Functions/Purchase order* to access the Pending vendor invoice form for the purchase order. In the Pending vendor invoice form, post the invoice as usual (→ Sect. 3.6.1).

If you decide not to post the approval of a particular invoice currently, click the button *Remove vouchers* in the action pane of the invoice approval journal to remove the selected invoice before posting. With the button *Find vouchers*, you can select the invoice again at any time.

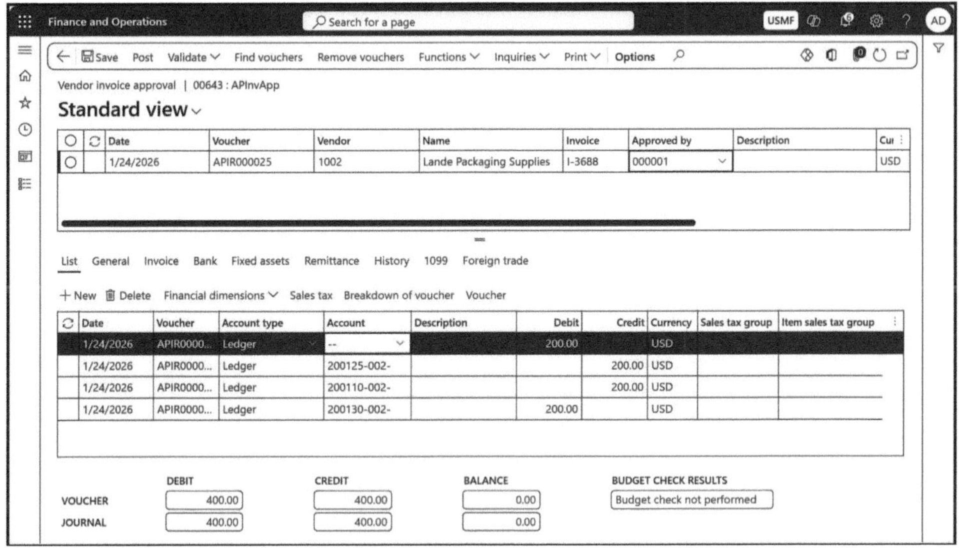

Fig. 9.18 The invoice approval journal lines after fetching an invoice register

9.3.2.6 Rejecting Invoice Approval

If you do not want to approve a vendor invoice, which has been posted in the invoice register (e.g., because it does not match the applicable purchase order, or because of other reasons), you have to post a cancellation.

For this purpose, open the invoice approval journal, create a new header, and in the journal lines, retrieve the applicable invoice register in the same way as for approval. But before posting the approval journal, click the button *Functions/Cancel* in the action pane. Then click the button *Post* or *Post/Post* in the action pane of the invoice approval journal header or lines to post the cancellation.

9.3.2.7 Invoice Pool

The invoice pool (*Accounts payable > Invoices > Invoice pool*) shows all pending invoice register approvals. You can use the invoice pool to post the approval for invoice registers, which refer to a purchase order (as an alternative to the invoice approval journal). For this purpose, select the respective line in the invoice pool and click the button *Purchase order* in the action pane to access the Pending vendor invoice form for the purchase order (similar to the corresponding button in approval journals).

9.3.3   Payments

Posting an invoice creates an open transaction with the vendor liability or the customer debt.

9.3.3.1 Open Transactions

In order to view the open transactions, click the button *Customer/Transactions/Transactions* in the Customer form, or *Vendor/Transactions/Transactions* in the Vendor form, and make sure to select the option "Open" in the lookup *Show* above the grid (applying a filter on open transactions). With the option "All" in the lookup *Show*, you can view all customer (or vendor) transactions.

If you want to print the open transactions, run the report *Accounts receivable > Inquiries and reports > Open transactions report* for customers, and the report *Accounts payable > Inquiries and reports > Vendor open transactions report* for vendors.

9.3.3.2 Customer Payments

You can register a customer payment which you have received, in the Customer payment journal page (*Accounts receivable > Payments > Customer payment journal*), or with the tile *Record customer payment* in the workspace *Customer payments*.

In the Customer payment journal page, create a record with a journal name in the journal header and switch to the lines. In the lines, enter the payment with the customer number (column *Account*), the transaction text (column *Description*), the payment amount (column *Credit*), and the offset account. If the customer has paid to your bank account, select the *Offset account type* "Bank".

If you want to settle the invoice that is paid when entering a payment line, select the invoice number in the column *Invoice* of the journal line—the journal line then receives the payment data (including the amount) from the invoice. Alternatively, you can enter the customer in the column *Account* and click the button *Settle transactions* in the toolbar of the lines to apply one or more invoices to a payment line (→ Sect. 9.3.4).

Apart from entering a payment in the journal lines, you can use the button *Enter customer payment* in the journal header to open the Enter customer payment form. In this form, you can select the open invoices which are paid and, with the button *Save in journal*, create and settle the payment lines. Another option for creating payment lines, which you can use for direct debiting (withdrawing from the bank account of the customer), is the customer payment proposal in the payment journal lines (similar to the vendor payment proposal, see below).

Once you have completed the payment lines, post the customer payment journal with the button *Post* or *Post/Post* in the action pane of the journal header or lines.

> *Note:* If the *Advanced bank reconciliation* (slider on the tab *Reconciliation* in the Bank accounts detail form) is activated for a bank account, you can also generate customer and vendor payment journals from the bank statement of the respective bank account.

9.3.3.3 Vendor Payments

In a similar way to customer payments, you can record payments to vendors in the vendor payment journal (→ Fig. 9.19), which you can access with the menu item *Accounts payable > Payments > Vendor payment journal*.

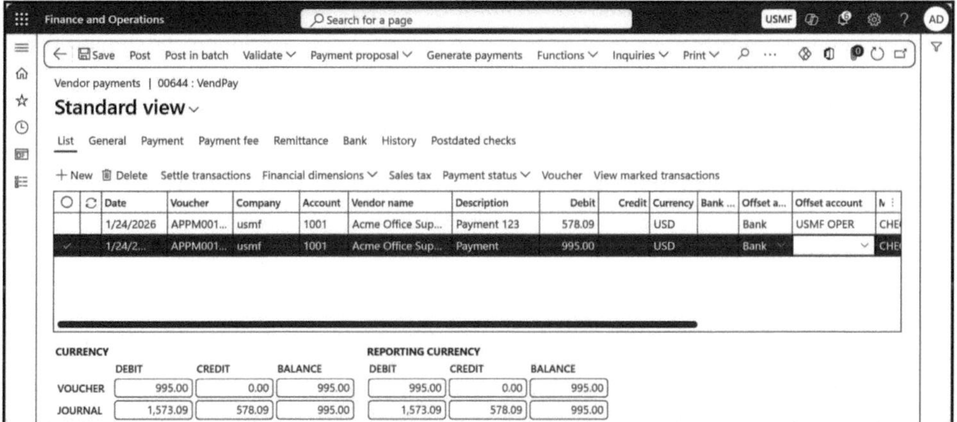

Fig. 9.19 Entering a payment line in a vendor payment journal

Manually registering a vendor payment works like registering a customer payment (including the settlement, → Sect. 9.3.4). But in most cases, outgoing payments require additional support and control. In Dynamics 365, the payment proposal and the payment status are available for this purpose. In addition, you can set up the process automation for vendor payments (*Accounts payable > Payment setup > Process automations*) to create payment journals automatically.

If you want to prevent paying a particular invoice, open the vendor transaction in Edit mode and switch to the tab *General*. On this tab, you can set the slider *Approved* to "No" or enter an *Invoice payment release date*. The payment proposal does not include the invoice until you set the approval in the transaction to "Yes", or until the release date has passed.

9.3.3.4 Methods of Payment

Methods of payment (*Accounts payable > Payment setup > Methods of payment*) are an important setting for processing vendor payments. Usually, there are at least two methods of payment: One for manual transfers and one for electronic banking.

In the methods of payment for electronic payment, the option "Approved" or "Sent" should be selected in the field *Payment status* to prevent posting a payment before the payment export file has been generated. More settings for electronic payments (e.g., file formats) are included in the further tabs of the Methods of payment form.

The lookup field *Period* in the upper pane of the Payment methods form specifies whether the invoices that are selected in a payment proposal are collected to one payment (e.g., *Period* = "Week" for one payment per week, or *Period* = "Total" for one payment which covers all selected invoices), or if you want to generate a separate payment per invoice (*Period* = "Invoice").

The field group *Posting* on the tab *General* of the Payment methods form controls the bank account or the ledger account from which you pay. This account is the default for the offset account when you select the payment method in a payment journal.

In the Vendor form, you can select the *Method of payment* for the vendor on the tab *Payment*. The payment method of the vendor is the default for purchase orders, vendor transactions, and payment journals.

9.3.3.5 Vendor Payment Proposals

The purpose of payment proposals is to support selecting vendor invoices for payment. In order to run a payment proposal, click the button *Payment proposal/Create payment proposal* in the action pane of the vendor payment journal.

In the *Vendor payment proposal* dialog, select the applicable option in the field *Select invoices by* (options "Due date", or "Cash discount date", or both) and enter a date range for this date (*From date* and *To date*) to select the invoices which should be paid. If you select the option "Cash discount date" in the parameter *Select invoices by*, invoices without cash discount are not included in the proposal. In the field *Minimum payment date*, you can enter a date (e.g., tomorrow's date if preparing the payment for the next day) to make sure that the payment date in the proposal is on or—for invoices with a later due date or cash discount date—after that date.

On the tab *Records to include* of the dialog, you can filter on vendor and transaction data. The *Summarized payment date* on the tab *Advanced parameters* in the dialog is used if the method of payment refers to the *Period* "Total".

Once you close the dialog with the button *OK*, a second dialog is shown in which you can check and edit the payment proposal. In this dialog, the *Payment date* (from the invoice due date, or the cash discount date, or the *Minimum payment date*) is shown in the respective column. You can remove invoices or change the payment date (with the button *Multiple change*) as applicable before you click the button *Create payments* to transfer the proposal to the payment journal.

The payment proposal applies a settlement (→ Sect. 9.3.4) for the selected invoices. Depending on the method of payment in the particular invoices, there is one payment line for multiple invoices or a separate payment line per invoice.

Before posting the vendor payment, you can still edit the proposal—click the button *Payment proposal/Edit invoices for selected payment* for this purpose.

9.3.3.6 Exporting and Posting Payments

In order to check the payment before generating and posting it, you can optionally print the payment journal with the button *Print/Journal* in the header or lines.

If an export file for electronic payment is required, make sure to generate the file before posting the payment. For this purpose, click the button *Generate payments* in the payment journal lines once you have completed the lines. When generating the payment, Dynamics 365 sets the payment status of the journal lines to "Sent". If required, you can also update the payment status in the appropriate column manually (or with the button *Payment status* in the toolbar of the lines).

Finally, click the button *Post* or *Post/Post* in the action pane of the journal header or lines to post the payment from the selected bank or ledger account.

9.3.3.7 Centralized Payments

Centralized payments are required in a company structure with headquarters which process the payments of an affiliated group. Before you can use centralized payments, you have to set up intercompany accounting (*General ledger > Posting setup > Intercompany accounting*) for the concerned legal entities. In addition, appropriate permission settings in an organization hierarchy with the purpose "Centralized payment" are required.

Payment journal lines and payment proposals show the column *Company* (*Company accounts* in the payment proposal). When you post a centralized payment, you can settle invoices in other companies.

9.3.4 Settlement of Transactions

When viewing customer or vendor invoices, you might want to know which invoices have been paid already. In order to answer this question, you need to register the settlement of invoices with payments.

9.3.4.1 Settling Vendor Transactions

If you want to apply a posted payment (or a credit note) to an invoice, open the Settle transactions dialog with the button *Invoice/Settle/Settle transactions* in the Vendor form. In the *Settle transactions* dialog (→ Fig. 9.20), select the checkbox *Mark* in the transaction lines which you want to settle. You can settle one or more invoices with one or more payments or credit notes.

If there are transactions in foreign currencies, you can specify the settlement date (for calculating exchange rate gain or loss) in the field group *Settlement posting date* at the top of the dialog. The field group *Date used for calculating discounts* determines the date for cash discount calculation. It includes the following options:

- **Transaction date**—Select the payment line that contains the date for discount calculation and click the button *Mark as primary payment* in the toolbar.
- **Selected date**—Enter the discount calculation date in the date field on the right.

Before you post the settlement with the button *Post* in the dialog, you can check the balance of the marked transactions on the tab *Totals* at the bottom of the dialog.

If you do not want to post the settlement as a separate step, you can register the settlement already when entering a payment. For this purpose, click the button *Settle transactions* in the toolbar of the payment journal lines when entering the payment. The Settle

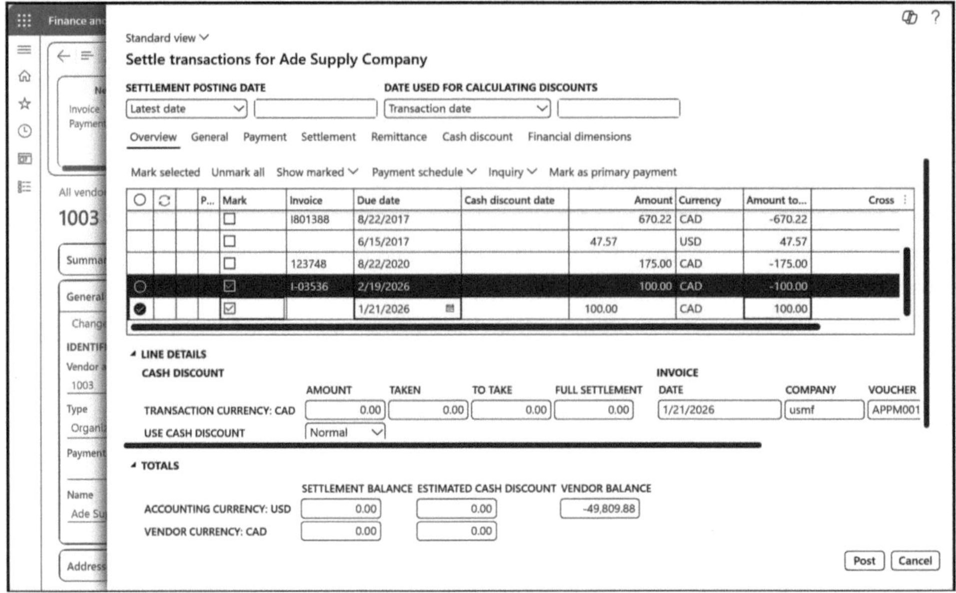

Fig. 9.20 Settling a vendor payment and an invoice in the Settle transactions dialog

transactions dialog which is shown then works similar to the Settle transactions dialog accessed from the Vendor form, but you only mark the invoices (the payment is no posted transaction yet) which you pay. With the button *OK* in the dialog, you transfer the marked invoice amount total to the payment journal line. The settlement is then posted when posting the payment.

With a payment proposal, a settlement is created automatically when generating the payment lines.

In case you have to cancel a posted settlement, open the Closed transactions form with the button *Invoice/Settle/Undo settlement* in the Vendor form. In the Closed transactions form, you can reverse settlements.

When working with settlements, be aware that there is no manual settlement if an automatic settlement is enabled in the applicable vendor posting profile (tab *Table restrictions*) or the Accounts payable parameters (section *Settlement*).

9.3.4.2 Settling Customer Transactions

Settling customer invoices and payments works similar to vendor transaction settlements. For customer transaction settlements, click the button *Collect/Settle/Settle transactions* in the Customer form to access the *Settle transactions* dialog. In this dialog, select the checkbox *Mark* in the transaction lines which you want to settle before you post the settlement with the button *Post*.

You can also mark settlements already when entering a customer payment—automatically in the background with the *Enter customer payment* form or when selecting an invoice number in the column *Invoice* of the payment journal line, or manually in the *Settle transactions* dialog which you access with the button *Settle transactions* in the toolbar of the payment journal lines. The settlement is then posted when posting the payment.

9.3.5 Working with Prepayments

Sometimes, it is required to make a payment before you accept an order from a customer or a vender accepts your order. In Dynamics 365, there are two options for processing such a prepayment—prepayments with a payment journal, and prepayment invoices.

9.3.5.1 Prepayment with Payment Journals

If a vendor asks for a partial or complete prepayment before accepting an order and shipping items, the simple way to deal with this is creating and posting a vendor payment which is marked as prepayment.

In a vendor payment journal (*Accounts payable > Payments > Vendor payment journal*), you can mark journal lines as prepayment—set the slider *Prepayment journal voucher* on the tab *Payment* in the journal line to "Yes". When posting the payment, the vendor summary account in the ledger transaction derives from a separate vendor posting profile (*Posting profile for payment journal with prepayment* in the Accounts payable parameters, section *Ledger and sales tax*, tab *Payment*). Optionally, you can settle a purchase order with the prepayment already before posting the product receipt or the invoice—register the settlement with the button *Invoice/Settle/Open transactions* in the Purchase order form.

After posting the product receipt and the vendor invoice for a prepaid purchase order, settle it (→ Sect. 9.3.4) with the prepayment—this is done automatically if the settlement has been registered on the purchase order already. Posting the settlement clears the prepayment on the vendor summary account for prepayments.

For customers, there is a similar process. If you ask a customer for a prepayment, you can process the prepayment in a customer payment journal and a sales order in the same way as vendor prepayments. For customer prepayments, the customer posting profile for prepayment is specified in the Accounts receivable parameters (section *Ledger and sales tax*, tab *Payment*).

9.3.5.2 Prepayment Invoices

If you don't want to register a payment without an explicit document which specifies the prepayment, you can ask the vendor for a prepayment invoice.

As a prerequisite for processing vendor prepayment invoices, the following setup is required:

- **Posting setup**—Main account for the option "Prepayment" on the tab *Purchase order* of the posting setup (*Cost management > Ledger integration policies setup > Posting*).

- **Accounts payable parameters**—*Posting profile with prepayment vendor invoice* (vendor posting profile for prepayments) and *Prepayment application policy* in the section *Ledger and sales tax*, tab *Prepayment invoice*.

Once you have entered and confirmed a purchase order for which the vendor wants a prepayment, you can enter the required prepayment with the button *Purchase/Prepay/Prepayment* in the Purchase order form. In the Prepayment dialog, enter the prepayment percentage or amount and select a procurement category for the prepayment.

When you receive the prepayment invoice from the vendor, click the button *Invoice/Generate/Prepayment invoice* in the Purchase order form. In the Vendor invoice form, enter the (prepayment) invoice number and post the invoice like any other vendor invoice. The invoice line is initialized with the prepayment entered in the purchase order.

The prepayment invoice is an open transaction which is ready for paying. In a vendor payment journal (*Accounts payable > Payments > Vendor payment journal*), post and settle the payment similar to the payment of a regular vendor invoice, including the option to use a payment proposal (→ Sect. 9.3.3). The vendor summary account in the posted ledger transaction for the payment derives from the vendor posting profile for prepayment invoices.

When you receive the regular vendor invoice at any time after posting the product receipt, enter and post it like any usual invoice. But if the *Prepayment application policy* in the Accounts payable parameters is set to "Notification" (and not to "Automatic"), click the button *Vendor invoice/Actions/Apply prepayment* in the Vendor invoice form and apply the prepayment invoice to settle it before posting the regular invoice. Applying the prepayment invoice inserts an offsetting line (with the procurement category entered in the prepayment) in the regular vendor invoice. If you do not apply the prepayment invoice when registering the regular invoice, apply it with the button *Invoice/Prepayment/Apply* in the Vendor form later.

If required for any reason, you can reverse a registered prepayment application with the button *Invoice/Prepayment/Reverse* in the Vendor form.

Customer prepayment invoices, which are available after activating the related feature, work similar to vendor prepayment invoices. The setup for customer prepayment invoices includes the main account for prepayment on the tab *Sales order* in the posting setup, and settings for the prepayment invoice in the Accounts receivable parameters (in the section *Ledger and sales tax*, tab *General*, and in the section *Updates*, the tab *Invoice*).

9.3.6 Transaction Reversal and Reversing Entries

In Dynamics 365, there are two different types of transaction reversals: Reversals that you enter manually (for corrections) and automatic reversals (for accruals).

9.3.6.1 Transaction Reversal

The transaction reversal, which is available for ledger transactions, vendor transactions, and customer transactions (including free text invoices), is a simple way to correct wrong vouchers in finance.

The transaction reversal is not available for transactions which refer to inventory, purchase orders, or sales orders. In order to reverse these transactions, register an appropriate document in the original module—for example, a return order in the Sales and marketing module.

You can start the transaction reversal from the Transaction inquiry. In order to access the Transaction inquiry for customer transactions, click the button *Customer/Transactions/ Transactions* in the Customer form. For the vendor transactions, click the button *Vendor/ Transactions/Transactions* in the Vendor form. For the ledger transactions, open the form *General ledger > Inquiries and reports > Voucher transactions* or click the button *Transactions* in the action pane of the Main accounts form.

In the Transaction inquiry, select the original transaction and click the button *Reverse transaction* or *Reverse/Reverse transaction* (for a customer payment, *Reverse/Cancel payment*). In the dialog (→ Fig. 9.21) which is shown next, you can edit the *Reversal posting date*. If you want to reverse a vendor invoice or customer invoice that has been settled already, cancel the settlement (→ Sect. 9.3.4) before reversing the invoice.

If you want to reverse a complete journal, you can start from the original journal. For this purpose, open the lines of the posted journal (general journal, invoice journal, payment journal) and click the button *Reverse entire journal* in the action pane.

The transaction reversal posts a new transaction which offsets the original transaction. If required, you can also reverse a reversal.

9.3.6.2 Automatic Reversal with Reversing Entries

Unlike manual transaction reversals, which you use to correct wrong transactions in most cases, reversing entries are transactions which are generated automatically to reverse accruals in a later period.

Reversing entries are available in the general journals (*General ledger > Journal entries > General journal*). In order to generate a reversing entry, select the checkbox

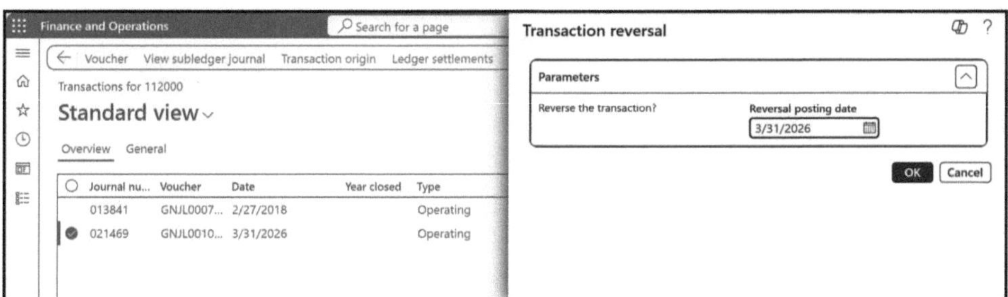

Fig. 9.21 Reversing a ledger transaction from the transaction inquiry

Reversing entry and enter a *Reversing date* (e.g., the first day of the next month) in the rightmost columns of the journal lines when entering the original transaction. In the journal header, the checkbox *Reversing entry* and the *Reversing date* provide a default for the lines.

When you post a general journal with reversing entries, a second transaction that reverses the original transaction is posted in parallel.

9.3.7 Case Study Exercises

Exercise 9.5—Segmented Entry in General Journals
An amount of USD 50 has been transferred from the account ZZ## and the first business unit to the account 111C## of exercise 9.1. Enter the transaction in a general journal with the journal name G-## of exercise 9.4.

Which segments are shown for the main account ZZ##? Review the lookup for these segments. Then post the journal and check the balance and the transactions of both accounts of the current exercise.

Exercise 9.6—General Journal Transaction
You withdraw USD 100 from the bank account B-## of exercise 9.3 and put it to the petty cash account 111C## of exercise 9.1. Register this transaction in a general journal with the journal name G-##.

Before posting, check the balance and the transactions for the bank account and the petty cash account. Then post the journal and check the balances and the transactions again.

Exercise 9.7—Vendor Invoice
The vendor of exercise 3.2 submits the invoice "VI907" with a total of USD 50. This invoice covers expenses, for which you have created the main account 6060## in exercise 9.1.

Record the invoice in an invoice journal with the journal name I-## of exercise 9.4. The invoice applies the terms of payment and the cash discount of exercise 3.1.

Before posting, check the vendor transactions and the vendor balance and—for the expense account—the ledger transactions and the ledger balance. Then post the invoice and check the balances and the transactions again.

Exercise 9.8—Vendor Payment
The invoice "VI907", which you have posted in the previous exercise, needs to be paid. Register the payment in a vendor payment journal with the journal name P-## of exercise 9.4. Pay from the bank account B-## of exercise 9.3. The payment amount should be reduced by the applicable cash discount.

Before posting, check the vendor balance and the bank account balance. Then post the payment and check the balances, the voucher transactions, and the transaction origin for the payment.

Exercise 9.9—Transaction Reversal
Your vendor of exercise 3.2 now submits the invoice "VI909" which is similar to the invoice "VI907" of exercise 9.7, but with a total of USD 30. Register and post this invoice.

After posting, you notice that the posted transaction is incorrect. You want to reverse it for this reason. Before reversing, check the vendor transactions and the vendor balance. For the expense account, check the ledger transactions and the ledger balance. Then reverse the invoice and check the balances and the transactions again.

9.4   Ledger Integration

One of the main advantages of an integrated business solution like Dynamics 365 is, that business transactions registered anywhere in the application are available in all other areas. Posting, for example, a sales order invoice does not only create the required document, but it also generates the following transactions:

- **Inventory transactions**—Affecting the inventory value.
- **General ledger transactions**—Revenue, COGS, stock, and customer accounts.
- **Customer transaction**—Open invoice in accounts receivable.
- **Sales tax transactions**—As applicable.

Depending on the transaction, invoice posting may include additional areas like commission, discount, or cash payment.

9.4.1   Basics of Ledger Integration

Ledger integration—the integration of the general ledger in finance with the other areas of the application—is one of the core characteristics of an integrated business solution (ERP solution). In Dynamics 365, a transaction in any area that is relevant to finance (e.g., sales, purchasing, inventory, or production) generates a transaction in the general ledger automatically.

9.4.1.1 Basic Settings
Several settings control, whether and which main accounts apply to the different transactions in business. For the areas of purchasing, sales, inventory, and production that are covered in this book, the following settings are relevant:

- **Summary accounts for vendor liabilities and customer debts**—In the posting profiles in accounts payable and accounts receivable.
- **Main accounts for inventory transactions**—In the posting setup.
- **Main accounts for resource usage in production**—In resources, cost categories, and production groups.

In addition, there are specific settings for particular transactions like sales tax, cash discount, indirect costs, or miscellaneous charges.

9.4.1.2 Vendors and Customers

Vendor posting profiles control the assignment of summary accounts for vendor transactions. Customer posting profiles for customer transactions work similarly. You can find more details on posting profiles in → Sect. 3.2.3.

9.4.1.3 Subledger Accounting

Subledger accounting in Dynamics 365 decouples posting in subledgers (e.g., in accounts payable) from posting to the general ledger. In this context, the subledger journal entry functionality provides the option to execute the transfer to the general ledger either asynchronous or in a batch job, and either detailed or summarized. Subledger accounting does not apply to all subledger transactions, but to some particular document types including (but not limited to):

- **Free text invoices**—Sales invoices not related to items (→ Sect. 4.5.3).
- **Product receipts**—Purchase order receipt (→ Sect. 3.5.4).
- **Vendor invoices**—Purchase order invoice (→ Sect. 3.6.1 and → 9.3.2).

In the General ledger parameters, settings in the section *Batch transfer rules* control the subledger transfer per company and document type. The *Transfer mode* specifies, when a subledger transaction is posted to the general ledger:

- **Asynchronous**—Posting as soon as sever capacity is available.
- **Scheduled batch**—In a separate batch job (e.g., in the nighttime), with the option to view subledger transactions before transferring to the general ledger. With this option, it is possible to summarize accounting entries.

If you set the option *Summarize accounting entries* in a batch transfer rule to "Yes", the ledger transactions of a batch are summarized per account and transaction type which means that you can't inquire the ledger transactions at the level of an individual invoice or product receipt.

Until the transfer to the general ledger has been executed (particularly for documents that use the scheduled batch transfer), you can view the posted subledger transactions in the menu item *General ledger > Periodic tasks > Subledger journal entries not yet transferred.* With the button *Transfer now* (for an immediate transfer) or *Transfer in batch* (for a scheduled transfer) in this form, you can immediately post the subledger transactions to the general ledger.

The button *View accounting* in the Subledger journal entries form and applicable source documents (e.g., free text invoices) provides access to the complete accounting information, including all applicable financial segments.

> *Note:* Apart from the setting for subledger transfer, the feature *Enhanced performance for source document accounting framework* also has an impact on when subledger transactions are posted to the general ledger. The Documents pending accounting form (*General ledger > Periodic tasks > Documents pending accounting*) shows pending transactions. You can click the button *Generate accounting* there to generate the ledger transactions rapidly.

9.4.2 Ledger Integration in Inventory

When you post inventory receipts and issues to the general ledger, there are two different types of transactions in Dynamics 365 (→ Sect. 7.2.4):

- **Physical transaction**—Posted with the product receipt or packing slip.
- **Financial transaction**—Posted with the invoice.

Depending on the structure of the chart of accounts in your company, you can use the same main accounts or different main accounts for the physical and the financial transaction.

9.4.2.1 Physical Transactions

It is an option, and not compulsory, to post physical transactions (product receipts and packing slips) to the general ledger.

As a primary prerequisite for posting physical transactions to the general ledger, the checkbox *Post physical inventory* must be activated in the item model group of the respective item. For purchase transactions, it is additionally required that the slider *Post product receipt in ledger* in the Accounts payable parameters (section *General*, tab *Product receipt*) is set to "Yes", and for sales transactions, the slider *Post packing slip in ledger* in the Accounts receivable parameters (section *Updates*, tab *Packing slip*).

For transactions in production control, you can find the relevant settings in the section *General* of the Production control parameters. Physical transactions in production control are picking lists and report as finished transactions.

9.4.2.2 Financial Transactions

For financial transactions, the checkbox *Post financial inventory* in the item model group determines whether inventory transactions are posted to the general ledger.

If this checkbox is cleared in an item model group, ledger integration is not active for the assigned items. For items with this setting, the purchase invoice does not post a ledger transaction to the stock account for inventory, but to the expense account for consumption. Accordingly, the sales invoice does not post a ledger transaction for inventory consumption. This is the appropriate setting for service items.

9.4.2.3 Posting Setup

The posting setup (*Cost management > Ledger integration policies setup > Posting*, or *Inventory management > Setup > Posting > Posting*) determines the main accounts for inventory transactions. It includes the following tabs with account settings ($\rightarrow$ Fig. 9.22):

- **Sales order**—Packing slips and invoices in sales.
- **Purchase order**—Product receipts and invoices in purchasing.
- **Inventory**—Journal transactions in inventory.
- **Production**—Picking lists, reporting as finished, and costing in production.
- **Standard cost variance**—Standard cost variances in inventory transactions.

Each of these tabs shows a list of available transaction types in the left pane. In order to view the related main accounts in the right pane, select the respective transaction type in the left pane. The posting setup is primarily depending on the combination of two relations:

- **Item relation**—Items or categories.
- **Account relation**—Customers or vendors.

In addition, main account settings optionally include the sales tax group and—for standard cost variance transactions—the cost group as applicable dimensions. In the item relation and the account relation (customer on the tab *Sales order*, vendor on the tab *Purchase order*), there are three levels for the assignment of accounts:

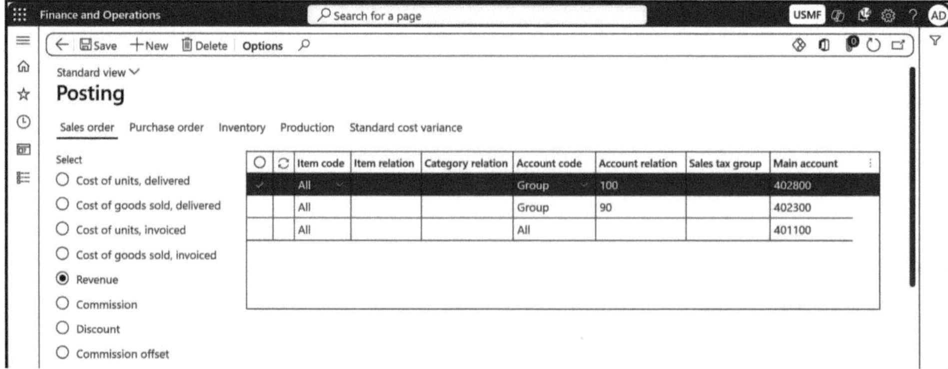

Fig. 9.22 Viewing the posting setup with the account settings for revenue posting

- **Table**—Particular item, customer, or vendor.
- **Group**—Item group, customer group, or vendor group.
- **All**– All items, customers, or vendors.

The *Item code* "Category"—an additional option in the item relation for sales and for purchasing—enables settings at the product category level.

When posting a transaction, Dynamics 365 always searches for the most specific setting ("Table") first, then for the group setting, and finally for the general setting ("All"). When you post, for example, a sales invoice, settings for the particular customer and item have the highest priority, followed by group settings. Settings in the Accounts receivable parameters (section *Ledger and sales tax*, tab *General*) control, whether the search should primarily use the item or the customer dimension. For purchasing, similar settings are available in the Accounts payable parameters.

As an alternative to the menu item, you can also access the Posting setup form with the button *Posting* in the Item group form, or with the button *Setup/Item posting* in the Customer group form or the Vendor group form. When you access the posting setup from a group form, it shows the main account settings filtered on the selected group.

9.4.2.4 Transaction Combinations and Ledger Reconciliation

The transaction combinations (*Cost management > Ledger integration policies setup > Transaction combinations*) control the available assignment levels in the posting setup.

Since reports for the reconciliation of the general ledger with inventory—for example, the Inventory value report (*Cost management > Inquiries and reports > Inventory accounting—status reports > Inventory value*, see → Sect. 7.3.1)—are usually based on item groups, the item group relation is usually activated in the transaction combinations.

9.4.2.5 Example—Transactions Related to Sales Order Processing

The following example for the automatic posting of ledger transactions based on ledger integration settings shows the transactions in sales order processing with activated ledger integration for packing slip and invoice posting (physical and financial transactions).

With the packing slip for the sales order, Dynamics 365 posts a ledger transaction that debits the account *Cost of units, delivered* and credits the account *Cost of goods sold, delivered* as specified in the posting setup. When posting the invoice, the ledger transactions that have been posted with the packing slip are reversed, and a ledger transaction is posted that debits the account *Cost of units, invoiced* and credits the account *Cost of goods sold, invoiced*. In parallel, a ledger transaction that credits the customer summary account (specified in the posting profile) and debits the account *Revenue* and—if applicable—the sales tax account is posted.

If the posting setup includes a setting for the transaction type *Discount*, sales line discounts are posted to this account. Otherwise, the discount is not posted separately but reduces the revenue amount.

Note: With pricing management (→ Sect. 4.8.3), there are additional options in the Pricing management parameters and the discounts (All discounts form) to specify the main account in ledger transactions.

9.4.2.6 Standard Cost Price and Moving Average

For items with an inventory model "Standard cost" (→ Sect. 7.3.1), essential settings are specified on the tab *Standard cost variance* of the posting setup. On this tab, you can find the main accounts for posting the difference between the actual cost price given by purchase order invoices (or production order costing) and the standard cost price (split by posting type, e.g., *Purchase price variance*).

For items that are assigned to an inventory model with a fixed receipt price, settings for posting a price difference are specified on the tabs *Purchase order* and *Inventory* of the posting setup.

For items with an inventory model "Moving average", settings for posting a price difference (for quantities that are not in stock anymore when posting the purchase invoice) or a revaluation are specified on the tab *Inventory* of the posting setup.

9.4.2.7 Service Items and Non-Stocked Items

Items that are not tracked in inventory (e.g., office supplies or consumables) can be linked to the product type "Service" and a particular item group and item model group for service items. In the item model group, ledger integration for physical and financial transactions should be deselected.

If you post a purchase invoice with such an item, a ledger transaction is posted that credits the expense account for consumption (instead of a stock account).

If you post a sales invoice, there is only a ledger transaction that credits the customer summary account and debits the revenue account (and no ledger transaction to the accounts *Cost of units, invoiced* and *Cost of goods sold, invoiced*).

You can assign non-stocked items to an item model group with a cleared checkbox *Stocked product* (→ Sect. 7.2.1). This setting prevents inventory transactions and deactivates the ledger integration for physical and financial transactions. But physical items and service items, which are included in a bill of materials, have to be assigned to an item model group in which the checkbox *Stocked product* is selected.

9.4.2.8 Changes of Settings

In order to avoid issues in the reconciliation of the general ledger with inventory, you should not change ledger integration settings in the item model group, in the parameters, and in the posting setup for items that are in stock or that have open inventory transactions. This includes both changing the setup itself and selecting a new item group in an active item.

9.4.3 Ledger Integration in Production

Unlike ledger transactions that are generated in purchasing, in sales, or in inventory, ledger transactions that are generated in production include the cost of resource operations (primarily from the working time).

9.4.3.1 Production Control Parameters

In line with this constraint, the lookup field *Ledger posting* in the section *General* of the Production control parameters includes the following options:

- **Item and resource**
- **Item and category**
- **Production groups**

The setting in the Production control parameters, which is not available in the Production control parameters by site, is the default for production orders. It is possible to override this default value in the individual production order—for example, if you want to apply specific settings for prototype production.

If the option "Item and resource" is selected in the *Ledger posting* parameter, item transactions apply the main accounts that are specified in the posting setup. For route consumption (resource usage), the main account settings in the resource (*Production control > Setup > Resources > Resource*s, tab *Ledger postings*) or—for transactions at the level of a resource group—in the resource group are used.

If the option "Item and category" is selected in the *Ledger posting* parameter, item transactions also apply the main accounts that are specified in the posting setup. But for route consumption, the account settings in the applicable cost category (*Production control > Setup > Routes > Cost categories*, tab *Ledger postings*) are used.

If the option "Production group" is selected in the *Ledger posting* parameter, the account settings in the production group (*Production control > Setup > Production > Production groups*) are used for item transactions and for route consumption. Production orders show the applicable production group on the tab *General* in the detail form (initialized from the tab *Engineer* in the released product).

9.4.3.2 Ledger Transactions in Production

When you process a production order and post a transaction, the following ledger transactions are posted (the main accounts depend on the selected option in the *Ledger posting* parameter):

- **Picking list**—Account "Estimated cost of materials consumed" against "Estimated cost of materials consumed, WIP" (WIP = "work in process").
- **Resource usage**—Account "Estimated manufacturing cost absorbed" against "Estimated manufacturing cost consumed, WIP".

- **Report as finished**—Account "Estimated manufactured cost" against "Estimated manufactured cost, WIP".
- **Indirect costs**—Settings in the costing sheet: "Estimated indirect costs absorbed" against "Estimated cost of indirect cost consumed, WIP".

The ledger transactions are posted when posting a production journal (picking list, route card, job card, or report as finished).

Costing the production order reverses all these transactions and posts the final financial receipt of the manufactured item, the consumption of materials and resources, and indirect cost transactions to main accounts that depend on the selected option in the *Ledger posting* parameter and on the related settings.

10

The organization of an enterprise determines the setup of its business application. For this reason, there needs to be an implementation project that includes the setup of the organization and of other core parameters before starting to work in Dynamics 365.

10.1 Organization Management

If you want to set up a new Dynamics 365 environment with its database, access the Power Platform Admin Center (PPAC) and deploy an environment that is hosted in Microsoft Azure. While on-premise implementations are still supported currently, it is recommended to migrate to Dynamics 365 cloud offerings.

Within a Dynamics 365 environment, the organization model represents the structure of the enterprise with its business processes. For this reason, the model has to be configured according to the operational and statutory structure of the enterprise. You can divide the organizational structures into the following types:

- **Statutory organization structures for legal reporting**—Hierarchies in line with the regulations of public authorities (e.g., for tax purposes).
- **Operational organization structures for management reporting**—Hierarchies in line with management requirements (e.g., divisional structures).
- **Informal structures**—Independent of organizational hierarchies.

In order to comply with the different reporting requirements, large enterprises often have multiple organizational structures and hierarchies in parallel. You can, for example, set up a hierarchy that matches the structure and the purpose of legal entities, another hierarchy that represents the divisional structure, and a third hierarchy that complies with regional structures.

For other enterprises, one simple hierarchy may be sufficient for all purposes.

10.1.1 Organization Model Architecture

The organization model in Microsoft Dynamics 365 meets the requirements of different kinds of organizations. Depending on the requirements, the organization setup includes multiple organization hierarchies in parallel (e.g., for decoupling the operational organization from the statutory organization), or only one simple hierarchy, which is used for all purposes.

10.1.1.1 Organization Types

The organization model includes the following organization types:

- **Legal entities**—Represent the statutory organization.
- **Operating units**—Represent the operational organization.
- **Teams**—Represent informal structures.

Only organization units with the type "Legal entity" and "Operating unit" are available in organization hierarchies. The type "Team" characterizes an informal type of organization, which is not included in hierarchies.

> *Note*: Legal entities are organizations that are recognized by the authorities. In Dynamics 365, companies are the only type of legal entities.

10.1.1.2 Using the Organization Model Within Dynamics 365

The organization model is used in many areas of the application, including the following purposes:

- **Company structure**—Legal entities represent the company organization.
- **Financial dimensions**—Operating units are an optional basis for financial dimensions, and with this assignment, you can use them in financial reporting (apart from the legal entities).
- **Data security**—Based on the organization hierarchy purpose *Security*, you can restrict user access to organizations separately from the company structure.
- **Business policies**—Business rules for areas like approval processes and centralized payments can apply a structure that is different from the hierarchy of legal entities.

Legal entities and operating units are not only part of the organization hierarchy, but they are also included in the global address book ($\rightarrow$ Sect. 2.4). For this reason, the addresses and contact details of legal entities and operating units are managed in the global address book.

10.1.2 Organization Units

The organization model includes organization units with the types "Legal entity", "Operating unit", and "Team" ($\rightarrow$ Fig. 10.1). Legal entities and operating units are the basic elements in the organizational hierarchies of an enterprise.

The Internal organizations page (*Organization administration > Organizations > Internal organizations*) shows all organization units with their type. Forms that are tailored to the specific requirements of the different organization types are available in the other menu items of the folder *Organization administration > Organizations*.

10.1.2.1 Legal Entities

Legal entities (*Organization administration > Organizations > Legal entities*) are company accounts in Dynamics 365 ($\rightarrow$ Sect. 10.1.4). They are the bottom level for legal reporting. Tax reports and financial statements, like balance sheets and income statements, are usually based on legal entities.

If multiple legal entities, typically the companies of an affiliated group, work in a common Dynamics 365 environment, you can manage the relations between these legal entities. Depending on the requirements, you use the following features:

- **Financial consolidation**—Manage financial consolidation of companies in an affiliated group.
- **Intercompany**—Automate business processes between the legal entities of a multi-company organization.
- **Organization hierarchies**—Use legal entities in the organization model (e.g., for the setup of data security or approval processes).

Internal Organization		
Legal Entities *Statutory organization* (Companies)	**Operating Units** *Operational organization* ➢ Departments ➢ Cost centers ➢ Business units ➢ Value streams ➢ Retail channels	**Teams** *Informal organization*

Fig. 10.1 Organization units in the organization model

10.1.2.2 Operating Units

Operating units (*Organization administration > Organizations > Operating units*) are used for reporting and for the internal control of business processes. The types of operating units that you use (e.g., business units as representation of divisions or regions) depend on the requirements of the enterprise.

In a standard Dynamics 365 environment, there are the following operating unit types:

- **Department**—Functional classification (e.g., "Finance").
- **Cost center**—For budgeting and expenditure control.
- **Value stream**—For production flows in lean manufacturing.
- **Business unit**—For strategic business objectives (e.g., divisions).
- **Retail channel**—Related to the Retail and commerce module.

When you create a new operating unit in the Operating unit form (→ Fig. 10.2), select the *Operating unit type* in the drop-down menu first. Then enter additional data like the name, address, and contact details in the detail form.

Once an operating unit is assigned to one or more hierarchies, you can click the button *View in hierarchy* to check the allocation within organizational structures.

If you want to report the financial performance of operating units (e.g., departments), link the operating units to financial dimensions (→ Sect. 9.2.3).

10.1.2.3 Teams

Teams (*Organization administration > Organizations > Teams*) represent informal organizations within an enterprise. A team simply is a group of people. There is no hierarchical organization structure that links the different teams.

Team types, which you can access with the button *Team types* in the Teams form, restrict the team members to different kinds of people (e.g., system users, employees, or vendor contacts).

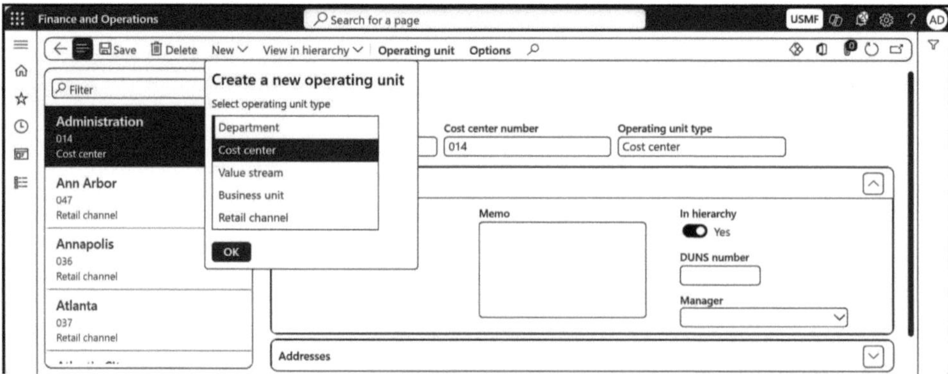

Fig. 10.2 Creating a cost center in the Operating unit form

When you create a new team, select the team type first. In order to assign people to the team, click the button *Add team members* in the toolbar of the tab *Team members*. Depending on the team type, available members are Dynamics 365 users, employees, or vendor contacts.

Teams are used in various areas of the application, for example, in the access permission setup for address books (select the applicable teams in the respective address books).

10.1.3 Organization Hierarchy Setup

An organization hierarchy shows the relationship between the organization units in line with the purpose of the hierarchy. Depending on the requirements, you can set up multiple hierarchies in parallel. The purpose(s) of a hierarchy determine its functional utilization—for example, a hierarchy with the purpose *Security* controls data access permissions.

10.1.3.1 Organization Hierarchies

The organization hierarchies in your enterprise are shown in the menu item *Organization administration > Organizations > Organization hierarchies*. If you want to create a new hierarchy, click the button *New* and enter the *Name* of the hierarchy. Then click the button *Assign purpose* on the tab *Purposes* to assign one or more hierarchy purposes to the hierarchy.

In order to view the hierarchy with its elements, click the button *View* in the action pane to open the hierarchy designer (→ Fig. 10.3). In the hierarchy designer, you can navigate within the hierarchy and switch the focus by clicking the respective element. You can change the hierarchy in the Edit mode and insert or remove organization units with the respective button in the toolbar. With the buttons *Cut* and *Paste*, you can move a unit and its subunits within the organization hierarchy.

Once you have finished editing the organization hierarchy, click the button *Publish* to activate the update. If you want to keep changes in a draft version, do not publish the update, but save the changes with the button *Save*.

The organization structure applies validity dates, which is why you enter an effective date when you publish the hierarchy after editing. It is not possible to modify a published version—you can only publish another version with a later date. For this reason, you should not publish a hierarchy with a future date as long as it is still possible that there are further changes in the hierarchy.

10.1.3.2 Organization Hierarchy Purposes

In case your enterprise requires different hierarchies for different purposes, set up multiple organization hierarchies. The organization hierarchy purposes (*Organization administration > Organizations > Organization hierarchy purposes*) refer to functional features in Dynamics 365. For this reason, available purposes (e.g., *Centralized payments* or *Security*) and the allowed organization types per purpose are determined by the application.

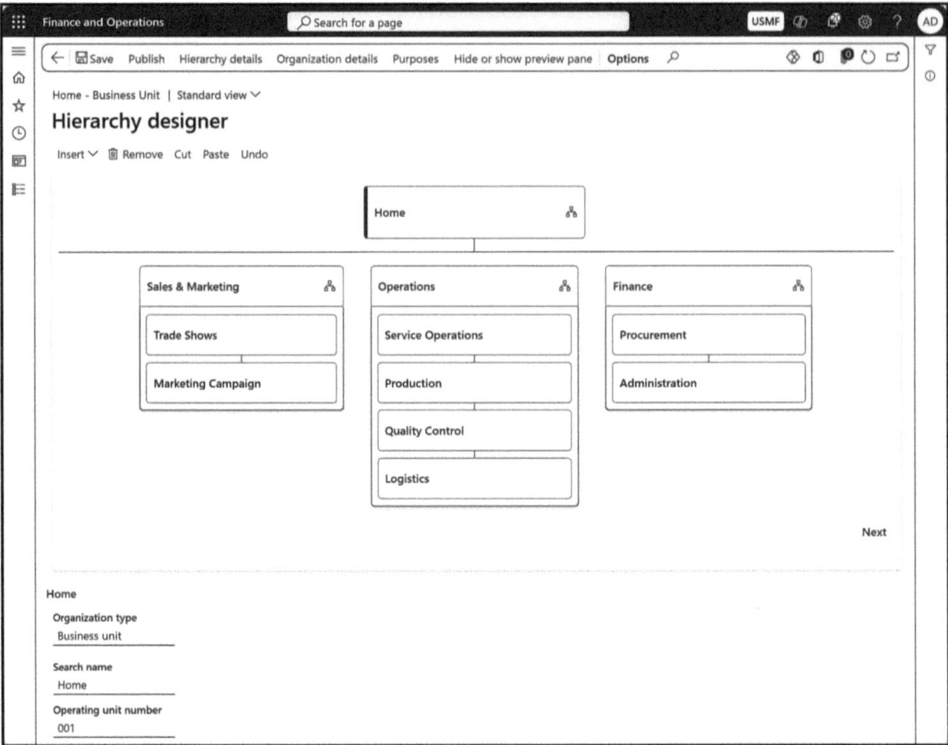

Fig. 10.3 Editing an organization hierarchy in the hierarchy designer

To assign the applicable organization hierarchy or hierarchies to a purpose, select the respective hierarchy purpose in the left pane of the Organization hierarchy purposes form and click the button *Add* on the tab *Assigned hierarchies* in the right pane. Depending on the requirements, you can assign one or more hierarchies to one purpose, and one hierarchy to one or more purposes.

10.1.4 Legal Entities (Company Accounts)

Once you log on to Dynamics 365, you work in a company account—the current company (legal entity) for the session. If not specified in the Dynamics 365 web address (parameter "cmp") when accessing the application, the current company is initialized from your user options.

The navigation bar of the Dynamics 365 web client always shows the current company. Depending on the setup of the company, the banner in the dashboard displays a company-specific image. If you want to switch from one current company to another, click the company field in the navigation bar and select the new company in the lookup.

10.1.4.1 Company Setup

You can manage the companies (legal entities) in the Legal entity form (*Organization administration > Organizations > Legal entities*). If you want to create a new company, click the button *New* in the action pane. In the *New legal entity* dialog (→ Fig. 10.4), enter the company name, the company ID (up to 4 digits), and the country/region (which by default determines applicable country-specific features).

All users with appropriate permissions can select this new company as the current company afterward. But before you can enter and post transactions in the new company, the setup of the company in all applicable areas and modules (like general ledger, accounts payable, and accounts receivable) has to be finished. A checklist of basic settings is given in the appendix of this book.

Core data in the Legal entity form include the company name (which is printed on documents and reports) and further settings like the primary company address (initialized with the country selected when creating the company). In order to edit the primary address or to enter an additional address (e.g., for invoicing or delivery), click the button *Edit* or *Add* on the tab *Addresses*. An example of an additional address is a default delivery address, which is different from the primary company address. This delivery address is the default for purchase orders (if no address is specified for the site or warehouse in the order header).

The tab *Contact information* contains the contact data of the company. Since the global address book includes the legal entities, company addresses with the contact data are shown in the global address book.

Further important settings in the Legal entity form include the primary bank account on the tab *Bank account information*. In a company located in the European Union, enter the VAT registration number (VAT exempt number) on the tab *Foreign trade and logistics*.

Fig. 10.4 Creating a company in the Legal entity form

10.1.4.2 Companies in the Data Structure

You can set up multiple company accounts (legal entities) within a Dynamics 365 environment. Except for shared application data like parties or products, company accounts establish a separate set of data within the database. The company is a key field in all relevant Dynamics 365 tables.

10.1.4.3 Company Banner in the Dashboard

In the Legal entity form, you can select a picture that is shown in the dashboard and another picture that is printed on reports. To specify the dashboard image, switch to the tab *Dashboard image* in the Legal entity form, select the option "Banner" or "Logo" in the field *Dashboard company image type*, and upload a picture with the button *Change* in the toolbar. The company image on reports is specified on the tab *Report company logo image* of the Legal entity form.

10.1.5 Cross-Company Data Sharing

In Dynamics 365, there are some areas in which data are shared across legal entities—e.g., parties in the global address book, charts of accounts, or products.

If you require common data management across companies in additional areas (e.g., if you want to enforce common payment terms), you can use cross-company data sharing.

10.1.5.1 Concepts for Cross-Company Data Sharing

In Dynamics 365, there are two concepts for data sharing:

- **Duplicate record sharing**—Records are stored per company, and any update in one company is duplicated across all companies in the policy.
- **Master company sharing**—Records are stored in a master company, and the companies in the policy directly update the record in the master company.

In general, duplicate record sharing is the preferred solution as it is more flexible. But if you share data across more than 300 companies or two million records in a table, use master company data sharing.

10.1.5.2 Setup of Cross-Company Data Sharing

In the Configure cross-company data sharing form (*System administration > Setup > Configure cross-company data sharing*), you can set up which tables are shared in which companies. If you want to create a new collection of shared data, click the button *New* in the action pane and enter a name for the data collection before you save the record.

For each shared table that you want to include in the collection, click the button *Add* in the toolbar of the pane *Tables and fields to share*, select the *Table name*, and click the button *Add table* in the drop-down menu. If you expand a node with a table in the pane *Tables and fields to share*, you can adjust the selection of fields that are shared. Then add the companies that should use the shared data collection in the pane *Companies which share the records in these tables* on the right.

In order to activate data sharing for a table collection, click the button *Enable* in the action pane of the Configure cross-company data sharing form.

10.1.5.3 Working with Cross-Company Data Sharing

If you insert, update, or delete records in a table and in a company, which is included in a shared table collection, the update of table data immediately applies to all companies in the table collection.

10.1.6 Sites and Production Units

Whereas company accounts represent legal entities in the organization structure, sites represent subsidiaries within a company (→ Fig. 10.5). Since sites are an inventory dimension (storage dimension), they are available in all areas of supply chain management within Dynamics 365.

If you want to calculate financial results at the site level, you can link the inventory dimension "Site" to a financial dimension. With a filter on the financial dimension, you can, for example, generate an income statement per subsidiary then.

10.1.6.1 Multisite Functionality
The multisite functionality in Dynamics 365 includes the following options:

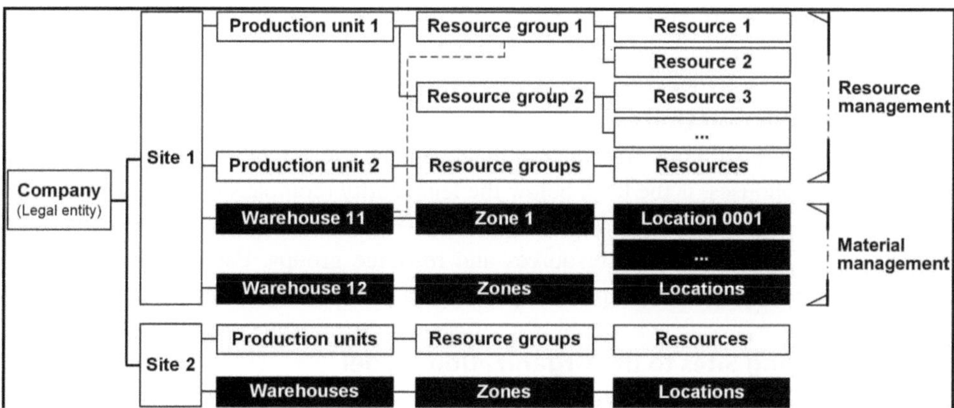

Fig. 10.5 Organization structure in resource management and material management

- **Master planning**—Per site or per company.
- **Bills of materials**—Per site or per company.
- **Production control parameters**—Per site or per company.
- **Item data (Released products)**—Default order settings per site or per company.
- **Transactions**—Sites in all inventory transactions, sales orders, purchase orders, and production orders.
- **Financial reporting**—Optionally for sites (if linked to a financial dimension).

10.1.6.2 Setup of Sites

In order to create a site in the current company, open the Site form (*Inventory management > Setup > Inventory breakdown > Sites*) and click the button *New*. In the new record, enter the ID, the name, and optionally the address. On the tab *Financial dimensions*, which is shown in case the inventory dimension "Site" is linked to a financial dimension, you can enter a dimension value for this dimension. This is mandatory if the dimension link is activated.

The link between the inventory dimension "Site" and a financial dimension is specified in the menu item *Cost management > Ledger integration policies setup > Dimension link*. In Edit mode, you can select a financial dimension which you want to use for sites. In order to use the dimension value that is entered in the Site form as a default in the financial transactions with the particular site, activate the link with the button *Activate link* in the action pane of the Dimension link form. With the button *Lock link*, you can prevent overriding the dimension value in transactions.

Sites are a mandatory storage dimension which is automatically activated in all storage dimension groups. For this reason, every inventory transaction includes a dimension value for the site. In addition, each warehouse has to be linked to a site.

If sites are not required in the organization of your enterprise, set up a single site which is selected in all transactions. You can enter this site as default value in the applicable settings—for example, in the *Default order settings* of released products. More details on inventory dimensions are given in → Sect. 7.2.2.

10.1.6.3 Production Units

In the organization structure for material management, the storage dimension *Site*, which groups the warehouses, is the level below the legal entity (company).

In resource management, the *Production unit* (→ Sect. 5.3.2) below the site is an additional level in the structure of resources and resource groups. Each production unit is linked to a site and represents a plant in production control and master planning.

10.1.6.4 Linking Sites to the Organization Model

It is not possible to include sites directly in the organization model. But you can link sites to a financial dimension, and financial dimensions to organization units, which in the end shows sites in the organization model.

In order to use sites in finance and in the organization model, complete the following implementation steps:

- **Operating units**—Create operating units with a common operating unit type (e.g., *Department* or *Business unit*) for the individual sites.
- **Financial dimension**—Set up a dimension related to this operating unit type.
- **Account structure**—Include this financial dimension in the account structure(s).
- **Dimension link**—Link the storage dimension *Site* to this financial dimension.

You can enter the name of the organization unit in the related site to visualize sites in the organization hierarchy. If the dimension link between the site and the financial dimension is activated, you can perform financial reporting per site.

10.2   User and Security Management

Business applications like Microsoft Dynamics 365 contain confidential data. In order to protect sensitive information, access to the application has to be limited in compliance with the requirements of your enterprise.

10.2.1 Access Control

Access control in Dynamics 365 is based on two elements:

- **Authentication**—Identification of users.
- **Authorization**—User permissions.

As a prerequisite for authenticating users, a system administrator has to create and to enable the users in Dynamics 365. User authentication is not only required for permission control. It is also the basis for logging user transactions and data updates. Further settings with reference to a Dynamics 365 user include the favorites, the user options, and the usage data, which enable a personalized workspace in Dynamics 365.

For authorization, Dynamics 365 applies a role-based security model. This means, that security roles control the access to application elements (e.g., menu items). A user in Dynamics 365 can have one or more roles, and these roles determine his permissions.

Permissions for application elements are not directly assigned to a role, but to duties and privileges. Duties and—below duties—privileges establish a grouping level for permissions in the structure of the security model.

The extensible data security framework additionally provides the option to restrict access based on effective dates or on application data (e.g., based on sales territories).

10.2.2 Users and Employees

Each person who accesses Dynamics 365 has to be set up as a Dynamics 365 user.

10.2.2.1 Managing User Accounts

In order to create a Dynamics 365 user, open the list page *System administration > Users > Users* and click the button *New*. In the new record, enter the *User ID* within Dynamics 365, the *User name*, the *Provider* (Microsoft Entra ID tenant of your organization) and the *Email* (Entra ID of the user) and make sure that the slider *Enabled* is set to "Yes" (enabling the user to log on to Dynamics 365).

> *Note*: As a prerequisite for creating a user, a user license must be assigned in the Microsoft 365 admin center.

10.2.2.2 Security Roles and Permission Assignment

In order to specify the permissions of the particular user, switch to the tab *User's roles* in the User detail form and assign the applicable security roles. Alternatively, you can use form *System administration > Security > Assign users to roles* to associate users with roles. In this form, you can also set up rules which assign new users automatically to security roles.

In the User form, the security roles of the selected user are shown in the FactBox *Roles for the selected user* on the right. If a user is assigned to multiple roles, the permissions of all selected roles are effective. In case of overlapping permission settings for an object, the higher access level applies.

You can restrict the security roles of a user at the organization level. For this purpose, select the user in the User detail form first. Then select the role that you want to restrict on the tab *User's roles*, and click the button *Assign organizations* in the toolbar of this tab. In the *Assign organizations* form, you can enable global access with the selected role, or restrict the role access to particular organizations. For permissions at the level of organizations, select legal entities (or elements of an organization hierarchy with the purpose *Security*) in the upper pane of the *Assign organizations* form and click the button *Grant* in the toolbar of the lower pane.

10.2.2.3 User Options

The button *User options* in the User form provides access to the user options of the selected user. Apart from accessing the user options from the user management, users with appropriate permissions can access their personal user options with the button *Settings* ⚙/*User options* in the navigation bar. Accessing the user options from the user management is a way to predefine settings like the language or the default for the current company.

10.2.2.4 Assigning Employees to Users

Apart from being a user, people who access Dynamics 365 are employees, contractors, or contact persons at external parties (e.g., a customer). The global address book contains both, workers (employees and contractors) and external contact persons.

In order to assign a Dynamics 365 user to a person in the global address book (worker or external contact), open the User detail form and, in the field *Person*, select the person that you want to assign to the user. The button *Maintain versions* provides the option to enter an effective date and an expiration date.

The worker assignment is used throughout the whole application. Examples are purchase requisitions, project accounting, warehouse management, case management, and sales order management. Once a user is assigned to a worker who is employed in the current company, the worker ID is used in all areas. It is, for example, the default for the field *Sales taker* in the order header when creating a sales order.

10.2.2.5 Employee Management

The User form contains the user settings for accessing Dynamics 365. Separately from the user setup, you can manage the enterprise staff in the Worker form ($\rightarrow$ Fig. 10.6).

Workers include employees and contractors, no matter whether they are Dynamics 365 users or not. Worker records are shared across companies, and the contact details are included in the global address book. The employment of a worker determines his assignment to one or more companies.

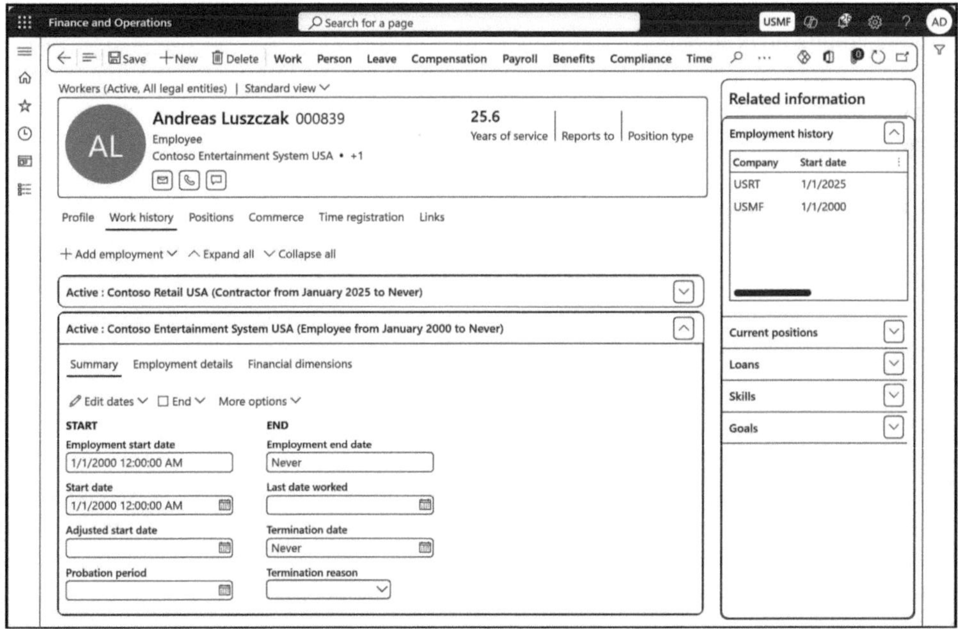

Fig. 10.6 Managing employment data in the Worker detail form

The Worker list page (*Human resources > Workers > Workers*) shows all employees and contractors in any company of the enterprise. With the button *View options* (on the right of the filter field above the grid), you can select to restrict the displayed records—to active, or past, or future employees, or contractors.

The Employee list page (*Human resources > Workers > Employees*) is a filtered view which shows only current employees (workers with the type "Employee") in the current company. If you want to view the workers who have been employed in the past, open the Past workers form. Workers with an employment in the future are shown in the Pending workers form.

General worker data are shared across companies, but some data—including the employment—are company-specific. In the FactBox *Employment history* on the right, and in the Employment form which you open with the button *Work/Work details/Employment history*, you can view the current and the past employments of the selected worker.

The tab *Work history* in the Worker detail form shows the company-specific employment data in one or more sub-tabs. For each employment, there is a separate sub-tab which displays the company of the employment in the tab header.

In order to create a new worker, click the button *New* and, in the *Hire new worker* dialog, enter at least the *First name*, the *Last name*, the company (*Legal entity*) employing the worker, the *Personnel number* (if not initialized from the number sequence), the *Worker type* (employee or contractor), and the *Employment start date*.

The default for the employing company is the current company. On the tab *Work history* in the Worker detail form, you can edit the employment or add an employment if the worker changes from this company to another company of the enterprise (or if he has a parallel employment in another company of the enterprise).

The required details of a worker primarily depend on the Dynamics 365 functionality that is used in your organization. These details include data for time registration, retail and commerce, project accounting, and human resources.

10.2.2.6 Online Users

If you want to know the users who are currently logged on to Dynamics 365, open the Online users inquiry (*System administration > Users > Online users*). This inquiry shows all client sessions that are connected to the application. If you have got appropriate permissions, you can click the button *End sessions* in the toolbar of the tab *Client sessions* to log off a user.

10.2.2.7 User Groups

User groups (*System administration > Users > User groups*) are not used in the role-based security setup, but for some particular settings. You can, for example, open ledger periods, which are on hold, for a specific user group. In workflows or financial journals, you can optionally apply user groups for the workflow task assignment, for approval, and for posting restrictions.

In order to assign users to a user group, select the respective group in the User group form and switch to the tab *Users*. On this tab, assign the applicable users by moving them from the left pane to the right pane.

10.2.3 Role-Based Security

In line with the security model in Dynamics 365, permissions are not directly assigned to individual users, but to security roles.

10.2.3.1 Security Model

The role-based security model includes the following elements (→ Fig. 10.7):

- **Role**—Group of duties required for a job function (e.g., "Accountant").
- **Duty**—Group of privileges necessary for a task (e.g., "Maintain fixed assets").
- **Privilege**—Permissions at the level of objects (e.g., "Post fixed assets journal").
- **Permission**—Low-level access restriction to securable objects (user interface elements, reports, tables, and fields, service operations).

The assignment of a user to one or more roles (depending on his job functions) determines his permissions. In general, roles refer to duties, and duties refer to privileges. But if required, you can also assign a privilege directly to a role.

A role is a set of access permissions that are required to perform a job function. Apart from functional roles, which refer to the functional tasks, there are additional role types. In general, there are the following role types:

- **Functional roles**—For example, "Buying agent".
- **Organizational roles**—For example, "Employee".
- **Application roles**—For example, "System user".

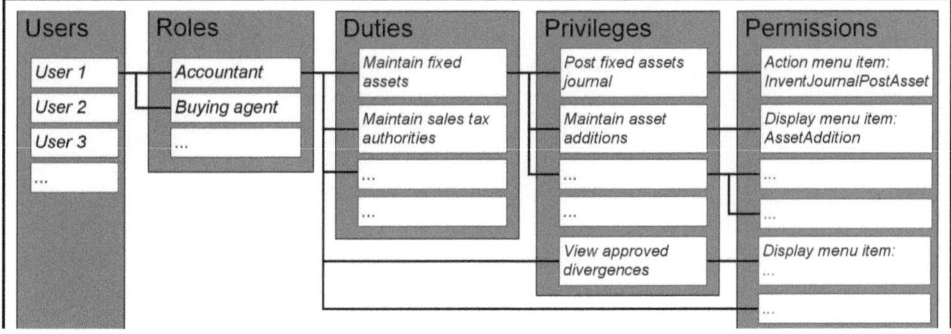

Fig. 10.7 Components of the security model

The role "System administrator" has access to all areas of the application. The access settings for this role are not editable.

10.2.3.2 Managing the Security Configuration

You can manage the security roles, duties, and privileges in the Security configuration form (*System administration > Security > Security configuration*). This form contains the tabs *Roles*, *Duties*, and *Privileges* with the related elements (→ Fig. 10.8).

On the tab *Roles*, the left pane shows the available roles in your environment. For the selected role in the left pane, you can view the duties and directly assigned privileges—for this purpose, click the respective element in the pane *References* in the middle of the form. If you want to add a duty or privilege to the selected role, select the respective node (e.g., "Duties") in the pane *References* and click the button *Add references* in the toolbar of the tab. If you want to create a completely new role, click the button *Create new*.

A duty is a group of privileges that are required for a particular task—e.g., for maintaining fixed assets. If you want to view or edit the duties, switch to the tab *Duties* of the Security configuration form. Select a duty and click the respective element in the pane *References* in the middle of the form to view the related privileges (and roles). If you want to add a privilege to the selected duty, select the respective node *Privileges* in the pane *References* and click the button *Add references* in the toolbar of the tab.

A privilege contains all permissions which are required for a particular application object. You can view and edit the security privileges on the tab *Privileges* of the Security configuration form. Select a privilege and click the respective element in the pane

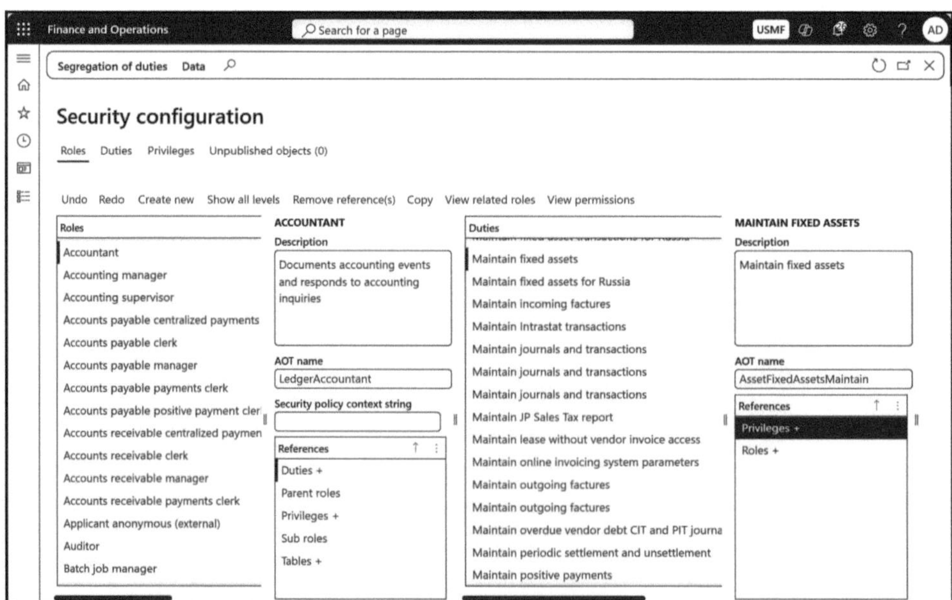

Fig. 10.8 Viewing the duties of the security role "Accountant"

References to view the related application objects (e.g., *Action menu items*). If you want to add a permission to the selected privilege, select the node in the pane *References* and click the button *Add references* in the toolbar of the tab.

Permissions specify access restrictions at the lowest level, based on application objects. The permissions, which you can select in the security privileges, are determined by the application development.

While editing the security configuration, updated elements are shown on the tab *Unpublished objects*. In order to activate the changes, click the button *Publish all* (or *Publish selection*) in the toolbar of this tab.

10.2.3.3 Security Diagnostics

In the Dynamics 365 pages and forms, the button *Options/Page options/Security diagnostics* displays a dialog that shows the roles, duties, and privileges which grant access to the respective form. The button *Add roles to user* in the dialog provide access to the form *Assign users to roles* (if a role is selected in the dialog). If you select a duty, you can assign a role, and for a privilege, you can assign a duty.

10.2.3.4 Segregation of Duties

The aim of the segregation of duties is to ensure, that major tasks which depend on each other, are not executed by the same person, but by different users (e.g., creating purchase orders and paying vendor invoices). As a prerequisite for using the segregation of duties functionality, enter applicable rules in the menu item *System administration > Security > Segregation of duties > Segregation of duties rules*.

Segregation rules determine duties, which may not be assigned to one user at the same time. They do not prevent permission settings which are in conflict with a rule. But you can validate a segregation rule when you set it up, and you can execute the periodic activity *System administration > Security > Segregation of duties > Verify compliance of user-role assignments* to verify compliance.

10.3 Common Settings

Various settings are required before an enterprise can start using Dynamics 365. Core settings in this respect include:

- **Organization management** → Sect. 10.1.
- **Security management** → Sect. 10.2.
- **Finance management** → Sect. 9.2.

Each module which is used in your enterprise also needs to be configured according to the particular requirements. As an example, the required terms of payment have to be set up in purchasing and in sales. In addition, there are some basic settings that are used in all areas of the application. You can find a short description of these settings below.

10.3.1 Number Sequences

Number sequences control the allocation of numbers throughout the whole application. In particular, number sequences are used in the following areas:

- **Master data**—For example, vendor numbers.
- **Journals and orders**—For example, purchase order numbers.
- **Posted transactions**—For example, invoice numbers.

Dynamics 365 includes company-specific number sequences and number sequences on the enterprise level. In a number sequence, the scope parameters control whether it is shared, or specific to a company.

10.3.1.1 Number Sequence Setup

In order to manage the number sequences, open the menu item *Organization administration > Number sequences > Number sequences*. The FactBox *Number sequence segments* on the right of this page shows the company and other applicable segments of the selected number sequence. If you want to create a new number sequence, click the button *Number sequence/New/Number sequence* in the action pane. Then enter a unique *Number sequence code* and a *Name*, and switch to the tab *Scope parameters* of the detail form. On this tab, you can specify whether the number sequence is shared, or restricted to a company or organization unit.

On the tab *Segments* of the detail form, specify the number format for the number sequence. Segments of a number include the following types:

- **Alphanumeric**—Number which increases every time the number sequence is used, replacing the number signs (#) in the format with the next number. The length of the alphanumeric segment must cover the largest number (specified on the tab *General*).
- **Constant**—Segments for prefixes (e.g., for a format "INV#####" or "12#####") and for suffixes (e.g., for a format "#####-INV"). In general, prefixes are preferable since they are easier to use (e.g., for filtering).
- **Other types**—Segments with the type *Company*, *Legal entity*, *Operating unit*, or *Fiscal calendar period* are only available if they are included in the *Scope* of the number sequence.

When you set up number sequences for document and transaction numbers, it is a good idea to avoid overlapping number sequences for the different documents in order to facilitate the tracking of transactions.

Note: With the button *Number sequence/New/Generate* in the Number sequences form, you can create a basic set of number sequences and the related number sequence references.

10.3.1.2 Number Sequence References

The number sequence references ($\rightarrow$ Fig. 10.9) determine the assignment of a number sequence to specific master data or transactions. You can edit the number sequence references on the tab *References* in the Number sequence detail form or in the section *Number sequences* of the Parameters form of each module.

A single number sequence can be assigned to multiple number sequence references at the same time. You can, for example, assign one common number sequence to invoices and to credit notes. This setting does not generate duplicate numbers, but assigns numbers to invoices and credit notes in line with the chronological order of the transactions.

10.3.1.3 General Settings in Number Sequences

The numeric first (*Smallest*) and last (*Largest*) number of a number sequence are specified on the tab *General* of the Number sequence detail form. The field *Next* shows the next number that will be provided by the number sequence. You can change the next number, but make sure to avoid duplicate keys and gaps in continuous numbers.

The slider *Manual* controls whether numbers are entered manually. If the slider *To a lower number* or *To a higher number* is set to "Yes", you can change the numbers which are assigned from the number sequence. Gaps in a number sequence are prevented with the slider *Continuous*. Set this slider only in number sequences to "Yes", which actually require continuous numbers. Voucher numbers often require continuous numbering, since it is a statutory requirement in many countries.

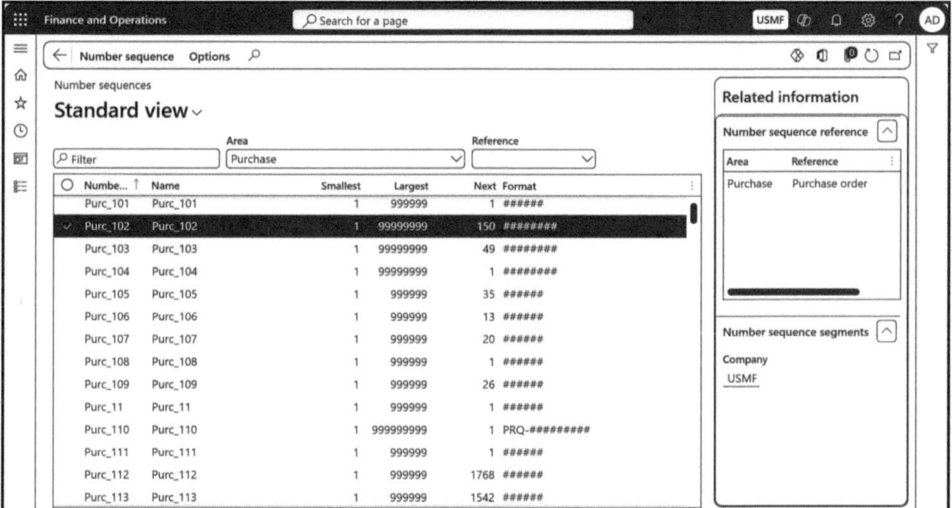

Fig. 10.9 Viewing the FactBox *Number sequence reference* in the Number sequence form

10.3.1.4 Preallocation of Numbers

On the tab *Performance* in the Number sequence detail form, you can set the slider *Preallocation* to "Yes" to enable preloading numbers from the database to the local buffer. Preallocation should not be selected for continuous numbers, but it improves the system performance for other number sequences. With the button *Number sequence/ Administration/Status list*, you can check the preallocated numbers. In order to remove (free) the preallocated numbers, select the applicable option in the button *Number sequence/Administration/Manual cleanup*.

10.3.2 Calendars

As a prerequisite for posting any transaction in Dynamics 365, an open ledger period which includes the respective posting date is required.

10.3.2.1 Ledger Calendars

Ledger calendars (*General ledger > Calendars > Ledger calendars*), which refer to the fiscal calendar that is linked to the current company, determine the open periods in which you can post transactions ($\rightarrow$ Sect. 9.2.1).

10.3.2.2 Other Calendars

Apart from the calendars in finance, other areas within Dynamics 365 have got separate period and calendar definitions.

The Working time templates form (*Organization administration > Setup > Calendars > Working time templates* or *Production control > Setup > Calendars > Working time templates*) contains default settings for the weekly working times. Working time templates are a basis for the calendars in the Calendars form (*Organization administration > Setup > Calendars > Calendars*). These calendars ($\rightarrow$ Sect. 5.3.1) are used in all areas of the supply chain management—including master planning, production, purchasing, sales, and inventory management.

The Project accounting module uses separate calendars, which you can access in the menu item *Organization administration > Setup > Calendars > Period types*. These calendars are a basis for project invoicing and required for estimates, invoice subscriptions, and the project-related employee setup.

10.3.3 Address Setup

The address setup is a prerequisite for entering and printing addresses correctly. In order to access the address setup, which is shared across companies, open the form *Organization administration > Global address book > Addresses > Address setup*.

On the tab *Country/region* of the Address setup form, you can view the available countries. Microsoft Dynamics 365 already includes a standard list of countries, but you can enter additional countries with the button *New* in the toolbar of this tab.

On the tab *Parameters*, sliders specify whether *ZIP/postal code*, *District*, *City*, or *County* are validated when entering an address. If set to "Yes", you cannot enter an address with, for example, a new ZIP code before the new ZIP code is entered on the tab *ZIP/ postal codes* in the address setup.

The address format on the tab *Address format* determines the way in which street, ZIP/ postal code, city, and country are shown in the address field of addresses. In order to comply with the regulations in different countries, an individual format per country is possible. The field *Address format* in the country setup (on the tab *Country/region* in the address setup) controls the address format per country.

If you want to set up a new format, click the button *New* in the toolbar of the tab *Address format*. In the pane *Configure address component* on the right, enter how the address segments (including *Street* and *City*) should be shown on printed documents. The segment selection is also used when you enter an address: Only fields that are included in the address format of the particular country are shown.

When you set up address formats, take into account that Dynamics 365 not only stores the individual fields of the address, but also the formatted address. If you change the address format and there are already addresses with the old format, you can update the existing addresses with the button *Update addresses* in the toolbar of the tab *Address format* in the Address setup form.

10.3.4 Parameters

With Dynamics 365, you can run business processes in different ways. Parameters are basic settings that select the way, which fits best to your organization—as a simple example, there is a parameter whether to use vendor approvals.

The definition of correct parameter settings is a core task when implementing Dynamics 365. Depending on the respective parameter, it is not easily possible to change a parameter setting at a later stage. Before you change any basic setting in an operational environment, make sure that you are aware of the consequences. Depending on the circumstances, read the online help or ask an expert to avoid data inconsistency or other issues.

The System parameters (*System administration > Setup > System parameters*) contain global parameters like the system language (default language for language texts in shared data, like product descriptions) or the default basic currency.

In addition, a parameter form that controls the company-specific settings is included in each module of the application. In order to access the parameters of a module, open the respective menu item in the folder *Setup* of the module—for example, the Accounts payable parameters in the menu item *Accounts payable > Setup > Accounts payable parameters*.

10.4   Alerts and Workflow Management

A workflow, which is a sequence of operations in a routine business process, contains the necessary activities for processing a document. Typical examples of workflows are approval processes—e.g., for purchase requisitions.

Microsoft Dynamics 365 provides the required functionality for configuring and processing workflows, including automated workflow processes. You can, for example, configure workflows to approve low-value purchases automatically while high-value purchases require manual approval.

Alerts within Dynamics 365 are automatic notifications that are based on alert rules and triggered by selected events (e.g., inserting a record). Compared to workflows, which support a sequence of activities including automatic actions, alerts are simple notifications without further functionality.

10.4.1 Alert Rules and Notifications

If you want to notify a user of an event that occurs within Dynamics 365, create an alert rule in the respective form. You can, for example, set up a rule to notify the responsible person when an agreed delivery date has passed, or when a new vendor is created.

10.4.1.1 Alert Rules

To create an alert rule, click the button *Options/Share/Create a custom alert* in the action pane of detail forms and list pages. A dialog is shown next, in which you can enter the details of the alert rule (→ Fig. 10.10).

In the field *Event* of the dialog, select the trigger for the alert—for example, creating or deleting a record, or modifying the content of a particular field. In alert rules that refer to a field, first select the respective field in the lookup *Field* of the dialog. If the basis of an alert rule is a date field, the field *Event* provides the option to generate alerts when the date is due. On the tab *Alert me with*, the *User ID* who receives the alert is initialized with your user, but you can change it.

If you want to edit your alert rules related to a particular form (e.g., the Vendor form), click the button *Options/Share/Manage my alerts rule* in the action pane of this form.

In the common Alert rules form (*System administration > Setup > Alert rules*), you can manage the alert rules of all users.

10.4.1.2 Alert Processing and Notifications

Alert notifications are only shown after executing the periodic activity *System administration > Periodic tasks > Alerts > Change based alerts* or, for alert rules that refer to a due date for a date field, *System administration > Periodic tasks > Alerts > Due date alerts*. These activities are usually periodic batch jobs.

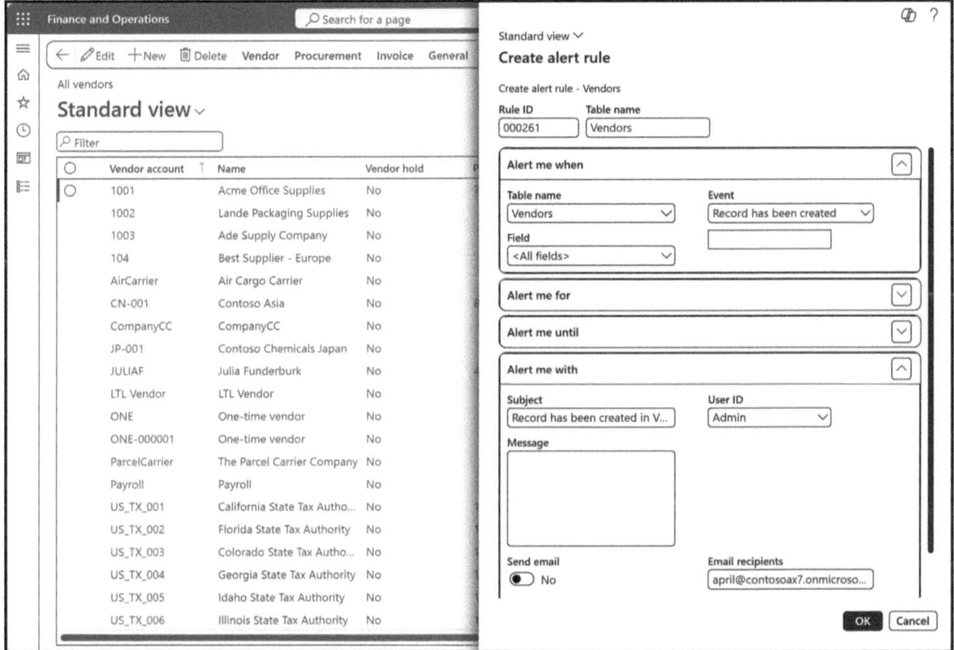

Fig. 10.10   Entering details in the dialog for a new alert rule

Once an event triggers an alert, a notification is sent to the action center (message center). Click the button ▣ (*Show messages*) in the navigation bar, which indicates the number of unread notifications, to view the notification. In the notification, a link to the origin of the alert provides access to the record triggering the alert.

10.4.2 Configuring Workflows

Workflows are available in many areas of Microsoft Dynamics 365, including but not limited to:

- **Purchase requisitions**
- **Purchase orders**
- **Vendor invoices**
- **Free text invoices**
- **Financial journals**

In each applicable menu, the folder *Setup* contains a menu item with the workflows in the particular module. The Procurement and sourcing workflows page (*Procurement and sourcing > Setup > Procurement and sourcing workflows*), for example, contains the workflows in the Procurement module.

10.4.2.1 Graphical Workflow Editor

In order to view and edit a workflow that is shown in a Workflow list page, click the workflow *ID* shown as a link in the grid. Dynamics 365 then downloads the *Workflow editor*, which is an application that communicates with the Dynamics 365 environment.

After signing in with your Dynamics 365 user account, you can view the graphical Workflow editor with the selected workflow. It includes the following panes (→ Fig. 10.11):

- **Canvas** [1]—Design area for the workflow, with elements and connections.
- **Toolbox** [2]—On the left, containing available workflow elements.
- **Error pane** [3]—Displaying error messages and warnings.

If you want to access the properties of the workflow, right-click in an empty space in the canvas and select the option *Properties* in the context menu (or click the button *Properties* after selecting an empty space in the canvas). Basic workflow settings include the *Owner* of the selected workflow.

In the toolbox on the left of the Workflow editor, the workflow elements are grouped by type (e.g., *Approvals*). Depending on the selected workflow, the toolbox contains different elements. You can hide or show the toolbox with the button *Toolbox* in the action pane.

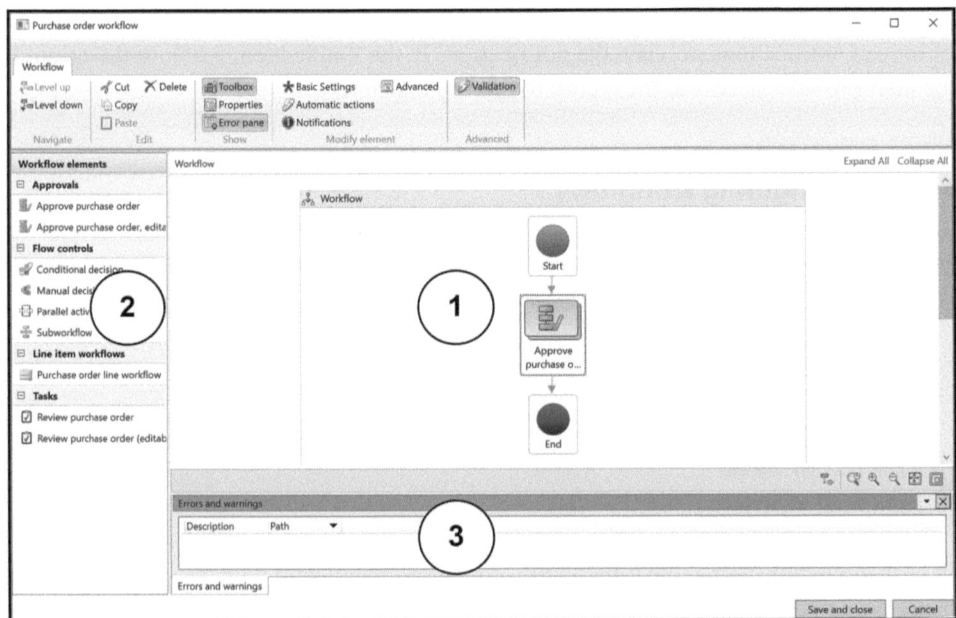

Fig. 10.11 Editing the purchase order workflow in the Workflow editor

If you want to add a workflow element to the workflow, click the respective element in the toolbox and drag it to the canvas. In order to edit the properties of the element, select the option *Properties* in the context menu (right-click the element to open the context menu for the respective element) or click the appropriate button in the button group *Modify element* of the action pane. The available options for the element depend on the element type.

For elements that require a manual activity (e.g., *Tasks* or *Manual decision*), the properties include a tab or button *Assignment* for assigning responsible persons. The *Assignment type* defines the search path for the responsible person. Applicable assignment types are "Participant" (related to user roles and user groups), "Hierarchy" (related to the position hierarchy in human resources), "Workflow user" (related to the user who starts or owns the workflow), "User" (direct assignment of respective user accounts), or "Queue" (work item queues, see below). If multiple users are assigned to an approval step, the settings on the tab *Completion policy* of the *Assignment* control whether a single user may approve, or if the approval of the majority or all assigned users is required. On the tab *Time limit* of the *Assignment*, you can specify the maximum duration for the decision whether to approve or to reject.

Workflow elements with the type "Approval" contain a lower workflow level with the approval steps. The responsible persons for approval are assigned at the level of the approval steps. In order to access the approval steps, double-click the particular approval element or click the button *Level down* in the action pane of the Workflow editor. If you want to access the upper level again, click the button *Level up* or click the link *Workflow* in the path shown in the header line of the canvas.

In the *Escalation* settings of an approval step or a task, you can activate and configure an automatic reassignment in case the assigned user exceeds the specified time limit. The tab *End action* in the escalation settings includes an automatic action if there is also no decision within the time limit for the escalation.

Settings for *Automatic actions* provide the option to automatically execute an action if the condition entered for the automatic action is met—for example, approving a requisition if the total amount is below a predefined maximum.

In order to connect the workflow elements in the canvas, create a line between the different elements. For this purpose, click on the border of one element and drag the line to the subsequent element (similar to the way of working in Microsoft Visio). In a valid workflow, all elements between *Start* and *End* have to be linked.

10.4.2.2 Work Item Queues

The option "Queue" in the assignment of the responsible person is only available with particular workflow element types (e.g., *Tasks*). As a prerequisite for the queue-based assignment, set up work item queues (*Organization administration > Workflow > Work item queues*).

Work item queues are used to pool workflow activities and to assign an activity to a group of people instead of a single person. If a work item is assigned to a work item queue, all members of the queue may claim the work item and work on it.

When you create a new work item queue, select the workflow type in the lookup field *Document* to specify the workflows in which the work item queue is available. Once the status of the work item queue is set to "Active", you can use it in the applicable workflows.

Apart from manually adding users to a work item queue (on the tab *Users* of the work item queue), you can apply an automatic assignment that is based on filter criteria. In order to access the setup for automatic assignment, click the button *Work item queue assignment rule* in the Work item queue form, or open the menu item *Organization administration > Workflow > Work item queue assignment rules*.

10.4.2.3 Workflow Versions

When you save a workflow with the button *Save and close* in the Workflow editor, Dynamics 365 creates a new version. A dialog is shown then in which you select whether to activate the new version or to keep the previous version activated.

If you want to access the versions of a workflow, click the button *Workflow/Manage/Versions* in the Workflow list page. In the *Workflow versions* dialog, you can activate a new version or an old version as applicable.

The active version is used in new workflows, which are submitted after activation. Work items of workflows in progress have to be finished with the original version.

10.4.2.4 Creating Workflows

In order to create a new workflow in a Workflow list page, click the button *New* in the action pane. A dialog is shown next, in which you have to select the applicable *Workflow type* (e.g., "Purchase requisition review") before you access the Workflow editor described above.

If there are two workflows of the same type in the Workflow list page, you can click the button *Workflow/Manage/Set as default* to specify a default.

10.4.2.5 Basic Setup for Workflows

Workflow processing is an asynchronous batch job, which is why the next activity in a workflow is not available immediately, but only after the respective workflow element has been processed. Depending on the batch configuration, this may take some time.

In order to set up the workflow infrastructure initially, an administrator can use the menu item *System administration > Workflow > Workflow infrastructure configuration*. This wizard generates batch jobs, which are shown in the menu item *System administration > Inquiries > Batch jobs*. As a prerequisite for the use of workflows, these batch jobs have to be processed repeatedly.

10.4.3 Working with Workflows

If there is an active workflow related to a Dynamics 365 form, the button *Workflow* is shown in the action pane of this form. This button indicates that workflow processing is necessary and provides the option to start workflow processing.

When working with workflows, you should keep in mind that workflow tasks are processed in a batch process. For this reason, work items are not available before the batch process has finished processing the submitted workflow.

10.4.3.1 Start of Workflow Processing

Once you have entered a record in a form that is assigned to a workflow, you can start workflow processing with the button *Workflow/Submit* in the action pane (e.g., in the purchase requisitions shown in → Fig. 10.12). In the following dialog, you can optionally enter a comment before you click the button *Submit* at the bottom. Submitting starts workflow processing, which generates work items that are based on the workflow elements of the workflow (specified in the Workflow editor).

After starting the workflow, the button *Workflow* does not show the option *Submit* anymore, but other options which are depending on workflow settings and on the current status of the workflow.

If you want to check the current status of workflow processing, click the button *Workflow/Workflow history* in the action pane. In the Workflow history form, you can refresh the screen with the shortcut *Shift + F5* or with the button ▢ (*Refresh*) in the action pane from time to time—in particular, if the workflow batch job has not processed the workflow yet.

> *Note*: If a workflow shows the status "Unrecoverable" because of an issue, you can click the button *Recall* in the workflow history to reset it to the status "Draft".

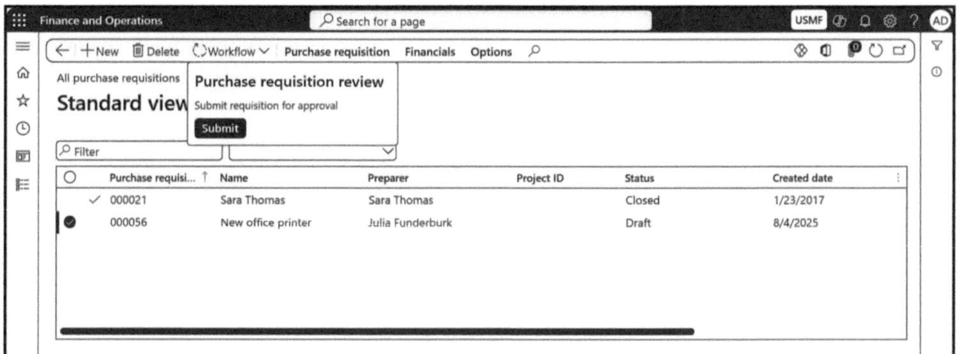

Fig. 10.12 Submitting a purchase requisition for approval (starting a workflow)

10.4.3.2 Work Items in Approval Workflows

Depending on the settings of the related workflow element, work items are either assigned to a work item queue or individual users.

If necessary, you can change the assigned approver (appropriate permissions required). For this purpose, open the Workflow history form and click the button *Reassign* on the tab *Work items*.

The work items that are assigned to a user are shown in the left pane of the homepage (Immersive home or dashboard) and in the Work item page (*Common > Work items > Work items assigned to me*). Available options in the button *Workflow* of the Work item page depend on the workflow element properties of the selected work item (as specified in the Workflow editor on the tab *Advanced settings/Allowed actions* in the *Properties* of the respective workflow element). Possible options include:

- **Approve**—Approve the request.
- **Reject**—Reject the approval finally (which does not prevent resubmitting).
- **Request change**—Reject, but promise approval if the request is changed.
- **Delegate**—Transfer the decision to another user.

The additional option "Recall" is not available to the approver, but to the person who has submitted the request. Recalling is an option to stop workflow processing before approval (e.g., if you want to modify the request).

If you are an approver and need to know more details before deciding on approval, you can access the original request straight from the Work item form—click the button *Open* in the action pane or click the request ID shown as a link in the column *ID*. In the original request (e.g., the purchase requisition), you have the same approval options as in the Work item list page.

Depending on the settings in the particular workflow (specified in the Workflow editor), there are additional workflow activities or multiple approvers.

> *Note*: Apart from the option of approving a request in the Dynamics 365 web client (Work item page), you can use the Approval Management mobile app.

10.4.3.3 Working with Work Item Queues

If a work item is assigned to a work item queue, it is shown in the list page *Common > Work items > Work items assigned to my queues*. As a prerequisite, you have to be a member of the work item queue to which the work item is assigned.

In the work item queue, you can click the button *Workflow/Accept* in the action pane to claim a work item on which you want to work. Accepting a work item moves the item to your work item list (among the other work items that are directly assigned to you) and prevents other queue members from working on the same item.

In the Work item page (*Common > Work items > Work items assigned to me*), you can subsequently execute applicable workflow actions like in any other directly assigned work item. In addition, the workflow button contains the options *Reassign* (for reassigning the work item to other persons) and *Release* (for releasing it back to the queue).

10.5 Additional Common Features

Advanced features, which are available across the whole application, include document management, case management, and the task guides.

The license configuration and the feature management determine the features that are available in Dynamics 365.

10.5.1 Document Management

In daily business, you work with structured data that are represented by data records in the business application (e.g., customer records). In parallel, there are data with reference to these records which are only available in an unstructured format (e.g., files or emails). These unstructured data are often hard to find.

With the document management in Microsoft Dynamics 365, you can solve this issue by appending files to data records. The attached files are directly accessible from within Dynamics 365. If you use the document management to attach, for example, all related notes and files to the respective customer in the Customer form, Dynamics 365 provides access to all relevant data on the customer—business data within Dynamics 365, and the related files—directly from the Customer form.

10.5.1.1 Document Types and Document Management Setup

As a prerequisite for accessing the document management in the Attachment form, the slider *Enable document handling* in the user options (in the section *Preferences*, on the tab *Miscellaneous*) has to be set to "Yes" for the users who work with document management.

In addition, the required document types have to be configured in the menu item *Organization administration > Document management > Document types*. The document types are divided into the following classes:

- **Simple note**—For plain text, which you enter directly in the Attachment form.
- **Attach file**—For attaching a file.
- **Attach URL**—For a web link, entered in the field *Description* of the document.

You can create multiple document types per class. The field *Class* in the document type determines whether assigned documents are notes, attachments, or URLs. For the class "Attach file", the selected option in the field *Location* determines whether attached files are stored inside the Dynamics 365 database, in the Azure Blob storage, or SharePoint.

The Document parameter form (*Organization administration > Document management > Document management parameters*) specifies core settings for document management, including the file types that are available in document management (in the section *File types*). If the slider *Use active document tables* in the section *General* of the parameters is set to "Yes", document management is only available for the tables that are included in the active document tables (*Organization administration > Document management > Active document tables*).

10.5.1.2 Attachment Form for Document Handling

In every list page or detail form, you can access the Attachment form for document handling (→ Fig. 10.13) with the button 🖼 in the action pane (the icon shows the number of attached documents) or with the shortcut *Ctrl + Shift + A*. In the Attachment form, you can edit notes and append documents as applicable. The documents are attached to the record that has been selected in the original form when opening the Attachment form.

With the button *New* in the action pane, you can create a new document in the Attachment form. The *Type* that you select in the drop-down menu of the button *New* determines if the new document is a note, a file attachment, or a URL. If the type is a file attachment, you can upload the document in a dialog that is shown next. If the type is a note, you can enter a multiline text in the field *Notes* on the tab *General*. In the field *Restriction* on tab *General*, select the option "External" if the document should be visible for external parties and if it should be printed on external documents (e.g., sales invoices).

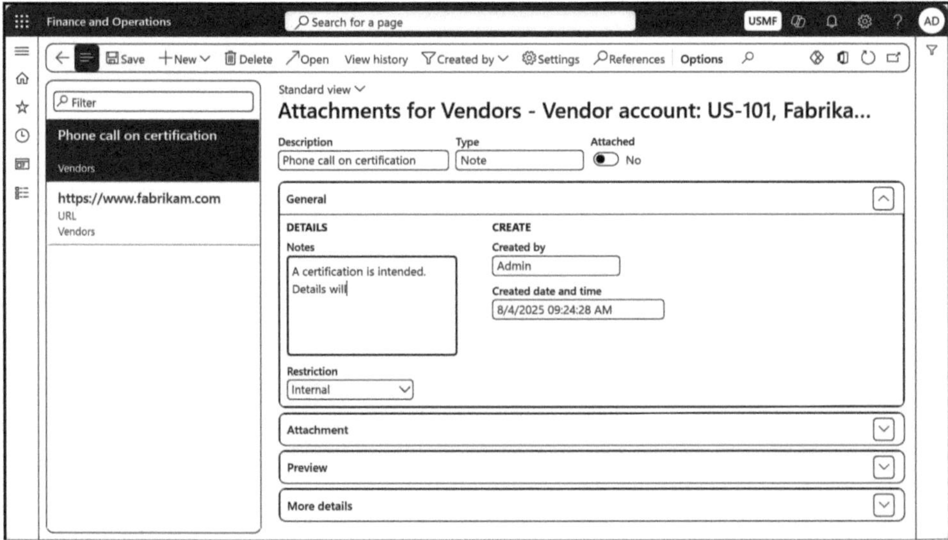

Fig. 10.13 Entering a simple note in the Attachment form

In case the document is an attachment, you can view the attached document with the button *Open* (which downloads the attachment) or directly on the tab *Preview* in the Attachment form.

10.5.1.3 Document History and Recycle Bin

In the Document management parameters, the slider *Enable document history* in the section *General* activates tracking of document handling activities. If enabled, you can view the past activities with the button *View history* in the Attachment form.

The slider *Deferred deletion enabled* in the Document management parameters activates a recycle bin for document handling. If enabled, you can view the recycle bin with the button *Deleted attachments* in the Attachment form.

10.5.2 Case Management

The purpose of case management in Dynamics 365 is to manage any kind of question or issue centrally. You can use it in many areas—for example, in customer service, collections, purchase management, and product management.

10.5.2.1 Setup for Case Management

Apart from the number sequence for cases, there is the following setup for the case management:

- **Case categories**—Classify cases by functional area.
- **Case processes**—Specify the activities for processing a case (optional).

Case categories (*Organization management > Setup > Cases > Case categories*) group cases in a hierarchical structure. In order to set up a new case category, click the button *New* in the action pane and select the *Category type*. If you do not select the top-level node in the left pane, but an existing category group, the new category is a subcategory with the category type of that group. On the tab *General* of the category, you can enter default values for the owner and for the *Case process*. These defaults are used when creating a case with the respective category.

Case processes (*Organization management > Setup > Cases > Case processes*), which are an optional setup, determine the necessary steps for processing a case. When you set up a new case process, enter the *Name*, the *Description*, and make sure that the *Type* is "Case process" (if you don't create a case process for following up a specific process type like a marketing campaign) before saving the record. The slider *Active* should be set to "Yes" to activate the case process. In order to define the steps (stages) for case processing, click the button *Process/View/Details*. In the process details, you can create a process stage with the button *New/Create level* (enter the name of the stage in the field *Purpose*). If required, you can create a multi-level hierarchy of stages.

For a simple case process, it may be sufficient to set up stages. But if required, you can create activities (e.g., *Appointments*) for the stages in the process details. Click the button *New/Create appointment* (or one of the other options in the *New* button) for this purpose, and—in case you want to make sure that a particular activity is executed when working on a case—set the slider *Required* in the activity to "Yes".

In case of required activities, additionally set the slider *Check for required activities* on the tab *Exit criteria* of the related stage to "Yes".

Note: For CAPA cases in the advanced quality management (→ Sect. 7.4.7), there are separate settings in the Inventory management parameters and in the menu items of the folder *Inventory management > Setup > CAPA management.*

10.5.2.2 Processing Cases

You can create a new case with the appropriate button in the action pane of any list page or detail form that refers to case management—for example, in the Sales order form (click the button *General/Customer/Cases/Create case*), the Customer form, the Vendor form, or the Released product form.

Cases that you create in a sales order are assigned to the respective customer and the order. In the *New case* dialog, select the *Case category* (only categories with the category type "General" or "Sales" are available) and enter a *Description*. On the tab *Other* of the dialog, you can override the *Employee responsible* (owner) and the *Case process,* which are initialized from the selected *Case category*.

If you want to follow up on a case, open the Case form (*Common > Cases > All cases*) and click the respective case ID (shown as a link in the column *Case ID*) to switch to the detail form (→ Fig. 10.14). Present assignments of the case—e.g., to a sales order—are shown on the tab *Associations*. If there are later additional associations, you can add them on this tab in the Case form—for example, if you want to assign a return order case also to the original sales order. The FactBox *Process tree* displays the process steps as specified in the applicable case process. The current status of the stages is shown in the Case process form, which you can access with the button *Case/Process/Case process* in the action pane of the Case form.

When you start working on a case, click the button *Case/Maintain/Change status/In process* in the Case form (if the status "In process" has not already been selected when creating the case).

If the case is attached to a *Case process* and you proceed with the case, click the button *Case/Process/Case/Change stage* and select the applicable stage to which you want to move. If the case process includes activities (e.g., *Appointments*), click the button *General/ Activities/Activities/View activities* in the Case form (or open the menu item *Common > Activities > All activities*) to access the related activities. Required activities of a case have to be completed by the responsible person.

On the tab *Case log*, you can view all interactions (e.g., a product receipt) that refer to the case. The case log facilitates getting an overview of the status of a case.

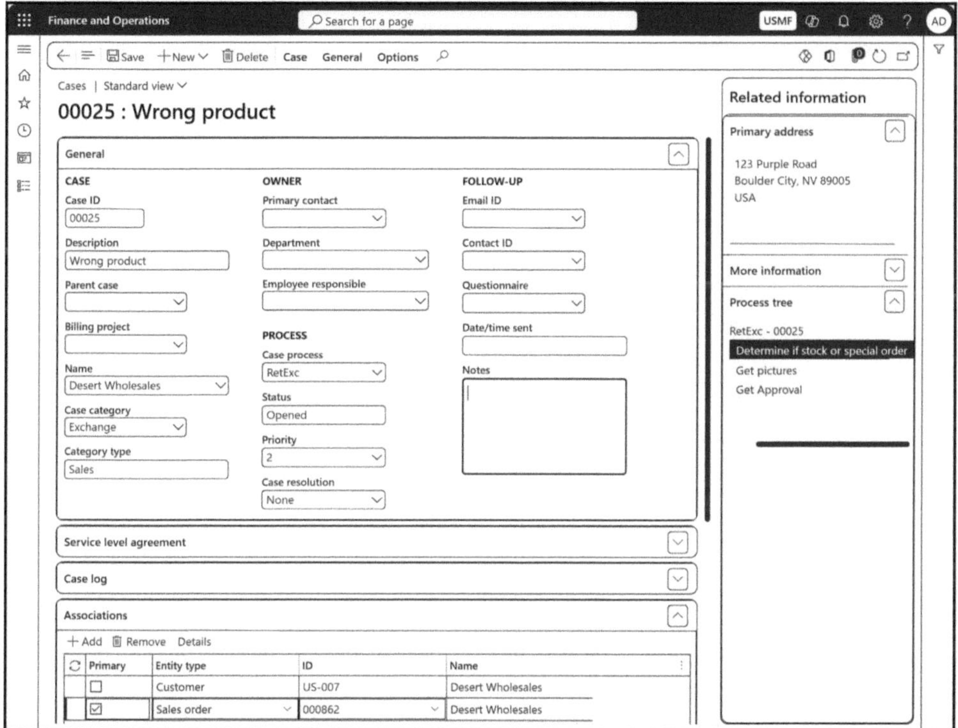

Fig. 10.14   Editing the details in a case associated with a sales order

To close a case, click the button *Case/Maintain/Change status/Closed* in the Case form.

Note: A standard filter prevents showing CAPA cases in the common Case form. They are shown in the CAPA cases form (*Common > Common > CAPA management > All CAPA cases*).

10.5.3 Task Recorder and Task Guide

Task guides are step-by-step instructions that explain how to perform a business process in Dynamics 365. In order to create a task guide, use the task recorder (→ Fig. 10.15).

You can open the task recorder with the button ⚙/*Task recorder* in the navigation bar. In the *Task recorder* dialog, click the button *Create recording* to create a recording. Then enter a *Recording name* in the next dialog and click the button *Start*. Once the recording is started, execute the steps that you want to record in the Dynamics 365 web client. You can edit the instructions with the button ☑ next to each step in the task recorder pane.

Once you have finished the recording, click the button *Stop* in the task recorder banner at the top. The task recorder subsequently shows a dialog with the option to save the recording to your PC, to the Lifecycle Services, or to export it as a Word document. When

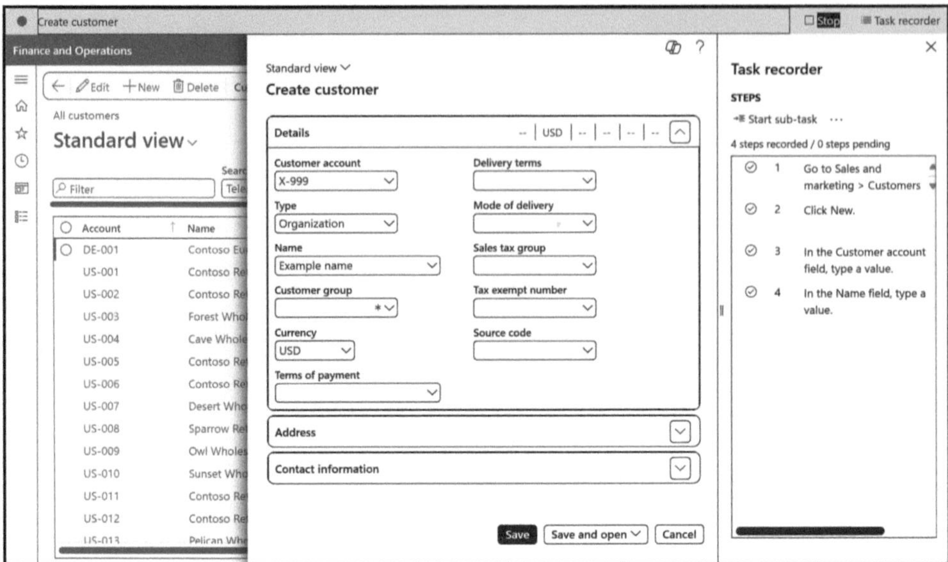

Fig. 10.15 Recording a guide in the task recorder

you are finished, click the button *Return to main menu* at the bottom of the dialog to return
to the task recorder pane.

   If you want to play a recording as a task guide, click the button *Play recording as guide*
in the task recorder pane and open the recording that has been saved to your PC or the
Lifecycle Services. If you have saved the recording to a Business Process Library in the
Lifecycle Services that is selected on the tab *Help* in the System parameters, you can view
the recording on the tab *Task Guides* in the help pane of the pages that are covered by the
recording.

10.5.4 Feature Management and License Configuration

When a new feature is available after a Microsoft service update, it is shown in the Feature
management workspace ($\rightarrow$ Fig. 10.16). In this workspace, which you can access with the
corresponding tile on the homepage (Immersive home or dashboard), the drop-down
below the workspace name provides the option to enable new features automatically.
Usually, it is set in a way that new features are only available after they have been manually enabled with the respective button in the workspace.

   The feature management is intended to delay new features temporarily—for example,
if you don't want to use Preview features until they are officially supported in production
environments.

   Unlike the feature management, the license configuration (*System administration > Setup > License configuration*) is designed to control the available functional

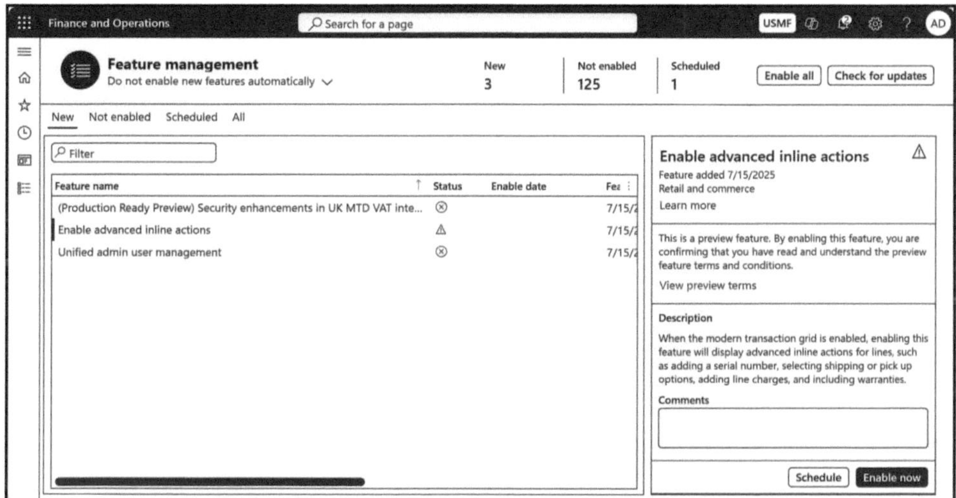

Fig. 10.16 Managing new features in the Feature management workspace

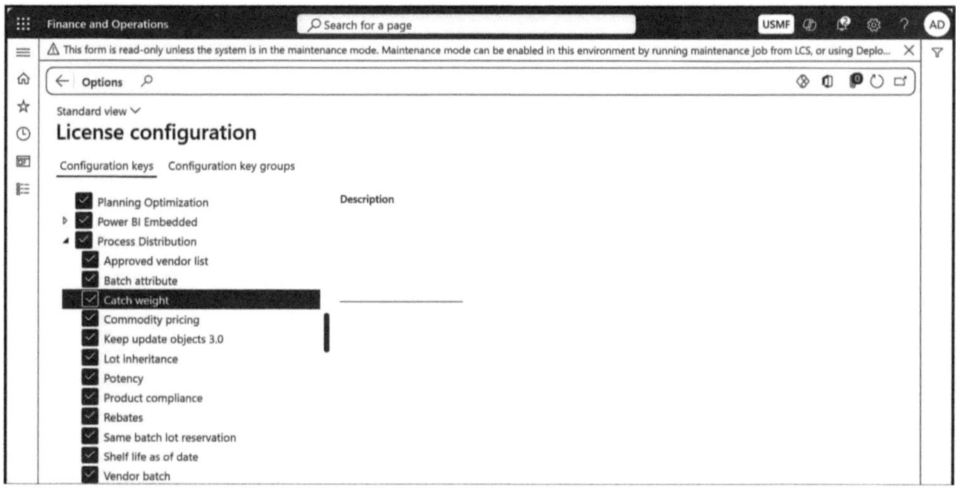

Fig. 10.17 Viewing the active license configuration

components on a long-term basis. If, for example, your enterprise doesn't need the catch weight functionality and wants to get rid of the related fields and functions, deselect the corresponding configuration key (→ Fig. 10.17). Changing the license configuration is only possible in maintenance mode.

Appendix

Setup Checklist

The checklists below cover the core setup of Dynamics 365 Finance and Operations. The tables on the basic setup include the necessary configuration steps for the functional areas that are covered by the book. They have to be finished before you can start working in any module. Master data and other essential settings of the individual modules are included in the subsequent tables.

Depending on the requirements, an additional setup is necessary in most cases.

Table A.1 Basic system setup

No.	Name	Menu item	Section
1.1	Configuration	*System administration > Setup > License configuration*	→ 10.5.4
1.2	Parameters	*System administration > Setup > System parameters*	→ 10.3.4
1.3	Legal entities	*Organization administration > Organizations > Legal entities*	→ 10.1.4
1.4	Users	*System administration > Users > Users*	→ 10.2.2
1.5	Features	Workspace *Feature management*	→ 10.5.4

Table A.2 Basic setup of a legal entity

No.	Name	Menu item	Section
2.1	Operating units	*Organization administration > Organizations > Operating units*	→ 10.1.2
2.2	Dimensions	*General ledger > Chart of accounts > Dimensions > Financial dimensions*	→ 9.2.3
2.3	Fiscal calendars	*General ledger > Calendars > Fiscal Calendars*	→ 9.2.1
2.4	Currencies	*General ledger > Currencies > Currencies*	→ 9.2.2
2.5	Rate types	*General ledger > Currencies > Exchange rate types*	→ 9.2.2
2.6	Exchange rates	*General ledger > Currencies > Currency exchange rates*	→ 9.2.2
2.7	Chart of accounts	*General ledger > Chart of accounts > Accounts > Chart of accounts*	→ 9.2.4

A. Luszczak, *Using Microsoft Dynamics 365 Finance and Operations*,
https://doi.org/10.1007/978-3-658-50563-9

No.	Name	Menu item	Section
2.8	Account structures	*General ledger > Chart of accounts > Structures > Configure account structures*	→ 9.2.4
2.9	Ledger	*General ledger > Ledger setup > Ledger*	→ 9.2
2.10	Sites	*Inventory management > Setup > Inventory breakdown > Sites*	→ 10.1.6
2.11	Warehouses	*Inventory management > Setup > Inventory breakdown > Warehouses*	→ 7.4.1
2.12	Bank accounts	*Cash and bank management > Bank accounts > Bank accounts*	→ 9.2.5
2.13	Address setup	*Organization administration > Global address book > Addresses > Address setup*	→ 10.3.3
2.14	Address book parameters	*Organization administration > Global address book > Global address book parameters*	→ 2.4.2
2.15	Number sequences	*Organization administration > Number sequences > Number sequences*	→ 10.3.1
2.16	Units	*Organization administration > Setup > Units > Units*	→ 7.2.1
2.17	Unit conversion	*Organization administration > Setup > Units > Unit conversions*	→ 7.2.1

Table A.3 Basic setup for general ledger and sales tax

No.	Name	Menu item	Section
3.1	Default descriptions	*General ledger > Journal setup > Default descriptions*	→ 9.2.4
3.2	Accounts for aut. transactions	*General ledger > Posting setup > Accounts for automatic transactions*	→ 9.2.4
3.3	Tax posting group	*Tax > Setup > Sales tax > Ledger posting groups*	→ 9.2.7
3.4	Tax authorities	*Tax > Indirect taxes > Sales tax > Sales tax authorities*	→ 9.2.7
3.5	Sales tax settlement periods	*Tax > Indirect taxes > Sales tax > Sales tax settlement periods*	→ 9.2.7
3.6	Sales tax codes	*Tax > Indirect taxes > Sales tax > Sales tax codes*	→ 9.2.7
3.7	Sales tax groups	*Tax > Indirect taxes > Sales tax > Sales tax groups*	→ 9.2.7
3.8	Item sales tax groups	*Tax > Indirect taxes > Sales tax > Item sales tax groups*	→ 9.2.7
3.9	Journal names	*General ledger > Journal setup > Journal names*	→ 9.2.8
3.10	Parameters	*General ledger > Ledger setup > General ledger parameter*	→ 9.2.8

Table A.4 Basic setup for procurement and accounts payable

No.	Name	Menu item	Section
4.1	Terms of payment	*Accounts payable > Payment setup > Terms of payment*	→ 3.2.2
4.2	Vendor groups	*Accounts payable > Vendors > Vendor groups*	→ 3.2.3
4.3	Posting profiles	*Accounts payable > Setup > Vendor posting profiles*	→ 3.2.3

No.	Name	Menu item	Section
4.4	Accounts payable parameters	*Accounts payable > Setup > Accounts payable parameters*	
4.5	Procurement parameters	*Procurement and sourcing > Setup > Procurement and sourcing parameters*	

Table A.5 Basic setup for sales and accounts receivable

	Name	Menu item	Section
5.1	Terms of payment	*Accounts receivable > Payments setup > Terms of payment*	→ 3.2.2
5.2	Customer groups	*Accounts receivable > Setup > Customer groups*	→ 4.2.1
5.3	Posting profiles	*Accounts receivable > Setup > Customer posting profiles*	→ 4.2.1
5.4	Form setup	*Accounts receivable > Setup > Forms > Form setup*	→ 4.2.2
5.5	Accounts receivable parameters	*Accounts receivable > Setup > Accounts receivable parameters*	
5.6	Sales and marketing parameters	*Sales and marketing > Setup > Sales and marketing parameters*	

Table A.6 Basic setup for product and inventory management

No.	Name	Menu item	Section
6.1	Storage dimension groups	*Product information management > Setup > Dimension and variant groups > Storage dimension groups*	→ 7.2.2
6.2	Tracking dimension groups	*Product information management > Setup > Dimension and variant groups > Tracking dimension groups*	→ 7.2.2
6.3	Item groups	*Inventory management > Setup > Inventory > Item groups*	→ 7.2.1
6.4	Transaction combinations	*Cost management > Ledger integration policies setup > Transaction combinations*	→ 9.4.2
6.5	Posting setup	*Cost management > Ledger integration policies setup > Posting*	→ 9.4.2
6.6	Item model groups	*Inventory management > Setup > Inventory > Item model groups*	→ 7.2.3
6.7	Costing versions	*Cost management > Inventory accounting > Costing versions*	→ 7.3.3
6.8	Inventory journal names	*Inventory management > Setup > Journal names > Inventory*	→ 7.4.1
6.9	Warehouse journal names	*Inventory management > Setup > Journal names > Warehouse management*	→ 7.4.1
6.10	Parameters	*Inventory management > Setup > Inventory and warehouse management parameters*	→ 7.4.1

Table A.7 Basic setup for production control

No.	Name	Menu item	Section
7.1	Production units	*Production control > Setup > Production > Production units*	→ 5.3.2
7.2	Cost groups	*Cost management > Inventory accounting policies setup > Cost groups*	→ 7.3.3
7.3	Working time templates	*Production control > Setup > Calendars > Working time templates*	→ 5.3.1
7.4	Calendars	*Production control > Setup > Calendars > Calendars*	→ 5.3.1
7.5	Route groups	*Production control > Setup > Routes > Route groups*	→ 5.3.3
7.6	Shared categories	*Production control > Setup > Routes > Shared categories*	→ 5.3.3
7.7	Cost categories	*Production control > Setup > Routes > Cost categories*	→ 5.3.3
7.8	Resource capabilities	*Production control > Setup > Resources > Resource capabilities*	→ 5.3.2
7.9	Resource groups	*Production control > Setup > Resources > Resource groups*	→ 5.3.2
7.10	Resources	*Production control > Setup > Resources > Resources*	→ 5.3.2
7.11	Journal names	*Production control > Setup > Production journal names*	→ 5.5.1
7.12	Calculation groups	*Cost management > Predetermined cost policies setup > Calculation groups*	→ 7.3.3
7.13	Costing sheet	*Cost management > Ledger integration policies setup > Costing sheets*	→ 7.3.3
7.14	Parameters	*Production control > Setup > Production control parameters*	→ 5.4.1
7.15	Parameters by site	*Production control > Setup > Production control parameters by site*	→ 5.4.1

Table A.8 Basic setup for master planning

No.	Name	Menu item	Section
8.1	Coverage groups	*Master planning > Setup > Coverage > Coverage groups*	→ 6.3.4
8.2	Forecast models	*Master planning > Setup > Demand forecasting > Forecast models*	→ 6.2.2
8.3	Master plans	*Master planning > Setup > Plans > Master plans*	→ 6.3.3
8.4	Parameters	*Master planning > Setup > Master planning parameters*	→ 6.3.3
8.5	Plg. Optim. parameters	*Master planning > Setup > Planning Optimization parameters*	→ 6.3.2

Table A.9 Other key settings

No.	Name	Menu item	Section
9.1	Employees	*Human resources > Workers > Workers*	→ 10.2.2
9.2	Terms of delivery	*Procurement and sourcing > Setup > Distribution > Terms of delivery*	→ 3.2.1
9.3	Modes of delivery	*Procurement and sourcing > Setup > Distribution > Modes of delivery*	→ 3.2.1
9.4	Cash discounts	*Accounts payable > Payment setup > Cash discounts*	→ 3.2.2
9.5	Payment methods (Purchasing)	*Accounts payable > Payment setup > Methods of payment*	→ 9.3.3
9.6	Activate trade agreements (Purchasing)	*Procurement and sourcing > Setup > Prices and discounts > Activate price/discount*	→ 4.8.1
9.7	Vendor price/ discount groups	*Procurement and sourcing > Prices and discounts > Price/ discount groups > Vendor price/discount groups*	→ 4.8.1
9.8	Trade agreement journal names	*Procurement and sourcing > Setup > Prices and discounts > Trade agreement journal names*	→ 4.8.1
9.9	Item discount groups	*Procurement and sourcing > Prices and discounts > Price/discount groups > Item discount groups*	→ 4.8.1
9.10	Activate trade agreements (Sales)	*Sales and marketing > Setup > Prices and discounts > Activate price/discount*	→ 4.8.1
9.11	Customer price/ discount groups	*Sales and marketing > Prices and discounts > Customer price/discount groups*	→ 4.8.1
9.12	Charges codes (Purchasing)	*Accounts payable > Charges setup > Charges code*	→ 4.3.4
9.13	Charges codes (Sales)	*Accounts receivable > Charges setup > Charges code*	→ 4.3.4
9.14	Return action (Purchasing)	*Procurement and sourcing > Setup > Purchase orders > Return action*	→ 3.7.1
9.15	Disposition codes (Sales returns)	*Sales and marketing > Setup > Returns > Disposition codes*	→ 4.6.1
9.16	Category hierarchies	*Product information management > Setup > Categories and attributes > Category hierarchies*	→ 3.3.1
9.17	Procurement categories	*Procurement and sourcing > Procurement categories*	→ 3.3.1
9.18	Sales categories	*Sales and marketing > Setup > Categories > Sales categories*	→ 4.2.3
9.19	Document management parameters	*Organization administration > Document management > Document management parameters*	→ 10.5.1
9.20	Document types	*Organization administration > Document management > Document types*	→ 10.5.1

No.	Name	Menu item	Section
9.21	Workflow configuration	*System administration > Workflow > Workflow infrastructure configuration*	→ 10.4.2

Table A.10 Master data

No.	Name	Menu item	Section
10.1	Vendors	*Accounts payable > Vendors > All vendors*	→ 3.2.1
10.2	Customers	*Accounts receivable > Customers > All customers*	→ 4.2.s1
10.3	Products	*Product information management > Products > All products and product masters*	→ 7.2.1
10.4	Released products	*Product information management > Products > Released products*	→ 7.2.1
10.5	Bills of materials	*Product information management > Bills of materials and formulas > Bills of materials*	→ 5.2.2
10.6	Operations	*Production control > Setup > Routes > Operations*	→ 5.3.3
10.7	Routes	*Production control > All routes*	→ 5.3.3

Commands and Keyboard Shortcuts

Table A.11 Basic commands and keyboard shortcuts

Shortcut	Button in action pane	Description
Alt+N	*New*	Create a record
Alt+Del(Alt+F9)	*Delete*	Delete a record
Alt+S(Ctrl+S)	*Save*	Save record (in Edit mode)
F2	*Edit (or Options/Edit/Read mode)*	Switch between Read mode and Edit mode
Esc		Close form (optionally without saving)
Shift+Esc		Close form and save record
Ctrl+Shift+F5	*Options/Edit/Revert*	Restore record (Undo pending changes)
Shift+F5	⟳ (Refresh)	Refresh (Save and synchronize record)
Ctrl+F2	ⓘ (in the right sidebar)	Show the FactBoxes
Ctrl+Shift+H	*Header* (in the title line)	Switch to the Header view (in transaction forms)
Ctrl+Shift+L	*Lines* (in the title line)	Switch to the Lines view (in transaction forms)
Ctrl+F10	(Right-click)	Open the Dynamics 365 context menu
Ctrl+G	(Click the column header)	Open the grid column filter for the current column

Shortcut	Button in action pane	Description
Ctrl+F3	(in the right sidebar)	Open the filter pane
Ctrl+Shift+F3	*Options/Page options/Advanced filter or sort*	Open the advanced filter
Ctrl+Shift+A	(Attach)	Attach document
Alt+F1	(in the left sidebar)	Show the navigation pane
Alt+G	(in the navigation bar)	Navigation search
Ctrl+?	*/Help* (in the navigation bar)	Help on forms

The option *View shortcuts* (in the context menu of controls, like a field name, or a button in a form) and the Dynamics 365 help explain all available keyboard shortcuts.

References

Adrià Ariste Santacreu: Extending Dynamics 365 Finance and Operations Apps with Power Platform (Packt Publishing, 2024)

Ludwig Reinhard: Special Finance Applications in Microsoft Dynamics 365 for Finance and Operations (Independently published, 2019)

Microsoft documentation (*https://learn.microsoft.com/dynamics365/finance/* and *https://learn.microsoft.com/dynamics365/supply-chain/*)

Simon Buxton: Extending Microsoft Dynamics 365 Finance and Supply Chain Management Cookbook (Packt Publishing, 2020)

Index